The neuropsychology of anxiety:
an enquiry into the functions
of the septo-hippocampal system

Jeffrey A. Gray

CLARENDON PRESS · OXFORD
OXFORD UNIVERSITY PRESS · NEW YORK

Oxford University Press, Walton Street, Oxford OX2 6DP

Oxford   New York   Toronto
Delhi   Bombay   Calcutta   Madras   Karachi
Petaling Jaya   Singapore   Hong Kong   Tokyo
Nairobi   Dar es Salaam   Cape Town
Melbourne   Auckland

and associated companies in
Beirut   Berlin   Ibadan   Nicosia

Oxford is a trade mark of Oxford University Press

Published in the United States
by Oxford University Press, New York

First published in hardback, 1982
Reprinted in paperback, with corrections, 1987

British Library Cataloguing in Publication Data
Gray, Jeffrey A.
The neuropsychology of anxiety.—(Oxford
psychology series)
1. Anxiety
I. Title
616.85'223   RC531

ISBN 0-19-852109-X
ISBN 0-19-852127-8 (pbk)

Printed and bound in Great Britain by
Biddles Ltd, Guildford and King's Lynn

OXFORD · PSYCHOLOGY · SERIES

OXFORD PSYCHOLOGY SERIES

EDITORS   Donald E. Broadbent
             James L. McGaugh
             Nicholas J. Mackintosh
             Michael I. Posner
             Endel Tulving
             Lawrence Weiskrantz

Contents

Acknowledgements

I am deeply grateful to Professor Jean Scherrer for the kindness and hospitality he extended to me during my stay in his laboratory in the Faculté de Médicine, Université de Paris VI, in 1979–80, when this book was written. My thanks are also due to the Nuffield Foundation for the award of a Social Science Research Fellowship which, in 1975–76, allowed me to start working on the book, and for help in the preparation of the manuscript. I am indebted to all of my colleagues and students at Oxford for innumerable ideas and points of information which have influenced my thinking over the years. Particular thanks are due to Dr Neil McNaughton, for his invaluable help in reviewing the enormous literature on the behavioural effects of septal and hippocampal lesions; to Dr Marianne Fillenz, for educating me in the mysteries of the noradrenergic neuron; to Dr Nicholas Rawlins, for clarifying many points in hippocampal physiology; to Mrs S. Digby-Firth and Mrs M. Penning-Rowsell for their care in preparing the manuscript; and to my sons, Ramin and Babak, for editorial assistance. The paperback edition was revised while I enjoyed the hospitality of the Department of Psychology and Philosophy, Virginia Military Institute, Lexington, Virginia.

For my wife, without whom this book could not have been written.

Preface to the paperback edition

Five years have passed since the completion of the text for the hardcover edition of this book. In some of the fields that the book reviews, five years is a long time. This is so, for example, in the case of research on the benzodiazepine receptor; this was discovered only in 1977, yet it is already succumbing to genetic cloning. Other fields move more slowly; but there is none that has failed to yield significant new data which would surely find a place in the text if it were being written today. In preparing the paperback edition, however, I have resisted the temptation to add new material piecemeal. The argument the book presents is too complex to respond to such local engineering without distortion of more distal parts. In any case, none of the new developments (so far as I can judge) seriously compromises or alters the main thrust of the argument. (For other views, the reader is referred to an issue of *The Behavioral and Brain Sciences* in which a précis of *The neuropsychology of anxiety* was the subject of comments from 27 workers in the field; see Gray *et al.* 1982.) I shall confine myself here, therefore, to a few reflections upon major developments, as judged from the perspective of the book, which have taken place in the areas that it covers.

An important contribution to our understanding of the anatomy of the septo-hippocampal system is the report of a major projection from the subicular region to the ventral striatum (Kelley and Domesick 1982). This discovery goes far to remove the mystery of the way in which the septo-hippocampal system manages to influence motor behaviour. The sub-iculo-striatal projection may be of particular importance in the inhibition of rewarded behaviour (including active avoidance), since the ventral striatum appears to play a key role in the transmission of incentive motivation to motor systems (see Willner 1985, who reviews, in particular, the functions discharged by the dopaminergic projection from nucleus A 10, in the ventral tegmental area, to the nucleus accumbens in the ventral striatum).

As noted above, work on the benzodiazepine receptor proceeds apace. Much more is now known about its biochemistry, anatomy, and physiology (e.g. Bowery 1984). However, the major issues that in 1981 clouded interpretation of the role of the benzodiazepine receptor in anxiety and anti-anxiety drug action remain unresolved today. The endogenous ligand (assuming it exists) for the benzodiazepine receptor has still not been positively identified, although Costa's group has reported a promising candidate possessing anxiogenic action (Alho *et al.* 1985). It also remains uncertain whether the enhancement of the inhibitory action of γ-aminobutyrate (GABA), known to be caused by both benzodiazepines and barbiturates, is able to account for the anxiolytic action of these compounds. Experiments from my own laboratory have generally supported this hypothesis for the benzodiazepines, but not for the barbiturates (Gray, Quintero, Mellanby, Buckland, Fillenz, and Fung 1984; Buckland, Mellanby, and Gray 1986). Whether or not anxiolytic drug action is due to enhancement of GABA-ergic transmission, there is still no convincing biochemical account of the selective behavioural action of these compounds. If anything, the case for basing such selectivity upon the heterogeneity of either benzodiazepine or GABA receptors has weakened (Trimble 1983; Bowery 1984). Indeed, the best available account of the selective action of anti-anxiety drugs (proposed by Haefely) places this, not in their biochemistry at all, but in the situation in which the animal is tested (Gray 1985*a*).

The heart of the book is the theory of septo-hippocampal function developed in Chapter 10. On the whole, this theory met with favourable comment in the issue of *The Behavioral and Brain Sciences* cited above. However, it has done nothing to halt the fever of psychological theorizing to which the field of 'hippocampology' is especially prone. An important new twist to this theorizing has been added by Rawlins (1985), who has adduced much data in support of his view that the hippocampus acts as an intermediate-term, high-capacity memory buffer. This hypothesis is not necessarily incompatible with the theory developed in this book. Indeed, Gray and Rawlins (in press) have shown that the same neural machinery is in principle capable of acting both as a comparator (Chapter 10) and as a memory buffer in Rawlins's sense.

This is a potentially fruitful development, since there is as yet no adequate explanation for the close links that apparently exist between the limbic circuits that mediate emotion and cognition respectively (Gray 1984). Clinically, the existence of such links has been reaffirmed by two recent developments. First, it has become clear that degeneration of the cholinergic septo-hippocampal projection (Rossor *et al.* 1982) and loss of cells in the subicular area (Hyman *et al.* 1985) are important features of the pathological process that underlies the dementia of Alzheimer's disease. Second, a study using positron-emission tomography to scan the brains of patients suffering from panic anxiety has shown—in striking confirmation of the major claim made in this book—that the principal site at which these patients differ from controls is the region containing the main input to the septo-hippocampal system, i.e. the entorhinal area, and the main output from this system, i.e. the subicular area (Reiman *et al.* 1984). It would seem, then, that the clinical pay-off for a proper understanding of the functions of the septo-hippocampal system is likely to be great.

Additional clinical evidence that the theory of anxiety developed in this book is along the right lines has come from Charney *et al.* (1984). Redmond and I independently proposed that the locus coeruleus, origin of the ascending noradrenergic projection to the septo-hippocampal system, plays a major role in anxiety (Chapter 11). It is possible to assess the activity of this nucleus by measuring the levels of the major metabolite of noradrenaline, 3-methoxy-4-hydroxyphenylethylene glycol (MHPG), in plasma. In agreement with the Redmond–Gray hypothesis, Charney *et al.* (1984) showed that yohimbine (an α_2-noradrenergic receptor blocker that increases locus coeruleus firing by interrupting auto-receptor-mediated inhibition) gave rise to self-reports of anxiety in human subjects. Furthermore, the degree of anxiety so provoked was well correlated with the rise in plasma MHPG also produced by yohimbine administration; and both self-reported anxiety and the rise in plasma MHPG were higher in patients suffering from panic attacks than in controls.

Although the major aim of the theory developed in this book is to account for anxiety, some consideration has also been given to the neural basis of depression and to the relations between depression and anxiety. This is a field in which points of view are liable to change with dizzying speed. It is in particular difficult to choose between the view that depression is due to underactivity in monoaminergic systems and the diametrically opposed view that it is due to monoaminergic overactivity (see Chapter 12). In the time since this book was written, Weiss, for example, has moved from the former to the latter position; and (impressed by the data with which he supported this move) I developed an alternative account of depression to the one advanced in this book (Weiss *et al.* 1982; Gray 1985*a*). But those who, like myself, have experienced mental amblyopia in the attempt to grasp the literature on depression now have an invaluable guide, in the shape of Willner's (1985) masterly exposition of the subject. Willner has convinced me (at least for the time being) that depression is due to an impairment in monoaminergic transmission (as in the original Schildkraut–Kety hypothesis; Chapter 12). This has the advantage that the account of depression offered here may stand essentially unchanged.

Much of my treatment of the neurology of depression in Chapter 12 is concerned with the helplessness that may be produced in animals by régimes of uncontrollable stress. It is important, therefore, that recent work has demonstrated that helplessness responds to anti-depressant and other drug treatments in the manner that one would predict from the assumption that it is a valid model of human depression (Willner 1985). At the same time, other work has implicated in helplessness many of the same structures (in particular, the septo-hippocampal system and its ascending noradrenergic innervation) that are also implicated in anxiety (Gray 1985*b*). The problems of interpretation that are posed by these two developments are discussed by Gray (in press).

There are, of course, many points of detail or emphasis which five years' further accumulation of data would require me to change or add to the text if I were to attempt a complete revision. But the main lines of the argument and the main conclusions I reached would not, I think, be much changed by this exercise. A number of findings cited in the text had not yet been published when the book was originally prepared for press. To help the reader trace the published reports I have included a list of additional references at the end of the book and have annotated the text accordingly. Further developments of some of the ideas contained in the book can be found in Gray (1984, 1985*a*), Gray *et al.* (1982), and Gray and Rawlins (in press). In addition, Gray (in press) has considered the relations between the theory developed here and a number of other issues in the psychology and neurology of aversively motivated behaviour.

Lexington, Virginia   J.A.G.
November 1985

References

Alho, H., Ferrero, P., Guidotti, A., and Costa, E. (1985). Neuronal location of a brain neuropeptide putative precursor of the endogenous ligand for brain beta-carboline recognition sites. *Soc. Neurosci. Abst.* **11,** 1122.

Bowery, N. G. (ed.) (1984). *Actions and interactions of GABA and benzodiazepines.* Raven Press, New York.

Buckland, C., Mellanby, J., and Gray, J. A. (1986). The effects of compounds related to γ-aminobutyrate and benzodiazepine receptors on behavioural responses to anxiogenic stimuli in the rat: extinction and successive discrimination. *Psychopharmacology* **88,** 285–295.

Charney, D. S., Heininger, G. R., and Breier, A. (1984). Noradrenergic function in panic anxiety. *Arch. Gen. Psychiatry* **41,** 751–63.

Gray, J. A. (1984). The hippocampus as an interface between cognition and emotion. In *Animal cognition* (ed. H. L. Roitblat, T. G. Bever, and H. S. Terrace) pp. 607–26. Erlbaum, Hillsdale, N.J.

—— (1985*a*). Issues in the neuropsychology of anxiety. In *Anxiety and the anxiety disorders* (ed. A. H. Tuma and J. D. Maser) pp. 5–25. Erlbaum, Hillsdale, New Jersey.

—— (1985*b*). Emotional behaviour and the limbic system. In *Interface between neurology and psychiatry* (ed. M.R. Trimble) pp. 1–25 (*Adv. Psychosom. Med.* 13). Karger, Basel.

—— (in press). *The psychology of fear and stress,* 2nd edn. Cambridge University Press, Cambridge.

—— *et al.* (1982). Précis and multiple book review of 'The Neuropsychology of Anxiety: An Enquiry into the Functions of the Septo-Hippocampal System'. *Behav. Brain Sci.* **5,** 469–534.

—— and Rawlins, J. N. P. (in press). Comparator and buffer memory: an attempt to integrate two models of hippocampal function. In *The hippocampus* Vol. IV (ed. R. L. Isaacson and K. H. Pribram). Plenum, New York.

—— Quintero, S., and Mellanby, J. (1983). Gamma-aminobutyrate, the benzodiazepines and the septo-hippocampal system. In *Benzodiazepines divided* (ed. M. Trimble) pp. 101–27.

——————— Buckland, C., Fillenz, M., and Fung, S. C. (1984). Some biochemical, behavioural and electrophysiological tests of the GABA hypothesis of anti-anxiety drug action. In *Actions and interactions of GABA and benzodiazepines.* (ed N. G. Bowery) pp. 239–62. Raven Press, New York.

Hyman, B. T., Van Hoesen, G. W., Kromer, L. J., and Damasco, A. R. (1985). The subicular cortices in Alzheimer's disease: neuroanatomical relationships and the memory impairment. *Soc. Neurosci. Abstr.* **11,** 458.

Kelley, A. E. and Domesick, V. B. (1982). The distribution of the projection from the hippocampal formation to the nucleus accumbens in the rat: an anterograde- and retrograde-horseradish peroxidase study. *Neuroscience* **10,** 2321–35.

Rawlins, J. N. P. (1985). Associations across time: the hippocampus as a temporary memory store. *Behav. Brain Sci.* **8,** 479–96.

Reiman, E. M., Raichle, M. E., Butler, F. K., Hersovitch, P., and Robins, E. (1984). A focal brain abnormality in panic disorder, a severe form of anxiety. *Nature* **310,** 683–5.

Rossor, M. N., Garrett, N. J., Johnson, A. L., Mountjoy, C. Q., Roth, M., and Iversen, L. L. (1982). A post-mortem study of the cholinergic and GABA systems in senile dementia. *Brain* **105,** 313–30.

Trimble, M. (ed.) (1983). *Benzodiazepines divided.* Wiley, Chichester.

Weiss, J. M., Bailey, W. H., Goodman, P. A., Hoffman, L. J., Ambrose, M. J., Salman, S., and Charry, J. M. (1982). A model for neurochemical study of depression. In *Behavioral models and the analysis of drug action* (ed. M.Y. Spiegelstein and A. Levy) pp. 195–223. Elsevier, Amsterdam.

Willner, P. (1985). *Depression: a psychobiological synthesis.* Wiley, New York.

UN COUP DE DÉS

JAMAIS

N'ABOLIRA LE HASARD

Toute Pensée émet un Coup de Dés

Stéphane Mallarmé

———

'The hippocampus—an organ of hesitation and doubt'

P.V. Simonov, 1974

Preface

This book presents a theory of the psychological nature of anxiety and the neural basis on which it rests. The theory is based principally on the effects observed in experimental animals of drugs which, in Man, are used successfully to control anxiety — the benzodiazepines, barbiturates, and alcohol. A central feature of the argument lies in the remarkable similarities between the behavioural effects of the anti-anxiety drugs, on the one hand, and those of damage to the septo-hippocampal system (part of the limbic forebrain), on the other. These similarities have prompted the hypothesis that the drugs affect anxiety by influencing in some way the activity of the septo-hippocampal system. The route by which this influence is brought to bear probably includes the long noradrenergic and serotonergic pathways which ascend from the brain stem to innervate much of the forebrain, including the septo-hippocampal system. Thus, in the search for the neural basis of anxiety, it became necessary to examine existing theories and evidence as to the behavioral functions of these and related structures in the brain. The search has not been confined to questions merely of the location in the brain of the systems that mediate anxiety. On the contrary, I believe that this excursion into neurology has resulted in a much richer understanding of the *psychology* of anxiety. Thus the theory presented here is truly neuropsychological, not a neural and a psychological part glued together merely by statements of identity.

In the course of the book it is necessary to consider many rival theories that have been proposed to account for the functions of the particular parts of the brain which are here allotted a role in anxiety: theories, for example, of the functions of the hippocampus or the dorsal ascending noradrenergic bundle. This in turn has required an extensive review of the available empirical data. I have tried to do justice to alternative hypotheses, and either to incorporate them into the present theory where they seem to be correct, or to substantiate my rejection of them where they do not. Thus the book ranges over many issues that are not themselves directly related to anxiety. This is particularly so in the analysis of the functions of the septo-hippocampal system, to which a large portion of the book is devoted. I hope that this portion will be of value to readers who wish to acquaint themselves with this part of the brain, even if they have no particular interest in anxiety: hence the broken-backed title of the book, held together with an ambiguous colon. Let me here dispel some of that ambiguity. It is not claimed that the septo-hippocampal system is concerned only with anxiety, nor that anxiety depends solely on that system. It *is* claimed, however, that the kinds of information processing that go on in the septo-hippocampal system are of central importance in the state of anxiety; that the perspective this hypothesis offers on the functions of the septo-hippocampal system can help clarify what these functions are; and that the perspective the hypothesis also offers on anxiety can help us penetrate some way into this mysterious state of mind.

I have been concerned with the analysis of anxiety for more than fifteen years. Thus this book is an extension of ideas that I have expressed on many previous occasions. However, the central theoretical model that I propose is largely new, forced into being by the very effort of trying to integrate the great diversity of data on which it rests. I had hoped to apply the theory not only to the symptoms and treatment of human anxiety (as, at the end of the book, I do), but also to the closely related problem of the personality of individuals who are particularly susceptible to anxiety. However, one year of sabbatical leave proved inadequate for the task, and I have been able only to touch upon this problem in the final chapter. I hope one day to return to it.

Oxford,   J.A.G.
May 1981

Introduction: the behavioural inhibition system

This century's dark continent is the brain or mind, two names for what, so far as we can at present tell, is one mysterious entity inside our skulls. Like the early explorers of Africa, we know quite a lot about the coastline of our continent: the sensory systems of vision and audition that bring the mind news of what is going on in the outside world, and the motor systems that act upon the world. But we know next to nothing certain about its interior. This book is a preliminary map of one of the most mysterious regions of that interior. In the language of mind, this region is called 'anxiety'; in the language of the brain, it is probably located somewhere in the limbic system.

In constructing this map I have been guided by one major premiss. A number of substances (the anti-anxiety drugs) are used routinely, and apparently with success, to reduce anxiety. It follows that a description of the psychological processes which are altered by the anti-anxiety drugs should be a description of the psychology of anxiety. Furthermore, to change behaviour, the anti-anxiety drugs must act on the brain. It should therefore also follow that a description of the neural processes which are altered by these drugs is a description of the neurology of anxiety. This argument sounds simple enough, but it contains many assumptions which will need careful examination in the pages that follow; and to carry it through empirically is, of course, far from simple. But, if it is correct, it can lead us not just to a theory of the psychology of anxiety nor only of its neurology, but to an integrated neuropsychology of anxiety which will blur (as blurred it must one day be) the division which at present separates our two languages, of brain and mind.

That is our destination; but it is far from our starting point. And, until we are certain that we have set up the right translation rules between brain and mind, it will be wise to keep the two languages as far as possible separate. It is for this reason that the theory of anxiety presented here is structured at two separate, though intimately related, levels.

At the psychological level it is a theory of the processes involved in the emotion of anxiety without reference to the neural structures which mediate them. At this level the problem is to define the inputs — stimuli — which give rise to the state of anxiety, the outputs — responses — which derive from this state, and the internal processes which relate outputs to inputs. It is these processes which, at the psychological level, constitute anxiety. Thus 'anxiety' is a theoretical concept, not a description of any particular pattern of stimuli or responses. As such it cannot be given a satisfactory definition independently of the theory in which it is embedded. So, like Little Red Riding Hood, we must plunge into the forest not knowing what the wolf looks like. (Readers impatient to meet him, warts and all, are invited to glance at the final chapter, which contains a short résumé of the theory developed in this book.)

The second level occupied by the theory is neurological. At this level it is a theory of the neural processes which do the job attributed to anxiety at the psychological level. Put like this, the neurological level is in a sense secondary to the psychological one. If the psychological component of the theory gets anxiety wrong, there can be no success in finding neural processes to match its supposed functions. Moreover, the converse is not true: one might get the neurological component completely wrong, but the psychological component none the less right. But, though it is in principle correct that the psychological component is in this sense primary, things in practice are not so simple. Frequently, when a neuropsychological experiment produces an unexpected result, the consequence is a modification of the relevant part of psychological theory rather than a change in our understanding of the function discharged by a particular part of the brain. Thus the relations between the psychological and neurological components of neuropsychological theories involve a great deal of mutual give and take to make the two levels fit each other as well as possible. The theory presented in this book is no exception: as we shall see, the results of physiological experiments have forced considerable elaboration upon a conception of anxiety that was derived initially from behavioural data.

There is, however, a serious danger lurking in this kind of dialectical relationship between psychological and neurological theorizing: one may make part of the theory immune from falsification, and thus useless. For one can often choose to protect one part of the overall neuropsychological theory from falsification at the expense of the other, by saying for example (when an experiment goes wrong) that anxiety does after all reside in this part of the brain, but we misunderstood the behavioural consequences of anxiety; or, conversely, that the psychology of anxiety is as we have said it to be, but it resides elsewhere in the brain. It is in part to avoid this danger that I have to a large extent separated the psychological and neurological components of the theory; in this way the reader may at least see the data bases on which each component rests independently of the other. To this end much of the psychological component has been described in some detail in an earlier book (Gray 1975), in which very little attention was paid to the results of experiments on the brain or experiments with drugs. In the present book, conversely, our attention will in the main be devoted to the neurological component.

My earlier book was concerned with wider issues in the theory of learning than just that part which is relevant to us here. But within that wider concern considerable attention was paid to what I called there the 'behavioural inhibition system'; this is identical to what has been called above the 'psychological component' of the theory of anxiety. We begin the present book with an outline of the behavioural inhibition system as it has already been described on the basis of purely behavioural data (Gray 1975). We then go on to consider (Chapter 2), within the conceptual framework provided by the notion of the behavioural inhibition system, the behavioural effects of the anti-anxiety drugs. Next (Chapters 3–13) we consider the functions (as deduced from lesion studies, stimulation studies, etc.) of those regions of the brain which, it is suggested, mediate the behavioural effects of the anti-anxiety drugs. This is the core of the book. I have called the brain areas concerned the 'septo-hippocampal system', although, as we shall see, it contains several other structures besides the septal area and hippocampus. Finally (Chapters 14–16), the concept of the behavioural inhibition system, now greatly enriched by its contact with the real brain, is applied to the symptoms and treatment of anxiety in Man.

Learning theory and the emotions

Whatever else anxiety is, it is undoubtedly an emotion; sometimes, reading the work of psychologists, one is tempted to think that it is the only emotion. Unfortunately, this statement does not take us much further forward, since it is a moot point whether 'anxiety' or 'emotion' is the more opaque concept. However, some kind of a consensus appears to have emerged among at least those psychologists who base their understanding of emotional behaviour on research with animals. This treats emotions as 'central' states (that is, in the head, but only ambiguously in the brain or mind) which are elicited by primary or secondary reinforcing stimuli (e.g. Mowrer 1960; Plutchik 1962; Millenson 1967). I have discussed this approach elsewhere (Gray 1972a) and subsequently embedded it in a more general treatment of the 'two-process' theory of learning (Gray 1975) with which, since the pioneering work of Mowrer (1947, 1960), it has usually been associated. In this chapter I wish only to summarize my own treatment of two-process theory insofar as it concerns the emotions and the behavioural inhibition system; for fuller details the reader is referred to Gray (1975).

The two processes of two-process theory are those of classical (or Pavlovian) and instrumental (or operant) conditioning. Whether or not these processes are fundamentally distinct from each other remains a matter of controversy (Mackintosh 1974), although I believe that a strong case can be made for the claim that they are (Gray 1975). In any particular situation, however, the behaviour actually acquired by the subject is normally the outcome of an interaction between both processes.

Classical conditioning is the process whereby the subject learns the associative relationships between discrete stimulus events (i.e. it is stimulus–stimulus, or S–S, learning). Consider two stimuli, of which the first (S_1) precedes the second (S_2) in time. Suppose that S_2 has some independent probability of occurrence (P_2) on occasions when it is not preceded by S_1. There are now three possible cases for the probability of occurrence of S_2

on those occasions when it is preceded by S_1 ($P_{2/1}$): $P_{2/1}$ may be greater than, equal to, or less than P_2. Experiments using the basic paradigm introduced by Pavlov (1927) have demonstrated that animals are sensitive to all three of these relationships, and that their behaviour in response to S_1 (the conditioned stimulus, or CS) changes accordingly (Dickinson 1980). Roughly speaking, if $P_{2/1}$ is greater than P_2, the animal responds to the CS in a manner that is appropriate to the anticipated occurrence of S_2 (the unconditioned stimulus, or UCS). In such cases the CS is said to be excitatory or positive (CS+) and the behaviour it elicits, a conditioned response (CR). Conversely, if $P_{2/1}$ is less than P_2, the animal responds to the CS in a manner that is appropriate to the anticipated non-occurrence of the UCS; in particular, it inhibits responses that would be elicited by a CS+. In such cases the CS is said to be inhibitory or negative (CS−) and the behaviour it elicits, conditioned inhibition. Finally, if $P_{2/1}$ is equal to P_2, the occurrence of S_1 neither elicits nor inhibits behaviour appropriate to S_2; furthermore, in subsequent tests, the animal behaves as though it has learnt that the occurrence of S_1 is irrelevant with respect specifically to the occurrence of S_2 ('learned irrelevance'; Mackintosh 1973).

Instrumental conditioning is the process whereby the subject acquires new behaviour patterns which affect its exposure to stimulus events (i.e. it is response–stimulus, or R–S, learning). An important feature of the particular version of two-process theory preferred by the present writer is that the instrumental learning process is further subdivided into two varieties, one concerned with maximizing reward, the other with minimizing punishment.

Consider a response, R, which the animal emits with some probability, P_R, and a stimulus, S, which occurs with some independent probability, P_S, when it is not preceded by R. As in the case of classical conditioning, we may distinguish three possible relations between P_S and the probability of occurrence of S when it is preceded by R ($P_{S/R}$): $P_{S/R}$ may be greater than, equal to, or less than P_S. Again as in the case of classical conditioning, the animal learns different things depending on which of these relationships in fact holds. This learning is manifested as a change in P_R. However, in order to describe what the animal learns in an instrumental conditioning experiment, it is necessary also to distinguish between kinds of stimuli. For, depending on the type of stimulus used, the change observed in P_R (for a fixed relation between P_S and $P_{S/R}$) may take opposite directions. The complexities that this introduces into the analysis of instrumental learning are set out in Table 1.1. The rows in this Table correspond to different relationships between P_S and $P_{S/R}$, the columns to different directions of change in P_R.

Table 1.1 may be read in two ways.

First, it defines different experimental operations. Thus, if we take the top row (stimulus presentation, i.e. $P_{S/R}$ greater than P_S), we see that the operation of reward is one in which the presentation of a stimulus contin-

Table 1.1. Instrumental reinforcing procedures with unconditioned reinforcing events. The abbreviations and symbols are as defined by the intersection of row (procedure) and column (outcome). $p(R)\uparrow$: outcome is an increase in the probability of the response on which the reinforcing event is made contingent. $p(R)\downarrow$: outcome is a decrease in the probability of this response. Crosshatching indicates those procedures-plus-outcomes which define a stimulus as an S^{R+} or an S^{R-}, respectively. Bracketed phrases refer to typical learning situations in which the various reinforcing procedures are employed. Rew: reward; Pun: Punishment; !: termination; $^{-}$: omission

OUTCOME

PROCEDURE	$p(R)\uparrow$	$p(R)\downarrow$
Presentation	Rew (approach)	Pun (passive avoidance)
Termination	Pun ! (escape)	Rew ! (time out)
Omission	Pun̄ (active avoidance)	Rēw (extinction)

☐ S^{R+}　　　■ S^{R-}

gent upon a response leads to an increased probability of emission of the response; a typical example would be the increased rate of bar-pressing or of running in an alley shown by a hungry rat if either of these responses is followed by food. Similarly, the operation of punishment is one in which stimulus presentation contingent upon a response leads to a decreased probability of emission of the response; this typically happens if, for example, bar-pressing or running in an alley is followed by foot-shock.

Before going on to examine the bottom two rows of Table 1.1, it is necessary to give some thought to the way in which the classical and instrumental conditioning processes interact.

We suppose that, for a given animal species, there exist stimuli which may act without prior learning as rewards and other stimuli which may act without prior learning as punishments. These stimuli ('reinforcers') may also act as UCSs in a classical conditioning paradigm. The responses elicited by UCSs are termed 'unconditioned responses' (UCRs), and the result of classical conditioning (to a rough approximation) is that the CS comes to acquire the property of eliciting some portion of the total pattern of UCRs elicited by the UCS. When the UCS is provided by a rewarding ('appetitive') or punishing ('aversive') stimulus, classical conditioning may in this manner confer on CSs, not themselves initially rewarding or punishing, 'secondary' or 'conditioned' appetitive or aversive properties. These secondary appetitive or aversive properties fall into two general classes: 'reinforcing' and 'motivational'. The reinforcing property corresponds to the reinforcing (i.e. rewarding or punishing) property of the UCS with which the CS has been paired. Thus a secondary rewarding stimulus increases the probability of recurrence of responses which it follows; and a secondary punishing stimulus (often called a 'warning signal') decreases the probability of responses which it follows. The motivational properties of secondary reinforcers are observed when the relevant stimulus is presented to the animal independently of its responses. They correspond to some degree (though they are not identical with) the eliciting properties of the UCS with which they have been paired; however, they are still very much the subject of empirical research and their exact nature is not entirely clear (Mackintosh 1974; Gray 1975).

The central states elicited by secondary rewarding and punishing stimuli, and which presumably underlie their reinforcing and motivational effects, have played a key role in theories of emotion. Thus Mowrer (1960) treats 'hope' as the state elicited by secondary appetitive stimuli, linked (as of course it is by common sense) to the anticipation of reward; and 'fear' similarly as the state elicited by secondary aversive stimuli and linked to the anticipation of punishment. These states of anticipation form the necessary background to the behavioural effects of the operations listed in the bottom row of Table 1.1. For it is only when an animal anticipates reward (hopes) that the omission of reward (Amsel's 1962 'frustrative non-reward') affects its behaviour; and only when it anticipates punishment (fears) that it is affected by the omission of punishment.

More formally, frustrative non-reward is the operation whereby reward is omitted after a particular response, given that reward has previously followed the same or similar responses and/or that reward is predicted to occur by secondary appetitive stimuli to which the animal is currently exposed. The usual effect of this operation is a decline in the probability of emission of the non-rewarded response ('extinction'); although, as we shall see, frustrative non-reward also has other effects on behaviour. Similarly, relieving non-punishment (Gray 1975) is the omission of punishment after a particular response, given that punishment has previously followed the same or similar responses and/or that punishment is predicted to occur by secondary aversive stimuli to which the animal is currently exposed. The usual consequence of this arrangement is that the response followed by non-punishment increases in probability, a phenomenon known as 'active' avoidance learning in contrast to the 'passive' avoidance learning seen when a response is punished and therefore declines in probability. The operations listed in the middle row of Table 1.1 are similar to those in the bottom row, except that the animal's response is followed, not by the omission of the reinforcer, but by its termination. This paradigm has been widely used with aversive reinforcers, in which case it is termed 'escape' learning; but it has not been much used with appetitive reinforcers.

It would be tidy if we could relate the bottom two rows of Table 1.1 straightforwardly to the two probabilities, P_S and $P_{S/R}$. But the complexities of experimental procedure do not permit this. The two paradigms in the left-hand column (escape and active avoidance) fit neatly enough: in both, $P_{S/R}$ is less than P_S, giving the opposite relationship to the one that holds for stimulus presentation (top row). However, nearly all experiments on the omission of reward (right-hand column, bottom row) use an extinction procedure, in which reward is simply discontinued ($P_{S/R} = P_S = 0$); the critical ingredient in this procedure, almost certainly, is a reduction in $P_{S/R}$ from the value it has before extinction begins. The procedure in which $P_{S/R}$ is lower than P_S, and the probability of emission of the response consequently declines, is known as omission training, but this has been used relatively little. Procedures involving termination of reward (right-hand column, middle row), often termed 'time out', also keep $P_{S/R}$ lower than P_S, but they too have been little studied. Recently, there has been much interest in the procedure in which $P_{S/R} = P_S$ and the stimulus is aversive; that is, the animal is exposed to aversive stimuli and has no way of controlling them. This procedure has been claimed to produce a particular cluster of psychological effects ('learned helplessness') which have been related to the emotional state of depression (Seligman 1975); we shall consider these phenomena in Chapter 12.

We have considered Table 1.1 so far as a set of definitions of experimental operations. A second way to read this Table is as a way of classifying *stimuli*. Thus there are three ways in which one may test for the appetitive properties of a stimulus. Such a stimulus should increase response probability when it is presented contingently upon that response, but decrease response probability when its termination or omission is so contingent. Empirically, it is normally the case that any stimulus which passes one test will pass all three. Such a stimulus may be called (using Skinner's 1938 terminology) a 'positive reinforcer'. Similarly, there are three ways in which one may test for the aversive properties of a stimulus. It should decrease response probability when its presentation is contingent upon the response, but increase response probability when its termination or omission is so contingent. Again it is normally the case that any stimulus which passes one test will pass all three. This kind of stimulus is called a 'negative reinforcer'. (The Skinnerian terminology also uses the phrases 'positive and negative *reinforcement*'. 'Positive reinforcement' is the top left-hand cell in Table 1.1, reward learning; 'negative reinforcement' covers the bottom two left-hand cells, escape and active avoidance.)

Table 1.1 contains three different recipes for parcelling out behaviour. One may focus on the different relations between response and stimulus (the rows), on the different directions of change in response (the columns), or on the distinction between positive and negative reinforcers (dotted versus dashed cells). It is an empirical question as to which, if any, of these classifications reflects real distinctions in the way the nervous system processes information in different learning situations. As we shall see in the next chapter, however, the behavioural effects of the anti-anxiety drugs appear to respect the distinction between directions of change in response probability: they alleviate response suppression whatever its source (the right-hand column of Table 1.1), while not affecting the acquisition of responses (the left-hand column). Conversely, the anti-anxiety drugs appear to ignore the distinctions between different kinds of relation between response and stimulus, or between positive and negative reinforcers.

Further relevant postulates of the present version of two-process theory concern frustrative non-reward. This is held to have effects on behaviour which are in certain respects identical to those produced by punishment, and there is much evidence to support this hypothesis (Wagner 1966; Gray 1967, 1975). Just as the simple operations of reward and punishment may combine with the classical conditioning component of the total learning process to produce secondary rewarding and punishing stimuli, so the more complex operation of frustrative non-reward may work in the same way. Thus, if an initially neutral stimulus is paired in a stimulus–stimulus sequence with non-reward (e.g. a tone is made to sound just before a non-rewarded entry into a goal-box at the end of an alley), it acquires by classical conditioning some of the properties of the event of non-reward itself. Such a stimulus becomes, among other things, aversive (i.e. the animal will treat it as a negative reinforcer, as defined in Table 1.1), just as it does if it is paired with a punishment, such as an electric shock. There are many other similarities between such 'secondary frustrative' stimuli and secondary punishing stimuli, so much so that the two kinds of stimuli may for most purposes be regarded as functionally equivalent.

Although both secondary punishing and secondary frustrative stimuli derive their properties from classical conditioning with the corresponding unconditioned event, there is good reason to believe that different systems mediate responses to conditioned and unconditioned stimuli, respectively. It is generally true of classically conditioned responses that these conform to a modified version of Pavlov's (1927) original stimulus substitution hypothesis, namely, that the properties acquired by a CS as a result of classical conditioning are properties also possessed by the UCS employed to establish the CR. The case where the UCS is an aversive stimulus is, however, a clear exception to this rule. In the rat, for example, an electric shock elicits as UCS a great deal of activity (running, jumping, etc.) and noise (squealing); but a CS which has been followed by such a UCS elicits exactly the reverse — immobility (freezing) and silence (Myer 1971). Similarly, a shock may elicit aggressive behaviour if a suitable object of aggression is present, but a CS paired with shock inhibits aggressive behaviour (Baenninger 1967; Myer 1971). Heart rate and respiration have also been seen to follow a similar pattern of inverse sign of change. In human subjects, for example, the cardiac response to shock is acceleration but to a CS signalling shock it is deceleration (Notterman *et al.* 1952; Obrist *et al.* 1965). Thus CSs signalling punishment appear to activate a different behavioural system from the one which mediates responses to punishment itself. There is less evidence for the same distinction in the case of primary and secondary frustrative events; some of it is from experiments using the anti-anxiety drugs, and we shall consider this in Chapter 2 (Section 2.9).

Just as the theory holds that frustrative non-reward is functionally equivalent to punishment, so it holds that relieving non-punishment is equivalent to reward. Thus, on this view, escape and active avoidance learning are both mediated by the system which also underlies simple reward learning. Like non-reward, non-punishment may serve as a UCS for the process of classical conditioning. If a CS is paired with non-punishment, it acquires secondary appetitive properties (i.e. the animal treats it as a positive reinforcer, as defined in Table 1.1); such a stimulus is often called a 'safety' signal. There are indications that safety signals are in many respects functionally equivalent to secondary rewarding stimuli; but the evidence on this score is less extensive than that which relates to the equivalence between secondary punishing and secondary frustrative stimuli.

The behavioural inhibition system

We are now in possession of the main distinctions which are required to describe, to a first approximation, the behavioural inhibition system. As set out in detail by Gray (1975), this system mediates responses to secondary punishing and secondary frustrative stimuli (Fig. 1.1). Thus the functional equivalence which appears to hold between these two types of stimuli (Wagner 1966, 1969; Gray 1975) is, on this view, due to their both acting on the same central system. In the language of the emotions, as forged by learning theorists, the state elicited by secondary punishing stimuli is usually termed 'fear' (Miller 1951; Mowrer 1947, 1960) and the state elicited by secondary frustrative stimuli, 'conditioned frustration' (Amsel 1962). Thus the functional equivalence between secondary punishing and secondary frustrative stimuli may also be expressed as an equivalence between fear and conditioned frustration (Gray 1967). In the theory developed in this book, both these states are subsumed into the more inclusive emotion, 'anxiety'.

It is as important to define the stimuli which do not act upon the behavioural inhibition system as those which do. The behavioural inhibition system is not affected by reward, conditioned or unconditioned. Nor, more interestingly, is it concerned with the mediation of responses elicited by unconditioned punishment or non-reward. These two kinds of stimuli are treated as functionally equivalent to each other, but as acting upon a different system from the one that responds to conditioned punishment and non-reward; as noted above, the patterns of behaviour elicited by

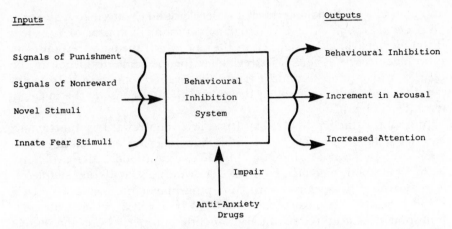

Figure 1.1. The behavioural inhibition system. This responds to any of its adequate inputs with all of its outputs, and (Chapter 2) comprises the hypothetical substrate on which the anti-anxiety drugs act to reduce anxiety.

unconditioned and conditioned punishing stimuli, respectively, are very different from each other. I have termed this second system, which mediates the behavioural effects of unconditioned punishment and non-reward, the 'fight–flight system' (Gray 1971a, 1975). In addition, I have postulated a third, 'approach' system, separate from both the others, which mediates behavioural responses to secondary appetitive stimuli (paired with either reward or non-punishment). Table 1.2 sets out the main distinguishing features of the three postulated systems (Gray 1972a). In this book, however, we are concerned only with the behavioural inhibition system.

Among the class of reinforcing stimuli (primary and secondary), then, the behavioural inhibition system responds only to secondary punishing and secondary frustrative stimuli. But there are two further classes of stimuli to which, according to the theory, the behavioural inhibition system is specialized to respond.

The first is the class of novel stimuli. Thus the phenomena described by Sokolov (1963) as the 'orienting reflex' and by Pavlov (1927) under the rubric of 'external inhibition' are closely related to the activities of the behavioural inhibition system.

The second is the class of 'innate fear stimuli' (Gray, 1971a, Chapter 2; Gray 1976); Seligman (1971) has used the term 'prepared' for essentially the same type of stimulus, but, as we shall see in Chapter 14, the theoretical nuances of the two terms are rather different. This class includes in particular stimuli that are associated with special dangers to the species (e.g. snakes for primates; Hebb 1946), and stimuli that arise during social interaction with conspecifics (e.g. threatening looks or calls). Since there

Table 1.2. Three major emotional systems

Emotional system	Reinforcing stimuli	Behaviour
Approach	conditioned stimuli for reward and non-punishment	approach learning; active avoidance; skilled escape; predatory aggression
Stop or behavioural inhibition	conditioned stimuli for punishment and non-reward	passive avoidance; extinction
Fight/flight	unconditioned punishment and non-reward	unconditioned escape; defensive aggression

has been very little experimental work on the pharmacology or neurology of the behaviour evoked by this class of stimuli, we shall have little to say about them in this book, although they will occupy our attention in Chapter 14.

So much for the stimuli that activate the behavioural inhibition system. But what does the system then do? This question can be understood in two ways.

The first, and simpler, way is as a request to list the outputs of the behavioural inhibition system (Fig. 1.1). Understood in this way, the question may be answered as follows (Gray 1975, p. 354). 'The functions of the behavioural inhibition system are: (a) to inhibit all ongoing behaviour, whether instrumental or classically conditioned or innate; and (b) to perform the maximum possible analysis of current environmental stimuli, especially novel ones. The orienting responses would then be one consequence of activity in this system. The other major outputs are an initial inhibition of all previously operative behaviour patterns; coupled with an increment in arousal level, i.e. an increment in the intensity of whatever behaviour finally does occur.'* Note that behavioural inhibition and increased arousal may, and probably usually do, co-exist. This seems to occur, for example, in the partial reinforcement acquisition effect (Goodrich 1959; Haggard 1959; see Section 2.7); that is to say, animals exposed to occasional non-reward both hesitate more (behavioural inhibition in the narrow sense) and run faster (higher arousal) than continuously rewarded controls (Amsel 1962; Gray and Smith 1969).

---

*This is an inadequate definition of the concept of arousal in general, but it is appropriate for most of the research on animal behaviour to which the concept can reasonably be applied (e.g. Gray 1971a, p. 185). In research on human subjects 'arousal' has acquired a much more complex significance (though one which is compatible with the more restricted definition given here), and includes among other things an increase in the capacity for sensory analysis (Gray 1964a; Eysenck 1967; Broadbent 1971). This wider definition of arousal enters into some of the arguments encountered later in the book (see Chapters 11 and 12).

The second, and harder, way is as a request for a description of the internal machinery by which the behavioural inhibition system performs these functions. An answer to the question, understood in this way, might be given at the level of software (mind) or hardware (brain). The major purpose of this book is to construct such an answer at both these levels.

By the behavioural inhibition system, then, we mean (at the outset of our enquiry) a system, neurology as yet unspecified, which produces the outputs listed to the right of Fig. 1.1 when it is challenged by one of the adequate stimuli listed to the left of this Figure. Note that, although two of the four kinds of stimuli to which the behavioural inhibition system responds are learnt (conditioned punishing and conditioned frustrative stimuli), this system does not itself play any role in the learning process as such. The formation of conditioned punishing and frustrative stimuli is thought to take place according to the same general processes as are involved in other forms of classical conditioning (with the exception, noted above, that there is a departure from the stimulus substitution rule); and this is the business of other brain systems. Note also that the way in which the behavioural inhibition system responds to these learnt stimuli is not itself learnt. The animal, as it were, knows innately how to respond to threat (of punishment, failure, or uncertainty), but it has to learn what is threatening. And sometimes it does not even need to learn this, since there appear to exist certain 'innate fear stimuli' (Gray 1971*a*, 1976) to which the behavioural inhibition system responds (as it does to novel stimuli) more or less automatically. This is a feature of the behavioural inhibition system which will assume a particular importance when we come to deal, in Chapter 14, with the symptoms of anxiety in man.

Figure 1.1 shows the behavioural inhibition system as it can be deduced from behavioural experiments (Gray 1975), although knowledge of the results of neuropsychological and especially psychopharmacological experiments has undoubtedly had a formative influence on some of the inferences drawn from the behavioural data. In the remainder of this book we shall seek the behavioural inhibition system in the real brain. But first we must see how well this concept can accommodate the data on the behavioural effects of the anti-anxiety drugs. That is the concern of the next chapter.

2

The behavioural effects of anti-anxiety drugs

The central argument of this book is that one can infer the nature of anxiety from the action of drugs that reduce anxiety. This argument rests upon a number of assumptions.

The first is that there exists a class of drugs which have the effect of reducing anxiety in man. There is a substantial clinical literature that supports this assumption (Rickels 1978), and we shall not examine it here. Clinically, the most important contemporary members of this class of anti-anxiety drugs are the benzodiazepines. These include a number of drugs in exceptionally wide use, such as Librium (chlordiazepoxide) and Valium (diazepam); more than sixty million of these tablets are prescribed annually in the United States alone (Tallman *et al.* 1980). But these are not the only substances used for the relief of anxiety. Before the benzodiazepines came into use, in the early 1960s, another family of drugs, the barbiturates, was widely prescribed for the same purpose; these are now principally used as sleeping pills. The barbiturate that is in widest use is known as 'Sodium Amytal'; its scientific name is sodium amylobarbitone in England and sodium amobarbital in the United States. The barbiturates were displaced by the benzodiazepines because the latter have less pronounced sedative effects and a greater margin ot safety between the clinically effective dose and the dose at which you can kill yourself. The benzodiazepines are also marginally more effective than the barbiturates at controlling anxiety (Rickels 1978), but the similarities between the clinical effects of the two groups of drugs far outweigh their differences. A third drug which was in vogue for a while before the benzodiazepines came to dominate the clinical scene is known as 'Miltown' (meprobamate). But the oldest anti-anxiety drug of all is one that needs no credentials: alcohol.

Chemically these substances are very different from each other, a fact that has its uses. All drugs have multiple effects. The effects that are therapeutically undesirable are termed 'side-effects', though from a physiological point of view there is, of course, no reason to suppose them to be any less closely related to the drug's principal mode of action than is its therapeutic effect. The benzodiazepines, for example, usually act as muscle-relaxants and anticonvulsants (Tallman *et al.* 1980), as well as reducing the subjective state of anxiety. If we are to use the pattern of action of the anti-anxiety drugs to deduce the nature of anxiety, what are we to say about these 'other' effects of the benzodiazepines? Are we to conclude that a susceptibility to convulsions is part of anxiety, for example? And, if not, what criterion can we use to decide that the anticonvulsant effect of the benzodiazepines is, in some sense, separate from their action on anxiety? It is here that the existence of other drugs which reduce anxiety is a great help. We can use them, as it were, to triangulate anxiety. It is the common action of the benzodiazepines, the barbiturates, etc., which (according to this argument) constitutes their effect on anxiety; where they differ we are dealing with 'side-effects' so far as anxiety is concerned. Thus, to follow up the convulsion example, alcohol is not an anticonvulsant, although some barbiturates are; so that we can conclude that a heightened susceptibility to seizures is not part of anxiety as deduced from the pattern of action of the anti-anxiety drugs.

This 'triangulation' strategy will be of particular importance when we come to consider the neurological mode of action of these drugs. For example, it has recently been discovered that the brain contains receptors that are specific for the benzodiazepines (Squires and Braestrup 1977; Möhler and Okada 1977). These receptors do not bind either the barbiturates or alcohol. Precisely for this reason we can infer that, although they are no doubt critical for the action of the benzodiazepines, they cannot be critical for anti-anxiety action in general.

The first assumption on which our argument depends, then, is that there are drugs which reduce anxiety; and, fortunately, there are several different kinds of such drugs. The second assumption is that the clinical action of these drugs is specific to anxiety.

If anti-anxiety drugs also reduced joy, anger, and the sex drive, we should make little progress in deducing anything about anxiety from studying them. Similarly, if the benzodiazepines were as effective in controlling schizophrenic thought disorder or manic elation as they are in alleviating phobic anxiety, this would not detract from their psychiatric usefulness — on the contrary — but it would greatly limit their value as scientific tools. Fortunately, this second assumption is also relatively well founded. For example, the anti-anxiety drugs are of little use in the treatment of schizophrenia or mania. Nor are they effective in the control of anger or aggression; indeed, they may actually facilitate aggressive behaviour, and this can be an important clinical hazard (Lynch *et al.* 1975). Thus the effects of the anti-anxiety drugs are relatively specific to anxiety; and this conclusion will be much strengthened when we have considered the behavioural effects of these drugs in experimental animals.

This conclusion needs, however, two qualifications.

First, at large doses alcohol and the barbiturates become anaesthetics, while at moderately large doses all the anti-anxiety drugs have strong sedative effects and disturb motor co-ordination. Thus, at elevated doses, behavioural specificity is no longer preserved. This qualification is of comparatively little importance, so long as we make our inferences only from studies which have employed small doses of the anti-anxiety drugs.

The second qualification is more fundamental. At the clinical level it has proved extremely difficult, and perhaps impossible, to distinguish between the effects of the anti-anxiety drugs on anxiety and on certain kinds of depression (Kellner *et al.* 1979; Frith *et al.* 1979; Johnstone *et al.* 1980); and, conversely, some drugs which are principally thought of as antidepressants are effective also in the treatment of anxiety (Frith *et al.* 1979; Paykel *et al.* 1979). This problem allows, in principle, of two solutions. Either one can conclude that the anti-anxiety drugs are not, after all, specific to anxiety; or that anxiety and the kind of depression against which the anti-anxiety drugs and the antidepressants are equally effective are not clinically distinct entities. The former solution, if it is correct, would greatly weaken the arguments deployed in this book. However, as we shall see in Chapter 12, there are good reasons to believe that the second solution is correct.

A third important assumption is that human anxiety, or something very like it, exists also in animals and responds in much the same way to anti-anxiety drugs. This assumption is critical, not only for the arguments pursued in this book, but also for the whole research endeavour to which it belongs. For it is impossible to perform the great majority of the relevant experiments without using animal subjects. Yet many people will undoubtedly find this assumption hard to accept. It is commonly believed that anxiety is an almost uniquely human state, dependent on such complex cognitive capacities as the ability to foresee the future, to form a self-image, or to imagine one's own mortality. To the extent that this belief is correct, the present approach to the study of anxiety is totally misconceived, for the major inferences on which it rests have been drawn from experiments with rats, mice, cats, or, at best, monkeys. Nor is it a belief that can be lightly brushed aside. Although the general continuity of human and animal behaviour is not open to serious dispute on biological grounds, this does not dispense with the need to demonstrate that continuity in each particular case. For at some point, not known in advance, the continuity will break down. Like every other species, man is in some ways unique, and common sense may be right to give him an especially large share of uniqueness. Thus we must be particularly careful to demonstrate that this third assumption is correct.

This demonstration will be made in two stages. In this Chapter I hope to show that the observed effects of anti-anxiety drugs in animals are consistent with the view that these agents act upon a state that is closely similar to the human state of anxiety. Later, in Chapters 14–16, we shall apply a theory of anxiety based on animal experiments to the phenomena of anxiety in man. In the last analysis, this is the touchstone of the theory's success: the understanding it brings, or fails to bring, of human anxiety.

It is by now evident that a careful description and analysis of the effects of the anti-anxiety drugs on the behaviour of experimental animals is essential for the argument pursued in this book. There have been many hundreds of experiments investigating these effects, starting with the pioneering work of Jules Masserman (Masserman and Yum 1946) on alcohol and Neal Miller (1951) on sodium amylobarbitone. I have recently reviewed these experiments in considerable detail (Gray 1977), so I shall

in the main confine myself here to a summary of the conclusions reached
in that paper, bringing them up to date where necessary. At the same
time as setting out these conclusions, I shall take the opportunity to describe a number of key experimental tasks which will recur in later chapters when we look at the behavioural effects of other treatments. The
description of these tasks is theoretically loaded in the following sense:
for each task I shall indicate the roles probably played by the different
processes distinguished in Chapter 1, and I shall do this within the theoretical framework developed in that chapter.

The first points that must be made are in one sense preliminary to the
detailed conclusions which will occupy most of our attention, but in another sense they are the most important points of all: it turns out that, in
summarizing the behavioural effects of the anti-anxiety drugs, it is hardly
ever necessary to add any qualifications concerning either the drug used
or the species investigated. The significance of these conclusions will be
apparent from what has already been said; we shall return to them at the
end of the chapter.

With these preliminaries, important as they are, behind us, we turn to
a detailed consideration of the behavioural effects of the anti-anxiety
drugs. If no references are given for the points made, they can be found
in Gray (1977). Unless otherwise stated, the following summary refers
equally to the benzodiazepines, the barbiturates, and alcohol; although I
have not reviewed the effects of meprobamate, these seem generally to be
similar to those of the other anti-anxiety drugs. Only the effects of low
doses of the drugs are considered, before sedative, motor, or anaesthetic
effects become prominent (for the actual doses, see Gray 1977). Since this
review is undertaken with theoretical issues in mind, it concentrates on
tasks from which important inferences can be drawn rather than attempting to be exhaustive. None the less, it is based on a survey of the great
majority of experiments in this field (some 400 reports are reviewed by
Gray 1977).

2.1. Rewarded behaviour

We consider in this section tasks in which the subject is required to perform a response for a reward, such as food or water, given on a continuous reinforcement (CRF) schedule, that is, a reward for every response.
As soon as intermittent reinforcement is employed, the animal's behaviour becomes a function of non-reward as well as reward. We shall therefore delay consideration of the effects of the anti-anxiety drugs on such
behaviour until we deal with non-reward in Section 2.7.

The anti-anxiety drugs are without systematic effect on simple rewarded behaviour. This generalization applies across a wide variety of
different tasks. In particular, it is unaffected by the distinction between
'spatial' tasks (such as running in an alley or learning to go to one side of
a T-maze) and non-spatial tasks (such as pressing a lever or pecking at a

key in a Skinner-box). This distinction will be important to us later in the book, when we examine the suggestion that the hippocampus is especially concerned with the analysis of spatial information and the control of behaviour in spatially complex environments (O'Keefe and Nadel 1978). Since we shall need eventually to compare the behavioural effects of the anti-anxiety drugs with those of hippocampal lesions, it is necessary also to bear in mind the spatial characteristics of different tasks as we examine drug effects. The only indication that these characteristics play any role in determining the effect of the anti-anxiety drugs on rewarded behaviour applies to the benzodiazepine, chlordiazepoxide, which usually reduces running speed in the alley but does not impair bar-pressing in a Skinner-box. However, since comparable effects are not usually seen after administration of barbiturates or alcohol, this pattern of results is probably unrelated to the anti-anxiety action of the benzodiazepines.

The conclusion that anti-anxiety drugs do not affect rewarded behaviour is supported by studies of electrical self-stimulation of the brain, a technique that has often been regarded as directly measuring central reward processes (though this is a view we shall have occasion to question later, in Chapter 11). None of the anti-anxiety drugs appears consistently to alter this type of behaviour.

Within the conceptual framework of two-process theory, simple rewarded behaviour typically depends on the action both of primary reward and of secondary rewarding stimuli derived from a classically conditioned association with the primary reward. Since the discovery of the autoshaping phenomenon (Brown and Jenkins 1968), it has become clear, however, that, under certain conditions, what appears to be instrumental rewarded behaviour can be maintained entirely by classically conditioned associations (Gray 1975, Chapter 2). In an autoshaping experiment a pigeon comes to peck at a lighted disc simply because the visual stimulus is correlated with the delivery of food, with no response contingency operative at all. Thus it is possible that some of the tasks in which the effects of the anti-anxiety drugs have been investigated tap, not instrumental reward learning, but principally the formation of a classically conditioned approach response to stimuli associated with an appetitive UCS. This possibility exists even in the widely used straight alley; the role played by classical conditioning in the behaviour of an animal running to a goal-box which contains food or water has never been properly evaluated. In other tasks, however, the observed behaviour is unlikely to reflect only classical conditioning. In a bar-pressing experiment with rats, for example, autoshaping occurs only under rather special conditions, and even then the rat's behaviour is normally very sensitive to response–reinforcement contingencies as well.

These ambiguities imply that, were the anti-anxiety drugs to impair rewarded behaviour, considerable experimental and theoretical analysis would be required to determine where in the chain of conditioning and performance they might work. Since rewarded behaviour is not consistently affected by the anti-anxiety drugs, this problem does not arise. On the contrary, the fact that the tasks on which this generalization is based consist of a rather indeterminate mixture of appetitive classical conditioning and instrumental positive reinforcement allows us to conclude that neither of these processes is affected by the anti-anxiety drugs.

2.2. Passive avoidance

Passive avoidance covers cases in which the subject is punished for making a designated response, and the response then declines in probability of emission. The response may be unconditioned (e.g. stepping from an exposed platform to the floor of the apparatus) or a previously learnt one (e.g. bar-pressing or running in an alley). As used here it covers both spatial and non-spatial tasks, although in some uses 'passive avoidance' is kept for the former case and 'punishment' for the latter. The distinction between passive and active avoidance (Table 1.1) turns on whether the animal can avoid punishment by *refraining* from making a specified response, all others going unpunished (passive avoidance); or whether it can avoid punishment by *making* a specified response, all others being punished (active avoidance).

The importance of this distinction is not self-evident, and theories of learning before the early 1960s usually treated active and passive avoidance as substantially identical. Experiments in that decade, however, strongly suggested that separate brain mechanisms mediate the two kinds of avoidance behaviour. These experiments were concerned with the effects of lesions to the septal area (McCleary 1966) and hippocampus (Douglas 1967), and we shall consider them in more detail in Chapter 6. At much the same time, although it did not attract so much attention, a similar pattern of results began to emerge from experiments using anti-anxiety drugs.

In this section we deal only with passive avoidance. Note that this depends on secondary aversive stimuli, derived from a classically conditioned association with the primary punishment, as well as on the primary punishment itself, for otherwise it would not be possible for the subject to suppress the punished response in advance of punishment (Gray 1975, Chapter 8). Furthermore, such secondary aversive stimuli acquire a very general capacity to suppress ongoing instrumental behaviour, even if their association with primary aversive UCSs is established under conditions in which instrumental behaviour is not punished. This phenomenon was first described by Estes and Skinner (1941), and is known as conditioned suppression; it is the best established example of what, in Chapter 1, I called the 'motivational' properties of secondary reinforcers.

The phenomenon of conditioned suppression makes it particularly difficult to determine the degree to which passive avoidance behaviour depends on instrumental or classical conditioning contingencies. Consider, for example, two kinds of experiment. In the first (discriminated punishment) a rat in a Skinner-box is given foot-shock in the presence of a distinctive signal only if it presses a bar; the consequence of such an arrangement is that bar-pressing declines in probability of occurrence in the presence of the signal. In the second experiment (conditioned suppression) a rat in a Skinner-box is again given foot-shock in the presence of the signal, but independently of its bar-pressing behaviour; the consequence of this arrangement is the same as before — bar-pressing declines in probability in the presence of the signal. Given that the first experiment, like the second, contains a stimulus–stimulus association (between the signal and foot-shock), and given that the second experiment demonstrates that such an association is sufficient to suppress bar-pressing, it is not possible without further analysis to attribute any of the suppression of bar-pressing seen in the first experiment to the instrumental contingency between bar-pressing and shock. Thus, even more than in the case of rewarded behaviour, if an experimental treatment alters passive avoidance, it is not usually clear whether this effect should be attributed to an alteration in the behavioural control exercised by classical or instrumental contingencies or both. We shall examine this issue in more detail in the next section.

The anti-anxiety drugs all impair passive avoidance in spatial tasks; that is, the drugged animals emit the punished response at a higher rate than controls. This effect is less dramatic with the benzodiazepines than with the barbiturates or alcohol, a fact which is perhaps connected to the more marked depressant effects of the former on running speed (Section 2.1). In the Skinner-box and other non-spatial tasks the barbiturates and benzodiazepines again reduce passive avoidance. The data on the effects of alcohol in such situations are less consistent, but more recent reports have demonstrated a lessened effect of punishment on bar-pressing behaviour in the drugged animals (Falk 1971; Cook and Davidson 1973; Leander *et al.* 1976). There is no reason to suppose that the observed effects depend on whether the punished response is learned or innate, although most of the data come from studies of the former kind. Nor is there any reason to suppose that the increased rate of emission of the punished response after drug administration is part of a general increase in responding. This possibility has been excluded by experiments in the Skinner-box which have used multiple schedules of reinforcement based on the one introduced by Geller and Seifter (1960). In this, periods of relatively low-density positive reinforcement (usually on a variable interval, VI, schedule*) without punishment alternate with periods of relatively high-density positive reinforcement (e.g. CRF) coupled with punishment, the two kinds of period ('components') being signalled by distinctive stimuli. In experiments of this kind, it has regularly been found that the anti-anxiety drugs

*For a description of this and related intermittent schedules, see Section 2.7.

increase the rate of punished, but not unpunished, responding.

Although the Geller–Seifter schedule controls for general changes in response rate, it does not control for the possibility that an increased response rate in the punished component of the multiple schedule results from a drug effect on low response rates *per se*, whether produced by punishment or by some other influence. There is in fact considerable evidence that some drug-induced changes in response rate may depend in just this way on pre-existing response rates, a phenomenon known as 'rate dependence' (Kelleher and Morse 1968). Thus it is important to exclude rate dependence as a possible account of the impaired passive avoidance seen after administration of the anti-anxiety drugs. Careful controls of this kind have been reported for the barbiturate, pentobarbitone, by McMillan (1973) and for the benzodiazepine, chlordiazepoxide, by Jeffery and Barrett (1979). In both experiments response rates were equated within the same animal between one component of a multiple schedule maintained by positive reinforcement alone and a second component in which responses were both rewarded and punished. The drug increased response rates in both components (a rate-dependent effect), but more so in the punished component even with response rate equated.

Recently Waddington and Olley (1977) have demonstrated an important potential source of confusion in experiments on passive avoidance. These workers studied the effects of chlordiazepoxide on 'step-down' passive avoidance under two training conditions. The animal's task was to refrain from stepping down from a safe, elevated platform to an electrified grid floor. In the first training condition the rat was removed from the apparatus immediately after it had been shocked and replaced later on the platform. In the second the rat was shocked until it returned of its own accord to the safe platform. This apparently trivial difference in procedure is theoretically of the greatest importance. As we shall see in Section 2.4, the anti-anxiety drugs have no effect on escape behaviour, that is, behaviour which is reinforced by the termination of a punishment to which the animal is already exposed (Table 1.1). Waddington and Olley's (1977) second procedure deliberately confounded an escape contingency (returning to the safe platform) with a passive avoidance contingency (refraining from stepping down to the floor), whereas their first procedure was one purely of passive avoidance. Given the other evidence that the benzodiazepines impair passive avoidance, we would expect chlordiazepoxide to have this effect in Waddington and Olley's first procedure, but not necessarily in the second. Prediction here would depend on the degree to which the response of staying up on the platform is based on the passive avoidance and escape contingencies, respectively. The results of the experiment confirmed this theoretical analysis: the drugged rats stepped down from the platform more rapidly than controls in the first procedure, but were not different from controls in the second.

2.3. Classical conditioning of fear

As we saw in the previous section, passive avoidance behaviour depends on both primary punishment and secondary punishing stimuli. According to two-process theory, secondary punishing stimuli become so as the result of classical conditioning. Thus it is possible that the impairment produced in passive avoidance by the anti-anxiety drugs is due to a disruption in aversive classical conditioning. We are thus led naturally to ask whether these drugs impair Pavlovian CRs to stimuli which have been paired with aversive UCSs in the absence of instrumental contingencies relating the animal's behaviour to such UCSs. Unfortunately, the data do not allow any very clear answer to this question.

There are three kinds of relevant experiment. The first is the one originally used by Pavlov (1927) himself, in which one measures a specific response (e.g. a change in heart rate, defecation) elicited by a CS after pairing with an aversive UCS. The other two employ variants of the conditioned suppression procedure described in the previous section. In this and analogous methods the effect of classical conditioning is evaluated by measuring the interference produced by the CS in instrumental behaviour, for example, bar-pressing. The CS–UCS pairing may be conducted while the subject performs the instrumental response used to assay the effect of conditioning, an 'on-the-baseline' procedure; or it may be conducted in a separate experimental situation where the response is impossible, an 'off-the-baseline' procedure.

There is no good evidence that the anti-anxiety drugs affect classical aversive conditioning when this is measured by discrete responses directly elicited by the CS. This suggests that the effects of the anti-anxiety drugs on passive avoidance are not mediated by an alteration in classical conditioning processes. On the other hand, there have been several reports of a reduction in on-the-baseline conditioned suppression after administration of these drugs, especially the benzodiazepines. It is possible that these results are due to a contamination of the measured classical conditioning by 'adventitious' punishment effects; that is to say, although the delivery of the aversive UCS is in fact independent of the instrumental response, the animal may none the less form a spurious association between this response and the UCS, in addition to the association between the CS and UCS. The benzodiazepines might then reduce on-the-baseline conditioned suppression by eliminating that part of it which arises from the spurious response–shock association. This would be consistent with the failure of the anti-anxiety drugs to affect straightforward Pavlovian CRs and with the impairment they produce in the suppression of responses that are explicitly punished. If this hypothesis is correct, we would not expect the anti-anxiety drugs to have any effect on conditioned suppression established with an off-the-baseline procedure; for in this there is no opportunity for adventitious punishment. The data on this issue are few and contradictory (Dantzer and Mormede 1976; Dantzer *et al.* 1976; and see the references in Gray 1977); but they do not in general show a reduction in conditioned suppression when anti-anxiety drugs are administered under these conditions.

The hypothesis that the anti-anxiety drugs affect response suppression only when this is due to a response–shock contingency (whether real or adventitious) carries the important implication that these agents may have a specific affinity for the mechanisms which mediate instrumental as distinct from classical conditioning (Gray, Rawlins, and Feldon 1979).

This possibility was investigated by Huppert and Iversen (1975). Rats were first trained to press a bar for sugar pellets. They were then divided into three groups. Animals in the 'master' group were shocked for pressing the bar. Each animal in the 'yoked control' group was paired to one in the first group, and shocked whenever its master was shocked, independently of its own bar-pressing behaviour. The third group received no shock at all. On the next day the latency to press the bar and the number of bar-presses were measured in all animals, no shocks now being delivered. Both shocked groups showed suppression of bar-pressing, but the group with the explicit response–shock contingency was significantly more suppressed than their yoked controls. This result is in agreement with other reports (e.g. Church *et al.* 1970) that response-contingent shock produces greater suppression of the punished response than response-independent shock. The interesting question addressed by the Huppert and Iversen (1975) experiment concerned the effects on the two kinds of response suppression of chlordiazepoxide, injected before the no-shock test session. Their results showed that the drug attenuated response suppression in both groups, but more so in the master than the yoked control group; in consequence the degree of response suppression no longer differed between the two groups. This result is consistent with the hypothesis that chlordiazepoxide exercises a special antagonism against the response suppression produced by training with instrumental punishment, as distinct from aversive classical conditioning.

There is one feature of Huppert and Iversen's (1975) results, however, which weakens this conclusion (J. N. P. Rawlins, personal communication). These workers also tested their animals in an open field immediately after the session in which they had been shocked. The shocked animals showed reduced activity ('ambulation') in the open field, as is commonly observed in fearful rats (Gray 1971*a*), and the reduction was greater in the group that had received response-contingent shock than in their yoked controls. This observation is rather surprising, for it suggests a greater generalization of fear to a different situation in the animals given a more precise signal of shock, namely, pressing the bar. One wonders, therefore, whether the animals in the response-contingent shock group had in fact formed an appropriate association between this act and the delivery of shock, a point about which Huppert and Iversen offer no evidence. If they had not formed such an association, the rationale of the experiment is destroyed.

In an effort to throw further light on this issue, Rawlins, Feldon, and Gray (1980a) trained rats to discriminate between response-contingent and response-independent shock. The animals were first trained to bar-press on a random interval (RI) schedule for sucrose reward. They were then exposed to a multiple schedule in which, during each session, there were two kinds of intrusion period, each associated with a distinctive stimulus. During one kind of intrusion period ('conditioned suppression'), shocks were delivered on a second RI schedule, independently of the animal's behaviour; during the other ('punishment'), shocks of the same intensity were programmed according to the same RI schedule, but they were delivered only if the animal pressed the bar. The majority of the rats learned to discriminate between the two kinds of intrusion period in that they displayed significantly different response rates in them. Rates were suppressed (relative to the baseline when no shocks were delivered) in both kinds of intrusion period, but most animals responded significantly less in the punishment than in the conditioned–suppression component. This result, like Huppert and Iversen's (1975), confirms earlier conclusions that response-contingent shock produces greater response suppression than response-independent shock. In addition, it shows that rats can detect the difference between the two modes of shock delivery and associate each with a distinctive stimulus.

After the animals had been trained in this way we injected them with chlordiazepoxide. As in Huppert and Iversen's (1975) experiment the drug attenuated response suppression whether this was due to response-contingent or response-independent shock, but significantly more in the former case; in consequence, the discrimination between the two modes of shock delivery which was present in the undrugged condition was eliminated. This finding is compelling evidence for an antagonism by the drug of the behavioural consequences of the response contingency itself. However, the design of the experiment leaves open the possibility of an alternative interpretation. Since response rates were lower in the punishment than in the conditioned–suppression component, the greater effect of the drug on the former might simply be an instance of rate dependency, that is, the lower the pre-drug rate, the greater is the increase in rate produced by the drug. This interpretation is also applicable to Huppert and Iversen's (1975) results.

To test this possibility Rawlins, Feldon, Salmon, Garrud, and Gray (1980c) trained separate groups of rats with either punishment or conditioned–suppression intrusion periods only. We matched the groups trained in these ways either for shock intensity (in which case the degree of response suppression was greater in the punishment than in the conditioned–suppression group) or for response rates during the intrusion periods (in which case the punished animals had lower shock intensities than those trained with response-independent shock). We then re-investigated the effects of chlordiazepoxide. Our results were entirely concordant with the rate-dependency hypothesis: in the groups matched for response rate, the degree to which the drug attenuated suppression was identical; in those matched for shock intensity, there was significantly greater attenuation of suppression in the punishment group (which had the lower pre-drug response rates) than in the conditioned–suppression group.

These results make it much harder to suppose that there is any special affinity between the anti-anxiety drugs and the mechanisms that mediate response suppression produced specifically by response–punishment con-tingencies. But in that case we are left, overall, with a pattern of results which speaks clearly neither for nor against the proposition that the anti-anxiety drugs affect aversive classical conditioning. *For* this view is the fact that on-the-baseline conditioned suppression is apparently no more nor less susceptible to the effects of the anti-anxiety drugs than is punishment-produced suppression, once response rates have been matched between the two procedures. *Against* it, is the failure of these drugs to alter specific Pavlovian CRs to aversive CSs, or (usually) off-the-baseline conditioned suppression (Gray 1977).

The situation is still more complicated if we take into account a recent experiment by M. Davis (1979), who used an off-the-baseline procedure to study the 'potentiated startle response'. In this experiment the rat's startle response was measured using a loud tone. On some trials the tone was preceded by a light which had previously been paired in a different apparatus with foot-shock. As a result of this pairing the light acquired the capacity to augment ('potentiate') the startle response to the tone, a phenomenon which may be regarded as an expression of the arousing effect of conditioned fear. Two benzodiazepines, diazepam and fluraze-pam, were administered either before the conditioning session or before the startle-test session or both. The drugs had no effect on the startle response to the tone itself; but both diminished the potentiation of the startle response produced by the light. They caused this effect only if administered prior to the test session; given during the conditioning ses-sion, they had no effect on the potentiated startle response measured sub-sequently. The effect of the drug was not due to a change in the animal's state between conditioning and testing, since the potentiated startle-response was reduced by the drug given before the test session whether drug or placebo had been given at the time of conditioning. Thus the pattern of results obtained by M. Davis (1979) was identical to the pattern reported by Tenen (1967) in an investigation of the effects of chlordiaze-poxide on off-the-baseline* conditioned suppression: a blockade of the

---

*Tenen's (1967) experiment is wrongly described by Gray (1977) as using an on-the-baseline design. I am grateful to P. Salmon for pointing this out to me.

expression but not the acquisition of conditioned fear (see Gray 1977, for other relevant studies).

It appears from these results that the anti-anxiety drugs sometimes block the effects of classical fear conditioning but sometimes do not; and that the outcome depends, in a complex and as yet unclear manner, both on the response measured and on the paradigm used to measure it. Thus response suppression is alleviated by the anti-anxiety drugs if it is established using an on-the-baseline procedure, but not (or not clearly) if it is established using an off-the-baseline procedure. Conversely, using an off-the-baseline procedure, conditioned suppression is not reliably affected by the anti-anxiety drugs, but the potentiated startle response (M. Davis 1979; Chi 1965; Williams, cited by Miller and Barry 1960) is.

When the results of experiments become difficult to summarize within the confines of a particular theory, it is probable that the theory is wrong or inappropriate. We shall attempt later to fit the results of the experiments reviewed in this section into a different framework (Chapter 10). For the moment, the safest conclusions we can reach are the following.

First, it seems unlikely that the effects of the anti-anxiety drugs on passive avoidance are due to a disturbance in the Pavlovian conditioning process itself. Specific Pavlovian CRs are not usually affected by these drugs; and when they do affect classically conditioned behaviour (as in the case of Tenen's experiment on off-the-baseline conditioned suppression, or Davis's on the potentiated startle response), this is due usually to a disruption in the expression, not the conditioning, of fear.

Second, the effects of the anti-anxiety drugs are not limited to the case in which behaviour is principally controlled by response–punishment contingencies: these drugs appear to reduce conditioned fear whether this results from exposure to response-contingent or response-independent aversive stimuli. This conclusion is a reversal of the position I adopted in my 1977 review; but it is a return to a simpler position held earlier (Gray 1971*a*). In reaching it I have been guided most strongly by the results of our own experiments on response-contingent and response-independent suppression matched for response rate between separate groups (Rawlins *et al.* 1980*c*) and by M. Davis's (1979) experiment on the potentiated startle response.

Third, although a response contingency is not necessary for the anti-anxiety drugs to produce their effects, the emission or otherwise of a motor response at the time that shock occurs does influence some of these effects. The disinhibition of response suppression by the anti-anxiety drugs usually occurs only if stimulus–shock associations are established using an on-the-baseline procedure. This suggests that these drugs alter the expression of an association which (while it is not instrumental in nature) depends for its formation on the joint occurrence of an aversive UCS and an ongoing motor response. In the experiments on the potentiated startle response, however, off-the-baseline procedures were used.

In this case, then, the association whose expression is blocked by the anti-anxiety drugs apparently depends only on stimulus–stimulus relationships.

2.4. Escape

The data reviewed in the preceding two sections make it clear that the anti-anxiety drugs reduce the behavioural effects of primary punishment and/or secondary punishing stimuli when appropriate experimental paradigms are used, and especially when punishment is used to suppress a response upon which it is contingent. They do not, however, permit one to decide whether the effect of the drug is on the response to the unconditioned punishment, the response to secondary punishing stimuli, or both. The data reviewed in this and the next two sections make it clear that the anti-anxiety drugs do not attenuate responses to unconditioned aversive stimuli as such.

Escape responses (e.g. bar-pressing, running in an alley or from side to side of a two-compartment box known as a shuttle-box) terminate a shock to which the animal is already exposed. If the anti-anxiety drugs reduce the effects of shock as such, one might expect them to impair escape behaviour. But no consistent effects have been observed, except for a tendency for chlordiazepoxide to reduce running speed to the same degree that it reduces rewarded running speed (Barry and Miller 1965) and which is probably therefore non-specific. We have already discussed (Section 2.2) Waddington and Olley's (1977) demonstration of the importance of the difference between escape and passive avoidance procedures in determining the effects of chlordiazepoxide: in a step-down passive avoidance task which allowed no escape back to the platform, this drug markedly reduced step-down latencies, but when an escape contingency was added the drug no longer had any effect. Thus the brain mechanisms which mediate escape seem to be sufficiently independent of those that mediate passive avoidance to take over when the latter are blocked by a drug.

2.5 Active avoidance

As indicated earlier, the distinction between active and passive avoidance is that the former requires the animal to make a designated response to avoid punishment, whereas the latter requires it to refrain from making one. The usual distinction between spatial and non-spatial tasks can be applied to active avoidance; but in addition it is necessary to distinguish within the spatial category between 'one-way' and 'two-way' tasks.

One-way active avoidance is the case in which one area is always dangerous (i.e. it is there that punishment is delivered), while another area is always safe. An example is an alley in which shock is delivered in the start-box and runway, but not in the goal-box. In a typical experiment of this kind the animal is put in the start-box, which is not yet electrified (as it would be in an escape procedure), and given a limited time (e.g. five seconds) to reach the goal-box before the shock is turned on. None of the anti-anxiety drugs has any consistent, specific effects on this kind of be-haviour. This negative result is important. Escape differs from passive avoidance in that it requires no anticipation of shock. Thus one might try to account for the fact that the anti-anxiety drugs impair passive avoid-ance, but not escape, by postulating a disruption in the ability to anticipate punishment. But one-way active avoidance also requires the animal to an-ticipate punishment, and it is not impaired by the anti-anxiety drugs. Thus these agents cannot generally disrupt the ability to anticipate pun-ishment.

Two-way active avoidance is the case in which the dangerous and safe areas are constantly interchanged. The shuttle-box is the classic example. In a typical shuttle-box experiment the animal is on one side of the two-compartment apparatus when a warning signal is presented. At some time after the onset of this stimulus shock is delivered, unless the animal has by then moved to the other side of the apparatus. If it is still on the original side, it can terminate (escape) shock by now running to the other side. The warning signal is itself normally terminated by a cross to the other side, whether on successful avoidance or on escape trials. The avoidance response, then, consists of crossing to the other side of the box than the one in which the animal finds itself when the warning signal is presented ('shuttling'). But this response takes the animal back to the side from which it ran away on the previous trial.

The complexity of this task, both from the animal's point of view and that of theoretical analysis, is evident. There are at least three potential sources of reinforcement for shuttling: termination of shock on escape trials, termination of the warning signal on both escape and avoidance trials, and avoidance of shock on avoidance trials. The evidence suggests that all three play a role in the control of shuttling (Bolles, Stokes, and Younger 1966; Gray 1975, Chapter 10). In addition, there is a conflict between active and passive avoidance, since the stimuli making up the now-safe side of the box, owing to their association with shock on pre-vious trials, must themselves become secondary punishing stimuli and so deterrents to approach behaviour. A different analysis of the complexities of the shuttle-box has been advocated by O'Keefe and Nadel (1978), as part of their overall approach to spatial behaviour; we shall consider this analysis when we deal with the effects of septal and hippocampal lesions on avoidance behaviour (Chapter 6). For the moment we shall suppose, as have several previous writers (e.g. McCleary 1966; Lubar and Numan 1973), that the most important feature of two-way avoidance procedures is the conflict they involve between active and passive avoidance.

On this view, the passive avoidance tendency should interfere with per-formance of the shuttling response, and we would expect in general a negative correlation between the strength of this tendency and the efficiency of shuttling. This expectation is supported both by direct experimental manipulation of factors in the shuttle-box situation (Freedman, Hennessy, and Groner 1974), and by the fact that a great variety of factors have been found to affect passive and shuttle-box avoidance in opposite directions. Thus Maudsley Reactive rats bred for high fearfulness in the open field test (Broadhurst 1960; Gray 1971*a*) show greater passive avoidance (Weldon 1967; Ferraro and York 1968) than Maudsley Nonreactive rats (bred on the same test for low fearfulness) but poorer shuttle-box avoidance (for references, see Gray and Lalljee 1974). Fuller (1970) has similarly reported a negative correlation between the efficiency of passive and shuttle-box avoidance across four inbred strains of mice. The role of genetic factors in the determination of shuttle-box avoidance has been further demonstrated by Wilcock and Fulker (1973). These workers showed that in the rat there are two independent genetic influences, each with directional dominance (and therefore each probably of Darwinian survival value), one for poor performance on early training trials, the other for good performance on later trials. They suggest that the first of these influences favours the development of a conditioned emotional response leading to freezing behaviour. This is essentially the same suggestion as the one advanced here (see Chapter 1, and the discussion of the behavioural inhibition system in Gray 1975, Chapter 8). Other factors which affect fearfulness and shuttle-box avoidance in opposite directions are sex, the less fearful females (Gray, 1971*b*, 1979*a*) showing poorer passive avoidance and better shuttle-box avoidance (for references, see Gray and Lalljee 1974); early handling, which reduces fearfulness (Levine 1962) and improves shuttle-box avoidance (for references, see Gray and Lalljee 1974); and lesions to the hippocampus (Douglas 1967) and septal area (McCleary 1966), which have the same effects and which first drew attention to this general pattern of relationships.

These findings allow us to make a firm prediction of the effects of the anti-anxiety drugs on two-way active avoidance. This prediction is derived in two ways. First, since passive avoidance appears to interfere with shuttling, and since the anti-anxiety drugs impair passive avoidance but do not affect one-way active avoidance, they should improve shuttle-box avoidance by reducing the interfering effects of passive avoidance. Second, we expect animals injected with an anti-anxiety drug to resemble animals which are low in fearfulness for other reasons. In each of the relevant comparisons given above animals low in fearfulness are relatively good at shuttle-box avoidance: Maudsley Nonreactive relative to Maudsley Reactive rats, females relative to males, early handled relative to unhandled animals. Again, therefore, we predict that the anti-anxiety drugs should improve shuttle-box avoidance. This indeed is the case, as has been demonstrated for the benzodiazepines, the barbiturates, and alcohol, and not only in the shuttle-box, but also in automated Y-mazes in which the safe arm is randomly varied from trial to trial. Furthermore, the drugs improve shuttle-box avoidance especially during early acquisition, when, according to Wilcock and Fulker's (1973) genetic findings, the passive avoidance tendency is at its strongest; and especially in highly fearful animals (Powell, Martin, and Kamano 1967; Martin, Powell, and Kamano 1966), as would be expected if the drug works by reducing fear. Remarkably, the same facilitation of two-way active avoidance that is seen in mammals is also produced by giving alcohol to goldfish (e.g. Scobie and Bliss 1974).

Rather similar findings have been reported in studies of non-spatial active avoidance. This has usually been studied in the Skinner-box using Sidman avoidance schedules. Such a schedule is defined by two parameters, the shock–shock and the response–shock intervals, of which the former is usually substantially shorter than the latter. In the absence of a response, shocks occur regularly at the shock–shock interval; each response postpones the next shock by the time defined by the response–shock interval. Notice that there is no explicit warning signal in this procedure, other than the passage of time since the last shock or the last response. When anti-anxiety drugs are given to animals that have learnt a bar-pressing response on this schedule, high doses impair performance, but this is probably a non-specific sedative effect. At low doses both the barbiturates and the benzodiazepines have been found to improve performance, especially in animals which perform poorly in the undrugged state. As suggested by Bignami *et al.* (1971), this effect is best understood as arising from a reduction in the response-suppressant effects of the secondary aversive stimuli constituted by the general experimental environment. This analysis has been examined less carefully, however, than the corresponding analysis of two-way avoidance tasks.

In summary of the last two sections, then, the anti-anxiety drugs do not affect escape or one-way active avoidance, they improve two-way active avoidance, and they tend to improve non-spatial avoidance in the Skinner-box; the latter two effects are probably due to lessened interference from the response-suppressant influence of secondary aversive stimuli.

2.6. Responses elicited by aversive stimuli

The pattern of results summarized at the end of the previous section more or less rules out the possibility that the anti-anxiety drugs generally lessen the effects of painful stimuli. This conclusion is also supported by direct studies of the responses elicited by such stimuli. However, there have been surprisingly few studies of this kind. Measurement of the threshold electric current at which flinching or jumping is provoked has failed to reveal any sign of analgesia. In the case of alcohol, there is even evidence of a reduction in the flinch and jump thresholds to shock. Complementary observations have been made in experiments on known analgesic drugs, such as morphine. These do not typically reduce passive avoidance in the manner of the anti-anxiety drugs (Geller, Bachman, and Seifter 1963; Kelleher and Morse 1964), although they do of course reduce responses directly elicited by painful stimuli. This double dissociation between the effects of the two classes of drugs is important evidence for the hypothesis (Gray 1967, 1975; see Chapter 1) that different brain systems mediate responses to unconditioned and conditioned aversive stimuli respectively.

A larger number of studies have been devoted to the effects of the anti-anxiety drugs (especially the benzodiazepines) on aggressive behaviour. This is sometimes elicited by shocking pairs of animals, which very reliably provokes an aggressive encounter, and sometimes simply by pairing previously isolated animals, usually males. The barbiturates and alcohol reduce aggressive behaviour, however provoked, only at relatively high doses, presumably as the result of general sedation or motor inco-ordination. At low doses, both kinds of drug actually facilitate aggression (Gray 1977; Kršiak 1976). The data on the benzodiazepines are much more variable. It is clear that they too are capable of facilitating aggressive behaviour at low doses, though it may also be necessary for them to be administered chronically for this effect to be observed. At higher doses there is conflicting evidence as to whether the benzodiazepines can reduce aggressive responses in a specific manner not due to sedation or loss of co-ordination. If such a specific anti-aggressive action exists, it is possible that it is confined to types of aggression in which fear is a prominent component, as when the animal is provoked by the experimenter. Since effects of this kind have not been reported after barbiturate or alcohol administration, they are probably not an essential feature of anti-anxiety action.

2.7. Effects of frustrative non-reward

We defined non-reward in Chapter 1 as the operation whereby reward is omitted after a particular response, given that it has previously followed the same or similar responses, and/or that it is predicted to occur by secondarily rewarding stimuli to which the animal is currently exposed. There are many different experimental situations in which the behavioural effects of non-reward can be observed and measured (Mackintosh 1974; Gray 1975). The most careful analyses of the action of the anti-anxiety drugs in such situations have used sodium amylobarbitone, although there has recently been an accumulation of data concerning the benzodiazepines. Both classes of drug have been shown to reduce the behavioural effects of non-reward across a wide variety of tasks; in contrast, the available data on alcohol are sparse and inconclusive.

The simplest situation involving non-reward is the extinction of a response previously rewarded on a continuous reinforcement schedule. Injected during extinction the anti-anxiety drugs reduce the rate of extinction. This effect is seen in the Skinner-box as well as the alley, so the spatial/non-spatial distinction is irrelevant. More complex, but theoretically intelligible, effects are observed when the drugs are administered to animals trained on various kinds of intermittent reinforcement schedules, that is, schedules on which responses are sometimes followed by reward and sometimes not. If a random 50 per cent schedule (partial reinforcement, or PRF) is used in the alley, it is often found that at the end of training partially rewarded rats run faster than continuously rewarded rats, especially in the start and run sections of the alley (Goodrich 1959; Haggard 1959. This 'partial reinforcement acquisition effect' is abolished by the anti-anxiety drugs, which reduce running speeds in animals trained on PRF but have no consistent effect in those trained on CRF. If the undrugged animals in this kind of experiment are then subjected to extinction, it is regularly observed that the PRF group takes much longer to extinguish than the CRF group. This 'partial reinforcement extinction effect' (PREE) is reduced or abolished in animals trained under sodium amylobarbitone or chlordiazepoxide (Feldon *et al.* 1979; Feldon 1977; Feldon and Gray 1981*a,b*; Willner and Crowe 1977; and see references in Gray 1977). As in the case of the partial reinforcement acquisition effect, this is due to changes confined to the partially reinforced animals. One may summarize these experiments, then, by saying that, whatever the effects of non-reward, the drug counteracts them.

Intermittent schedules of reinforcement have also proved sensitive to the effects of the anti-anxiety drugs in the Skinner-box. Consider first interval schedules. On these a response is rewarded only after some interval has elapsed since the last reinforcement. On a fixed interval (FI) schedule this interval is constant. As pointed out by Staddon (1970, 1972), this means that the delivery of reward is a reliable signal that, for some time, responses will not be rewarded again; in other words, the delivery of reward can itself serve as a conditioned frustrative stimulus. Behaviourally, the control exercised by this property of an FI schedule is manifest in the so-called 'FI scallop'. This is a distinctive pattern of responding in which the rate of response is low just after reward and gradually increases as the time for the next available reward approaches. What would we expect to be the consequences for such behaviour of a reduction in the effects of non-reward? It seems clear that the inhibitory effect of reward delivery should be reduced, with a consequent increase in response rate in the early part of the fixed interval, disruption of the scallop, and therefore an increase in the overall response rate. Just these changes are seen after administration of barbiturates, alcohol (McDonough *et al.* 1975) or benzodiazepines. Compare this pattern of change with the one observed using variable interval (VI) or random interval (RI) schedules. The only difference between these and the FI schedule is that successive intervals between programmed reinforcements vary randomly. But this has the effect that the animal no longer has a reliable signal of periods of low probability of reinforcement. In consequence response rates remain steady, with no pause after reward is delivered. And, as would be expected, the anti-anxiety drugs have no consistent effects on the rate of response.

Similar considerations apply to fixed ratio (FR) as to FI schedules. On these the animal must make a specified number of responses for reward to be obtained. Once this number becomes large, the delivery of a reward necessarily becomes a signal that some time will pass (the time required to complete the fixed ratio) before a response will again be rewarded. In consequence there develops a pronounced pause in responding after each reward, the length of which is proportional to the size of the FR. Arguing from the FI analogy, we would therefore expect the anti-anxiety drugs to reduce this post-reinforcement pause. It is consistent with this expectation that these drugs increase FR response rates; but it is not clear from the published data whether they do this by shortening the post-reinforcement pause or in some other way.

Another schedule which contains a definite signal of non-reward is known as 'differential reinforcement of low rates' (DRL). On this the subject is required to let a specified time (typically about 20 seconds) elapse between successive responses to obtain a reward. Thus the making of a response (or the delivery of reward for a successful response) is a reliable signal that any further response before the specified interval has passed will go unrewarded. Using the same arguments as before, we would predict that the anti-anxiety drugs will disrupt DRL performance by shortening inter-response times. Just this pattern has been observed after administration of all three kinds of anti-anxiety drug.

The anti-anxiety drugs also antagonize the behavioural effects of non-reward when reward is not removed completely, but merely reduced in quantity. Large rewards sustain higher levels of performance than small rewards. If animals that are accustomed to receiving large rewards are unexpectedly switched to a small reward, their performance drops to a level lower even than that sustained by accustomed low reward. This undershoot or 'depression effect' has been seen in alleys (Crespi 1942) and Skinner-boxes (Baltzer and Weiskrantz 1970), and in both apparatuses it is blocked or attenuated by barbiturates and benzodiazepines (Baltzer, Huber, and Weiskrantz 1979; and references in Gray 1977). Differences in the levels of performance sustained by *accustomed* large and small reward, respectively, are not affected by these drugs, so the blockade of the depression effect is not due to a failure to perceive reward size as such.

When animals accustomed to small rewards are unexpectedly switched to large ones, there is an overshoot or 'elation effect' which is symmetrical with the undershoot, although usually smaller and less reliable. The elation effect is also reduced by the anti-anxiety drugs, but to a smaller extent than the depression effect (Rabin 1975; Baltzer *et al.* 1979). This finding has prompted Baltzer *et al.* (1979) to suggest that these drugs, rather than having a restricted antifrustration action, are more adequately described as having an 'emotional flattening action' on responses to change in reward, whether the change is positive or negative. This suggestion raises an issue of obvious importance, but there are too few relevant data to evaluate it further.

2.8. Discrimination learning

A lessened effect of non-reward would be expected to impair discrimination learning, but not necessarily under all conditions. In this connection we must distinguish between simultaneous and successive discrimination tasks. In the former the animal is presented simultaneously with the positive (S+) and negative (S−) stimuli and it must choose between them. There is no reason to suppose that non-reward plays an important role in this kind of discrimination, since the subject can correctly solve the problem by learning simply that the positive stimulus is associated with reward. In a successive discrimination S+ and S− are presented separately, and the animal's task is to respond in the presence of S+ and to refrain from responding in the presence of S−. Thus correct performance depends on inhibiting responding in the presence of the non-rewarded stimulus, as well as associating S+ with reward. If the anti-anxiety drugs attenuate the effects of non-reward, then, we would expect them to impair successive discrimination learning by causing over-responding in the presence of S−, but not to alter simultaneous discrimination learning. This is indeed the pattern of results obtained in both spatial (alley) and non-spatial (Skinner-box) tasks.

There is a more complex variant of the successive discrimination known as a 'conditional discrimination'. An example will bring out the the essential features of this paradigm. It comes from a report by Iwasaki *et al.* (1976), who made an explicit comparison between the effects of chlordiazepoxide on simultaneous and conditional discrimination learning. For this purpose they used a choice-box in which, for the simultaneous task, the rat had to choose between black and grey doors. In the conditional task both doors were the same brightness (black or white) on a given trial, and the animal had to learn to go left when they were one brightness and right when they were the other. Animals injected with saline as a control found the two tasks equally difficult. (Had the two tasks used stimuli of the same brightness, say black and white in both cases, the conditional discrimination would have been harder than the simultaneous one.) Animals injected with chlordiazepoxide were no different from controls on the simultaneous task, but were impaired on the conditional discrimination.

The explanation offered above for the effects of the anti-anxiety drugs on simpler forms of successive discrimination learning is inadequate to account for this result. In a conditional discrimination the animal has to choose trial by trial between competing responses, not choose between responding and not responding, as in other successive discriminations. Thus it is not obvious that one can account for the impairment produced by anti-anxiety drugs simply by the supposition that these agents disinhibit responses suppressed by non-reward.

Simultaneous discriminations share with conditional discriminations the requirement to choose between alternative responses trial by trial. But they differ in two respects: (i) the correct response does not change from trial to trial and consequently (ii) the correct response rapidly develops a stronger excitatory potential than any competing response. In a conditional discrimination, by contrast, the correct response does change from trial to trial, with the consequence that the excitatory potentials of the two competing responses are likely to be roughly equal. Thus, to perform efficiently in a conditional discrimination, the animal must be able to suppress interference from the response which, on a given trial, happens to be incorrect. The fact that the anti-anxiety drugs impair conditional and other successive, but not simultaneous, discriminations, suggests that the mechanisms responsible for the suppression of non-rewarded and interfering responses, respectively, are the same or similar, and that both are sensitive to the action of these drugs.

Although simultaneous discrimination is itself unaffected by anti-anxiety drugs, the reversal of such a discrimination (the old S − becoming S + and *vice versa*) has been shown to be impaired by barbiturates (Caul 1967; Bindra and Reichert 1967). It is unfortunate that more experiments of this kind have not been reported, since, as we shall see, reversal learning is particularly sensitive to the effects of septal and hippocampal lesions (Section 6.22). It is possible to account for the effects of the barbiturates on reversal learning either in terms of a reduced capacity to withhold non-rewarded responses (which would retard extinction of the response to the old S +), or in terms of a reduced capacity to suppress interfering responses (since the strengths of the tendencies to respond to the two stimuli will be about equal during at least part of the period of reversal training). These two accounts, of course, are not mutually exclusive.

This analysis of the effects of the anti-anxiety drugs on discrimination learning is not limited to the case in which correct responses are followed by reward. The same patterns hold if the correct response is reinforced by shock avoidance, as for example in the Iwasaki *et al.* (1976) experiment on conditional discrimination, or shock escape, as in Bindra and Reichert's (1967) experiment on reversal learning. The fact that there is no need to distinguish between positive and negative reinforcement for the correct response is in accord with the assumption (Chapter 1) that active avoidance and escape depend on the same mechanisms as rewarded approach learning.

2.9 Responses elicited by frustrative non-reward

Just as passive avoidance is controlled by both primary punishment and secondary punishing stimuli, so the behaviour considered in the last two sections results from exposure to both primary non-reward and secondary frustrative stimuli. In the case of experiments using aversive reinforcement it was possible to show that the anti-anxiety drugs impair the control of behaviour by secondary punishing stimuli but not the effects of primary punishment (Sections 2.4–2.6). To demonstrate a similar dissociation is experimentally much harder in the case of non-reward. None the less, the available data suggest that the unconditioned effects of non-reward, like those of punishment, are immune to the influence of the anti-anxiety drugs.

The best evidence for this conclusion is the failure of these drugs to influence the 'frustration effect' in the double runway (Amsel and Roussel 1952). In this experiment the rat is run in two sequential alleys with reward always available in the second goal-box but only sometimes in the first. It is found that the animal runs faster in the second alley after non-reward in the first goal-box than after reward there; and suitable control groups show that this effect is due to an increase in running speed elicited by non-reward rather than a reduction in running speed produced by reward. The frustration effect is usually interpreted as reflecting an increased level of arousal directly produced by non-reward, though other interpretations are possible (Gray 1975, p. 283). Several experiments have now shown that sodium amylobarbitone, which so powerfully antagonizes the effects of non-reward considered in the previous two sections, has no influence on the double-runway frustration effect (for references, see Gray 1977).

If one trains groups of rats with continuous or partial reinforcement in the double runway and subsequently extinguishes them in the first alley only, it is possible to study the frustration effect and the PREE in the same animals. Gray and Dudderidge (1971) made use of this fact to demonstrate the different sensitivity of these two phenomena to the action of sodium amylobarbitone. During training half the animals were given this drug and half saline; during extinction, no animals were drugged. The drug did not alter the frustration effect during training, but it attenuated the PREE (i.e. resistance to extinction was reduced in the animals trained on PRF). Note that the frustration effect is measured at a point in time *after* the occurrence of non-reward, whereas the PREE is measured in the first alley in anticipation of non-reward. Thus this pattern of results is consistent with the hypothesis (Gray 1967, 1977) that sodium amylobarbitone has no effect on responses elicited by the event of non-reward itself, but reduces responses controlled by conditioned frustrative stimuli (i.e. those constituting the startbox and stem of the first alley, and which presumably control the behaviour of running towards the first goal-box).

A similar set of observations has been reported by Soubrié, Thiébot, Simon, and Boissier (1978a). These workers accustomed rats to drink from a bottle and then subjected them to an extinction test (the bottle empty). Shortly after, the animal was again given a full waterbottle. This led to an increased water intake relative to occasions when drinking was not preceded by the extinction test. The authors interpret this phenomenon along the lines of the Amsel and Roussel frustration effect, that is, as reflecting an increased level of arousal produced by primary non-reward. If this interpretation is correct, we would not expect the phenomenon to be altered by administration of anti-anxiety drugs. This is indeed what Soubrié *et al.* (1978a) found, using several benzodiazepines, meprobamate, and sodium amylobarbitone; only a rather high dose of chlordiazepoxide (16 mg kg^{-1}) had any effect. Soubrié *et al.* (1978a) also observed the effects of these drugs during the extinction test. They all increased resistance to extinction, i.e. the amount of licking at the empty bottle. Thus, as in Gray and Dudderidge's (1971) experiment, there was a dissociation between behaviour measured in advance of non-reward (impaired by by the anti-anxiety drugs) and behaviour measured after non-reward (unaffected).

One cannot measure a flinch or jump response to non-reward, as one can to shock (Section 2.6), but it is possible to measure the aggressive response elicited by non-reward (e.g. Gallup 1965; Azrin 1967). Thus Miczek and Barry (1977) investigated the effect of alcohol on the aggressive behaviour of pairs of male rats induced by the omission of an accustomed food reward. The results of this experiment exactly paralleled the results of similar experiments which have examined the effect of alcohol on aggression induced by electric shock (Weitz 1974): a low dose of the drug (0.5 g kg^{-1}) facilitated aggression whereas higher doses (1–1.5 g kg^{-1}) suppressed it. The enhanced aggression seen at the lower dose is inconsistent with the hypothesis that the anti-anxiety drugs weaken the impact of primary non-reward; while the parallel effects of the drug on aggression elicited by punishment and non-reward, respectively, support the hypothesis that these two unconditioned events act upon a common system (Chapter 1; and Gray 1975). It would be valuable to have similar data on other anti-anxiety drugs, especially since alcohol is the one which has been least studied in other situations involving non-reward.

More indirect evidence for the immunity of responses elicited by non-reward to the influence of the anti-anxiety drugs comes from a series of studies of their effects on the PREE as a function of intertrial interval (ITI) and number of training trials. The importance of these parameters stems from the different theories of the PREE proposed by Amsel (1962) and Capaldi (1967).

A detailed discussion of these theories can be found in Mackintosh (1974). Briefly, Capaldi has suggested that an animal trained in the alley on a PRF schedule learns on reward trials to run in the presence of some kind of trace of non-reward experienced on a preceding non-rewarded trial. Resistance to extinction is then increased because the PRF-trained animal encounters these same traces of non-reward during extinction. At short ITIs (seconds or minutes) the trace postulated by Capaldi can be regarded as a direct after-effect of non-reward, of a kind which (if the arguments pursued in this section are correct) is unaffected by the anti-anxiety drugs. At longer ITI's (e.g. 24 hours) Capaldi treats the trace as a memory of non-reward. It is still controversial whether such long-lasting memories of non-reward play a role in the determination of the PREE at long ITIs. If they do, it is almost certainly a weak one compared to other processes involved, and we shall therefore ignore it here. Amsel's theory of the PREE also supposes that PRF-trained animals learn to run in the presence of stimuli that are related to non-reward, but these are now seen as internal stimuli characteristic of the state of conditioned frustration elicited by secondary frustrative stimuli (e.g. those that make up the start-box and stem of the runway and which precede non-reward in the goal-box). The increased resistance to extinction then follows along much the same lines as it does in Capaldi's theory. There is no reason to regard the two theories as mutually exclusive. On the contrary, Capaldi's after-effect of non-reward can readily be identified with the primary state of frustration which Amsel supposes to be directly elicited by non-reward; and the PRF-trained rat might well learn to run in the presence both of traces of primary frustration from the previous trial and stimuli characteristic of conditioned frustration elicited during the current trial.

The available evidence suggests, in fact, that both theories are tenable, but that their optimal range of application is different (Mackintosh 1974; Feldon *et al.* 1979). It seems probable that Capaldi's theory holds better at short ITIs and Amsel's at long. This follows from the fact that after-effects of non-reward decline in strength as the ITI increases, while there are neither theoretical nor empirical grounds for believing that conditioned frustration differs as a function of ITI. Rather more equivocally, there is evidence that, at short ITIs, the contribution of the processes postulated by Amsel grows as the number of training trials increases.

If these arguments are correct, there are two ways to produce a PREE, one (Capaldi's) dependent on after-effects directly elicited by non-reward, the other (Amsel's) dependent on conditioned frustration elicited by secondary frustrative stimuli. Thus, if the anti-anxiety drugs affect responses to secondary frustrative stimuli but not responses to the primary event of non-reward, we would expect them to have a more complete effect on the PREE, the closer the experimental conditions approximate to those that favour Amsel's process over Capaldi's. In particular, we would expect a large effect of the anti-anxiety drugs on the PREE when the ITI is long. This prediction has been verified for sodium amylobarbitone by Feldon *et al.* (1979) and for chlordiazepoxide by Feldon and Gray (1981a). Conversely, it would be expected that the anti-anxiety drugs would have no effect on the PREE at short ITIs with few training trials (less than about 10). This prediction has been verified for sodium amylobarbitone by Ziff and Capaldi (1971). When the ITI is short but the number of training trials relatively large (40–100), mixed and intermediate effects are observed (see references in Feldon *et al.* 1979), as would again be expected.

2.10. Responses to novelty

Responses to novelty have played a substantial role in investigations of individual differences in fearfulness and their genetic (Broadhurst 1960), ontogenetic (Levine 1962), and hormonal (Gray 1971*b*) bases (see Gray 1971*a*, for a review). In the open-field test, for example, the animal is taken from its home cage and placed in a large arena, usually brightly lit and sometimes located under a source of loud noise. Measures are taken of its exploratory behaviour (ambulation, and rearing on the hind legs) and of its level of defecation and urination. There is good evidence that high fearfulness is accompanied by high defecation scores (Broadhurst 1960, 1975; Gray 1971*a*, 1979*a*). The relation between ambulation and fearulness is more complex. Apparently, ambulation is positively related to fearfulness when the animal is first exposed to the open field, but subsequently this relation becomes negative. Thus Whimbey and Denenberg (1967) tested rats for a few minutes a day for five days in the open field and took a variety of measures of behaviour which were then factor analysed (Harman 1960). Two factors were extracted, one apparently related to fearfulness, the other to activity or exploration. Ambulation on the first day of testing loaded positively on the fearfulness factor, but on subsequent days its loading was negative. On all days of testing ambulation also loaded positively on the exploration factor. Thus ambulation in the open field is a complex measure of both exploratory activity and fearfulness (at least), and the relation it bears to other measures of fear is not constant. When ambulation is measured over a fairly long time of testing, and the kind of detailed breakdown of scores over time undertaken by Whimbey and Deneberg (1967) is not reported, the overall score is usually negatively related to fear. Thus, out of 26 reported correlations between ambulation and defecation in the open field reviewed by Archer (1973) for the rat, 22 were negative; and out of nine such correlations for the mouse, seven were negative.

With this background, then, we would expect a drug that reduces fear to decrease defecation and, in general, to increase ambulation; but the latter change should be composed of a decrease in ambulation during the first few minutes of testing, followed by an increase subsequently. The fate suffered by these predictions when tested against the data on the anti-anxiety drugs is mixed.

With regard to defecation, there are few usable data. Chlordiazepoxide reduces defecation and urination in the open field (Fukuda and Iwahara 1974), as we would expect, but it does so also in the home cage (Oishi *et al.* 1972), so this result cannot be attributed to an effect specifically on fear. McNaughton (1977) failed to produce consistent changes in open-field defecation with sodium amylobarbitone, but he used a test which was kept deliberately unstressful, and the control defecation scores were very low. The second prediction, that overall ambulation should be increased, is strongly supported by data on both the benzodiazepines and the barbiturates obtained in several test situations, including the open field (see Simon and Soubrié 1979, for a review). Furthermore, this increase is not seen if the environment is familiar (Marriott and Spencer 1965; Simon and Soubrié 1979), nor if the open field is relatively unstressful, lacking bright lights or loud noise (N. McNaughton, personal communication), suggesting that it is indeed due to an anti-anxiety effect. If, however, the drug effect is examined as a function of test duration, we find a pattern of results exactly contrary to prediction: ambulation is increased *only* in the first two or three minutes in the open field and several other test situations (Iwahara and Sakama 1972; Fukuda and Iwahara 1974; Rushton and Steinberg 1966; Boissier and Simon 1969; Soubrié, Thiébot, Simon, and Boissier 1977).

A second contradiction between data on individual differences in fearfulness and those on the anti-anxiety drugs concerns the rearing response. Maudsley Nonreactive rats rear more than Reactives (Gray 1965; Broadhurst 1975) and females more than males (Gray 1965; Hughes and Symes 1972); so, following arguments used when we discussed two-way active avoidance (Section 2.5), we might predict that the anti-anxiety drugs will increase rearing. The data clearly support the opposite conclusion: these drugs reliably and specifically reduce rearing (Thiébot *et al.* 1973, 1976). As with ambulation, any tendency for the drugs to increase rearing is restricted to the first few minutes of the test (Fukuda and Iwahara 1974); but this tendency is weak and often absent (Iwahara and Sakama 1972), and it is followed by a substantial fall in rearing scores which is not paralleled by a fall in ambulation unless high doses are used (Thiébot *et al.* 1976).

It is possible that these contradictions between data on individual differences and drugs, respectively, arise from the use of different test procedures. N. McNaughton (personal communication) has obtained increased rearing and ambulation after administration of sodium amylobarbitone to rats tested in a stressed open field (bright lights and loud noise), but reduced rearing and only inconsistent changes in ambulation when the rats were tested in an unstressed open field. Only a direct comparison between the effects of individual differences in fearfulness and those of the anti-anxiety drugs on exploratory behaviour tested under identical conditions could resolve this point; and, as far as I know, such a comparison has not been reported. A further, and likely, possibility is that the effects of the anti-anxiety drugs on ambulation and rearing are confounded by changes in motor coordination, which are not involved when fearfulness is manipulated by selective breeding or choice of sex. Note in this connection that rearing is apparently more sensitive than ambulation to the depressant effects of the anti-anxiety drugs on motor coordination (Thiébot *et al.* 1973, 1976).

A further test of exploratory behaviour produces results which are more in accord with expectations derived from the literature on individual differences. This is the emergence test, in which the time to emerge from a relatively familiar to an unfamiliar environment is shorter both in rats bred for low fearfulness and in females relative to males (Gray 1971*a*). As expected from this pattern of results, emergence time is also shortened by administration of benzodiazepines (Simon and Soubrié 1979).

Ambulation, rearing, and emergence time are complex functions of fearfulness, directed exploratory behaviour, and general activity. Thus it is difficult to deduce from these measures anything about the way in which the animal absorbs information about the novel environment to which it is exposed. One way to approach this problem is to measure the exploratory behaviour that is evoked by discrete novel elements in the environment (as distinct from locomotion in a generally novel environment). Behaviour of this kind is generally decreased by the anti-anxiety drugs.

Hughes (1972; Hughes and Syme 1972; Hughes and Greig 1975), for example, put rats into one half of a two-compartment box, then removed them and injected them with chlordiazepoxide or placebo before returning them to the apparatus with both halves now open. The drug reduced entries into the novel side of the box even though it increased overall locomotion. In a similar experiment with sodium amylobarbitone, Ison, Glass, and Bohmer (1966) placed rats in the stem of a T-maze separated by glass partitions from the two arms, of which one was black and one white. After three minutes the rat was removed, one of the arms was changed so that they were both now the same brightness (black or white), and the rat returned to the stem of the maze. As in other experiments using this technique, normal rats chose to enter the changed arm about 75 per cent of the time; the rats drugged with sodium amylobarbitone chose at random. This finding may be related to the blockade of spontaneous alternation that has been reported for several anti-anxiety drugs (Gray 1977; Douglas and Truncer 1976). In this procedure the animal is simply placed in the stem of a T-maze and allowed to explore freely. The first choice of arm (left or right) is recorded, and the procedure repeated. On the second trial about 70 to 80 per cent of normal animals typically choose the arm opposite to the one chosen on the first trial; drugged animals choose at random. Alternation in normal animals is in part due to a tendency to vary the arm chosen ('stimulus alternation') and in part to a tendency to vary the direction of body turn ('response alternation'). It is possible to distinguish between these two tendencies by comparing behaviour in the T-maze with that in a cross-shaped maze in which the animal is alternately placed at opposite ends of one piece of the cross. When this is done, it transpires that different experimental treatments can reduce stimulus alternation, response alternation, or both. An analysis along these lines of the action of sodium amylobarbitone shows that it affects only response alternation (McNaughton and Feldon 1980).

A lone experiment by McGonigle *et al.* (1967) has taken this type of analysis further by measuring the degree to which a drugged animal *learns* about a novel element in its environment. These workers trained rats on a random 50 per cent PRF schedule to choose the positive cue (black or white) in a choice-box, choice of the negative cue never being rewarded. The rats were then shifted to a combined-cue discrimination (black vs. white and horizontal vs. vertical stripes, both cues being presented together) in which the old positive cue remained positive. During this stage of the experiment half the animals received sodium amylobarbitone and half placebo. Finally, transfer tests were conducted with only horizontal vs. vertical stripes and no drug. Controls chose correctly on 81 per cent of these transfer trials, but the animals that had received the drug showed no learning about the novel cue. Notice that the task was a simultaneous discrimination, which (Section 2.8) is normally unaffected by the anti-anxiety drugs. We may reasonably suppose, therefore, that the critical element was the requirement that the animal switch control of its behaviour to the novel cue.

It is unfortunate that other workers have not followed the lead set by McGonigle *et al.* (1967). There is a rich theoretical and experimental literature on the role of attention in animal learning (Sutherland and Mackintosh 1971), from which many tests of learning about novel cues similar to theirs might easily be derived. Instead there have been several attempts to deduce something about the efficiency of stimulus analysis from the rate at which motor responses elicited by novel environments habituate. Experiments along these lines have shown that habituation rate is increased, in the sense that there is a steeper decline in locomotion as the test continues in the drugged animals (Iwahara and Sakama 1972; Fukuda and Iwahara 1974; Rushton and Steinberg 1966). This, of course, is a necessary consequence of the fact, mentioned above, that the anti-anxiety drugs increase locomotor behaviour differentially in the initial phase of an animal's exposure to a novel environment. But it is not clear what, if anything, this tells us about the processsing of information concerning the novel environment. Other, more elaborate experiments based upon the same principle allow of no clearer interpretation, and have in any case produced contradictory results (Ahtee and Shillito 1970; Nolan and Parkes 1973; File 1976).

The findings reviewed in this section are less clearcut and less readily interpretable than those summarized earlier in this chapter. This is perhaps because experiments in this field have been designed with less attention to theory than has been the case when paradigms closer to the heart of learning theory have been used. In trying to bring some order into the data it is necessary to distinguish between two kinds of effect of novelty.

In the first instance, novel stimuli may act simply as general stressors. Thus a bright light in Broadhurst's (1960) open-field test is not necessarily any more novel than a dim one, but it suppresses ambulation to a greater extent. Inhibitory effects of this kind can be seen in many test situations. Thus an unfamiliar situation suppresses eating, drinking, and social interaction; like open-field ambulation, the suppression of social interaction is greater the brighter the illumination (File 1980). All these effects are reversed by the anti-anxiety drugs (Simon and Soubrié 1979; Soubrié *et al.* 1975, 1976; Thiébot *et al.* 1979; File 1980). From this point of view, novelty is one element among others that increase the general level of fear. Often, but not invariably, one consequence of an increased level of fear is an inhibition of motor behaviour, which in the extreme takes the form of freezing. The anti-anxiety drugs counteract the effects of the increased level of fear and thus often, but not invariably, disinhibit behaviour, including exploratory behaviour. The major exception to this generalization is rearing, which, for unknown reasons, is reliably reduced by the anti-anxiety drugs.

The second way in which novel stimuli act is by drawing the animal's attention directly to themselves. The anti-anxiety drugs appear to impair this process, although interpretable data are scarce. The drugged animal devotes less specific exploratory behaviour to the novel elements in its environment, and probably learns less about them.

In both cases, then, the anti-anxiety drugs generally block the behavioural effects of novelty.

2.11. Conclusion: the action of the anti-anxiety drugs

We have now completed this behavioural profile of the anti-anxiety drugs. The extent to which it is applicable to all of these drugs is remarkable (although, to be sure, there are lacunae in the data). The only major qualifications that it has been necessary to make with respect to particular drugs concern the benzodiazepines, which appear to slow running speed and sometimes to antagonize aggressive behaviour in a manner that is not characteristic of the other anti-anxiety drugs. These similarities between the different classes of anti-anxiety drugs strongly imply that they act upon a common neural mechanism.

Central to this profile is the impairment produced by the anti-anxiety drugs in passive avoidance behaviour. This then gives rise to the improvement seen in two-way active avoidance and probably also to the improvement in active avoidance in the Skinner-box. The impairment in passive avoidance is not due to a loss of effectiveness of the punishing UCS itself. Thus it must reflect some change in the behavioural control exercised by secondary punishing stimuli. This change takes place whether these stimuli are established by association with response-contingent or response-independent aversive UCSs; but the process of classical conditioning is not itself affected by the anti-anxiety drugs. Thus we may conclude that the anti-anxiety drugs reduce the expression of conditioned fear (that is, responses to secondary punishing stimuli). Although the association whose expression is blocked in this way is not instrumental (i.e. does not depend on response contingencies), it does appear to depend on the joint occurrence of an aversive UCS and an ongoing motor response, since the anti-anxiety drugs attenuate on-the-baseline but probably not off-the-baseline conditioned suppression. This is a problem to which we shall return in Chapter 10.

A similar picture emerges when we consider the effects of the anti-anxiety drugs on responses to non-reward. In general such responses are reduced or blocked completely by these drugs. It is probable that, in the same way that unconditioned responses to painful UCSs are unaffected by the anti-anxiety drugs, so also are unconditioned responses elicited by non-reward. The strongest evidence for this conclusion comes from the immunity of the double-runway frustration effect to these drugs. Thus, as in the case of paradigms using painful stimuli, the effects of the anti-anxiety drugs are due to an alteration in the control of behaviour by secondary aversive stimuli. There are no reported experiments which allow one to judge whether the anti-anxiety drugs alter the conditioning process whereby secondary frustrative stimuli are formed. But there is clear evidence that these drugs can impair the control over behaviour exercised by such stimuli after they have been formed. Feldon *et al.* (1979), for example, trained rats in the alley on a single alternating schedule of reward and non-reward, with the consequence that the animals learned to run fast on rewarded trials and slow on non-rewarded trials ('patterned running'). After they had been trained for over 700 trials, and had displayed consistent patterned running for over 300 trials, the rats were injected with sodium amylobarbitone. As expected, this drug increased running speed on non-rewarded trials (presumably by reducing the inhibitory control exercised by secondary frustrative stimuli) without altering running speeds on rewarded trials.

Finally, as we saw in the previous section, the anti-anxiety drugs attenuate the behavioural effects of novelty, whether these take the form of inhibiting ongoing behaviour or the elicitation of specific investigatory responses.

Thus the anti-anxiety drugs attenuate responses to secondary punishing stimuli, secondary frustrative stimuli, and novel stimuli. Since these three classes of stimuli are all adequate inputs to the behavioural inhibition system as defined by Gray (1975) and in Chapter 1, we may summarize the behavioural effects of the anti-anxiety drugs most succinctly by saying that these agents *impair the functioning of the behavioural inhibition system.*

This formulation is also consistent with what the anti-anxiety drugs do *not* do: they do not alter behaviour that is controlled by reward or by non-punishment (as in escape and active avoidance), stimuli that *ex hypothesi* do not act upon the behavioural inhibition system. According to the theory outlined in Chapter 1, escape and active avoidance are mediated by the same mechanism that produces rewarded approach behaviour. It is consistent with this theory that the anti-anxiety drugs do not affect either kind of behaviour. The role of aversive conditioning, on this view, is to establish a dangerous environment or set of stimuli by comparison with which a safe environment or set of stimuli can be recognized. Active avoidance is itself then reinforced by attainment of these safety signals (Gray 1975, Chapter 10). Provided, therefore, that the process of fear conditioning is sufficiently intact for the set of danger signals to be established — and we have seen that it is — there is no reason to expect the anti-anxiety drugs to impair active avoidance behaviour.

In the previous chapter I listed the outputs of the behavioural inhibition system as inhibition of ongoing behaviour, increased attention to novel features of the environment, and increased level of arousal. Does the impairment in the functioning of the behavioural inhibition system produced by the anti-anxiety drugs extend to all three of these outputs?

It will be clear by now that the anti-anxiety drugs lift behavioural inhibition when this is produced by any of the adequate inputs to the behavioural inhibition system. We saw instances of this in connection with secondary punishing stimuli (alleviation of passive avoidance or on-the-baseline conditioned suppression), secondary frustrative stimuli (increased resistance to extinction), and novelty (disinhibition of exploratory behaviour or social interaction). Response suppression caused by other stimuli is not alleviated by the anti-anxiety drugs. Thus Miczek (1973) compared the effects of chlordiazepoxide on the on-the-baseline conditioned suppression produced by a signal for shock and by a signal for free food, respectively; the drug alleviated the former but not the latter.

Attention has been studied only in connection with novelty; although the use by McGonigle *et al.* (1967) of a partial reinforcement schedule (see Section 2.10) was no accident, since it is known (Sutherland and Mackintosh 1971) that non-reward increases the spread of attention. This problem requires much more research, but the available data are consistent with the view that the anti-anxiety drugs decrease the spread of attention otherwise produced by stimuli which act upon the behavioural inhibition system.

There are several examples of a blockade by the anti-anxiety drugs of the increment in level of arousal which has been attributed to the functioning of the behavioural inhibition system, but this too is a neglected problem. In part this is because the concept of arousal is much less firmly embedded in animal learning theory than in human experimental psychology (e.g. Gray 1964a; Eysenck 1967; Broadbent 1971), so that there are few experimental paradigms which unambiguously address this issue. One paradigm which comes close to this ideal is the partial reinforcement acquisition effect (Section 2.7); this has been explicitly treated as reflecting an increased level of arousal arising from exposure to secondary frustrative stimuli (Amsel 1962; Gray and Smith 1969). As we have seen, it is blocked by several anti-anxiety drugs. The potentiation of the startle reflex which may be produced by preceding the startle stimulus by either a secondary punishing (Brown 1961) or a secondary frustrative (Wagner 1963) stimulus is a second example. As we saw in Section 2.3, the potentiation produced by a secondary punishing stimulus has been reported to be blocked by both benzodiazepines and barbiturates (M. Davis 1979; Chi 1965). A further example comes from an experiment by Sanger and Blackman (1976), who paired a CS with a shock UCS in an on-the-baseline paradigm, but with a DRL schedule as the baseline instead of the commonly used VI. On this schedule an aversive CS produces, not conditioned suppression, but an acceleration of the low rates of response normally maintained by a DRL schedule (Blackman 1968). This conditioned acceleration was attenuated by chlordiazepoxide (Sanger and Blackman 1976), as it is also by sodium amylobarbitone (De Villiers, Dent, and Gray, unpublished). A final example depends on the use of a novel stimulus. Simon *et al.* (1968) used a puff of air to increase the exploratory activity of mice in a box; this increased activity was diminished by diazepam at doses which did not affect the exploratory behaviour of animals not subjected to air puffs.

Although these last two examples (Sanger and Blackman 1976; Simon *et al.* 1968) have not been so well analysed theoretically as the partial reinforcement acquisition effect and the potentiated startle response, these results are sufficiently consistent with one another for us to conclude that the anti-anxiety drugs block the arousing effects of all three classes of input to the behavioural inhibition system.

These findings also make it clear that the changes produced by the anti-anxiety drugs in motor behaviour are not exclusively disinhibitory. Rather, they counteract whatever is the effect of a secondary aversive or a novel stimulus: if the stimulus suppresses behaviour, the anti-anxiety drugs facilitate it; if the stimulus facilitates behaviour, the anti-anxiety drugs suppress it. This pattern of findings rules out an action directly on motor systems.

Other data rule out an action on perceptual systems. As we have seen (Section 2.8), the anti-anxiety drugs do not produce any impairment in discrimination learning, provided the discriminanda are presented simultaneously, not successively. Since responses directly elicited by painful stimuli are also not impaired, we must suppose that the perception of pain is unaltered. It is less straightforward to conclude that the perception of non-reward is unaltered, but the effects of the anti-anxiety drugs on the Crespi (1942) depression effect and its operant analogue (Baltzer and

Weiskrantz 1970) strongly suggest that this is so. As described in Section 2.7, these drugs attenuate the undershoot that is produced by an unexpected change from high to low reward; but the drugged animals maintain the same differential as controls between the speeds or rates of responses reinforced by large and small *expected* rewards, respectively (Rosen, Glass, and Ison 1967; Ridgers and Gray 1973).

The anti-anxiety drugs, then, do not act directly on motor or perceptual systems; nor, as we saw above, do they change the capacity for learning or conditioning as such. Formally, their effects are well described by the formula we have already used: they impair the functioning of the behavioural inhibition system (Fig. 1.1); and this description applies as well to the outputs of the system as to its inputs. Informally, the description that seems to apply best is that of a change in mood or disposition. The drugged animal cares less about threats of punishment, omens of failure, or disappointment, or the uncertainties of a novel environment. This description is surely one that applies also to people who have drunk a glass of whisky or swallowed a Valium. Thus it is reasonable to conclude that *these drugs reduce anxiety in animals as in man.*

I have largely described experimental tasks in this chapter with reference to the rat, both because it is the most widely used species in this type of research and because, from a theoretical point of view, it is the one for which the most interesting tasks have usually been designed. But this should not mislead the reader into thinking that all of the data have been gathered with rats. On the contrary, the species that have served in these experiments include fish, birds, mice, cats, dogs, pigs, and monkeys. It is a striking feature of the data (Gray 1977) that, in spite of this diversity of experimental subjects, there is virtually no need to qualify any of the conclusions reached with respect to species. Furthermore, there is no sign of change, qualitative or even quantitative, in the nature of anti-anxiety drug action as one approaches, phylogenetically speaking, our own species. This implies that the substrate upon which the anti-anxiety drugs act is phylogenetically very old, old enough to be present (so far as we know) in all contemporary mammalian species and perhaps even in all vertebrates, since birds and fish apparently respond to anti-anxiety drugs in much the same way as rats and monkeys. This conclusion, based on behavioural experiments, is supported by recent studies of the benzodiazepine receptor, which also appears to be generally present in the brains of vertebrates, including fish (Nielsen, Braestrup, and Squires 1978).

From these data, two inferences can be drawn. First, if the action of the anti-anxiety drugs in these diverse species is to reduce anxiety (and the conclusions we have reached in this chapter strongly suggest that it is), it follows that anxiety itself is phylogenetically very old. This at once rules out of court any attempt to explain human anxiety in terms that are specific to man (by recourse, say, to the vagaries of the Oedipus complex), let alone specific to the pressures of modern life. Second, we now have an important clue as to the brain structures which mediate anxiety and on which the anti-anxiety drugs act. These must include as major components structures which are common at least to most mammals, rather than structures (such as the cerebral cortex) which have achieved particular prominence only in man or the other primates; although this does not necessarily mean that phylogenetically more recent structures play no role in anxiety among creatures that possess them (see Chapter 13).

We may conclude, then, that there is much in common between human anxiety and the anxiety experienced by a rat or a mouse, enough at any rate for it to be reasonable to search in the brains of these small creatures for the neural mechanisms that mediate anxiety. In conducting this search, as we shall in the next few chapters, the behavioural effects of the anti-anxiety drugs described above will be our most important guide.

3

The septo-hippocampal system: anatomy

In the previous chapters the behavioural inhibition system has been specified in purely functional terms. We now start upon the search for structures in the brain with functions corresponding to those attributed to this system. It is possible, of course, that nothing in the real brain corresponds to a system deduced in this way from behavioural and psychopharmacological data. In that case, we shall have to conclude that our deductions so far have been in error. If, however, our search is successful, the theory which guided this search will be greatly strengthened. A more likely outcome is that we shall find structures whose functions correspond in part, but not entirely, to those of the behavioural inhibition system. In that case, there will be a number of options; but these are better left until we have seen how close a fit can be made between psychological theory and neural tissue.

The centrepiece of our search will be the septo-hippocampal system, that is, the hippocampal formation (hippocampus proper, dentate gyrus, and subicular cortex), the septal area, their interconnections, and the afferent and efferent pathways which relate them to other parts of the brain. The main reason for this choice is the remarkable parallel that exists between the behavioural effects of lesions to the septal area and hippocampal formation, on the one hand, and those of the anti-anxiety drugs, on the other. We shall consider this parallel in detail in Chapter 6. But we must first learn something of the anatomy and physiology of the septo-hippocampal system. That is the business of this and the next chapter.

As we saw in Chapter 2, it is unlikely that the anti-anxiety drugs act directly on motor or sensory systems. Nor is their action completely non-specific; on the contrary, their effects depend in a remarkably precise manner on the type of reinforcement controlling behaviour and the mode in which this control is exercised. Thus one cannot capture the action of the anti-anxiety drugs by speaking of a change in the general level of alertness or arousal. This is an important conclusion, since it was at one time thought that the barbiturates acted as general 'depressant' drugs (a term still found in textbooks of pharmacology), reducing all forms of behaviour indiscriminately. Correspondingly, the chief site of action of these drugs was thought to lie in the ascending reticular activating system of the midbrain, a system which apparently plays a critical role in regulating arousal level (Magoun 1963; Gray 1964a). While this hypothesis may be correct with respect to the sedative and anaesthetic effects of relatively large doses of barbiturates, it is clearly inappropriate as an account of the effects reviewed in Chapter 2.

Since the sedative and anaesthetic properties of the benzodiazepines are less pronounced than those of the barbiturates, the 'general depressant' hypothesis is even less attractive as an account of the action of this newer group of anti-anxiety drugs. However, a rather similar hypothesis has recently been advanced, based on research into the physiological mode of action of these drugs. It has been shown that the benzodiazepines, after binding to a specific receptor in the brain, increase the effectiveness of the postsynaptic action of the neurotransmitter, γ-aminobutyric acid (GABA) (Guidotti, Toffano, and Costa 1978; Macdonald and Barker 1978). Although the barbiturates do not bind to this receptor, they also increase the effectiveness of GABA-ergic neural transmission (Ransom and Barker 1976; Barker and Ransom 1978). Thus it has been proposed that anti-anxiety action depends on this facilitation of GABA-ergic transmission (Costa and Greengard 1975). But GABA is found virtually everywhere in the brain, and appears to play a role (inhibitory) at more synapses than any other neurotransmitter (Mandel and DeFeudis 1979). Thus we might expect a drug which generally increases GABA-ergic transmission to have sedative or anticonvulsant properties (as do the benzodiazepines and the barbiturates), but not to produce the very specific behavioural changes we reviewed in the last chapter.

We shall return to the GABA-ergic hypothesis of anti-anxiety action in Chapter 11. For the moment, guided by the behavioural effects of the anti-anxiety drugs, we shall assume that, in searching for a site of anti-anxiety action in the brain, we should not look in the first instance at mechanisms which regulate the general level of arousal, any more than at motor or sensory mechanisms. The septo-hippocampal system fits this negative prescription well. It does not lie on any of the primary sensory routes, with the possible exception of olfaction (Wilson and Steward 1978; Habets *et al.* 1980*a*,*b*), nor on a motor pathway; and while it has close relations with midbrain systems that regulate arousal level, these do not appear to be any closer than those possessed by many other forebrain structures. Over 40 years ago it was proposed by Papez (1937) that the hippocampus is well placed to participate in a neural circuit concerned with the elaboration of emotional experience. Although very different in detail, the present model of hippocampal function starts from the same assumption.

O'Keefe and Nadel (1978) have recently advocated a very different approach to the septo-hippocampal system, stressing its cognitive functions, especially in the analysis of spatial information. We shall have more to say later about their theory and its relation to the one proposed here. But no serious student of septo-hippocampal function should fail to read their forceful and lucid argument for himself, nor will it be possible to examine the present theory critically without doing so. Since these authors have presented a thorough review of the anatomy and electrophysiology of the septo-hippocampal system, there is no need to go into excessive detail here. I shall therefore summarize only those features of septo-hippocampal anatomy (this chapter) and physiology (Chapter 4) which will be essential for the behavioural arguments that follow. For further details, the reader may consult (besides O'Keefe and Nadel, Chapters 3 and 4), the volumes edited by Isaacson and Pribram (1975), DeFrance (1976a), and Elliott and Whelan (1978; see especially the chapter by Swanson).

The anatomy of the septo-hippocampal system

Since most of the behavioural experiments have been performed with rats or other animals (e.g. rabbit, cat, mouse) in which the anatomy of the septo-hippocampal system is similar to that of the rat, I shall concentrate on this group of species. Figure 3.1 shows a photograph of the hippocampal formation and septal area excised from the brain of a rat. This piece of tissue seems to call forth culinary similes. O'Keefe and Nadel (1978) liken its shape to a sausage. I prefer to think of it as a pair of bananas joined at the front. The region where the bananas join is the septal area; *in vivo* it lies near the front of the brain, towards the animal's snout. The two bananas are symmetrical about the midline of the brain; this passes vertically through the middle of the septal area. Because of the complex curvature of the hippocampi (the two bananas when they separate) as they retreat from proximity to the septal area, the usual anatomical distinctions of anterior/posterior, dorsal/ventral, etc., have to be used with caution. Blackstad (1956) has suggested, therefore, that in describing locations along the body of the banana one should use a septo-temporal axis: points close to the septal area lie at the 'septal' pole; points close to the other extremity of the banana (which *in vivo* is deep inside the temporal lobe of the cerebral cortex) lie at the 'temporal' pole. As one goes from the septal to the temporal pole, the hippocampi first rise higher in the brain and then descend; at the same time, they move from the medial location of the septal area to become steadily more lateral. Although, as we shall see, the internal structure of the hippocampal formation is essentially the same throughout its septo-temporal extent, it is often convenient to consider only a portion of the total length of the banana. For this purpose it is useful to distinguish the dorsal hippocampus (the part closest to the septal area and highest in the brain); the hippocampal flexure or arch (where the hippocampus sweeps downward in its most caudal aspect); and the ventral hippocampus (the part furthest from the septal area and deepest in the brain). Notice that, by the time one reaches the ventral hippocampus, movement towards the temporal pole is now in the anterior direction, back again towards the front of the brain.

The fibres which connect the septal area and the hippocampal formation travel in two bundles: the fimbria, which sweeps along the outside edges of the two bananas; and the dorsal fornix (*fornix superior*), which keeps to the midline and courses in the hollow between the two bananas. The two bundles (which probably do not differ functionally) come together close to the septal area, where they are termed the 'fimbria-fornix'. Other fibres connect the hippocampi of the two hemispheres. These

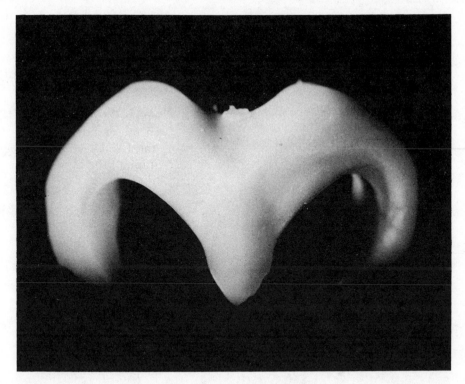

Figure 3.1. The hippocampal formation and septal area dissected from the brain of a rat. (Photograph by J. P. Broad, from Rawlins (1977).)

travel in the ventral and dorsal hippocampal commissures or *psalteria*. The ventrally directed commissural fibres enter the fimbria on one side and cross the midline at the bottom of the fimbria-fornix to join the fimbria on the other side. The smaller dorsal psalterium runs above the top of the hippocampal flexure, at the point where the hippocampus begins to turn down.

The hippocampal formation has a beautifully ordered internal structure which has made it a favourite target for anatomists and physiologists alike. A section transverse to the septo-temporal axis reveals two major interlocking U-shaped rows of large cells which (to mix culinary metaphors) give the appearance of a slice of Swiss roll (Fig. 3.2). If the section is through the dorsal hippocampal formation, the upper U is the hippocampus proper or 'Ammon's horn' (*cornu Ammonis*); the lower U, the dentate gyrus or *fascia dentata*. (The term 'hippocampus' strictly speaking refers only to Ammon's horn; but it is loosely used as a synonym for the entire hippocampal formation, as will already be evident from my own usage.) But, owing to the way the hippocampal banana curves along its septo-temporal extent, when we reach the ventral hippocampal formation

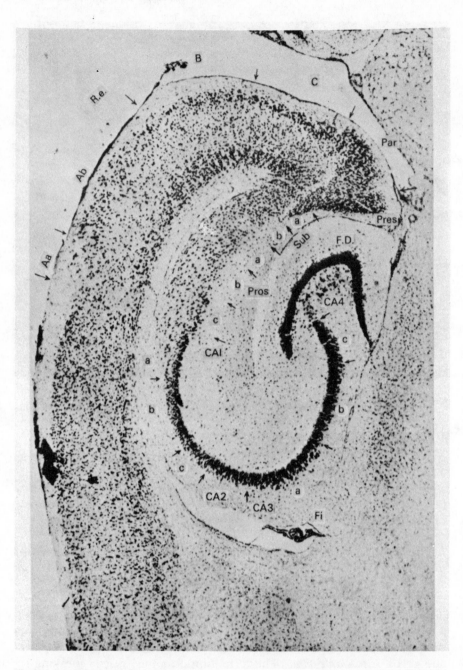

Figure 3.2. Photograph of a horizontal section of the right side of the adult mouse brain as seen from above. The section passes through the posterior arch of the hippocampus and entorhinal cortex (R.e.). Caudal is up. Note the gradual transition from the six-layered entorhinal cortex through the parasubiculum (Par), presubiculum (Pres), subiculum (sub), prosubiculum (Pros), to the three-layered cor-

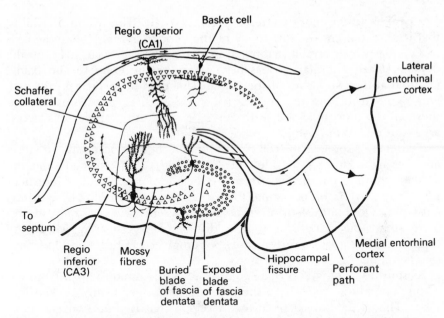

Figure 3.3. Schematic diagram of intrahippocampal connections. Horizontal section through the right hippocampus as in Fig. 3.2 except that caudal is on the right. (From O'Keefe and Nadel (1978).)

these relations are exactly reversed, if we continue to define 'up' and 'down' with respect to the location of the brain inside the skull; that is, the upper U is now the dentate gyrus and the lower U, Ammon's horn. If the transverse section is made at the level of the hippocampal flexure (where it is a horizontal section), Ammon's horn is more anterior, the dentate gyrus more posterior. At all levels the arch of the hippocampal U lies close to the fimbria, the arch of the dentate U furthest from the fimbria.

On the basis of cytoarchitectonics (i.e. cell morphology) further subdivisions are made within the hippocampus. If we follow the hippocampal U round, starting with the tip furthest from the *fascia dentata* (Fig. 3.3), there is first a double row of medium-sized pyramidal cells which define the *regio superior* or CA 1 (for *cornu Ammonis*, field 1). The next major subdivision is the *regio inferior,* consisting of the semicircle of giant pyramidal cells running from the arch of the U to within the dentate gyrus. The *regio inferior* was further subdivided by Lorente de Nó (1934) into CA 2, 3, and 4, but Blackstad (1956) finds no difference between CA 2 and 3;

tex of the hippocampus proper (CA₁–CA₄) and the fascia dentata (F.D.). Lorente de No further subdivided some of these areas (a, b, c). Fi is the fimbria. Nissl stain. (From O'Keefe and Nadel (1978), after Lorente de No (1934).)

CA 4 refers to the more scattered pyramidal cells lying within the hilus, that is, the area enclosed by the U of the dentate gyrus. Unlike the cells of CA 1–4, which are all pyramidal in shape, the cells that make up the dentate U are granular. It has been suggested by O'Keefe and Nadel (1978) that the two halves of the dentate U should be termed the 'buried' and 'exposed' blades, the former lying within the hippocampal U; but there are no morphological differences between the granule cells associated with this distinction.

Examples of some of the cell types found in the hippocampal formation are shown in Fig. 3.4. Besides the CA 1 and CA 3 pyramids and the dentate granule cell, this illustrates the most important kind of interneurone found in the hippocampal formation, the basket cell. These different types of cell, and their afferents and efferents, are packaged so regularly that they give rise to the distinctive layering by which the hippocampal formation can so easily be recognized in histological sections (see Fig. 4.6).

As shown in Fig. 3.2, if one extends the U of Ammon's horn from CA 1, one enters an area where the cells are no longer neatly packed into rows. This is the subicular cortex, a region that is transitional in morphology between the simple cortical structure of the hippocampus and the six-layered neocortical mantle. As we shall see, this area occupies a nodal point in the hippocampal formation, since it is the source of nearly all the output from the septo-hippocampal system. On the basis of cytoarchitectonics, Lorente de Nó (1934) divided this region into the prosubiculum (closest to CA 1), the subiculum proper, and the pre- and parasubiculum (which follow the subiculum as one reaches, and then bends round into, the rhinal sulcus at the top of Fig. 3.2). As shown in Fig. 3.3, the subicular area and *regio superior* of the hippocampus are separated from the dentate gyrus by the hippocampal fissure.

The parasubiculum abuts onto the entorhinal cortex, which is as important an input station to the hippocampal formation as the subicular area is for output. The entorhinal area is part of the neocortex. It too is further subdivided into medial and lateral areas, the former lying next to the parasubiculum within the rhinal sulcus, the latter lying on the exposed surface of the cerebral cortex. The afferents from the entorhinal cortex, both medial and lateral, take a route known as the 'perforant path'; this first travels in the upper layers of the subiculum (near the surface of the hippocampal banana) and then perforates the *regio superior* to innervate the dentate granule cells (Fig. 3.3). Most of the projection is ipsilateral, but there is also a small contralateral contribution.

The interconnections between the different cell fields of the hippocampal formation are as regular as their appearance. For the most part these interconnections are organized in strips or 'lamellae' transverse to the septo-temporal axis of the hippocampus (Andersen, Bliss, and Skrede 1971; Rawlins and Green 1977; Fig. 3.5). The starting point for the pas-

(a)

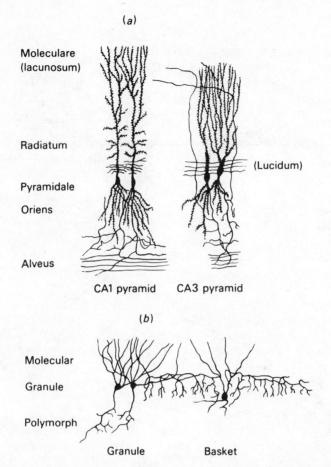

Moleculare
(lacunosum)

Radiatum

Pyramidale

Oriens

Alveus

(Lucidum)

CA1 pyramid   CA3 pyramid

(b)

Molecular

Granule

Polymorph

Granule   Basket

Figure 3.4.(*a*) Examples of CA1 and CA3 pyramidal cells. (After Ramon y Cajal (1955) Fig. 475.) (*b*) Examples of dentate granule cells and a basket cell of Cajal. (After Lorente de No (1934) Fig. 10.) The regular packaging of these cells in the hippocampus gives rise to the distinctive layers whose names are shown to the left (compare Fig. 4.6). (From O'Keefe and Nadel (1978).)

sage of information round a lamellar strip is an input from the entorhinal cortex along the perforant path to the dentate granule cells. The granule cells in turn send impulses along their axons (the 'mossy fibres') to the CA 3 and 4 pyramids. The CA 3 pyramids have bifurcating axons, of which one branch exits from the hippocampus in the fimbria, destined for the septal area, while the other (the 'Schaffer collateral') synapses with the dendrites of the CA 1 pyramidal cells. Finally, the CA 1 pyramids send their axons out of Ammon's horn in the alveus, a sheet of fibres which covers the outside of the hippocampal banana like a gleaming white skin (dorsally in the dorsal hippocampus, ventrally in the ventral hippocam-

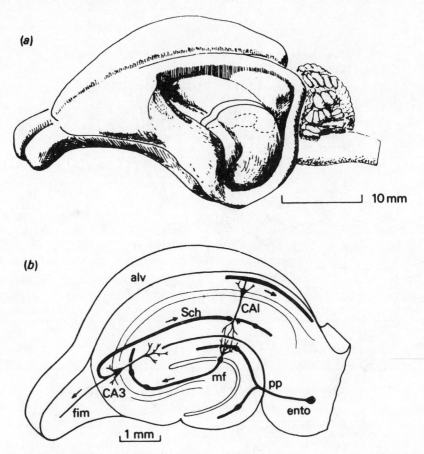

Figure 3.5. Lamellar organization of the hippocampus. (*a*) Lateral view of the rabbit brain with the parietal and temporal neocortex removed to expose the hippocampal formation. The lamellar slice indicated has been presented separately in (*b*) to show the proposed circuitry. alv, alveus; ento, entorhinal cortex; fim, fimbria; pp, perforant path; Sch, Schaffer collateral. (Modified by J. N. P. Rawlins, from Andersen *et al.* (1971).)

pus). It used to be thought that CA 1 was the source of the massive efferent pathway which travels in the fornix. But both electrophysiological (Andersen, Bland, and Dudar 1973) and anatomical (Hjorth-Simonsen 1973; Swanson and Cowan 1975) experiments have now shown that the CA 1 axons are destined for the subiculum (Fig. 3.2), and that it is this region which is the origin of the hippocampal outflow in the fornix.

The flow of information around this circuit, from the entorhinal input to the output along the CA 1 axons, is organized along strictly topographical lines, in the sense that activity that starts in one lamella remains largely confined to that lamella. There is some evidence that this is in part due to an inhibitory influence of one lamella upon adjacent lamellae, perhaps mediated by the basket cells (Stuble, Desmond, and Levy 1978), in a manner reminiscent of lateral inhibition in sensory systems. But, in addition, there are excitatory connections between CA 3 cells in different lamellae (Lebovitz, Dichter, and Spencer 1971; Hjorth-Simonsen 1973; Rawlins and Green 1977); these make up the rather poorly characterized longitudinal association pathway described by Lorente de Nó (1934). Further complication in what is otherwise an essentially unidirectional circuit is the existence of direct projections from the entorhinal cortex to CA 3 and CA 1, bypassing the dentate granule cells (Steward 1976); and return pathways from CA 3 to the dentate gyrus (Zimmer 1971), and from the temporal one-third of fields CA 3 and CA 4 to the entorhinal cortex (Hjorth-Simonsen 1971). CA 3 is also the source of the commissural fibres that connect the hippocampi of the two hemispheres via the ventral and dorsal *psalteria;* these fibres terminate in all major fields (CA 1, CA 3 and the dentate gyrus) of the opposite hemisphere (Gottlieb and Cowan 1973; Segal and Landis 1974). The extensive connections of the CA 3 pyramids would seem to make of these a nodal point of co-ordination for the whole hippocampal circuit: ipsilaterally, they project to CA 1 and the dentate gyrus; contralaterally, they project to both these fields and to CA 3 itself; and they are the source of return pathways to both major sources of input to the hippocampal formation, the entorhinal cortex and the septal area.

The septal area is much smaller than the hippocampal formation and much less regular in its anatomy. It contains a number of different nuclei and is traversed by a variety of different fibre pathways. Although it is in spatial proximity to the hippocampal formation and is easily dissected out together with it (as shown in Fig. 3.1), not all its relations are with the hippocampus. Indeed, the diverse connections of the nuclei found in the septal area make it unlikely that it is a functional unity at all. This has not prevented it from becoming a major target of research in physiological psychology. I fear that the main reason for this, though it has never been stated, is not entirely respectable: owing to the disposition of the structures that bound the septal area, it is rather easy to make reproducible lesions by passing current through an electrode placed there. As shown in Fig. 3.6, the septal area is bounded on either side by the lateral ventricles and, above and below, by two bundles of commissural fibres, the corpus callosum and the anterior commissure (although the septal area extends both anterior and posterior to the crossing of the latter). The electrical properties of these structures limit the spread of current, so that the entire area lying between them, and only that area, can reproducibly be destroyed. If electrical homogeneity were a guarantee of functional unity, this would be a splendid technique; unfortunately, it is not.

The septal area may be regarded as consisting of four major divisions (Swanson and Cowan 1976; Swanson 1978): medial, lateral, ventral, and posterior. Most closely related to the hippocampus are the medial and

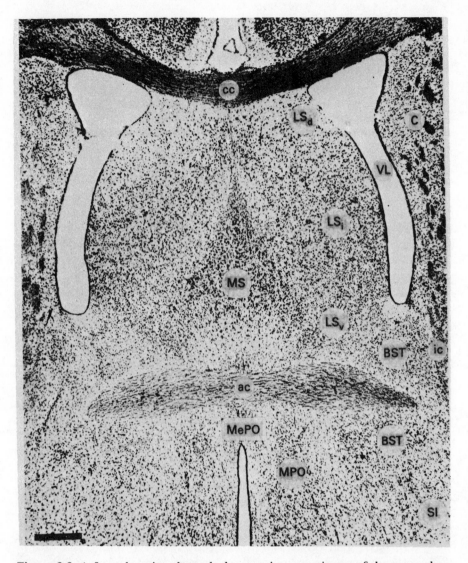

Figure 3.6. A frontal section through the anterior commissure of the rat to show the major divisions of the septal region, except for the posterior group, which lies more caudally in the vicinity of the ventral hippocampal commissure. Kluver–Barrera stain; scale: 0.5 mm. BST, bed nucleus of the stria terminalis; C, caudate nucleus; LS$_d$, LS$_i$, and LS$_v$, dorsal, intermediate, and ventral parts of lateral septal nucleus; MePO, median preoptic nucleus; MPO, medial preoptic area; MS, medial septal nucleus; SI, substantia innominata; VL, lateral ventricle; ac, anterior commissure; cc, corpus callosum. (From Swanson (1978).)

lateral divisions. These are located anteriorly, i.e. furthest away from the hippocampus, from which they are separated by the posterior division.

The medial septal area is further subdivided into the medial septal nucleus dorsally and the nucleus of the diagonal band of Broca ventrally, but this division appears to be somewhat arbitrary. As shown in Fig. 3.7, both these nuclei stain heavily for the enzyme acetylcholinesterase, part of the considerable evidence that they consist largely of cholinergic cells, i.e. cells whose transmitter is acetylcholine. These cells are the origin of an extensive projection to virtually all parts of the hippocampal formation, and also to the entorhinal cortex. This projection travels in both the fimbria and the dorsal fornix; fibres taking the former route terminate in the dorsal hippocampus, those taking the latter route terminate in the ventral hippocampus (Meibach and Siegel 1977a; Rawlins, Feldon, and Gray 1979). Within the medial septal area there is a topographic organization such that, as one proceeds ventrally and laterally, the terminal areas within the hippocampus move septo-temporally (Segal and Landis 1974; Meibach and Siegel 1977a). The medial septal projection to the hippocampal formation is largely ipsilateral, but a small contralateral projection also exists (Mellgren and Srebro 1973; Lynch, Rose, and Gall 1978). As we shall see in the next chapter, this septo-hippocampal projection controls the slow electrical activity known as the hippocampal theta rhythm.

The lateral division of the septal area is further subdivided, on the basis of neuronal size and packing density, into dorsal, intermediate, and ventral parts (Fig. 3.6). All parts of this division receive a projection from the hippocampus. This projection travels in the fimbria, where it is topographically organized such that, the closer the cell of origin to the temporal pole of the hippocampal formation, the more lateral in the fimbria the fibre travels. Its termination in the lateral septal area is also topographically organized: as one proceeds dorsal to ventral in the lateral septum, one encounters terminals from progressively more temporal sites in the hippocampus. Thus the dorsal lateral septal area receives input principally from the dorsal hippocampus, the intermediate lateral septal area principally from the region of the hippocampal flexure, and the ventral lateral septal area principally from the ventral hippocampus (Meibach and Siegel 1977b; Swanson and Cowan 1977). The majority of these terminals have their cells of origin in CA 3. However, it appears that some CA 1 cells also project to the septal area although there is disagreement on this point between anatomical and physiological data (see the discussion in Elliott and Whelan 1978, pp. 46–7 and 138–41). There is also controversy as to whether any hippocampal fibres terminate in the medial, rather than the lateral, septal area (Elliott and Whelan, *loc. cit.*), and whether any of them reach the septal area by way of the dorsal fornix in addition to the well-known route in the fimbria (Meibach and Siegel 1977b). In addition to its hippocampal afferents, the lateral septal area

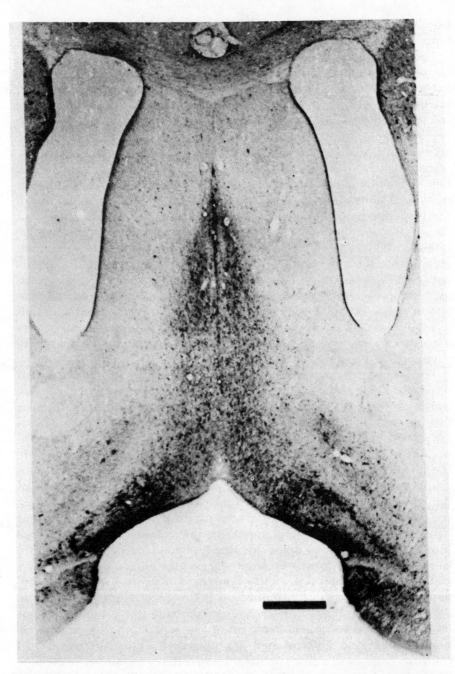

Figure 3.7. Low-power photomicrograph of the septum stained by AChE histo-chemistry in a rat previously treated with diisopropylfluorophosphate. At this co-ronal level the various AChE-positive cell types appear in separate fields. The cells of the central portion of the medial septal nucleus (MSN) are noticeably more

receives a projection from the subicular area. This is topographically organized in the same way as the hippocampal projection, that is, the septo-temporal axis along the subiculum corresponds to a dorsal–ventral axis in the lateral septal area. Like the small CA 1 projection, this is unilateral, whereas the projection from CA 3 terminates in the lateral septal area of both hemispheres. Although, as we shall see below, the lateral septal area projects outside the septo-hippocampal system, it projects also to the medial septal area, thus closing the septo-hippocampal loop (Raisman 1966; Swanson and Cowan 1976; DeFrance 1976*b*; Krayniak *et al.* 1980).

With the few reservations expressed above, then, the major relations between the hippocampus and the medial and lateral divisions of the septal area are as follows: (i) the septal projection to the hippocampus has its origin in the medial septal area, travels in both the fimbria and dorsal fornix, is probably predominantly cholinergic, and terminates throughout the hippocampal formation; (ii) the hippocampal projection to the septal area has its origin principally in CA 3 and the subiculum, travels principally in the fimbria, and terminates principally in the lateral septal area; (iii) the lateral septal area projects to the medial septal area, closing the septo-hippocampal loop.

The posterior division of the septal area is less central to the septo-hippocampal system than the medial and lateral divisions, but its relations with the hippocampus are none the less close. It consists of two cell groups, the septo-fimbrial and triangular nuclei. Both lie within the fibres of the fimbria-fornix, the septo-fimbrial nucleus more laterally, the triangular nucleus more medially; and both receive a similar projection from the hippocampus and the subiculum to that received by the lateral septal area.

The ventral division of the septal area comprises the bed nucleus of the stria terminalis, a heterogeneous region separating the septal area from the preoptic region ventrally and from the caudate nucleus laterally. Its relations are principally with the amygdala, though it also receives afferents from the ventral part of the subiculum, about which we shall have more to say later. Thus, although it is part of the septal area, the ventral division is only marginally part of the septo-hippocampal system and will receive correspondingly little attention in this book. Also located ventrally in the vicinity of the septal area, and sometimes included within it, is the nucleus accumbens; but this is now thought to relate more closely to the ventral caudate than to the septal area proper (Heimer and Wilson 1975), and it too will largely be ignored.

faintly stained than those of the dorsal MSN 'cap'. The cells of the diagonal band region, seen in an ovoid configuration near the ventral face of the section, are similarly distinct from central MSN cells on the basis of staining intensity and gross morphology. A small population of intensely stained 'midline cells' comprise the fourth distinct AChE-positive subgroup. Bar = 500 μm. (From Lynch *et al.* (1978).)

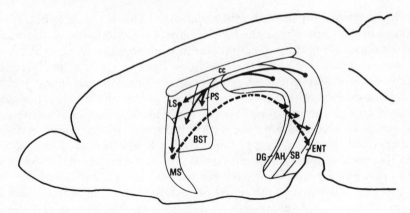

Figure 3.8. The major fibre systems interrelating the septum and hippocampal formation. AH, Ammon's horn; BST, bed nucleus of the stria terminalis; DG, dentate gyrus; ENT, entorhinal area; LS, lateral septal nucleus; MS, medial septal nucleus; PS, posterior septal nuclei; SB, subicular complex; cc, corpus callosum. (From Swanson (1978).)

This highly condensed survey of the connections between the septal area and the hippocampal formation is summarized in Fig. 3.8. It is clear from this Figure and Fig. 3.5 that the septo-hippocampal system is remarkably well equipped for talking to itself. Unfortunately, we do not know what it talks about. The usual way to get an anatomical clue to the kind of information that a neural structure deals with is to ask about its connections: where does its information come from, and where does it go to? But many parts of the septo-hippocampal system appear to talk *only* to other parts of the system (for example, the dentate granule cells and the CA 1 pyramids). Even the CA 3 pyramids, with their extensive connections, do not venture further than the lateral septal area, the contralateral hippocampus, and the entorhinal area.

Connections of the septo-hippocampal system

It is, in fact, only at a few points that the septo-hippocampal system makes contact with the outside world. The two major points of input are the entorhinal and medial septal areas; the major points of output are the subicular area and the septal nuclei.

The afferents to the entorhinal area have been described in detail in the rhesus monkey by Van Hoesen, Pandya, and Butters (1972, 1975; Van Hoesen and Pandya 1975); it is not clear to what extent the same afferents exist also in the rat (Beckstead 1978). In the monkey the entorhinal area apparently receives information from all sensory systems, but only after it has undergone extensive elaboration by the neocortical association areas. A summary of Van Hoesen's results is presented in Fig. 3.9.

As O'Keefe and Nadel (1978, p. 126) comment, 'This figure makes it clear that there is a cascading of inputs from a number of cortical areas through all adjacent regions leading ultimately to the entorhinal cortex. This pattern of inputs to the entorhinal area strongly suggests that the hippocampus is concerned not with information about any particular modality, but rather with highly analysed, abstracted information from all modalities.'

The data summarized in Fig. 3.9 refer to the visual, auditory, and somaesthetic systems. A rather more direct olfactory input to the entorhinal cortex, originating in the olfactory bulb itself or relaying in the prepyriform cortex, has been described in rats and cats (Swanson 1978; Wilson and Steward 1978; Habets *et al.* 1980*a, b*). Besides these sensory inputs, Van Hoesen's group has described a projection from the orbital region of the prefrontal cortex; this may have a particular significance for the theory developed in this book (see Chapter 13). There are also projections from certain thalamic nuclei (the nucleus reuniens, and the paratenial and periventricular nuclei), and from the amygdala (Krettek and Price 1977; Segal 1977*e;* Beckstead 1978). Within the septo-hippocampal system itself, there are projections to the entorhinal cortex from the medial septal area, hippocampal fields CA 3 and 4, and the subicular area

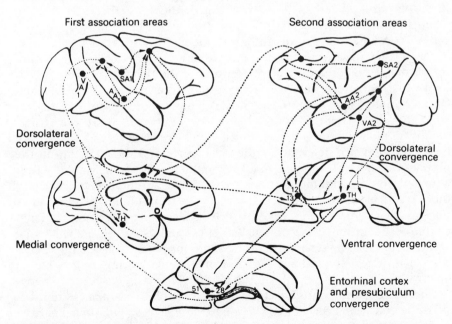

Figure 3.9. Convergence of afferent information onto the entorhinal cortex from primary (SA1, AA1, VA1) and secondary (SA2, AA2, VA2) association areas of the neocortex in the monkey. (From Van Hoesen, Pandya and Butters (1972); copyright 1972 by the American Association for the Advancement of Science.)

(Köhler *et al.* 1978; Segal 1977*e*; Beckstead 1978). Since the subicular area is the chief output station of the hippocampal formation, the latter projection closes a long loop around the hippocampal circuit illustrated in Fig. 3.5. There also exists a short subiculo-entorhinal loop, since the entorhinal cortex projects directly to all divisions of the subicular area (Van Hoesen *et al.* 1979).

To describe the information received by the entorhinal area as 'highly analysed and abstracted from all modalities' does not tell us much; but it is more than we can say about the information received by the medial septal area. Functional studies, especially of the hippocampal theta rhythm (see Chapter 4), which is controlled by cells in the medial septal area, have suggested to many workers that this region receives inputs from lower brain centres that are in some way related to the overall level of arousal. Lindsley's group (Lindsley and Wilson 1975), for example, has described areas in the midbrain or hypothalamus, the stimulation of which either elicits or disrupts the theta rhythm, and has attempted to deduce from these observations which pathways converge on the septal area to produce these effects. The difficulty with this approach is that a great variety of sensory and motor influences affect the theta rhythm (Chapter 7), so a change in theta when a particular brain region is stimulated does not necessarily indicate a direct pathway from that region to the septal area. There is, moreover, some doubt whether it is the site stimulated or the parameters of stimulation which determine the hippocampal response, theta or disruption of theta (Paiva *et al.* 1976).

Direct anatomical evidence for brainstem or hypothalamic afferents to the medial septal area capable of controlling the theta pacemaker cells is in any case not strong. There is a projection from the lateral preoptic and lateral hypothalamic areas to the medial septum, but it is not particularly large (Swanson 1978). With regard to the brainstem, there are clearly identified monoaminergic projections, which we shall consider in a moment; but they are not vital for the occurrence of a theta rhythm in the hippocampus, which suggests that their influence on medial septal cells is a limited one. In addition to these hypothalamic and brainstem afferents, there is a projection to the medial septal area from the medial habenular nucleus (Segal and Landis 1974), which itself receives a projection from the posterior group of septal nuclei. These inputs to the medial septal area are all more mysterious than the septo-hippocampal system itself, so they give us few clues about the kind of information this system has to deal with.

There are other points of entry to the septo-hippocampal system besides the entorhinal cortex and the medial septal area. The subicular area is rich in afferents, but we shall discuss these at the same time as considering the efferents from this region. The projection from the prefrontal cortex is not confined to the entorhinal area; there is evidence in monkeys for a direct projection of the orbitofrontal cortex to fields CA 1 and CA

3 of the hippocampus (Leichnetz and Astruc 1976), and for a projection to the lateral septal area from the dorsolateral prefrontal cortex (Tanaka and Goldman 1976). There is also evidence for a direct projection from the cingulate cortex to the hippocampal formation (Wyss, Swanson, and Cowan, cited by Swanson in Elliott and Whelan 1978, p. 45). A thalamic nucleus whose function is obscure, the nucleus reuniens, has been shown to project to CA 1, as well as to the entorhinal and subicular areas (Herkenham 1978; Segal 1977e; Beckstead 1978). And there is a projection from cell groups in the area of the mammillary bodies in the hypothalamus (the supramammillary and submammillothalamic nuclei) directly to the hippocampus (Pasquier and Reinoso-Suarez 1976). Since the mammillary bodies are the target for an important part of the hippocampal outflow from the subicular area, these afferents from the same region may again close a loop between hippocampal input and output. But none of these projections brings further insight into the functions of the septo-hippocampal system.

The remaining important projections to the septo-hippocampal system originate in the brainstem and use as their neurotransmitter one of the three monoamines, noradrenalin (called 'norepinephrine' in the United States), dopamine, or 5-hydroxytryptamine (also called 'serotonin').

The principal noradrenergic projection originates in the locus coeruleus (A 6 in the nomenclature for nuclei containing monoamines introduced by Dahlström and Fuxe 1964; see Fig. 3.10). This projection travels in the dorsal ascending noradrenergic bundle (Fig. 3.11), entering the septum in the medial forebrain bundle to terminate in both the medial and lateral septal areas, although Segal (in Elliott and Whelan 1978, p. 128) finds a heavier innervation in the medial nuclei. Fibres from the same source also terminate diffusely throughout the hippocampal formation, but especially heavily in the hilus of the dentate gyrus. To reach the hippocampus the locus coeruleus fibres take three routes (Elliott and Whelan 1978, pp. 125–30). The most round-about passes through the septal area, rises anterior to the corpus callosum to join the cingulum bundle, and then travels in a posterior direction until it reaches the splenium of the corpus callosum, where it descends again to enter the hippocampal formation from above. A second bundle of fibres, quantitatively the least important, also passes via the septal area, but then takes a more direct route through the fornix and fimbria. Finally, a third group of fibres takes a ventral route, passing through the ventral amygdaloid bundle and the region of the amygdala and pyriform cortex to innervate the ventral hippocampus.

The locus coeruleus is the sole source of noradrenergic innervation of the hippocampal formation. But the septal area also receives a projection from two cell groups (A 1 and A 2) in the medulla oblongata whose fibres travel in the ventral noradrenergic bundle (Fig. 3.11). The noradrenergic innervation of the septal area seems to be about equally due to cells in the

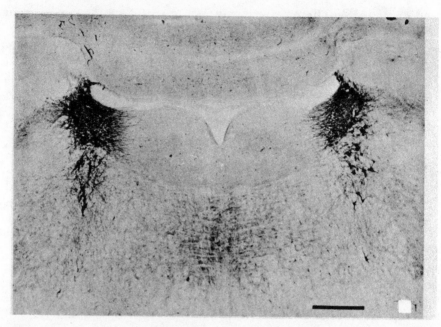

Figure 3.10. The locus coeruleus. The photograph shows a transverse section through the rat brainstem at the level of maximal cross-sectional extent of the locus coeruleus, stained (dark cells) for the enzyme, dopamine-β-hydroxylase (which catalyses the synthesis of noradrenalin from dopamine). Bar = 500 μm. (From Grzanna and Molliver (1980).)

locus coeruleus and cells in A 1 and A 2 (Moore and Bloom 1979); thus, after destruction of the dorsal noradrenergic bundle, levels of noradrenalin in the septal area are reduced by about 50 per cent (Owen, Boarder, Fillenz, and Gray 1982). Like the locus coeruleus fibres, the afferents from A 1 and A 2 terminate in both the lateral and medial septal areas (Björklund, in Elliott and Whelan 1978, p. 127).

The serotonergic innervation of the septo-hippocampal system originates in the raphe nuclei of the brainstem (Fig. 3.12), mainly in B 8 (Dahlström and Fuxe 1964), the median raphe (Bobillier *et al.* 1976; Kellor *et al.* 1977), but with a small contribution from B 7, the dorsal raphe, as well (Pasquier and Reinoso-Suarez 1977). Efferents from the raphe nuclei follow essentially the same three routes as those from the locus coeruleus to reach the septo-hippocampal system (Azmitia, in Elliott and Whelan 1978, pp. 80–2; Fig. 3.13). Those that take the ventral route to innervate the ventral hippocampus originate in the dorsal raphe. Fibres from the median raphe enter the septal area in the medial forebrain bundle and then take both the fornix-fimbria route and the supracallosal route in the cingulum bundle to reach the dorsal hippocampus (Azmitia and Segal 1978). The median raphe, in addition, innervates the medial septal area and the dorsal part of the lateral septal area; the dorsal raphe innervates the anteroventral part of the lateral septal area and the nucleus accumbens.

The dopaminergic innervation of the septo-hippocampal system is less extensive. The lateral septal area receives a projection from cell group A 10, located in the ventral tegmental area; like the noradrenergic and serotonergic projections, this arrives in the medial forebrain bundle. There may be a small dopaminergic innervation of the hippocampus from the same source (Wyss 1977; Schwab *et al.* 1978; Simon, Le Moal, and Cardo 1979), but this remains controversial. A 10 also projects to the entorhinal area (which, in addition, receives afferents from the locus coeruleus and the dorsal and median raphe) and to the nucleus accumbens (Segal 1977*e;* Beckstead 1978; Lindvall and Björklund 1978).

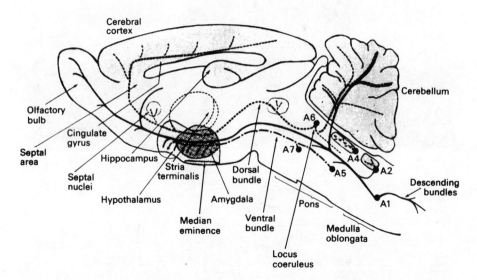

Figure 3.11. Saggital representation of the rat brain, showing the principal ascending and descending noradrenergic pathways. Cell bodies in the locus coeruleus (A6) give rise to pathways (– – –) innervating all cortical areas of the brain. The dorsal bundle arising from A6 also innervates areas of the amygdala and anterior hypothalamus, while a short descending pathway innervates lower brainstem nuclei. Cell group A1 (——) gives rise to a descending bulbo-spinal pathway, and a major ascending ventral pathway, which follows the course of the medial forebrain bundle all the way to the olfactory bulb. This ventral bundle, which comprises ascending fibres from cell groups A5 and A7 (– · – · –) as well as from A1 and A2, gives off branches to the lateral mammillary nuclei, the lateral and ventral hypothalamus (the latter providing terminals to the median eminence and infundibulum), and to large parts of the limbic forebrain (including the anterior medial amygdaloid complex, the ventral medial septum, and cingulum). Shaded areas indicate regions of noradrenergic terminals. (From Livett (1973).)

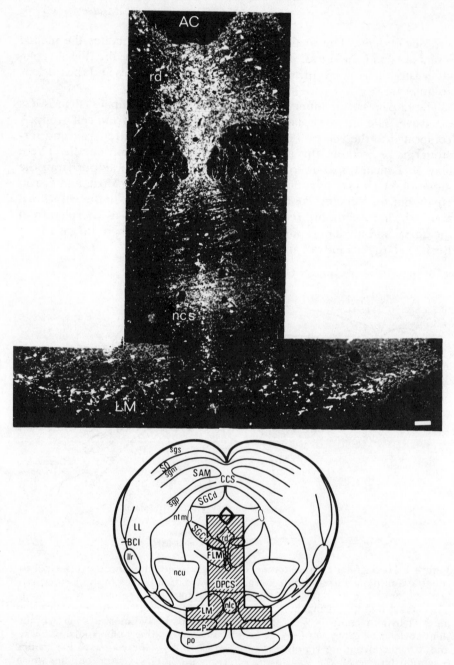

Figure 3.12. The raphe nuclei in the brainstem of the rat as shown by an immuno-histofluorescent technique. rd, dorsal raphe (B 7); ncs, nucleus centralis superior or median raphe (B 8); LM, lemniscus medialis (B 9); AC, cerebral aqueduct. Bar: 50 μm. For abbreviations in the schematic diagram of the brain region to which the photograph corresponds, see Steinbusch (1981), from which the figure is taken.

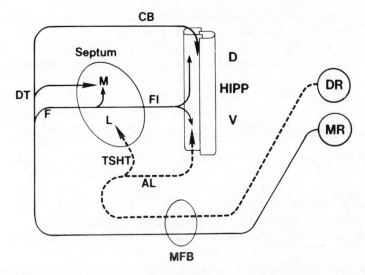

Figure 3.13. Diagrammatic representation of the main projections of the serotonin axons to the septo-hippocampal complex. AL, ansa lenticularis; CB, cingulum bundle; D, dorsal and V, ventral hippocampus; DR, dorsal raphe; DT,
diagonal tract; F, fornix column; FI, fimbria; L, lateral and M, medial septal nucleus; MFB, medial forebrain bundle; MR, median raphe; TSHT, septohypotha-
lamic tract. (From Azmitia, in Elliott and Whelan (1978, p. 81).)

These, then, are the principal monoaminergic inputs to the septo-
hippocampal system. If we knew their functional significance, this might
put some constraints upon the role of the septo-hippocampal system itself. But we do not. Indeed, when we discuss the noradrenergic and serotonergic systems in greater detail (Chapter 11), we shall find that the
tables are turned: our knowledge of septo-hippocampal function will be
our best guide in interpreting the data on monoaminergic pathways. Even
if we knew the information carried by these pathways, we should be little
better off in trying to decide what the septo-hippocampal system does
with it. For the same information is apparently carried from the locus
coeruleus and the raphe nuclei to other wide regions of the brain (neocortex, amygdala, caudate nucleus, etc.), each of which presumably does
something rather different.

All in all, then, we have gleaned singularly little insight into the functions of the septo-hippocampal system by enquiring about its afferents.
Can we do better from a knowledge of its efferents?

As Swanson (1978) points out, the number of sites in receipt of direct
septal and hippocampal projections is relatively small. The efferent projections of the hippocampal formation (apart from those from CA 3 to
the septal area, and from CA 3 and CA 4 to the entorhinal cortex) appear
to arise exclusively from the subicular complex. This projection goes

largely by way of the post-commissural fornix, a massive continuation of the fimbria-fornix that sweeps down in two columns, one in each hemisphere, through the septal area posterior to the anterior commissure (hence 'post-commissural'). The targets of the subicular efferents are the mammillary bodies in the hypothalamus, and the anterior thalamus, particularly the anteroventral thalamic nucleus but perhaps also the anterodorsal and anteromedial nuclei (Swanson and Cowan 1977). The mammillary bodies themselves also project to the anterior thalamic nuclei (along the mammillothalamic tract), so another loop is closed. Further convergence is provided by the output from the septal area, for both the medial and lateral septal nuclei project to the mammillary bodies, as well as projecting diffusely to the lateral hypothalamus. In addition to the subicular efferents in the post-commissural fornix, Meibach and Siegel (1977c) have recently described a supracallosal projection from the dorsal subiculum to the cingulate cortex. This connection introduces still further loops into the circuitry of the septo-hippocampal system. For the anteroventral nucleus of the thalamus (to which, as we have seen, the subiculum projects both directly and via the mammillary bodies) also projects to the cingulate cortex; and the cingulate cortex in turn projects back to both the subicular area and the anteroventral nucleus of the thalamus. Some of these loops and projections are illustrated in Figs. 3.14 and 3.15.

Other outputs from the septo-hippocampal system originate in the posterior division of the septal area. Both the septo-fimbrial and triangular nuclei project through the stria medullaris to the habenular nuclei; and the triangular nucleus also projects via the fasciculus retroflexus to the interpeduncular nucleus in the midbrain (Swanson 1978). These connections are illustrated in Figs. 3.14 and 3.16.

The ventral part of the subicular complex gives rise to a pattern of outputs that is very different from the projections of the remainder of the subiculum. It is not clear how germane these outputs are to the theme of this book. In general, there is a remarkable homogeneity in the anatomy, connections and physiology of the hippocampal formation throughout its septo-temporal extent. An exception to this rule is the pathway to the entorhinal cortex from CA 3 and CA 4, which originates only in the temporal one-third of the hippocampal formation. But a much bigger exception is the ventral subicular output summarized in Fig. 3.17. This travels in the medial corticohypothalamic tract, which winds round the medial side of the descending columns of the fornix, then descends vertically through the preoptic area towards the anterior and middle regions of the hypothalamus (Raisman, Cowan, and Powell 1966). As Swanson (1978) points out, the output of the ventral subiculum suggests that this part of the hippocampal formation is more closely related to the amygdala than to the rest of the septo-hippocampal system. Thus, like the amygdala, the ventral subiculum projects to the bed nucleus of the stria terminalis and to the ventromedial nucleus of the hypothalamus; in addition, it receives a projection from the amygdala itself.

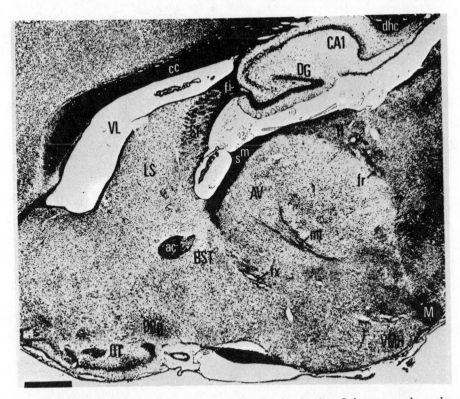

Figure 3.14. A parasagittal section through the forebrain of the rat to show the close relationship between the septum and hippocampus, which are reciprocally interconnected by fibres running in the fimbria. This section also shows the major sites in direct receipt of septo-hippocampal projections, including the habenula, anterior thalamic nuclei, mammillary body, and ventromedial nucleus of the hypothalamus. Klüver–Barrera stain; scale: 1.0 mm. AV, anteroventral nucleus of thalamus; BST, bed nucleus of stria terminalis; DBB, nucleus of the diagonal band; DG, dentate gyrus; H, habenula; LS, lateral septal nucleus; OT, olfactory tubercle; M, mammillary body; VL, lateral ventricle; VMH, ventromedial nucleus of the hypothalamus; ac, anterior commissure; cc, corpus callosum; dhc, the dorsal hippocampal commissure; fi, fimbria; fr, fasciculus retroflexus; fx, fornix; mt, mammillo-thalamic tract; sm, stria medullaris. (From Swanson (1978).)

As well as these anatomical reasons for regarding the ventral subicular projection as something apart from the rest of the septo-hippocampal system, there is a practical reason. The corner-stone of the arguments by which we shall try, in Chapter 6, to gain some insight into the functions of the septo-hippocampal system is the pattern of behavioural change seen after lesions to the septal area or hippocampus. But lesions of the hippocampal formation almost always spare the ventral subiculum. Thus we have very little idea at present what the functions of the ventral subicular area are, nor whether they are the same as those of the rest of the hippocampal formation.

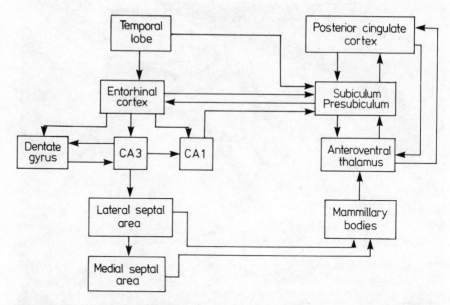

Figure 3.15. Some efferents from, and return projections to, the septo-hippocampal system. The subicular complex also projects (not shown) to the mammillary bodies.

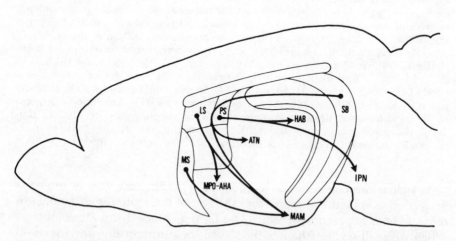

Figure 3.16. The major sites in receipt of direct septo-hippocampal projections. The efferent connections of the ventral part of the subiculum and the bed nucleus of the stria terminalis are shown in the next figure. ATN, anterior thalamic nucleus; HAB, habenula; IPN, interpeduncular nucleus; LS, lateral septal nucleus; MAM, mammillary bodies; MPO–AHA, medial preoptic and anterior hypothalamic area; MS, medial septal nucleus; PS, posterior septal nuclei; SB, subicular complex. (From Swanson (1978).)

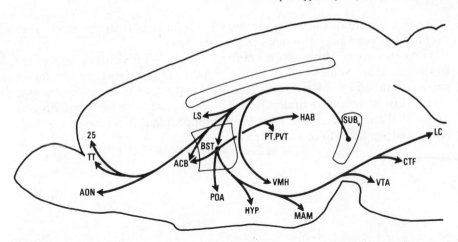

Figure 3.17. The efferent connections of the ventral part of the subiculum and the bed nucleus of the stria terminalis, two parts of the septo-hippocampal complex which are closely related to the amygdala on both topological and connectional grounds. ACB, nucleus accumbens; AON, anterior olfactory nucleus; BST, bed nucleus of the stria terminalis; CTF, central tegmental field; HAB, habenula; HYP, hypothalamus; LC, locus coeruleus; LS, lateral septal nucleus; MAM, mammillary body; POA, preoptic area; PT, parataenial nucleus; PVT, paraventricular nucleus of the thalamus; SUB$_v$, ventral subicular complex; TT, taenia tecta; VMH, ventromedial nucleus of the hypothalamus; VTA, ventral tegmental area; 25, infralimbic area. (From Swanson (1978).)

It would seem that the outputs of the septo-hippocampal system do not offer any greater insight into septo-hippocampal function than its inputs. As when we considered its internal organization, the overwhelming impression is of a system superbly well equipped for talking to itself — loops abound, exits are few.

In the disposition of these loops a nodal point seems to be occupied by the subicular cortex (Fig. 3.15). The strange thing is that this region apparently starts out in receipt of the same information that is then recirculated to it in several different ways, some longer, some shorter. For Van Hoesen *et al.* (1979) report extensive inputs to the subicular cortex from the same areas in the temporal lobe (Fig. 3.9) that project also to the entorhinal area, as well as an input from the entorhinal area itself. Thus the subicular cortex receives information from the neocortex via the temporal lobe; information from the entorhinal area which has reached the latter structure from the same source; and information from CA 1 which has been circulated round the hippocampal circuit (Fig. 3.5) after setting out again from the entorhinal area. It then sends this information out along the descending columns of the fornix, only to have it come back yet again after a long trip through the mammillary bodies, the anterior thalamus and the cingulate cortex. Of course, it is not 'the same' information.

If it were, we should need to suppose that a large part of the brain does nothing but echo back the news that it receives.

The existence of these reverberating loops makes it virtually impossible to deduce from anatomical considerations alone the nature of the information handled by the septo-hippocampal system, or the transformations which this information undergoes. To explain what these loops do is a major challenge to any theory of septo-hippocampal function; it is a challenge that we take up in Chapter 10.

4

The septo-hippocampal system: electrophysiology

The orderliness of its structure has made the hippocampal formation a favourite target for electrophysiological study. In consequence, much is known about its basic physiology. But it is not the intention of this brief chapter to review septo-hippocampal physiology in any detail. Rather, it concentrates on just a few phenomena which will be particularly important for the behavioural arguments encountered later in the book. Among these phenomena pride of place is occupied by two: the hippocampal theta rhythm (Green and Arduini 1954); and the remarkable plasticity of response which is characteristic of the circuit from the entorhinal area through the hippocampus to the subiculum.

The hippocampal theta rhythm

The theta rhythm (Fig. 4.1) is an unusually regular, almost sinusoidal, high-voltage rhythmic activity which can be recorded through gross electrodes placed almost anywhere in the hippocampal formation. It can be observed under a wide variety of different experimental and behavioural conditions. Depending on these conditions and upon species, its frequency ranges from 4 to about 12 or occasionally even 14 Hz (Vanderwolf, Kramis, Gillespie, and Bland 1975). Since 'theta' is conventially defined in human electroencephalography (EEG) as the 4–7-Hz band, this term can occasion some ambiguity when it is applied to hippocampal slow activity. To get round this problem the Canadian psychologist, Vanderwolf, who has done much to clarify the behavioural correlates of theta, prefers the term 'rhythmic slow activity'; but 'theta' is shorter and widely used by European workers, and I shall continue to use it here.

The theta rhythm is easily recorded in rats, rabbits, cats, dogs, and other small mammals. It is not certain whether a homologous rhythm exists in primates, but computer analysis of the human hippocampal EEG shows a peak in the resulting power spectrum lying in the 4–7-Hz band (Brazier 1968). Among animals with a well-defined theta rhythm, it is not clear to what extent its frequency range varies as a function of species. Since, as we shall see in Chapter 7, observed frequency depends critically on behaviour, and the behavioural conditions in which different species have been observed have rarely been identical, this is not a simple issue. Earlier descriptions of the theta rhythm were obtained in acute experiments under anaesthetics and/or the paralysing drug, curare, and both of these affect theta. The widely used anaesthetic, urethane, for example, reduces theta frequency in the rat (rarely below 6 Hz when the animal is free-moving) to a remarkably steady 4 Hz. Vanderwolf's group (see Chapter 7) has shown that there is a close positive correlation between the frequency of theta and the extent of the animal's movements, a parameter which, of course, is reduced to zero in acute experiments. It is for reasons

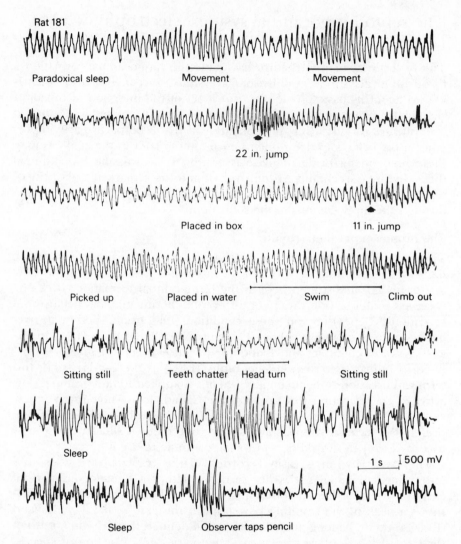

Figure 4.1. Electrical activity at a single hippocampal site during sleep and various types of behaviour in the rat. Note the following: theta during paradoxical sleep, struggling when held in the hand, swimming and head movement; large-amplitude irregular activity during sitting still while alert and while chattering the teeth; irregular slow activity and 'spindling' during slow-wave sleep and small-amplitude irregular activity when the rat was awakened but did not move about. Note also the following: increased theta frequency and amplitude associated with twitching during paradoxical sleep and with jumping in avoidance tasks; different frequencies and amplitudes of theta associated with head movements, swimming, jumping 11 in, and jumping 22 in. Calibration: 1 s, 500 μV; half-amplitude filters, 0.3 and 75 Hz. Electrode placement: Ca1, hippocampus. (From Whishaw and Vanderwolf (1973).)

like these that earlier observations of theta generally reported frequencies in the 4–6-Hz band, so that the term 'theta' was correctly applied to them. These earlier experiments were usually carried out with rabbits or cats, whereas work with free-moving animals has relied much more on the rat. The frequency range seen in the free-moving rat is typically 6–12 Hz, although frequencies above 10 Hz are seen only under special conditions (Chapter 7). Thus one might have concluded that there is a major species difference, the rabbit's theta range being, say, 4–7 Hz and the rat's, 6–12. However, observations of theta in the free-moving rabbit (Harper 1971; Kramis, Vanderwolf, and Bland 1975) demonstrate essentially the same frequency range as in the free-moving rat, and essentially the same relationship between frequency and behaviour.

None the less, there does seem to be a genuine difference in the theta frequency range between rats and rabbits, on the one hand, and cats and dogs, on the other. In free-moving cats (Elazar and Adey 1967; Brown 1968; Grastyan and Vereczkei 1974) and dogs (Lopes da Silva and Kamp 1969; Arnolds *et al.* 1979 *a, b, c*) the observed frequencies have rarely risen above 7–8 Hz. Kemp and Kaada (1975) saw a highest theta frequency in the free-moving cat of 8.5 Hz, accompanying visual searching. Since the highest theta frequencies are seen in rats or rabbits when movement is most vigorous, this observation might suggest that the right experimental conditions for very high-frequency theta have not been set up in research on cats and dogs. On the other hand, low frequencies of theta (4–5 Hz) have been seen in cats (e.g. Elazar and Adey 1967) and dogs (e.g. Black and Young 1972) under conditions where the frequency in the rat would almost certainly be higher. Thus it is probable that there are true species differences in the frequency band covered by theta: in rats and rabbits, as well as guinea pigs (Sainsbury 1970) and gerbils (Whishaw 1972), theta generally lies between 6 and 10–12 Hz; in cats and dogs it lies between 4 and 8–9 Hz. This conclusion is supported by the extensive review given by O'Keefe and Nadel (1978, Table A6) of the theta frequencies observed under various conditions in these species: those seen in cats and dogs are typically about 2 Hz lower than those seen in rats and rabbits in roughly comparable experiments.

Besides the theta rhythm, two other major patterns of activity have been distinguished in the hippocampal EEG. Vanderwolf (1969) has termed these 'large irregular activity' and 'small irregular activity'. Examples of both are shown in Fig. 4.1. It is the theta rhythm, however, which will occupy our attention, and this for two reasons. First, and more important, a great deal of research has been devoted to the behavioural significance of the theta rhythm, so that it has become a major source of theory about hippocampal function and a major method of testing theory. Second, research has been directed equally intensively at the physiological mechanisms which underlie the theta rhythm. Thus knowledge of the behavioural significance of this rhythm can to some extent be related to the structure and organization of the septo-hippocampal system.

In spite of the intensive research on the physiology of the theta rhythm, however, there is much that is still unknown. I shall start this brief review with the facts that seem most certain.

Theta can be recorded in most parts of the hippocampal formation. Most research has been confined to the more easily accessible dorsal hippocampus, but theta can also be recorded from the ventral hippocampus (McGowan-Sass 1973; Rawlins, Feldon, and Gray 1979). The distribution of theta has been mapped by lowering an electrode gradually through the dorsal hippocampus, or by moving electrodes along the septo-temporal extent of the dorsal hippocampus. The first kind of mapping study (Winson 1974, 1976*a,b;* Bland, Andersen, and Ganes 1975; Bland and Whishaw 1976; Green and Rawlins 1979; Bland, Sainsbury, and Creery 1979) has revealed two maxima of theta amplitude (Fig. 4.2). The first is located near the pyramidal cells of CA 1; more precisely, with reference to the different layers, or 'strata', produced by the regular packaging of cells in the hippocampal formation, it lies in *stratum oriens* and *stratum pyramidale* (Fig. 4.6). The second maximum, which is 180° out of phase with the first, lies just above the dentate granule cells, in *stratum lacunosum-moleculare* of field CA 1 and *stratum moleculare* of the dentate gyrus (Fig. 4.6). The regions in which these maxima are found have been termed the 'generators' of the hippocampal theta rhythm. The dentate maximum is greater than the one in CA 1. Between the two there is a 'null zone' (in *stratum radiatum*) at which theta is small or absent. The reversal of phase between the two generators takes place abruptly in the free-moving or curarized rabbit and in the curarized rat, but more gradually in the free-moving rat (Winson 1974; Fig. 4.2), and the null zone is correspondingly shorter or longer. There is doubt as to whether theta can be found at all in CA 3 (O'Keefe and Nadel 1978, p. 146; Green and Rawlins 1979).

There is also uncertainty concerning the relation between theta recorded simultaneously at different points along the septo-temporal axis of the dorsal hippocampus. Petsche and Stumpf (1960) reported a systematic phase shift as one goes from the septal to the temporal pole, or from medial to lateral hippocampus, with the theta waves acting as though they originate in the septal area and travel in a posterolateral direction at a rate of about 30–40 cm s⁻¹. But Bland, Andersen, and Ganes (1975) found the theta waves to be in phase over large areas of the hippocampal formation. Green and Rawlins (1979) report results like those of Bland *et al.* (1975) for the upper generator, but results like those of Petsche and Stumpf (1960) for the lower one; in addition, they find that sites closer to the fimbria lag behind more posteromedial sites.

Although the two maxima of theta amplitude have been called 'generators', it is not clear how they generate theta. What is certain is that they do not do this on their own. They are critically dependent on the input

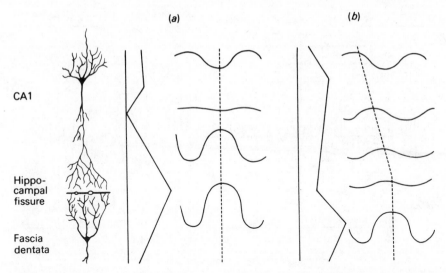

Figure 4.2. Changes of theta amplitude and phase at different depths in the hippocampus of different preparations: (*a*) rabbit and curarized rat; (*b*) the freely moving rat. In each panel the left graph shows relative amplitude on the abscissa, and the right shows a single theta wave at each level and the phase relations amongst them. (From O'Keefe and Nadel (1978), after Winson (1976*b*).)

that the hippocampus receives from the medial septal area. This conclusion is based on several lines of evidence, much of it gathered in the first instance by the Vienna group working with Petsche and Stumpf (see Stumpf 1965, for a review).

There are cells in the medial septal nucleus and the nucleus of the diagonal band which fire in bursts that are steadily in phase with the theta rhythm simultaneously recorded in the hippocampus (Petsche *et al.* 1962; Stumpf 1965; Apostol and Creutzfeldt 1974), although there is no theta in the septal area itself. Disruption of the firing of these cells disrupts the hippocampal theta rhythm. This can be done temporarily, by injection into the medial septal area of procaine, a local anaesthetic, or chronically, by destruction of medial septal tissue (Green and Arduini 1954; Petsche and Stumpf 1960; Stumpf 1965). The latter effect is permanent (Gray 1971*c*; Rawlins *et al.* 1979). There are other brain regions, damage to which disrupts theta temporarily, but a permanent loss of theta has been demonstrated only after destruction of the medial septal area or its efferents. A further way of disrupting theta is by electrical stimulation of the medial septal area at frequencies above about 70 Hz (Fig. 4.3). This gives rise to a pattern of small irregular activity which, in the best case, lasts as long as the stimulation but not longer (Stumpf 1965; Ball and Gray 1971), and is presumably due to blockade of the normal pattern of low-frequency bursts seen in medial septal neurones. Conversely, one may

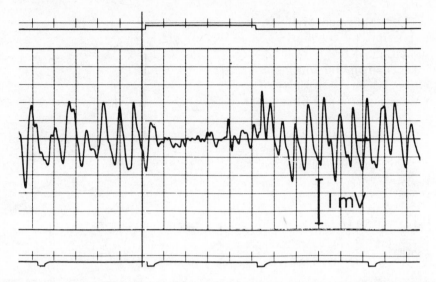

Figure 4.3. Blocking of hippocampal theta rhythm by high-frequency septal stimulation in the free-moving rat. The recording site was in the dorsomedial subiculum. Septal stimulation (77 Hz, 0.5 ms pulse width, about 100 μA) was applied during upward deflection of top pen marker; bottom pen marker, time in seconds. (From Ball and Gray (1971).)

artificially elicit ('drive') a theta rhythm in the hippocampus by low-frequency stimulation of the medial septal area, i.e. using frequencies that lie within the naturally occurring theta range (Fig. 4.4). There is an important difference between theta elicited in this way from the septal area and theta elicited (as it can be) by stimulation of many other brain regions. In the latter case, theta is elicited by *high*-frequency stimulation, and the elicited theta frequency often rises as the voltage of the applied current increases (Sailer and Stumpf 1957; Stumpf 1965; McNaughton and Sedgwick 1978). Only with septal stimulation does each pulse produce a corresponding wave in the hippocampal EEG, so that the elicited theta frequency is identical to the frequency of the applied current (Stumpf 1965; Gray and Ball 1970; James *et al.* 1977; Wetzel *et al.* 1977a).

It is well established, then, that cells in the medial septal area are the pacemakers for the hippocampal theta rhythm (Brücke *et al.* 1959; Stumpf 1965). Until recently, because research has concentrated almost exclusively on the dorsal hippocampus, there has been some obscurity about how impulses from the pacemakers reach the hippocampus. Dorsal hippocampal theta is unaffected by section of the fimbria, but is eliminated by section of the *fornix superior*, i.e. the dorsomedial portion of the fimbria-fornix (Myhrer 1975a). This is a surprising finding, since the bulk of the medial septal efferents appear to travel in the fimbria. We have recently confirmed Myhrer's (1975a) observations with regard to dorsal hippocampal theta; but we have shown in addition that in the ventral hippocampus theta is eliminated by fimbrial section and unaffected by destruction of the fornix (Rawlins *et al.* 1979). Thus the medial septal outflow which controls theta travels in the *fornix superior* to the dorsal hippocampus but in the fimbria to the ventral hippocampus. Neither Myhrer (1975a) nor Rawlins *et al.* (1979) distinguished between CA 1 and dentate theta. Andersen *et al.* (1979) report that the septal fibres controlling theta in the dentate generator take a medial route to the dorsal hippocampus, but travel more ventrally than those interrupted by the dorsal fornix lesion used by Rawlins *et al.* (1979); this suggests a dorsal-to-ventral organization of septal fibres controlling CA 1 and dentate theta respectively.

These observations are consistent with the known anatomy of the cholinergic projection from the medial septal area to the hippocampus (Chapter 3). Furthermore, Rawlins *et al.* (1979) report good agreement

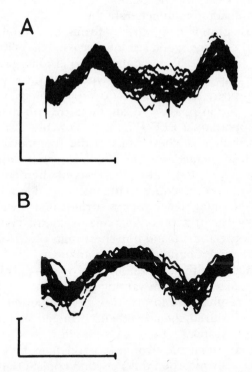

Figure 4.4. Two examples of driven theta waves in response to septal stimulation in the free-moving rat. The recording site was in the dorsomedial subiculum. Calibration: 0.5 mV and 100 ms. Each panel is the superimposition of about 10 successive sweeps on an oscilloscope. Stimulation parameters: 0.5 ms pulse width, 130 ms inter-pulse interval and intensities 100 (A) and 80 (B) µA. (From James *et al.* (1977).)

between the disappearance of staining for acetylcholinesterase and the loss of theta in the dorsal, ventral, or flexure regions of the hippocampus, depending on the lesion used. Thus it seems probable that the septo-hippocampal cholinergic projection is responsible for conveying instructions from the medial septal pacemakers to the hippocampal generators of theta. It has been suggested by McLennan and Miller (1974a, 1976) that the medial septal projection to the hippocampus is itself controlled by the hippocampal projection to the lateral septal area via the fimbria. However, Rawlins *et al.* (1979) report normal theta in both the dorsal and the ventral hippocampus after destruction of the lateral septal area, and normal theta in the dorsal hippocampus after destruction of the fimbria. Thus, although it is possible that the hippocampus influences the theta-controlling cells in the medial septal area, the hippocampo-septal projection is not essential for theta.

So far, then, two points are firm: the existence of the CA 1 and dentate generators of theta; and their control by the medial septal pacemaker. What is much less clear are the cellular mechanism by which the pacemaker causes the generators to generate theta.

One hypothesis, proposed in various forms by a number of authors (Lynch, Rose, and Gall 1978; and see the discussion in O'Keefe and Nadel 1978, pp. 146–50), is that hippocampal interneurons, probably the basket cells, play an important role. This hypothesis turns critically on the identity of the so-called 'theta units' in the hippocampus, that is, cells that fire in bursts that are in phase with the theta rhythm simultaneously recorded in the hippocampal EEG (Fig. 4.5). Fox and Ranck (1975) have mapped the distribution of these units in the free-moving rat and find them in the main in *stratum oriens* of CA 1, in *stratum lucidum, radiatum,* and *moleculare* of CA 3, and within the hilus of the dentate gyrus (Fig. 4.6). This distribution corresponds to the histological localization of interneurons, so that Fox and Ranck (1975) suggest that theta units are cells of this kind. However, this proposal remains controversial, as does the very distinction between theta and non-theta units on which it rests. Thus neither Andersen nor Vinogradova (in Elliott and Whelan 1978, pp. 130–36) believe that there are theta and non-theta cells — only theta *states,* into which a given cell may enter with varying probability.

Very different results have in any case been reported by Bland *et al.* (1980), working with urethane-anaesthetized rabbits in which units were identified by their response to synaptic and/or antidromic activation. These workers found that the strongest correlations between unit firing and the simultaneously recorded theta rhythm applied to dentate granule cells and CA 1 pyramids; much poorer correlations were found for CA 3 pyramids (of which, however, only six units were studied) and basket cells. It is possible that the different results reported by Fox and Ranck (1975) and Bland *et al.* (1980) turn on their use of the free-moving rat and the anaesthetized rabbit, respectively. Bland *et al.* (1980) suggest that, if this

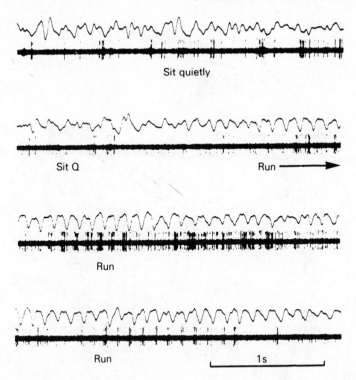

Sit quietly

Sit Q   Run ———➤

Run

Run   1s

Figure 4.5. A 'theta unit' with good phase relation to the theta recorded from the same microelectrode. (From O'Keefe and Nadel (1978).)

is the case, the difference between the two preparations may correspond to the two types of theta identified by Vanderwolf on behavioural and pharmacological grounds (see Chapter 7).

Whichever neurons fire in phase with theta, the relationship between their firing and the slow rhythm in the EEG is unclear. One would like to think that changes in neuronal firing give rise to the EEG rhythm, since this would at last bring slow waves into contact with the anatomy of the nervous system that creates them. But so far there has been no clear demonstration that this is so. Bland *et al.* (1980) suggest that theta represents a summation of 'nearly synchronous rhythmical postsynaptic potentials in hippocampal formation neurons generated by rhythmical septal cell discharges.' This is possible, but needs testing. It remains puzzling on any account that CA 3 participates in theta less than other hippocampal regions, although it is no less densely innervated by the medial septal area.

If the basket cells play a critical role in the generation of theta, as proposed by Fox and Ranck (1975), they must be the target of the medial septal innervation. This too is not certain. The distribution of the medial septal projection to the hippocampus has not been accurately described at

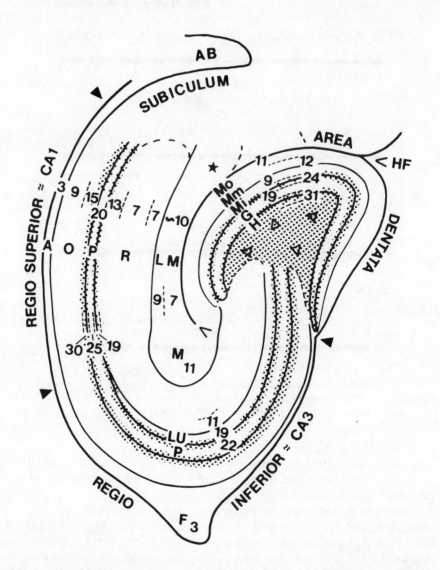

Figure 4.6. Schematic drawing of a section transverse to the septo-temporal axis of the rat hippocampal formation. In area dentata and hippocampus stippling indicates the zones with the highest intensities of staining, corresponding to activity per volume, for acetylcholinesterase and choline acetyltransferase. The numbers indicate the choline acetyltransferase activity as measured biochemically in microdissected samples, the unit being 1/10 of the activity in strips of tissue cut at right angles through all layers of CA1 — about 20 μmol $h^{-1}g^{-1}$ dry weight. *, part of molecular layer in CA1/subiculum having relatively high acetylcholinesterase and choline acetyltransferase activity, partially resistant to lesions of afferent pathways. ▼, limits between the cortical subfields: area dentata, hippocampus regio inferior (≈CA3), hippocampus regio superior (≈CA1), and subiculum; > <, bottom and orifice of the hippocampal fissure (HF). Other symbols: A, alveus; AB, angular bundle (psalterium dorsale); F, fimbria; G, granular cell layer of area

the ultrastructural level. Lynch *et al.* (1978) report autoradiographic results which suggest that afferents of medial septal origin terminate on a population of interneurons in regions of the hippocampal formation that stain heavily for acetylcholinesterase. This is consistent with Fox and Ranck's (1975) hypothesis. Similarly, Storm-Mathisen (1978) has reviewed studies in which the distribution of acetylcholinesterase and choline acetyltransferase has been mapped in the hippocampal formation, and his findings reveal a good correspondence with the distribution of theta units reported by Fox and Ranck (1975): the two enzymes are heavily concentrated in the *stratum oriens* and *pyramidale* of CA 1, the *stratum lucidum* and *pyramidale* of CA 3, and the hilus and inner zone of *stratum moleculare* of the dentate gyrus (Fig. 4.6). These findings are consistent with the notion that the cholinergic projection from the medial septal area terminates on interneurons; but they by no means prove it. Electrophysiological studies have also so far been unable to resolve this issue. Results obtained by McNaughton and Miller (in preparation)* suggest that, in the dentate gyrus, medial septal afferents have a complex termination at three different sites: directly on the granule cells, directly on a population of cells in the hilus, and finally on a population of interneurons which also receive collateral innervation from the granule cells.

Further uncertainty clouds the nature of the receptor upon which the medial septal cholinergic projection acts. Two classes of cholinergic receptor, 'muscarinic' and 'nicotinic', have long been established, based upon their special sensitivity to muscarine and nicotine, respectively. Both muscarinic (Kuhar and Yamamura 1976) and nicotinic (Dudai and Segal 1978) receptors are found in the hippocampus. According to Segal (in Elliott and Whelan 1978, pp. 130–6), the distribution of the nicotinic receptor fits the distribution of septo-hippocampal terminal fields much better than does that of the muscarinic receptor. Segal (*loc. cit.*) also reports that theta cells respond to nicotinic agonists and antagonists, whereas non-theta cells are responsive to muscarinic substances. This might account for the curious effect of curare (an antinicotinic drug) on the abruptness of the phase reversal between the two generators of theta (Winson 1974; Fig. 4.2). But if the whole of the septal effect on theta has to pass through a nicotinic receptor one might expect this drug to abolish theta entirely, yet it does not (Black, Young, and Batenchuk 1970; Winson 1974).

A further complication concerning the nature of the septo-

dentata; H, hilus fasciae dentatae; LM, lacunosal and molecular parts of stratum lacunosum-moleculare of hippocampus CA1; LU, stratum lucidum (mossy fibre layer) of CA3; M, stratum lacunosum-moleculare of hippocampus; Mi, Mm, and Mo, inner, middle, and outer zones of stratum moleculare of area dentata; O, P, and R, stratum oriens, pyramidale, and radiatum of hippocampus. For layering, compare Fig. 3.4. (From Storm-Mathisen (1978).)

*See McNaughton and Miller (1984) in additional references.

hippocampal pacemaker projection will become apparent in Chapter 7, when we deal with the behavioural correlates of theta. Vanderwolf's group (Vanderwolf *et al.* 1975, 1978) has presented strong evidence that there are two types of theta rhythm, with different behavioural correlates and different characteristic frequency ranges. One of these types of theta is blocked by systemic injections of the anticholinergic (predominantly antimuscarinic) drugs, atropine and scopolamine, but the other is not. It is not clear whether the effect of systemic atropine and scopolamine on theta is exercized within the hippocampus or at some point afferent to the medial septal pacemaker. If these drugs act intrahippocampally, it is puzzling that they affect one type of theta, rather than all theta; for all theta is eliminated by surgical destruction of the medial septal area (Gray 1971c; Rawlins *et al.* 1979). Thus there are difficulties in the way of supposing that the medial septal projection controlling theta is either nicotinic or muscarinic.

If, in spite of these uncertainties, we accept the notion that the first target of the septal pacemaker is the hippocampal basket cell, what happens next?

Here again we are in the realm of speculation. There is evidence (O'Keefe and Nadel 1978, pp. 117–18 and 146–7) that each basket cell is capable of inhibiting hundreds of pyramidal cells (in CA 1 and CA 3) or granule cells (in the dentate gyrus); this inhibition is probably mediated by GABA (Stefanis 1964; Curtis, Felix, and McLennan 1970). Thus, as Lynch *et al.* (1978) point out, 'By innervating the interneuron population the numerically inferior septal inputs to the hippocampus could exert an influence which would be far greater than could be achieved by their direct termination on hippocampal pyramidal or granule cell dendrites'. The repeated inhibition of the firing of the latter classes of cells would, on this view, constitute the major consequence of the septal input to the hippocampus. In agreement with this view, Andersen (in Elliott and Whelan 1978, p. 312) concluded from observations of intracellular membrane potential oscillations in dentate granule cells, occurring in phase with the extracellularly recorded theta rhythm, that 'The rhythm is caused by regularly occurring inhibition, cutting into the ongoing steady background activity'. One consequence of this would be that the theta rhythm would maintain 'large areas of the hippocampus (and perhaps other parts of the brain as well) in the same, or related, phases of excitability' (O'Keefe and Nadel 1978, p. 148). It is not surprising that a phenomenon such as this, calling as it does for functional interpretation, has attracted so much attention from physiologist and psychologist alike.

These arguments lead one to expect that the medial septal cholinergic projection would excite the inhibitory basket cells or directly inhibit the pyramidal or granule cells. But Segal (in Elliott and Whelan 1978, p. 131) found that cells with nicotinic receptors (which he presumed to be theta units and interneurons) were *inhibited* by nicotine, while cells with muscarinic receptors (presumed to be non-theta pyramidal cells) were *excited* by acetylcholine. Once again, therefore, the data on cholinoceptive cells in the hippocampus are difficult to integrate with other data. In view of these difficulties, it is perhaps premature to exclude the possibility that, in addition to the well-established cholinergic projection to the hippocampus, the medial septal area is the origin of a second, non-cholinergic projection which is responsible for the control of theta. In support of this possibility, Lynch *et al.* (1978) observed medial septal cells which projected to the hippocampus but did not stain for acetylcholinesterase. Similarly, Fantie (1979) stimulated the medial septal area and observed electrophysiological effects in the hippocampus which survived both muscarinic and nicotinic blockade (see below). If such a non-cholinergic projection exists, however, it appparently follows the same route as the cholinergic one and terminates in the same regions of the hippocampal formation (Lynch *et al.* 1978; Rawlins *et al.* 1979).

However the theta generators in the hippocampus are constructed, they do not function without instruction from the septal pacemaker. It therefore becomes important to know what causes the pacemaker to make paces. I have already alluded to our profound ignorance on this point in the previous chapter. It is possible to elicit theta by stimulation in many parts of the brain, including, for example, the lateral hypothalamus and the midbrain reticular formation (e.g. Stumpf 1965; Whishaw, Bland, and Vanderwolf 1972; Anchel and Lindsley 1972; Robinson and Vanderwolf 1978); but, as pointed out in Chapter 3, it is difficult to deduce from such observations anything about the specific inputs that activate the septal pacemaker. At most of these sites, when high-frequency stimulation is used, the frequency of the elicited theta increases with voltage (Stumpf 1965; Sailer, and Stumpf 1957; McNaughton and Sedgwick 1978). Since this relationship disappears (along with spontaneous theta) after destruction of the medial septal area (Stumpf 1965), it follows that the septal area acts as an intensity–frequency transducer: the higher the intensity of the neural input that it receives, the higher is the frequency of theta that it instructs the hippocampus to generate. At some sites, however, stimulation elicits a theta rhythm that does not rise above quite a low frequency, between 7 and 8 Hz in the free-moving rat (Robinson and Vanderwolf 1978; Graeff, Quintero, and Gray 1980). We shall consider the psychological significance of these observations in Chapter 7; but they do not help us to specify more precisely the inputs to the septal area which control the theta pacemaker.

If we ask about the inputs to the medial septal area that are established on anatomical grounds, we are not much better off. As we have seen, transection of the fimbria, eliminating the hippocampal projection to the lateral, and thence to the medial, septal area, does not affect dorsal hippocampal theta, and affects ventral hippocampal theta only in virtue of the destruction of medial septal afferents to the hippocampal formation

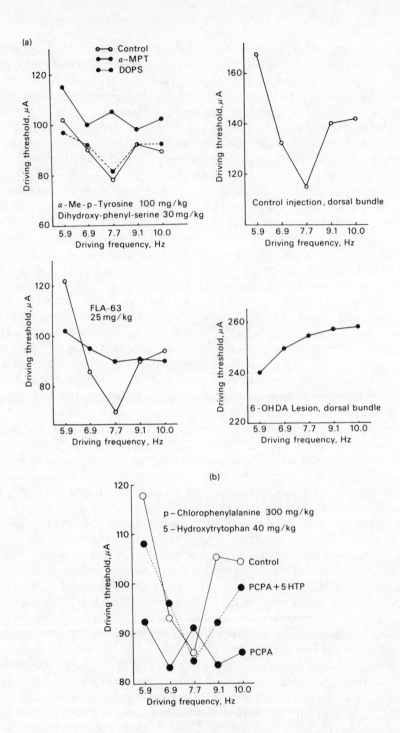

that it also causes (Rawlin *et al.* 1979). Thus the hippocampal projection to the septal area is unnecessary for theta. Theta also survives destruction of the ascending noradrenergic (Gray *et al.* 1975; Robinson, Vanderwolf, and Pappas 1977) or serotonergic (McNaughton *et al.* 1980*a*) projections to the medial septal area. Of the known projections to the medial septal area (Chapter 3), this leaves the input from the lateral preoptic and lateral hypothalamic regions. This may have some special influence on the septal pacemaker, but there is no convincing evidence for this suggestion.

Although elimination of the noradrenergic or serotonergic afferents to the septo-hippocampal system does not eliminate theta, these treatments do produce more subtle changes.

If one elicits hippocampal theta by low-frequency stimulation of the septal area (Fig. 4.4) in the free-moving male rat, one can demonstrate a characteristic function relating (i) the threshold current able to drive theta to (ii) stimulation frequency (which is identical to the frequency of the elicited theta). As shown in Fig. 4.7, there is a minimum in the resulting 'theta-driving curve' at a frequency of 7.7 Hz, corresponding to an inter-pulse interval of 130 ms. This function (whose possible behavioural significance will be discussed later) is reliably observed in individual males of several rat strains (Gray and Ball 1970; James *et al.* 1977). Females do not manifest a 7.7-Hz minimum in the theta-driving curve, but only a shallow fall in threshold as frequency rises from 6 to 10 Hz. The difference between the sexes depends on circulating testosterone, since castration of the male eliminates the 7.7-Hz minimum, while injection of testosterone propionate either to castrated males or to females produces it; ovariectomy is without effect (Drewett *et al.* 1977). In male rats the 7.7-Hz minimum appears abruptly between 15 and 16 days of age (Lanfumey, Adrien, and Gray 1982).

The characteristic shape of the theta-driving curve in the male rat depends on the integrity of both noradrenergic and serotonergic projections to the septo-hippocampal system. Pharmacological blockade of either nor-

Figure 4.7. Threshold currents for septal driving of hippocampal theta rhythm (see Fig. 4.4) as a function of stimulation frequency in the free-moving male rat. In the undrugged animal (open circles) the minimum threshold is at 7.7 Hz (130 ms interpulse interval). This minimum is eliminated by blockade of either noradrenalin (a) or serotonin (b). (a) shows the effects of systemic injection of alpha-methyl-*p*-tyrosine (α-MPT), which blocks the synthesis of both dopamine and noradrenalin, together with the restoration of the curve to normal by subsequent administration of dihydroxyphenylserine (DOPS), which acts as a substrate for the synthesis of noradrenalin only; of systemic FLA-63, which blocks the synthesis of noradrenalin only; and of destruction of the dorsal ascending noradrenergic bundle by local injection of the selective neurotoxin, 6-hydroxydopamine (6-OHDA). (b) shows the effects of systemic *p*-chlorophenylalanine (PCPA), 300 mg kg^{-1}, which blocks the synthesis of serotonin, followed by 5-hydroxytryptophan (5-HTP), 40 mg kg^{-1}, to act as a substrate for renewed synthesis of this transmitter. (Data from McNaughton *et al.* (1977) and Gray *et al.* (1975).)

adrenalin or serotonin eliminates the 7.7-Hz minimum (McNaughton *et al.* 1977; Fig. 4.7). Blockade of noradrenalin does this by selectively increasing the theta-driving threshold at 7.7 Hz. This effect can be reproduced by destruction of the dorsal ascending noradrenergic bundle by local injection of the selective neurotoxin, 6-hydroxydopamine (Ungerstedt 1968). This treatment reduced hippocampal levels of noradrenalin by more than 90 per cent (see Chapter 11) and, as shown in Fig. 4.7, completely eliminated the 7.7-Hz minimum in the theta-driving curve (Gray *et al.* 1975). Pharmacological blockade of serotonin has more complex effects, lowering the thresholds for theta-driving at all frequencies other than 7.7 Hz (McNaughton *et al.* 1977; Valero *et al.* 1977). Again, it is possible to reproduce these effects by destruction of the ascending serotonergic fibres by local injection of a specific neurotoxin, 5,7-dihydroxytryptamine (Baumgarten *et al.* 1978; see Chapter 11). Using this technique we have shown that a moderate destruction of serotonergic terminals in the hippocampus gives rise to a lowering of the theta-driving threshold at about 9 Hz, while a more complete destruction lowers the threshold at about 7 Hz (McNaughton *et al.* 1980*a*). The latter effect can also be produced by interventions in the adreno–pituitary system (Valero *et al.* 1977) or by foot-shock (Valero and Gray, unpublished), so it may be related to a stress response. Since septal serotonergic terminals were unaffected in these experiments (the injection of 5,7-dihydroxytryptamine was made into the fornix-fimbria and/or the cingulum bundle), these changes in the theta-driving curve are probably due to the loss of a serotonergic influence on the production of theta within the hippocampus itself (McNaughton *et al.* 1980*a*). This inference does not necessarily apply, however, to the noradrenergic input to the septo-hippocampal system, since, in the experiment using 6-hydroxydopamine, the dorsal noradrenergic bundle was destroyed before its entry into the septal area (Gray *et al.* 1975).

In summary, then, the noradrenergic input to the septo-hippocampal system from the locus coeruleus selectively lowers the threshold for septal driving of theta at a frequency of 7.7 Hz by an action which may be within the septum or within the hippocampus; while the serotonergic input from the median raphe selectively raises the threshold for septal driving of theta at frequencies above and below (but especially below) 7.7 Hz by an action which is probably intrahippocampal. It is possible that the action of testosterone (necessary for the appearance of a 7.7-Hz minimum in the theta-driving curve) is exercized by way of the dorsal noradrenergic bundle, since it has been shown that a majority of cells in the locus coeruleus take up this hormone (Heritage *et al.* 1980).

The characteristic shape of the theta-driving curve also seems to depend upon the integrity of the feedback from the hippocampus to the septal area. Section of the fimbria eliminates the 7.7-Hz minimum, substituting a flat function similar to the one seen after destruction of the dorsal noradrenergic bundle (Rawlins *et al.* 1979). McLennan and Miller (1974*a*, 1976) reported electrophysiological observations suggesting that feedback via the fimbria from the hippocampus activates a frequency-gating mechanism in the lateral septal nucleus. They suggested that this could be an essential link in the generation of the hippocampal theta rhythm. As we have seen, this is not so, since theta survives destruction of either the fimbria or the lateral septal area (Rawlins *et al.* 1979). But it is possible that the frequency-gating mechanism described by McLennan and Miller (1974*a*, 1976) plays a role in the modulation of theta frequency, along with the noradrenergic and serotonergic afferents to the septo-hippocampal system.

One final word about theta before we pass on to other topics. Although theta is generated in CA 1 and the dentate gyrus, these are not the only regions from which it can be recorded. Within the hippocampal formation itself there is a prominent theta rhythm in the subicular area (Gray 1972*b*), but this is probably volume-conducted from adjacent areas of the hippocampus and dentate gyrus (Bland and Whishaw 1976; James *et al.* 1977). The entorhinal area also displays a theta rhythm (Adey, Dunlop, and Hendrix 1960), and this is generated locally (Mitchell and Ranck 1980). However, entorhinal theta also depends on the septal pacemaker, since destruction of the medial septal area eliminates it (Rawlins, Mitchell, Olton, and Steward 1980*d*). Theta can also be recorded from the thalamus (indeed, it was once called the 'thalamic rhythm') and the neocortex. Since these lie respectively above and below the hippocampal formation, volume conduction is likely in both cases, and has indeed been demonstrated in the case of rat neocortex (Gerbrandt, Lawrence, Eckhardt, and Lloyd 1978). A hippocampal origin for neocortical theta in the rat is also supported by the report that it can be driven in the same way as hippocampal theta by low-frequency septal stimulation (Landfield 1977). A final region from which theta has been recorded is the ventral tegmental area in the vicinity of the A10 dopaminergic cell group (Le Moal and Cardo 1975). It is not clear exactly how this relates to hippocampal theta. But Winson (1974) has shown that theta recorded in the brain stem may arise from a hippocampal generator; and Le Moal and Cardo (1975) were able to abolish ventral tegmental theta by medial septal lesions. Thus there are no clear instances to date of theta generated elsewhere than in the hippocampal formation or not under medial septal control.

Evoked potentials and unit responses

I have concentrated so far on the hippocampal EEG because of the significance that the behavioural correlates of theta have had for theories of hippocampal function. Recently, however, studies of single-unit activity in the hippocampus have assumed a comparable importance, especially for the spatial theory of hippocampal function developed by O'Keefe and his associates (O'Keefe and Nadel 1978). In principle the investigation of single-unit responses should afford much more direct inferences than EEG studies to the functional roles of different morphological elements in the nervous system. On the positive side, the units from which one records are identical to (and in the best case identified with) the morphological elements whose function one hopes to determine; on the negative side, the relationship of slow-wave activity either to neuronal firing or to anatomical structure remains obscure, to say the least. And indeed the single-unit approach to the study of nervous function has paid enormous dividends in, say, the visual system. However, there are peculiar difficulties in applying this approach to the septo-hippocampal system. It turns out (perhaps for reasons that derive directly from the functions in fact performed by the septo-hippocampal system) that the characteristic stimuli to which hippocampal units respond depend critically on the experimental environment in which the animal is placed. This in turn tends to relate rather closely to the kind of unit response the experimenter expects to find. In consequence it is virtually impossible to discuss the available data on unit neuronal responses in the septo-hippocampal system without bringing in psychological theory, an undertaking we shall therefore postpone until Chapter 7.

About the only non-controversial remark that can be made about the types of stimuli to which septal or hippocampal units respond is that units in the medial septal area are multimodal, that is, each unit responds to a variety of different kinds of sensory input, e.g. visual, auditory, sciatic (Hayat and Feldman 1974; Zin et al. 1977). These observations are consonant with the generally held view that the medial septal input to the hippocampal formation is non-specific with regard to the sensory information that it conveys. That it does convey this information to the hippocampus is demonstrated by the fact that medial septal lesions reduce the number of hippocampal units responding to simple sensory stimuli, such as lights, clicks or foot-shock (Miller and Groves 1977). Interestingly, there was a particular loss in this experiment of hippocampal *inhibitory* unit responses after medial septal lesions; this offers some support for the hypothesis, discussed above in connection with the theta rhythm, that the septo-hippocampal projection is predominantly inhibitory. In iontophoretic experiments Segal (1974a, 1975a; Segal and Bloom 1974a, b) has shown that both noradrenalin and serotonin also produce predominantly inhibitory responses in the hippocampus and septal area. Furthermore, these responses were mimicked by electrical stimulation of the brainstem nuclei (the locus coeruleus and the median and dorsal raphe) from which the monoaminergic afferents to the septo-hippocampal system originate. Segal and Bloom (1974a) also showed that the hippocampal response to iontophoretically applied noradrenalin is mediated by a β-noradrenergic receptor, a fact which will achieve some importance in Chapter 11.

It remains to consider one further class of phenomena which have been influential in shaping theory about septo-hippocampal function. If one follows the passage of a neural event which commences in the entorhinal area and then travels around the hippocampal circuit shown in Fig. 3.5, one observes a remarkable plasticity of response (Andersen 1978). To a repeated, constant input both increased responses ('potentiation') and decreased responses ('habituation') have been observed. Potentiation can be observed either during a train of stimuli, in which case it depends critically on the frequency of stimulation, and is known as 'frequency potentiation'; or at quite long intervals after a period of high-frequency ('tetanizing') stimulation, when it is known as 'post-tetanic' or 'long-term' potentiation. These phenomena have been detected using several different methods of measurement: single-unit responses; population spikes (the current generated by the action potentials of many similar cells firing simultaneously); or field potentials, a less well-defined extracellular event picked up from a large population of neurons (Andersen 1978). And they have been detected in a variety of different preparations, ranging from the free-moving animal to a lamellar slice cut transverse to the septo-temporal axis of the hippocampal formation and investigated *in vitro*. Long-term potentiation has made a particularly great impression on students of hippocampal function, because of its possible relation to memory. It is therefore of particular importance that this phenomenon has been observed in free-moving animals. Moreover, the effect can last up to three days (Bliss and Gardner-Medwin 1973), a time span that is a long way from the millisecond scale on which most physiology works and well into the psychological domain.

Research on potentiation is in a very active phase at the moment, and much is still controversial. I shall summarize here only the main features of the data, without much regard to the preparation from which they were gleaned.

The links in the trisynaptic chain, perforant path to dentate, mossy fibres to CA 3, and Schaffer collaterals to CA 1 (see Fig. 3.5), are all excitatory, the transmitters probably being the amino acids, glutamate or aspartate (Storm-Mathisen 1978). If electrical stimulation is applied to the perforant path, frequency potentiation is greatest at rates of stimulation of 10–20 Hz, and the process progresses round the neuronal chain, first appearing in the dentate response, then in CA 3 and last in CA 1 (Fig. 4.8). A somewhat lower optimum frequency (8 Hz) has been reported when stimulation is applied to the mossy fibres and the responses recorded in CA 3 or CA 1 (Alger and Teyler 1976). It is difficult to know, however, how precisely to treat these values, since, according to Andersen (1978), the optimal stimulus frequency rises as the level of anaesthesia falls; how one is to apply this observation to the hippocampal slice *in vitro* (used for example by Alger and Teyler 1976) is unclear.

Long-term potentiation also depends on stimulus frequency, but it is not directly related to the degree of frequency potentiation seen during the period of stimulation itself. Andersen (1978) observed bigger effects

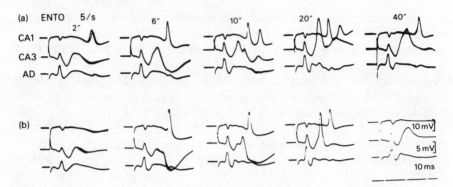

Figure 4.8. Frequency potentiation in the hippocampal formation. Records from dentate area (AD), CA3, and Ca1 during (a) and after (b) tetanic stimulation at 5 Hz to perforant path. Labels on top indicate time after onset and stop of the tetanus. Note sequence of recruitment, largest responses after 20 and smaller after 40 seconds of tetanus. (From Andersen (1978).)

after a 50-Hz train than after 10 Hz. This author makes the important point that the stimulation parameters necessary to produce long-term potentiation (which lasted for 30–75 minutes in his experiments) are not too different from those likely to be encountered under physiological conditions. Thus long-term potentiation was observed with a 10-Hz stimulus applied for 10 seconds, and observations of hippocampal and entorhinal cells in the free-moving animal show that they fire spontaneously at these or higher rates for comparable periods of time (e.g. O'Keefe 1976; Segal 1973*b*).

For potentiation to occur, it is generally not sufficient for the presynaptic fibre to fire at the appropriate rate for the appropriate time; in addition, normal synaptic activation must take place (Andersen 1978; Dunwiddie *et al.* 1978; Hesse 1979). However, B. McNaughton *et al.* (1978), working with anaesthetized rats, have reported contrary observations: discharge of the dentate granule cells at the time of the tetanizing stimulation was neither necessary nor sufficient in their experiment for long-term potentiation to occur in response to later stimulation. This experiment is also unusual in finding that, under certain conditions, potentiation occurred if two separate input pathways were simultaneously tetanized (the lateral and medial perforant paths, which innervate respectively the outer and middle one-thirds of the molecular layer of the dentate gyrus), but not if only one of these pathways was stimulated. In other experiments it has been sufficient to stimulate only one input line (Andersen 1978).

Potentiation has usually been found to be confined to the tetanized pathway (Steward *et al.* 1977; Andersen 1978; Deadwyler *et al.* 1978; N. McNaughton and Miller 1979*), the response to other synaptic inputs

*See also McNaughton and Miller (1984) in additional references.

onto the same target cells either being unchanged (Andersen *et al.* 1977) or depressed (Lynch *et al.* 1977). There are two reports, however, of potentiation also extending to other synapses terminating on the same cell (Yamamoto and Chugo 1978; Misgeld *et al.* 1979). It is possible that this discrepancy depends on the particular population of postsynaptic cells studied (P. Andersen, personal communication), since Yamamoto and Chugo (1978) and Misgeld *et al.* (1979) worked with the mossy fibre input to CA 3, whereas the other reports concerned the response in CA 1 or in the dentate granule cells. Potentiation may also be specific to a particular collateral of a branching neurone. Thus Miller and McNaughton (1979*) stimulated CA 3 in anaesthetized rats, simultaneously activating the pathway to the lateral septum and the Schaffer collaterals to CA 1; no potentiation occurred in the former pathway, as previously reported by Andersen, Teyler, and Wester (1973), although the CA 1 response recorded at the same time was potentiated. Although the hippocampal input to the septal area does not apparently display potentiation, the septal input to the hippocampal formation (specifically, to the dentate granule cells) does (McNaughton and Miller 1979*). As in the case of potentiation from entorhinal or intrahippocampal stimulation (see above), the phenomenon is confined to the tetanized pathway: medial septal stimulation potentiated the dentate response to subsequent medial septal stimulation, but not to perforant path stimulation, and vice versa (McNaughton and Miller 1979*).

Potentiation consists in an increased response after a repetitive input. But exactly the opposite has also been reported: a reduction of the response with repeated stimulation. Using natural stimuli (lights, tones, and the like), Vinogradova (e.g. 1970) and her colleagues have studied this phenomenon — habituation — in considerable detail; but we shall postpone consideration of this work until we deal with behavioural experiments in Chapter 7. The more purely electrophysiological experiments have used essentially the same techniques as those used to demonstrate potentiation.

So far habituation has been reported only in the dentate granule cells in response to stimulation of the perforant path, both in the hippocampal slice (Alger and Teyler 1976; Teyler and Alger 1976; White *et al.* 1979) and in the intact rat (Harris *et al.* 1978). In Alger and Teyler's (1976) experiment this synapse was directly compared with the CA 3 response to stimulation of the mossy fibres, and with the CA 1 response to stimulation of the Schaffer collaterals. All three of these synapses displayed long-term potentiation (lasting at least 30 minutes). But, whereas the CA 3 and CA 1 responses showed frequency potentiation (maximum increase at 8 Hz over the range 0.1 to 15 Hz), the dentate response decreased during stimulation and the amount of this decrease grew as frequency increased from 0.1 Hz to a maximum at 8 Hz, habituation still being observed even at 15 Hz. There is a contradiction between this observation of habituation at

*See also McNaughton and Miller (1984, 1986) in additional references.

frequencies as high as 8–15 Hz and other observations, described above, that at these frequencies potentiation occurs in the perforant path–dentate synapse. To some extent, at least, this is a problem of measurement, and both processes — habituation and potentiation — can occur at the same time. This is illustrated by the findings reported by White *et al.* (1979). These workers delivered pairs of pulses to the perforant path and varied the interval both between the pairs and between members of the pair. Their results demonstrated changes in response magnitude which were a complex function of both intervals. At frequencies of presentation of *pairs* of stimuli above 0.05 Hz, habituation was observed, in the sense that response to the first member of the pair gradually declined. But, at the same time, potentiation was observed, in the shape of a greater response to the second than to the first member of the pair, with the greatest effect occurring at an inter-stimulus interval of 40–50 ms (corresponding to a frequency of 20–25 Hz). Thus habituation appears to occur preferentially at relatively low frequencies of stimulation, potentiation at relatively high ones.

The perforant path–dentate synapse, then, seems to play a rather special role in the hippocampal circuit, in that it may show habituation as well as potentiation of the response to repeated stimulation. But the use of the term 'habituation' to describe this phenomenon begs a number of important questions. In particular, we need to know whether the response decrement observed in response to electrical stimulation in the hippocampus (not to say the hippocampal slice) is the same phenomenon as the behavioural habituation described by Sokolov's (1960) group in Moscow.

Teyler and Alger (1976) go some way to meeting this point by showing that response decrement in the dentate granule cells shares a number of features with behavioural habituation, including spontaneous recovery (but over the very short period of 30 seconds), dishabituation, habituation of dishabituation, and the distinction between chronic and acute habituation (Sokolov 1960, 1963; Gray 1975, Chapter 1). Winson and Abzug (1978) also report findings which suggest that blockade of the entorhinal input to the hippocampal formation at the level of the dentate granule cells may play a role in normal behaviour. They stimulated the perforant path in free-moving rats and recorded the response one, two, or three synapses around the hippocampal circuit during different stages of alertness or sleep. They found transmission to be better during slow-wave sleep than during still alertness, with transmission during two other stages accompanied by theta (rapid-eye-movement sleep, and awake-moving) occupying an intermediate position. These differences in the efficiency of transmission were almost entirely due to changes at the perforant path–dentate synapse. Since Winson and Abzug's (1978) frequency of stimulation (0.1 Hz) was in the range where Alger and Teyler (1976) and Teyler and Alger (1976) observed habituation in the hippocampal slice, it is possible that the two phenomena are related and that both may justly be described as 'habituation'.

These observations suggest that there is an important gating of neural transmission in the dentate gyrus. Given the potential significance of this phenomenon for behaviour, it would be valuable to know how it works. Andersen (1978) has discussed possible synaptic mechanisms underlying frequency and long-term potentiation, and concludes that these may be based on an increased amount of liberated transmitter or on local post-synaptic changes near the tetanized synapse. Morphological changes may also be involved. Van Harreveld and Fifková (1975) observed a swelling in dendritic spines after tetanizing stimulation of the perforant path; this would presumably have the effect of increasing the efficiency of synaptic transmission, since the synaptic cleft now becomes smaller.

More distant influences are also involved. Winson and Abzug (1978) note that the hilus is rich in noradrenergic and serotonergic terminals and speculate that these inputs may play a role in determining the passage of a neural message through the dentate gate. There is evidence to support this suggestion. Assaf and Miller (1978) studied the effects of stimulation of the median raphe on the dentate response to perforant path stimulation. The raphe stimulation inhibited the spontaneous firing of the granule cells, as in Segal's (1975a) earlier observations of CA 1 and CA 3 pyramidal cells; but at the same time it facilitated the population spike recorded in response to perforant path stimulation. Thus it seems that the serotonergic innervation of the hippocampal formation is able to open the dentate gate. Segal (1977a, b, c, d) has reported indirect evidence that the noradrenergic afferents to the hippocampal formation are similarly able to facilitate transmission round the hippocampal circuit. His experiments do not necessarily implicate the perforant path–dentate step in the chain (see Chapter 7). But Assaf (1978) and Assaf, Mason, and Miller (1979), studying the effects of locus coeruleus stimulation on the dentate response to perforant path stimulation, showed changes at this synapse of the same kind as those seen by Assaf and Miller (1978) after median raphe stimulation: an inhibition of the spontaneous firing rate in dentate granule cells coupled with an increased response to perforant path stimuli. Thus both monoaminergic inputs to the hippocampal formation apparently facilitate passage through the dentate gate.

There is also evidence that the septo-hippocampal projection plays a similar role; recall that the cholinergic innervation of the hippocampus, like the noradrenergic and serotonergic innervation, is particularly dense in the hilus (Fig. 4.6). As noted above, Winson and Abzug (1978) found transmission around the hippocampal circuit during both walking and sleeping theta to be intermediate between the levels noted during slow-wave sleep and still alertness. They also reported that transmission is more variable during theta than at other times. Segal (1978a), working with the hippocampal response to stimulation of the contralatera-hippocampus (the 'commissural' response), also found that the initial response (10–15 ms latency) was smaller during awake theta than during non-theta states (still-alertness and slow-wave sleep). But in addition he recorded a late potential (30–40 ms latency) which was greater during theta than non-theta. As we shall see in Chapter 7, Segal (1977*b, c, d*) has demonstrated that this late potential is specifically enhanced by procedures, such as classical conditioning, which cause the animal to pay particularly close attention to its environment at the time the commissural response is tested. Thus it is possible that theta facilitates transmission round the hippocampal circuit only for stimuli which are important in the control of the animal's behaviour.

Alvarez-Leefman and Gardner-Medwin (1975) conducted a more direct investigation of the interaction between septal and entorhinal inputs to the hippocampus. They report that a single conditioning pulse applied to the septal area just before another test pulse applied to the perforant path facilitates the dentate granule response to the latter. This facilitation was maximal at two intervals of separation between the two stimuli: there was a rapid effect (inter-stimulus interval about 2 ms) and a slow one (about 15–300 ms), interrupted by a period of inhibition maximal at an inter-stimulus interval of 4–6 ms. It is possible that the slow facilitation is related to the theta rhythm; the time scale is of the right order. This inference is supported by the location of effective stimulation sites in the septal area; these were in the medial nucleus or the nucleus of the diagonal band (Alvarez-Leefman 1977; J. D. Dudar and A. R. Gardner-Medwin, personal communication). These findings have been confirmed by Fantie (1979) and McNaughton and Miller (in preparation*). McNaughton and Miller (in preparation*) also showed that a conditioning pulse applied to the perforant path facilitated the response to a subsequent test stimulus applied to the medial septal nucleus, although (as noted earlier) trains of stimuli applied to the medial septal area and perforant path, respectively, did not interact insofar as long-term potentiation was concerned.

It would be satisfying to relate these observations to the well-known cholinergic projection from the medial septal area to the hippocampus. Surprisingly, however, Fantie (1979) was unable to alter the effect of a septal conditioning pulse on the response to a perforant path test pulse by systemic injections of either muscarinic (atropine, scopolamine) or nicotinic (tubocurarine, dihydro-β-erythroidine) antagonists. Dudar and Gardner-Medwin (personal communication) similarly failed to change the septal stimulation effect by injection of atropine through the intrahippocampal recording electrode. These findings make it implausible that the septo-hippocampal cholinergic pathway is involved in the effects described by these workers; but no other septal afferents to the hippocampus have yet been described.

Recently, however, Rudell, Fox, and Ranck (1980) have provided evidence that the septally controlled theta rhythm does indeed gate transmission of stimuli round the hippocampal circuit. Chronically implanted electrodes were used to deliver pulses to the entorhinal cortex in the free-

*See also McNaughton and Miller (1984) in additional references.

moving rat. The size of the population spike recorded in the dentate granule cells varied systematically with the phase of the simultaneously recorded dentate theta rhythm, being at a maximum 110° after its positive peak. Similarly, CA 1 population spikes were recorded in response to pulses delivered to commissural fibres coming from the contralateral hippocampus. Again the size of the response varied systematically in relation to theta; surprisingly (since theta in CA 1 is 180° out of phase with theta in the dentate) the location of the maximum response remained at 110° after the positive peak of the dentate theta wave. Thus it appears that a stimulus reaching the hippocampus at about this time is likely to receive privileged transmission through all points on the hippocampal circuit. These findings suggest that the theta rhythm could play an important role in the selection of stimuli for entry into the hippocampal circuit, and/or in timing the entry of successive stimuli.

It is surprising that there has not been more research along these lines. Anatomically speaking, the hippocampus seems to serve as a point of confluence between two major neural streams, one entering from the septal area, the other from the entorhinal cortex. One might have expected that physiologists would pay particular attention to what happens when these streams intermingle. It is intriguing, moreover, that both streams are exquisitely sensitive to small differences in low frequencies of stimulation. On the septal side of the divide, we have the theta rhythm, with a frequency which varies very precisely in relation to the animal's behaviour (Chapter 7); on the entorhinal side, we have the phenomena of frequency potentiation and habituation. In both cases, there seems to be some kind of nodal point at frequencies around 8 Hz. Thus the minimum in the theta-driving curve (Fig. 4.7) lies exactly at 7.7 Hz, and a change in the inter-pulse interval of as little as 5 ms is sufficient to give rise to a significant change in the threshold for septal elicitation of theta (James *et al.* 1977); furthermore, the two types of theta described by Vanderwolf's group (Chapter 7) have frequency bands which meet at roughly this same value. On the entorhinal side it is not so clear, but there appears to be some kind of transition, as stimulation frequency rises above 8 Hz, from effects that consist predominantly in habituation to effects that consist predominantly in potentiation. It would be particularly valuable to know whether there is any relationship or interaction between these effects of frequency on the septal and entorhinal inputs, respectively, to the hippocampal formation.

Research on the pure electrophysiology of the septo-hippocampal system has not so far been able to answer these questions; nor can it yet elucidate the basic functions served by the phenomena (theta rhythm, potentiation, habituation) described in this chapter. These are issues to which we return in Chapter 7, when we shall take a look at more behaviourally oriented electrophysiological research.

5

Approaches to septo-hippocampal function

I began this book by likening our journey to that of the explorers of the last century. By now the reader may perhaps feel the aptness of the analogy. We have quite good maps of the internal circuitry of the septo-hippocampal system; indeed, in some respects this is the best mapped part of the brain. But when we ask where we are in relation to the rest of the brain, we find that we are indeed in darkest Africa. Neither the known inputs to the septo-hippocampal system nor its known outputs tell us much about the kind of information it receives or what it does with it. Potentials move busily around the hippocampal circuitry, sometimes meeting an intrepid electrode on the way. The electrode can tell us that the potential is there and sometimes where it has come from — but not what it is *for*. It is hardly surprising that, under these circumstances, imagination reigns supreme: each scrap of information that our explorers bring back, it sometimes seems, is the basis of a new theory of hippocampal function. In this chapter I shall briefly describe the main hypotheses that have been proposed and the major sources of data on which they rest. More detailed discussion of their respective merits is reserved for later, when we know more about the behavioural investigations of septo-hippocampal function which, in the end, will have to decide between them. For the moment, we shall simply bring the different theories on stage and indicate their pedigree.

One of the striking features about theory in this area is its close dependence on method. Each major hypothesis is based largely on data gathered in only one particular way, and unfortunately those who espouse it rarely look at data gathered in other ways. It will come as no surprise to learn that none of the methods is without serious problems. One would therefore expect that, though a theory based on data obtained with one method may get something right, it is unlikely to get it all right; and this indeed is the case. Thus, to make the most of the theories that have been advanced, and to transcend them if we can, we must consider carefully the limitations of the methods on which each depends. For this reason the present chapter also briefly describes the major methods that have been used to study septo-hippocampal function and their relation to the theories that each has spawned.

Clinical data

The earliest theory to gain wide acceptance relates the hippocampus to memory. It was based on the striking changes observed in patients treated for epilepsy by bilateral resection of the medial temporal lobe, including the hippocampus (Scoville and Milner 1957; Penfield and Milner 1958). After surgery such patients appear to be incapable of forming new memories, although they remember much about their lives before the operation. As Weiskrantz (1978, pp. 375–6) puts it, 'In confronting these patients informally in the clinical situation, the conclusion is practically irresistible that they cannot form a durable record of their new experiences. . . . Their most striking disability is in remembering incidents in daily life, even after a gap of just a few minutes, and even when the incident (such as seeing the experimenter) is experienced on several occasions.' To account for this syndrome, and for similar observations made in more formal experimental tests, Milner (1968) proposed the hypothesis that patients of this kind fail to 'consolidate' memories, that is, transfer them from short-term to long-term storage. We shall consider in Chapter 9 the extent to which this general description of the consequences of temporal lobe damage in man is correct, especially in the light of the accumulating evidence (Weiskrantz and Warrington 1975; Weiskrantz 1978) that, under some conditions at any rate, these 'amnesic' patients are in fact capable of forming new long-term memories.

The observations on which the memory hypothesis is based suffer from the kind of limitation usually associated with clinical data. The lesion made in these patients was neither limited to the hippocampus, nor did it destroy all the hippocampus. Only indirectly therefore can the inference be made that damage to the hippocampus was critical for the behavioural effects observed after surgery (Weiskrantz and Warrington 1975; Weiskrantz 1978; Butters and Cermak 1975; Horel 1978). Furthermore, the patients who underwent this operation were, of course, not normal beforehand — they were epileptic. Isaacson (1972) has demonstrated in animal experiments that removal of the hippocampus after it has been rendered epileptic for a period before surgery can affect behaviour quite differently from the removal of a normal hippocampus.

A further problem is rather more peculiar to this operation. Precisely because it has such drastic effects on memory it is rarely if ever used now, so that the population of patients available for further research is somewhat limited. In consequence, most of the relevant research is now performed with other patients suffering from the amnesic syndrome, particularly those in whom a chronically high consumption of alcohol produces the condition known as 'Korsakoff's psychosis' (Victor *et al.* 1971). There appear to be striking similarities between the memory impairments seen in these cases and those produced by temporal lobe resection, so this strategy is perhaps justified (see the discussion in Elliott and Whelan 1978, pp. 394–6). But, since Korsakoff patients do *not* normally have damage in the hippocampus (although they often have damage in structures closely associated with the hippocampus), it is even harder to make inferences to hippocampal function from their behaviour than from the behaviour of patients with resection of the temporal lobe.

It was partly the dramatic nature of the memory impairment seen in these surgical cases that prompted the great growth of interest in the 1960s in the effects of hippocampal lesions on the behaviour of experimental animals. Very rapidly these experiments converged on the conclusion that hippocampectomy does *not* produce any obvious signs of memory impairment in species such as the rat, cat or monkey. This raised the problem, not yet resolved, that there may be a quite different behavioural function for the hippocampus in man and other animals. If so, the enterprise on which we are engaged is, of course, fundamentally misconceived. There are at least three other possibilities, however. The first is that the human amnesic syndrome has nothing much to do with the hippocampus; as we have seen, the clinical data, to say the least, do not exclude this possibility. The second (argued recently by Weiskrantz and Warrington 1975) is that the 'amnesic' syndrome in man has been misunderstood, and that when it is understood correctly it resembles the syndrome seen in animals after hippocampal damage. The third is that the early animal experiments set the subject the wrong problem, and that when the right problem is set memory deficits *do* ensue after hippocampal damage; this point of view has been advanced in different forms by, for example, Winocur and Mills (1970), Iversen (1976), and Gaffan (1972). To set the 'right' problem, of course, requires that we understand the nature of the deficit produced by hippocampal lesions, and this takes us right back to theory. These are issues we shall take up in Chapter 9.

Experimental lesions

Although the early experiments on the effects of hippocampal lesions in animals failed to disclose a memory deficit, they did reveal reliable and substantial changes in behaviour. By the mid-sixties the most promising hypothesis to account for these changes postulated a loss in the animal's capacity to inhibit behaviour. Essentially the same hypothesis was proposed in respect of the septal area; this is hardly surprising, given that the behavioural syndromes produced by lesions to the hippocampus and the septal area, respectively, resemble each other closely (Chapter 6). The behavioural inhibition hypothesis was proposed in two different forms. In the first the function of the hippocampus is seen as that of gating out stimuli to which it is maladaptive to respond (Douglas and Pribram 1966; Douglas 1967). In the second, the function of the septal area (McCleary 1966) or the hippocampus (Kimble 1969) is seen as more directly that of inhibiting a dominant, but now maladaptive, response. In the latter form essentially the same hypothesis had been proposed earlier by Kaada (1951) on the basis of observations of the effects of electrical stimulation of the septal area, fornix, and hippocampus on motor and autonomic responss. With respect to the hippocampus the behavioural inhibition hypothesis is essentially the only one to which the literature on experimental lesions has given birth; its rivals owe their existence to data gained by other methods. But the data on the effects of septal lesions have also spawned several other hypotheses of a rather diverse character, e.g. increased incentive motivation (Harvey and Hunt 1965) or changed emotional reactivity (Brady and Nauta 1953); for reviews see Caplan (1973) and Ursin (1976). A consideration of why this should be so brings us up against the limitations of the lesion method.

The general limitations of the lesion method have often been rehearsed. Pride of place is usually occupied by the remark that, when you destroy the area whose functions you hope to discover, you then study not that area but the rest of the brain. Furthermore, the rest of the brain is no longer in its normal state. It reacts in unpredictable ways to the loss of one of its parts. It may, for example, sprout new connections that are not normally there, and this appears to happen particularly easily in the septo-hippocampal system (e.g. Raisman 1969; Gerbrandt, Rose, Wheeler, and Lynch 1978); or a region that is normally devoted to other things may take over the function of the damaged tissue; or, again, a problem that is solved by an intact animal in one way may be solved by one whose brain is damaged in quite a different way. So that it is hazardous to deduce the function of the missing part by simple subtraction of the behaviour of the lesioned animal from that of an intact one. These problems exist for any lesion experiment. But they are compounded by still greater problems when there are serious uncertainties concerning the anatomy of the area and virtually total ignorance even of its general functions, as is the case for the septo-hippocampal system.

The problems posed by lesion experiments are less acute in the case of the hippocampal formation than in that of the septal area, for two reasons: first, the anatomy of the hippocampal formation is better understood; second, morphologically speaking, the hippocampal formation is much more homogeneous. Thus, one has some licence to believe that the hippocampal formation constitutes a particular organ delimited from the rest of the brain, and some way of estimating the degree to which one has removed it. This is a much less reasonable position to adopt in the case of the septal area. Unlike the hippocampal formation, which is for the most part marked out by its own boundaries, the limits of the septal area are established in the main by extrinsic structures: the corpus callosum, the lateral ventricles, the anterior commissure, and the descending columns of the post-commissural fornix. It is also these other structures which, for the most part, determine the shape of a lesion produced electrolytically, by far the most common method of damaging the septal area.

The great majority of lesion experiments aim to destroy the entire septal area lying between these boundaries, and for the most part they succeed in doing so (Fig. 5.1). But, as we saw in Chapter 3, this area contains a diversity of nuclei; and to those which have close connections with the hippocampus can be added others which do not. Thus, in a typical large septal lesion of this kind, the damage often includes the bed nucleus of the stria terminalis and the nucleus accumbens or even, when the lesion extends ventrally below the level of the anterior commissure, the preoptic region of the hypothalamus (Fig. 3.6). In addition — and again in con-

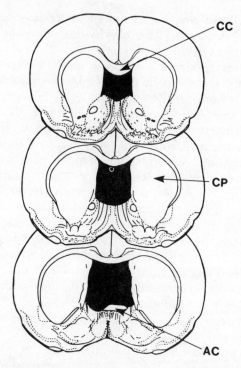

Figure 5.1. A typical large electrolytic lesion (shaded black) of the septal area, bounded by the corpus callosum (CC), the lateral ventricles (which separate the septal area from the caudate–putamen, CP), and the anterior commissure (AC). The diagrammatic frontal sections of the rat brain are modified from Mabry and Peeler (1972).

trast to hippocampal lesions — damage to the septal area disrupts a number of fibre pathways that traverse it. These include to a greater or lesser extent (depending on the particular lesion) the subicular output travelling in the fornix; the noradrenergic and serotonergic fibres which enter the septal area through the medial forebrain bundle on their way to the hippocampus and to large regions of the neocortex; and other fibre pathways, whose nature is still obscure, entering the septal area with the median forebrain bundle. It would be remarkable indeed if destruction of an area as complex and diverse as this produced a unitary change in function.

This conclusion has become commonplace (e.g. Fried 1972*b*; Ursin 1976), but only after many efforts at unitary accounts of the 'septal syndrome' have been tried and failed. This is not to imply that unitary explanations should not be sought; on the contrary, the whole thrust of scientific research is towards the strongest generalization which will explain the largest number of observations. But it seems clear that some parcellation of the septal area should first be made on anatomical grounds. Unfortunately, this is easier said than done. For it is difficult to make small lesions of discrete nuclei within the septal area and so investigate their functions one by one; difficult, but not impossible, and we shall consider in Chapter 10 some of the progress that has been made along these lines.

Much of the relevant research has stemmed from the hypothesis (Donovick 1968; Gray 1970a) that the similarities between the behavioural effects of septal and hippocampal lesions (Chapter 6) are due to the fact that septal lesions eliminate the hippocampal theta rhythm. It follows from this hypothesis that lesions confined to the medial septal pacemakers for theta should affect behaviour in the same way as hippocampectomy. It turns out, however, that this simple 'theta' hypothesis is inadequate: some of the behavioural effects of hippocampal lesions can be reproduced by damage to the medial septal area, but others by damage to the lateral septal area (Chapter 10). This is hardly surprising, given the role of these two regions as input and output stations for the hippocampus, respectively. Only if the hippocampus did nothing to transform the information that it receives would we expect the effects of damage to its inputs and outputs to be identical. Indeed, one way to gain some insight into what transformations the hippocampus performs is by establishing the different effects of lesions to the medial and lateral septal areas.

There remains, however, the problem of deciding how many distinct functions the septal area itself performs. For our purposes it will be sufficient to separate out from the total septal syndrome that part which is due to its connections with the hippocampus. In this dissection our clearest guide will be the hippocampal syndrome. This approach rests on the assumption that behavioural sequelae of large septal lesions which closely resemble the effects of hippocampectomy are due to the joint destruction of the hippocampal input and output in the medial and lateral septal areas respectively. Those parts of the septal syndrome which cannot be attributed to septo-hippocampal connections will not then concern us further. To this end Chapter 6 is devoted to a detailed comparison between the septal and hippocampal syndromes.

Although hippocampal lesions pose fewer problems of interpretation than septal lesions, they none the less present problems of a practical order. The convoluted shape of the hippocampus makes it hard to remove completely or simply. There are two major ways of trying to do so. The less satisfactory, but more widely used, is by making electrolytic lesions. To destroy all or most of the hippocampus by this method it is necessary to insert an electrode at multiple points along its septo-temporal axis. Even so, it is common for much hippocampal tissue to remain intact, especially the ventral portion. The alternative is to suck the hippocampus out, usually starting near the septal pole. Because of the way the hippocampal formation is surrounded by the fibres of the alveus, this method is surprisingly effective and, in the best case (Fig. 5.2), most of the hippocampal banana comes out with its skin. But there is a price to pay: the

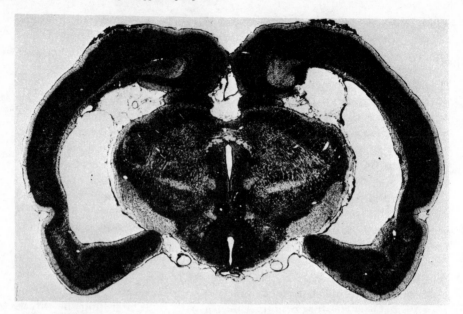

Figure 5.2. An aspiration lesion of the hippocampus made by Dr J. N. P. Rawlins.

method also produces extensive cortical damage. One can control for this by using a group with cortical damage only, but even so one ends up studying the effects of hippocampal plus cortical damage and comparing this to the effects of cortical damage alone. If both lesions produce similar behavioural changes but for different reasons (not an impossible situation), one would erroneously conclude that the hippocampal damage has been without effect. And even with an aspiration lesion there is almost always some ventral hippocampal tissue left intact.

Because of the widespread use of electrolytic lesions in experiments on the hippocampus and the greater accessibility of the dorsal hippocampus, the majority of studies of the behavioural effects of hippocampal lesions have actually been concerned with the *dorsal* hippocampus only. This is only an important problem if there are major differences of function between the dorsal and ventral hippocampus. With the exception of the rather special pattern of projections from the ventral tip of the subiculum (Fig. 3.17), and the pathway from CA 3 to the entorhinal area which is confined to the temporal one-third of the hippocampus (Hjorth-Simonsen 1971), the anatomy of the hippocampal formation is in fact remarkably homogeneous throughout its septo-temporal extent. Furthermore, damage in the dorsal region of the hippocampus frequently disconnects the ventral hippocampus from the septal area by severing the fimbria. Thus such a lesion is probably functionally equivalent, or nearly so, to a total hippocampectomy. Experiments which have explicitly sought for different effects of dorsal and ventral hippocampal lesions have generally yielded mixed and rather unsystematic results. Thus, although the extent to which there are functional differences between dorsal and ventral hippocampus remains a live issue, we shall pay little attention to it in this book (see, however, Chapter 10).

The difficulties posed by lesions to the hippocampus have encouraged some investigators to destroy instead its afferent and/or efferent pathways. This has the advantage that the overall insult to the brain is usually much smaller. But problems are posed by uncertainties in the anatomy. Sometimes it is not even realized until too late that these uncertainties exist. Thus we only know about the mistakes of interpretation that have been made in the past and which (we hope) have now been cleared up. Two examples of such past mistakes will serve to illustrate the problem.

Until recently it was believed on apparently good anatomical grounds that the major outflow of the hippocampus originated in CA 1 and from there directly entered the fornix *en route* for the mammillary bodies and anterior thalamus. It followed that, by severing the fornix-fimbria, one could almost totally de-efferent the hippocampus. Since this is a much smaller surgical intervention than removal of the entire hippocampus, it seemed preferable as a way of investigating hippocampal function. It turns out, however, that fornix section has much less severe behavioural effects than hippocampectomy, at least in some situations (see, for example, the discussion of passive avoidance in Chapter 10). The mystery was solved when it became clear that CA 1 projects to the subiculum, and that the subiculum is the source of the descending fibres in the fornix (Swanson and Cowan 1975; Chapter 3). Since the subiculum also projects to the cingulate cortex (Meibach and Siegel 1977*c*) and the entorhinal area (Beckstead 1978; Segal 1977*e*; Köhler *et al.* 1978), and since there is in any case a direct projection to the latter region from *regio inferior* (Zimmer 1971), fornix section falls very far short of a hippocampal de-efferentation.

The second example also concerns the fornix. It was reported by Myhrer (1975*a*) that section of a circumscribed region in the *fornix superior* eliminated the hippocampal theta rhythm. This lesion seemed suitable therefore for investigations of the functional significance of the theta rhythm, and it was used for this purpose in behavioural experiments (Myhrer 1975*a*, 1977; Gray *et al.* 1978, Fig. 7). Unfortunately, further research (Rawlins *et al.* 1979) has shown that this lesion eliminates theta only in the dorsal hippocampus; ventral hippocampal theta is intact. Once again, therefore, what was thought to be a total lesion is only partial; and inferences drawn from these experiments about the functional significance of theta are invalid.

Recording methods

The hypotheses of septo-hippocampal function discussed so far — consolidation of memory and behavioural inhibition — derive from studies of damaged brains. The hypotheses to be considered next originate in experiments on essentially normal brains. These experiments rely upon observations of the electrical activity of the septo-hippocampal system (usually the hippocampus) under a variety of environmental and behavioural conditions. Two kinds of observations have been made: slow-wave activity (mainly theta) and single-unit firing. In each case no damage is done to the brain other than by the implantation of electrodes. This damage is not entirely negligible, and (especially where small brains are concerned, such as that of the mouse) it may sometimes act like a restricted lesion (Zornetzer, Boast, and Hamrick 1974); but the damage is small compared to that produced in a deliberate lesion experiment, and unlikely to produce a drastic reorganization of brain circuitry. However, the price paid for the privilege of working with the normal brain is the virtual renunciation of the manipulative experiment. One is left, therefore, with correlations between environmental conditions and patterns of electrical activity, but little power to choose between the many possible reasons, some of them trivial, why such correlations might exist.

This limitation on the power of the correlative experiment can be put in another way. In a large railway station both the station-master and the porters are likely to have copies of the time-table of train arrivals, but the actions they base on it are very different; and knowing that he possesses a time-table does not help you pick out the station-master from the porters. Similarly, if you observe that hippocampal electrical activity changes in response to a particular environmental input, this tells you that the hippocampus has access to information about that input, but not what it does with the information, nor even that it does anything at all. And many other brain structures doing quite different jobs have access to the same information.

These problems are not insurmountable; A. H. Black (1975) and O'Keefe and Nadel (1978, p. 161) offer illuminating discussions of how to overcome them. But their reality is shown by the plethora of different hypotheses that observational research of this kind has thrown up, especially research on the behavioural correlates of theta. There is no need to catalogue these hypotheses here (they make the hippocampus the home of just about every process found in a handful of psychology textbooks). Only three have achieved widespread currency.

The first attributes to the hippocampus a role in the production and habituation of orienting responses to novel stimuli. This hypothesis has been proposed on the basis of observations of both theta (Grastyan *et al.* 1959) and single-unit activity (Vinogradova 1970).

The second attributes to the hippocampus a role in the execution of voluntary movement (Vanderwolf 1969), and is based on observations of the behavioural correlates of theta. The observations are solid: the correlation between theta and movement exists. But the moment this hypothesis is confronted with the data from lesion studies, it runs into trouble. For almost the only behaviour that no-one has claimed to be disturbed in animals without a hippocampus, or without the septal pacemaker for theta, is voluntary movement.

The third hypothesis has been proposed by O'Keefe and Dostrovsky (1971) and O'Keefe and Nadel (1978) on the basis of single-unit research. It attributes to the hippocampus a role in the analysis and use of spatial information. One of the virtues of this hypothesis is its ability to incorporate the careful observations of Vanderwolf's group (the correlation between theta and movement now being attributed to the spatial analysis that necessarily accompanies movement through space) without running into quite such flagrant opposition to the lesion data.

It will be noticed that these hypotheses do not bear very much relation to the first two we have considered (memory consolidation and behavioural inhibition), nor indeed to one another. Evidently we are still some way from universal agreement.

Stimulation methods

Another method which has been widely used in the study of septo-hippocampal function is that of electrical stimulation. This shares with recording methods the advantage that the brain remains largely normal; although, especially when it produces epileptic seizures, stimulation can sometimes disrupt brain function for shorter or longer periods. But it also allows experimental manipulation of the structures stimulated.

The greatest problem of interpretation posed by this method is that of determining whether the stimulation acts like a temporary functional lesion (by 'jamming' the stimulated neurones), or whether it activates in a more or less normal manner the neurones lying close to the electrode tip. Obviously the inferences one can draw from a stimulation experiment depend critically on this point. A second major problem is that of deciding which neuronal pathways are affected by the stimulation, for there is no place in the brain which helpfully offers only one pathway, segregated from all others, as the target for the electrode. Thus one might simultaneously jam some routes and activate others. One can increase the selectivity and precision of the applied stimulation by varying its parameters (pulse duration, pulse frequency, current intensity, etc.) so that they are optimal only for the desired effect. But one does not usually know in advance what the best parameters are, and the number of possible combinations to choose from is enormous. One way to choose an optimal combination is to join recording to stimulation, provided one has a suitable electrophysiological criterion by which to assess the efficiency of the applied stimulus. We have tried to combine the two methods in this way by stimulating the septal area so as to drive or block theta (Figs. 4.3 and 4.4) while observing the behavioural effects of the stimulation (Gray 1972*b*; Gray, Araujo-Silva, and Quintão 1972); and Segal (e.g. 1977*c*) has ingeniously combined behavioural methods with observations of changes in the intrahippocampal response to stimulation of the commissural pathway (see Chapter 7). But the resulting experimental procedures are complex and difficult.

By and large stimulation experiments have not given rise to new hypotheses about the nature of septo-hippocampal function. In the main they have been addressed to the memory hypothesis. In particular there has been widespread use of the method of post-trial stimulation. In this, one applies the stimulation only after a learning trial has been completed and examines its effects on performance of the learned responses during a nonstimulated test trial some time later. If one observes a change in responding, it is argued that (since stimulation was not applied during the training or test trials themselves) this cannot be due to effects of the stimulation on motivation, registration of information, motor ability, etc., but must be due specifically to an alteration in memory processes (McGaugh 1966). This argument is a cogent one, but with two important reservations.

The first is related to the difficulty of knowing whether stimulation jams or activates normal neuronal function. As we shall see (Chapter 8), when post-trial stimulation is applied to the hippocampus the results of the experiment are frequently positive. But they are positive variably in two directions: sometimes retention is improved by post-trial stimulation, sometimes it is impaired. On its own, either of these findings can be interpreted as favourable to the memory hypothesis of hippocampal function. One would account for the former result by saying that stimulation activated a process normally involved in the consolidation of memory, and for the latter by saying that it jammed such a process. But a hypothesis which can be supported by either of two diametrically opposed outcomes in the same experiment is on inherently weak ground.

The second reservation concerns the phenomenon of state dependency (Overton 1966). It is known from psychopharmacological experiments that access to memory can become restricted to the drug state in which learning took place. Thus, if one wishes to argue that a drug present during learning blocks memory processes, it is necessary to demonstrate that retention is impaired both when the drug is absent during testing and when it is present. There is evidence that brain stimulation can similarly create a 'state' to which memory becomes restricted (Phillips and Le Piane 1980; Rawlins 1980), and it is possible that this occurs even when stimulation is applied post-trial. Yet virtually none of the experiments on the effects of post-trial stimulation of the septo-hippocampal system has controlled for the possibility of state dependence.

Although stimulation experiments have not given rise to new hypotheses about septo-hippocampal function, they have been the source of an important theory of the behavioural functions of the dorsal ascending noradrenergic bundle, by which the septo-hippocampal system is innervated (Fig. 3.11). In the relevant studies, it is not the experimenter, however, who applies the stimulation; he merely sets things up so that the animal can, if it wishes, 'self-stimulate'. It turns out that electrical self-stimulation is well maintained by electrodes located all along the dorsal noradrenergic bundle and perhaps also (though this is disputed) in the locus coeruleus itself (Crow 1972a, b; Wise 1978; Routtenberg and Santos-Anderson 1977). Findings such as these, allied to pharmacological evidence suggesting a role for noradrenalin in self-stimulation (Stein, Wise, and Belluzzi 1977; Rolls 1975; Wise 1978), have prompted the hypothesis that the dorsal bundle mediates the behavioural effects of reward (Stein 1968) or learning in general (Kety 1970; Crow 1973). In the latter form, this hypothesis resembles the consolidation hypothesis of hippocampal function, but in the former it is yet a further theory to add to our growing arsenal. We shall consider these hypotheses and the evidence that relates to them in Chapter 11. To anticipate the conclusions we shall reach there, it turns out that there is again a gross conflict between the results obtained using different methods. For the evidence from lesion experiments is virtually unanimous: destruction of neither the dorsal bundle nor the locus coeruleus impairs learning for conventional rewards (food, water, etc.).

Two other hypotheses have emerged from research on the ascending noradrenergic and serotonergic projections to the septo-hippocampal system. These are in part based upon an important innovation in lesion techniques: the use of selective neurotoxins injected in particular regions of the brain to destroy pathways which use only a particular neurotransmitter. In this way one can selectively destroy the dorsal noradrenergic bundle using 6-hydroxydopamine (Ungerstedt 1968), or the ascending serotonergic fibres using 5, 6- or 5, 7-dihydroxytryptamine (Baumgarten *et al.* 1978). We shall discuss these methods more fully in Chapter 11. Experiments using this technique to destroy the dorsal noradrenergic bundle have given rise to the hypothesis that this pathway performs the function of excluding from attention stimuli of low relevance to ongoing behaviour (Mason and Iversen 1979); this has much in common with Douglas's (1967) version of the behavioural inhibition theory of hippocampal function. A second hypothesis which is similar to the behavioural inhibition theory has been proposed for the ascending serotonergic pathways, namely, that these mediate the behavioural effects of punishment (Graeff and Schoenfeld 1970; Graeff and Silveira Filho 1978; Stein, Wise, and Berger 1973; Tye *et al.* 1977). This hypothesis has a broader base than most of the others described above, and finds support in pharmacological and stimulation experiments, as well as in lesion studies. We shall consider it in Chapter 11.

The anxiety hypothesis

Most of the *dramatis personae*, both theoretical and methodological, that we shall meet in later chapters of this book are now on stage. The close relation between method and theory noted above must make us suspect that none of the hypotheses advanced so far can be completely correct, for a successful theory transcends method. But it is probable that each method has led research workers closer to some aspect of the truth. Note that the theory of anti-anxiety drug action developed in Chapter 2 already represents in some degree a synthesis between the different views of septo-hippocampal function canvassed in this one. It is closest to the behavioural inhibition theory proposed for the septal area by McCleary (1966) and for the hippocampus by Douglas (1967) and Kimble (1969); and to the view that the septo-hippocampal system mediates orienting responses to novel stimuli (Grastyán *et al.* 1959; Vinogradova 1970). As we shall see, it can also keep company with certain versions of the memory hypothesis (Chapters 9 and 10). The hypotheses that are most different from the view advocated in this book are those that attribute to the septo-hippocampal system a role in the execution of voluntary movement (Vanderwolf 1969), spatial analysis (O'Keefe and Nadel 1978) or the consolidation of memory (Milner 1968); or to the dorsal noradrenergic bundle a role in learning (Kety 1970; Crow 1973) or the mediation of responses to reward (Stein 1968).

As we have seen, all methods have their limitations. But we have to start somewhere. For the argument pursued in this book it is necessary to link the action of the anti-anxiety drugs with the septo-hippocampal system. We can be reasonably certain that drugs impair the functioning of whatever systems they act on in the brain. In this respect they may be said to act like a temporary lesion. Thus the most convenient way to make the case that anti-anxiety drugs alter behaviour, at least in part, by acting on the septo-hippocampal system is to demonstrate a parallel between their effects and those produced by destruction of the septal area or the hippocampus. This starting point is also dictated by the sheer volume of data on the behavioural effects of large septal or hippocampal lesions. This allows a reasonably stringent test of the proposition that the effects of these lesions resemble those produced by the anti-anxiety drugs. Accordingly, the next chapter reviews the evidence on this point.

6

The behavioural effects of septal and hippocampal lesions

The purpose of this chapter is threefold. First, we shall compare the behavioural effects of septal lesions with those of lesions to the hippocampus. As argued in the previous chapter, this should allow us to dissect out from the syndrome produced by damage to the septal area that part which is due to destruction of its connections with the hippocampus. In this way we should be able to delineate a 'septo-hippocampal syndrome' common to lesions of both structures. Second, we shall consider how these data bear on the theories of septo-hippocampal function sketched briefly in the previous chapter. Finally, we shall compare the septo-hippocampal syndrome to the effects of the anti-anxiety drugs reviewed in Chapter 2. In this way we can begin to test the hypothesis that these agents alter behaviour by impairing the normal functioning of the septo-hippocampal system.

Many hundreds of experiments have examined the effects of septal or hippocampal lesions on behaviour in a wide variety of different situations. These experiments have been reviewed before a number of times; see, for example, on the hippocampus Altman *et al.* (1973) and O'Keefe and Nadel (1978), and on the septal area Lubar and Numan (1973), Dickinson (1974), Ursin (1976), and Grossman (1978). However, none of these reviews has explicitly compared the septal and hippocampal syndromes to each other, nor either of them to the effects of the anti-anxiety drugs. Gray and McNaughton (1983) have made a detailed comparison between the septal and hippocampal syndromes, a task which required a complete re-evaluation of the literature on the effects of each of these lesions taken on its own. This chapter is therefore based on the Gray and McNaughton (1983) review; detailed references for the statements made, if they are not given below, can be found in that paper.

Very few experiments have been directly concerned with the parallels between the effects of septal or hippocampal lesions, on the one hand, and anti-anxiety drug action, on the other. For the most part the two lines of research have gone their separate ways. In consequence, for some kinds of behaviour we have information on drug effects but none on the effects of lesions, and for other kinds of behaviour the reverse is the case. Moreover, the theoretical preoccupations which have guided research in the two fields have been largely different. Thus a certain strain is likely to be evident in applying to this review of the lesion data the same format that was used in Chapter 2 to structure the review of the effects of the anti-anxiety drugs. None the less, since our overriding purpose is to compare the drug and lesion effects, I shall keep to this format as far as possible. Under each behavioural heading I shall describe the effects of septal and hippocampal lesions separately, compare them to each other, and comment (if it is appropriate) on their bearing on the different hypotheses of septo-hippocampal function. I shall leave comparison between the lesion and drug effects, respectively, until the end of the chapter. Unless otherwise indicated, all statements refer to the effects of large lesions to the septal area or hippocampus; more discrete lesions are discussed later in the book.

6.1. Rewarded behaviour

Septal lesions

When CRF schedules are used a difference emerges depending on whether the straight alley or the Skinner-box is used. In the former apparatus about half the studies have found no effect, and this is the case whether food or water reward was employed. When septal lesions do affect running speed, this is usually increased (in all but one report). But an experiment by Henke (1977) illustrates the unreliability of this finding. He used a double runway with food available on CRF in both goal-boxes. Septal animals ran faster than controls in the first alley but not in the second, and even this effect disappeared after 30 trials. Similarly, Feldon and Gray (1979*a*) observed faster speeds in the start but not the goal section of a single alley. Increased running speed has been seen after septal lesions with both food and water reward. The only experiment to find a reduction in running speed was by Wolfe *et al.* (1967) using water reward. In the Skinner-box, in contrast, the majority of studies have found elevated responses rates in septal animals trained on CRF. Type of reward does not seem to be an important variable in distinguishing the few studies which failed to produce this outcome. Among the studies using water reward, however, there are two demonstrations that level of deprivation may be important: Harvey and Hunt (1965) were able to eliminate the increment in response rates by preloading with water before the test session; and Sagvolden (1975*a*) observed an increased response rate at 48 hours' water deprivation, but a decreased response rate at 12 hours' deprivation.

The elevated response rates in the Skinner-box are also seen with interval schedules, both FI and VI.* There have been fewer experiments using ratio schedules (FR and VR), and these have also shown a tendency for response rates to increase after septal lesions. Among the few failures to find that septal lesions increase response rates on interval schedules, two have been due to manipulation of water drive: Harvey and Hunt (1965) eliminated the difference in FI rate between septals and controls by preloading with water, and Sagvolden (1979) observed reduced VI rates at levels of water deprivation up to 24 hours.

---

*For definitions of these and other intermittent reinforcement schedules, see Section 2.7.

Hippocampal lesions

When CRF schedules are used hippocampal lesions do not generally affect either running speed in the alley or response rates in the Skinner-box. The exceptions to this generalization are in the direction of increased or decreased responding about equally often. Among the reports of reduced running speed, Cohen's (1970) was the only experiment which used sucrose reward. The two exceptional experiments to find increased response rates on CRF schedules in the Skinner-box were also the only ones to use water reward (Rabe and Haddad 1968; Van Hartesveldt 1973); in Van Hartesveldt's (1973) experiment the rate increment was seen with a small (0.01 ml) but not a large (0.08 ml) reward. There have been fewer experiments on the effects of hippocampal lesions on free-operant behaviour under intermittent schedules. These have found rate increases under most conditions studied (FI, VI, and FR schedules; food, water, and sucrose reinforcement). The exceptions to this trend do not appear to be due to any obvious variable.

Septal and hippocampal lesions compared

The two lesions are alike in their general lack of effect on running in the alley and in their tendency to increase free-operant responses under intermittent schedules. They apparently differ in that septal but not hippocampal lesions also produce elevated response rates on CRF schedules in the Skinner-box. But this difference may be confined to food reward, since the two studies which have used water reward on CRF in the Skinner-box after hippocampal lesions both found rate increments (Rabe and Haddad 1968; Van Hartesveldt 1973).

Comment

It is clear that neither septal nor hippocampal lesions impair basic reward processes. On the contrary, it seems possible that reward has a supranormal effect on the behaviour of the lesioned animal. This possibility is supported by numerous observations of increased water intake after septal lesions, and rather less consistent observations of increased food intake. However, hippocampal lesions do not generally alter either food or water intake (O'Keefe and Nadel 1978, Table A27). The role played by water drive in determining the effects of septal lesions (Harvey and Hunt 1965; Sagvolden 1975a, 1979), and by size of water reward in determining those of hippocampal lesions (Van Hartesveldt 1973), also suggests an alteration in incentive or motivational processes (Caplan 1973; Jarrard 1973). It is difficult to see, however, why changes in food or water drive should affect responding in the Skinner-box more consistently than running in the alley. If anything, running speed is more sensitive to drive variables than is free-operant response rate, except when interval schedules are used (Mackintosh 1974, p. 151).

If the observed septal and hippocampal over-responding is not due to increased incentive effects, to what else might it be due? O'Keefe and Nadel (1978, p. 325) relate over-responding in the Skinner-box to the reduced exploration seen after hippocampal lesions (see below, Section 6.12). On this account, the hippocampal animal responds more on the bar because it spends less time poking about in other parts of the Skinner-box. This is plausible, and it could apply to septal lesions as well, since these too reduce exploration (Section 6.12). However, it is difficult to see why reduced exploration would give rise to the combination of normal running speed and elevated operant response rate seen after both septal and hippocampal lesions. On the face of it, the spatial hypothesis (O'Keefe and Nadel 1978) should predict that the effect of a hippocampal lesion is greater, the greater the spatial element in the experimental task. While this is not always easy to determine, on any reasonable interpretation an alley offers a more 'spatial' problem than a Skinner-box. Thus one might expect that, if a hippocampal rat over-responds in a Skinner-box because it engages less often in spatial exploration, then it would over-respond to an even greater degree in the alley. Alternatively, one might expect a hippocampal rat to have difficulty in solving the more spatial alley task at all, so that one now predicts the opposite — a hippocampal impairment in the alley. These ambiguities in the spatial hypothesis limit its usefulness in the present context.

It is possible, in any case, that the critical difference between alley and Skinner-box experiments lies, not in the apparatus, but in the type of schedule used. Alley experiments almost invariably use discrete-trial schedules, that is, the experimenter determines when the animal has an opportunity to make its response, whereas Skinner-box experiments almost invariably use free-operant schedules, that is, the animal responds as and when it will. The measurement made is also different: speed of traversing the alley once the response is initiated in the one case, rate of bar-pressing in the other. It seems probable that any tendency to explore the environment instead of performing the measured response will have more effect on free-operant response rate than on discrete-trial running speed. Thus a reduced tendency to engage in exploratory behaviour, as is produced by both septal and hippocampal lesions (Section 6.12), might differentially increase responding in the Skinner-box, without this having anything to do with differences in the spatial characteristics of this apparatus and the alley respectively.

A further possibility is that the increased response rates seen with intermittent schedules in the Skinner-box reflect a change in the control of behaviour by stimuli associated with non-reward; we consider this possibility below (Section 6.18).

6.2. Passive avoidance

The data on passive avoidance after hippocampal lesions have served as ground for a particularly fierce battle between defenders of the behavioural inhibition theory (Altman *et al.* 1973) and their spatially-minded assailants (Black, Nadel, and O'Keefe 1977; O'Keefe and Nadel 1978, pp. 313–15). Since this is an important issue, both with regard to the theory presented here and for the spatial hypothesis of hippocampal function, I shall consider the relevant experiments in some detail. The conclusions I shall come to differ in certain respects from those of O'Keefe and his collaborators. Part of the reason for this difference is that they lump together experiments on hippocampectomy with others in which only partial hippocampal lesions were made, or in which afferents and efferents to the hippocampus (especially those in the fornix-fimbria) were damaged. Since these other lesions do not always produce the same behavioural effects as hippocampectomy, this is a dangerous practice. The conclusions summarized below are mainly based on the effects of large lesions only.

Septal lesions

There is clear agreement in the literature that septal lesions impair passive avoidance in runways or other types of apparatus in which locomotion is punished after first being rewarded with food or water.

Among the few exceptions to this rule are two interesting reports by Fried (1969, 1972a). In his 1969 experiment rats were trained to run in the alley for CRF food, then they received CRF food plus 30 per cent random PRF shock, and finally CRF food and CRF shock. The lesion was made either before any training, or after a small number of trials of PRF shock, or after long exposure to PRF shock. If made at either of the two earlier times, the lesion produced a deficit in passive avoidance; the late lesion, however, was without effect. In Fried's 1972a experiment the rats were trained with CRF food, followed by an eight-day 'vacation' and then CRF food together with PRF shock. The lesion was made either before any training (when it again produced a passive avoidance deficit) or during the vacation. In the latter case passive avoidance was actually *increased* by the lesion. This was the only case in this series of experiments in which the lesion intervened between the experience of reward only and experience of shock. Thus it is possible that the increased passive avoidance was an instance of state dependence (Overton 1966), that is, the change in the animal's state resulting from the loss of the septum might have allowed it the more easily to form a habit (inhibiting locomotion) opposite to the one learnt (approaching the goal) in the former state (septum intact).

It is unlikely that the impaired passive avoidance seen in the alley is due to increased incentive motivation since, as we have seen (Section 6.1), septal lesions only inconsistently increase baseline running speed for food or water reward. Even when unpunished running speed is increased by the lesion, this does not necessarily account for the passive avoidance deficit. Thus Beatty *et al.* (1973) adulterated the food reward given to septal animals (with quinine) until their running speeds were reduced to a level equal to that of controls; the passive avoidance deficit seen when shock was introduced was lessened by this procedure, but it was still present.

A further way round the incentive problem is to use an innate response requiring no explicit positive reinforcement. Two principal techniques have been used for this purpose: 'step-through', in which the animal spontaneously enters one box (usually dark) from another (usually bright); and 'step-down', in which the animal descends from an elevated platform. After either of these responses the animal receives foot-shock and passive avoidance is measured as an increased latency to respond on subsequent trials. In both kinds of experiment passive avoidance is normally reduced by septal lesions (Table 6.1). An exception to this rule is Beatty *et al.*'s (1973) investigation of the effects of repeated shock on step-down behaviour. In rats without prior exposure to shock the usual effect of septal lesions — impaired passive avoidance — was obtained. But if the rats were tested a second time in the step-down task or if they had had prior experience of shock, the lesion had no effect. Similar effects were also seen in the alley (Beatty *et al.* 1973). Together with Fried's (1969) experiment, discussed above, these results suggest that the passive avoidance deficit normally seen in septal animals can be overcome if there is repeated experience of shock either before (Fried) or after (Beatty) the lesion. Beatty *et al.*'s (1973) experiment also showed another variable to be important: the interval between acquisition of the passive avoidance response and retention testing. At an interval of one hour, the septal rats (provided they had not had previous experience of shock) were impaired; at intervals of 24 hours or more, they did not differ from controls.

As well as controlling for incentive effects, the step-down and step-through techniques minimize the importance of spatial information in the control of the animal's behaviour. This is also achieved in experiments in which the punished response is bar-pressing or a similar operant. Three out of five such experiments found deficits in response suppression after septal lesions. In one of the exceptions (Sodetz and Koppell 1972), rats were exposed to VI food reward schedule, followed by VI food together with FR shock, starting at FR 250 and gradually increasing in shock density until it became CRF. Only then were the rats lesioned, and the whole behavioural sequence repeated. There was no effect of the lesion. It will be seen that this experiment is similar to Fried's (1969) in suggesting that there is no passive avoidance deficit if the animals have had extensive pre-lesion experience of punishment. This, rather than the particular task used, appears to be the critical variable. In contrast to long exposure to

Table 6.1. Effects of septal lesions on step-through and step-down passive avoidance as a function of the presence or absence of an escape component in the task

	Escape		No escape	
	Impairment	No impairment	Impairment	No impairment
Step-through	Glick et al. (1974) Thomas (1972a)* Thomas (1973)		Winocur and Mills (1969)	
Step-down	Beatty et al. (1973)†	Beatty et al. (1973)†	Novick and Pihl (1969)	Frank and Beatty (1974)‡

*Two experiments.
†Prior experience of shock eliminated the impairment.
‡Lesioned animals superior to controls; punishment by immersion in water.

shock, long experience of the to-be-punished response appears to magnify the effects of septal lesions on passive avoidance. This inference is drawn from an experiment in which rats were shocked after either 25 or 250 unpunished bar-presses (Schwartzbaum and Spieth 1964). There was a passive avoidance deficit under both conditions, but it was more pronounced after the larger number of unpunished responses.

Further evidence that the septal deficit in passive avoidance is not confined to spatially complex environments comes from experiments in which consummatory behaviour is punished and one measures the extent to which it is suppressed. However, this type of experiment may also reflect the increased food and water intake which results from septal lesions. Nearly 20 experiments of this kind have been reported, two-thirds of them finding a smaller suppression of consummatory behaviour in animals with septal lesions (Table 6.2). Usually water has been used, but the same effect has been found with milk or solid food. The exceptions to the rule do not present a systematic picture. It is possible that the interval between shocks is important. Thus Bengelloun, Burright, and Donovick (1976a) observed a passive avoidance deficit after septal lesions if the animal was left to take as many shocks as it wished before giving up drinking at an electrified water spout; but if the animal was removed after a single shock per daily session, there was no effect of the lesion.

A lessened sensitivity to punishment is also observed in septal animals when the punished response is initially acquired as an active avoidance response. This result has been obtained with several different kinds of active avoidance response: two-way avoidance in the shuttle-box, one-way avoidance in a two-compartment apparatus or in the runway, and non-spatial avoidance in the Skinner-box. These findings virtually eliminate incentive effects as a general explanation of the septal passive avoidance deficit, since the reinforcer for the punished response and the punishment are both in the same modality. Since one-way active avoidance is itself frequently impaired by septal lesions (Section 2.5, below), the weakened effect of punishment in this design is not due to a stronger active avoidance component. Thus, for example, in the experiments reported by McNew and Thompson (1966) and Thomas and McCleary (1974a), the septal animals were initially poorer at one-way active avoidance, but once this response was punished they performed it better than controls. There is no apparent pattern in the experiments which failed to find a passive avoidance deficit using this paradigm.

One final technique which has been used to bring out the septal passive avoidance deficit is to punish movement. Three out of four experiments of this kind have demonstrated a passive avoidance deficit, i.e. increased movement in spite of shock, after septal lesions. This was not a consequence of differences in pre-shock activity levels, which were actually lower in the lesioned animals (Slotnick and Jarvik 1966; Slotnick and McMullen 1973).

Table 6.2. Effects of septal lesions on passive avoidance of feeding and drinking as a function of shock to the mouth or feet

	Shock to mouth	Shock to feet
Impairment	Bengelloun *et al.* (1976a)† Kaada *et al.* (1962) Kelsey (1975) McCleary (1961)* McCleary *et al.* (1965)* Miczek *et al.* (1972)§ Middaugh and Lubar (1970) Ross *et al.* (1975) Van Hoesen *et al.* (1969)*	Bengelloun *et al.* (1977)‡ Capobianco *et al* (1977) Endröczi and Nyakas (1971) Heybach and Coover (1976)‖ Singh 1973
No effect	Bengelloun *et al.* (1976a)† Hamilton *et al.* (1970) Holdstock (1972) Miczek *et al.* (1972)§	Bengelloun *et al.* (1977)‡

* Feeding; unless thus indicated, the punished response was drinking.
† Impairment with many shocks per session, not with single shocks per session.
‡ Impairment in 400-day-old rats, not in 80-day-old rats.
§ Impairment at 2 and 5, but not 10, days after the lesion.
‖ Impairment on only one of three measures.

Hippocampal lesions

As in the case of septal lesions, there is overwhelming agreement that passive avoidance is impaired by hippocampal lesions when responses in a spatially extended situation (e.g. a runway or two adjacent boxes) are learned for positive reinforcement (food or water) and then punished with shock. The factors that give rise to the few discrepant results (5 out of 19), where they are known, are diverse. Fried and Goddard (1967) demonstrated effects of the amount of pre-lesion experience of shock similar to those reported by Fried (1969) for septal lesions. They obtained the usual impairment of passive avoidance if hippocampal lesions were made either before acquisition of the food-rewarded running response or during the conflict phase (after the introduction of shock but before total suppression of running). But if the lesion was made after suppression of running was complete there was no effect either on extinction of passive avoidance or on its re-acquisition. Cogan and Reeves (1979) report that the passive avoidance deficit depends jointly on shock intensity and inter-trial interval. They obtained the deficit with 0.18 mA and a 60-second ITI, but not with 1.8 mA and a 60-minute ITI; the other combinations of shock intensity and ITI (0.18 mA – 60-minute ITI, and 1.8 mA – 60-second ITI) produced intermediate results. These results suggest that the hippocampal animal can overcome its deficit in passive avoidance if the shock is sufficiently intense and/or it has sufficient time to digest the ex-

perience of shock. The role played by ITI in these results recalls the observation by Bengelloun *et al.* (1976*a*) that the septal passive avoidance
deficit disappears if only one shock is given a day (see above).

In a further analysis of this type of experiment, Black, Nadel, and
O'Keefe (1977) have suggested that the hippocampal passive avoidance
deficit is confined to measures made at a distance from the goal (e.g. start
and running times, but not goal times, latencies to eat, or numbers of
shocks taken). From this they infer (in support of the spatial theory) that
the underlying reason for the deficit is an inability correctly to locate in
space the place where the shock is received. In general, the data support
the generalization advanced by Black *et al.* (1977; see their Table 6). In
addition, this group has published observations which fit the same pattern. Thus Winocur and Black (1978) first rewarded running in an alley
and then shocked the rat in the goal-box; subsequent to shock hippocampals ran faster than controls in the first, but not the second half of the
alley. Similar results were reported by Okaiche *et al.* (1978) studying rats
with fornix lesions.

However, in spite of the general concordance of the data with the analysis advanced by Black *et al.* (1977), there are several reports which conflict with it. Thus Stein and Kirkby (1967) and Stein *et al.* (1969) found a
hippocampal deficit in passive avoidance as indexed by the latest possible
measurement, the number of shocks actually taken. In the first of these
reports the number of shocks taken was increased by the lesion after a
long (60 trials) but not a short (30 trials) period of initial rewarded training; in the second report, 100 trials were used. This pattern of results
recalls the effect of pre-shock training on the septal passive avoidance
deficit (Schwartzbaum and Spieth 1964; see above). Using fornix lesions,
Greene and Stauff* (1974) also found that the lesioned animals took
more shock than controls. A further experiment that runs counter to the
Black *et al.* (1977) analysis was reported by Winocur and Bindra (1976).
Although the hippocampal animals in this experiment did not take more
shocks than controls, the difference between the two groups (measured
by running speed in the alley) was greater, the *nearer* the animal was to
the goal.

There is less reason to attempt to exclude the possibility that the hippocampal passive avoidance deficit is due to incentive changes than in the
case of septal lesions. For, as we have seen, hippocampal lesions do not
normally alter running speed for food or water reward, or food or water
intake. Thus the simple step-down and step-through experiments (without positive reinforcement) have not had this particular theoretical significance for the study of hippocampal function. They have, however, had

---

*This experiment is wrongly entered in Black *et al.*'s (1977) Table 6 as having shown no
deficit after fornix lesions. In fact, not only did the lesioned animals take more shocks on
the single day when shock was presented, they also showed more rapid approach to the
goal-box (in which shock had occurred) on the next day.

significance in other contexts. First, it has been suggested that hippocampal lesions reduce the animal's capacity to withhold learned, but not innate responses (Kimble *et al.* 1966). Second, it has been claimed by Black *et al.* (1977) that the hippocampal passive avoidance deficit is not seen in situations that do not require spatial analysis, and that simple step-down and step-through tasks belong to this class. The latter authors also suggest that, if the task includes an escape as well as a passive avoidance component, efficient performance does require spatial analysis. Examples of tasks of this kind are ones in which, after descending from a platform to an electrified floor, the animal is shocked continuously until it retreats (escapes) back onto the platform; or ones in which the animal is placed on an electrified floor and must first find a safe area and then stay in it. We shall consider the relevance of these procedural details to the O'Keefe and Nadel (1978) spatial theory below; for the moment, note simply that the Black *et al.* (1977) analysis predicts that a hippocampal deficit will be seen in step-down or step-through passive avoidance only if there is also an escape component in the task.

As shown in Table 6.3 (and see Black *et al.* 1977) the data offer strong support for this prediction. If one simply groups together all experiments using step-through or step-down, the effects of hippocampal lesions are extremely variable. But a large measure of order is brought into the data if these experiments are separated into those which include an escape component, and those which do not. In the former group, all reports except one show a hippocampal impairment in passive avoidance. The exception (Dawson *et al.* 1973) also finds an impairment, but only if the interval between acquisition and the retention test was short (3 minutes); at 24 hours hippocampal lesions were without effect. (Note the concordance between this result and the role played by test-retention interval in Beatty *et al.*'s 1973 experiment with septal animals; and by ITI or intershock interval in the experiments by Cogan and Reeves 1979, with hippocampal animals and by Bengelloun *et al.* 1976*a*, with septals, discussed above.) Conversely, in the experiments in which there was no escape component in the passive avoidance task, almost none of the experiments listed in Table 6.3 found an impairment after hippocampal lesions. The exception is a report by Isaacson, Olton, Bauer, and Swart (1966).* In this experiment the rat had to cross a gap to descend from a shaking, elevated runway and was given 0, 20, or 40 training trials before being shocked for doing so. Hippocampal lesions attenuated the suppressive effects of the shock, and pretraining magnified this effect. (Note the concordance between this result and the role played by pre-punishment training in determining the hippocampal passive avoidance deficit in the runway, and the septal passive avoidance deficit in the Skinner-box; Stein

---

*Isaacson *et al.* (1966) is wrongly classified by Black *et al.* (1977, Table 5) as 'escape followed by step-down'. There is no mention of any escape component in the published description of the method.

and Kirkby 1967; Schwartzbaum and Spieth 1964.) In addition, Dokla (1979) obtained equivocal results: his hippocampal rats showed a passive avoidance deficit in a simple step-through task when compared to sham operates, but not when compared to cortical controls; the latter were intermediate between the other two groups.

Other data which are relevant to the role of space in determining the effects of hippocampal lesions on passive avoidance concern punished consummatory behaviour. Black *et al.* (1977) conclude in their review that hippocampal animals 'inhibit the drinking response as readily as do normal rats'. But this conclusion is based on a *pot-pourri* of experiments which used lesions of the fornix and the perforant path, as well as lesions to the hippocampus itself. If only experiments which have involved major hippocampal damage are considered, the picture is less clearcut than Black *et al.* (1977) would have us believe. As shown in Table 6.4, there are four positive reports and four negative ones. In addition, Myhrer (1981) finds a deficit in the inhibition of punished drinking in rats with combined dorsal hippocampal damage and section of the ventral perforant path (severing the connection between the ventral hippocampus and the entorhinal area).*

In an effort to bring order into these mixed results, Capobianco *et al.* (1977) suggest that the critical variable may be the site of shock delivery — to the feet or the mouth. As shown in Table 6.4, too few experiments have used foot-shock for a careful evaluation of this hypothesis to be possible at present. All three experiments using foot-shock, however, have found a deficit in passive avoidance (Capobianco *et al.* 1977, with both hippocampal and fornical lesions; Brunner and Rossi 1969, with hippocampal lesions), while only three of the seven experiments using mouth-shock with hippocampal animals, and none of the six experiments using this technique after fornix lesions, did so. Thus there is some indication in the data that a hippocampal deficit in the inhibition of pun-

*Since this is an important point with regard to the O'Keefe and Nadel (1978) spatial hypothesis, it is worth entering into detail concerning the discrepancy between the conclusions reached here and those reached by Black *et al.* (1977). First, out of the nine experiments given by Black *et al.* (1977, Table 3) as showing no effect of hippocampal lesions on the punishment of consummatory behaviour, five are in fact concerned with lesions to the fornix or perforant path (De Castro and Hall 1975; Myhrer 1975*a*, *b*; Myhrer and Kaada 1975; Ross, Grossman, and Grossman 1975). Second, Black *et al.* (1977) exclude two of the experiments included in the present Table 6.4 because of a lack of 'relevant statistical analyses'. This point is hard to accept. In one case (Snyder and Isaacson 1965), it is true that no significance test was conducted, but the summary statistics that were presented strongly suggest that, had one been conducted, an acceptable level of significance would have been attained. In the other (Holdstock 1972) numerous significance tests are presented. It is possible that Black *et al.* (1977) were concerned either about the fact that scores (lap-rates at an electrified water supply) were adjusted for body weight, or about the fact that there were differences in the unpunished lap-rate between some lesioned groups and controls. But at least one of the findings reported by Holdstock (1972) escapes these problems: his dorsal hippocampal group in Experiment 2 did not differ from controls in body weight or unpunished lap-rate, but showed a significantly higher punished lap-rate ($p < 0.02$ by a Mann–Whitney U-test).

Table 6.3. Effects of hippocampal lesions on step-through and step-down passive avoidance as a function of the presence or absence of an escape component in the task

	Escape		No escape	
	Impairment	No impairment	Impairment	No impairment
Step-through	Blanchard et al. (1970) Blanchard and Fial (1968) Boast et al. (1975) Dawson et al. (1973)* Glick and Greenstein (1973) Glick et al. (1974) Miller et al. (1975) Zornetzer et al. (1974)	Dawson et al. (1973)*		Dokla (1979)[†] Kimble et al. (1966) Riddell (1968) Sideroff (1977) Winocur and Mills (1969)
Step-down	Plotnik et al. (1977) Teitelbaum and Milner (1963)		Isaacson et al. (1966)	Brunner et al. (1970)[‡] Riddell (1968) Riddell (1972)

*Impairment when animals tested 3 minutes after training, not when tested 24 hours after training.

[†]Impairment with respect to unoperated but not cortical controls.

[‡]Lesioned animals superior to controls.

Table 6.4. Effects of hippocampal (H) and fornical (F) lesions on passive avoidance of drinking as a function of shock to the mouth or feet

		Shock to mouth	Shock to feet
Impairment	H	Holdstock (1972) Snyder and Isaacson (1965) Myhrer (1981)*	Brunner and Rossi (1969) Capobianco *et al.* (1977)
	F		Capobianco *et al.* (1977)
No effect	H	Boitano and Isaacson (1967) Boitano *et al.* (1968) Kaada *et al.* (1962) Kveim *et al.* (1964)	
	F	De Castro and Hall (1975) Myhrer (1975a) Myhrer and Kaada (1975) Kaada *et al.* (1962) Ross *et al.* (1975) Van Hoesen *et al.* (1969)	

*Combined dorsal hippocampal ablation and section of ventral perforant path; but Myhrer (1981) also cites unpublished data showing the same effect after hippocampal lesions.

ished drinking is easier to observe with foot-shock than with mouth-shock.*

The hippocampal deficit in passive avoidance is also evident when the punished response has itself been acquired as a one-way (McNew and Thompson 1966; Coscina and Lash, 1969) or two-way (Papsdorf and Woodruff 1970; Lovely *et al.* 1971) avoidance response. Black *et al.* (1977) state that persistence of punished one-way active avoidance occurs only if there is also a deficit in the acquisition of this behaviour, a correlation they relate to the disturbance in spatial behaviour supposedly produced by hippocampal lesions. It is true that deficits in active avoidance occurred in the experiments by McNew and Thompson (1966) and Coscina and Lash (1969) cited above. But a correlation requires negative as well as positive instances. The negative instances provided by Black *et al.* (1977) concern either fornix or ventral hippocampal lesions. There is one report of a failure of a full hippocampal lesion to affect either acquisition of one-way active avoidance or its subsequent punished extinction (Coscina and Lash 1970), but there was only one punished trial in this experiment. Thus further data are needed before one can accept the view that a hippocampal deficit in the inhibition of punished active avoidance appears only if there is also a deficit in the acquisition of this response.

*A determined defender of the spatial hypothesis might try to make the case that shock to the feet is more easily related to a spatial map than is shock to the mouth, as suggested in fact (somewhat half-heartedly) by Capobianco *et al.* (1977).

Septal and hippocampal lesions compared

It is clear that the two syndromes are very similar. Both lesions produce passive avoidance deficits in a variety of situations but have their most pronounced effects in tasks requiring locomotion towards a positive reinforcer. In neither case is it likely that the passive avoidance deficit depends critically on changes in the incentive value of the positive reinforcer. The two lesions apparently differ in that the septal effect is more reliable in tasks which involve a minimum of prior learning of the to-be-punished response. As shown in Table 6.3, about half the experiments using hippocampal lesions have found deficits in step-down or step-through passive avoidance. The corresponding table for septal lesions (Table 6.1) has many fewer entries, but most of the published reports find passive avoidance deficits. Furthermore, Winocur and Mills (1969), in a direct comparison of simple step-through passive avoidance after hippocampal and septal lesions, respectively, found no change after the former but a deficit after the latter. Similarly, there is a more reliable effect of septal lesions on the inhibition of punished drinking (Kaada *et al.* 1962; Table 6.2); however, this may be due to the increased water intake also produced by these, but not normally by hippocampal lesions.

Tables 6.1 and 6.2 may be examined to see whether the same variables which influence the effects of hippocampal lesions on the inhibition of unlearnt responses also do so where septal lesions are concerned. With respect to step-down and step-through tasks (Table 6.1), the data are limited; but overall they show no sign that the addition of an escape component plays a role in determining the effects of septal lesions on passive avoidance, as it does in the case of hippocampal lesions (Table 6.3). However, there is concordance between the two kinds of lesion when we examine the influence of the mode of shock delivery (to the feet or the mouth) on the inhibition of punished drinking (Table 6.2): like hippocampal lesions (Table 6.4), septal lesions have a more reliable effect if foot-shock is used. There is no sign in the data on septal lesions that the impairment in the inhibition of active avoidance responses depends on the presence or absence of an impairment in the acquisition of this type of response; but, as we have seen, there is little evidence that this variable is important for hippocampal lesions either.

The date we have reviewed suggest that three other variables are important in determining the effects of both kinds of lesion. Prolonged experience with shock prior to the lesion reduces the passive avoidance deficit in both septal (Fried 1969) and hippocampal (Fried and Goddard 1967) animals. A long interval between shocks, or between training with shock and retention testing, has a similar effect: for septal lesions, see Beatty *et al.* (1973) and Bengelloun *et al.* (1976a); for hippocampal lesions, Cogan and Reeves (1979) and Dawson *et al.* (1973). Conversely, a prolonged period of rewarded training before the introduction of shock magnifies the effect of both septal (Schwartzbaum and Spieth 1964) and hippocampal (Stein and Kirkby 1967; Isaacson *et al.* 1966) lesions.

Thus such differences as exist between the septal and hippocampal deficits in passive avoidance are apparently quantitative only: the septal deficit is somewhat wider and more robust, especially when simple, unlearnt responses are punished. But even this difference may be more apparent than real. Consider, for example, the effects of the two lesions on punished drinking (Tables 6.2 and 6.4). If we confine ourselves to experiments using shock to mouth, there have been reports of a deficit in the inhibition of punished drinking after septal lesions in six out of 11 cases; the comparable figures for hippocampal (excluding fornix) lesions are three out of seven. This slight difference is then increased by the greater number of positive reports using foot-shock with septal than with hippocampal animals; but this reflects the habits of the experimenter, not the behaviour of his subjects. The only variable which appears to affect the outcome of one lesion but not the other is the presence or absence of an escape component in the passive avoidance task: this has a strong effect on the hippocampal passive avoidance deficit (Table 6.3), but apparently none on the septal deficit (Table 6.1).

Comment

It is possible that the O'Keefe and Nadel (1978) spatial theory applies to the hippocampal passive avoidance deficit; it certainly does not apply to the septal syndrome. Septal lesions produce passive avoidance deficits when simple step-down, simple step-through, bar-pressing, eating, or drinking are punished. None of these findings is compatible with the hypothesis that the primary effect of the lesion is to cause a difficulty in spatial analysis. It is precisely these observations, however, which are less clear where hippocampal lesions are concerned. There appears to be no report of the effect of hippocampal lesions on punished bar-pressing. With respect to punished drinking, the data summarized in Table 6.4 hardly inspire confidence in the existence of a hippocampal deficit in the inhibition of this response. However, as we have seen, the apparent difference between the septal and hippocampal syndromes at this point may turn entirely on the greater use with hippocampal animals of mouth-shock rather than foot-shock.

The strongest evidence for the spatial theory, insofar as passive avoidance is concerned, lies in the unreliability of the effect of hippocampal lesions on step-through and step-down passive avoidance, coupled with the role played by the addition of an escape component to these tasks (Table 6.3). In accounting for this pattern of results, Black *et al.* (1977) make two assumptions. First, step-down or step-through is supposed not to need spatial analysis; the animal can solve the problem simply by inhibiting movement. Second, the addition of an escape component encourages the intact animal to use a 'place strategy', that is, to identify part of its environment as a safe place, rather than movement as a dangerous act. Since, according to the spatial theory, such a strategy is unavailable to hippocampal animals, it is predicted that these will be impaired if the task contains an escape component. But conversely, since hippocampal animals are as good as controls at inhibiting movement, they should not be impaired in simple step-through or step-down. And these are the results obtained (Table 6.3).

This account is plausible. But there is an alternative possibility. Note first that in experiments on simple step-down or step-through it is common to introduce shock after a minimum of experience of the experimental situation, and also to test passive avoidance at a 24-hour interval. But these are exactly the conditions which minimize the passive avoidance deficit after both hippocampal and septal lesions in several other tasks (see above). Thus it is possible that these variables (which have nothing necessarily to do with space) account for the difficulty in observing a passive avoidance deficit in the simple step-down and step-through tasks. This explanation can also account for the effects of adding an escape component. For in experiments of this kind the inter-shock interval is typically short (seconds or minutes), depending on the animal's frequency of return to the shock area. Consider, for example, the experiment by Bengelloun, Burright, and Donovick (1976a) on the inhibition of punished drinking in septal animals. As we have seen, these workers observed a passive avoidance deficit if the animal was left to take as many shocks as it wished before giving up drinking at an electrified tap; but there was no deficit if the rat was given only one shock per daily session. It is difficult to see why this difference in procedure should have any effect on the requirement for spatial analysis. But, with regard to the interval between shocks, it is equivalent to the difference between step-down with escape (many shocks per session) and step-down without escape (one shock per session). Thus an account in terms of inter-shock interval integrates Bengelloun *et al.*'s (1976a) findings using punished drinking with those obtained in step-down and step-through paradigms. Further experiments are needed to determine whether this analysis, or the analysis proposed by Black *et al.* (1977), is better able to accommodate the data.

Whichever explanation is correct, there is a discrepancy between the effects of an added escape contingency on the passive avoidance deficit seen after hippocampal lesions and injection of chlordiazepoxide, respectively. As we saw in Chapter 2 (Section 2.2), Waddington and Olley (1977) showed that an added escape contingency *eliminates* the deficit otherwise produced by this drug in simple step-down passive avoidance. This finding was fully in accord with the theory of anti-anxiety drug action developed in Chapter 2. By the same token, the opposite effect of an added escape contingency seen in animals with hippocampal lesions is not in agreement with that theory. It would be valuable to have a direct comparison between drug and lesion effects in the two kinds of behavioural paradigm; for, as we have now seen repeatedly, quite small changes in procedure can drastically alter the effects of an experimental treatment, making it hazardous to compare treatments across different experiments. With this exception, the data reviewed in this section are in generally good agreement with the data on anti-anxiety drug action; although for many variables the available data do not allow relevant comparisons to be made.

6.3 Classical conditioning of fear

Septal lesions

The evidence for impairment of classical conditioned responses with aversive unconditioned stimuli is slight. Experiments measuring discrete responses (heart rate, galvanic skin response, nictitating membrane closure) have been negative or, at best, mixed. When more diffuse responses have been measured, some evidence for impaired fear conditioning has been reported. Four of these positive reports concern conditioned freezing, which is reliably reduced by septal lesions (Brady and Nauta 1953; Trafton 1967; Duncan 1971; Mattingley *et al.* 1979). A deficit in on-the-baseline conditioned suppression was reported in two early studies, but only under limited conditions: Harvey *et al.* (1965) found a deficit with a 1 mA but not with a 0.5 mA shock, and Brady and Nauta (1955) found one at 3 but not 60 days post-operatively. These two experiments used water reward for the baseline response, so the results may have been due to the increased water intake generally produced by the very large lesions employed. Two other studies using food failed to find any effect of septal lesions on conditioned suppression (Duncan 1972; Molino 1975). Off-the-baseline procedures do not appear to have been used to study conditioned suppression after septal lesions. Dickinson and Morris (1975), however, studied off-the-baseline conditioned acceleration. In this paradigm a CS, previously paired with shock, is presented to an animal engaged in active avoidance behaviour, and causes this to increase in its rate of emission. In Dickinson and Morris's (1975) experiment there was no effect of septal lesions on conditioned acceleration of a wheel-turning avoidance response maintained on a Sidman schedule (see Chapter 2, Section 2.5, for a description of this schedule).

The robustness of the passive avoidance deficit caused by septal lesions (Section 6.2) contrasts strongly with these weak effects on conditioned fear. This contrast has prompted two attempts directly to compare the effects of septal lesions on the response suppression produced by response-contingent and response-independent shock respectively. Dickinson (1975) used separate groups allocated to each behavioural condition; septal lesions alleviated response suppression in both. Feldon, Rawlins, and Gray (in press *a, b*)* used the within-group design described in Chapter 2 (Section 2.3). Rats were trained to discriminate between two stimuli, presented on the baseline, of which one signalled response-

*See additional references.

contingent shock and the other, response-independent shock of the same intensity and on the same RI schedule. Response suppression occurred in the presence of both stimuli, but it was greater in the stimulus signalling response-contingent shock. Rats with septal lesions (either medial, abolishing theta, or lateral, preserving it) discriminated between the stimuli at least as well as controls. Only the lateral septal lesions clearly alleviated response suppression, and this occurred equally in both types of shock period. Thus the experiments of both Dickinson (1975) and Feldon *et al.* (in press *a, b*)* suggest that, when on-the-baseline procedures are used, the role of the septal area in promoting response suppression is equally strong whether shock is delivered according to an instrumental or a classical conditioning paradigm.

These experiments represent the most careful attempt to date to compare the effects of septal lesions on passive avoidance and on conditioned suppression. The similarity of the effects observed is strongly at odds with the impression created by assembling together the experiments which have studied the one or other kind of response suppression separately. Two conclusions seem possible. The first is that the robustness of the septal effect on passive avoidance and the general weakness of the effect on conditioned fear are due to other procedural differences artefactually linked with the two kinds of paradigm. The second is that passive avoidance and on-the-baseline conditioned suppression share some feature which is susceptible to septal lesions and which is lacking in other methods of measuring conditioned fear.

Hippocampal lesions

There have been few studies of classical aversive conditioning after hippocampal lesions, and there is little evidence of any impairment. There are reports of reduced (Blanchard and Blanchard 1972) or more rapidly extinguished (Kaplan 1968) freezing. In studies of conditioned suppression off the baseline all three possible outcomes have been reported: increased suppression (Antelman and Brown 1972), no change, and reduced suppression (Freeman *et al.* 1974). The discrepancy between the two findings reported by Freeman *et al.* (1974) was a function of magnitude of reward (no change with 4 percent sucrose, reduced suppression with 32 per cent). The increased suppression reported by Antelman and Brown (1972) is likely to have been an artefact of their procedure. They tested conditioned suppression to the CS from a shuttle-box avoidance task after asymptotic learning had been reached. Since hippocampals learned the avoidance response sooner (4 vs. 8 days in controls), they had fewer exposures to the CS. As shown by Kamin, Brimer, and Black (1963) in normal rats, there is a curvilinear relation between number of presentations of a CS in the shuttle-box and the magnitude of the conditioned suppression that it produces. Thus the hippocampals and controls in Antelman and Brown's (1972) experiment could not strictly be compared.

*See additional references.

Two studies of on-the-baseline conditioned suppression reported no change (Solomon 1977) or at best a non-significant trend to reduced suppression (Rickert *et al.* 1978) after hippocampal lesions. One study has investigated off-the-baseline conditioned acceleration of Sidman avoidance (Micco and Schwartz 1971); again there was no effect of hippocampal lesions.

Finally, a number of experiments have examined the effects of hippocampal lesions on conditioned taste aversion. In this procedure the animal is made ill (by a poison such as lithium chloride or by X-irradiation) shortly after ingestion of a distinctively flavoured substance and it subsequently shows reluctance to ingest substances flavoured in the same way. Reduced taste aversion has been reported after hippocampal lesions by Miller, Elkins, and Peacock (1971), Krane *et al.* (1976) and McFarland *et al.* (1978), though not by Thomka and Brown (1975). More rapid extinction of taste aversion has also been reported (Miller *et al.* 1975; Krane *et al.* 1976). The most important departure from this picture* is one report of retarded extinction of taste aversion after hippocampal lesions (Kimble *et al.* 1979). In this experiment the rats were given five days' pre-exposure to the to-be-conditioned flavour; as we shall see, this may have been critical in producing the anomalous result.

Septal and hippocampal lesions compared

Neither septal nor hippocampal lesions produce the consistent changes in conditioned fear that they both produce in passive avoidance experiments. Septal and probably hippocampal lesions reduce conditioned freezing. On-the-baseline conditioned suppression is reduced by septal lesions, but off-the-baseline conditioned suppression has not been studied. The two experiments devoted to on-the-baseline conditioned suppression in hippocampals found no effect (Solomon 1977; Rickert *et al.* 1978). A further possible point of divergence between the two syndromes concerns conditioned taste aversion. This is usually reduced by hippocampal lesions; but McGowan *et al.* (1969, 1972) have observed *increased* aversion after both lateral and medial septal lesions. On the other hand Siegel (1976) observed a more rapid recovery from taste aversion after medial septal lesions, as also reported after hippocampal lesions by Miller *et al.* (1975) and Krane *et al.* (1976).

Comment

The failure of either septal or hippocampal lesions to reduce conditioned fear favours those interpretations of the passive avoidance deficit which

---

*O'Keefe and Nadel (1978, p. 315 and Table A23) paint exactly the opposite picture, and conclude that 'the hippocampus is not integral to this type of passive avoidance learning'. Since this disagreement is not vital to the argument pursued here, I shall not go into the reasons for it.

minimize the role of emotional processes. However, we have already noted (Chapter 2) that the anti-anxiety drugs also produce only inconsistent effects in experiments on conditioned fear; thus, unless these drugs also work by altering non-emotional processes, the force of this argument is much weakened. The absence of lesion effects in experiments on conditioned fear is consistent with the spatial theory of hippocampal function, since the techniques used to measure conditioned fear usually minimize the role of spatial analysis. This theory handles the observation of reduced freezing by supposing that this is (in part) a response to the perception of a dangerous place, a perception which *ex hypothesi* is impaired by damage to the septo-hippocampal system (O'Keefe and Nadel 1978, pp. 304–6); but reduced freezing is also of course consistent with a loss of behavioural inhibition. The spatial hypothesis is also strengthened by the failure to observe consistent effects of septal or hippocampal lesions when off-the-baseline procedures are used. It is typical in such procedures to test the reaction to the CS in a different place from the one in which conditioning was established; thus, on the spatial hypothesis, there is no reason to expect the reactions of lesioned animals to differ from those of controls.

There are, however, a number of features of the data from classical conditioning experiments which fit equally ill with the spatial theory and with the emotional approach to septo-hippocampal function. These features suggest, rather, a direct loss of inhibitory function, whether at the motor level or at that of stimulus selection.

Thus Lockart and Moore (1975) and Powell *et al.* (1976) used a differential conditioning paradigm to study the rabbit's nictitating membrane response after septal lesions. In both experiments the lesion disinhibited responses to the CS–. In a similar experiment with hippocampal rabbits Solomon (1977) saw no change in Pavlovian conditioned inhibition. However, Micco and Schwartz (1971), studying conditioned inhibition of a Sidman avoidance response in the rat, found this to be impaired by hippocampal lesions. It is difficult to see how these observations can be related to space. Nor can they be interpreted as a reduced response to conditioned aversive stimuli; on the contrary, in each of these cases the lesion gives rise to an increased response.

Similar inferences can be drawn from experiments on other forms of inhibition. 'Latent' inhibition is the loss of capacity to control behaviour which accrues to a stimulus when it is repeatedly presented without reinforcement at the start of a conditioning experiment (Lubow and Moore 1959; Gray 1975, pp. 111–13). An impairment in latent inhibition has been reported after septal lesions by Weiss *et al.* (1974), who pre-exposed a stimulus subsequently used as the warning signal in a shuttle-box avoidance task; and after hippocampal lesions by Ackil *et al.* (1969), using the same design, and by Solomon and Moore (1975), who pre-exposed a stimulus subsequently used as the CS for a nictitating membrane response. A loss of latent inhibition may also account for the otherwise anomalous report (see above) of *increased* taste aversion after hippocampal lesions (Kimble *et al.* 1979); for in this experiment the to-be-conditioned flavour was pre-exposed for five days before conditioning began.

Another way to rob a stimulus of the capacity to control behaviour is to pair it with a UCS only in the presence of an additional, previously conditioned, CS for the same UCS. This is Kamin's (1968) 'blocking' effect. In two experiments it has been reported that the blocking effect is itself blocked by hippocampal lesions (Solomon 1977; Rickert *et al.* 1978).* Since these experiments, like those on latent inhibition, used aversive UCSs (electric shock), it is difficult to describe them in a manner that fits the emotional theory of hippocampal function; for in each case the consequence of the lesion is that the animal responds *more* to a stimulus that predicts shock. As to the spatial theory, this has no natural application to these paradigms.

In all these cases (loss of conditioned inhibition, loss of latent inhibition, disruption of the blocking effect) the lesioned animal continues to respond actively to a stimulus which has lost its effectiveness for the normal animal. This general kind of result is predicted by theories which emphasize the inhibitory functions of the septo-hippocampal system. Douglas's (1967) theory, according to which the hippocampus excludes non-reinforced stimuli from the control of behaviour, handles the first two of these phenomena particularly well. Disruption of the Kamin blocking effect, however, would seem to call for a more complex analysis.

6.4. Escape behaviour

Septal lesions

There is evidence for an increase in unconditioned escape behaviour when septal cotton rats (Bunnell and Smith 1966) or mice (Slotnick and McMullen 1972) engage in agonistic encounters with conspecifics. No consistent pattern of change emerges from studies of skilled escape. An impairment in jump-up escape reported by Beatty *et al.* (1975) may be related to the reduction in spontaneous rearing produced by septal lesions (Section 6.12, below).

Hippocampal lesions

Unconditioned escape is generally increased by hippocampal lesions during agonistic encounters with conspecifics (Kolb and Nonneman 1974), predators, or a shock-prod (Blanchard and Blanchard 1972). There are no consistent changes in skilled escape behaviour. Strong and Jackson (1970) observed a reduced tendency for hippocampals to jump out of an open-field test; as in the case of septal lesions, this may reflect a reduction in spontaneous rearing.

---

* However, P. Garrud, J. N. P. Rawlins, J. Feldon, and N. J. Mackintosh (personal communication) have failed to replicate this observation. See additional references.

Septal and hippocampal lesions compared

The similarities between the two syndromes are evident.

6.5. One-way active avoidance

Septal lesions

There is a very general impairment in one-way active avoidance in animals with septal lesions. This result has been obtained when the avoidance response is locomotion from one box to another, along a runway, along the sides of a square runway, or in a running wheel; when it is a jump to a safe platform; or when it is a choice response (position or brightness) in the T maze. No general difference in procedure appears to distinguish the exceptions to this overall pattern of impairment. Bengelloun (1979) was able to eliminate the deficit in jump-up avoidance by removing the need to handle septal animals during the inter-trial interval. Since septal animals are hyperreactive to handling (Fried 1972b), this observation raises the possibility that the active avoidance deficit is due to a disturbance in behaviour provoked by handling (McCleary 1966; Bengelloun 1979). However, Ross, Grossman, and Grossman (1975) used an automated one-way avoidance task (traversing the four sides of a square) and found the usual septal deficit. Conversely, inter-trial handling does not disturb the performance of septal animals in the alley when the response is rewarded with food or water, but one-way avoidance is impaired in this apparatus.

Hippocampal lesions

There tends also to be an impairment in one-way active avoidance after hippocampal lesions, but it is less reliable than the septal deficit. However, there have been fewer studies of one-way avoidance after hippocampal than after septal lesions. There appears to be only one report of a deficit in jump-up avoidance in hippocampal animals (Rich and Thompson 1965), though this technique has been used frequently after septal lesions. In the two-box apparatus, only three out of eight experiments have shown an impairment in hippocampals; in two of the other experiments there was a deficit compared to unlesioned but not to cortical controls. In Olton and Isaacson's (1969) experiment a deficit appeared if avoidance training was preceded by a pseudoconditioning procedure in which the future CS was presented in random association with shock, but this was transformed into a hippocampal superiority if avoidance training was preceded by ten trials of fear conditioning (paired presentations of CS and shock). The evidence for a one-way avoidance deficit is marginally stronger (two out of three experiments) in the alley.

Septal and hippocampal lesions compared

There is a clearcut deficit in one-way active avoidance after septal lesions, and rather more equivocal evidence of a similar change after hippocampal damage.

Comment

The deficit in one-way active avoidance is unexpected on the behavioural inhibition hypothesis, as it is on the hypothesis that the effects of septal and hippocampal lesions should resemble those of the anti-anxiety drugs. On the face of it, the spatial hypothesis can account for it simply by the supposition that the lesioned animal has difficulty in locating the safe part of its environment; but in that case one would expect similar deficits when the same response (e.g. running to the end of an alley) is rewarded with food, and these are not seen (Section 6.1).

O'Keefe and Nadel (1978, p. 307) have suggested that the occurrence of a one-way active avoidance deficit in hippocampal animals depends on the absence of an explicit CS for the avoidance response. According to this view, the absence of a CS makes it more important for the animal to use a place strategy to solve the avoidance problem, and *ex hypothesi* it is just such strategies that hippocampal animals lack. They should therefore be deficient in one-way avoidance only when there is no explicit CS. Most experiments of this kind (10 out of 11) employ a CS; four of these (Coscina and Lash 1969; Duncan and Duncan 1971; Olton and Isaacson 1969; Rich and Thompson 1965) found a deficit, contrary to O'Keefe and Nadel's position, as did the sole experiment which did not use a CS (McNew and Thompson 1966). It would hardly seem from this pattern of results that the existence of an explicit CS is a critical factor.

O'Keefe and Nadel (1978, p. 307) also seek support for the spatial theory in observations reported by Olton and Isaacson (1968, 1969). In the first of these studies pre-habituation to the CS retarded the subsequent learning of the hippocampal* but not the normal animals; in the second (as we saw above) prior fear-conditioning by pairing the CS with shock facilitated learning in the hippocampals, but not in the normals. Thus in both cases the hippocampals appeared to be more sensitive to manipulations affecting the salience of the CS, a finding which O'Keefe and Nadel (*loc. cit.*) attribute to the lack of competition in these animals from place hypotheses. However, other data in Olton and Isaacson's (1968) report contradict this interpretation. These workers also investigated the effects of pre-habituation of the CS on two-way active avoidance, using identical procedures, the same apparatus, and the same CS (offset of a light in the shuttle-box) as in their experiment on one-way avoidance. Under these conditions the performance of normal animals was significantly improved by pre-exposure of the CS, whereas that of the hippocampals was unaffected. Furthermore, as we saw in Section 6.3 above, other experiments have shown rather generally that hippocampals are less sensitive than normals to manipulations which affect the salience of the CS. This has appeared in experiments on conditioned inhibition (Micco and Schwartz 1971), latent inhibition (Ackil *et al.* 1969; Solomon and Moore 1975), Ka-

---

*In fact, while the trend of the data was in this direction, Olton and Isaacson (1968) offer no statistical support for this assertion.

min's blocking effect (Solomon 1977; Rickert *et al.* 1978), and perhaps pre-exposure of the flavour used in conditioned taste aversion (Kimble *et al.* 1979).

6.6. Non-spatial active avoidance

Septal lesions

Two kinds of bar-press avoidance have been studied after septal lesions: the Sidman schedule, and the discriminated bar-press with an S− that is either explicit or implied (the inter-trial interval). Improved Sidman avoidance is a very robust effect of septal lesions; the number of responses emitted is reduced, the number of shocks received is reduced, there is a consequent increase in efficiency (shocks avoided/responses emitted), and there is a reduction in bursting (i.e. very short inter-response intervals, usually elicited by shock). Of two experiments using the discriminated bar-press response, one found improved performance after septal lesions.

Hippocampal lesions

Fewer experiments have been performed using bar-press avoidance with hippocampal animals. Two out of three experiments on Sidman avoidance found improved performance, as did one of the two experiments on discriminated bar-press avoidance. Identifiable special factors were at work in the exceptional Sidman case, since it involved reversal learning (Ellen and Wilson 1963; see Section 6.22 below).

Septal and hippocampal lesions compared

- Septal lesions certainly and hippocampal lesions probably improve bar-press avoidance, especially if a Sidman schedule is used.

6.7 Two-way active avoidance

Septal lesions

The facilitation produced by septal lesions in shuttle-box avoidance is well known. In the material surveyed by Gray and McNaughton (1983) there were 51 reports of this facilitation. This must go far to establishing the effect as the best replicated phenomenon in physiological psychology. Most experiments have used an escape-avoidance schedule with a warning signal. However, facilitation has also been observed with Sidman schedules; as in the bar-press Sidman schedule considered in the previous section, the septal animals receive fewer shocks, but this is accompanied by a rise rather than a fall in response rate. Most experiments have been with the rat, but similar findings have been reported in hamsters, mice, guinea pigs, cats, and squirrel monkeys. In both rats and guinea pigs the effect is obtained when the lesion is made in infancy and testing not conducted until adulthood. Thus the phenomenon is of impressive generality.

Hippocampal lesions

The improvement produced by hippocampal lesions in shuttle-box avoid-ance is as reliable as that produced by septal lesions, though there have been fewer experiments (about 15). Again, most of these have used an escape-avoidance schedule, but there are also reports of facilitation on Sidman schedules. Positive findings have been reported for rats, rabbits, and guinea pigs.

Septal and hippocampal lesions compared

The similarity between the two syndromes extends beyond the mere fact of improved shuttle-box avoidance, since the exceptions to this rule ap-pear to be due to the same factors in both cases. Thus enhanced perfor-mance is not seen if either septal (Moore 1964; Van Hoesen *et al.* 1969) or hippocampal (Andy *et al.* 1967; Olton and Isaacson 1968) lesions are made after acquisition of the response. The use of darkness as a safety signal may militate against the usual facilitation in the case of both septal (Kasper-Pandi *et al.* 1969) and hippocampal (Lovely *et al.* 1971) lesions. Another variable which appears to eliminate the usual septal facilitation of two-way avoidance is the use of discontinuous shock (Dalby 1970; Sagvolden 1975*b*); unfortunately, there appear to be no data on the influ-ence of this variable on the performance of hippocampal animals. In a direct comparison of the effects of the two lesions on Sidman avoidance in the shuttle-box Capobianco *et al.* (1977) could not distinguish between them. In an exception to this generally concordant picture, Lovely (1975) found that hypophysectomy abolished the effect of hippocampal but not septal lesions on shuttle-box avoidance; the significance of this finding is obscure.

Comment

Although the fact of improved shuttle-box performance is not in dispute, its interpretation is. One possibility is that it is not a learning phenomenon at all, merely a consequence of increased spontaneous shuttling. Both sep-tal and hippocampal lesions increase initial (pre-shock) and inter-trial re-sponding. Thus it is possible that the lesioned animal acquires shuttle-box avoidance faster because it comes into contact with the relevant reinforce-ment contingency more often, especially in the initial stages of training. It is consistent with this account that lesions made after acquisition do not improve shuttle-box performance. Also consistent with it is Matalka and Bunnell's (1968) observation in an experiment on septal lesions of a sig-nificant negative correlation between the number of inter-trial responses and trials to criterion. However, there are several reports of superior avoidance in the absence of increased spontaneous shuttling: in septal an-imals, Buddington *et al.* (1967), Van Hoesen *et al.* (1969), and Johnson (1972); in hippocampals, Jarrard (1976). In two experiments inter-trial responding was punished to eliminate differences in response rate between septals and controls: none the less performance of the avoidance response was still superior in the lesioned animals (Kenyon and Krieckhaus 1965; Schwartzbaum *et al.* 1967).

Neither increased initial nor increased inter-trial responding, then, is necessary for the superior performance of the lesioned animals. But this might still result from an increased probability of shuttling under conditions in which shocks occur, whether or not shuttling is effective in avoiding shock. This view is supported by the observation 'in both septal (Schütz and Izquierdo 1979) and hippocampal (Lovely *et al.* 1971; Calderazzo Filho *et al.* 1977) animals that the increased shuttling is at least as pronounced when a pseudoconditioning procedure is used as when the avoidance contingency is added; indeed, the septal superiority is even more pronounced under these conditions. There seems to be no reason, therefore, to suppose that the lesioned animals are better at *learning* avoidance in the shuttle-box. Rather, they appear to lack some factor — freezing or response suppression or behavioural inhibition, as it is variously expressed with differing theoretical nuances — that interferes with the performance of intact animals.

Most investigators probably accept some version of this hypothesis. There are three ways in which particular versions differ. First, there is disagreement as to whether the interference with active locomotion (which *ex hypothesi* is removed in lesioned animals) is a specific motor pattern (freezing), i.e. a species-specific defensive reaction as defined by Bolles (1972); or whether it emanates from a central inhibitory system (as defined, e.g., by Gray 1975; see Chapter 1) of which freezing is simply one manifestation. Second, there is disagreement as to whether the inhibitory influence is directed against a specific response (entry into the opposite side of the shuttle-box), or whether it is an undirected interference with all locomotion. Third, there is disagreement as to whether septal and hippocampal lesions disrupt response suppression directly, or disrupt other behavioural propensities to which this is closely connected.

To illustrate these dichotomies, let us contrast the view advocated by Black *et al.* (1977) and O'Keefe and Nadel (1978) with the notion of the behavioural inhibition system developed by Gray (1975). O'Keefe and his collaborators hold that (i) freezing is a species-specific defence reaction, which (ii) is undirected in the sense defined above, and which (iii) is elicited by the perception of a dangerous and inescapable place. They then propose that hippocampal lesions disrupt the perception of space, so that freezing is reduced and active avoidance facilitated. In addition, they hold that, since place hypotheses are inappropriate in the shuttle-box (there is no safe place), the absence of such hypotheses in the lesioned animal removes a second potential source of interference with learning the correct response (O'Keefe and Nadel 1978, p. 308). In contrast to this position is the view that (i) freezing is one manifestation of the activity of a central behavioural inhibition system, and (ii) this activity is directed to the inhibition of a specific response under conditions in which (iii) secondary aversive stimuli warn the animal of possible punishment for making that response. On this view, lesions of the septo-hippocampal system directly damage the behavioural inhibition system. This approach is close to that proposed by McCleary (1966) and several subsequent workers (e.g. Altman *et al.* 1973).

There are several features of the data which support the behavioural inhibition view rather than the spatial hypothesis.

First, Garber and Simmons (1968) examined the effects of septal lesions on avoidance in a shuttle-box in which the shock level was much higher (0.9 mA) on one side than on the other (0.2 mA). The septals had significantly faster entries into the high-shock compartment but significantly slower entries into the low-shock compartment than the controls. The controls showed a pronounced passive avoidance of the high-shock compartment, and the septal facilitation stemmed from a reduction in this passive avoidance component. So far the data are in accord with either of the views advanced above. But Garber and Simmons' (1968) data also show that the septals discriminated between the two sides of the apparatus, inasmuch as they entered the high-shock compartment consistently more slowly than the low-shock compartment. Thus the lesion left intact the perception of space, but reduced passive avoidance of the high-shock side.

Second, one condition which eliminates the septal facilitation of two-way active avoidance is the use of discontinuous shock (Dalby 1970; Sagvolden 1975b). For unknown reasons discontinuous shock produces less freezing than continuous shock (Moyer and Chapman 1966). If the controls freeze less when discontinuous shock is used, and if the septal effect is due to reduced freezing, it follows that there is less likelihood that the septal facilitation will be observed. It is difficult to imagine, however, that discontinuous shock could weaken the perception of a dangerous place, as the spatial theory must presumably suppose.

Third, there are two experiments which run directly counter to the hypothesis of reduced spatial ability in septal animals in two-way avoidance situations. Dalby (1970) used a square alley in which, on each trial, the animal could avoid shock by running to either adjacent arm. On the hypothesis of a loss of spatial perception, it might be predicted that a lesioned animal would show either a greater tendency than controls to return to the arm from which it had just escaped or a greater randomness in its choice of arm. In fact the septals showed a greater tendency to progress in an orderly manner round the square. A similar result was reported by Thomas (1974) in an experiment of similar design, except that a cross-shaped maze was used; the septals showed a greater tendency to progress round the arms of the cross. As against these two results, however, Hamilton (1972) used a two-compartment apparatus on a turntable which enabled him to put intrabox and extrabox cues in conflict with each other. He found that septals were less affected by such conflict than controls, suggesting (in agreement with the spatial hypothesis) that they were not solving the problem in terms of the location of the apparatus in the general experimental environment, but by responding to particular intrabox cues.

A final point which is easier to reconcile with the behavioural inhibition hypothesis is the observation that neither the septal (Kasper-Pandi *et al.* 1969) nor the hippocampal (Lovely *et al.* 1971) facilitation of two-way avoidance is seen when darkness is used to signal the safe side of the apparatus. For the well-known tendency of rats to prefer darkness, especially under conditions of danger, will reduce the passive avoidance tendency in controls and with it the usual advantage of the lesioned animals. But there seems to be no reason why this arrangement of the stimuli should weaken the role attributed in O'Keefe and Nadel's (1978) theory to the animal's spatial hypotheses.

6.8. Responses elicited by aversive stimuli

As we have seen, both septal and hippocampal lesions reduce passive avoidance while septal (and perhaps hippocampal) lesions also impair one-way active avoidance. A possible explanation for these deficits is a lowered reactivity to shock. Such an explanation might also be applied to the improvements produced by both lesions in bar-press and shuttle-box avoidance, since increases in shock intensity often produce less efficient performance in these tasks (Sagvolden 1976; Levine 1966; McAllister *et al.* 1971; Moyer and Korn 1964; Theios *et al.* 1966). In this section, therefore, we review experiments which have directly measured responses elicited by shock in septal and hippocampal animals (except for aggressive responses, which are dealt with in Section 6.15 below).

Septal lesions

If one just asks the question, 'was reactivity to shock increased, decreased, or unchanged by septal lesions?', a complex picture emerges. Order can be brought into this picture, however, if one takes into account the degree to which the shock-elicited response consists of increased or decreased movement. Thus, out of a dozen or so observations of increased reactivity to shock after septal lesions, all but two involved an increase in motor behaviour (jumping or general activity); out of five reports of no change, four measured the detection threshold for shock, i.e. the current intensity at which flinching is first seen; and when Blanchard and Fial (1968) used crouching as a measure of reactivity to shock, this was decreased by septal lesions, i.e. the animal moved more. Thus these data suggest that the effect of septal lesions is simply to increase movement in response to shock. There are some observations, however, to which this type of classification does not apply. Thus Holdstock (1970) reported a reduction in the galvanic skin response (GSR) and in heart-rate acceleration after septal lesions. Since movement is normally accompanied by an increased heart rate, the latter finding is unlikely to be secondary to changes in the amount of movement.

Hippocampal lesions

The few observations on hippocampal animals conform to the same pattern: the flinch threshold to shock is unaltered, the jump threshold is lowered and the amount of crouching is reduced (Blanchard and Fial 1968; Eichelmann 1971).

Septal and hippocampal lesions compared

It is clear that neither lesion decreases reactivity to shock; thus their effects on avoidance behaviour cannot be accounted for by such a change, although this has been suggested (Sagvolden 1976). On the contrary, the general picture is one of increased reactivity to shock. However, this does not appear to involve lowered thresholds for the perception of shock. Rather, both lesions seem generally to increase motor reactions to shock.

6.9. Responses elicited by non-aversive stimuli

Given the pattern of change described in the previous section, the question arises whether increased motor reactions are seen also when one measures responses elicited by non-aversive stimuli. A great diversity of observations fall under this heading. The stimuli used have belonged to many modalities (auditory, visual, olfactory, thermal, tactile), and the responses measured have been very diverse (the startle response, locomotion, GSR, EEG changes, bar-pressing for sensory reinforcement, etc.). Gray and McNaughton (1983) have classified the reported effects of septal and hippocampal lesions according to each of these variables, and also according to the direction of change in motor behaviour produced by the lesion.

Septal lesions

There appear to be no systematic effects of stimulus modality or the particular response measure used. The same pattern which holds for aversive stimuli is found again. Virtually all the reports of increased reactivity to stimulation in the septal animal have involved an increase in motor activity in the lesioned group. There are only two reports of reduced reactivity to stimulation in septal animals; both used a measure — the GSR — with no motor involvement (Holdstock 1969, 1970). These results are not easily explained in terms of increased preference for, or aversion to, stimulation. For example, there have been reports of increases both in operant responding reinforced by light (Feigley and Hamilton 1971; Zuromski *et al.* 1972) and in shuttling to escape from light (Schwartzbaum *et al.* 1967; Bengelloun, Nelson, Zent, and Beatty 1976*b*). Thus septal lesions appear to increase motor reactions to stimuli whether or not they are aversive and irrespective of modality. The GSR, however, is reduced whether audiotory, visual, or shock stimuli are used (Holdstock 1969, 1970).

Hippocampal lesions

There are fewer relevant reports dealing with hippocampal lesions, so the picture is less clear. However, whenever increased reactivity to stimulation has been reported in hippocampal animals, this has involved an increase in motor behaviour. But there are few observations of decreased reactivity to stimulation after hippocampal lesions. Rogozea and Ungher (1968) observed reduced EEG and motor orienting responses to auditory stimuli in hippocampal cats; thus the direction of change in motor behaviour was opposite to the one expected. On the other hand, the observation by Krane *et al.* (1976) of reduced neophobia (i.e. increased drinking of a novel-flavoured fluid) fits the general pattern.

Septal and hippocampal lesions compared

Once again the two syndromes are very similar. Both kinds of lesion lead to increased motor responses to stimuli in a number of modalities. The increased motor reactivity to shock is thus part of a more general change.

6.10. Distraction experiments

The experiments reviewed in the previous section used simple responses (e.g. startle, the GSR). This section is concerned with the effects of novel stimuli presented to animals while they are engaged in other behaviour. In such experiments one may measure either the effect of the new stimulus in distracting the animal away from its ongoing behaviour, or the direct response to the stimulus.

Septal lesions

There have been few experiments of this kind with septal animals, and there appears to be no report of the effect of the ongoing behaviour on the direct response to the distractor. In experiments in which the septal animal's response to the distractor is measured by change in the baseline (distracted) behaviour, the lesion has been reported about equally often to produce an increase, a decrease or no change in this response. However, when we consider the direction of change in motor behaviour involved in these effects, order once more emerges. In every case in which the septal lesion has had an effect, motor behaviour has been increased.

P. E. Gray (1976) reported a particularly instructive pattern of results. He trained rats to bar-press for sucrose on an FI schedule and then presented a distractor (lights or clicks) early or late during the fixed interval. Presented early, the distractor increased bar-pressing rate in intact controls (presumably owing to a disinhibitory action); this effect was increased by septal lesions. Presented late during the interval, the distractor decreased bar-pressing rate; this effect was unchanged by septal lesions. In a somewhat similar experiment De Noble and Caplan (1977) superimposed free reinforcement on two different operant schedules, on one of which (DRL) it gave rise to a rate acceleration and on the other (DRH, differential reinforcement of high rates of response*) to a rate deceleration. The rate acceleration was larger in septals than controls, the rate deceleration was no different. In two other experiments in which bar-pressing rate was reduced when a distractor was presented to controls, the extent of the reduction was lessened by septal lesions (Harvey *et al.* 1965; Schwartzbaum and Kreinick 1974). Thus the only generalization which can accommodate these data is that septal lesions tend to increase motor responding.

Hippocampal lesions

Observations of changes in the baseline behaviour in hippocampal animals show more clearly the same picture as that seen after septal lesions. There have been many reports of reduced distraction after hippocampal lesions, but in every case this takes the form of increased motor activity (bar-pressing, panel-pressing, running).

There are also several observations of the response directly elicited by the distractor in hippocampal animals. Five out of nine of these show a *reduced* response to the novel stimulus, the direct opposite of the usual result obtained when the animal is not engaged in other behaviour at the time of presentation of the novel stimulus (previous section). That this difference is indeed due to the fact that the animal is 'otherwise engaged' is shown by three experiments which have directly investigated this variable. Hendrickson *et al.* (1969) found a reduction in motor orienting responses after hippocampal lesions if a click was presented to the rat while it was drinking, but not if it was either sated for water or thirsty but not drinking. Means *et al.* (1971) used a cross maze with one arm shut off to form a T. If this arm was opened up after a simple spontaneous alternation test, hippocampals explored it as much as controls. But if it was opened after the rats had been trained on left-right single alternation, hippocampals explored it less than controls. Finally, Crowne *et al.* (1969) found no effect of hippocampal lesions on the cardiac response to a compound auditory and visual stimulus unless the rat was pressing a panel. Note that, in this experiment, the effect of the lesion on an autonomic response was determined by the animal's motor behaviour at the time of stimulation. This suggests that the confused picture otherwise seen when non-motor responses to stimuli have been measured (Gray and Mc-Naughton 1983) might appear more orderly if the animal's behaviour at the time of measurement was better recorded or controlled.

---

*On this schedule only responses separated by less than a minimum interval (typically of the order of one or two seconds) are reinforced.

Septal and hippocampal lesions compared

Distraction has frequently been reported to be reduced after hippocampal. lesions (about 10 reports), but only occasionally after septal lesions (Harvey *et al.* 1965; Schwartzbaum and Kreinick 1974; Raphelson *et al.* 1965). However, this difference between the two syndromes is more apparent than real, since in both cases the pattern of results appears to fit the general rule, seen in the two previous sections, that there is increased motor activity in the lesioned animal. This interpretation gains support from the fact that changes in distraction are easily seen in the lesioned animals if the baseline response has a large motor element (bar-pressing, running), whereas a licking baseline is relatively refractory to change after either septal (Weiss, Friedman, and McGregor 1974) or hippocampal (Gustafson 1975) lesions.

Comment

The data reviewed in this and the previous two sections make it clear that septal and hippocampal lesions rather generally increase motor reactions to stimulation. This phenomenon offers good support for versions of the behavioural inhibition theory which emphasize relatively direct suppression of motor behaviour (e.g. McCleary 1966; Altman *et al.* 1973).

However, the experiments in which one measures the response directly elicited by a distractor suggest that, in addition, other processes are involved. For under these conditions the motor response to the distractor is usually reduced by hippocampal damage; whereas, if the same sort of response is measured when the animal is not engaged in instrumental behaviour, it is usually increased. Thus in predicting the effect of novel stimuli on hippocampal animals, one has to take account of the animal's dominant activity or 'set'. The principle which appears to operate is this: the lesioned animal displays the dominant motor activity with greater vigour than controls. If this activity is that directly elicited by the novel stimulus, the lesioned animal displays this directly elicited response to a more marked degree. But if some other behaviour is dominant, this is performed with greater vigour by the lesioned animals, and the directly elicited response is weakened. In this connection an experiment by Raphelson *et al.* (1965) is of particular interest. These workers changed the visual cues in an alley in which rats were running for a food reward; this slowed controls down, but speeded hippocampals up. This result shows that the difference between the lesioned and intact animals is not a matter of stimulus detection: both groups detected the novel stimulus, but they reacted to it differently. In terms of arousal theory (Gray 1964a; Gray and Smith 1969), a novel stimulus causes normal animals to alter the direction of their behaviour (so that it is controlled by the novel stimulus) and also increases arousal level. Raphelson *et al.*'s (1965) experiment suggests that the increment in arousal takes place in hippocampals as in normals, but not the change in direction of behaviour.

6.11. General activity

Given the general increase in the vigour of motor responses to specific stimuli produced by septal and hippocampal lesions, it is natural to ask whether general motor activity is also increased when specific stimuli are not presented.

Septal lesions

The effects of septal lesions on general activity are very mixed. There is a slight preponderance of observations of increased activity, but that is about all one can say.

Hippocampal lesions

Here the picture is much clearer. In a substantial majority of studies increased activity has been reported after hippocampal lesions. Furthermore, the exceptions to this rule are almost all with a single apparatus, the running wheel. It is also pointed out by O'Keefe and Nadel (1978, p. 259) that studies employing an ultrasonic device to measure movement have failed to find hyperactivity in hippocampal rats. The reasons for these two exceptions are not known.

Septal and hippocampal lesions compared

Classification of the data on septal animals according to the apparatus used (Gray and McNaughton 1983) suggests that the two lesions are alike in increasing activity in the shuttle-box and in not increasing it in the running wheel. But hippocampal lesions produce a rather general increase in activity which is not apparently seen after septal lesions.

6.12. Exploratory behaviour

Section 6.11 was concerned with experiments in which the total amount of activity in a given environment is measured. This section is concerned with experiments in which the distribution of activity is measured in different parts of an environment. It should be noted, however, that the distinctions between measures of general activity, reactivity to stimulation, and exploration, respectively, are, to say the least, cloudy, and that all of them may in addition be confounded with changes in affectivity (see below, Section 6.14).

Septal lesions

Spontaneous alternation is reliably reduced by septal lesions. Using a cross maze Dalland (1970) found that septal animals perseverate goal-boxes ('stimulus perseveration') rather than body-turns ('response perseveration'). Thomas (1972b) confirmed this and showed that the cues perseverated by septal animals include intramaze visual and olfactory but not extramaze stimuli. However, McNaughton and Feldon (1980), studying medial and lateral septal lesions, found that medial lesions caused perseveration of body-turns while lateral lesions had no effect. Loss of spontaneous alternation results in less flexible exploration of the environment. Changes of the same kind have been seen in experiments which offer the animal several goal-boxes baited with food (Winocur and Mills 1969), or several levers which may be pressed to get food (Cherry 1975). In each case, septal animals showed stronger preferences than controls for one of the possible routes to reward.

The remaining experiments considered in this section do not make the distinction between amount and direction of locomotion which is inherent in tests of spontaneous alternation. Perhaps for that reason they present a very confused picture. Most of them have used the open-field test, where there is the added difficulty that locomotion ('ambulation') is influenced in a complex manner by fear of the test situation (Whimbey and Denenberg 1967; Mos, Lukaweski, and Royce 1977). If one simply counts heads, ambulation was increased by septal lesions in twelve cases, decreased in four, and unaffected in nine.

Order can be brought into this picture if we take account of the complex loading of ambulation on Whimbey and Denenberg's (1967) emotionality factor (see Chapter 2, Section 2.10) and assume that septal lesions reduce emotionality in the open field; this assumption is justified by the data (see below, Section 6.14) showing that septal lesions reduce open-field defecation. Arguing from Whimbey and Denenberg's (1967) factor-analytic results, we would expect reduced emotionality to decrease ambulation upon early exposure to the open field, but to increase it later (Chapter 2, Section 2.10). Scrutiny of the reported effects of septal lesions from this point of view yields the following pattern of results (Gray and McNaughton 1983). In experiments with a single testing session up to 5 minutes long or with two 3-minute sessions, septal lesions have reduced ambulation or left it unchanged. In experiments with a longer single session (15 minutes) or more than two sessions, septal lesions have increased ambulation. In two experiments in which measures were taken sufficiently frequently and over long enough periods, both effects were seen, i.e. a reduction in ambulation for the first 2–5 minutes of the first test session followed by an increase in ambulation for the remaining periods of observation (Donovick and Wakeman 1969; Gomer and Goldstein 1974). These results are exactly as would be predicted if we assume that septal lesions decrease an animal's score on Whimbey and Denenberg's (1967) emotionality factor.

In contrast to the complexity of the findings with ambulation, the effects of septal lesions on rearing behaviour are simple and consistent: rearing is reliably reduced.

Hippocampal lesions

Spontaneous alternation is clearly reduced by hippocampal lesions. The impairment can be overcome if the period of exposure to the goal-box (Kirkby *et al.* 1967) or arm (Stevens 1973) of the T-maze is increased from the usual minute or so to 50 minutes, or if the inter-trial interval is kept sufficiently short (Gross *et al.* 1968). Thus the lesioned animal apparently takes longer to become sufficiently familiar with one arm for it then to choose the other, and loses this familiarity more rapidly during the inter-trial interval. Experiments using the cross maze show that hippocampals perseverate body-turns, not goal-boxes or extramaze stimuli (Dalland 1970, 1976; Lash 1964). A lessened flexibility of exploratory behaviour has also been seen when a previously closed arm is opened up in a maze (Cohen 1970; Means *et al.* 1971).

In the open-field test there is a clear augmentation of ambulation. Rearing, however, has been studied less often; in two out of four experiments it was reduced (Strong and Jackson 1970; Murphy *et al.* 1975).

Septal and hippocampal lesions compared

The two lesions are alike in reducing spontaneous alternation and other measures of the animal's tendency flexibly to explore its environment. There is evidence, however, that hippocampal lesions produce perseveration of the same body-turns, whereas septal lesions produce perseveration of behaviour directed to the same stimuli (Dalland 1970; but see McNaughton and Feldon 1980). In the open-field test hippocampal lesions clearly increase ambulation, whereas septal lesions have more mixed effects. There are two possible reasons for this discrepancy. First, as we have seen, the effects of septal lesions can be understood by supposing that they reduce emotionality or fear; hippocampal lesions apparently do not have this effect (Section 6.14, below). Second, the increase in ambulation produced by hippocampal lesions may be related to the clearer increase in general activity produced by hippocampal than by septal damage (previous section). Finally, rearing is definitely decreased by septal lesions; the effects of hippocampal lesions, though not so clearly established, tend to be the same.

Comment

The disturbance in spatial exploration produced by the two lesions is good support for the spatial theory. But note that the anti-anxiety drugs also reduce spontaneous alternation (Gray 1977; Chapter 2, Section 2.10).

The anxiety hypothesis receives support from several features of the data. Besides the impairment in spontaneous alternation, the reduction in rearing and the increase in ambulation seen after the lesions all figure in the syndrome created by the anti-anxiety drugs. However, the detailed pattern of change in ambulation seen after septal lesions raises a problem.

This, as we have seen, can be predicted accurately from experiments on individual differences in fearfulness (Whimbey and Denenberg 1967). But the effects of the anti-anxiety drugs depart from this pattern. These agents increase ambulation only in the first few minutes of exposure to the open field (Chapter 2, Section 2.10); but this is precisely the time at which septal lesions decrease ambulation. Further data are needed to resolve this problem. It would be particularly valuable to measure the effects of septal lesions, the anti-anxiety drugs and individual differences in fearfulness in the same test.

6.13. Habituation

Septal Lesions

Habituation has been studied in a variety of different situations. Generally it has been reported to be retarded by septal lesions. But examination of these reports (Gray and McNaughton 1983) shows that they nearly always conform to the now general pattern that the changes observed after septal lesions consist in a greater vigour of motor activity. This holds true also for the one experiment which obtained more rapid habituation after septal lesions, for the response measured was *suppression* of running in the alley (Raphelson *et al.* 1965). There is, however, one study of habituation which cannot be classified in terms of motor activity. Sanwald *et al.* (1970) found that septal lesions retarded habituation of the cardiac deceleration produced by a novel tone. Since the initiation of movement is normally accompanied by cardiac acceleration, this finding is unlikely to be secondary to altered motor behaviour. A second report which suggests that retarded habituation is a genuine feature of the septal syndrome, independent of changes in motor activity, comes from De Noble and Caplan (1977). These workers trained rats to barpress for food on either a DRL or a DRH schedule, and then superimposed free food on a variable time* (VT) schedule. This gave rise to a rate acceleration in the DRL condition and a rate deceleration in the DRH condition. In both cases, the effect of the superimposed VT schedule habituated in the controls, but not in the septals. Note that, in the DRH condition, septals displayed retarded habituation by responding *less* than controls.

Hippocampal lesions

Retarded habituation is equally apparent after hippocampal lesions; and once again nearly all the changes recorded took the form of increased motor activity in the lesioned animals. This holds also for the one observation of more rapid habituation after hippocampal lesions, since the response measured was suppression of drinking (Köhler 1976*a*). There are, however, two cases in which retarded habituation was observed even though this involved reduced motor activity on the part of the lesioned

*That is, a variable interval schedule in which the delivery of reward is independent of the animal's responses.

animals: habituation of suppression of panel-pressing in hippocampal monkeys (Douglas and Pribram 1969), and of suppression of bar-pressing in hippocampal rats (Gustafson and Koenig 1979). The latter result was obtained, however, only when a second novel stimulus was tested; habituation of the response to the first one showed no differences between lesioned and control rats. There are also two reports of retarded habituation with non-motor responses, EEG (Rogozea and Ungher 1968) and cardiac deceleration (Sanwald *et al.* 1970).

Septal and hippocampal lesions compared

Both lesions retard habituation when the measured response involves increased motor activity. In such experiments it is difficult to disentangle a genuine effect on habituation rate from increased motor reactivity. But there is evidence (from experiments measuring decreased motor activity or non-motor responses) that both lesions may have such an effect.

6.14. Fearful behaviour

The term 'fear' is used in this section in a narrow sense to cover the type of behaviour discussed in Chapter 2, Section 2.10; some of the relevant observations have already been described in Section 6.12, above (open-field ambulation, rearing).

Septal lesions

One of the best validated measures of fear is defecation (Gray 1971*a*, 1979*a*). There are several reports that septal lesions reduce defecation in the open field, the runway, and in the shuttle-box during avoidance training. There are also reports that emergence time (Thomas *et al.* 1959) and the latency to eat in a novel environment (Ross *et al.* 1975) are reduced by septal lesions. Although open-field urination is not reduced, there is much less of a case for considering urination a measure of fear (Mos *et al.* 1977; Gray 1979*a*).

Hippocampal lesions

Hippocampal lesions have generally been reported to be without effect on presumed measures of fear, including defecation, urination, and wall-clinging behaviour in the open field. The sole indications of reduced fear after hippocampal lesions are the reports by Jarrard (1968) of increased eating in the open field, and by Krane *et al.* (1976) of reduced neophobia.

Septal and hippocampal lesions compared

Tests of fear discriminate between septal lesions (which reduce fearfulness) and hippocampal lesions (which do not).

Comment

The failure to find concordance between the effects of septal and hippocampal lesions on tests of fear is an embarrassment for the hypothesis that the septo-hippocampal system plays a role in anxiety. But note that the effects of the anti-anxiety drugs on such tests are also discrepant at several points with expectation from the literature on individual differences in fearfulness, where they have so far found their major application (see Chapter 2, Section 2.10).

6.15. Aggressive behaviour

Septal lesions

Shock-induced fighting between pairs of rats is reliably increased by septal lesions. A more confused picture emerges when other techniques of inducing intraspecific aggression (simple pairing, or competition over food) are examined. These have yielded reports of increased and decreased aggression about equally often. It is probable that this confusion is at least in part due to species differences. Most of the reports of increased aggression have concerned the hamster. In the rat there appears to be a clear difference between the results obtained when shock is used to induce aggression and those obtained using other methods. In the latter case the preponderance of experiments have found reduced aggression after septal lesions. The special role played by shock is also indicated by experiments on mouse-killing, which is increased by septal lesions if it is induced by shock (Miley and Baenninger 1972) but not if rats and mice are simply placed together (Malick 1970; Paxinos 1975). A direct comparison of the two methods of inducing aggression confirms this view: septal rats showed both increased shock-induced aggression and reduced aggression in a food-competition situation (Miczek and Grossman 1972). The reduced aggression seen when shock is not used occurs only if the lesion is made in a previously dominant animal, not in a subordinate (Lau and Miczek 1977; Blanchard, Blanchard, Takahashi, and Takahashi 1977; Gage, Olton, and Bolanowski 1978).

It is probable that there is a close relation between the increase in shock-induced aggression and the 'septal hyper-reactivity' syndrome. I shall not review this syndrome in detail here, since it is so well known (Fried 1972b). Essentially it consists in exaggerated reactions (startle, jumping, biting) to mild tactile stimuli (typically, poking, picking up, and puffs of air). A careful description of these reactions by Blanchard, Blanchard, Lee, and Nakamura (1979) and Albert and Wong (1978) suggests that the syndrome is better described as one of hyperdefensiveness, since it closely resembles the behaviour of an animal defending itself against a threatening opponent. Under these conditions defence may also involve attack, as will seem plausible to the many experimenters whose fingers have been bitten when they handled septal rats too freely. The aggression elicited by foot-shock is probably part of the same pattern.

Hippocampal lesions

The few experiments which have investigated aggressive behaviour after hippocampal lesions (mostly in rats) have fairly consistently found reduced aggression, no matter how this is produced.

Septal and hippocampal lesions compared

The two lesions differ in their effect on shock-induced aggression (increased after septal lesions, probably decreased after hippocampal lesions). This conclusion is confirmed by a specific comparison between septal and hippocampal rats (Eichelmann 1971). When shock is not used, both lesions reduce aggression in the mouse and rat. This kind of aggression is increased by septal lesions in the hamster, but this species has not been studied after hippocampal lesions. The increase in shock-elicited aggression seen after septal lesions may be related to the septal hyperreactivity syndrome. This syndrome is not usually reported in hippocampal animals, although a mild version was observed by Harley (1972) and Nonneman *et al.* (1074); it is possible that, for this effect, damage to the ventral hippocampus is necessary (McGowan *et al.* 1972).

6.16. Social interaction

Septal lesions

There have been several investigations of gregarious behaviour in the open field. In this test two animals are put together into the open field and the time they spend in contact is measured. Septal lesions usually increase contact time in rats, mice, and deer mice. Other measures have shown increased social contact in septal hamsters, cats, and cotton rats. In a study of mice Booth *et al.* (1979) took a number of behavioural measures which they divided into pro-social (increasing the probability of further social contact), anti-social (decreasing this probability) and non-social. Septal lesions specifically increased pro-social behaviour. Thus septal lesions facilitate social interaction very generally.

Hippocampal lesions

There is very little information about social behaviour after hippocampal lesions. Ely *et al.* (1976, 1977) found that hippocampal lesions prevented the formation of social hierarchies in groups of five male mice. This may reflect similar changes in gregariousness and dominance to those seen after septal lesions.

Septal and hippocampal lesions compared

Septal lesions increase social interaction; there are insufficient data to determine whether hippocampal lesions have this effect.

Comment

The area of affective behaviour, which has roughly been covered by this and the preceding two sections, is one in which the septal and hippocampal syndromes differ relatively strongly. Septal lesions have more pronounced effects than hippocampal lesions. These effects are of two apparently contradictory kinds. First, there is an increase in defensive responses to tactile and painful stimuli, as seen in the hyper-reactivity syndrome and the increase in shock-elicited aggression. It is plausible to see this as a lifting of inhibition of aggressive–defensive responses. Second, there is a cluster of changes — reductions in fear, social dominance, and social agression — which perhaps underlie the increase in pro-social interaction. Hippocampal lesions apparently do not produce the increase in defensive responses or the reduction in fear, but they too reduce social aggression.

6.17. Non-reward: resistance to extinction

Septal lesions

Septal lesions regularly give rise to increased resistance to extinction of previously rewarded responses, both in alleys and in the Skinner-box.

In the alley there are several reports of increased resistance to extinction after acquisition on CRF. Septal lesions also increase resistance to satiation (Henke 1975), running speed being measured with the goal-box baited but the animal sated. This parallel is consistent with the general behavioural similarities between non-reward and satiation (Morgan 1974). It is possible to block the normal increase in resistance to extinction by interpolating a satiation test between acquisition and extinction (Henke 1975). This may be the same kind of phenomenon that we encountered in Section 6.2, where we saw that the passive avoidance deficit normally produced by septal lesions disappears with repeated exposure to shock (e.g. Beatty *et al.* 1973). In agreement with this interpretation, Rawlins (1977) found that rats with medial septal lesions tested in the alley after previous experience with non-reward failed to show increased resistance to extinction, though they did when tested before this experience.

When a running response is acquired under partial reinforcement quite different results are obtained. On the hypothesis that septal lesions block the behavioural effects of non-reward, this is to be expected (Chapter 2, Section 2.7). This hypothesis predicts that septal lesions will block the partial reinforcement extinction effect, so that resistance to extinction should be reduced in PRF-trained animals. This result was reported by Gray, Araujo-Silva, and Quintão (1972) and Henke (1974, 1977). Henke (1974) further showed that abolition of the PREE by septal lesions depends on the number of acquisition trials. With 48 trials there is a total abolition of the PREE and, as predicted, this is due both to an increase in resistance to extinction after CRF and a decrease in resistance to extinction after PRF. With 96 trials, the PREE is intact and septal lesions produce no change in resistance to extinction after PRF training. This pattern of results was confirmed by Feldon and Gray (1979*b*) in an experiment using lateral septal lesions. Thus septal lesions do not block completely the effects of non-reward, but rather attenuate or delay them. This interpretation is supported by observations during the course of acquisition: Henke's (1974) PRF group with septal lesions developed the variability in running times which is characteristic of this training condition (Amsel

1962) later than controls. These results with the PREE paradigm are consistent with those described in the previous paragraph: given enough experience with non-reward, septal animals overcome their deficit. All these experiments used an ITI of a few minutes. Septal lesions also abolish the PREE when the ITI is set at 24 hours (Feldon and Gray 1979*a*).

In the Skinner-box acquisition schedule is apparently unimportant in determining the effect of septal lesions on resistance to extinction. This is increased whether training is on CRF, FR, FI, VI, or DRL schedules. This difference between Skinner-boxes and alleys is more likely to be related to the use of free-operant (as distinct from discrete-trial) schedules than to the spatial characteristics of the apparatus, since no clear equivalent to the PREE has been described when free-operant schedules are used. Septal lesions did not affect the change in bar-pressing rate produced by a shift from response-contingent to free reinforcement in experiments by Atnip and Hothersall (1975) and Manning and McDonough (1974); but in the former experiment septal animals over-responded when there was a shift from VI to differential reinforcement of other behaviour (DRO), i.e. reward for any behaviour other than the previously reinforced response. This is intelligible if the septal deficit consists in responding appropriately to the omission of reward; for responding causes no loss of reward on free-reinforcement schedules, but it does on DRO. Another way of eliminating responding is to gradually increase the requirement imposed by a FR schedule, which then becomes a "progressive ratio' schedule. There are several reports of higher response rates in septal animals tested on this schedule.

The increase in resistance to extinction normally seen in septal animals tested in the Skinner-box may be blocked by an interpolated satiation test (Henke 1975), and the increased responding on a progressive ratio schedule is not seen on a second occasion of testing (Rawlins 1977), parallelling in both cases effects seen in the alley. Fallon and Donovick (1970) demonstrated that the usual septal effect could even be converted into a reduction in resistance to extinction if drive was changed from food to water deprivation between acquisition and extinction. This may indicate that the usual septal effect is closely tied to the context in which the response is acquired (see the discussion of Winocur and Olds's 1978 experiment in Section 6.22 below). Carey (1967) also found a reduction in resistance to extinction after septal lesions if these were made between acquisition and extinction; this may have been an instance of state dependency (Overton 1966).

Hippocampal lesions

Hippocampal lesions give rise to increased resistance to extinction with as much regularity as septal lesions.

In the alley after CRF training there have been eight reports of increased resistance to extinction. As in the case of septal lesions, the use of a PRF schedule alters this result. Rawlins, Feldon, and Gray (1980*b*) used acquisition and extinction conditions identical to those used by Henke (1974, 1977) and Feldon and Gray (1979*b*) to display clearly the effects of septal lesions on the PREE: 48 acquisition trials with an ITI of a few minutes. The same results were obtained: the lesion increased resistance to extinction after CRF training, but decreased it after PRF training and abolished the PREE. Earlier experiments on the PREE after hippocampal damage have not obtained such clear results, but in each case there are reasons why this should have been so (see the discussion in Rawlins *et al.* 1980*b*).

In apparatus other than the alley (most often the Skinner-box) there have been consistent reports of increased resistance to extinction after CRF training. There are also reports of increased resistance to extinction after training on FR (Amsel *et al.* 1973) and FI (Manning and Mc-Donough 1974) schedules. As in the case of septal lesions, Manning and McDonough (1974) found no effect of hippocampal lesions on respond-ing when free reinforcement was substituted for FI. Nonneman *et al.* (1974) also found no effect of hippocampal lesions on resistance to ex-tinction after acquisition on DRL, although septal lesions have been shown to increase resistance to extinction after this form of training (El-len, Gillenwater, and Richardson 1977). Since animals must already learn to restrain their responding on a DRL schedule, it is not clear that extinc-tion is the same process after this as after most other schedules. The ef-fect of hippocampal lesions on resistance to extinction apparently lasts through repeated testing to a greater extent than the comparable septal effect. Thus Henke and Bunnell (1971) found increased resistance to ex-tinction in a second test after interpolated CRF reacquisition, and Schmaltz and Isaacson (1967) found the same effect in three such tests. Given these findings, it is surprising that experiments using progressive ratio schedules have found no effect of hippocampal lesions or, at best, a transient increase in response rate (Schmaltz *et al.* 1973).

Increased resistance to extinction after hippocampal lesions has also been seen in several discrimination tasks, including simultaneous tactile, brightness, and position discriminations, choice of the correct one of two bars or panels, or running in a complex maze. These discrimination ex-periments are important in showing that the increased resistance to ex-tinction is not simply a consequence of the increased motor activity caused by hippocampal lesions (Sections 6.8–6.11). For the lesioned animals dis-played a greater persistence of the correct choice, as well as simply a greater tendency to respond (Webster and Voneida 1964; Kimble and Kimble 1970; Means and Douglas 1970; Niki 1965). Persistence was also shown by Kimble (1969) in hippocampal rats trained on a brightness dis-crimination for water reward and then satiated for water; thus, like sep-tals (Henke 1975), hippocampal rats are more resistant to satiation as well as extinction.

Septal and hippocampal lesions compared

Septal and hippocampal lesions both cause increased resistance to extinction under a wide variety of conditions. Many detailed points of similarity between these conditions have been noted above. After discrete-trial training on PRF schedules, however, both lesions, under appropriate conditions, reduce resistance to extinction and abolish the PREE. The data on both lesions are consistent with the hypothesis of a reduced sensitivity to non-reward. In the case of hippocampal lesions data from discrimination tasks eliminate the possibility that the increased resistance to extinction is a secondary consequence of increased motor activity. Comparable data have not been reported for septal lesions. However, it is difficult to see how increased motor activity could give rise both to increased resistance to extinction after CRF training and to reduced resistance to extinction after PRF training.

Comment

The data on increased resistance to extinction fit naturally with the behavioural inhibition approach to septo-hippocampal function. However, the *decreased* resistance to extinction produced by septal or hippocampal lesions when animals have been trained on PRF in the runway requires one to interpret this approach in the sense of a lowered sensitivity to the stimuli which normally provoke behavioural inhibition (i.e. stimuli associated with non-reward), rather than simply as a loss of the capacity to inhibit responding.

There are several features of the data to which the spatial theory finds no natural application. Two examples are the increased resistance to extinction seen regularly in the Skinner-box, and in Webster and Voneida's (1964) experiment; in the latter, cats were trained on a simultaneous tactile discrimination for which they were required to palpate raised patterns at the bottom of a tube. In these cases the spatial element is minimal. O'Keefe and Nadel (1978, Chapter 10) attempt to resolve this difficulty by attributing to the rest of the brain (after the hippocampus has been removed) a 'taxon' system which has just those properties necessary to account for the behaviour of the lesioned animal. This approach is too *ad hoc* to carry much conviction. At the least their theory should predict that the increased persistence seen after hippocampal lesions should be more apparent in spatial than non-spatial tasks. But the data offer no support for this inference.

If the increased resistance to extinction seen in non-spatial tasks is not due to a spatial deficit, it lacks parsimony to appeal to such a deficit in spatial tasks. If none the less we apply to the data on resistance to extinction in the alley the same arguments as those used by Black *et al.* (1977) in their treatment of the passive avoidance deficit in this apparatus (Section 6.2, above), we would expect the effects of the lesion to be more marked, the further the animal is from the goal (on the assumption that it has difficulty in relating the frustrating event of non-reward to the spatial lay-out of its environment). This possibility was specifically examined by Rawlins *et al.* (1980*b*) in their experiment on the PREE. Neither the increased resistance to extinction in the hippocampal CRF group nor the reduced resistance to extinction in the PRF group showed any sign of decline in going from the start to the goal section of the alley. Winocur and Bindra (1976) similarly found that resistance to extinction after CRF was increased by hippocampal lesions most in the section of the alley closest to the goal.

6.18. Non-reward: intermittent schedules

We have already seen (Section 6.1) that septal and hippocampal lesions tend to increase response rates on intermittent free-operant schedules of reinforcement. Here we explore these and related phenomena further for their relevance to the hypothesis that these lesions alter responses to non-reward (Chapter 2, Section 2.7).

Septal lesions

As pointed out in Chapter 2, it is possible to treat the characteristic FI scallop as a consequence of the inhibitory control over responding exercized by the delivery of reward (which acts as a signal for a temporary period of non-reward); a similar argument applies to the post-reinforcement pause seen on FR schedules. We therefore expect that a treatment that disrupts the normal behavioural effects of stimuli associated with non-reward should disrupt the FI scallop by increasing response rates early in the fixed interval, and similarly that it should reduce the post-reinforcement pause on FR schedules. The data on septal lesions are generally in agreement with these expectations: there are several reports of a reduction in the FI scallop or in the post-reinforcement pause on both FI and FR schedules. In two experiments (Beatty and Schwartzbaum 1968; Ross and Grossman 1975), however, there was also an increase in the rate at the end of the fixed interval ('terminal rate'), which is not predicted by the non-reward hypothesis.

Another schedule to which similar arguments apply is DRL. Here it is the making of a response which signals the temporary unavailability of reward for further responding (Chapter 2, Section 2.7). Thus, on the non-reward hypothesis, we would expect septal lesions to shorten interresponse times, with a consequent loss of reinforcement and a higher response/reinforcement ratio (decreased efficiency). This, indeed, is one of the best-replicated features of the septal syndrome. The disruption in DRL performance can be overcome if the animal is very gradually shaped through successive increments in the DRL interval (De Noble and Caplan 1977), or if a cue, used to signal the end of the DRL interval, is gradually faded out of the procedure (Ellen, Dorsett, and Richardson 1977).

Hippocampal lesions

Three out of five experiments on FI performance have found rate increases after hippocampal lesions, but of these only one (Beatty and Schwartzbaum 1968) conforms to the pattern outlined above, that is, a reduction in the gradient of the FI scallop with no change in terminal rate. In contrast, Haddad and Rabe (1969) and Jackson and Gergen (1970) found an increase in the steepness of the scallop, and the latter authors also report an increase in terminal rate. Ellen and Powell (1962) saw no change in the scallop and an *increase* in the post-reinforcement pause. There are no published data on the effects of hippocampal lesions on the post-reinforcement pause on FR schedules.

DRL performance is as clearly impaired by hippocampal as by septal lesions. The pattern of change is the same: shorter inter-response times with a consequent loss of reinforcement. One important variable is training paradigm. Schmaltz and Isaacson (1966) showed that the impairment is only obtained if rats are trained on CRF before being shifted to DRL (the usual procedure), not if they are at once trained on DRL. This may be because the usual procedure contains an element of extinction or reversal of the initially learnt habit of rapid responding. When the rats were put straight on to DRL an increased response rate was still seen in the lesioned animals, but without loss of reinforcement. However, Riddell *et al.* (1973) were able to demonstrate the hippocampal impairment in DRL efficiency even if the lesion was made after acquisition and with pre-lesion CRF training given on a different response and for a different reinforcer. Braggio and Ellen (1976) showed that the hippocampal deficit could be 'repaired' by a period of training with a cue to signal the end of the DRL period; unlike septal animals, for which the cue must be faded out gradually (Ellen, Dorsett, and Richardson 1977), this therapy works for hippocampals even when the cue is removed abruptly.

Septal and hippocampal lesions compared

On both FI and FR schedules septal lesions usually produce the pattern of change which would be expected if there is a loss of behavioural control by signals of non-reward. This is not so for hippocampal lesions. Both lesions impair DRL performance in the way that is predicted by the non-reward hypothesis. The septal effect appears to be somewhat more robust than the hippocampal one: it does not depend on CRF preceding DRL training (Kelsey and Grossman 1971), and it is less readily eliminated by training on cued DRL.

6.19. Discrimination learning: simultaneous

In this and the next section we deal with simultaneous and successive discriminations respectively. A reduction in the ability to withhold non-rewarded responses would be expected to disrupt successive but not simultaneous discrimination learning (Chapter 2, Section 2.8). Spatial discriminations are treated separately in Section 6.21, below, because of their relevance to the spatial hypothesis. Simple position habits, however, are treated as belonging to the simultaneous rather than the spatial category.

Septal lesions

The majority of experiments have concerned brightness or position discriminations, although there have been occasional studies of other stimulus dimensions. Septal lesions are generally without any effect on performance in these tasks. The exceptions consist about equally often of reports of impairment and improvement. No particular role appears to be played by stimulus dimension.

In the case of some of the exceptions it is possible to detect special features at work.

Singh (1973), for example, reports that septal rats were superior to controls in a position discrimination. He trained the animals to go to their preferred side; this might have aided septals because of their reduced spontaneous alternation (Section 6.12). Conversely, Chin *et al.* (1976, Experiment 2) report an impairment in septal rats trained on a brightness discrimination in a sequential choice-box (four choices, each between two paths), with black positive. The impairment appeared only if training on this task was preceded by a series of trials in which the animal was forced to go to white. It is easy to relate this result to the reversal learning deficit produced by septal lesions (Section 6.22, below). In another experiment in the same apparatus, training was preceded by 12 trials in which the rat was forced equally often to go to black and white and to left and right. Under these conditions septals were superior to controls when subsequently required to go to black (Chin *et al.* 1976, Experiment 3). This suggests that septal lesions may block 'learned irrelevance' (Mackintosh 1973; Dickinson 1980), that is, learning that certain cues are relatively poor predictors of reinforcement. If so, this finding is perhaps related to those reviewed in Section 6.3, above, and which show that septal and hippocampal lesions attenuate latent inhibition (Weiss *et al.* 1974; Ackil *et al.* 1969; Solomon and Moore 1975), Kamin's blocking effect (Solomon 1977; Rickert *et al.* 1978) and perhaps the pre-exposure effect in taste aversion conditioning (Kimble *et al.* 1979).

A further important factor is the presence of additional cues. A septal impairment in position discriminations has been reported when there is a competing brightness cue. Thus Dabrowska and Drzewiecka (1975) found normal acquisition in the absence of such a cue, but an impairment if one was present but irrelevant. Similarly, Sikorsky *et al.* (1977) observed impaired acquisition of a position habit in septal rats which had previously been trained in the acquisition and four serial reversals of a brightness discrimination in the same apparatus (a T-maze).

In these cases the additional cue cannot help solve the discrimination and may hinder solution. The opposite outcome — a septal superiority —

has been observed when two cues are perfectly correlated, so that the animal may use either or both to solve the problem. Thus, using the same sequential choice-box as Chin *et al.* (1976; see above), Donovick *et al.* (1978) tested rats on discriminations in which brightness was perfectly correlated with position (left or right) or with a left–right alternation sequence; septals acquired both habits faster than controls. There have also been two reports of septal superiority when the animal is transferred from a single-cue to a two-cue discrimination, the initial cue retaining its earlier significance (Donovick *et al.* 1978; Liss and Lukaszewska 1966). However, in both cases this finding was heavily dependent on the exact stimuli used and may have been an artefact of different levels of learning of the initial discrimination in the lesioned and control groups. None the less it appears that under some conditions (though their exact nature is unclear) septals may solve a discrimination involving two perfectly correlated cues more readily than controls.

Under other conditions, however, septal lesions appear to impair the animal's ability to cope with two stimulus dimensions simultaneously. Donovick *et al.* (1979) report an experiment in which rats were trained with one dimension relevant (brightness or position) in stage 1, and with both dimensions relevant and perfectly correlated in stage 2; finally, in stage 3, they were tested with either the original positive cue or the positive cue added in stage 2. Septals were no different from controls in stage 3 when tested with the original positive cue, but they were impaired when tested with the cue added in stage 2. This result is very similar to the effect of sodium amylobarbitone described by McGonigle, McFarland, and Collier (1967; Chapter 2, Section 2.10). In both cases the experimental treatment apparently prevented an added redundant cue from gaining control over the animal's behavior.

Hippocampal lesions

Discrimination learning has been a much more popular subject of investigation after hippocampal than after septal lesions, and a wide variety of stimulus dimensions has been studied. Most commonly the lesion has no effect. There are many more exceptions to this generalization, however, than there are after septal lesions. Roughly one third of the reports find a difference between hippocampal and control groups, always in the direction of an impairment. But in many of these cases it is possible to identify a special factor. The most important of these is the existence of an initial bias which works against the solution of the problem. It is likely that such a bias would handicap hippocampal animals, given the difficulty they have in extinction (Section 6.17) and reversal learning (Section 6.22). This factor comes into play in two slightly different ways. First (conceptually closer to the extinction deficit) the lesioned animals are impaired on simultaneous discriminations if they start with a response preference opposed to the correct choice. Second (conceptually closer to reversal learning) they are impaired if they have previously learned a discrimination different from the one on which they are currently tested.

There are fewer reports of impairment in position discriminations than other simultaneous discriminations. Among those that have been reported are several cases in which the animals were trained to choose the side of the apparatus opposite to their initial preference. The loss of spontaneous alternation in hippocampal animals (Section 6.12) implies that they will take longer than controls to abandon this preference and so contact the relevant reinforcement contingency. In several other cases the animals had initially acquired a potentially conflicting habit, for example, left–right alternation (Means *et al.* 1971) or a brightness discrimination (Samuels 1972).

There are more cases of impairment in brightness discrimination learning after hippocampal lesions. Even so, there is a clear preponderance of reports of no change (16 out of 25; Gray and McNaughton 1983). Among the exceptions Samuels and Valian (1968) found greater negative transfer in hippocampal animals when the discrimination was changed from correlated brightness-and-position to brightness alone, and Winocur and Breckenridge (1973) found a hippocampal deficit only if the rats had first been trained on left-right alternation. In Harley's (1979) report of a hippocampal deficit an irrelevant tactile cue (acrylic vs. wire mesh floor) was also present. This finding may conform to the principles we saw at work in the case of septal lesions (Dabrowska and Drzewiecka 1975; see above). However, there was no evidence that responses were controlled by the tactile cue in hippocampals any more than in controls; and when Harley (1979) subsequently trained his rats to discriminate between the tactile cues, there was no hippocampal deficit whether the previous brightness cue was now absent or present but irrelevant. A particularly interesting case of impaired brightness discrimination was reported by Han and Livesey (1977) in an experiment testing Douglas's (1967) hypothesis that hippocampals have difficulty in gating out negative stimuli. Rats were trained to choose the brighter of two patches of light under three conditions: in the control condition both lights were turned off as soon as the animal made its response; in the 'enhanced positive' condition S+ remained lit for a short time after the response; and in the 'enhanced negative' condition S− similarly remained lit. Hippocampals were impaired only in the enhanced negative condition, fitting Douglas's hypothesis.

The most serious indication that hippocampal lesions impair simultaneous discrimination learning comes from experiments using visual patterns. This is the one case in which there have been more reports of impairment (eight) than of no change (seven). However, some of the reported impairments are of dubious interpretation; in Spevack and Pribram's (1973) experiment, for example, the amygdala was removed along with the hippocampus. Winocur and Mills (1970) and Winocur (1979) have provided evidence of the role played by previously acquired habits.

In the first of these experiments hippocampal rats were impaired on pattern discrimination only if they had first learned a brightness discrimination. In the second they were impaired in a discrimination between horizontal and vertical stripes only if they had first been exposed to an insoluble problem (both discriminanda associated with 50 per cent random PRF) using diagonal stripes; no impairment was seen if there was either no pre-exposure, or pre-exposure with no stimuli in the choice box and all choices rewarded. A further condition which apparently favours the appearance of a hippocampal impairment is an excess of discriminanda. Thus Douglas *et al.* (1969) used one positive cue and one, two or four negative cues; hippocampal monkeys were impaired only when more than one negative cue was used. This finding is consistent with Douglas's (1967) theory of hippocampal function, and may be related to the deleterious effects of irrelevant cues on septal (Dabrowska and Drzewiecka 1975) and hippocampal (Harley 1979) performance noted above. There remain, however, a few reports of impaired pattern discrimination in hippocampal animals for which no special reason is discernible. Olton (1972), for example, reports an impairment in discriminating between vertical and horizontal rectangles in a choice box. Note, however, that in this experiment, though the lesioned animals developed an incorrect position habit, their response latencies discriminated between the positive and negative stimuli. Thus, even when a deficit in pattern discrimination is present after hippocampal lesions, this appears to be due to difficulties in controlling the choice response, not to perceptual difficulties.

Septal and hippocampal lesions compared

Neither septal nor hippocampal lesions affect simultaneous discrimination learning in any general way. There are many reports of impairment after hippocampal lesions (though these are in a clear minority compared to reports of no change) but hardly any after septal lesions. However, nearly all the hippocampal impairments can be explained without positing any difficulty in forming the simultaneous discrimination itself. The most important factor favouring the appearance of an impairment, after either kind of lesion, is the existence of an initial response bias or a previously acquired habit which must be overcome if the discrimination is to be solved. A second factor is the existence of an excess of irrelevant stimuli or multiple negative cues. If there is any disturbance of simultaneous discrimination *per se* after hippocampal lesions, it is confined to visual pattern discriminations. Unfortunately, this has hardly been studied after septal lesions.

A possible discrepancy between the effects of the two lesions is suggested by a comparison between Chin *et al.*'s (1976) experiment on septal animals and Winocur's (1979) on hippocampals. In the former experiment septal lesions *facilitated* a brightness discrimination after pretraining with random exposure to the cues subsequently used for the discrimination. In the latter, pretraining of a similar kind gave rise to an *impairment* in hippocampal performance in a pattern discrimination. It is possible, however, that this discrepancy is due to a difference in the reinforcement schedule used during pre-training. Chin *et al.* (1976) reinforced all pre-training choices, whereas Winocur (1979) used a random PRF schedule. The latter schedule is known to encourage the formation of irrelevant position habits in a spatial situation; and Winocur (1979) reports that the hippocampal impairment indeed took the form of a persistent position habit.

Comment

The failure of lesions to the septo-hippocampal system to affect simultaneous discrimination is consistent with the non-reward hypothesis. At first sight the fact that these lesions cause no disruption in the acquisition of position discrimination is a threat to the spatial hypothesis. However, for the purposes of this theory (O'Keefe and Nadel 1978), space has a highly abstract and theoretical definition, and it is held that simple position habits can be acquired without recourse to spatial analysis as such. This view is not unreasonable, especially when one takes into account the results of experiments on spontaneous alternation (Section 6.12), which have shown that, in the T-maze, septal animals largely approach goal-box stimuli and hippocampals repeat body-turns, while neither appears to situate the different parts of the apparatus within the extramaze environment (see O'Keefe and Nadel 1978, p. 266 *et seq.*). None the less, it is surprising on the spatial account that brightness, and certainly visual pattern, discriminations are more fragile in hippocampal animals than position discriminations. If anything, the spatial theory should predict that, having lost one class (spatial) of possible competing strategies, the hippocampal animal should be superior to normals in the solution of visual discriminations in spatial situations.

As we have seen, simultaneous discriminations appear to be particularly susceptible to the interfering effects of irrelevant stimuli in animals with septal and hippocampal lesions. This pattern of results is in agreement with Douglas's (1967) theory of hippocampal function, as are several particular features of the data (see the descriptions of Han and Livesey's 1977, and Douglas *et al.*'s 1969, experiments above). However, there is an apparent discrepancy between this generalization and the inference we drew earlier (Section 6.10) that lesioned animals are more resistant than normal to distraction. The important variable may be the degree to which the response whose distraction is measured has been learned. In the distraction experiments (Section 6.10), this response is typically simple and well acquired at the time the distractor is applied. In the experiments reviewed in the present section (Dabrowska and Drzewiecka 1975; Douglas *et al.* 1969) the distracted behaviour was a complex choice response and still being learned.

6.20. Discrimination learning: successive

The prediction from the non-reward hypothesis (Chapter 2, Section 2.8) is that septal or hippocampal lesions should impair successive discriminations by disinhibiting responding in the presence of the negative stimulus.

Septal lesions

The results of experiments on successive discrimination in septal animals have been very mixed. There have been about equal numbers of reports of impairments or no change. In addition, three experiments actually obtained improved successive discrimination after septal lesions. Two of these (Vom Saal *et al.* 1975; Carlson and Vallante 1974) used olfactory cues, and in Carlson and Vallante's experiment septals were not different from controls if visual or auditory stimuli were used. In the third (Carlson *et al.* 1972) the stimulus consisted of the presence or absence of a food pellet, which may perhaps also have acted as an olfactory cue. Thus it appears from these experiments that septal lesions may increase the effectiveness of odour in the control of discriminatory behaviour. The impairments in successive discrimination after septal lesions generally take the predicted form of increased responding in the presence of S−.

A single alternation schedule is a species of successive discrimination in which (provided direct cues of the availability of reinforcement have been eliminated) the relevant cue is the outcome of the previous response; that is, the animal learns that reward signals non-reward on the next trial and vice versa. On the hypothesis that septal lesions release non-rewarded responses from inhibition, these would be expected to increase responding on non-rewarded trials but to leave responding on rewarded trials unchanged, as does sodium amylobarbitone (Feldon *et al.* 1979). Two experiments of this kind, one in a runway and one in a Skinner-box with a retractable lever, have produced results opposite to the one just predicted: the septal animals were superior to controls, responding faster on rewarded trials and slower on non-rewarded trials. In the runway experiment (Carlson *et al.* 1972) this might have been due to an improvement in olfactory discrimination of the kind noted above, since the reward was wet mash and no precautions were taken to prevent this from providing differential odour cues on rewarded and non-rewarded trials. But it is difficult to see how this could occur in the bar-pressing task (Carlson and Norman 1971).

Hippocampal lesions

The effects of hippocampal lesions on successive discrimination are much less variable than those of septal lesions, and there is a clear preponderance of reported impairments. As with septal lesions, these have usually taken the form of increased responding in the presence of S−. Freeman *et al.* (1973) demonstrated that the presence of the hippocampal deficit is affected by the allocation of stimuli to the role of S+ or S−: hippocampals over-responded when S− consisted in the absence of the tone used as S+, but not when the tone itself served as S−. Thus an explicit signal for non-reward apparently helps hippocampals to overcome their difficulty in withholding responses. Plunkett and Faulds (1979) investigated the dependence of the hippocampal deficit on stimulus modality in the runway: hippocampals were significantly impaired on two visual problems (orientation of stripes, and brightness), non-significantly on a thermal problem (hot vs. cold floor) and not at all on a tactile problem (rough vs. smooth floor). This pattern of results is consistent with Harley's (1979) report that hippocampal lesions impaired a simultaneous brightness but not tactile discrimination (Section 6.19).

Conditional discriminations have some features of simultaneous and some of successive discrimination (Chapter 2, Section 2.8). In the presence of one stimulus the animal must make one response, and in the presence of another it must make the opposite response. There is a consistent hippocampal deficit in such tasks, usually studied in T- or Y-mazes. Lash (1964) used three different kinds of T-maze. He found that the performance of the hippocampal animals was poorer, the lower their rate of spontaneous alternation. Thus the hippocampal deficit may be due, at least in part, to a difficulty in varying responding so as to sample reinforcement contingencies efficiently. A rather unusual stimulus dimension was studied by Hsiao and Isaacson (1971). Rats were tested in a Y-maze with food in one goal arm and water in the other; on alternate days they were deprived of food or water and required to make the corresponding choice. Hippocampals were impaired on this task as in more conventional conditional discriminations.

The results of experiments on single alternation after hippocampal lesions have been very mixed. In the Skinner-box the important variables appear to be the inter-trial interval and the type of lever, retractable or non-retractable. With a retractable lever hippocampals are inferior to controls at an ITI of 80 or 40 seconds, the same as controls at an ITI of 20 seconds, and better than controls at a 10-second ITI (Walker *et al.* 1970; Means *et al.* 1970; Walker *et al.* 1972). With a non-retractable lever a hippocampal impairment has been seen with ITIs from 5 to 30 seconds (Warburton 1969; Walker and Means 1973; White 1974). The hippocampal impairment in the latter experiment was exacerbated by the presence of a second lever on which the rat could work for continuous reinforcement. In the alley Franchina and Brown (1970) found a hippocampal impairment at a 20-second ITI. Under very similar conditions, Cogan *et al.* (1976) found no effect of hippocampal lesions; however, they did observe an impairment using a single alternating schedule of reward and delayed reward. Thus hippocampal lesions impair performance on single alternation schedules only inconsistently. On the occasions when impairments are seen, they conform to the predicted pattern, i.e. a specific difficulty in withholding responses on non-rewarded (or delayed) trials

(Warburton 1969; Franchina and Brown 1970; Cogan *et al.* 1976). But in some of the cases in which the lesioned group was superior to controls exactly the opposite was seen, that is, a reduction in responding on non-rewarded trials (Brown *et al.* 1969; Means *et al.* 1970). The latter results imply that the lesion *increased* the inhibitory effect of non-reward.

Septal and hippocampal lesions compared

In straightforward successive discriminations hippocampal lesions consistently and septal lesions rather less consistently impair performance by increasing the tendency to respond in the presence of the negative stimulus. Exceptionally, septal lesions appear to improve the learning of olfactory discriminations; these have not been studied after hippocampal lesions. Hippocampal lesions consistently impair conditional discriminations; comparable tasks have not been studied after septal lesions. On single alternation schedules both lesions have been shown under some conditions to produce a surprising facilitation of performance which none of the major existing theories of septal or hippocampal function would predict. The conditions which facilitate single alternation in hippocampal animals tested in the Skinner-box include a retractable lever combined with an ITI not greater than 10 seconds; these were also the conditions used in the one comparable report with septal animals (Carlson and Norman 1971). Under other conditions hippocampal lesions impair single alternation performance by disinhibiting responding on non-rewarded trials; this has not been reported after septal lesions, but there has been only one relevant experiment (Carlson *et al.* 1972).

Comment

The release of non-rewarded responses in successive discrimination tasks is consistent with the non-reward hypothesis. The most serious challenge to this hypothesis, in the data reviewed in this section, comes from the experiments on single alternation. These have, on several occasions, produced results which run directly counter to prediction.

6.21. Discrimination learning: spatial

Septal lesions

There have been very few investigations of maze learning after septal lesions. Impairments have been reported in a Lashley maze (Thomas *et al.* 1959), Olton's radial-arm maze (Olton, Walker, and Gage 1978) and Maier's three-table 'reasoning' task (Hermann *et al.* 1978). Spatial (left-right) alternation is reliably reduced by septal lesions in several different situations.

Hippocampal lesions

It has been known for a long time that there is a severe impairment in spatial learning after hippocampal lesions (e.g. Thomas and Otis 1958;

Kaada *et al.* 1961), but the spatial theory of hippocampal function has recently made experiments of this kind very fashionable. Thus there are at least 24 reports of this type of change after hippocampal lesions (O'Keefe and Nadel 1978, Table A20). The apparatus used to demonstrate the deficit has included Lashley, Hebb-Williams, Dashiell, sunburst, multiple T, multiple U, and radial-arm mazes, as well as Maier's three-table task.

Spatial alternation tasks have produced a more mixed picture. Although a majority of studies has found an impairment after hippocampal lesions, there have also been reports of no change and even of improvements. Among the latter cases Stevens and Cowey (1972) used a visual cue to indicate the correct one of two levers to press; hippocampals were superior to controls only if this visual cue was spatially separate from the lever. It is suggested by O'Keefe and Nadel (1978, p. 268) that the use of place strategies by normal animals would be a handicap when cue and manipulandum are separated in this manner; the superiority of the hippocampals then arises from their supposed lack of place hypotheses. The most surprising result is that of Jackson and Strong (1969), who used rats in a two-lever task in which the basic unit was a pair of responses, one left and then one right, with reward consequent on the second. Hippocampals were superior at learning this basic unit, and also at learning repeated sequences of such units (up to five) with reward following only the final response. Furthermore, when a third lever was added and the animal required to learn a chain of the form, A–B–A–B–C, the hippocampals were still superior. It is difficult to see what feature of Jackson and Strong's (1969) situation can account for the difference between their results and those of other, simpler spatial alternation experiments in the Skinner-box in which an impairment was seen after hippocampal lesions (Riddell *et al.* 1973; Niki 1966; White 1974).

One factor which favours the appearance of a hippocampal deficit in spatial discrimination tasks is a delay interposed before the opportunity to respond. Thus Racine and Kimble (1965) reported a profound impairment in hippocampal rats tested on single alternation at only a 5- or 10-second delay between successive responses; pre-operatively the same subjects had coped successfully with delays of 40 minutes or more. Sinnamon *et al.* (1978) placed rats in one of four boxes on an 'information trial' with water present in the box. The rat was then given an opportunity to choose between the four boxes. The longer the interval between the information trial and the opportunity to choose, the greater was the hippocampal deficit. The effects of a delay can be magnified by providing the animal with a potentially interfering activity in the delay interval. Thus Jarrard (1975) reported that hippocampal rats were unimpaired at spatial alternation even with delays up to 4 minutes; but an impairment was produced if they ran in a running wheel during this interval.

Septal and hippocampal lesions compared

Hippocampal lesions cause a very general impairment in spatial discrimination learning. Septal lesions have not been studied in these situations to
anything like the same extent; but they too appear to impair spatial discriminations. Both lesions also generally impair spatial (left–right) alternation; but there are several surprising reports of hippocampal superiority in operant spatial alternation tasks. This finding is perhaps related to
the superior hippocampal performance also sometimes seen in operant
single (go no-go) alternation experiments (Section 6.21). It is suggested by
O'Keefe and Nadel (1978, p. 325) that this type of result is due to the
general tendency of hippocampal animals to acquire bar-pressing responses easily and to execute them rapidly. If so, we would expect to see
similar phenomena in septals, since, if anything, operant over-responding
is seen even more frequently in these animals (Section 6.1). However, neither spatial nor single alternation has been much studied in the Skinner-
box after septal lesions.

Comment

The findings reviewed in this section offer strong support for the spatial
theory. However, they are also open to other interpretations. They might
be explained in terms of an increased susceptibility to interference, since
the tasks used are open to substantial retro-active and/or pro-active interference. In that case the spatial character of the task would be incidental
rather than critical. This interpretation is supported by Olton's recent
work (Olton, Becker and Handelmann 1979a) using the radial-arm maze.
He converted this into a non-spatial task by (i) defining each arm very
clearly in terms of intramaze stimuli, (ii) minimizing extramaze stimuli,
and (iii) altering the topographical relation between arms by interchang-
ing them between trials. The impairment produced by lesions to the
fimbria-fornix in performance on this task was as severe as the impairment seen in the normal task, in which the animal's choices are controlled
by extramaze, spatial cues. Olton *et al.*'s (1979a) own interpretation of
these findings is in terms of their theory of working memory; this is an
approach we shall consider later (Chapter 9).

It is not clear what the relation is between the deficit in spatial discrimination and the changes in exploratory behaviour noted in Section 6.12.
Niki (1966), in an investigation of the effects of hippocampal lesions on
performance in the Dashiell maze, noted that the lesioned animals chose
fewer paths and switched between them less often. This would clearly
reduce the animal's chances of hitting on the correct path. But it is not
clear whether a deficit in flexible exploration underlies the impairment in
spatial learning, or whether both these impairments result from the same
underlying change, e.g. a loss in the capacity to handle spatial information.

6.22. Reversal learning

Septal lesions

Experiments on reversal learning require the animal to reverse a (usually simultaneous) discrimination, the old S+ becoming S− and vice versa. Septal lesions produce a highly reliable impairment in position reversal and 'serial' position reversal (i.e. several successive reversals). Since there is no impairment in simple position learning (Section 6.19), this effect is specific to the reversal element.

Experiments on brightness reversal have produced a much more mixed picture. Schwartzbaum and Donovick (1968) and Dabrowska and Drzewiecka (1975) found no effect of the lesion, even though position reversal was impaired in both experiments. There are, however, several recent reports from Donovick's laboratory of impaired brightness reversal after septal lesions. These reports are in part due to the introduction of a new and evidently more sensitive measure of discrimination learning in the sequential four choice-point maze used by this group (Section 6.19). As well as measuring errors upon first entering each section of the maze ('initial errors'), they measure repeated attempts to enter the incorrect alternative in each section ('repeated errors'). As measured by repeated errors septals were inferior to controls in four experiments on brightness reversal reported by Sikorsky *et al.* (1977) and Chin *et al.* (1976). These impairments appeared whether septals had been better, worse or no different than controls in initial acquisition of the discrimination. Another experiment from this group investigated the effect of an irrelevant dimension on reversal (Donovick *et al.* 1978). In the acquisition phase of this experiment rats learned a discrimination with black and right as perfectly correlated positive cues; they were then reversed to white positive with position irrelevant or to left positive with brightness irrelevant. Septals were impaired on both reversals, and to a greater extent on brightness than position reversal.

Hippocampal lesions

The impairment produced by hippocampal lesions in position reversal is as reliable as that produced by septal lesions and is again independent of impairment in the acquisition of the position habit.

Hippocampal animals also show an impairment in reversal learning when tested with a variety of other dimensions.

There are several reports of impaired brightness reversal without an acquisition deficit (Silveira and Kimble 1968; Nonneman and Isaacson 1973). In Samuels's (1972) experiment the impairment in brightness reversal was limited to the first of three reversals, was less persistent and required larger lesions than the deficit in position reversal noted in the same experiment. This suggests that brightness reversal is less vulnerable to hippocampal damage than is position reversal. There are also reports of impaired visual pattern reversal with no acquisition deficit (Douglas and Pribram 1966; Winocur and Olds 1978). In Winocur and Olds's (1978) experiment the reversal deficit appeared only if the animals were tested in the same apparatus and under the same deprivation conditions as prevailed during acquisition. If reversal was conducted in a different apparatus and with drive shifted from hunger to thirst, the deficit, though still present, was no longer significant. This finding is to be compared with the retention deficit observed in the same experiment (when the original habit was retested after a seven-day interval). Such a deficit was found in rats tested under the changed, but not in the original acquisition conditions. Thus the initial learning was apparently more closely tied to the conditions of original acquisition in hippocampals than in controls: a change in these conditions produced a retention deficit but facilitated reversal learning in the lesioned animals.

Other modalities have also been used to demonstrate the hippocampal deficit in reversal learning. Impaired tactile reversals have been reported by Webster and Voneida (1964) and Harley (1979). In Harley's (1979) experiment the deficit appeared only if there was an irrelevant brightness cue also present during reversal. Webster and Voneida's (1964) experiment is particularly difficult to accommodate within the spatial theory because of its total lack of any spatial element: cats were required to palpate raised patterns at the bottom of a tube, position randomized between right and left. Also problematic for the spatial theory is Ellen and Wilson's (1963) report of a deficit in the reversal of shock–escape bar-holding to shock–avoidance bar-pressing. The only type of reversal which appears to be immune to the effects of hippocampal damage is that of object reversal in the rhesus monkey (Mahut 1971; Jones and Mishkin 1972). Weiskrantz and Warrington (1975) suggest that this may be due to the use in these experiments of 'junk' objects, which by definition differ from each other along many stimulus dimensions. Thus the animal might solve a reversal problem by shifting stimulus dimensions rather than by altering its response to a cue on a given dimension (Sutherland and Mackintosh 1971). This suggestion has not been tested directly.

Septal and hippocampal lesions compared

Both lesions impair position and brightness reversals, and there is some indication in each case that brightness reversals are less susceptible to the effects of the lesion. Hippocampal lesions have also been shown to impair visual pattern and tactile reversals, but not junk object reversal in the rhesus monkey; there are no comparable data on septal lesions with these discriminations.

Comment

The deficit in position reversal might be seen as support for the spatial theory. But the impairment also seen in other kinds of reversal, including some with minimal spatial content (e.g. Webster and Voneida 1964; Ellen and Wilson 1963), greatly weakens this account. The non-reward hypothesis treats reversal deficits as analogous to extinction deficits: the animal is treated as having difficulty in inhibiting non-rewarded responses in both cases. Some of the detailed error patterns seen after lesions are compatible with this account. There are several reports of perseverative errors at the start of reversal training (Silveira and Kimble 1968; Jones and Mishkin 1972; Singh 1973; Nonneman *et al.* 1974). Riddell *et al.* (1973) noted that, in a serial position reversal, the hippocampal deficit was particularly marked if the first response of the day happened to be incorrect; the animal then had difficulty in abandoning it. In other experiments, however, the lesioned animal has abandoned the old response as rapidly as controls, but has then adopted an inappropriate and persistent position habit (Isaacson, Nonneman and Schmaltz 1968).

It would be wrong, however, to suppose that perseveration in the lesioned animal is a simple matter of failing to inhibit the motor response. Consider for example Silveira and Kimble's (1968) analysis of error patterns during reversal of a simultaneous brightness discrimination in hippocampal rats first trained to go to the lighted arm of a Y-maze. During reversal the lesioned animals showed an increase in light-going responses relative to controls up to the first correct response. But after this point the hippocampals no longer differed from controls in this respect. Rather, they persisted longer in whatever hypotheses they adopted, and they adopted fewer such hypotheses than controls (a 'hypothesis' was defined by consistencies between successive choices). Thus hippocampal lesions resulted in a more general behavioural inflexibility than would be conveyed by the notion of an impairment in motor inhibition.

6.23. Contrast effects

The experiments grouped in this section are of heterogeneous design. They have in common the measurement of responses to one reinforcement condition which is contrasted with a second (usually more favourable) one.

Septal lesions

We saw in Chapter 2 (Section 6.9) that part of the evidence that antianxiety drugs do not impair responses to unconditioned non-reward (as distinct from stimuli associated with non-reward) is their failure to alter the frustration effect in Amsel and Roussel's (1952) double runway. The same lack of effect is reported for septal lesions (Mabry and Peeler 1972; Henke 1977). In Henke's (1977) experiment an important double dissociation was demonstrated between septal and amygdaloid lesions: the former abolished the PREE (tested in the first half of the double runway) but left intact the frustration effect tested in the same animals; the latter abolished the frustration effect but left intact the PREE. The effects of septal lesions closely resembled those reported for sodium amylobarbitone in the same situation (Gray and Dudderidge 1971). There is an operant analogue of the frustration effect, in which the reinforcer is omitted intermittently at the termination of the fixed interval of an otherwise standard FI schedule. Normal animals respond faster after such reward omission than after reward, but this effect may have nothing to do with frustration (Staddon 1970, 1972). The 'FI omission' effect was unaltered by septal lesions in an experiment by Manning and McDonough (1974); an increase was reported by Poplawsky and Cohen (1977), but they did not control for the increased baseline response rate also produced by septal lesions. Further evidence that the anti-anxiety drugs act on conditioned but not unconditioned frustration was seen in the fact that they block the PREE at a 24-hour ITI, but not at short ITIs (Chapter 2, Section 6.9). However, septal lesions block the PREE equally completely under both conditions (Feldon and Gray 1979a, b).

Another phenomenon which has been linked with frustration (Gray and Smith 1969) is behavioural contrast (Reynolds 1961). This is an increase in response rate in the presence of S+ which occurs when an operant response is reinforced on a multiple schedule of which one component is either extinction or relatively low in reinforcement density. According to Gray and Smith (1969) behavioural contrast reflects conditioned frustration, and should therefore (on the anxiety hypothesis of septo-hippocampal function) be attenuated by septal lesions. However, these lesions are without effect on behavioural contrast (Dickinson 1973; Davison *et al.* 1975; Henke 1976). In the experiments by Dickinson (1973) and Henke (1976) the animal was also provided with a second lever, responses on which terminated S− without otherwise altering reinforcement contingencies; septal lesions increased response rate on this lever. Henke (1976) interpreted this finding to indicate that the aversiveness of S− was increased by septal lesions. However he had no control for the general increase in response rate caused by septal lesions; nor was there any evidence that responding on the second lever was genuinely reinforced by the termination of an aversive S−. C. Preston (personal communication) has used Henke's paradigm with normal rats and failed to obtain such evidence.

Finally, there have been four experiments on the Crespi depression effect, in which responding for a reward of relatively low incentive value is reduced below a control level by previous experience of a reward of higher value (Chapter 2, Section 2.7). Three of these experiments found no effect of septal lesions (Pubols 1966; Flaherty and Hamilton 1971; Hammond and Thomas 1971). In the fourth (Flaherty *et al.* 1973) lick rate was measured when sucrose concentration was shifted from 32 to 4 per cent; septal lesions reduced the depression effect if there was a four-day interval between the pre- and post-shift exposures to sucrose, but not with a one-day interval.

Hippocampal lesions

Hippocampal lesions have been reported to leave the double-runway frustration effect unchanged (Swanson and Isaacson 1969) and to increase the FI omission effect (Manning and McDonough 1974). Of four experiments on the Crespi depression effect two found no change (Van Hartesveldt 1973; Kramarcy *et al.* 1973), but Murphy and Brown (1970) and Franchina and Brown (1971) both report that it is absent after hippocampal lesions. In Murphy and Brown's (1970) experiment hippocampal rats shifted from 32 to 4 per cent sucrose lowered their lick rate to a level appropriate to the lower reward, but did not display the under-shoot that constitutes the depression effect proper. This is the same pattern of results that is produced by the anti-anxiety drugs (Gray 1977). However, in Franchina and Brown's (1971) experiment the hippocampal group did not change their running speed at all when shifted from 12 to one pellet reward in the alley. They also showed no change in running speed when the reward was increased from one to 12 pellets. Thus there was no evidence in this experiment that hippocampal animals noticed the change in reward size in either direction. There appears to be no report of the effect of hippocampal lesions on behavioural contrast; but Gaffan (1973) found no effect of fornix lesions.

Septal and hippocampal lesions compared

Neither lesion alters the double-runway frustration effect; the putative operant analogue of this (the FI omission effect) may be increased by both lesions. The Crespi depression effect is inconsistently impaired after hippocampal lesions, but there is little evidence of such a change after septal lesions.

Comment

The results reviewed in this section offer only slight support for the hypothesis that damage to the septo-hippocampal system reduces the behavioural effects of stimuli associated with non-reward, but not those of non-reward itself. It is consistent with the second limb of this hypothesis that septal and hippocampal lesions do not reduce the double-runway frustration effect or the FI omission effect. But the completeness with which the PREE is disrupted by both septal (Feldon and Gray 1979*b*) and hippocampal (Rawlins *et al.* 1980*b*) lesions when short ITIs are used is not consistent with an effect on conditioned frustration only (Chapter 2, Section 2.9; Feldon *et al.* 1979). Conversely, if conditioned frustration is reduced, we would expect a reduction in the Crespi depression effect to follow more reliably from damage to the septo-hippocampal system. The failure to affect behavioural contrast is less surprising, since recent analyses of this phenomenon suggest that it is not related to frustration (Schwartz and Gamzu 1977).

6.24. Comparison between septal, hippocampal, and anti-anxiety syndromes

Table 6.5 summarizes the septal and hippocampal syndromes as they have been described in this chapter. It is not surprising, given the extensive interconnections between the hippocampus and the septal area, that they should resemble each other; but in view of the numerous pitfalls of the lesion technique it is surprising that they resemble each other so closely. There is no need to go further into the details of this resemblance, since we have commented on them in the appropriate sections above. Those effects which are seen after both kinds of lesions may provisionally be taken to define a 'septo-hippocampal syndrome'; although one cannot exclude the possibility that in part the resemblance between the effects of septal and hippocampal lesions is fortuitous, or due to the interruption by septal lesions of hippocampal afferents or efferents rather than to communalities between hippocampal and septal function as such.

Some of the dissimilarities between the septal and hippocampal syndromes call for special comment (for references to the relevant sections of this chapter, see Table 6.5).

One-way active avoidance is impaired by septal but not clearly by hippocampal lesions. It has been shown by Ross and Grossman (1977) that the effect of septal lesions is reproduced by transection of the stria medullaris, but not by section of various other pathways afferent to or efferent from the septal area. Since the stria medullaris carries fibres from the septofimbrial and triangular nuclei to the habenular nuclei, Ross and Grossman's (1977) findings suggest that the effect of septal lesions on one-way active avoidance may not be related principally to septo-hippocampal connections. This inference is supported by the fact that transection of the fornix-fimbria does not normally impair one-way active avoidance (Woody and Ervin 1966; Uretsky and McCleary 1969; Thomas and McCleary 1974b; Myhrer 1975a; Ross et al. 1975; Liss 1968). But note that the data on hippocampal lesions are far from clear, and the divergence from the effects of septal lesions may be more apparent than real.

The biggest differences between the septal and hippocampal syndromes appear in the realm of affective behaviour. The well-known hyperreactivity which occurs after septal lesions (Fried 1972b) is seen, if at all, only mildly after hippocampal lesions. Note, however, that it is also only a transient feature of the septal syndrome, disappearing within one or two weeks after the lesions (Yutzey et al. 1964), especially if the animals are handled (Brady and Nauta 1955) or caged in groups (Ahmad and Harvey 1968). As in the case of the septal one-way avoidance deficit, investigations of the septal connections responsible for hyper-reactivity suggest the importance of relations other than those with the hippocampus. In particular, experiments by Albert and his colleagues have pointed to the importance of descending septal control over the ventromedial hypothalamus. The relevant pathway appears to pass through or originate in the lateral septal area and then descend ventral to the anterior septal area (Albert, Brayley, and Milner 1978*a;* Brayley and Albert 1977*a, b;* Albert and Richmond 1977; Albert and Wong 1978; see also Grossman 1978; and Chapter 8 below). The increase in shock-induced aggression also seen only after septal lesions may depend on the same mechanisms as the hyper-reactivity syndrome (Grossman 1978).

The most embarrassing finding for the theory developed in this book is that hippocampal lesions do not reproduce the effects of septal lesions on fear, as measured by open field defecation and related measures. As noted in Sections 6.12 and 6.14 above, this divergence between the two syndromes is possibly related to the somewhat different effects produced by the two lesions on open-field ambulation: a consistent increase after hippocampal lesions, mixed increases, and decreases after septal lesions. As shown in Section 6.12, the effects of septal lesions on ambulation can be understood on the assumption that these reduce the contribution of fear to the control of locomotion in the open field. Another fact which perhaps enters into the different effects of septal and hippocampal lesions on open-field ambulation is the more consistent increase in general activity produced by hippocampal lesions. Unfortunately, nothing is known about the particular pathways which underlie the effects of septal and hippocampal lesions on open-field behaviour.

One notable feature of the differences between the septal and hippo-campal syndromes is that these consist virtually entirely of added features in the septal syndrome. This is to be expected, given the greater anatom-ical diversity of the septal area (Chapter 3). Thus septal lesions produce, in addition to the effects common to hippocampal lesions: increased re-sponding on operant CRF schedules; decreased fear in the open field with its probable consequence of mixed effects on ambulation; the hyper-reactivity syndrome and the probably related increase in shock-induced aggression; perhaps impaired one-way active avoidance (though this may also be produced by hippocampal lesions); and possibly an increased sen-sitivity to olfactory cues (but this has not been studied after hippocampal lesions). In contrast, there are no clear instances of hippocampal effects that are not in the septal syndrome. Hippocampal lesions reduce shock-induced aggression; but since both kinds of lesion reduce socially induced aggression, this may be the basic 'septo-hippocampal' effect which is then masked in septal animals by their hyper-reactivity to shock. Hippocampal lesions are apparently more likely to reduce the Crespi depression effect and to steepen the FI scallop; but the effects on these phenomena of neither lesion have been clearly established. Similarly, hippocampal le-sions have been shown to impair single alternation under some condi-tions, but septal lesions have been inadequately studied in this paradigm. Between them these findings do not suggest that either lesion has more consistent effects on responses to non-reward; for an attenuation of such

Table 6.5. Comparison between the behavioural effects of septal (S) and Hippocampal (H) lesions and anti-anxiety drugs*

Section Ch. 2	Ch. 6	Task	Syndrome common to S and H lesions	Features in S, not H, syndrome	Features in H, not S, syndrome	Effects of anti-anxiety drugs
1	1	Rewarded running, CRF	o			o
1	1	Rewarded bar-pressing, CRF	o	+		o
7	1	Rewarded bar-pressing, intermittent reinforcement	+			+†
2	2	Passive avoidance	−			−
3	3	Classical conditioning with aversive UCS	o			o
3	3	On-the-baseline conditioned suppression	−	−		−
3	3	Off-the-baseline conditioned suppression		?.?	?o	?o
3	3	Taste aversion	o		−	?.?
4	4	Agonistic escape	+			o
4	4	Skilled escape	o			o
5	5	One-way active avoidance	+	−		+
5	6	Non-spatial active avoidance	+			+
5	7	Two-way avoidance	o			+
6	8	Threshold of detection of shock	+			o
	8	Movement elicited by shock	+			?.?
9, 10, 13		Movement elicited by novel stimuli	−			?.?
	10	Distraction			+‡	?.?
	11	General activity	−	?		?.?
10	12	Exploration of novel stimuli			+	−
10	12	Spontaneous alternation	−§			−
10	12	Open-field ambulation		−/+‖		+/−‖
10	12	Rearing	−			−
10	13	Habituation rate	?.−			?.?
10	14	Open-field defecation		−		?.?

Chapter	Chapter 2	Behaviour*				
10	14	Emergence time				—
6	15	Shock-induced aggression	+		?.	?¶
6	15	Hyperreactivity syndrome	+		—	?.
6	15	Social aggression	—			o
10	16	Social interaction	+	+	?.	?+¶
7	17	Resistance to extinction	—			?+**
7	17	Partial reinforcement extinction effect			?.	+
7	18	Partial reinforcement acquisition effect	?.o#		?.	—
7	18	Performance on DRL schedule	—		?+	—‡
7	19	Fixed-interval scallop				—
8	20	Simultaneous discrimination	o			—
8	20	Successive discrimination	−§§			o
8	21	Single alternation				—
8	22	Spatial discrimination	—		?−	?.
8	23	Reversal learning	−	?.	?−	—
9	23	Double runway frustration effect	o			o
7	23	Crespi depression effect		?.	?−	—

*This comparison is based on the information in the sections of this chapter and Chapter 2 listed in column 1, together with the more detailed reviews given by Gray (1977) and Gray and McNaughton (1983). +, facilitation; −, impairment; o, no consistent change; ?, insufficient data. If an entry in columns 4 or 5 is accompanied by a question mark in the other column, the difference between the septal and hippocampal syndromes cannot be established because of insufficient data.

†An exception is the VI schedule, on which rates are not increased by anti-anxiety drugs but are increased by both lesions.

‡The apparent difference between the effects of the two lesions may be an artefact of the available data, since both lesions increase activity in the shuttle-box and decrease activity in the running wheel.

§It is possible that septal lesions increase stimulus perseveration and hippocampal lesions, response perseveration; but this apparent difference has been questioned by McNaughton and Feldon (1980).

||Septal lesions reduce ambulation upon early exposure to the open field but increase ambulation with continued exposure; the pattern of change with anti-anxiety drugs is the reverse.

¶In this case the question mark indicates, not insufficient data, but major inconsistencies in the data (see Gray 1977).

**The anti-anxiety drugs increase social interaction only (see Gray 1977).

||Anti-anxiety drugs are relatively ineffective with short inter-trial intervals, but the two lesions have very large effects under these conditions (Feldon et al. 1979; Feldon and Gray 1979a, b; Rawlins et al. 1980b).

#Feldon and Gray (1979a, b).

§§Septal lesions improve successive discrimination with olfactory cues.

responses should give rise to a reduced Crespi effect, a reduced FI scallop and impaired single alternation.

As noted in the comments on individual sections, several different theories of septo-hippocampal function find support at different points in the data, but none of them finds support at all points. It would be otiose to go over this ground again, and also premature, since, before we attempt to produce any kind of theoretical integration of the data, it will be necessary to look at the results of other kinds of experiments besides those which use lesions. Note that we have so far given no attention to the hypothesis that the hippocampus is concerned with memory; we shall delay consideration of the data relevant to this hypothesis until Chapter 9.

The anatomical interconnections between the septal area and hippocampus provide strong *a priori* grounds for expecting the septal and hippocampal syndromes to resemble each other, irrespective of any particular theory of their behavioural functions. This is not so for the resemblances which exist between the septo-hippocampal syndrome and the effects of the anti-anxiety drugs. But it is clear from Table 6.5 that these too are remarkably strong. As before I shall devote most attention to the exceptions to the rule.

Consider first those cases in which the septal and hippocampal syndromes themselves diverge. The hypothesis that the anti-anxiety drugs act on a joint septo-hippocampal system must predict conservative effects for the drugs in these instances, that is, that they will fail to produce the added features found only in the septal syndrome. This is the case for the increased operant CRF response rate, the one-way active avoidance deficit and the hyper-reactivity syndrome seen in septal animals, none of which is found after administration of the anti-anxiety drugs (Gray 1977; Chapter 2). There is no clear evidence concerning the effects of the anti-anxiety drugs on open field defecation, which is decreased by septal lesions; this is an important lacuna in the data. Emergence time is reduced by both the benzodiazepines (Simon and Soubrié 1979) and septal lesions (Thomas *et al.* 1959); but this test has not been used with hippocampal animals. Ambulation in the open field is consistently increased by anti-anxiety drugs (Simon and Soubrié 1979), which resemble in this respect hippocampal rather than septal lesions. Thus none of these data suggests any resemblance of anti-anxiety drug action to the special features of the septal syndrome.

The cases in which hippocampal lesions (somewhat questionably; see above) produce special effects of their own reveal a more mixed picture. Although both septal and hippocampal lesions impair spontaneous alternation, there is evidence (Dalland 1970) that they do so differently, septal lesions by increasing perseveration of goal-arms, hippocampal lesions by increasing perseveration of body-turns. Sodium amylobarbitone has the latter effect; but it should be noted that the difference between the effects of septal and hippocampal lesions in this situation may not be clearcut

(McNaughton and Feldon 1980). On the assumption that hippocampal lesions reduce the Crespi depression effect, whereas septal lesions do not, there is again a resemblance between anti-anxiety drug action (Gray 1977; Chapter 2) and the hippocampal effect. The same is true if we assume that hippocampal but not septal lesions impair single alternation in the alley, since this is impaired by sodium amylobarbitone (Feldon *et al.* 1979). On the other hand, if we assume that septal but not hippocampal lesions reduce the FI scallop, this effect is reproduced by the anti-anxiety drugs (Chapter 2; Gray 1977), so that in this respect the drug acts like a septal lesion. This, and the reduction in on-the-baseline conditioned suppression, appear to be the only cases in which the effects of the anti-anxiety drugs resemble those of a septal rather than a hippocampal lesion.

Aggressive behaviour presents a rather special case, on which it is difficult to obtain a clear perspective because the effects of the anti-anxiety drugs are themselves so variable (Gray 1977). But there is some reason to suppose that there is a real divergence at this point between the effects of the drugs and those of either kind of lesion. Both septal and hippocampal lesions usually reduce aggression induced by means other than shock (most commonly, by pairing previously isolated animals). If such an effect is seen after administration of the anti-anxiety drugs, it is confined to the benzodiazepines; furthermore, it appears that the reduction in aggressive behaviour is more evident when aggression is induced by shock. When shock is not used, all the anti-anxiety drugs have been reported (though not invariably) to increase aggression, especially in low doses. This effect seems to have no counterpart after either septal or hippocampal lesions. Thus, to the extent that conclusions are possible about aggressive behaviour, the anti-anxiety syndrome resembles neither that produced by septal nor that produced by hippocampal lesions.

With this exception, the most striking feature of Table 6.5 is that, wherever the effects of septal and hippocampal lesions are the same as each other, those of the anti-anxiety drugs (if they are known, for there are many lacunae in the data) are again the same. In common to the effects of drugs and lesions are: lack of change in rewarded running; increased response rate on operant intermittent schedules; reduced passive avoidance; lack of effect on aversive Pavlovian conditioning; lack of effect on skilled escape; improved non-spatial avoidance; improved two-way active avoidance; no change in the threshold for detection of shock; reduced spontaneous alternation; reduced rearing; increased resistance to extinction; decreased resistance to extinction after PRF training in the alley; impaired performance on DRL schedules; lack of effect on simultaneous discriminations; disinhibition of responding to S− in successive discriminations; impaired reversal learning; and no change in the double-runway frustration effect. In addition there is one other similarity which is less clearly established than these: under certain conditions there is a reduction after all three treatments in the animal's capacity to attend to and take in information about novel features of its environment; although for the most part this conclusion is based on different experimental tasks in each case (see Sections 6.10, 6.12, and 6.19, above; and Chapter 2, Section 2.10). This is a formidable list of similarities, and it offers strong support for the hypothesis that the anti-anxiety drugs act in some way by impairing the functioning of the septo-hippocampal system.

At a more theoretical level, there is one feature of the effects of the anti-anxiety drugs which appears to be missing from the septo-hippocampal syndrome. As we saw in Chapter 2, these drugs impair all three normal outputs of the behavioural inhibition system: behavioural inhibition itself, increased attention to novel stimuli, and increased level of arousal. There is evidence that septal and hippocampal lesions produce the first two of these changes, but none that they lower the level of arousal.

Two experiments suggest more positively that they do not have this effect.

Dickinson (1975) trained rats on a discrete-trial task in which bar-presses were rewarded with food on a VR 2 schedule (i.e. random 50 per cent PRF). Shock was delivered for bar-pressing on the same schedule. In one condition it was perfectly positively correlated with food delivery, in another negatively. Among control animals bar-pressing was more suppressed by shock in the negatively than in the positively correlated condition, a phenomenon attributed to the counter-conditioning of the effects of shock by the immediately following food in the positively correlated condition (Dickinson and Pearce 1977); in fact, in the positively correlated condition, bar-pressing was not suppressed in controls at all. In both conditions response rate was increased by septal lesions: in the negatively correlated condition, there was less suppression among the lesioned animals than among controls, in agreement with other data summarized in Section 6.2 above; but in the positively correlated condition there was an actual increase in response rate relative to the *unsuppressed* control baseline. One interpretation of these findings (Dickinson 1974, 1975; Gray and Smith 1969) is that the level of suppression seen in the controls represented an algebraic summation between two separate effects of punishment, one (behavioural inhibition proper) rate-decreasing, the other (increased arousal) rate-increasing, and that septal lesions selectively eliminated the former only.

A second experiment which lends itself to the same interpretation was described in Section 6.10 above. In a study of the effects of distraction on the behaviour of rats in the alley, Raphelson *et al.* (1965) showed that a novel stimulus caused running speeds to decrease in normal animals, but to increase in hippocampals. As in the Dickinson (1975) experiment, this result may reflect a loss after hippocampal lesions of behavioural inhibition, but with preservation of the arousal increment caused by novel stimuli. This account may also explain why behavioural contrast is immune to the effects of septal (Dickinson 1973; Davison *et al.* 1975; Henke 1976) or fornix (Gaffan 1973) lesions; for this phenomenon, assuming it to be due to conditioned frustration at all, reflects an increment in level of arousal (Gray and Smith 1969).

The data we have reviewed clearly call for some kind of theoretical integration. Given the complexities we have encountered in this chapter, it is doubtful that the theory presented in Chapter 2, when we had to cope only with the anti-anxiety drugs, can survive without change or development. But before we embark on theory construction, there are other data to review, dependent on other methods of investigation. We deal with these in the next three chapters.

7

Hippocampal electrical activity and behaviour

The experiments reviewed in the last chapter all imposed severe insults on the brain. Those we consider now do much less damage. One simply implants electrodes in the hippocampus or related structures and records the signals these pick up: slow waves in the EEG, field potentials, or the firing of single neurones (Chapter 4). By varying the behavioural and environmental conditions under which the recordings are made, and looking for concomitant variation in the signals received, one hopes to deduce something about the functions of the septo-hippocampal system.

The behavioural correlates of theta

The results of lesion experiments are compatible, as we have seen, with many hypotheses of septo-hippocampal function. But they are unlikely to give rise to the idea that the septo-hippocampal system is concerned with the execution of movements. This hypothesis was suggested by Vander-wolf (1969, 1971) on the basis of studies of the behavioural correlates of the theta rhythm, and this has remained the chief — perhaps the only — source of its support. There is no need to review these studies in the kind of detail we devoted to lesion experiments in Chapter 6, since there is little disagreement as to the major facts (as distinct from their interpretation), and O'Keefe and Nadel (1978, Chapter 4 and Tables A5 to A12) have in any case recently summarized much of the relevant material. This harmony is in large measure due to the careful and thorough investigations reported by Vanderwolf and his group. By showing how well theta is correlated with movement, at least under some experimental conditions, these workers have made it much more difficult to cling to hypotheses which have associated theta with a variety of psychological processes of a more or less recondite nature. Rather than go into all these hypotheses, and the reasons for their probable demise (Vanderwolf *et al.* 1975; Black 1975), I shall concentrate here only on the major facts and the theories which continue to be compatible with them.

The movement hypothesis is based on observations of conscious rats and rabbits showing that, whenever the animal engages in more or less vigorous movements, the hippocampal EEG normally contains a prominent theta rhythm; conversely, when the animal is still or its behaviour involves little movement, theta is usually absent (see Fig. 4.1). Vanderwolf *et al.* (1975) have summarized these observations in the manner shown in Table 7.1. They raise several questions. How should we best describe the correlation between theta and movement? How absolute is it? Does it indicate that the hippocampus participates in the execution of movements?

In its early form the movement hypothesis claimed that theta occurs to the extent that the animal engages in *voluntary* movement (Vanderwolf 1971). This hypothesis had to be abandoned for two reasons.

Table 7.1. Normal relation of hippocampal activity to behaviour in the rat. (From Vanderwolf *et al.* (1975))

HIPPOCAMPUS	BEHAVIOUR
	Type 1. walking, running, swimming, rearing, jumping, digging, manipulation of objects with the forelimbs, isolated movements of the head or one limb, shifts of posture. Related terms: voluntary, appetitive, instrumental, purposive, operant, or 'theta' behaviour.
	Type 2. (a) alert immobility in any posture. (b) licking, chewing, chattering the teeth, sneezing, startle response, vocalization, shivering, tremor, face-washing, scratching the fur, pelvic thrusting, ejaculation, defecation, urination, piloerection. Related terms: automatic, reflexive, consummatory, respondent, or 'non-theta' behaviour.

First, the notion of voluntariness has proved elusive of any definition other than 'correlated with theta', rendering the whole exercise irredeemably circular. The most important attempt to exit from the circle was the proposal (Vanderwolf 1971) that voluntary behaviour can be used to accomplish different types of goal, whereas involuntary behaviour is associated with only one particular motivational state. Thus a rat can run (theta) to obtain food or water or to avoid shock, but it normally licks (non-theta) only for water. This proposal was defeated by the demonstration that, when rats are trained to lick at a tube to avoid shock (thus meeting the criterion for 'voluntary' behaviour), the hippocampal record contains predominantly large irregular activity (Fig. 4-1), just as it does when the rat drinks normally (Black and Young 1972; Young 1976). Note, however, that, while this demonstration weakens the hypothesis that theta is related to *voluntary* movement, it further strengthens the association between theta and movement from which this hypothesis was derived. For it appears not to matter *why* an animal performs a given movement; the fact that it is performed is sufficient to guarantee the correlated appearance of theta. It is observations like these which limit most drastically the usefulness of hypotheses relating theta to psychological processes (e.g. learning, attention, frustration) which might underlie the observed movement (A. Black 1975).

But a second kind of observation went to the heart of the association between theta and movement. For it is now clear that movement is not necessary for theta to occur. To begin with, it has long been known that theta is a prominent feature of so-called 'paradoxical' sleep (O'Keefe and Nadel 1978, Table A11), that is, sleep accompanied by low-voltage fast-wave activity in the neocortex, rapid eye movements (hence also 'REM' sleep), and in man reports of dreaming. More recently it has become clear that, in species other than the rat, and especially in the cat and rabbit, theta is frequently seen in states of alert immobility (e.g. Harper 1971; Kemp and Kaada 1975; Kramis, Vanderwolf, and Bland 1975; Arnolds *et al.* 1979*c*; and see O'Keefe and Nadel 1978, Table A8, *b*). In the rat, on data from which Vanderwolf's movement hypothesis was originally based, this point has been more controversial. However, there are several reports of theta during immobility in the rat while sniffing (Gray 1971*c*), preparatory to jumping (Whishaw and Vanderwolf 1973), or when presented with a CS signalling foot-shock (Whishaw 1972; Graeff, Quintero, and Gray 1980).

Faced with these observations Vanderwolf has had to retreat on two fronts (Vanderwolf *et al.* 1975, 1978). First, in describing the correlation between theta and movement, it was necessary to abandon the theoretically interesting but indefensible distinction between 'voluntary' and 'automatic' behaviour, in favour of the impregnable but theoretically empty position that there exist 'Type 1' and 'Type 2' forms of motor activity (Table 7.1) which are, respectively, associated and not associated with theta. There remained the problem of the exceptions to the rule, however phrased. For a while Vanderwolf flirted with the notion that theta occurs in immobile animals which are in a state of readiness to move; but this proposal is almost impossible to disprove, and so scientifically weak. More recently he has suggested that there are two kinds of theta, one associated with Type 1 motor activity and which never occurs in association with immobility, the other capable of occurring during immobility.

The distinction between 'movement' and 'non-movement' theta has been backed up by an important series of observations of pharmacological and other differences between them. 'Movement' theta is resistant to systemic injections of antimuscarinic drugs (e.g. atropine, scopolamine), is abolished by anaesthetics (e.g. urethane, ether), and is normally of relatively high frequency (in the rat, more than 7–8 Hz); in addition, of course, it occurs in association with Type 1 behaviour patterns. 'Non-movement' theta is abolished by systemic treatment with antimuscarinics, it can occur in anaesthetized animals, and it is normally of relatively low frequency (in the rat, less than 7–8 Hz); in addition, it occurs in awake, immobile animals (Vanderwolf *et al.* 1975, 1978). Note, however, that both types of theta are abolished by medial septal lesions; thus they both depend on the same pacemaker. Given the differential susceptibility of the two kinds of theta to anticholinergic drugs, this poses something of a mystery, since (as we saw in Chapter 4) the septo-hippocampal fibres which control theta are themselves almost certainly cholinergic (Lewis and Shute 1978). It is possible that the effects of antimuscarinic drugs on non-movement theta are exercized by way of a muscarinic input (direct or indirect) to the septal pacemaker.

So as not to beg any functional questions, let us refer to these two kinds of theta (following Vanderwolf's example) as 'atropine-resistant' and 'atropine-sensitive' respectively. Can we say anything more precise about their functional correlates than that the former is associated with movement and the latter with absence of movement?

With regard to atropine-resistant theta some clues have been afforded by studies of variation in the frequency of theta within this band. There is good agreement that vigorous movements which cause the animal to move from one place to another (walking, running, swimming, jumping), or which have been temporarily perverted from this function (running in a running wheel), are associated with higher frequencies of theta ($>$ 8 Hz in the rat and rabbit, 5–7 Hz in the cat and dog) than less vigorous movement which does not normally cause spatial displacement (bar-pressing); the latter is accompanied by frequencies around 6–7 Hz in the rat and 3.5–5.5 Hz in the cat and dog (O'Keefe and Nadel 1978, Tables A6, *a* and *c*). Note, however, that these observations were made for the most part before Vanderwolf's group distinguished between the two types of theta, and that the frequencies associated with bar-pressing fall generally within the range that the two-theta hypothesis allots to atropine-sensitive theta. Thus it is possible that the theta seen in association with bar-pressing is of this kind. If one considers only the class of vigorous locomotor behaviour which is accompanied by high-frequency theta, theta frequency is higher, the greater the amplitude of the movement, whether this occurs naturally (Whishaw and Vanderwolf 1973) or is provoked by electrical stimulation of the hypothalamus (Bland and Vanderwolf 1972*a*).

Following up this type of observation, Morris, Black, and O'Keefe (1976; see O'Keefe and Nadel 1978, pp. 179–82) studied theta frequency in the seconds just before and during a vertical jump. They varied independently the distance the rat had to jump and (by attaching to its back weights of different magnitudes) the force it had to exert. Their results eliminated various possible correlates of theta frequency during this type of movement, including force and rate of acceleration. The major remaining candidates were velocity of movement and the size of the displacement the movement produces. These are important observations, but it is not yet clear how far they can be generalized. If, for example, the animal is forced to run in a running wheel at different speeds, the frequency of theta observed when movement is initiated is positively correlated with speed of movement of the wheel, suggesting again that the critical variable may be velocity; however, as movement continues, theta frequency settles down to a value (7–8 Hz) which is independent of the speed of revolution of the wheel (Whishaw and Vanderwolf 1973). Arnolds *et al.* (1979*b*) report observations which suggest that the animal's own motor behaviour is unimportant: theta frequency was positively correlated with speed of movement whether the subject (a dog) was forced to step along a conveyor belt moving in the opposite direction, or was pulled along in a cart.

Although much remains to be clarified, experiments of this kind have begun to suggest some quite precise behavioural correlates for theta frequency during what O'Keefe and Nadel (1978) call 'displacement' movements. In contrast, suggestions as to the correlates of Vanderwolf's atropine-sensitive theta have remained largely negative, stressing simply the absence of movement. It is possible, however, that this type of theta conforms to the earliest hypothesis proposed, namely, that it is associated with increased arousal and/or attention provoked by novel sensory stimuli (Green and Arduini 1954; Grastyán *et al.* 1959).

In the cat, in which theta during immobility has been seen particularly often (O'Keefe and Nadel 1978, Table A8, *b*), it is clearly associated with attentive postures and visual exploration (e.g. Kemp and Kaada 1975; Bennett and French 1977). In the rabbit the strong theta response to novel sensory stimuli formed the basis of Green and Arduini's (1954) classic description of slow-wave activity in the hippocampus. Several recent studies (O'Keefe and Nadel 1978, Tables A8, *b*, and A9) have confirmed this description, showing in addition that the unanaesthetized animal may be completely immobile during such a theta response and that the observed theta is abolished by atropine (Vanderwolf *et al.* 1975). In the immobile rat theta has been observed during vigorous movement of the vibrissae (Gray 1971*c*) or in response to presentation of an aversive CS (Whishaw 1972; Graeff *et al.* 1980). If one disregards the question of immobility, there is an impressive cross-species unanimity in the data (O'Keefe and Nadel 1978, Table A5): theta is invariably seen during exploratory behaviour which involves active searching. In the rat the theta associated with such behaviour tends to be of an intermediate frequency, typically 7–8 Hz; in the cat theta frequency remains low (4–5 Hz). As suggested by Bennett, French, and Burnett (1978), if there is any difference between the rat, on the one hand, and the cat and rabbit, on the other, this is likely to reflect species-specific modes of exploratory behaviour. The rat tends to explore by moving slowly round its environment so that it can make use of information received via the vibrissae; the cat and rabbit, in contrast, tend to explore visually, remaining immobile. It may be for this reason that theta frequencies during exploratory behaviour are usually intermediate in the rat but near the lower end of the range in the cat. Lower theta frequencies may be seen in the rat under conditions in which it is presented with a CS for unavoidable shock. During such stimulation the animal remains almost totally immobile and theta (abolished by scopolamine) has a frequency of about 6 Hz (Graeff *et al.* 1980).

It is probable, then, that in all the species studied atropine-sensitive theta is related to attentive immobility. It is not clear, however, whether searching behaviour involving active locomotion belongs with atropine-resistant or atropine-sensitive theta, supposing that it must belong with one or the other. Nor is it clear whether, within the atropine-sensitive band, there is any particular correlate of theta frequency, as there appears to be in the atropine-resistant band.

As we have seen, the data forced Vanderwolf to abandon his original hypothesis that theta relates solely to movement. The same data render untenable any unitary hypothesis relating theta solely to arousal, attention, the orienting reflex or similar constructs. More elaborate proposals, according to which theta has different functional correlates in different frequency bands, were made by Adey (1967) and Gray (1970*a*). Vanderwolf's two-theta proposal represents in certain respects a convergence with Gray's (1970*a*) position. This grew out of observations made during the course of experiments concerned with the wider theory, to which this book is devoted, that the anti-anxiety drugs affect behaviour by acting on the septo-hippocampal system. We saw in Chapter 2 that these drugs block the behavioural effects of stimuli associated with non-reward; and similar observations made after septal or hippocampal lesions were reviewed in Chapter 6. As a parsimonious account of the similarities between the behavioural effects of these three treatments, it was proposed that the anti-anxiety drugs affect behaviour by impairing septal control of the hippocampal theta rhythm. However, observations of the theta rhythm during behaviour sensitive to the effects of the anti-anxiety drugs required this hypothesis to be modified and made more precise (Gray and Ball 1970; Gray 1970*a*).

In these experiments it was found that, running in the straight alley for water reward, rats display theta at most times, but that the frequency of theta depends on the exact behavioural conditions. Upon first entry into the alley, during exploratory behaviour, the observed theta had a mean frequency of 7.7 Hz. When the animal was well trained and running fast towards the goal, theta frequency rose to about 8–10 Hz. When it entered the goal and consumed water, theta frequency fell to 6–7.5 Hz. Finally, on non-rewarded trials (either during extinction or on a random PRF schedule), the mean theta frequency was 7.7 Hz. Given the extensive documentation that has appeared since 1970 on the motor correlates of theta, the most obvious interpretation of these observations would relate them simply to the amount of motor activity involved (little during consumption of water, more during exploration and the agitated behaviour called forth by non-reward, most during fast running towards the goal). But at the time these observations were made the motor hypothesis of theta was poorly established, and a different interpretation seemed warranted. According to this interpretation, there are three bands of theta. A high-frequency band (>8.5 Hz) is related to the performance of instrumental behaviour (note the similarity of this view to Vanderwolf's original voluntary movement hypothesis). A low-frequency band (<7.5 Hz) is associated with the performance of fixed action patterns (e.g. eating, drinking). Finally, in a narrow frequency band centred on 7.7 Hz, theta is related to the activity of the behavioural inhibition system as defined in Chapters 1 and 2; that is, theta in this band reflects (among other things) the inhibition of ongoing behaviour caused by signals of non-reward, punishment, or novelty. On this hypothesis, the anti-anxiety drugs impair septal control of theta only in this narrow, middle-frequency band.

The chief point of difference between this 'frequency-specific' hypothesis and Vanderwolf's two-theta proposal is the special significance it accords to frequencies lying close to 7.7 Hz. This feature of the hypothesis has received support from a number of sources.

As we saw in Chapter 4, it is possible to drive theta by low-frequency stimulation of the septal area, the frequency of the elicited theta being identical to that of the applied current. If one plots the threshold current able to drive theta as a function of stimulation frequency in the free-moving male rat, one obtains a characteristic function with a minimum threshold at 7.7 Hz (Fig. 4.7). This 7.7-Hz minimum in the theta-driving curve is normally maintained by several special systems, including the ascending noradrenergic fibres from the locus coeruleus, the ascending serotonergic fibres from the median raphe, circulating testosterone and hormones of the pituitary–adrenocortical system, and the hippocampo-septal projection travelling in the fimbria (Gray *et al.* 1975; McNaughton *et al.* 1977, 1980a, b; Drewett *et al.* 1977; Valero *et al.* 1977; Rawlins *et al.* 1979; see Chapter 4).

Three lines of evidence relate the 7.7-Hz minimum in the theta-driving curve to anxiety. First, there is clear confirmation of the prediction that the anti-anxiety drugs should impair control of theta only in the 7.7-Hz band: as shown in Fig. 7.1, sodium amylobarbitone, chlordiazepoxide, diazepam, and alcohol all abolish the 7.7-Hz minimum by a selective increase in the threshold at this frequency (Gray and Ball 1970; Gray *et al.* 1975; McNaughton *et al.* 1977). Second, the 7.7-Hz minimum is absent in males of a strain of rats selectively bred for low emotionality (the Maudsley Nonreactive strain), though it is present in males of at least six other strains (Wistar, Sprague–Dawley, Sherman, Long–Evans, Brattleboro, and Maudsley Reactive). This observation (Drewett *et al.* 1977) is consistent with an association between blockade of the 7.7-Hz minimum and low fearfulness, and thus reinforces the observations made with anti-anxiety drugs. Third, the 7.7-Hz minimum is absent in females of all these strains, owing largely to insufficient levels of circulating testosterone (Drewett *et al.* 1977); since female rats are in general less fearful than males (Gray 1971b, 1979a), this finding too is consistent with an association between the 7.7-Hz minimum and fearfulness. In addition to this evidence from experiments on the theta-driving curve, the behavioural effects of driving theta at 7.7 Hz are also in general agreement with prediction; these effects are described in the next chapter.

There is considerable evidence, then, that some kind of special significance attaches to theta in a middle-frequency band which in the rat (the only species so far studied from this point of view) lies close to 7.7 Hz. However, it is clear that Gray's (1970a) frequency-specific hypothesis cannot be correct as initially formulated. There are several reasons for this conclusion.

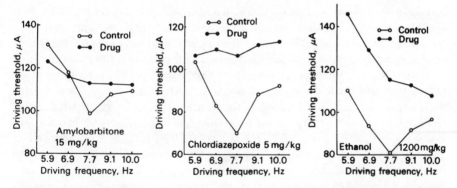

Figure 7.1. Threshold currents for septal driving of hippocampal theta rhythm (see Fig. 4.4) as a function of stimulation frequency in the free-moving male rat before (control) and after (drug) injections of three anti-anxiety drugs. (Data from McNaughton *et al.* (1977).)

First, the same data which preclude *voluntary* movement as the correlate of high-frequency theta in Vanderwolf's scheme (see above) also preclude it in Gray's scheme. Whether licking occurs as a fixed action pattern or as behaviour instrumentally reinforced by food or the avoidance of shock, its correlate in the hippocampal EEG remains the same: large irregular activity or low-frequency theta (Black and Young 1972; Young 1976). But according to Gray's (1970*a*) hypothesis, licking as an instrumental act should be accompanied by high-frequency theta.

Second, and by the same token, the correlate of low-frequency theta cannot correctly be described as the performance of a fixed action pattern, or licking would change its theta pattern when it comes to be used as an operant. There is in any case disagreement about the type of hippocampal activity observed during fixed action patterns (O'Keefe and Nadel 1978, Table A7). There are rather more reports of large, irregular activity than of low-frequency theta. O'Keefe and Nadel (1978, p. 164) suggest that these discrepancies may in part reflect species differences, the rabbit and dog being more likely to display low-frequency theta during fixed action patterns than the rat. But the number of reports of low-frequency theta accompanying fixed action patterns in the rat makes this suggestion unlikely. It is in any case unclear whether there is a true difference between large, irregular activity and low-frequency theta. Black and Young's (1972) results, for example, are included by O'Keefe and Nadel (1978) as an example of large, irregular activity during licking; but Young (1976), in a more extensive analysis of the same data, reports a spectral peak at 6 Hz. It seems probable in fact that large, irregular activity is merely theta of low frequency and great variability (Arnolds *et al.* 1979*a*). Both regular theta and large, irregular activity disappear after septal lesions, leaving only low-voltage, desynchronized fast-wave activity (Gray 1971*c;* Rawlins *et al.* 1979). Thus we might ignore this problem and conclude that fixed action patterns, whether used instrumentally or not, are always accompanied by an EEG pattern which we can call low-frequency theta or large, irregular activity as the mood takes us. But there are exceptions even to this loosely formulated rule, since regular theta of, relatively high frequency accompanies the sexual behaviour of the male rat (Kurtz and Adler 1973) and dog (Arnolds *et al.* 1979c); and if this does not count as a fixed action pattern, it is difficult to know what does.

Third, but more arguably, an objection has been raised by Morris and Black (1978) to the proposed association between middle-frequency theta and responses to non-reward. These workers showed that it is possible to predict to a high degree of accuracy the theta frequency elicited by non-reward if one takes into account (i) the motor patterns observed on such occasions (sniffing, walking, rearing, turning, and holding still), and (ii) the theta frequencies associated with the same motor patterns when they are not elicited by non-reward. Convincing as these data are, the argument based on them — that the correlation between non-reward *per se* and any particular theta frequency is therefore artefactual — is misconceived. Non-reward, of course, elicits specific patterns of behaviour, and these occur also in response to other events. Given the theoretical equivalence between stimuli associated with non-reward, stimuli associated with punishment and novel stimuli (Chapter 1), this indeed is to be expected. The problem is to determine what relations exist between the observed motor behaviour, the central states that produce this behaviour and its accompanying theta frequency. Observational methods alone are probably incapable of solving this problem.

A more important objection against the proposed association between 7.7-Hz theta and non-reward is that the frequency seen in response to this event is quite variable depending on the particular conditions of the experiment. Gray and Ball's (1970) original observations in the runway have been replicated in this apparatus (Kimsey, Dyer, and Petri 1974; and personal observations) and when a thirsty rat is exposed to an empty water tube (Soubrié, Thiébot, Simon, and Boissier 1978a); but non-rewarded lever-pressing in the Skinner-box is accompanied by theta at about 7 Hz (James and Gray, unpublished) and non-reward for a jump-up response elicits theta at 8.0 Hz (Morris and Black 1978). Conversely, theta between 7.5 and 8.5 Hz has been seen under conditions which have nothing obvious to do with any of the stimuli thought to activate the behavioural inhibition system (e.g. during walking, running in a wheel, or swimming: Whishaw 1972; Whishaw and Vanderwolf 1973).

If we reject the frequency-specific hypothesis as originally formulated (Gray 1970a), there none the less remains strong evidence that there is something special about intermediate frequencies of theta (see above). Might there be some relation between these and the two types of theta described by Vanderwolf? One possibility is that 7.7 Hz represents a transition point between Vanderwolf's atropine-sensitive (low-frequency) and atropine-resistant (high-frequency) theta.

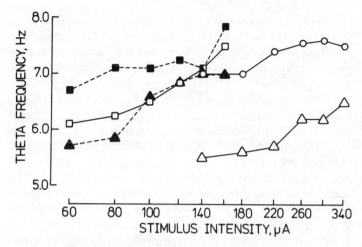

Figure 7.2. The frequency of the hippocampal theta rhythm in the free-moving rat as a function of intensity of stimulation of the median raphe; each symbol corresponds to a different individual animal. (From Graeff *et al.* (1980).)

This possibility is suggested by the results of a recent experiment in which we used chronically implanted electrodes to stimulate the median raphe nucleus in the rat (Graeff *et al.* 1980). Stimulation at this site elicits behavioural immobility (Robinson and Vanderwolf 1978), a crouching posture, defecation, and other visible signs of fear (Graeff and Silveira Filho 1978). At the same time a theta rhythm is elicited in the hippocampus. Stimulation at most sites in the brainstem gives rise to a continuous increase in theta frequency as current intensity is increased. Stimulation in the median raphe, however, produces an increase of this kind only up to a limiting frequency which lies very close to 7.7 Hz (Fig. 7.2). Two observations indicate that the theta elicited in this way belongs to Vanderwolf's atropine-sensitive class. First, the rat continued to show behavioural immobility up to the maximum theta frequency elicited; for this result to be obtained, it appears to be essential that the electrodes be well located within the median raphe nucleus. Second, the threshold for elicitation of theta was increased by scopolamine. It should be noted in this connection that the median raphe appears to contain serotonergic (Dahlström and Fuxe 1965) as well as cholinergic (Lewis and Shute 1967) cell-bodies, and that both project to the septo-hippocampal system, the former directly, and the latter indirectly. However, the threshold for elicitation of theta was unaffected in Graeff *et al.*'s (1980) experiments by the administration of antiserotonergic drugs. Thus these observations are consistent with the view that stimulation of the median raphe activates a cholinergic input to the septo-hippocampal system which elicits low-frequency theta associated with behavioural immobility; and that the limiting frequency up to which this type of theta can dominate the hippocampal EEG is approximately 7.7 Hz.

A transitional role for theta at frequencies near 7.7 Hz is also suggested by other observations. A. H. Black (1975) required rats simultaneously to stand still and to produce theta in order to gain reinforcement (water or shock avoidance). The rats were able to meet these conditions only up to a theta frequency of about 7 Hz (Morley and Black, cited in Black 1975). Conversely, Whishaw, Bland, and Bayer (1978) report that the *lowest* theta frequency observed in free-moving rats given atropine or scopolamine was about 7.7 Hz. Thus the special significance of 7.7-Hz theta may arise, not because it is additional to the two types of theta described by Vander-wolf's group, but because it is a frontier at which these two meet.

The observations we have considered so far attempt to relate the occur-rence of theta or its frequency averaged over some period of time to the behaviour by which it is accompanied. There have also been more ambi-tious attempts to relate the occurrence of individual motor acts to partic-ular theta waves or to a particular instant (phase) within a train of theta waves. Thus Komisaruk (1970) and Macrides (1975) noted that move-ments of the rat's vibrissae tend to stay in phase with hippocampal theta over relatively long periods of time. This suggests the possibility that there is an optimal time of arrival in the brain of sensory information and that the theta rhythm is in some way concerned with ensuring that this optimum is attained. Further observations along the same lines show that septal lesions which abolish theta may also cause a pronounced loss of the rhythmicity of vibrissae movement seen in the intact rat and disrupt the normal synchrony between movements of the vibrissae on the two sides of the snout (Gray 1971c). However, the phase relations between vibrissae movements and theta are not constant, and the association between loss of theta and disruption of vibrissae movement after septal lesions is not perfect. More recently phase-locking has been reported between theta and the moment at which a rat presses a bar for either food reward (Semba and Komisaruk 1978) or hypothalamic self-stimulation (Buño and Velluti 1977); while Arnolds *et al.* (1979b) have reported a close relation between momentary changes in theta frequency and amplitude, on the one hand, and individual acts of sighing or stepping in the dog, on the other. These observations suggest that theta might be concerned with ar-ranging an optimal time for the initiation of a motor act. In the absence of further data, however, suggestions such as these must remain in-triguing speculations.

The close correlation established by Vanderwolf's group between at least one kind of theta and motor processes poses a dilemma when it is viewed in conjunction with the data from lesion experiments reviewed in the previous chapter. Those data showed no sign of disturbance in motor behaviour. On the contrary, there is considerable evidence for disinhibi-tion of motor responses after either septal or hippocampal lesions. Thus it is not possible to attribute to the theta rhythm an active role in the production of movement. If one is guided by the lesion data, one might propose that the hippocampus has the task of inhibiting movement.

There are then two possible ways of making sense of the correlation between theta and movement. One way is to say, with Altman, Brunner, and Bayer (1973), that the theta seen when an animal is in full flight indicates a readiness to 'slam on the brakes', in Nadel *et al.*'s (1975) graphic phrase; this has little more attraction than the proposal once made by Vanderwolf that the theta seen when an animal is not moving indicates that it is thinking of doing so. The second is to suppose that theta is a sign of an inhibited or inactive hippocampus, which is therefore *not* performing its allotted task, namely, that of inhibiting movement. But this proposal runs counter to evidence, described in the next chapter, which shows that theta represents an active state of hippocampal function.

A further possibility is that the hippocampus neither produces nor inhibits movement, but that it uses information gathered during locomotor behaviour for other purposes. A specific version of this approach is the spatial theory advanced by O'Keefe and Nadel (1978). In its general form this theory is able to make a reasonably good job of accounting for some (though by no means all) of the lesion data, as we saw in the last chapter; and it can clearly take comfort from the observation that the best correlate of theta frequency in the atropine-resistant band appears to be the velocity of movement or the distance travelled, variables which can plausibly be regarded as affecting map-making. In O'Keefe and Nadel's (1978, p. 220) model, theta is used during displacement movements to help in the construction of spatial maps. We shall return later to this and other proposals concerning the functions discharged by theta (Chapter 10). But first let us consider the degree to which the spatial theory is supported on its home ground, that of the single-unit study.

Single-unit studies

The search for behavioural correlates of the firing of single neurons in the hippocampus has had a much shorter history than the corresponding investigations of slow-wave activity. But limited time has not limited controversy (see e.g. Elliott and Whelan 1978, p. 309 *et seq.*), and there are almost as many hypotheses as research workers in this field. This numerical equivalence may not be a coincidence. On one view of hippocampal function, this is to distinguish between novel and familiar events, irrespective of the nature of these events (Vinogradova 1970, 1975; Vinogradova and Brazhnik 1978). It follows that the hippocampus must gain temporary access to whatever stimuli are present at a given time in the animal's environment, and must have some means of establishing whatever regularities exist in that environment. If so, the hippocampus will appear to possess cells which are specialized to respond to whatever stimuli or regularities the experimenter chooses to build into his experiment. These in turn are likely to depend on what he thinks the hippocampus does. Thus each research worker can find support for his own theory, and the fires of controversy are well stoked.

Before we come to these problems of interpretation, however, let us first review the major findings. It is clear that neither the septal area nor the hippocampal formation possesses units with permanent, well-defined sensory fields. This is to be expected on Vinogradova's novelty hypothesis; but, given the distance between the hippocampal formation and the primary sensory pathways, it would be surprising on any count if it were otherwise. What is in question is the nature of the stimuli which are *temporarily* able to elicit unit responses in the hippocampus. Since no consensus free of theoretical bias is yet possible, I shall describe separately the results reported in the three major kinds of investigation so far undertaken before I attempt to bring them all under one umbrella. These investigations have been concerned with habituation, with classical and instrumental conditioning, and with movement in spatially complex environments.

The habituation studies are largely from Vinogradova's laboratory near Moscow. The present account follows closely two reviews she has herself recently written (Vinogradova 1975; Vinogradova and Brazhnik 1978). The experiments were done with unanaesthetized, slightly restrained rabbits, kept in a box in which the presentation of stimuli was under rigorous experimental control. The unit responses are described according to certain parameters of their spontaneous firing rates and initial responses to the stimuli used, and also according to the particular region of the hippocampal formation and septal area in which they were recorded. The stimuli consisted of simple sensory events (lights, clicks, tones, and sometimes tactile or olfactory stimuli) which were either novel to the animal or had been repeatedly presented for differing numbers of previous trials. Since the details of the particular observations made in different regions of the septo-hippocampal system will be important for arguments encountered later in the book, I shall describe them separately for each region. However, for the purposes of the argument followed in the present section, the major points which emerge from these experiments are three. First, a majority of units in the septal area and hippocampus are multimodal, that is, they respond to stimuli of more than one sensory modality. Second, in some parts of the septo-hippocampal system, unit responses are elicited by novel stimuli and are then subject to habituation with a time course which closely resembles the one described by Sokolov (1960) for the orienting reflex in the intact organism. Third, the nature of the experimental situation imposed on Vinogradova's rabbits permits a conclusion relevant to the spatial hypothesis: it is possible to observe reliable single-unit responses in the hippocampal formation under conditions in which spatial information is of minimal significance to the animal.

Field CA 3

The majority of neurons respond to stimuli in all modalities tested. The observed responses are usually of long latency (50–200 ms) and consist of diffuse, tonic changes of firing rate which outlast the stimulus by several seconds, with a gradual return to the background level (typically 15–30 spikes s^{-1}). Both increased and decreased firing rates are elicited by the applied stimuli, but a given neuron responds regularly in one way or the other. Neurons with inhibitory reactions are somewhat more numerous than those with excitatory reactions. The adequate stimulus in either case is novelty. With repeated presentation of the same stimulus the response gradually decreases in duration and, by the eighth to twentieth trial, disappears. Reappearance of the response can be produced by changes in the parameters of the stimulus or the conditions of its presentation (e.g. a change in pitch, an increase or decrease in stimulus intensity, stimulus duration or repetition rate). Repeated presentation of the same stimulus over several experimental sessions results in the complete disappearance of the response, even when the stimulus is applied at the beginning of the day's session; responses to other stimuli, not previously used, however, remain normal. The dynamics of these changes in response are closely similar to those described for the orienting reflex by Sokolov (1960). Essentially the same results are obtained in the dorsal and ventral hippocampus.

Field CA 1

The spontaneous firing rate of the cells recorded in CA 1 was lower (3–25 spikes s^{-1}) than in CA 3, and 44 per cent responded to stimuli in only one sensory modality (as against 5 per cent in CA 3). Furthermore, among multimodal cells, there were some in which different types of response were seen depending on stimulus modality. Thus CA 1 appears to preserve more information about the specific characteristics of the stimulus than CA 3. Given our current understanding (see Chapters 3 and 4) of the flow of information around the hippocampal circuit, this result is surprising, since it is generally believed that CA 3 (less specific, according to Vinogradova's observations) is the source of the input to CA 1 (more specific), rather than the reverse. It is possible, however, that the greater specificity of CA 1 responses is due to the direct entorhinal projection to CA 1 (Steward 1976). Many responses consisted of 'phasic' changes in activity, limited to the duration of the applied stimulus, rather than the longer-lasting 'tonic' reactions seen in CA 3. These sometimes took the form of a combined 'on' and 'off' response at the start and end of the stimulus. Tonic reactions were also observed, but these were a little shorter (by 1–2 seconds) than those observed in CA 3. Both excitatory and inhibitory reactions were observed in about equal proportions. Habituation occurred as in CA 3, but in fewer cases (74 per cent). Before habituation took place, there was often a short-lived build-up of the reaction, so that the greatest response was typically to the second or third stimulus presentation in the series.

Dentate gyrus

Spontaneous firing rates are either very low ($1-2$ s^{-1}) or very high ($30-40$ s^{-1}). The reactions observed fell into three, roughly equal classes: tonic inhibitory, phasic excitatory, and 'on' effects, i.e. a short burst of pulses at stimulus onset. The shortest latencies seen were about $3-4$ ms longer than those seen in the entorhinal cortex (see below), consistent with transmission from this structure along the perforant path. Some cells showed a relatively high selectivity of response (e.g. to tones in a limited frequency band), but most were multimodal. Habituation of the kind seen in CA 3 was absent. The duration of tonic inhibitory reactions sometimes became less, but they never completely disappeared. Even after $200-300$ stimulus repetitions unit responses were still evoked. Some transformations of reaction, however, from inhibitory to excitatory or the reverse, were observed. In addition, many cells (42 per cent) came only gradually to respond after the same stimulus had been repeated $15-20$ times.

Entorhinal cortex

Spontaneous firing rates are $20-30$ s^{-1}. The majority of responses were of the phasic and on–off varieties, mostly excitatory. Only 17 per cent of responses were of the tonic kind. Both short-latency ($12-20$ ms) and long-latency ($40-100$ ms) responses were seen. The level of multimodal convergence was high (64 per cent), but as a rule stimuli in different modalities produced reactions of different kinds. Considerable differentiation of responses was also seen within modality, e.g. to tones of different pitch. Habituation was virtually absent; on the contrary, there was a tendency for reactions to become clearer after several stimulus repetitions. These results are in general agreement with the widely held view, supported by the known connections of the entorhinal area (Chapter 3), that this is the source of a relatively specific sensory input to the hippocampal formation.

Medial septal nucleus

Spontaneous activity was high ($20-30$ spikes s^{-1}) and often grouped into bursts whose repetition rate lay within the theta range; these observations agree with those of others (Stumpf 1965; Apostol and Creutzfeldt 1974). Reactions were usually tonic and multimodal, with inhibitory responses slightly more numerous than excitatory ones. These observations conform to the generally held view that the information transmitted from the medial septal area to the hippocampus is non-specific. Whether the reactions were excitatory or inhibitory, they tended to group into theta bursts. Signs of habituation were seen in only a minority of neurons (31 per cent), and this tended to be much more protracted and less complete than in CA 3.

Lateral septal nucleus

Most features of the firing of lateral septal neurons, including the tendency to fire in theta bursts, were the same as those observed in medial septal neurons. But there was one important difference. Practically all lateral septal neurons displayed habituation in the form of a gradual shortening and finally a complete disappearance of the response.

Vinogradova's important 1975 paper also contains similar data on many other limbic structures which are closely related to the septo-hippocampal system. We shall consider some of these other observations later, and also the theory that Vinogradova has developed on their basis (Chapter 10). For the moment, however, we shall pause only to draw the most obvious conclusions from the data summarised above.

First, it seems reasonably certain that CA 3 is the focus of the habituation process described by Vinogradova. Habituation is not seen in the three structures which project to CA 3 (the dentate gyrus, the entorhinal cortex, the medial septal nucleus), but it is present in the two structures to which CA 3 projects (the lateral septal nucleus and, less regularly, CA 1). Thus it seems that habituation takes place in CA 3 and is then passed on to the latter two structures. This inference receives strong confirmation with respect to the lateral septal area from the effects of destruction of the hippocampo-septal projection that runs in the fornix-fimbria. After this lesion habituation no longer occurred in the lateral septal area; on the contrary unit responses tended to increase with stimulus repetition (Vinogradova 1975; Vinogradova and Brazhnik 1978).

However, it should also be noted that habituation in CA 3 depends on its receiving both its normal inputs, from the medial septal and entorhinal areas. In animals that have had the septal area disconnected from the hippocampus by fornicotomy, Vinogradova and Brazhnik (1978) describe two different patterns of response depending on the period after the operation at which CA 3 neurons are recorded. Ten to fourteen days after the operation habituation is abnormally rapid (3–5 stimulus presentations); at 3–6 months after surgery habituation is absent and there is instead a gradual build-up of response as also seen in the lateral septal area. An incremental process of this kind is also seen after transection of the perforant path. When habituation is disturbed in CA 3 after these operations, similar changes are seen in CA 1. Thus habituation apparently depends on a transformation performed in CA 3 on joint inputs from the medial septal area and the entorhinal cortex; the results of this transformation are then passed on to CA 1 and back to the lateral septal area.

Habituation consists in the disappearance of the response to a familiar stimulus. But Vinogradova's experiments also demonstrate the opposite phenomenon: a build-up in the response to a familiar stimulus. In the intact animal this was observed in the entorhinal area and the dentate gyrus. The build-up of response in these regions took about as many stimulus presentations (2–12 in the entorhinal area, 15–20 in the dentate gyrus) as did habituation in CA 3 (8–15). The fact that the build-up is quicker in the entorhinal area than in the dentate gyrus is consistent with transmission of the relevant information along the perforant path. Thus,

with repeated presentation of a stimulus lacking in behavioural significance, two changes take place simultaneously in the septo-hippocampal
response: an augmentation of the reaction in the entorhinal area and
dentate gyrus coupled with a diminution in CA 3, CA 1 and the lateral
septal area.

Note that augmentation of the rate of firing of neurons projecting
from the entorhinal area to the dentate gyrus might be expected to bring
into play the processes of frequency and long-term potentiation described
in Chapter 4. Thus potentiation may correspond, in psychological terms,
to the build-up of 'familiarity' (Vinogradova and Brazhnik 1978). Vinogradova's treatment of potentiation along these lines has an important
advantage over the suggestion that this phenomenon might be the basis
of a mechanism of associational learning (see the discussion in Elliott and
Whelan 1978, p. 407 *et seq.*). Such a mechanism requires in principle information about two related events which, from a neuronal point of view,
might both be presynaptic or one pre- and one postsynaptic (Hebb 1949).
However, the bulk of the evidence (Chapter 4) suggests that potentiation
depends only on the application of stimulation of appropriate parameters
to a single input pathway (Andersen 1978). As pointed out by Bliss
(1980), this objection applies also to O'Keefe and Nadel's (1978, p. 230)
proposal that potentiation forms part of the process whereby the animal
builds up a spatial map, since their model of how this works requires the
simultaneous arrival of two or more inputs on the same dendrites. The
development of familiarity, in contrast, should require nothing more than
repetition of the same single input.

The results obtained by Vinogradova's group provide a satisfyingly coherent picture of how the hippocampus performs one of the many functions that have been attributed to it. But let us not forget her own warning: 'it is curious how we find in the brain what we are looking for' (in
Elliott and Whelan 1978, p. 197). To what extent do her observations
depend on the particular experimental conditions she used?

It has been suggested by Mays and Best (1975) and by Ranck (1973; see
also the discussion in Elliott and Whelan 1978, p. 309 *et seq.*) that Vinogradova's rabbits only respond as they do because they are asleep or
nearly so. This suggestion (which is not accepted by Vinogradova) is based
on observations in the rat that habituation to repeated tones occurred in
a majority of hippocampal units but only if the animal was sleeping, in
which case the stimulus woke it up (Mays and Best 1975). Thus, rather
than habituation of the specific response to sensory stimuli, Mays and Best
suggest that it is general arousal or waking up which habituates. Given
the close relations which are known to exist between habituation of the
orienting reflex and the general level of arousal (Sokolov 1960), this objection is not so radical as it first seems. None the less, if the mechanisms
described by Vinogradova operate only when the animal is extremely
drowsy, their general behavioural interest is limited. Unfortunately, there

is a dearth of other observations to settle this point. Although there have been some tens of experiments on single- or multiple-unit responses in the hippocampus of waking animals, they have not generally paid much attention to the course of habituation. Given the rapidity with which this occurred in Vinogradova's experiments (8–20 trials), it is very easy to miss it altogether and conclude simply that the hippocampal formation is unresponsive to the stimuli used. Segal (1974*b*) none the less observed habituation in CA 1 and CA 3 units when lights and tones were presented to rats. On the other hand, neither Lidsky *et al.* (1974*a, b*), working with awake (but curarized) rabbits, nor Hirano *et al.* (1970), working with rats, saw any decrement in the response to repeated sensory stimuli. This important issue requires more experimental attention.

The stimuli used in habituation experiments are necessarily devoid of any particular significance for the animal. In the next group of experiments we shall consider, the same kinds of simple sensory stimuli are employed, but they are given extra significance by the methods of classical or instrumental conditioning. These experiments establish that hippocampal unit responses may be preserved from habituation, and sometimes undergo more complex transformations, if the animal has some reason to be interested in the stimulus that elicits them.

Observations of this kind were first reported by Olds and his collaborators, mainly working with a technique which requires the animal (a rat) to remain motionless for a short period (1–2 seconds) upon presentation of a signal and then to take food or water from a magazine. It is difficult to classify this technique as classical or instrumental conditioning. Using a tone CS for foods Olds and Hirano (1969) found that the initial hippocampal inhibitory response to the tone was transformed by conditioning into an excitatory response. Olds, Mink, and Best (1969) required the rat to press a lever upon receipt of a signal and then remain motionless for about two seconds; during this interval some units showed changes in firing rate which depended on the nature of the reinforcement (food or water) which had been signalled. A degree of differentiation between the unit responses to the CS+ and CS− for a food reward (without barpressing) was reported by Hirano, Best, and Olds (1970); the firing rate of CA 1 and CA 3 units increased in response to both kinds of signal, but more so to the CS+. When the CS+ was subjected to extinction, the firing rate went down again, though it remained above the pre-conditioning baseline. Sideroff and Bindra (1976) similarly observed diffferential CA 1 responses to a CS+ and a CS− for water; the firing rate rose and remained elevated in response to CS+, but initially rose and then fell during presentation of the CS−. These responses persisted when the rat was satiated for water. Thus there is some differentiation (though it is none too impressive) between food and water, and between positive and negative signals for food or water. The differentiation between food and shock, surprisingly, appears to be more recalcitrant. Fuster and Uyeda

(1971) trained monkeys to press different levers for food or shock avoidance in response to different visual stimuli; both stimuli produced excitatory unit responses which could not be distinguished. Working with the rat, Segal and Olds (1973) found a differential response to CSs signalling food or shock, respectively, but only in the dentate gyrus, where firing rate increased to the CS for food but decreased to the CS for shock; in other hippocampal regions firing rate increased in response to both kinds of stimuli, though more to the CS for food.

Even though, in some of these experiments, the animal was required to remain immobile during the recording period, O'Keefe and Nadel (1978, pp. 214–16) suggest that the results may reflect the motor correlates of theta reviewed earlier in this chapter. This position is harder to maintain in respect to Berger and Thompson's (1978a, b) experiments with rabbits, since the animal was restrained throughout. Hippocampal and septal units were recorded during the course of conditioning of the nictitating membrane response (with a tone CS and an air-puff UCS). A control group received random pairings of the CS and UCS. Neither the tone nor the air-puff elicited much change in unit responses in this control group, nor in the experimental group before conditioning began. Conditioning gave rise to the rapid development of, first, an excitatory response to the air-puff (already present by the second conditioning trial), which on a given trial preceded the unconditioned closure of the nictitating membrane by approximately 35 ms; and then a similar response to the CS, appearing during the first daily session (117 trials day^{-1}). The same pattern was seen whether the recording electrode was in CA 1, CA 3, or the dentate gyrus. Lateral septal neurons behaved like hippocampal units, but lagged a little behind in the development of the conditioned response. Medial septal neurons, in contrast, showed the same responses to the the CS and the UCS in the truly random control group as in the classical conditioning group: there was no sign of conditioning, and only a small degree of habituation. Segal (1973a), using Olds's method with unrestrained rats, similarly found only non-habituating, short-latency (12–24 ms) unconditioned responses in the medial septal area when tones were used as CS+ and CS− for food.

These observations are in agreement with Vinogradova's experiments on habituation at several points: the resemblance between lateral septal and hippocampal activity; the indication that this is due to a transfer of information from the hippocampus to the lateral septum; and the unchanging nature of medial septal responses. But the type of information transferred from the hippocampus to the lateral septal area is diametrically different: loss of response in the habituation experiments, creation of a response after conditioning.

Two experiments by Hirsh (1973a, b), using Olds's method, provide a further rapprochement between the results of conditioning and habituation studies. Hirsh (1973a) found that a preliminary stage of pseudoconditioning (random presentation of CS and the food UCS) delayed the subsequent development of conditioned hippocampal unit responses to the CS. On the plausible assumption that pseudoconditioning activates processes that are identical or at any rate similar to those which underlie habituation, this observation is consistent with Vinogradova's in showing that hippocampal responses are sensitive to habituation. In a second experiment Hirsh (1973*b*) demonstrated that transection of the fornix-fimbria increased the number of hippocampal responses to the CS during preconditioning, in agreement with Vinogradova's report that this lesion disturbs habituation. Fornix transection also increased hippocampal unit responses to a CS− signalling the omission of the food UCS (Hirsh (1973*b*); this effect and the increased responding during pseudoconditioning resemble in certain respects the observations of behavioural disinhibition after septal and hippocampal lesions (Chapter 6, Section 6.3).

Between them, the habituation and conditioning experiments show that CA 3, the source of the hippocampo-septal projection, can transmit either a reduced or an augmented message to the septal area. These observations present an obvious parallel with those discussed in Chapter 4 and which gave rise to the idea of a 'dentate gate'. This parallel has been strengthened by the experiments of Segal, who has used a number of methods to investigate change in transmission round the hippocampal circuit as a function of conditioning.

In the earliest of these experiments Segal (1973*b*) studied unit responses to positive and negative CSs for food. Units in the entorhinal area showed differential responses to the CS+ and CS−, and in some cases the response to the CS+ was of very long duration, lasting up to a minute. In the hippocampus Segal noticed that, if the inter-trial interval (i.e. the interval betweeen successive presentations of the CS+) was less than a minute, there was an augmentation of the unit response to the CS+. He suggested that this might be due to the sustained entorhinal input to the hippocampus lasting over this interval. This suggestion was supported by the finding (Segal 1975*b*) that transection of the perforant path eliminated the augmented hippocampal response otherwise seen in CA 1 and CA 3 at inter-trial intervals less than a minute. Note that the rate of firing of entorhinal units (about 10 spikes s^{-1}) and the duration of their sustained response to the CS+ are about the same as the stimulation parameters necessary to produce frequency or long-term potentiation (Chapter 4). Thus these results suggest that potentiation may play a role in the formation of conditioned unit responses in the hippocampus. This suggestion is not necessarily at variance with the proposal already made that potentiation underlies the development of familiarity (Vinogradova and Brazhnik 1978), for of course a conditioned stimulus is one with which the animal must be familiar.

Somewhat surprisingly Segal seems not to have followed up this promising line of research. Instead he has switched his attention to the commissural response, that is, the response seen in one hippocampus after stimulation of the commissural pathway from the contralateral hippocampus. This too is subject to frequency potentiation. If pairs of pulses are applied and the interval between members of the pair is varied, there is a maximum response to the second pulse at an interpulse interval of 30 ms (Segal 1977d). Segal studied the effect on the magnitude of this potentiation of applying the two hippocampal pulses while simultaneously presenting a CS for a food or shock UCS. If tested in this way in the presence of the CS, potentiation of the commissural response was supranormal (Segal 1977d). Thus it seems that a conditioned stimulus facilitates transmission round the hippocampal circuit. The enhanced potentiation affected in particular a late (latency, 32–40 ms) and long-lasting negative component in the complex field potential evoked by paired contralateral hippocampal pulses. This same late component was present in the response to a single contralateral hippocampal pulse if, and only if, this pulse was applied during a CS (tone or light) for either a food or shock UCS (Segal 1977b, c). Control experiments showed that this response was absent if the hippocampal pulse was applied in the presence of the same stimuli but when they were not acting as CSs, or if they signalled a food UCS but the animal was sated for food.

These behavioural correlates of the late negative component in the commissural response make its physiology a matter of prime interest. Segal (1977a) showed that the late component can be produced if a single contralateral hippocampal pulse is preceded by priming stimulation (100 Hz for 100 ms) delivered to the locus coeruleus 100–200 ms earlier; if the priming-test interval is extended to 300–400 ms the effect is no longer obtained. Evidence that the effect of locus coeruleus stimulation is due to activation of the noradrenergic cell-bodies located there comes from the observation that systemic injection of the dopamine-β-hydroxylase inhibitor, diethyldithiocarbamate, blocked the late negative response (Segal 1977a). In the same experiments it was shown that stimulation of the median or dorsal raphe nuclei, 50–300 ms before the hippocampal test pulse, also gave rise to the late negative response; this effect was blocked by systemic p-chlorophenylalanine and reinstated by subsequent administration of 5-hydroxytryptophan, demonstrating its serotonergic nature.

The role of the noradrenergic fibres originating in the locus coeruleus is further emphasized by the experiments of Segal and Bloom (1976). These workers tested hippocampal unit responses to a tone presented to free-moving rats. Before conditioning the tone elicited inhibitory responses. Pharmacological experiments with drugs such as diethyldithiocarbamate suggested that this response was mediated by a noradrenergic pathway. When the tone was made a CS for food, the hippocampal unit responses became excitatory. Preceding the CS by locus coeruleus stimulation increased the size of these excitatory responses. Thus the direction of the effect of the noradrenergic innervation of the hippocampus on hippocampal unit responses depended on the functional characteristics of the stimuli which elicited them: if the stimulus was of no particular consequence, the effect was to deepen the inhibition of unit firing; if it was a CS, the effect was to increase the excitation of unit firing.

A final experiment in this series suggests a role for the theta rhythm. Segal (1978*a*) notes that the initial component of the commissural response is reduced, but the late negative component increased, when the rat displays hippocampal theta (during walking, struggling, exploration) relative to times when it does not (quiet awake or slow-wave sleep).

Results obtained with a rather different technique, but with similar implications, have been reported by Deadwyler, West, and Lynch (1979) and Lynch, Rose, and Gall (1978). They studied the field potential evoked in the outer molecular layer of the dentate gyrus (corresponding to the site of input from the perforant path) by a tone which the rat was required to use as a signal for water-rewarded bar-pressing. This potential appeared only after the animal had learned to use the tone as a signal for this response. Furthermore, it disappeared during extinction and reappeared during reconditioning, these changes taking place over about 20 trials and being in good agreement with the corresponding changes in the animal's behaviour. So far, these results are similar to the several other demonstrations noted above that conditioning facilitates the passage through the hippocampal formation of responses evoked by sensory stimuli. However, although the evoked potential indicated that a large signal was arriving in the dentate gyrus from the perforant path, this was not accompanied by reliable discharge of the dentate granule cells. For this to occur it was necessary also to present a second, non-rewarded tone, the animal now being required to discriminate between them. This had the consequence that, to the positive tone, there was a prolonged burst of firing in the granule cells, while to the negative tone there was an initial burst of spikes followed by a rapid return to background firing rates. Thus optimal passage of information through the dentate gate required not only the conditioning of a positive stimulus, but also the formation of a discrimination between positive and negative cues. This finding is perhaps related to the increased orienting reflex which is known to occur if a discrimination is substituted for a simple excitatory behavioural response (Sokolov 1960, 1963).

It would seem, then, that most of the data from both conditioning and habituation experiments converge on a plausible functional interpretation of the plasticity of response displayed by neurons in the dentate gyrus and CA 3. If a stimulus is of low intrinsic significance (tones, flashes, and the like) and is not associated with other events of greater importance, the response it elicits rapidly decreases (in about 10–20 presentations). The decrease occurs first in CA 3, which requires for this purpose inputs from both the entorhinal area, synapsing in the dentate gyrus, and the medial septal area. The decreased (habituated) response is then passed along to CA 1 and the lateral septal area. If, however, a stimulus is given significance, by pairing it with a biologically important UCS or by making it the signal for an instrumental response, the hippocampal unit responses are stabilized or even augmented. This process appears to be facilitated by noradrenergic and serotonergic afferents to the hippocampal formation. It may also be aided by the medial septal input to the hippocampus (see the discussion of Fantie's, Alvarez-Leefman's, and McNaughton and Miller's experiments at the end of Chapter 4). Like the decremental change of habituation, the augmented (conditioned) response is passed from CA 3 to the lateral septal area. The role played by frequency and long-term potentiation in these changes is not clear; but it is possible that these phenomena underlie the development of the familiarity (Vinogradova and Brazhnik 1978) which is common to habituated stimuli whether they are insignificant or conditioned. In agreement with this interpretation, there is a build-up of responses in the entorhinal area both when an insignificant stimulus undergoes habituation (Vinogradova 1975) and when a CS+ is repeatedly presented (Segal 1973*b*).

These data, evidently, are the stuff of which theories of attention are made, and theorists such as Douglas (1967), Grastyan *et al.* (1959), and Vinogradova (1975) who have emphasized this aspect of hippocampal function must find much comfort in them. But we must not be so persuaded as to ignore a third class of experiments on the behavioural correlates of hippocampal unit responses: those which seek these correlates in the places through which the animal passes. There is no need to review these experiments in great detail, since O'Keefe and Nadel (1978) have recently done so (to the virtual exclusion, it must be added, of any other kind of single-unit experiment). In any case, the major facts are not in dispute, although (in a phrase the reader has met before) their interpretation is. These facts have been gathered in experiments on free-moving rats observed in mazes or other spatially diverse environments.

It is common for workers in this tradition to distinguish between two types of units, 'theta' cells and 'complex-spike' cells, according to criteria established by Ranck (1973) and Fox and Ranck (1975). These criteria (Table 7.2) appear reasonably well-founded, although Vinogradova (in Elliott and Whelan 1978, p. 311) has been unable to apply them to the units she records in rabbits, and Andersen (*loc. cit.*) believes that the distinction is not between types of cell but between states of activity into which the same cell may pass at different times. If they are different cell types, much of the evidence (Ranck, in Elliott and Whelan 1978, p. 309) suggests that complex-spike cells are pyramids and theta cells interneurons (perhaps basket cells). But Bland *et al.* (1980) have described cells in anaesthetized rabbits which have a close correlation with theta but project out of the hippocampus. The nomenclature is in any case misleading, since it is agreed that theta and complex-spike cells may both fire in phase with the simultaneously recorded theta rhythm, but that the latter do so

Table 7.2. Differences between theta cells and complex-spike cells in the hippocampus

		Theta cells	Complex-spike cells
1(a)	Complex spikes	never	all have some
(b)	Simple action potentials	always	all have some
2	Duration of extracellular negative spike (distorted)	all 0.15–0.25 ms	all 0.3–0.5 ms in single spikes and spikes of complex spikes
3	Rate of firing most of the time awake and SWS	almost all >8 s⁻¹	all <12 s⁻¹, most <2 s⁻¹, many off*
4	Maximum rate of firing	29–147 s⁻¹, sustained for many seconds	all <40 s⁻¹, most <20 s⁻¹ sustained for less than 2 s*
5	Patterns of firing	comparatively regular	irregular
6	During theta rhythm in slow waves in paradoxical sleep or awake		
	(a) Rate	at maximum rate if and only if theta rhythm is present	no simple relation usually <1 s⁻¹*
	(b) Phase relations	most have clear phase relation	most have clear phase relation
7	Relations to LIA spike	almost all fire with bursts	sometimes fires
8	Spike heights	usually <200 μV ($\bar{x} = 164$ μV)	larger than theta units ($\bar{x} = 267$ μV)
9	Anatomical location		
	in CA1	stratum pyramidale / stratum oriens	stratum pyramidale
	in CA3	stratum pyramidale / apical dendritic layers	stratum pyramidale
	in FD	stratum granulosum / hilus of FD	stratum granulosum

*A complete spike is counted as a single potential.
From Ranck (1973), Fox and Ranck (1975), and O'Keefe and Nadel (1978).
Abbreviations: LIA, large irregular activity; FD, fascia dentata, SWS, slow-wave sleep.

less regularly (O'Keefe, in Elliott and Whelan 1978, p. 314). Other distinctions (Table 7.2), less theoretically loaded, between the two types of cell lie in their firing rates (high for theta cells, low for complex-spike cells) and the type of action potential they display; as their name indicates, complex-spike cells sometimes (and theta cells never) manifest a series of spikes of declining magnitude with inter-spike intervals of 2–7 ms.

There is good agreement that, when a rat is observed in a spatially complex environment, some hippocampal units fire principally when the animal is moving (with the concomitant high-frequency theta rhythm described earlier in this chapter), irrespective of its mode of movement or destination. O'Keefe and Nadel (1978) term these cells 'displace' units. Displace units commonly fire in bursts which are phase-locked to theta (Ranck 1973; Feder and Ranck 1973; O'Keefe and Nadel 1978; see Fig. 4.5), and according to O'Keefe and Nadel (1978) there is excellent agreement between the criteria proposed by Ranck (1973) for theta units and their own observations of displace units. Conversely, units which satisfy Ranck's criteria for complex-spike units have been observed to fire only when the animal is in a particular place. The part of the environment where such a 'place' unit fires, or fires maximally, has been defined as its 'place field'. It was the description of such units by O'Keefe and Dostrovsky (1971) that gave the major impetus to the spatial theory of hippocampal function, although similar suggestions have been made on the basis of lesion experiments (e.g. Olton and Isaacson 1968; Mahut 1971).

Convincing demonstrations of place units have been provided by O'Keefe and Conway (cited in O'Keefe and Black 1978) using the specially constructed environment shown in Fig. 7.3. Animals were trained inside a square enclosure.

The walls were formed by floorlength black curtains. Within the enclosure, there were four cues by which the rat could locate itself: a dim light, a white card, a buzzer and a fan. Four male hooded rats were made hungry and trained to go to one of the arms of a T-maze to obtain food. From trial to trial, the maze and the cues were randomly rotated by some multiple of 90° relative to the environment but maintained the same spatial relation to each other. In order to rule out other intra-maze cues as a means of solution, the arms were interchanged from trial to trial. Body turns were ruled out by randomly rotating the stem of the T-maze 180° relative to the cross-bar so that on one-half of the trials a right turn was required to reach the goal while on the other half, a left turn was required. After the rats had learned the task, they were further trained so that after running to the goal arm and consuming the reward they should run to the non-goal arm and thence back to the start arm, where they received a second reward. Thus on each trial they made a complete circuit of the maze, giving the hippocampal units an equal opportunity to fire on all parts of the maze. The place where the units fired on the maze was recorded by pulsing a light-emitting diode on the rat's head whenever an action potential occurred and photographing these light flashes with an overhead camera (O'Keefe and Black 1978, p. 184).

It will be obvious that, with this kind of careful investigation, it is not possible to gather data on large numbers of units. Thus O'Keefe and

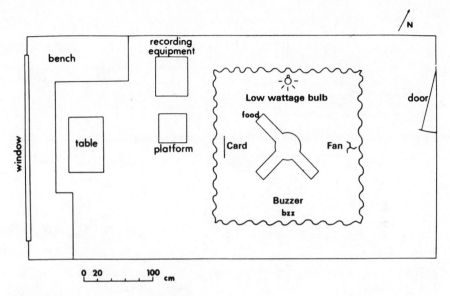

Figure 7.3. Layout of the experimental room in O'Keefe and Conway's single-unit experiment. The cue-controlled enclosure is the curtained-off area just to the right of centre. (From O'Keefe and Black (1978).)

Conway were able to describe the fields of only twelve units in this experiment. However, there was a great unanimity in their behaviour. They all fired in response to particular relations between the four controlled cues inside the enclosure (the light, card, buzzer, and fan); an example of such a place field is shown in Figure 7.4. On probe trials one or more of these cues was removed. Some place units responded, as in the example shown in Fig. 7.4, by increasing their firing over the whole of the test environment; others responded by ceasing to fire. In either event the place field (defined both by where the cell fires and where it does not) was lost. The former type of response to a missing cue may be related to the 'misplace' units also described by O'Keefe and Nadel (1978), that is, units which fire when the rat goes to a place and fails to find a particular stimulus (e.g. a light or food) which has previously been there. Both place and misplace units have also been described by other workers (Ranck 1973; Olton, Branch, and Best 1978; O'Keefe and Nadel 1978, p. 209).

There is something more than a little miraculous about constructing an *ad hoc* environment like the one shown in Fig. 7.3, which no rat has ever encountered before, sticking a wire into the middle of the brain and pulling out place fields just like that. Obviously the hippocampus cannot come pre-wired to respond, say, to 'a fan equidistant from a buzzer and a light, and 90° round from the light'. The place field that is made up of such esoteric stimuli can only be there because the hippocampus constructs it

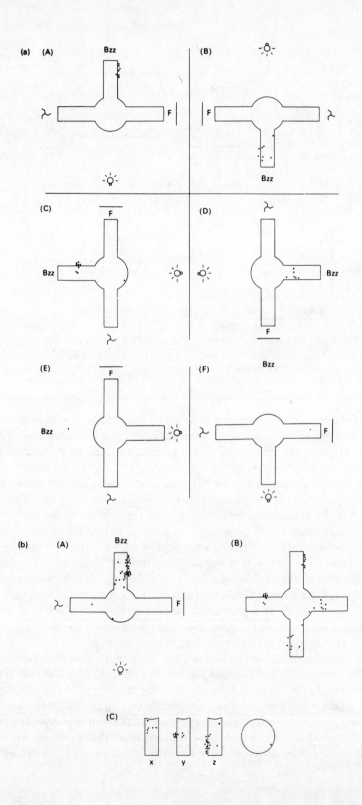

on the basis of the peculiar information with which it is provided. This construction, moreover, is accomplished extraordinarily rapidly. Hill (1978) trained rats to shuttle for food in a shuttle-box. He then implanted them with recording electrodes and placed them for the first time ever in a T-maze where shuttling between goal-arms was again rewarded with food. Place fields appeared *immediately* in this new apparatus for 10 out of 12 units tested.

The hippocampus contains an enormous number of neurons. A success rate of this kind implies that the great majority are at once devoted to the construction of place fields — if that is the kind of environment the experimenter provides. It also implies that in a different kind of environment they would construct some other kind of field. This point has recently begun to worry proponents of the spatial theory. Thus Ranck (in Elliott and Whelan 1978, p. 310) reports that the same cell has one behavioural correlate in a clearly spatial task (running in an eight-arm maze), another in a task which may or may not be spatial (retrieving pups in a nest-box), and yet a third in a task which is almost certainly not spatial (bar-pressing on a DRL schedule). And, of course, experiments such as Vinogradova's (1975) and Berger and Thompson's (1978*a*, *b*), described above, also find 'fields', but under conditions which are likely to inspire an interest in space in only a very contemplative rabbit.

These experiments, then, demonstrate that place can be a powerful determinant of responses in hippocampal cells. That is an important demonstration. But it is insufficient to satisfy the exigencies of the spatial theory. For these to be satisfied at least two other conditions must be met.

First, other types of stimuli should not be effective in eliciting hippocampal unit responses. It is for this reason that O'Keefe and Nadel (1978) have to argue out of court most of the data from the habituation and conditioning experiments. They try to do this, as we have seen, by suggesting that the responses observed in these experiments were due to changes in arousal level (and therefore non-specific), or to accompanying

Figure 7.4. (a) The firing of a place unit when a rat is on the T-maze inside the cue-controlled enclosure. Each dot represents one action potential. Four trials are shown in A–D in which the T-maze and the cues on the wall have four different orientations relative to the external world. The orientation of the external world is constant. Note that the unit fires when the rat is in the start arm when it is on the side close to the buzzer, regardless of the orientation relative to the external world. E and F show two trials with the start arm rotated 180° so that it is on the side close to the light. There is no unit firing in the start arm. (b) The same unit as in (a), showing the results of trials A–D superimposed in different ways. A: pictures aligned with the same orientation to the controlled cues on the wall; B: pictures aligned with the same orientation to the external world; C: physical components of the maze separated and superimposed. Note that the z-arm was used as the start arm *twice* while the other arms were used only *once* each. (From O'Keefe and Nadel (1978).

motor responses (allowed into their theory as part of the means by which the putative spatial map is constructed). But these arguments fail to carry conviction.

Second, for the spatial theory to be correct, the observed fields must not only be specific to places, they must also require the construction of a spatial map in the full sense given to this phrase within the O'Keefe and Nadel (1978) model. Since a large part of their book is devoted to explaining what this means, it would be presumptuous to offer a short definition here. For our present purposes it is sufficient to note that a response that is guided by some combination of stimuli does not require us to postulate a map and does not, therefore, provide evidence for the correctness of the spatial theory (see Olton, Becker, and Handelmann 1979*a*, *b*). But there is nothing in the observations reported by O'Keefe and Conway which cannot be explained as a unit response elicited by a combination or set of combinations of stimuli (e.g. the light at angle alpha plus the fan at angle beta or the card at angle gamma). Indeed, the experiment was almost perfectly designed to require the rat to respond to such combination of stimuli. Furthermore, just such responses to combinations of stimuli have been demonstrated by Brown (1982), recording hippocampal units in rhesus monkeys required to perform a non-spatial conditional discrimination; certain of these units would respond or not depending on the context in which a particular stimulus was presented.

If the experiments on place units do not establish the correctness of the spatial theory of hippocampal function, it is legitimate to set them alongside other single-unit studies and ask what new information they provide. First, they demonstrate the existence of cells that fire preferentially when theta occurs as the rat moves through space. Given the evidence for the behavioural correlates of high-frequency theta reviewed earlier in the chapter, it would have been something of a mystery if there were not cells that behave in this way. Second, they demonstrate the existence of misplace units. But this observation is also not unexpected, for the information to which these units respond is novelty (due to stimulus omission) in the particular context of space. And, although it would be difficult to regard the hippocampal response to novelty in an immobile rabbit as a subclass of responses to places, it is easy to treat misplace units as a subclass of responses to novelty; nor need this subclass have any special significance. Third, and much more interestingly, these experiments demonstrate that the stimuli to which the hippocampus responds cannot be pre-wired, a possibility that the habituation and conditioning experiments, using as they did very simple sensory stimuli, left open. Indeed, they show that the stimuli to which the hippocampus responds are allocated afresh to individual neurons each time the animal enters a new environment (Hill 1978; Ranck, in Elliott and Whelan 1978, p. 310). Furthermore, these allocations are both highly complex (as in O'Keefe and Conway's experiments) and very rapidly determined (as in Hill's).

These inferences, and those we have been able to draw from the other experiments reviewed in this chapter, will be important when we try to integrate the different approaches to the enigma of septo-hippocampal function into a single theory in Chapter 10. But there are still other data to absorb first.

8

The behavioural effects of stimulating the septo-hippocampal system

The methods whose results we have considered so far have given support to several different hypotheses of septo-hippocampal function. The behavioural inhibition and spatial hypotheses each found partial confirmation in the lesion experiments reviewed in Chapter 6; the abundant similarities between the effects of septal and hippocampal lesions, on the one hand, and those of the anti-anxiety drugs on the other strengthen the anxiety hypothesis; and the EEG and single-unit studies reviewed in the last chapter suggest roles for the hippocampus in attention, habituation, and spatial analysis. But there has as yet been little sign of support for the most widely known hypothesis of all: that the hippocampus subserves memory. We shall consider the clinical data which gave rise to this hypothesis in the next chapter. Here we examine the only method of experimental investigation which, so far, has tended with any consistency to confirm clinical impression: the method of electrical stimulation.

The difficulties inherent in this method were discussed in Chapter 5. A major problem is to know whether the stimulation is jamming the network into which the electrode has been placed or activating it in a more or less normal manner; and there is no reason why both types of effect should not be produced simultaneously, some networks being jammed and others activated. If one does not know which of these two effects is produced by the stimulation, any experimental result is necessarily open to (at least) two opposing inferences concerning the function of the stimulated pathway. One way round this problem is to compare the effects of electrical stimulation to those known to be produced by a lesion. If the two effects are the same, the stimulation presumably jams; if they are opposite to each other, it presumably activates; and if they are neither the same nor opposite, then something more complex is going on. If the effect of stimulation is like that of a lesion, the amount of addition information that the method can provide is limited; although it can be used to determine the critical site or time at which a functional impairment produces a change in behaviour. More interesting is the case in which stimulation produces effects opposite to those of a lesion. Under these conditions stimulation experiments can provide important new insights into the behavioural functions of the structure concerned.

Hippocampal stimulation

If one simply tallies all reported behavioural effects of stimulating the hippocampus directly (for a partial list of references, see O'Keefe and Nadel 1978, Table A 29) and classifies them into three groups, 'like lesion', 'opposite to lesion', and 'uninterpretable', one ends up with roughly equal numbers in each group. Thus, not surprisingly, it is not possible to say that hippocampal stimulation acts generally like a lesion or the converse. I have attempted to bring order into this confusion by considering the different behavioural paradigms used, but without success. Thus it seems unlikely that hippocampal stimulation tends normally to disrupt some functional systems but to activate others. Rather than review these studies in detail (see O'Keefe and Nadel 1978, Chapter 12, and Izquierdo 1975), I shall concentrate on experiments which demonstrate effects opposite in direction to those of a hippocampal lesion. Only two groups of studies consistently fit this pattern.

The first of these is quickly dealt with. In general, as we saw in Chapter 6, hippocampal lesions give rise to an increase in motor activity under a wide variety of conditions. Conversely, there are several reports that hippocampal stimulation causes an arrest of movement (Kaada, Jansen, and Andersen 1953; MacLean 1957; Vanegas and Flynn 1968; Bland and Vanderwolf 1972*b*; Byzsakaki, Grastyán, and Lénárd 1978). In combination, the lesion and stimulation effects offer good support for the hypothesis that the hippocampus is concerned with the inhibition of movement. The arrest of movement caused by hippocampal stimulation seems to be very general. Bland and Vanderwolf (1972*b*) were able to disrupt jumping, running, swimming, and struggling by stimulating the dentate gyrus; lapping, however, was unaffected, offering support for the distinction between Type 1 and Type 2 behaviour patterns (Table 7.1) developed by Vanderwolf on the basis of their relations to high-frequency theta (see Chapter 7). The arrest of movement produced in Bland and Vanderwolf's (1972*b*) experiment was not due to seizure activity (an ever-present hazard when the hippocampus is stimulated), but it required stimulation frequencies greater than about 10 Hz and current intensities capable of eliciting sizable evoked potentials bilaterally in the hippocampus.

The second group of studies is of greater interest, since it offers good support for the hypothesis that the hippocampus plays a role in the consolidation of memories (Milner 1968). This group consists of experiments in which stimulation of the hippocampus just after a learning trial has facilitated the subsequent retention of the behaviour learned. A particularly convincing series of experiments of this kind has been reported from Cardo's laboratory in Bordeaux. These have used mice trained in three different behavioural tasks, but stimulated in essentially the same way in each.

In the first task the mouse is initially trained for 15 minutes to bar-press for food on a CRF schedule. It is then removed from the box and stimulated 30 seconds later (100 Hz at half the threshold current for the production of seizures). During the retention test (usually 24 hours later) the effect of the post-trial stimulation is measured by the difference in bar-pressing rate between the experimental animals and unstimulated controls. Unfortunately, the effects of hippocampal lesions have not been reported for this task. Normally, such lesions do not affect CRF bar-pressing (Chapter 6, Section 6.1). But it may be important that the apparatus used in these experiments is different from the usual Skinner-box. Rather than being adjacent to each other, the lever and food magazine are at opposite sides of the box and separated by a partition. Since animals have a strong tendency to remain close to a source of reward, this is likely to introduce an element of conflict into the task: in order to press the lever the animal must overcome the tendency to stay by the food magazine. Thus it would not be surprising if hippocampal lesions, which regularly impair spatial reversal learning (Chapter 6, Section 6.22), were to have a deleterious effect on performance in this task. At any rate, there is no reason to suppose that they would improve performance, and certainly not in a manner that affected only the retention test.

The probable effects of hippocampal lesions are easier to describe for the other two tasks used by the Bordeaux group. One is step-through passive avoidance (with shock in the darker and larger of two boxes) and an escape component (that is, the animal is shocked until it exits from the dark box). This is reliably impaired by hippocampal lesions in the mouse (Table 6.3). There is a single trial, hippocampal stimulation being applied 30 seconds later, and a retention test next day. The other task is a successive discrimination in the same apparatus used for the simple CRF bar-pressing experiment. There are alternating 50-second components of CRF and extinction (i.e. a MULT CRF/EXT schedule); CRF is signalled by a buzzer and a bright light, extinction by white noise and a dim light. Hippocampal stimulation is applied after only the first of several daily sessions. Hippocampal lesions would be expected to impair behaviour in this task by increasing response rates selectively during the extinction component (Chapter 6, Section 6.20); precisely this effect is reported after simple electrode implantation, which presumably acts like a small lesion (Destrade and Jaffard 1978).

We first consider the effects of hippocampal stimulation in the two tasks for which we have clear predictions based on the known lesion effects. These effects differed according to the strain of mouse investigated, apparently in relation to different levels of activity of hippocampal choline acetyltransferase, which controls the synthesis of acetylcholine. Take first strain BALB/c. In mice of this strain tested in the passive avoidance task, 80 seconds of post-trial stimulation produced a marked facilitation in retention, as measured by an increased latency to enter the shock box and a shorter time spent there (Jaffard, Destrade, and Cardo 1976; Jaffard *et al.* 1977; Destrade and Jaffard 1978). In the successive discrimination task, stimulation for 4 seconds after the first daily session facilitated performance in subsequent sessions: the discrimination ratio (rate during S+/rate during S−) was increased, and this change was due to a fall in response rate during S− (Destrade and Jaffard 1978). Thus in both experiments the effect of stimulation was exactly opposite to those expected after a hippocampal lesion, and consistent therefore with the hypothesis that stimulation was activating processes normally discharged by the hippocampus. Furthermore, the specificity of the effect, especially in the successive discrimination experiment, coupled with the application of the stimulation *after* the learning trial, strongly implies that these processes relate in some way to memory.

In the CRF bar-pressing task mice of the BALB/c strain show a 'reminiscence effect', that is, the response rate observed 24 hours after the first training session (without brain stimulation) is higher than at the end of that session (Destrade *et al.* 1976). Post-trial hippocampal stimulation for 40 or 80 seconds enhances this effect; the stimulation is most effective if it commences 30–200 seconds after the training session; and at a training-stimulation interval of 600 seconds there is no effect (Destrade *et al.* 1973, 1976). This pattern of results is consistent with the hypothesis that there is a short period after learning during which memories are somehow strengthened ('consolidated'), and that hippocampal stimulation is able to facilitate this process. The assumption that these effects reflect the normal activity of the hippocampus is supported by the results obtained when the stimulation provokes seizure activity. Soumireu-Mourat *et al.* (1975) compared the effects of currents above and below the seizure threshold: when seizures occurred, retention of the bar-pressing response was impaired; the opposite result was obtained with sub-seizure stimulation.

The Bordeaux group has also studied two other strains of mice, C57 BL/6 and C57 BR. Neither of these strains spontaneously displays the reminiscence effect shown by BALB/c mice in the CRF bar-pressing task; on the contrary, after the 24-hour retention interval, their bar-pressing rates are lower than those recorded on the previous day (Jaffard *et al.* 1979). Post-trial hippocampal stimulation fails to alter performance on the retention test either in this task or in step-through passive avoidance in C57 BR mice; in C57 BL/6 mice it improves retention only slightly (Jaffard *et al.* 1976, 1977, 1979; Destrade *et al.* 1976).

There is evidence that these behavioural differences between the strains, and their different modes of response to hippocampal stimulation, are related to the level of cholinergic activity in the hippocampus. BALB/c mice have higher levels of hippocampal choline acetyltransferase than mice of either of the other two strains (Jaffard *et al.*, 1977). Three hours after hippocampal stimulation mice of the BALB/c strain show a further rise in hippocampal choline acetyltransferase, which the other strains show barely (C57 BL/6) or not at all (C57 BR) (Jaffard *et al.* 1977). Jaffard *et al.* (1979) report that hippocampal stimulation 24 hours *before* acquisition eliminated the higher choline acetyltransferase activity in the hippocampus of BALB/c mice, and also the spontaneous reminiscence effect in this strain. Pre-acquisition stimulation also eliminated the enhancement of reminiscence otherwise produced by post-trial stimulation in the BALB/c strain. Thus both spontaneous reminiscence and the enhancement of this effect by post-trial hippocampal stimulation apparently depend in some way upon elevated levels of hippocampal choline acetyltransferase, suggesting that these phenomena reflect the activity of intrahippocampal cholinergic terminals (presumably of septal origin).

These findings add up to a rather impressive case for a hippocampal involvement in the consolidation of memory. But there is a flagrant discrepancy between the results obtained by the Bordeaux group in their experiments on passive avoidance and those reported by other workers.

There have been a number of reports of retention *deficits* after post-trial hippocampal stimulation both in step-through passive avoidance (Lidsky and Slotnick 1971; Vardaris and Schwartz 1971; Wilson and Vardaris 1972; Zornetzer, Chronister, and Ross 1973), the task used by the Bordeaux group, and in other passive avoidance tasks: punished bar-pressing (Lidsky and Slotnick 1970; Kesner *et al.* 1975), punished drinking (Haycock *et al.* 1973) or eating (McDonough and Kesner 1971), punished locomotion to a water reward (Sideroff *et al.* 1974), and (with entorhinal stimulation) step-down avoidance (Collier and Routtenberg 1978). Results more like those of the Bordeaux group were reported by Landfield *et al.* (1973), who found that passive avoidance of the previously rewarded of a T-maze was impaired by electrode implantation and restored to normal levels by post-trial hippocampal stimulation which (as assessed by the neocortical EEG) elicited theta. These workers found the same pattern of results using a one-way active avoidance task, providing stimulation was applied 5 seconds rather than 5 minutes after foot-shock.

It is difficult to see any variable which might account for the difference between the results obtained by the Bordeaux group and Landfield *et al.* (1973), on the one hand, and the retention deficits seen in the other experiments cited above, on the other.

One obvious possibility is the presence or absence of seizure activity. As we have seen, the Bordeaux group, using the CRF bar-pressing task, has shown that the occurrence of seizures can transform the facilitation of retention produced by post-trial hippocampal stimulation into a retention deficit (Soumireu-Mourat *et al.* 1975). Of the other reports of such a deficit, seizure activity occurred in the experiments by Vardaris and Schwartz (1971), Wilson and Vardaris (1972) and Kesner *et al.* (1975); conversely, Zornetzer and Chronister (1973), who delivered only a single pulse to the hippocampus, causing no seizure activity, found only a non-significant deficit in the retention of step-through passive avoidance. Lidsky and Slotnick (1970, 1971) give no information about the effects of their stimulation on the hippocampal EEG. But in other experiments no seizures were detected in the EEG and retention deficits were nonetheless obtained (McDonough and Kesner 1971; Zornetzer *et al.* 1973; Sideroff *et al.* 1974). Sideroff *et al.* (1974), in their experiment on punished locomotion to water reward, were particularly careful to eliminate the possibility that their results could be due to seizure activity in the hippocampus.

A second possible variable, given its role in determining the effects of hippocampal lesions on step-through and step-down passive avoidance (Chapter 6, Section 6.2), is the presence or absence of an escape component in the task. The passive avoidance task used by the Bordeaux group has such a component. But, among the experiments reporting a retention deficit after post-trial hippocampal stimulation, so did the tasks used by Lidsky and Slotnick (1971) and Zornetzer *et al.* (1973).

There remain two possibilities of a more general nature.

The first is state dependency. Phillips and Le Piane (1980) have shown that, like drugs, brain stimulation can create a state which then constitutes a necessary context for the efficient retrieval of an association learnt during that state. Thus, if testing is conducted without brain stimulation, a deficit in retention will occur which can be misinterpreted as evidence for direct interference with a process necessary for memory consolidation. The control for this possibility is to test retention also during brain stimulation. This control has never been applied in experiments on the hippocampus. Thus it is possible that the observed retention deficits are all due to the non-specific effects of state change. Note, however, that this problem does not arise for facilitated retention: it is difficult to conceive of circumstances in which a change of state between learning and testing for retention could *enhance* performance.

The second possibility is one which might underlie either disrupted or facilitated retention. Presentation of a novel stimulus just after a learning experience can affect memory either favourably or deleteriously, the outcome depending on subtle and as yet only partially understood experimental parameters (Wagner 1978). Thus post-trial hippocampal stimulation might act simply like a novel stimulus. A control for this possibility is perhaps to use an exteroceptive stimulus in the same way as brain stimulation, exposing the animal to it just after the learning trial; although, of course, one has no idea of the qualities of hippocampal stimulation that it would be necessary to match in this way. No such control has ever been used.

It is clear from this discussion that we are a long way from understanding the mode of action of post-trial hippocampal stimulation, or the reasons why this sometimes facilitates retention and sometimes impairs it. Until these reasons are known, considerable uncertainty must attach to the interpretation of either kind of effect. None the less, the experiments in which retention has been facilitated by post-trial hippocampal stimulation give the memory hypothesis real support.

Septal stimulation

Research on the behavioural effects of septal stimulation has not generally been concerned with the memory hypothesis. For this reason the method of post-trial stimulation has been little used. Except for the few experiments which have deliberately attempted to manipulate hippocampal electrical activity, the hippocampal EEG has not usually been monitored. Since electrical stimulation of the septal area, especially when it is of high frequency, is a particularly effective way of provoking hippocampal seizures, this omission is as serious as when direct hippocampal stimulation is employed. A simple tally of reported effects of septal stimulation that are like, opposed to, or incommensurable with those of septal lesions reveals the same confusion as the comparable tally of experiments on the hippocampus. As before, therefore, I shall concentrate on those experiments which reveal interpretable effects opposite in sign to those of lesions.

In applying this strategy to the septal area, however, there is an additional variable to take into account. In the hippocampal stimulation experiments, as in the majority of those using septal stimulation, the frequency of the applied current has been high (typically, 50–100 Hz). However, there are also several reports of the behavioural effects of low-frequency stimulation of the medial septal area, used to drive the hippocampal theta rhythm (Fig. 4.4). The assumption underlying these experiments is that stimulation which elicits essentially the same pattern of electrical activity that the septal area normally controls in the hippocampus, i.e. the theta rhythm, must act in a more or less physiological manner. Conversely, since high-frequency stimulation of the medial septal area blocks the theta rhythm (Fig. 4.3), this can be regarded as jamming the normal septal input to the hippocampus. If these assumptions are correct, 'theta-driving' stimulation of the septal area should have behavioural effects opposite to those of a lesion (septal or hippocampal), while 'theta-blocking' stimulation should act in the same manner as a lesion. A further assumption underlying these predictions is that theta reflects an active state of hippocampal function. If, on the other hand, as suggested by Grastyán et al. (1959), theta indicates that the hippocampus is inhibited, the predictions are exactly reversed. Thus, by testing them against the available data, it should be possible to determine which of these views of theta is correct.

If one simply observes the behaviour elicited by theta-driving septal stimulation, there is not much to see (Gray 1972b; Wetzel, Ott, and Matthies 1977a; Kramis and Routtenberg 1977). Upon the first few occasions of stimulation the animal usually searches around as though something has excited its curiosity. This is consistent with the observations (Chapter 7) relating the spontaneous theta rhythm to orienting or attentive behaviour. However, the same type of searching behaviour is elicited by stimulation at many sites in the brain, and there is no reason to attach any special significance to it when it is elicited from the septal area. With repeated stimulation the animal rapidly habituates and comes to ignore it; it may even curl up in a corner and go into a light sleep.

It is relevant to the motor hypothesis of the function of theta (Chapter 7) that, after the initial searching reactions have habituated, there is no tendency for theta-driving stimulation to elicit movement. This is so whether the stimulating (and therefore theta) frequency is low or high; one may drive a high-amplitude theta rhythm at 10 or 11 Hz while the rat remains immobile (personal observations). This is in contrast to theta elicited by high-frequency hypothalamic or reticular stimulation, which is normally accompanied by movement whose vigour is positively correlated with the frequency of the elicited theta (Whishaw, Bland, and Vanderwolf 1972; Robinson and Vanderwolf 1978; McNaughton and Sedgwick 1978). The only occasion on which there appears to be any correlation between septally elicited theta and motor behaviour is after systemic injection of the anticholinergic drug, scopolamine, when driven theta is observed only if the animal simultaneously moves (McNaughton *et al.* 1977). This treatment also slightly raises the threshold for septal driving of theta; but, contrary to what one might expect from the relation of atropine-sensitive spontaneous theta to frequency, this increase in threshold does not affect low theta frequencies more than high. These observations are consistent with the hypothesis that the sensitivity of non-movement theta to anticholinergic drugs is due to an action on a cholinergic input to the medial septal pacemaker, rather than the septo-hippocampal final common pathway for theta (Graeff *et al.* 1980; see Chapter 7).

More formal behavioural observations are equally difficult to fit with the motor hypothesis of the function of theta. Klemm and Dreyfus (1975) saw no effect of driving theta (4 or 8 Hz) in the rabbit on activity in a box or ambulation in the open field. Gray (1972*b*) found that theta-driving at 7.7 Hz decreased the rat's speed of running for water reward in the alley; and Glazer (1974*a*) and Klemm and Dreyfus (1975) similarly found a reduction in the rate of FR bar-pressing for food and water reward, respectively. Since both septal and hippocampal lesions generally disinhibit motor responses (Chapter 6), these effects are consistent with the hypothesis that hippocampal theta reflects an active hippocampal state; but they conflict with the motor hypothesis of theta function. However, high-frequency theta-blocking stimulation may also disrupt movement, causing an arrest reaction (similar to the one produced by direct hippocampal stimulation) if it is applied while the rat is in motion (Gray, Araujo-Silva, and Quintão 1972) or pressing a bar (Ito 1966). These effects are consistent with the hypothesis that hippocampal desynchrony, rather than theta, reflects an active hippocampal state; and they may also be interpreted in a manner consistent with the motor hypothesis of theta function, but only if we take theta to indicate an inhibited hippocampus. There are in any case contrary findings with theta-blocking stimulation: Glazer (1974*a*) saw no effect on FR bar-pressing, and Klemm and Dreyfus (1975) none on activity in a box or ambulation in the open field. All in all the main conclusion that one can draw from these observations is that the direction of change in movement is a poor criterion by which to classify the effects of septal stimulation.

These experiments show that there is rather a loose coupling between theta and the motor patterns that it normally accompanies. Movement is normally accompanied by theta (Chapter 7); yet one may eliminate theta without disturbing movement (Glazer 1974*a;* Klemm and Dreyfus 1975) or elicit theta and not affect (Klemm and Dreyfus 1975) or even disrupt (Gray 1972*b;* Glazer 1974*a*) movement. Similar inferences flow from observations of behaviour that is not normally accompanied by clear theta. Drinking, for example, is normally accompanied by large, irregular activity (or low-frequency theta) in the hippocampal EEG. Gray (1972*b*) replaced this by theta at 7.7 Hz with no sign of change in drinking behaviour. Similar observations have been reported by Kramis and Routtenberg (1977). Another example concerns self-stimulation. Grastyán *et al.* (1966) observed a relationship between rewarding hypothalamic stimulation and the elicitation of hippocampal theta; they proposed therefore that the latter might be a sign of positive reinforcement. But, using septal self-stimulation, Ball and Gray (1971) found that rats were entirely indifferent to the effect that this behaviour had on the hippocampal EEG: when coulombs were kept constant, response rate, response duration, and the threshold reinforcing current were identical whether the septal stimulation drove or blocked hippocampal theta. This is a further warning, if one is still needed, against inferring cause from correlation.

When more complex behaviour is studied, one finds effects of both theta-driving and theta-blocking septal stimulation.

Results in experiments on one-way active avoidance have been conflicting, perhaps mirroring the inconsistent effects of hippocampal lesions on this form of behaviour (Chapter 6, Section 6.5). Klemm and Dreyfus (1975), using a two-compartment apparatus in which one side was safe and the other dangerous, disrupted both escape and avoidance by applying 8-Hz theta-driving stimulation while the rabbit was responding; the number of avoidances was reduced and both escape and avoidance latencies were increased. Stimulation at 4 Hz affected avoidance in the same way, but left escape unchanged. Theta-blocking stimulation, however, had no effect on behaviour in this task. In a similar experiment with rats Landfield (1977) again found that theta-blocking stimulation was without effect; but theta-driving at 7.7 Hz facilitated avoidance, reducing latencies of response.

Results which form a more coherent pattern have been obtained in a series of experiments on the extinction of rewarded behaviour. Gray (1970*a*) proposed that 7.7-Hz theta has a special association with the operation of the behavioural inhibition system and is specially sensitive to the effects of the anti-anxiety drugs (see Chapter 7). It follows from this hypothesis that, if the anti-anxiety drugs, septal and hippocampal lesions all have a common effect on behaviour, 7.7-Hz theta-driving should produce the opposite effect (Gray 1970*a*). As we saw in Chapters 2 (Section 2.7) and 6 (Section 6.17), the anti-anxiety drugs, septal and hippocampal

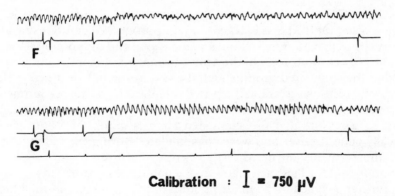

Calibration : $I = 750\ \mu V$

Figure 8.1. The electrical activity of the hippocampus recorded on two successive trials (F, G) on which a rat ran in a straight alley to a water reward. Bottom pen marker, time in seconds. Progress along the alley is shown by the middle pen marker: successive deflections indicate opening of the start-box door, breaking of two photobeams along the alley, and then of a third photobeam in the goal-box which operates a water fountain whose activity terminates at the final deflection. No stimulation was applied on trial F. On trial G septal stimulation (7.7 Hz, 0.5 ms pulse width, 125 μA) was applied throughout the time the rat drank (i.e. between the final two deflections of the middle pen marker). (From Gray (1972*b*).)

lesions all increase resistance to extinction after CRF training in the alley. It can be predicted, therefore, that driving theta at 7.7 Hz during extinction should decrease resistance to extinction. This prediction was confirmed by Gray (1972*b*). However, since the observed effects of septal stimulation consisted in slower running speed and enhanced exploratory behaviour (both, of course, part of normal behaviour during extinction), this finding could reflect simply the distracting effect of novel brain stimulation. Some evidence against this interpretation of Gray's (1972*b*) results comes from the observation that the stimulated rats continued to run more slowly than controls when tested without stimulation the next day.

This problem of interpretation was eliminated in a second experiment reported in the same paper (Gray 1972*b*). The design of this experiment was based on the assumption that 7.7-Hz theta-driving constitutes an internal signal of non-reward, one strong enough, moreover, to override the fact that, objectively, the animal gets a reward. Rats were trained to run in the alley for CRF water reward. An experimental group was also subjected to 7.7-Hz theta-driving on a random 50 per cent of trials, the stimulation being applied throughout the 5 seconds that water was available in the goal-box, but at no other time (the effect of the stimulation on the hippocampal EEG is shown in Fig. 8.1). On the assumption that the stimulation constituted a signal of non-reward, then, the experimental group was on a random 50 per cent schedule of partial reinforcement. Such a schedule normally produces an increase in resistance to extinction relative to CRF controls (the partial reinforcement extinction effect). As we have seen, the PREE is blocked under appropriate conditions by anti-anxiety drugs (Chapter 2, Section 2.7) and septal ahd hippocampal lesions (Chapter 6, Section 6.17). On the same argument as before, then, we predict that the stimulated group should be *more* resistant to extinction than controls (which were animals treated identically to the experimental group, except that they were never stimulated). This is the result obtained (Gray 1972*b*). Note that the stimulated animals drank the water reward normally on every trial, and were not stimulated during extinction testing. Thus theta-driving did not directly disrupt reinforcement during acquisition, nor could it have acted as a distraction during extinction.

A further prediction from the same set of arguments is that theta-blocking stimulation should reduce resistance to extinction if it is applied on the non-rewarded trials of a conventional PRF schedule; for it then blocks the 7.7-Hz theta which is normally elicited by non-reward in the alley (Gray and Ball 1970). This prediction was tested by Gray, Araujo-Silva, and Quintão (1972), in an experiment using the same basic procedures as those just described, except that experimental and control groups were now both on a random PRF schedule of water reward, and the experimental group were stimulated (200 Hz) when they entered the goal-box on non-rewarded trials during acquisition; no stimulation was delivered during extinction. Again the prediction was confirmed: the stimulated group was less resistant to extinction than unstimulated controls. Thus theta-blocking acted in the same manner as a septal or hippocampal lesion, agreeing with the observation in Gray's (1972*b*) experiment that theta-driving had the converse effect to a lesion.

These experiments offer an internally coherent pattern of findings which, taken together, are consistent both with the specific hypotheses that were under test, and with the general hypothesis that theta is an active state of hippocampal function which it is possible to elicit in a more or less physiological manner by septal stimulation. Confirmatory findings have been reported by Glazer (1974*a, b*).

In the first of these experiments Glazer '(1974*a*) drove theta at 7.7 Hz while rats bar-pressed for food on a discrete-trial FR 10 schedule. During acquisition the effect of this stimulation was to slow the rate of bar-pressing, as also found by Klemm and Dreyfus (1975) with rabbits working on a FR schedule. Since both septal and hippocampal lesions increase FR response rate (Chapter 6, Sections 6.1 and 6.18), an effect which is consistent with reduced responsiveness to stimuli associated with non-reward, these observations are in line with the hypothesis that theta reflects an active hippocampal state. During extinction (when there was no further septal stimulation) Glazer's (1974*a*) rats stimulated at 7.7 Hz were more resistant to extinction than unstimulated controls or animals stimulated at 200 Hz; the latter, theta-blocking, stimulation had no effect on either acquisition or extinction. Except for the failure of 200-Hz stimulation to increase FR rate during acquisition (which would be the probable effect of a septal or hippocampal lesion), these results are as predicted* and in good agreement with Gray's.

The design of Glazer's (1974*b*) second experiment was derived from Amsel's (1962, 1972) theory of the generalized PREE. This phenomenon is observed in experiments in which the animal is first trained on a PRF schedule of reward for one response, and then (sometimes long after) on a CRF schedule for a second response; the second response is then extinguished, and it is found that resistance to extinction is increased relative to controls given CRF training on both responses (e.g. Ross 1964). Thus the increased resistance to extinction produced by a PRF schedule is long-lasting and transfers to conditions other than those in which non-reward is initially encountered. It is possible to account for this phenomenon by supposing that, in the first phase of the experiment, the internal stimuli characteristic of anticipatory frustration become counter-conditioned so that they now serve as signals to persist in the partially reinforced behaviour (see Chapter 2, Section 2.9); during extinction of the second response anticipatory frustration occurs once more and the habit of persistence transfers to the new behaviour (Amsel 1962, 1972).

With this background, consider Glazer's (1974*b*) experiment. Rats were first instrumentally trained to produce theta in the 7.5–8.5-Hz band for food reward.. If theta in this band is equivalent to an internal signal of frustration, as supposed by Gray (1970*a*) and Glazer (1974*b*), it follows that this method of training is equivalent to a conventional PRF schedule, since in both cases anticipatory frustration is followed by reward and counter-conditioning should take place. If we now train these rats on a second response and then extinguish it, they should show increased resistance to extinction (a generalized PREE) relative to appropriate controls. This is the experiment Glazer (1974*b*) conducted. The second response was bar-pressing rewarded with food on a discrete-trial FR schedule. There were two control groups, one given initial instrumental reinforcement for producing low-frequency hippocampal activity (4–5 Hz) outside the critical 'frustration' band, the other simply given food independently of hippocampal electrical activity. The three groups did not differ in acquisition of the bar-press response, but the group initially rewarded for producing theta in the 7.5–8.5-Hz band was significantly more resistant to extinction than either of the two control groups.

Although this result is in good agreement with those reported by Gray (1972*b*) and Gray, Araujo-Silva, and Quintão (1972), and the arguments on which its interpretation depends are consistent with those used earlier,

---

*Glazer (1974*a*) himself predicted that 7.7-Hz stimulation would eventually give rise to faster bar-pressing during acquisition, on the grounds that a PRF schedule in the alley causes faster running than a CRF schedule. However, such a partial reinforcement acquisition effect has never been seen in the Skinner-box and it is only inconsistently found even in the alley, so the grounds for this prediction were weak.

the ratio of theory to observation is perhaps beginning to seem excessive. The length of time which elapsed between instrumental training of theta and the measured increase in resistance to extinction (20 days) in Glazer's (1974*b*) experiment made us wonder, therefore, whether some much more general, proactive effect of theta elicitation might be involved. This suspicion was strengthened by observations (see Chapter 12) showing that pro-active effects which can have nothing to do with counter-conditioning are also seen when animals are simply exposed to conventional aversive stimuli (e.g. foot-shock) in the first phase of experiments whose general design is like that used by Glazer (1974*b*).

To examine this possibility, Holt and Gray (unpublished)* repeated Glazer's (1974*b*) experiment, using septal stimulation at 7.7 Hz rather than instrumental training to elicit theta in the first phase of the experiment. This change allowed us to compare two conditions: one in which each episode of theta-driving (5 seconds in duration) was followed by delivery of a food pellet (in theory, allowing counter-conditioning to take place); the other a 'truly random' control procedure in which theta-driving and food-delivery were programmed independently of each other (so that counter-conditioning could not occur). A further control group received food only, with no brain stimulation. The rest of the experiment was identical to Glazer's (1974*b*). If we apply Amsel's (1962, 1972) theory of the generalized PREE to this design, we expect to produce increased resistance to extinction of the bar-press response (on which all animals were trained in the second phase of the experiment) in the condition in which 7.7-Hz theta was paired with food, but not in the truly random control group. In fact both groups showed increased resistance to extinction relative to unstimulated controls and, if anything, animals in the truly random condition were more resistant to extinction than those in the paired condition. As in Glazer's (1974*b*) experiment, there were no differences between any of the groups during acquisition; moreover, the detailed pattern of extinction performance was very similar in the two experiments. Thus it is likely that the effects of experimental manipulation of theta are the same whether this is achieved by septal stimulation or by instrumental training.

The demonstration that the experimental elicitation of theta can have unconditioned, pro-active effects — effects, moreover, which are rather long-lasting (3–4 weeks at least) — casts a new light on experiments which have used this technique. The hypothesis that 7.7-Hz theta is related to the activity of the behavioural inhibition system is not necessarily affected by this demonstration. For, as we shall see in Chapter 12, conventional stimuli which are presumed to act on this system also have pro-active effects of a similar kind. But the details of the interpretations we have advanced above are called into question at several points.† It is possible, for

---

*See additional references.

†In fact the implications of Holt and Gray's findings go well beyond the particular context in which they are considered here. The possibility of long-lasting pro-active effects of brain stimulation is rather generally ignored and rarely, if ever, controlled for.

example, that the precise time and circumstances under which septal stimulation is delivered are of relatively little importance, and that the outcome is determined simply by the type and amount of stimulation. But it is also possible that theta-driving or -blocking stimulation has two types of effect, one unconditioned and the other dependent on particular associations with other events in the animal's environment and/or reinforcement schedule. This appears to be the case for conventional reinforcers (Gray, Owen, Davis, and Feldon 1980).

If we disregard for the moment pro-active effects, and possibly even if we take them into account (see Chapter 12), the results of Gray's and Glazer's experiments are in good agreement with the hypothesis that theta is functionally related to a system which mediates the behavioural effects of anticipatory frustration (Gray 1970a). It is also possible, however, to interpret most of these data in conformity with the memory hypothesis. On this view, increased resistance to extinction is not due to changed reactions to non-reward, but is a sign of more complete consolidation of the initial learning. This point of view would receive little support from research in the general field of learning (Mackintosh 1974; Gray 1975), which has rather discredited the use of resistance to extinction as a measure of the strength of learning, but it is not entirely to be neglected. If we adopt it, we would interpret the more rapid extinction seen when the animal is subjected to 7.7-Hz theta-driving during extinction trials as better learning that the conditions of reinforcement have changed; the slower extinction after theta-driving has been applied during acquisition as better learning of the initial running or bar-pressing response; and the faster extinction after theta-blocking has been applied during acquisition as due to a blockade of consolidation. Thus, on this view (which has been forcefully advocated by Landfield 1976), theta is a correlate of the process of consolidation.

The notion that theta is related in some way to the storage of memories in fact has a fairly long history. It was first proposed during the 1960s on the basis of a series of experiments from Adey's laboratory in which theta and theta frequency were related to different aspects of the animal's behaviour in a variety of learning tasks (e.g. Adey, Dunlop, and Hendrix 1960; Elazer and Adey 1967; Adey 1967). These experiments were carried out before Vanderwolf's work on the motor correlates of theta was known, and little account was taken therefore of the possibility that the phenomena observed were related rather to movement than to learning or memory. With the publication of Vanderwolf's (1969, 1971) work, they have tended to be lost from view. But there are also other reasons for thinking that theta might be correlated with the consolidation of memory.

Landfield and McGaugh (1972) noted that electroconvulsive shock (ECS) — which is known under some conditions to give rise to retrograde amnesia — decreased theta in the neocortex (probably volume conducted from the hippocampus; see Chapter 4), while stimulation of the midbrain reticular formation, which can facilitate retention of material learned just before the stimulation is applied (Bloch 1970), increased theta, both these changes being observed in the period immediately following treatment. In a rather more complex experiment Nicholas *et al.* (1976) investigated so-called 'cue-dependent reinstatement amnesia' after ECS. It is possible to produce retrograde amnesia by subjecting an animal to ECS just after exposure to one of the cues involved in the learning situation, rather than immediately after learning itself. Nicholas *et al.* (1976) exploited this phenomenon to compare the effects of ECS on neocortical theta under two closely comparable conditions, one of which gave rise to amnesia and the other not. Rats were trained initially on a food-rewarded maze problem. There followed a seven-day retention interval, during which all animals were placed daily in a neutral box. On the seventh day half the rats were given ECS in the start-box and half in the neutral box; neocortical activity was measured over the succeeding 30 minutes, and a retention test was carried out in the maze 24 hours later. The group which received ECS in the start-box had more errors in the retention test (reinstatement amnesia); during the 30 minutes after ECS this group also manifested less theta than the neutral-box controls.

These observations, however, are correlational only. The most direct way to test the hypothesis that theta is related to consolidation is to manipulate theta just after learning and measure retention. Experiments using septal stimulation for this purpose have been reported by Landfield (1977) and Wetzel *et al.* (1977*b*).

Landfield (1977) used two frequencies of stimulation, 7.7 Hz to drive theta and 77 Hz to block it (monitored in the neocortical EEG), and two tasks, step-through passive avoidance with an escape component and one-way active avoidance in a two-compartment apparatus. In the passive avoidance task stimulation was applied for 20 minutes immediately after the single learning trial. On the retention test, 48 hours later, step-through latency was longer (passive avoidance greater) in the driving than the blocking group, consistent with the hypothesis that the occurrence of theta enhances consolidation; however, neither stimulated group was significantly different from either unoperated or implanted controls, which had intermediate latencies. Neither driving nor blocking stimulation had any effect if given during the retention test itself; on Gray's (1970*a*) behavioural inhibition hypothesis, it would have been expected that theta-driving should increase passive avoidance and theta-blocking impair it. In the one-way active avoidance task stimulation was applied for 10 minutes immediately after each of two daily acquisition sessions. On the retention test 48 hours later the implanted controls were significantly poorer than intact animals, in agreement with the general finding that septal lesions impair one-way active avoidance (Chapter 6, Section 6.5). Theta-driving stimulation restored performance (shortened response latencies) to normal levels, significantly above those of the implanted controls or theta-blocking group. Theta-blocking stimulation had no effect. If stimulation was applied during the retention test, performance was facilitated by theta-driving but unaffected by theta-blocking.

It cannot be said that these results give strong support to the consolidation hypothesis. The effects in the passive avoidance task were of marginal significance; and those in the active avoidance task were the same whether stimulation was applied during the putative phase of consolidation or during the retention test. The effects observed, however, continue to be in line with the hypothesis that theta-driving has effects opposed to those of a lesion: improved passive and one-way active avoidance.

Wetzel *et al.* (1977*b*) studied rats in a two-way active avoidance task in an automated Y-maze. Theta-driving stimulation was applied at 7 Hz during the period 5–15 minutes after an initial 40-trial session or during a 10-minute period 4 hours after this session. An additional group received 100-Hz stimulation at the earlier time; this blocked theta, but only incompletely. Controls were implanted but not stimulated. The results showed that theta-driving improved performance on the retention test (24 hours later), and only in the group stimulated 5 minutes after training; the stimulation was particularly effective in animals which had many errors during initial training. Stimulation at 100 Hz produced an insignificant impairment in retention.

These results are in good agreement with the consolidation hypothesis. Unfortunately the effects of septal stimulation *during* performance were not studied in this experiment. Given the known effects of lesions (Chapter 6, Section 6.7) and the general pattern of findings seen earlier in this chapter, we would expect theta-driving to impair performance and theta-blocking to improve it. The finding that post-trial theta-driving improved two-way active avoidance contradicts this expectation. Thus Wetzel *et al.*'s (1977*b*) results depart from the usual rule that the effects of theta-driving are opposite to, and the effects of theta-blocking the same as, those of a lesion.

The majority of other findings reviewed above, however, conform to this rule. With this conclusion in mind we can turn to other experiments in which the septal area has been stimulated but the hippocampal EEG not monitored, to see if the rule holds also for these. There are no reports of low-frequency stimulation of the septal area without monitoring of the hippocampal EEG. If high-frequency stimulation is applied to the medial septal area, it is likely (though by no means certain) that it will block theta; applied to the lateral septal area (outside the theta pacemaker), it is not likely to block and might even elicit theta. Thus we would expect high-frequency medial septal stimulation probably to act like a lesion, but prediction is not possible for lateral septal stimulation.

The effects of medial septal stimulation are generally in line with expectation. Goldstein (1966*a*) stimulated the medial septal area at 60 Hz during active avoidance in the shuttle-box; this increased the rate of acquisition and the number of spontaneous crossings, both effects seen also after septal or hippocampal lesions (Chapter 6, Section 6.7). Notice that this result is the opposite to that reported by Wetzel *et al.* (1977*b;* see above) using post-trial high-frequency stimulation in a two-way avoidance task. Goldstein (1966*b*) also reported an impairment in on-the-baseline conditioned suppression, which is inconsistently seen after septal lesions (Chapter 6, Section 6.3). A series of results reported by Donovick and Schwartzbaum (1966) are nicely consistent with the lesion data (Schwartz-baum and Donovick 1968; Chapter 6, Sections 6.19 and 6.22): medial septal stimulation at 100 Hz had no effect on simultaneous position or brightness discriminations, impaired position reversal and increased per-severative errors during this type of learning, and had no effect on brightness reversal.

Two studies, however, report contrary findings. Breglio *et al.* (1970) saw an elevation in the startle threshold to foot-shock with high-frequency stimulation (lesions usually lower this threshold: Chapter 6, Section 6.8). And Carder (1971), studying one-way and two-way active avoidance in the shuttle-box, applied medial septal stimulation either 5 seconds before or 5 seconds after trial onset. In the former case both kinds of avoidance were facilitated; post-trial stimulation had no effect. Predictions from the lesion literature (Chapter 6, Sections 6.5 and 6.7) are that one-way avoid-ance should be impaired and two-way avoidance facilitated. However, it is possible that the animal was able to use the pre-trial stimulation as an extra warning signal, which would improve performance, so the correct interpretation of Carder's (1971) findings is uncertain.

Lateral septal stimulation also acts most often like a lesion. Thus Schwartzbaum and Donovick (1965), studying punished bar-pressing, ob-served reductions in freezing and defecation and less suppression of bar-pressing during 100-Hz stimulation; and Kasper (1964), studying pun-ished drinking, similarly observed reduced freezing and defecation and an increase in the number of shocks taken (cf. Chapter 6, Sections 6.2 and 6.14). In the latter experiment medial septal stimulation was ineffec-tive, in agreement with Landfield's (1977; see above) observations in a step-through passive avoidance task. Kasper's (1964) differentiation be-tween lateral and medial septal sites is consistent with the effects of small lesions within the septum (see Chapter 10) in implicating the lateral septal area as the focus of the passive avoidance deficit seen after large septal lesions. Other results reported by Kasper (1964, 1965) are also consistent with the rule that high-frequency lateral septal stimulation acts like a tem-porary lesion: the learning of a position discrimination was unaffected, but reversal was impaired (cf. Chapter 6, Sections 6.19 and 6.22). Simi-larly, Kaplan (1965) found that stimulation of this kind increased the bar-pressing rate on a DRL schedule with a consequent loss of rewards (cf. Chapter 6, Section 6.18).

A series of studies from Albert's laboratory presents a contradictory pattern of results, high-frequency lateral septal stimulation acting in the *opposite* manner to a lesion. These studies have been concerned with the hyper-reactivity syndrome, seen after either septal or ventromedial hypothalamic lesions in the rat. Discrete lesions within the septum point to foci for this syndrome in the lateral septal area and the region ventrolateral to the anterior septal area (Paxinos 1976; Albert and Richmond 1976; Albert, Brayley, and Milner 1978a; Grossman 1978). The same conclusion is suggested by experiments in which the local anaesthetic, lidocaine, is injected into the septal area (Albert and Richmond 1977; Albert and Wong 1978); and intraseptal injections of drugs point to the importance of an α-noradrenergic synapse in the anteroventral septal area (Albert and Richmond 1977). The medial septal area is apparently not involved in the hyper-reactivity syndrome in the rat, since lesions confined to this region produce, if anything, an exceptionally placid animal (Clody and Carlton 1969; Gray 1971c).

If hyper-reactivity is created by a lesion to the ventromedial hypothalamus, this may be temporarily suppressed by stimulation of either the lateral or the anteroventral septal area; in the rat medial septal stimulation is without effect (Brayley and Albert 1977a, b; Albert et al. 1978a). However, in the cat, MacDonnell and Stoddard-Apter (1978) found that medial septal high-frequency stimulation *lowered* the threshold for intraspecific aggressive behaviour elicited concurrently by ventromedial hypothalamic stimulation. A lesion in the lateral septal area does not alter the effectiveness of anteroventral septal stimulation, but a lesion at the latter site eliminates the effect of lateral septal stimulation (Albert et al. 1978b). If hyper-reactivity is created by septal lesions, stimulation of the ventromedial hypothalamus does not affect it (Albert et al. 1978b). Thus information flows in a descending direction between the lateral and anteroventral septal areas, and this pathway probably inhibits elements in the ventromedial hypothalamus. In agreement with this inference, Maeda (1978) reports that, in the cat, the threshold for hissing provoked by electrical stimulation of the ventromedial hypothalamus is lowered by septal lesions.

The internal consistency of this series of observations leaves little doubt that lateral septal stimulation activates a descending pathway, destined probably for the ventromedial hypothalamus. There is no obvious reason why the stimulation used by Albert and his collaborators should be particularly apt to excite normal pathways. Their stimulation parameters (60 Hz and 20 μA) are very similar to those used, for example, by Schwartzbaum and Donovick (1965) and Kasper (1964, 1965). It is perhaps important that Brayley and Albert (1977b) took care to verify that their stimulation does not produce an after-discharge at the electrode site. Alternatively, there may be something about the particular pathway concerned which makes it respond to such stimulation in a relatively normal manner, while other systems tend rather to be jammed. It is particularly surprising that opposing patterns of results should have been obtained in experiments on passive avoidance (Schwartzbaum and Donovick 1965; Kasper 1964), on the one hand, and in Albert's experiments on hyper-reactivity on the other. Both the passive avoidance deficit and the hyper-reactivity syndrome seen after septal lesions seem to consist in a loss of behavioural inhibition, and both have their focus in the lateral septal area. It is natural, therefore, to seek a common mechanism underlying the two phenomena. Yet lateral septal stimulation disrupts passive avoidance (like a lesion) but inhibits hyper-reactivity (opposed to a lesion). These results are inconsistent with the hypothesis of a common mechanism. However, they do not refute it; for the variability of the effects of brain stimulation is so great, and our understanding of the reasons for this variability so small, that it is entirely possible that Kasper's (1964) stimulation jammed the same pathway that Albert's activated.

Conclusion

The experiments reviewed in this chapter permit several new and important inferences. First, theta reflects an active state of hippocampal function; this is clear from the experiments on theta-driving (which generally produces effects opposed to those of a lesion) and theta-blocking (which generally acts like a lesion). Second, the effects of experimental manipulation of theta offer no support for the motor hypothesis of the significance of this rhythm. Third, the same experiments strengthen the hypothesis that theta in the 7.5–8.5-Hz band is associated with the operation of the behavioural inhibition system, at least when this is activated by stimuli associated with non-reward. Fourth, several lines of evidence suggest that the septo-hippocampal system exercises a relatively direct inhibitory control over behaviour: the arrest of movement caused by hippocampal stimulation, the effects of lateral septal stimulation on passive avoidance, and Albert's experiment on hyper-reactivity (although, as we have just seen, the two last sets of experiments are difficult to integrate with each other). Finally, the experiments using post-trial hippocampal stimulation and, to a lesser extent, post-trial theta-driving offer, for the first time in this review of the experimental literature, good support for the memory hypothesis of septo-hippocampal function. Thus the gap that has existed at this point between the experimental and clinical data has to some extent narrowed. But this gap remains large. In the next chapter we shall attempt to narrow it further.

9

The hippocampus and memory

There appears to be a considerable difference between the effects of hippocampal lesions in animals and man. In man the most dramatic change is apparently the loss of the ability to form new memories. But we saw virtually no sign of such a change in the animal experiments reviewed in Chapter 6. In the present chapter we examine this discrepancy more closely. We shall ask two questions. First, did we miss anything in our review of the lesion literature in Chapter 6? Perhaps, by making use of a behavioural framework which was first developed to deal with the effects of the anti-anxiety drugs (Gray 1977), we failed to spot changes in memorial processes which are in fact produced by hippocampal damage in animals. The second question is addressed to the clinical data: is the evidence for loss of memory after hippocampal lesions what it seems? It is possible that the discrepancy between the animal and human data has arisen because the clinical picture has been misinterpreted. If neither of these strategies works, we shall have to conclude — with great reluctance, because it would cut much of the ground from beneath our feet — that the septo-hippocampal system does different things in man and the other animals.

Experiments with animals

There is a quite remarkable absence of any sign of disturbed retention after septal lesions. It is possible that this is because virtually no-one has thought that memory deficits might be a consequence of septal lesions, so no-one has looked for them. It is the hippocampus which figures so prominently in the literature on amnesia. Given the overwhelming similarities between the septal and hippocampal syndromes (Chapter 6) and the close anatomical and physiological relations between the septal area and hippocampus, it is surprising that memory does not figure in the long list of functions that at one time or other have been attributed to the septal area; but it does not. However, even if no-one has specifically looked for retention deficits after septal lesions, there have been many experiments in which such a deficit would almost certainly have been manifest, had it existed. There have been many reports of a deficit after septal lesions in that classic test of memory, one-trial passive avoidance with a 24-hour retention interval (Chapter 6, Section 6.2); but there is little reason to attribute this to a disturbance in retention rather than a difficulty with passive avoidance. If alley running is learned for food on a CRF schedule at a 24-hour inter-trial interval, septal rats are as good as controls (Feldon and Gray 1979a). About the only observation which suggests some kind of increased loss of information over a long retention interval comes from an experiment by Flaherty et al. (1973) on the Crespi depression effect: septal rats were not different from controls when tested one day after training, but showed a reduced depression effect when tested four or five days later.

There is rather more evidence that hippocampal lesions can lead to deficits in retention. Lesions made after acquisition have been reported to impair retention (Andy *et al.* 1967; Rich and Thompson 1965), as also sometimes found with septal lesions (Carey 1967; Moore 1964). But, since pre-acquisition lesions do not produce these impairments, they are more likely to reflect some form of state dependency (Overton 1966) than a role for the damaged structure in memory processes. More convincing is the report by Glick and Greenstein (1973), who trained mice in step-through passive avoidance (with an escape component) and destroyed the hippocampus either immediately (within 2 minutes) or one hour after the training trial. Retention was disturbed by the former lesion, but not by the latter; when the lesion was made immediately after training, there was also an increase in the rate of forgetting between retention trials conducted one day and one week after training. In the same vein Uretsky and McCleary (1969) lesioned the entorhinal area and the fornix in cats that had learned a one-way active avoidance response either 3 hours or 8 days previously; there was an impairment during retention testing only in the former case. These results cannot be attributed to state change, since the change between the occasions of learning and retention testing is no less if the lesion is made later rather than sooner after the training trial.

The results obtained by Glick and Greenstein (1973) and Uretsky and McCleary (1969) fit well with the consolidation hypothesis and with the results of the post-trial stimulation experiments reviewed in the previous chapter. But one wonders how specific these effects are to the hippocampus. It is likely that a variety of insults to the brain (and indeed to the body) occurring just after learning can affect retention simply in virtue of the non-specific interference they produce. It is consistent with this possibility that amnesia has been reported after post-trial electrical stimulation of a wide diversity of brain sites (e.g. Routtenberg and Holzman 1973; Wyers and Deadwyler 1971). Similarly, in Glick and Greenstein's (1973) experiment, retention was disturbed by immediate post-trial destruction of the caudate nucleus as well as destruction of the hippocampus.

A further possibility is that a hippocampal lesion or hippocampal stimulation just after learning both acts as a source of interference and renders the animal more susceptible to the effects of such interference. For there are several demonstrations that animals with hippocampal lesions *are* more susceptible to interference. Thus Jarrard (1975) showed that hippocampal rats were impaired in a delayed spatial alternation task if they were forced to run in a running wheel during the delay interval, but not otherwise. Thomas (1978) reported a similar effect in rats with lesions of the fornix-fimbria, severing the septo-hippocampal connections. In these cases the interference is present during the interval between stimulus and response. But hippocampal animals are also more susceptible to interference occurring between acquisition and a retention test, a design closer to Glick and Greenstein's (1973) experiment. Thus Winocur (1979) trained rats on a simultaneous discrimination between horizontal and vertical stripes. During the five-day training-retention interval, animals were given one of three kinds of experience: an insoluble problem with diagonal stripes and random 50 per cent partial reinforcement, reward for all choices with no stimuli present, or rest. Hippocampal animals were impaired in retention of the original habit only after the intervening insoluble problem. Note, however, that pre-training on the insoluble problem also gave rise to a hippocampal impairment in initial acquisition of the horizontal–vertical discrimination; thus Winocur's (1979) findings indicate that hippocampal lesions cause a general susceptibility to interference, not a retention deficit as such.

If hippocampal lesions produce retention deficits (for whatever reason), the question arises whether the deficit depends on the retention interval. The consolidation hypothesis (Milner 1968) proposes that it is specifically the laying-down of long-term memories which is disrupted by hippocampal damage. But the interference effects described by Jarrard (1975) and Thomas (1978) were found over comparatively short intervals (4 minutes). One report suggests that there may be some differentiation within the hippocampal formation of structures that subserve retention over relatively short or long intervals respectively: electrode implantation in the dentate gyrus impaired step-through passive avoidance tested either 15 minutes or 24 hours after acquisition, but electrodes in other parts of the hippocampal formation produced an impairment only at a 15-minute retention interval (Boast *et al.* 1975). As we saw above, Glick and Greenstein (1973) report data which suggest more rapid forgetting in hippocampal mice. The same construction can perhaps be put on Jarrard and Isaacson's (1965) observation that hippocampal rats displayed increased resistance to extinction at a 10-minute, but not a 10-second, ITI; or on the reports that the hippocampal deficit in certain spatial tasks is exaggerated by the introduction of a delay between trials (Racine and Kimble 1965; Sinnamon *et al.* 1978). But the effects of delay are task-specific. In the reports by Jarrard *et al.* (1964) and Jarrard and Isaacson (1965), for example, the *acquisition* of the running response was unaffected by ITI; so, if there was more rapid forgetting in the hippocampal animals, this affected only the non-rewarded trials of extinction.

Thus, even when retention deficits emerge after hippocampal lesions, they fail to support the view that the hippocampus acts as a *general* memory mechanism, they do not consistently implicate either long- or short-term memory, and they do not appear to be specific to the memory aspects of the task but to depend rather on other processes. Can we make any progress in defining what these processes are? Several suggestions have been made.

Winocur (1981) has proposed that, under conditions of high interference, hippocampal animals are unable (for unspecified reasons) to extract enough information from cues that are typically sufficient for controls. In consequence they become abnormally dependent on 'contextual cues', i.e. background stimuli that can be used to determine which of several possible responses to a common stimulus is correct in a particular context. In support of this view Winocur and Olds (1978) trained rats on a simultaneous discrimination between horizontal and vertical stripes and tested them after a seven-day retention interval either in the same or a different apparatus, and either under the same (food) or different (water) drive. There was a retention deficit only when conditions were changed between acquisition and retention testing. When reversal learning was substituted for retention testing, the opposite occurred: there was a large deficit in the unchanged conditions, only a non-significant one in the changed conditions. Thus, in accord with Winocur's hypothesis, hippocampal animals were excessively dependent on contextual cues for the maintenance of the behaviour they had first learned. A perhaps similar phenomenon was described by Fallon and Donovick (1970). Normally, septal lesions increase resistance to extinction (Chapter 6, Section 6.17); but Fallon and Donovick (1970) changed drive from food to water deprivation between the acquisition and extinction of a bar-pressing response, and the lesioned animals were now *less* resistant to extinction than controls.

A rather different suggestion, also concerning context, has been made by Hirsh (1974). According to this proposal, hippocampal lesions disrupt the 'contextual' retrieval of information from memory. Since this proposal has been somewhat neglected, and is rather technically defined, I shall go into it in some detail, largely in Hirsh's own words.

Contextual retrieval is defined as retrieval of an item of stored information initiated by a cue which refers to but is not necessarily described within the information that is retrieved. An example is indexing of library books according to their authors. This concept has strong implications for theories of how the brain controls behaviour. Understanding these implications requires defining and exploring the metaphysiological concept of the performance line. A performance line is defined as a system mediating the series of events or processes initiated by the overtly observable stimulus and resulting in the occurrence of the overtly observable response. It is considered to exist in real time and real space and ultimately to be physiologically observable.

S–R theories, as usually interpreted by physiological psychologists, hold that memory is stored upon the performance line. The stimulus is defined as activation by an environmental event of a neural system sensitive to it. Memory, or more exactly, learning, is held to result from the formation of a functional connection between the neural elements sensitive to the stimulus and those responsible for producing the response. This connection becomes the key part of the performance line for that particular combination of stimulus and response elements and is unique to it. . . .

When contextual retrieval is present it is no longer necessary to store acquired information upon the performance line. Information can be stored in a sequestered place or state free from interference by information processing being car-

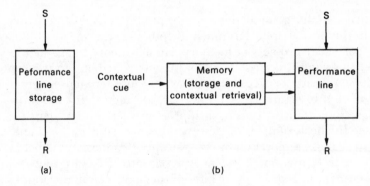

Figure 9.1. Schematic diagrams of systems using associative (a) and contextual (b) retrieval. S, stimulus; R, response. (From Hirsh (1974).)

ried out on the performance line. Schematic representations of systems with and without contextual retrieval are presented in Fig. 9.1. In a system with contextual retrieval, information can be moved from storage to the performance line independently, and thus before the occurrence, of the stimulus described within the retrieved information. . . .

It is assumed that when an item of information is contextually retrieved it is placed upon the performance line. Perceptual systems are adjusted to be particularly receptive to the stimulus described within the information. The object of attention is specified. In such a system behaviour is no longer completely controlled by environmental events because the perceptual systems are adjusted prior to the occurrence of the overtly observable stimulus. The potential of the retrieved stimulus description for controlling behaviour is considerably greater than that of non-retrieved descriptions. . . . By contrast, when memory is stored upon the performance line, no stimulus 'description' has more potential for controlling behaviour than any other until the event described actually occurs and initiates retrieval. . . .

It is also assumed that motor systems are adjusted to more readily produce the response described within the retrieved information as a result of contextual retrieval. . . .

When behaviour which conflicts with previous learning is acquired, the previous acquisition must be made inoperative when learning involves altering the performance line. The new and previous acquisitions cannot both be retained, as both would be activated by the stimulus. To avoid conflict at least part of the previously acquired learning must be removed from the performance line, usually by inhibiting one of its stages.

Systems utilizing contextual retrieval do not require deletion of previous learning. The conflicting items of information can be differentiated by the addition of a contextual label indicating that the previously acquired information was formerly true. . . .

The effects of hippocampal lesions are held to result from disruption of contextual retrieval. In the normal brain, storage is considered to be separate from the performance line. When the hippocampus is absent storage is held to occur within the performance line (Hirsh 1974, pp. 422–6).

We shall not at this stage follow Hirsh in applying this theory to the whole gamut of behavioural changes seen after hippocampal lesions; but, to anticipate, the general theory of septo-hippocampal function developed in the next chapter has much in common with his ideas. As applied to the particular problem of memory, Hirsh's theory treats the hippocampal deficit (when it occurs) as arising from an inability to use contextual labelling to decide between competing response tendencies under conditions of high interference. We have already seen that conditions of this kind are important in causing a hippocampal retention deficit; and we shall see further examples of this phenomenon later in the chapter.

Hirsh's (1974) application of the concept of context to the behaviour of animals with hippocampal lesions is apparently very different from Winocur's (1981); indeed, Winocur himself (personal communication) sees the two approaches as diametrically opposed. But a little reflection shows that Winocur and Hirsh use the term 'context' in different ways. For Hirsh, this is something the animal puts into the description of the stimuli to which it responds; for Winocur it is out in the environment. The processes that Hirsh ascribes to the hippocampus would play a particularly critical role in the control of behaviour when there are no large changes in the environmental context (discussed by Winocur) to assume this control. Thus Hirsh too would predict that a large difference in the environmental context of initial acquisition and reversal training would help the hippocampal animal to overcome its usual deficit in reversal learning, as found by Winocur and Olds (1978). So, from this point of view, rather than being opposed to each other, the two hypotheses are mutually complementary, and Hirsh's can be seen as specifying the reasons why, as postulated by Winocur, hippocampal animals are unable to extract enough information from cues that are typically sufficient for controls: they lack the process of contextual labelling and retrieval.*

It is not yet clear, however, that the concept of context takes us much further than the description of the hippocampal deficit as one of increased susceptibility to interference. Since interference effects have been studied most effectively with human subjects, we shall leave further examination of this topic until we deal with the clinical literature. Before we come to this, however, there remain two other approaches that have been applied to the animal data: Gaffan's (1972, 1974, 1977a, b) proposal that hippocampal damage disrupts 'recognition' memory, and Olton's (1978a; Olton, Becker, and Handelmann 1979a, b) that it disrupts 'working' memory. These two hypotheses, superficially rather different, turn out to have much in common, as becomes clear when one examines the experimental evidence that has been offered in support of each.

Gaffan distinguishes between, on the one hand, recognition memory or memory for familiarity and, on the other, the associative memory that is responsible for turning stimuli into secondary reinforcers, positive or neg-

---

*In line with this suggestion, Brown (1982) describes hippocampal units which, in rhesus monkeys trained on a conditional discrimination, responded or failed to respond to particular stimuli depending on the context in which these were presented.

ative (see Chapter 1). He proposes that hippocampal lesions disrupt only the former. This hypothesis is in many respects similar to Vinogradova's (1975), according to which the hippocampus subserves orienting responses to novelty and their habituation as the stimulus becomes familiar.

Olton also distinguishes between two kinds of memory. A task may require for its solution information which is constant from trial to trial or moment to moment; this is deemed to be held in 'reference' memory. The 'working' memory, by contrast, holds information which is also necessary for correct responding but which changes from trial to trial or moment to moment. A simple example is a delayed matching-to-sample task, in which the animal must (say) pick out of two stimuli the one that is the same as (or different from) a stimulus that it has seen some seconds, minutes or hours ago. From trial to trial the particular set of stimuli offered to the animal is altered, so that it must remember a different stimulus across each successive delay interval. This job is done by the working memory, and is attributed by Olton *et al.* (1979*a*) to the hippocampus. Conversely, according to this proposal, the hippocampus is not concerned with memory of those features of the matching-to-sample task which are constant from trial to trial (e.g. the nature of the reward, the required motor response, the matching-to-sample rule itself).

Let us deal first with Gaffan's hypothesis, that hippocampal lesions selectively disrupt recognition memory. In an initial experiment to test this hypothesis, Gaffan (1972) studied rats with lesions of the fornix-fimbria in a T-maze of which one arm was initially black and one white. One of the arms was then changed so that both were black or both white. As reported earlier (e.g. Ison, Glass, and Bohmer 1966), normal rats under these conditions chose the changed arm; but when a frightening stimulus (loud noise) was added on the choice trial, they preferred to enter the familiar arm. Animals with fornix lesions chose at random under both conditions. (Note the similarity of the result in the unstressed condition to the effect of sodium amylobarbitone described by Ison *et al.* 1966; see Chapter 2, Section 2.10.) Gaffan (1972) attributes these findings to a failure on the part of fornical rats to discriminate the familiar from the changed arm. But they are equally compatible with the spatial hypothesis of hippocampal function. Gaffan's later experiments avoid this problem by using nonspatial tasks.

In the first of these experiments (Gaffan 1974) fornix-lesioned monkeys were trained on delayed matching-to-sample with objects as discriminanda. The lesioned animals were as good as controls if the delay was set at 10 seconds, but there was a substantial impairment at 70 and 130 seconds. An impairment could also be produced at the 10-second interval if the animal was tested on a list of objects, rather than a single one. For example, at list length 3, with objects represented by letters, the animal was shown A, B, and C and then required to choose among A and D, B and E, and C and F, in that order. Fornix-lesioned monkeys were inferior to controls at all list lengths studied (3, 5, and 10). This finding is consistent with a disruption of recognition memory. But note that it is equally consistent with Olton's hypothesis; for, as we saw above, matching-to-sample is a paradigmatic example of a task involving working memory.

However, the remaining two tasks set to Gaffan's (1974) monkeys produced results which were more specifically in line with the distinction between recognition and associative memory. In one, the animal was initially presented with a set of 10 objects, one at a time, five of which were followed by reward (food) and five not. There then followed a retention test in which the monkey was faced with pairs of objects, of which one was constant and the other was one of the objects that had been presented initially. If the latter had initially been associated with reward, the animal's task was to choose it; if it had not, the animal was required to choose the constant object. Thus the animal was asked, 'Do you remember which objects were associated with reward, and which were not?'. As predicted by Gaffan, fornix-lesioned animals were not different from controls on this task. The other task was similar, except that the animal was initially presented with only five objects, all followed by reward. These five, and five others, were each then paired with the constant object; the animal was required to choose the previously presented object if it was a member of the pair, but the constant object otherwise. Thus it was asked, 'Do you remember seeing this object before?'. Again as predicted, fornix-lesioned monkeys were inferior to controls on this task. Furthermore, controls were better in the recognition task than in the test of associative memory, whereas the lesioned animals were better at association than recognition.

This kind of task is very similar to those used to study human memory. A subject may be presented, for example, with a list of words or pictures and later asked whether items on a second list did or did not figure in the first. Gaffan (1977a) designed another experiment to come even closer to this model. The monkey was shown 25 pictures (on slides) per daily session, each picture occurring twice. Order of presentation was randomized but the same slides were used each day. The monkey's task was to earn a food reward by pressing a panel only on the second appearance of each slide. This is analogous to asking a human subject to answer 'yes' or 'no' to the question, have you seen this picture earlier today?. Two rhesus monkeys achieved over 90 per cent accuracy even when an average of nine slides were presented between the first and second occurrence of any one slide. After fornix section they were able to achieve accurate performance only up to an average of three intervening slides. Note that it is precisely on this kind of yes–no recognition task that the human amnesic impairment is particularly pronounced.

In a final experiment Gaffan (1977b) explicitly compared a spatial and non-spatial versions of list learning. In the non-spatial version the monkey was successively shown three colours (transilluminated discs) followed three seconds later by one of six possible colours. Its task was to press one response panel if the test colour had been present in the sample set of three, and another panel if it had not. The spatial version consisted of the successive illumination of three out of six discs followed three seconds later by the illumination of one of them. The monkey's task was now to press one panel if the test disc was in the set of positions first illuminated, another panel if it was not. Fornix-lesioned monkeys were impaired on the two tasks to the same extent and in the same manner: they made a greater number of omission errors ('forgetting'), but only when the test stimulus was the first to have been presented in the initial list of three colours or positions. Both normal and lesioned monkeys showed a pronounced 'recency' effect, that is, their recognition was better the more recently the test stimulus had appeared (i.e., the later in the list). These results show the operation of retro-active interference (of the later stimuli with the earlier) and suggest that this was increased by fornix damage. Again this is similar to the human data which, as we shall see, clearly implicate an exaggerated susceptibility to interference in the amnesic syndrome.

A similar evolution in experimental design from more to less spatial tasks has taken place in Olton's work. The experiments were conducted in a radial-arm maze, an apparatus shaped like a wheel with the central hub and spokes but no outside rim. The rat's task in this apparatus is to retrieve a food reward from each arm. Once the food is taken, there is no point in revisiting the same arm for the duration of that trial, since it will not again contain food. The normal rat shows an impressive capacity to remember which arms it has already visited, even in a 17-arm maze (Olton 1978*a*). To achieve this high level of performance it appears not to rely on marking strategies (e.g. odour trails), response chaining or consistent response strategies (e.g. go to the next arm on the left). When intramaze cues are pitted against the general spatial environment provided by the experimental room, the latter usually dominates performance. Choice accuracy declines somewhat with successive choices within a trial. There is a recency effect, in that errors (revisiting an arm once visited) increase, the closer the first visit is to the start of the trial. But this recency effect is eliminated if the rat is confined to the centre platform of the maze for 20 seconds after each arm entry. There is no primacy effect (that is, no tendency for the first visit of the trial to be relatively immune to later error). If the animal is exposed to several trials within the same day (at a one-minute ITI), there is an increase in errors across trials; but the first visits at the start of each new trial are made with perfect accuracy. Thus, although there is pro-active interference between trials (earlier ones impairing performance on later), the rat distinguishes between the end of one trial and the start of the next. The distribution of errors in space is random.

From these observations Olton (1978*a*, p. 365) describes the characteristics of working memory as follows: 'Limited capacity, interference among contents, lack of decay for periods of up to several minutes, little if any serial ordering, and no generalization or confusion among items'. If the hippocampus is the site of this memory system, performance on the radial-arm maze should obviously be impaired after hippocampal lesions. But note that the same prediction follows from at least two other positions. The spatial theory would attribute to the rat the construction of a map of the maze which it uses to guide its responses: no hippocampus, no map. From Gaffan's point of view, Olton's maze offers the rat a list of spatial locations (established by the rat) and asks it to recognize those it has entered before (Gaffan, in Elliott and Whelan 1978, p. 403): no hippocampus, no recognition memory. It would be something of a disaster if such a well-founded prediction proved false. Fortunately, it does not. Lesions of the hippocampus, the fornix-fimbria, the entorhinal cortex or the septal area all profoundly impair performance in the radial-arm maze (Jarrard 1978; Olton, Walker, and Gage 1978; Olton and Werz 1978; Walker and Olton 1979). Evidence that the effects of entorhinal and fornix lesions are due to the resulting disturbance of hippocampal function comes from experiments in which each of these lesions was placed unilaterally. If they were both on the same side of the brain, performance was essentially normal; but unilateral destruction of the fornix and the contralateral entorhinal cortex produced as profound an impairment as a bilateral lesion of either structure alone or both combined (Olton 1978*b*). Thus, for successful performance in the radial-arm maze, the hippocampus has to have access, at least on one side of the brain, to both its major sets of connections, cortical and subcortical.

As in the case of Gaffan's experiments it is possible to eliminate at least one possible explanation of these results, the one offered by the spatial theory. This was demonstrated by designing a version of the task which depended for its solution on the use of intramaze, nonspatial cues (Olton, Becker, and Handelmann 1979*a*).

Intra-maze cues were made salient by having the sides of the arms 10 cm high and placing a unique set of visual and somatosensory stimuli in each arm. For example, one arm had black and white stripes in the floor and sides, and a groove 2 cm deep cut into the arm at each black stripe. Another arm had a diamond pattern painted on the sides and a smooth floor and sides. Extra-maze cues were minimised by lighting the inside of the maze, covering the top of the maze with cheese cloth and reducing room illumination to a low level. . . . An opaque guillotine door was placed between the centre compartment and the entrance to each of the arms. By lowering the doors, the experimenter could confine the rat to the centre.

All rats were first shaped to run out the arms with the maze in a stationary position in the room. They were then placed in an 'interchange' procedure as illustrated in Fig. 9.2. After the rat had chosen an arm and returned to the centre, the guillotine door in front of each arm was lowered confining him to the centre compartment. While the rat was confined, the arms were moved and their topological relationship changed. . . . After the arms were moved, the guillotine doors

TRIAL N   TRIAL N +1   TRIAL N + 2

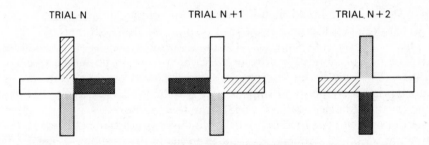

Figure 9.2. A diagram of the experimental design used in Olton, Becker, and Handelmann's (1979*a*) 'interchange' procedure. Each arm of the maze is indicated by a different pattern. After each choice the rat was confined to the centre compartment and the arms were moved while it was so confined.

were raised and the rat allowed to make a choice. When he returned to the centre, the guillotine doors were lowered and the arms interchanged again (Olton *et al.* 1979*a*).

These procedures ought effectively to have prevented the construction of any kind of spatial map. It follows that, if the spatial theory of hippocampal function is correct, animals with hippocampal damage should perform as well as controls in this task. But they do not: the impairment produced by destruction of the fornix-fimbria is as profound as it is in the usual radial-arm maze (Olton *et al.* 1979*a*).

The disruption caused by damage to the hippocampus or its connections, then, has nothing specific to do with memory for space. Is it specific to 'working' memory? In an effort to demonstrate specificity of this kind, Olton and Pappas (1979) made use of a 17-arm radial maze in which eight of the arms (the same on every trial) were never baited. Thus the rat had two things to remember: (i) the eight arms that were never, and the nine arms were always, baited at the start of a trial (reference memory); and (ii) the arms in the baited set that it had already visited on a particular trial (working memory). On Olton's theory, damage to the hippocampus should disrupt the latter but not the former. Lesions of the fornix-fimbria severely disrupted the working memory component of this task, as predicted. The reference memory component was also disrupted, but only transiently. Note that, as in Gaffan's (1974) experiment on association memory (see above), this finding contradicts any simple application of the hypothesis that hippocampal damage disrupts the ability to detect non-reward.* An animal with fornix lesions can learn not to enter arms that

---

*But note also that the discrimination between always-rewarded and never-rewarded arms in this experiment is a rather complex variant of a simultaneous discrimination; and we already know that this is not usually disrupted by hippocampal lesions (Chapter 6, Section 6.19).

are never rewarded (Olton and Pappas 1979), and it can remember which objects have been followed by reward or non-reward (Gaffan 1974).

These experiments, especially Gaffan's, bring us at last within hailing distance of the amnesic syndrome described after hippocampal damage in man. But only if the interpretation once placed on that syndrome — namely, that it is due to a complete and specific loss in the ability to form long-term memories (Milner 1968) — is wrong. For this interpretation does not apply to the memory deficits which are found in rats or monkeys after hippocampal damage. It is not even likely that memory *per se* is affected by such damage. As in tasks in which the hippocampal deficit is not centrally related to memory, the key factor which brings out a memory disturbance seems to be the existence of potent sources of interference. This is clearly apparent in Gaffan's (1977*b*) experiments on delayed matching-to-sample of colours and spatial positions. The deficit shown by the fornix-lesioned monkeys was confined to the item presented first in the list, the one most likely to suffer from retro-active interference. Although the role played by pro-active or retro-active interference in the hippocampal deficit in the radial-arm maze has not been investigated, it is evident that this technique is also one that provides multiple sources of interference.

If interference is a critical element, it is not one whose influence is limited to memory. On the contrary, we have seen several examples of a heightened susceptibility to interference in lesioned animals under conditions in which memory plays only a small role (see Chapter 6, Sections 6.19 and 6.22). Indeed, in some of these experiments the difficulty experienced by the lesioned animal seems to arise because it is *more* strongly affected than intact controls by what it first learned; thus, if anything, in these experiments the lesioned animal forgets rather than remembers too little. For example, Winocur and Mills (1970) showed that hippocampal rats were impaired in learning a simultaneous pattern discrimination only if they had first learned a brightness discrimination. Another example is Donovick *et al.*'s (1979) experiment on the effects of septal lesions. Rats were first trained on a simultaneous discrimination with either brightness or position as the relevant dimension. The other dimension was then used to add a second, redundant cue. Transfer of behavioural control to the added cue was impaired in septal animals. A third example is Kimble's (1975) analysis of the behaviour of hippocampal rats under various conditions of reinforcement in a Y-maze with one arm lit and the other unlit. Kimble scored his subjects as showing position or brightness hypotheses, depending on the consistencies linking their successive choices of arm. Hippocampal rats clung longer to whichever response strategy they first happened upon, and their subsequent behaviour in a changed environment was dominated by this strategy to an abnormal degree. And, of course, the extensive literature on the septal and hippocampal deficit in reversal learning (Chapter 6, Section 6.22) is abundant testimony to the difficulty the lesioned animal has in abandoning its old habits.

In the light of experiments such as these, it would be more reasonable to treat the retention deficits reported by Gaffan and Olton as part of a wider picture, in which susceptibility to interference plays a central role, rather than as indications that loss of memory (be it 'working', 'recognition', or some other kind) is itself the central feature of the hippocampal syndrome. If, in spite of this, one continues to speak of a memory impairment, it can hardly be specific to long-term memory. The difficulties of separating between long- and short-term memory in man are notorious (e.g. Baddeley 1981; Hitch 1980), and any attempt to transfer these concepts to the animal data is fraught with even greater problems. None the less, Gaffan's (1977*b*) monkeys were required to carry in their memory three colours for only about five seconds; if this is long-term, one wonders what short-term memory would look like.

What of the concepts of recognition and working memory favoured by Gaffan and Olton respectively? Do they help to account for the data? It is difficult not to be suspicious of both concepts, since they are formulated so differently, yet give rise to virtually identical experimental designs and can find support in essentially the same data (consider the descriptions, above, of Gaffan's experiments on matching-to-sample in terms of working memory, or Olton's radial-arm-maze in terms of lists of items to be recognized). None the less, it is possible to discriminate between the two concepts, as shown by Gaffan's (1974) experiment on associative memory. In that experiment (see above), the animal had to respond differentially to objects previously paired with reward or non-reward. Since these objects were presented in lists of 10, different each time, the task must have involved what Olton calls working memory. On Gaffan's theory, however, it does not involve recognition memory. Thus the fact that fornix lesions did not disturb performance on this task clearly favours Gaffan's view over Olton's. On the other hand, Olton's view has the advantage that it automatically takes account of the fact that retention deficits appear only when there are many changed items to be remembered. This feature was built into all of Gaffan's experiments, but it does not appear to have any basis in the concept of recognition memory. On the face of it, a disruption in this type of memory should affect a single item free from interference as easily as a list of items. Thus it is not clear that Gaffan's theory can account even for the findings in his own experiments. Recall, for example, that his fornix-lesioned monkeys were impaired on the recognition of a colour or position only if two other stimuli had intervened between presentation of the sample and the test stimulus. A disruption of the process by which one detects that a stimulus is novel or familiar should have affected items in any position on the list.

Even supposing that disruption of working or recognition memory could offer an account of all the observations in experiments directly concerned with retention, it is unlikely that either of these hypotheses can account for the great variety of other changes seen after septal or hippocampal lesions. Take but one example, the impairment in DRL responding (Chapter 6, Section 6.18). What is the requirement for recognition memory in this task which is not also present in many other bar-pressing experiments? And what is the requirement for working memory? The animal's task, *throughout* the experiment, is to delay pressing the bar until, say, 20 seconds has elapsed since the last press; but hippocampal or septal animals cannot wait. Olton *et al.* (1979*a*) try to apply their theory to this deficit in the following manner. 'The correct response changes during the course of the experiment. Within 20 seconds of the previous response, the rat should not press the bar. This flexible stimulus–response association is characteristic of working memory procedures.' Indeed, it is; and it may be that hippocampal lesions disrupt the animal's capacity to cope with 'flexible stimulus–response associations'. But to describe DRL as a working *memory* procedure is a purely verbal device. The flexibility required of the animal lies in the timing of its response, not in what it must remember.

The most general account of the hippocampal retention deficit that we can reach so far, then, is that this represents, and perhaps arises from, an excessive susceptibility to interference effects. This alters behaviour in a variety of situations, of which those that require retention of material over short or long periods constitute a subset. The impairment produced in this kind of task is not specific to space, nor to the need for long-term memory. To these tentative, and largely negative, conclusions, Gaffan's experiments permit us to add one that is equally tentative, but more positive: recognition memory is apparently more vulnerable to hippocampal damage than is memory for reinforcement. Armed with these conclusions, we can at last confront the clinical data.

The clinical data

The first problem is to know what the clinical data are. There are two major collections to choose from.

The first consists of observations on a few individuals who suffered extensive damage to the hippocampus. Reports concerning these individuals stem largely from the late 1950s and the 1960s (Milner 1970). There are few new subjects to study, precisely because the huge amnesic deficit described in the early cases more or less rules out this type of surgery for its original application, the relief of temporal-lobe epilepsy. Although there is some evidence that the critical focus for the amnesia indeed lies in the hippocampus (Milner 1970, 1971; Butters and Cermak 1975), the fact remains that all these patients had extensive damage to other temporal-lobe structures (including the overlying neocortex and amygdala). They had also been epileptic for a long time before surgery; although O'Keefe and Nadel (1978, p. 416) point out that there have been reports of amnesia associated with hippocampal damage but with no prior history of seizures. Thus the profound anterograde amnesia which followed surgery can only tentatively be related to hippocampal damage alone* (Weiskrantz 1978). The small number of patients who underwent the operation, and the lack of new cases, also makes it difficult to use them to test the various new hypotheses concerning the nature of hippocampal function which have emerged only in the last decade.

The second possible source of data is from patients suffering from Korsakoff's syndrome. Since these patients usually derive their symptoms from a history of prolonged heavy drinking, they are in moderately ample supply and likely to continue so. Thus they have provided the test bed for most of the newer approaches to the amnesic syndrome. It can be argued that their symptoms are sufficiently similar to those of patients with avowed hippocampal damage to make such experiments relevant to the enigma of hippocampal function (Weiskrantz 1978). But Korsakoff patients do not normally have visible pathology in the hippocampal formation; and the variable pathology which they do display is found in structures sometimes closely related to the hippocampus (e.g. the mammillary bodies; Mair, Warrington, and Weiskrantz 1979) but sometimes not (e.g. the dorsomedial and other nuclei in the thalamus; Victor *et al.* 1971). A recent report (McEntee and Mair 1978) has noted a specific reduction of metabolites of noradrenalin, largely of central origin, in the cerebrospinal fluid of Korsakoff patients. Since, as we shall see in Chapter 11, there is reason to link the behavioural deficits seen after lesions to the dorsal ascending noradrenergic bundle to its connections with the septo-hippocampal system, this report perhaps strengthens the case for considering the Korsakoff syndrome to be relevant to septo-hippocampal function; but the case remains tenuous.

Thus the relevance of either of these clinical groups to the hippocampus is clouded with uncertainty. It is for this reason that I have chosen to deal with the amnesic syndrome last in this survey of data relating to hippocampal function. For the same reason I shall not attempt a detailed review of the clinical literature, which has in any case been reviewed several times recently (Weiskrantz and Warrington 1975; Weiskrantz 1978; Butters and Cermak 1975; Baddeley 1981). Since our main interest is to determine the extent to which similar processes are at work in the animal with septo-hippocampal damage and in the human amnesic syndrome, we shall concentrate on recent experiments which have attempted to define

---

*In support of such a relationship, Gaffan (in Elliott and Whelan 1978, p. 396) points out that there are three reported cases of amnesia associated with bilateral damage to the fornix and no other bilateral damage to the brain. On the other hand, Horel (1978) marshals evidence implicating, rather, structures in the temporal lobe overlying the hippocampus.

more closely the fundamental impairment from which the amnesic patient suffers. For the reasons given above, these have largely used Korsakoff patients.

Three major principles emerge from this research. First, there is much that the amnesic patient remembers; furthermore, what he remembers is often what he might be expected to remember, given the animal data. Second, a powerful factor favouring the appearance of amnesic symptoms is the presence of sources of interference. Third, there does not appear to be any disruption in consolidation. These principles go a long way to bridge the gulf between the animal and human data. But before we allow ourselves to be seduced by them too readily, we should recall the 'practically irresistible' clinical impression that these patients 'cannot form a durable record of their new experiences' (Weiskrantz 1978). It is against this background that virtually any sign of learning is seized upon as evidence that amnesia is not complete.

Such signs of learning have now been seen under a diversity of conditions. The earliest reports concerned relatively simple motor tasks. Thus Corkin (1968) reported good learning to track on the pursuit rotor and to tap out a sequential pattern. These experiments were performed with 'H.M.', who, after his bilateral temporal lobectomy for the relief of epilepsy, has become one of the most closely studied patients in the history of medicine. Sidman *et al.* (1968), also studying H.M., used operant conditioning techniques (with money as the reinforcer) to establish good learning in a discrimination of circles from ellipses and in matching-to-sample with trigrams and ellipses. In the matching-to-sample tasks, however, H.M.'s performance deteriorated badly when a delay was introduced. With the ellipses, his deficit was severe at delays greater than 24 seconds; with the trigrams, his retention was normal for as long as 40 seconds, but he was noted to achieve this level of performance only with the aid of constant verbal rehearsal. Studying two amnesic patients, one with Korsakoff's syndrome and the other probably post-encephalitic, Weiskrantz and Warrington (1979) report successful eye-blink conditioning. In both this experiment and Sidman *et al.*'s (1968), retention lasted over a 24-hour interval. The two reports also have in common a striking dissociation between the learning and retention of a motor response, on the one hand, and verbal acknowledgement of learning, on the other: the patients could report no knowledge of the reinforcement contingencies controlling their behaviour, nor even of the general experimental arrangements in which they had taken part. This important observation must be borne in mind in any comparison of the effects of hippocampal damage in animals and man; for one obviously cannot demonstrate a disruption of verbal commentary on motor learning in animals that do not speak.

A further set of experiments in which relatively normal learning and retention have been seen in amnesic patients has used the method of cued recall (Weiskrantz 1978). In this paradigm the subject is given partial information about an item he is to recall and asked to identify the complete item. In different versions of the paradigm he is given fragments of a picture or word, the first few letters of a word, a semantic clue to the item, or the first of a pair of words that rhyme. With repeated exposure of the incomplete cue followed by the complete item, subjects require less and less partial information to identify the item, or identify it more rapidly, thus providing a learning curve. Alternatively, the cue can be presented at the time of retention testing. Using these techniques Warrington and Weiskrantz (e.g. 1970, 1974; Weiskrantz and Warrington 1970a, b) have demonstrated in Korsakoff amnesics learning which is not significantly slower than normal and which is durable over retention intervals of hours or days. Milner, Corkin, and Teuber (1968) reported a similar demonstration using incomplete pictures with H.M. The normal or nearly normal performance of the amnesic subjects is not simply due to the task's being easier, since they are disproportionately aided by the provision of cues (Warrington and Weiskrantz 1970, 1974).

These data prompted Weiskrantz and Warrington (1975) to propose an interference hypothesis to account for the amnesic syndrome. According to this hypothesis the amnesic does not forget or fail to consolidate what he learns. Rather, he cannot select the correct response out of a range of competing possibilities. When uncued free recall is tested, the poor performance of the amnesic is associated with a high rate of false positive responses. Thus Warrington and Weiskrantz (1968), testing memory for repeated lists of words, found that amnesics generated more false positives than controls, and that 50 percent of them were intrusions from previous lists. This observation is, of course, consistent with the animal literature (see above, and Chapter 6), which has frequently demonstrated that hippocampal lesions give rise to a difficulty in abandoning the response or strategy that is learnt first. On this view, the method of cued recall aids amnesic subjects by limiting the range of possible false positives. It is consistent wihth this hypothesis that the beneficial effect of cued recall is greater, the smaller the set of potential responses that it leaves open (Warrington and Weiskrantz 1974). When this set was reduced to one (by prompting with a set of three letters which can be completed by only one word in the English language), the so-called amnesics actually remembered better than controls over a retention interval of 24 hours (Warrington and Weiskrantz 1978).

In a test of the interference hypothesis, Warrington and Weiskrants (1974) designed an experiment to resemble the reversal learning paradigm which has been so consistently sensitive to hippocampal damage in animals (Chapter 6, Section 6.22). Recall was cued by sets of three letters which could each be the initial letters of only two English words. Subjects first learned a list consisting of one word from each of these pairs of alternatives; they were then reversed to the alternative list. Amnesics were not significantly different from controls in their retention of the first list; but they were severely impaired both on reversal to the alternative list and on reversal back again to the original one. Furthermore, this impairment was associated with an abnormal persistence in producing items from the first list learned. These results give good support to the interference hypothesis, and demonstrate that, under the right conditions, the behaviour of the human amnesic patient bears a striking resemblance to that of an animal with damage to the septo-hippocampal system.

Warrington and Weiskrantz (1978) have recently replicated these findings, but at the same time they point out a difficulty for the interference hypothesis. Reversal learning was tested on four successive trials, each with cued recall. As shown in Fig. 9.3, the amnesic group were as good as controls at remembering the first list but were impaired on reversal learning, replicating the earlier results. The problem for the interference hypothesis is posed by the fact that the amnesics were *not* impaired relative to controls on the *first* reversal trial, but only later. If their impairment were due to excessive interference from items learned on the first list, one might have expected the effect to be greatest on the first reversal trial. However, as Warrington and Weiskrantz (1978) suggest, 'it is possible that prior responses, while not stronger initially, may extinguish more slowly when a new response is required to the earlier cue, or indeed may decay more slowly over long intervals even when no response is demanded,' in the amnesic subjects.

Earlier in the chapter we considered Winocur's (1981) hypothesis that hippocampal animals are excessively dependent on contextual cues. This hypothesis has also been applied to the human amnesic syndrome (Kinsbourne and Wood 1975; Winocur 1981). It is difficult, however, to distinguish this approach from Weiskrantz and Warrington's (1975) interference hypothesis. Consider, for example, an experiment by Winocur and Weiskrantz (1976), in which amnesic subjects were tested on lists of paired associates (which they are usually very bad at learning), but with the possible set of responses constrained by a rule common to the whole list (e.g. that all pairs rhyme). One can regard such a rule as providing partial information, as in the cued recall experiments described above; or, equally naturally, as providing a context, namely, the one made up of the set of words with the same sound as the stimulus word. On either view, amnesics should learn a list made up in this way more effectively than they do usually; and this in fact was the case (Winocur and Weiskrantz 1976). As in Warrington and Weiskrantz's (1974, 1978) experiments on reversal learning, the patients were severely impaired when required to learn a second list sharing the same rule and initial words as the first; and they showed a strong tendency to produce false positive responses from among the associates learned in the first list.

A second experiment (Winocur and Kinsbourne 1978) derived more explicitly from the concept of context. Amnesics were tested on paired-

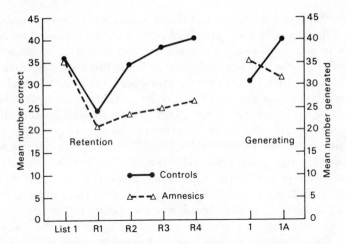

Figure 9.3. Left panel: 'reversal learning'. For each recall cue (the initial three letters) there were only two English words available as possible responses. Subjects were first taught one set of words (List 1) and then were given four trials with the alternative set (R1, 2, 3, 4). The same cues were used on all five trials. Right panel, generating scores: at the end of the reversal learning stage subjects were asked to produce two words in response to each cue. 1, recall of original list; 1A, recall of reversal list. (From Warrington and Weiskrantz (1978).)

associate learning under one of two conditions: in a standard experimental room with normal sound or illumination levels, or in a room illuminated only by a bright red lamp and with background music. When both learning and retention testing were carried out in the more unusual environment, the amnesic deficit was greatly reduced. Conversely, if amnesics learned two successive lists in two different experimental rooms, this reduced the degree to which their recall of the second list was impaired by prior learning of the first. In neither experiment was the behaviour of normal subjects affected by the context of learning. These results parallel those reported by Winocur and Olds (1978) using hippocampal rats (see above): the amnesic and hippocampal retention deficit is combatted by a strong context common to the conditions of learning and recall; the reversal deficit is combatted by a change in these conditions. In sum, the provision of a strong cue as to the correct response aids the amnesic to select it from among possible competitors. But there seems no good reason, either empirical or theoretical, to distinguish between the cases in which the cue is intrinsic to the item to be retrieved (cued recall by partial information) or extrinsic to it (contextual cueing).

Learning of one thing can interfere with the learning of another only if it is remembered. Thus it is implicit in the data and theories considered so far that there is no failure of consolidation in the amnesic patient. This assumption is supported by the fact that, as we have seen, under some conditions amnesics do learn and retain information over relatively long periods. A particularly long period of retention was reported by Milner *et al.* (1968) in an experiment in which H.M. had to learn a stylus maze with seven choice points. He was very slow to learn this task: but once he had learned it he showed 75 per cent savings over a two-year interval, in spite of the fact that (as in the experiments by Sidman *et al.* 1968, and Weiskrantz and Warrington 1979, described earlier) he had no verbally accessible memory of the maze at all. In general, rates of forgetting, if the level of learning is equated, do not appear to differ between amnesics and controls (Baddeley 1981). A further observation that is inconsistent with the consolidation hypothesis was reported by Warrington and Weiskrantz (1970, 1974) in their experiments on cued recall. If cues were provided only at the time of learning, recall was not aided; but if they were provided only at the time of retention testing, the amnesic deficit was greatly reduced. Thus cued recall aids retrieval, implying that the material has been stored, though not necessarily stored normally. A final point against the consolidation hypothesis is the evidence (Sanders and Warrington 1971) that amnesic patients have difficulty in recalling remote items antedating their illness; items such as these would presumably not only have been stored, but stored normally.

Amnesics, then, can learn and consolidate their learning; but their memories are excessively subject to interference from similar material. The trouble with this conclusion is that (given the ubiquitous role played in normal human memory by interference effects) it adds little to saying that amnesics have a bad memory. It would be comforting if we could delineate some more precise dysfunction in the amnesic syndrome.

Weiskrantz and Warrington (1975) have considered the possibility that interference arises because the amnesic subject is unable to suppress the response he first learns. This suggestion is closely related to the behavioural inhibition hypothesis as applied to the septo-hippocampal syndrome in animals. It has a number of advantages: it can account 'directly for intrusion phenomena, for the effectiveness of cued recall and other interference-limiting constraints, and for the preempting of present performance by earlier memories' (Weiskrantz and Warrington 1975, p. 424). Evidence against this hypothesis is the fact that false positive responses do not emerge on the first occasion when they can (as one would expect, if they are the primary cause of interference), but do so only gradually with repeated testing (Warrington and Weiskrantz 1978; see Fig. 9.3).

A second candidate is Gaffan's hypothesis that the hippocampus subserves the discrimination of familiarity. This accounts directly for the recognition deficit that is so prominent in amnesia. It can be applied to deficits in recall, if one assumes (plausibly) that this involves a stage in which an internally generated candidate memory is recognized as familiar or rejected as unfamiliar. But it has no natural application to the observation that amnesics are particularly strongly wedded to the first response they learn. And Warrington and Weiskrantz (1978), in their experiment on reversal learning (see above), present evidence against Gaffan's account of the deficit in recall. After reversal learning was complete, the subjects were asked to produce two words in response to each cue (recall that the cue consisted of the first three letters of only two words in the English language). As shown in the right-hand panel of Fig. 9.3, amnesics produced significantly fewer list 2 responses, although they actually produced more list 1 responses than controls. But if the amnesic deficit lies only in recognition, as proposed by Gaffan, there should have been no difference between amnesics and controls in *generating* items from either list. A further point against Gaffan's theory comes from an experiment by Brooks and Baddeley (cited by Baddeley 1981). They repeated Gaffan's (1974) experiments on recognition and association memory in the monkey (see above), using human subjects and pennies as rewards, but otherwise replicating his design. Unlike fornix-lesioned monkeys, amnesic humans were worse at associative than recognition memory.

A third proposal as to the nature of the underlying amnesic deficit is one that we have not met before. Butters and Cermak (1975) suggest that amnesic patients suffer from a disturbance in the process of 'semantic encoding'. Put like this, the encoding hypothesis is almost necessarily limited to the human case, since the notion of semantic encoding is closely tied to the details of experiments on verbal learning. It is supposed that, when a subject is presented with a word, he can commit it to memory after subjecting it to one or more of (at least) three different kinds of analysis: acoustic (what the word sounds like), associative (what it is associated with), or semantic (what it means). A link has been forged, it is true, between the notion of semantic encoding and the animal literature; for O'Keefe and Nadel (1978) suppose that the type of map which subserves spatial analysis in rats is used also to represent semantic and linguistic structure in man. But this link is a weak one, since a minimum condition for the application of the O'Keefe and Nadel (1978) theory to the human amnesic syndrome is that this should include a deficit in spatial ability; and this condition is not met (Milner *et al.* 1968; Weiskrantz 1978; Baddeley 1981). Thus, if semantic encoding were the chief deficit in the amnesic syndrome, the problem of relating the animal and human data would be acute indeed.

Much of the evidence on which the encoding hypothesis rests was gathered in experiments in which Korsakoff patients were required to learn serial lists of words (Cermak and Butters 1972; Cermak, Butters, and Gerrein 1973; Butters and Cermak 1975). In the earliest of these reports the list consisted of eight words, of which two were from each of four different semantic categories (animals, professions, etc.). Cueing by category name improved recall among controls, but not among Korsakoff patients. This is consistent with a failure of adequate semantic encoding at the time of learning in the patient group. Cermak *et al.* (1973) compared the effects on recall of rhyming and semantic cues respectively. Controls and patients were equally helped by rhyme, but the patients were less helped by category names. Associative cueing (e.g. 'table' as the cue for 'chair'), however, was as effective with amnesic subjects as with controls. Thus it appeared to be specifically semantic encoding that was deficient. A similar inference is suggested by an experiment in which the subject was asked to detect repetitions in a long list of words. Besides genuine repetitions, the list contained some homonyms, synonyms, and associates. Korsakoff patients made as many correct identifications as controls, and no more false recognitions of either synonyms or neutral words; but they made more false recognitions of both homonyms and associates. Butters and Cermak (1975, p. 393) take these results to indicate that 'The Korsakoff patients were encoding the words on acoustic and associative dimensions but were not encoding the semantic dimensions of the words to the extent that would allow the rejection of acoustically identical or highly associated words.'

Butters and Cermak (1975) pushed this analysis further by making use of the technique known as 'release from pro-active interference'. Wickens (1970) had shown that, in normal subjects, pro-active interference is reduced if the semantic category to which successive items belong is changed for a particular item in the list. Cermak, Butters, and Moreines (1974) showed that this held true also for Korsakoff patients, provided the change in category was relatively gross (from letter sets to number sets); but, unlike controls, the patients derived no benefit when the category shift was more subtle (from sets of animal names to a set of names of vegetables). If these results are generalized to all interference effects, they suggest that Korsakoff patients may suffer more from interference because they make fewer relevant distinctions between items.

Butters and Cermak (1975) make a strong case, then, for the view that a deficit in semantic encoding plays an important role in the amnesic syndrome. But, as pointed out above, if this case is accepted, it reopens a rather substantial gulf between the human and animal data. It is possible, however, that one further step in the analysis offered by Butters and Cermak (1975) can again close the gap.

This step is the suggestion that 'the Korsakoff patients' encoding deficits may be related to a general impairment in their ability to attend to the relevant dimensions of stimuli' (*loc. cit.*, p. 393). On this formulation, the deficit in semantic encoding is itself the manifestation of a wider difficulty, one that could in principle be found in other species. This proposal rests, however, on a slender evidential basis. Oscar-Berman and Samuels (1973, 1977) trained patients on a visual discrimination with stimuli differing simultaneously along four dimensions (form, colour, size, and position). After training was complete, transfer trials were conducted to determine which dimensions were controlling the subjects' choices. In comparison to other brain-damaged patients and normal controls, the Korsakoff patients made use of fewer stimulus dimensions, concentrating especially on colour to the exclusion of other possibilities. This may be the same phenomenon as the one described in hippocampal rats by Samuels and Valian (1968), who found that the lesioned animals were poorer than controls at transferring from a simultaneous discrimination in which brightness and position were perfectly correlated to brightness alone. A failure in multidimensional stimulus analysis might also underlie the excessive dependence on environmental context described in hippocampal rats by Winocur and Olds (1978) and in human amnesics by Winocur and Kinsbourne (1978). In these experiments, change in a dominant environmental cue produced a retention deficit, or conversely provision of such a cue eliminated the deficit. These findings are explicable if we suppose that, in hippocampal animals and human amnesics alike, a difficulty in multidimensional stimulus analysis prevents the subject from learning also about other, more subtle, cues in his environment.

Note that none of the stimulus dimensions studied by Oscar-Berman and Samuels (1973) was more 'semantic' than the others. Thus, if there is a common thread linking their findings to those of Butters and Cermak (1975), it has to be an impairment in multidimensional stimulus analysis that underlies a deficit in semantic encoding rather than the other way round. This view has the advantage that it offers a direct link to the animal data; for there are several indications that animals with septal or hippocampal lesions are deficient in the simultaneous analysis of several stimulus dimensions (see above, and Chapter 6, Sections 6.19 and 6.22). It is unlikely in any case that a deficit in semantic encoding is a necessary feature of the amnesic syndrome; for amnesics are sometimes helped by semantic cueing (Winocur and Weiskrantz 1976; Winocur 1981), and the benefit they derive from this is not necessarily less than that derived by controls (Mayes, Meudell, and Neary, cited by Baddeley 1981).

Our analysis of the human amnesic syndrome must rest there. As in the case of the comparable animal data, the only firm conclusion we can reach is that the amnesic patient is excessively sensitive to interference. But this leaves open the critical question of the origin of this sensitivity. Is it primary or secondary? If it is secondary, what gives rise to it?

A theory of septo-hippocampal function

The suspects are all in the living room, the clues all jumbled in our heads; but the plot remains obscure. The time has come to decide who did it, or rather what it — the septo-hippocampal system — does. As in all the best detective stories, the real culprit will emerge only when we have constructed a theory to account for 'all' of the evidence; but — as in most such stories — there are likely to be several messy loose ends that the theoretician conveniently overlooks. Let us begin where they always begin, by eliminating some of the suspects.

It is a good rule that the suspect you first think of is innocent. So it is with the hippocampus. The first suggestion to be taken seriously was Milner's consolidation hypothesis. But, apart from some of the studies using post-trial stimulation (Chapter 8), experimental work with animals has given it little support. And, even as an account of the human clinical data which engendered it, it is no longer as attractive as it once seemed. It seems clear that the hippocampus takes no direct part in the long-term storage of information. This conclusion is supported as strongly by the effects of lesions, which do not disrupt long-term memory as such (Chapters 6 and 9), as by single-unit studies, which demonstrate that hippocampal neurons are allocated afresh to novel environmental stimuli with a rapidity that is inconsistent with any obvious kind of storage function (Chapter 7). Both the animal and human deficits in recall or recognition after hippocampal damage now appear to arise from an excessive susceptibility to interference (Chapter 9). If this is so, the results of the post-trial stimulation experiments will need some other explanation than that offered by the consolidation hypothesis, if they are not to become the first of our loose ends.

Another good rule is that at least one of the late suspects is a false trail. In our case, this is Vanderwolf's voluntary movement hypothesis. The experiments on the behavioural correlates of slow-wave activity in the hippocampal EEG (Chapter 7) yield strong support for a relationship between theta, or more likely one kind of theta, and movement through space. Since the stimulation experiments (Chapter 8) show that theta is almost certainly an active state of hippocampal function, it follows that the hippocampus is doing something when the animal moves. However, the possibility that the hippocampus is concerned with the production or control of movement as such is excluded by the lesion experiments (Chapter 6). But, equally, the hypothesis that the septo-hippocampal system is concerned directly and exclusively with the inhibition of movement (which often receives support from the lesion data) looks much less plausible if the hippocampus is continuously active when the animal is in rapid motion.

The spatial theory offers a convenient way out of this impasse, since it allows the hippocampus to be doing something important (laying down and/or utilizing spatial maps) while the animal is moving, without requiring it either to produce or inhibit movement. This theory also receives support in its home base, among some of the single-unit studies of the behavioural correlates of hippocampal activity (Chapter 7). But consideration of *all* the single-unit studies makes it very unlikely that spatial mapping (if it occurs at all) is more than a specialized aspect of the general functions of the septo-hippocampal system. There are in any case data from other kinds of experiment which the spatial theory can accommodate only at the cost of quite acrobatic contortions. Thus lesions to the hippocampal formation disrupt behaviour in tasks from which all apparent spatial content has been removed (Chapters 6 and 9). Good examples are Webster and Voneida's (1964) report of impaired extinction and reversal of a simultaneous tactile discrimination; the many reports of an extinction deficit in the Skinner-box; and Gaffan's (1977*b*) experiment on the recognition of lists of colours.

Even when the task is a spatial one, the spatial theory cannot always offer an explanation of the detailed pattern of effects observed after damage to the septo-hippocampal system. Thus the loss of the PREE in the alley after septal (Henke 1974; Feldon and Gray 1979*a, b*) or hippocampal (Rawlins, Feldon, and Gray 1980*b*) lesions is not predicted by the spatial theory and contains features which run directly counter to O'Keefe and Nadel's (1978, p. 347) discussion of the phenomenon. And even when the predictions of the spatial theory are verified in a clearly spatial task, it turns out that elimination of the spatial element fails to alter the fundamental hippocampal deficit (Olton, Becker, and Handelmann 1979*a*). It remains true that spatial stimuli are powerful determinants of the firing of hippocampal neurons, and that spatially complex tasks are particularly good instruments with which to display the behavioural deficits produced by septal or hippocampal lesions. But this must be due to some feature of the relevant experimental situations other than space, a feature which can also be found in situations with a minimal spatial content.

We can reject, then, memory consolidation, voluntary movement and spatial analysis as accounts of septo-hippocampal function. Alas, no other suspect can be so readily eliminated. One problem is even to know how many other suspects there are. Several appear to shade rather easily into one another: is sensitivity to interference different from loss of contextual labelling, non-reward from novelty, detection of familiarity from recognition memory? Perhaps we are dealing with a master of disguises. Nor can we be certain that there is only one criminal: there could be a conspiracy. Non-reward or novelty might be responsible for the break-in, but behavioural inhibition for the break-out; and they might both use inside help (attention? multidimensional stimulus analysis?). Careful scrutiny of the distinguishing features of the remaining characters in the plot suggests, indeed, that we are dealing with a whole gang, of somewhat indeterminate membership, who work together rather than against each other.

When we consider this congeries of hypotheses, all more or less alike, a pattern recurs that we have seen before: they each explain some things well, but none can comfortably encompass more than a small portion of the data.

Consider first the motor version of the behavioural inhibition hypothesis, i.e. that the septo-hippocampal system inhibits motor output relatively directly. This is supported by many of the lesion experiments (see, for example, Chapter 6, Sections 6.2 and 6.7–6.13); and by certain observations (Chapter 8) of the effects of hippocampal stimulation (arrest of movement) and septal stimulation (inhibition of the hyper-reactivity produced by hypothalamic lesions). But it is difficult to make sense within the behavioural inhibition hypothesis of the continuous theta that an animal displays when it moves through space. And, even on its home ground of lesion effects, there are many results that this hypothesis cannot easily explain. Consider, for example, Donovick *et al.*'s (1979) experiment in which septal lesions prevented learning about a second redundant cue added to a simultaneous discrimination already controlled by a different cue; or the reports that septal or hippocampal lesions retard the habituation of a response with no motor component (Sanwald *et al.* 1970; Rogozea and Ungher 1968; Chapter 6, Section 6.13). Findings such as these suggest a difficulty in the intake of information rather than in the inhibition of responding. Note, however, that one has to search the literature carefully (or treat it with a strong bias, as in the Nadel, O'Keefe, and Black 1975 review) to find results which do not accord in some measure with the motor version of the behavioural inhibition theory. Thus it is likely that some aspect of this hypothesis will figure in any final theory of septo-hippocampal function.

The hypotheses that the septo-hippocampal system mediates the orienting response and its habituation (Vinogradova) and that it gates out redundant stimuli from the control of behaviour (Douglas) have much in common; and both are in many respects complementary to the motor version of the behavioural inhibition hypothesis. They gain support from the association of low-frequency theta with responses to novelty; while Vinogradova's (1975) observations of hippocampal and lateral septal unit responses to novel and familiar stimuli demonstrate that the septo-hippocampal system receives the information it would require if it is indeed to organize orienting behaviour or eliminate responses to unimportant stimuli (Chapter 7). But only a few of the findings in lesioned animals support this position, e.g. the loss of Kamin's blocking effect (Solomon 1977; Rickert *et al.* 1978) or of latent inhibition (Ackil *et al.* 1969; Weiss *et al.* 1974; Solomon and Moore 1975).

A critical point against Vinogradova's hypothesis is that there is very little evidence of change in simple orienting responses or their habituation after damage to the septo-hippocampal system. Most of the relevant data can be more easily accommodated by the generalization that motor responses to novel stimuli (as to stimuli of other kinds) are released from inhibition in the lesioned animal (Chapter 6, Sections 6.8–6.13). Thus it is probable that the apparently simple neuronal habituation described by Vinogradova (1975) underlies something more complex than simple habituation at the behavioural level. This inference is strengthened by a consideration of the experiments on Kamin's blocking effect. The normal animal fails to develop an association to a second CS if this is added to a first one which already predicts the same UCS (Mackintosh 1974); but animals with hippocampal lesions respond to the added CS (Solomon 1977; Rickert *et al.* 1978). This is probably not due to a simple delay in habituation of the response to the first CS, since Rickert *et al.* (1978) failed to alter the effect of hippocampal lesions by doubling the number of trials of training on the first CS. It is possible that, in the normal animal, blocking depends on a process that one might call 'instructed habituation'; that is, as a result of the discovery on the first compound-stimulus trial that reinforcement conditions have not changed, the redundant stimulus is identified as one to which attention need not be paid (Mackintosh 1978). Thus hippocampal lesions may disrupt this more complex kind of habituation. This hypothesis is consistent with Douglas's (1967) description of hippocampal function as that of gating out stimuli which are not predictive of reinforcement.

The Douglas–Vinogradova 'attentional' version of the behavioural inhibition theory easily shades over into at least two other hypotheses.

The first is the hypothesis that the septo-hippocampal system mediates responses to non-reward (Gray 1970*a*). Since non-reward must involve novelty (absence of the accustomed reward), this hypothesis is probably not fully dissociable logically from Vinogradova's; empirically, Amsel (1972) has in any case made out a strong case for the view that novelty and non-reward elicit essentially similar responses. Since these responses include inhibition of ongoing behaviour and increased attention to the environment (Chapters 1 and 2), the non-reward hypothesis is equally close to the motor and the attentional versions of the general behavioural inhibition theory. In the light of these similarities it is fruitful to apply the concept of habituation to the experiments on the PREE (Chapter 6, Section 6.17). It is possible to treat this effect as an instance of habituation to non-reward (Amsel 1962, 1972). In accord with this view, and with Vinogradova's (1975) observations on hippocampal and septal unit responses during repetitive sensory stimulation (Chapter 7), hippocampal (Amsel *et al.* 1973; Rawlins *et al.* 1980*b*), total septal (Henke 1974, 1977) and lateral but not medial septal (Feldon and Gray 1979*a*, *b*) lesions disrupt the PREE. This pattern of results suggests that, just as habituation of single-unit responses depends on the passage of information from the hippocampus to the lateral septal area (Chapter 7), so does the development of tolerance for frustrative non-reward. This suggestion is elaborated later in the chapter.

The second close relative of the Douglas–Vinogradova position is Gaffan's (1972) recognition memory hypothesis. Since this proposes that the hippocampus is a mechanism for detecting novelty/familiarity, it is at first sight indistinguishable from Vinogradova's orienting reflex hypothesis. It can be distinguished, however, from Douglas's (1967) position because, according to Gaffan, the hippocampus is involved in the recognition of familiarity whether this results in the production or the inhibition of a response, whereas Douglas supposes it to be concerned only with the latter. In practical terms, since Gaffan has largely been concerned with memory, the difference between the two hypotheses comes down to the question whether the recognition errors made after hippocampal lesions consist essentially in false positives (as predicted by Douglas) or equally often in false positives and omission errors (as predicted by Gaffan). The data (reviewed in Chapter 9) give clear support to Douglas on this point: the hippocampal memory deficit consists largely of false positives, and these are heavily influenced by sources of interference in the experimental task.

As we saw in the last chapter Olton's concept of working memory is operationally very close to Gaffan's concept of recognition memory. The feature which unites them, and sets them apart from Vinogradova's simpler treatment of novelty, is their concern with renewable lists (although, in Gaffan's case, this appears to be a matter of experimental practice rather than, as in Olton's, central to the theory). Such lists require the subject to answer, not just the question 'is this stimulus novel or familiar?', but also 'is it more or less familiar than that one?', or 'is it *relatively* novel (within the last day, hour, or few minutes)?' Thus, if the hippocampus is the organ responsible for successful performance in tasks of this kind, it must be given additional properties besides those necessary just to control the orienting reflex and its habituation. As a general account of hippocampal function, this approach cannot take us far, since it has no obvious application to the majority of simpler tasks which have regularly disclosed deficits in hippocampal rats or mice. On the other hand, there appears to be something about lists, and especially lists that require recognition memory as defined by Gaffan (1977a, b), which provokes a particularly profound and enduring deficit in the performance of hippocampal animals (Olton et al. 1979a, b).

Note that a natural link exists between Gaffan's recognition memory hypothesis and earlier research on the orienting reflex (Sokolov 1960). This research showed that, although the response to a repeated neutral stimulus habituates, habituation can be prevented for an indefinite period by turning the stimulus into a Pavlovian CS. Recall that this treatment also guarantees that the stimulus continues to evoke unit responses in the hippocampal formation (Chapter 7). Observations such as these imply that habituation of the orienting reflex (both behavioural and 'hippocampal') is under higher controls which are sensitive to the associative significance of stimuli. These controls might be of cortical origin (Sokolov 1960; see Chapter 13) or they might form part of the hippocampal circuitry itself; and there are of course other possibilities (see Chapter 11). Performance on a renewable list, of the kind used by Gaffan or Olton, might similarly depend on this type of higher control over a hippocampal circuit whose basic function is that of producing or habituating orienting responses under simpler conditions. For this kind of control to work it would be necessary that habituation of the orienting reflex could both be cancelled (at each new presentation of a previously encountered list) and expedited (when an item within a given list presentation has been processed sufficiently for that trial). It is possible that the second of these processes is also responsible for 'instructed habituation' in the Kamin blocking effect, as discussed above. By analogy, therefore, we can call the first process (cancellation of habituation) 'instructed dishabituation'.

The theory

In trying to integrate these different views and their supporting data, I shall make the following assumptions.

First, there is no long-term storage of information in the hippocampal formation. This assumption has been discussed above.

Second, the septo-hippocampal system plays no role in the initial learning of responses to new stimuli (provided there is no confusion with or interference from similar stimuli or responses). This assumption is justified by the data reviewed in Chapter 6, which provided no evidence of impairments in initial learning after either septal or hippocampal lesions.

Third, the septo-hippocampal system receives much information about behaviour which it does not at the time control. The single-unit studies reviewed in Chapter 7 showed that, if a stimulus achieves special significance for the animal (as when it is turned into a Pavlovian CS or the cue for an instrumental response), habituation of the unit responses it elicits is prevented; indeed, such stimuli appear to receive a privileged passage around the hippocampal circuit (Fig. 3.5). But the experiments reviewed in Chapter 6 demonstrate that precisely those tasks (simple classical or instrumental conditioning) which protect stimuli from habituation in the hippocampal circuit are immune to disruption by septal or hippocampal lesions. Similarly, the occurence of a pronounced theta rhythm during voluntary movements (Chapter 7) suggests that the hippocampus is extremely active at such times; yet destruction of the hippocampus or elimination of the theta rhythm by septal lesions leaves voluntary movement unaffected.

The fourth and central assumption is one which commanded maximum support at the recent Ciba symposium on septo-hippocampal function

(Elliott and Whelan 1978, pp. 418–19): that the septo-hippocampal system acts as a comparator.

The hypothesis that the hippocampus acts as a comparator has been developed most extensively by Vinogradova (1975). According to her (see Chapter 7) area CA 3 acts as a detector of novelty/familiarity. But the lesion evidence makes it clear that the hippocampus does both less and more than detect novelty: less, because at the behavioural level the orienting reflex and its habituation are not disturbed to any great degree after hippocampal lesions; more, because the kinds of behavioural disruption which *are* seen after such lesions suggest that the hippocampal formation makes other comparisons besides simple judgments of familiarity (consider, for example, experiments on reversal learning, or on two-way active avoidance). However, if the hippocampal formation makes other and perhaps more complex comparisons, it is unlikely that these are conducted exclusively in the CA 3 comparator described by Vinogradova. For, on her own evidence, the kind of information processing that is undertaken in CA 3 is insufficiently detailed to allow decisions that go much beyond 'novel' or 'familiar' (this point is amplified below). Thus, although the theory we shall develop here incorporates Vinogradova's CA 3 novelty comparator, it treats this as only part of a more extensive system.

According to the theory, the function of this system is to compare, quite generally, actual with expected stimuli. In this monitoring capacity, it functions continuously; but it controls behaviour directly only under special conditions. Thus it has two modes of operation: 'just checking' (not controlling behaviour) and 'control' mode (directly controlling behaviour). The main part of the system is a second comparator (described below), additional to Vinogradova's; the CA 3 novelty comparator is seen as auxiliary to this one, sending on to it for further, more detailed analysis only signals that have special importance. The function of the second comparator is, so to speak, trouble-shooting. It is called into play when the animal's normal routine (or 'plan', in Miller, Galanter, and Pribam's 1960 term) is interrupted by one of several adverse conditions, notably, novelty, non-reward, error, or punishment. Its task is then to work out what has gone wrong so that existing plans can be applied again or new ones substituted. The relationship of these ideas to the behavioural inhibition system described in Chapters 1 and 2 will be clear, as also their resemblance to commonsense notions of anxiety. But the purpose of the theory is to account for the data on the septo-hippocampal system, not for anxiety, and it must stand or fall in the first instance by its success in this endeavour.

Before we search for such a comparator in the hardware of the septo-hippocampal system, let us consider what kinds of information processing are necessary for it to be able to perform its functions (Fig. 10.1).

Clearly the comparator must have access to information about both current sensory events ('the world') and expected ('predicted') events. These

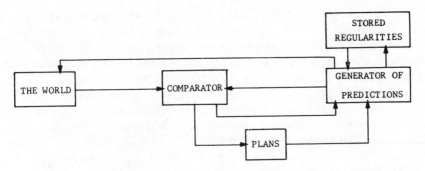

Figure 10.1. The kinds of information processing required for the successful functioning of the hypothetical comparator. (See text for further explanation.)

two classes of information must, however, themselves be closely inter-related. Predictions can only be generated in the light of information about the world. Thus current sensory events must be transmitted to the 'generator of predictions'. In addition, the latter must have access to information about past environmental regularities which, in conjunction with the current state of the world, determine the content of the next prediction. But this will be sufficient only if the environment is one over which the subject has no control (for example, in one of Vinogradova's habituation experiments). If, as in most cases, the subject's behaviour affects its world (as when it runs in a maze or presses a bar), the generator of predictions must also have access to information about the next intended set of movements, i.e. plans or motor programmes (Brooks 1979). Prediction will now depend on the conjunction of the present state of the world, stored past environmental regularities, the next intended step in the motor programme, and stored past relationships between such steps and changes in the environment.

In either event, once made the prediction must be tested against the world. For this to be possible, the right sensory inputs must be chosen. If the next predicted event is a card bearing horizontal stripes, it cannot usefully be compared to information received along auditory or olfactory channels; and if the prediction further states that the card will be at the northern end of an alley, it is no use looking in the southern end. It follows that the sensory information fed to the comparator must be selected in the light of what is predicted. This implies that selection is controlled by the generator of predictions and/or the comparator itself. The selection can be accomplished in principle in one of two ways. The subject's motor behaviour can be left under the control of other systems, and selection accomplished by choosing among the sensory events which occur anyway as a result of that motor behaviour; this must be the predominant method of selection when the comparator operates in the 'just checking' mode. Alternatively, the selection mechanism can take active control of the animal's motor behaviour and command appropriate exploratory action. This might range from simple adjustments of sensory organs (e.g. dilation of the pupils) to complex patterns of locomotion. In certain cases a compromise might be possible (e.g. the animal might continue to run towards the goal-box of an alley to obtain food, while sniffing at the sidewalls to verify a prediction for the comparator). However selection is accomplished, it must be accomplished at the right time. A comparator can work only if the elements it compares reach it more or less simultaneously. Thus the system must have some way of quantizing time and serially ordering both predicted and actual events.

According to the theory presented here, the septo-hippocampal system is responsible for both the generation of predictions and the comparison between these and actual events. It follows from the arguments presented above that it must also be responsible for selecting the sensory input that is appropriate to the prediction under test. Along with virtually all students of hippocampal function we shall assume that the entorhinal area, via the perforant path, is the source of this sensory input; this is supported both by the anatomical evidence (Chapter 3) and the single-unit studies (Chapter 7). Other major assumptions of the theory are that the septo-hippocampal system does not normally exercise control over behaviour when a series of expectations is confirmed by actual events (except when these include punishment); that it normally does take control when expectations are disconfirmed ('mismatch'); and (following Vinogradova 1975, and O'Keefe and Nadel 1978) that the theta rhythm quantizes the operation of the comparator in time.

In order to see how this theory can be applied to the available data it is necessary first to distinguish between four grossly different cases; for ease of exposition I shall call them 'scenarios'.

Scenario 1   The animal is in a totally new environment. Under these conditions there can as yet be no predictions for the comparator to match against current stimulation. It follows that the only task in which the septo-hippocampal system can engage is the gathering of information which will make subsequent prediction possible.

Scenario 2   There exists a set of expectations which continue to be verified by current sensory input. Under these conditions, according to the theory, the septo-hippocampal system exercises no control over behaviour.

Scenario 3   The comparator detects a mismatch between expected and actual events. Under these conditions the septo-hippocampal system assumes direct behavioural control. Major features of this control consist in the active inhibition of motor behaviour and the execution of information-gathering behaviour with the aim of resolving the discrepancy that has emerged between expectation and outcome. It is supposed that (except under special circumstances) an animal would not intend to execute a behaviour pattern that eventuates in aversive stimulation; thus the occurrence of stimulation of this kind constitutes a 'mismatch' for the purposes of the theory, even when it is predicted.

Scenario 4 After the discrepancy has been resolved behavioural control passes back to other systems which may, however, receive updated information as a result of the activities of the septo-hippocampal system.

We now consider each of these scenarios in more detail.

Scenario 1: exposure to a novel environment

I have already commented on the lack of change in simple orienting responses or their habituation after septal or hippocampal lesions (Chapter 6, Sections 6.9, 6.10, and 6.13). Leaving aside the frequently observed phenomenon of motor disinhibition in novel environments, the few reports of a slight retardation in habituation or of a reduction in the GSR in lesioned animals can hardly be considered as evidence of a fundamental disruption in the intake of information about novel stimuli, as required by Vinogradova's hypothesis. Yet at the same time it is clear from the EEG and single-unit experiments (Chapter 7) that the hippocampus is engaged at such times in registering novel events, and, if they have no special significance, in registering this fact as well, by habituating the neural responses they evoke. Assuming that the hippocampus does not do this out of idle curiosity, we may suppose that the information so registered will be of value to its later activities. This does not mean that the hippocampus *stores* this information for future use; and we have already made the contrary assumption. This assumption is supported by the rapidity with which hippocampal units picked out at random by the experimenter's electrode respond to stimuli in a totally new environment (Hill 1978); this could not happen if many units were already dedicated to the storage of previously acquired information. Thus it is more likely that the hippocampus passes on the information it receives for storage elsewhere, perhaps after tagging it in ways we shall consider later. Much the same arguments apply if we consider the earliest learning of simple classical or instrumental conditioned responses. The single-unit data make it clear that such associational connections are registered by the hippocampus; the lesion data make it clear that the septo-hippocampal system plays no role in the acquisition of the learned response. Given the anatomical connections of the septo-hippocampal system, the most likely site of storage (whether of information about familiarity or about simple conditioned associations) is the temporal lobe, to which the hippocampus has access via its projections to the entorhinal cortex from CA 3 and the subiculum

(Chapter 3). The temporal lobe has been implicated in storage processes, in part by the same evidence which apparently implicates the hippocampus, but also by other evidence (Horel 1978).

The major functional disturbance found when septal or hippocampal animals are tested in novel situations is a disruption in the patterning and flexibility of active exploration of spatially extended environments (Chapter 6, Section 6.12). This is a major point of support for the spatial theory of hippocampal function. Unfortunately, there appear to be no reports of the effects of septal or hippocampal lesions on the active exploration of complex, but non-spatial environments. How would a hippocampal rat differ from a normal one, for example, if different patterns of responding on a bar produced different patterns of visual, auditory, or olfactory stimulation? Without such information it is not possible to judge whether the deficit in exploratory behaviour observed in spatial tasks is specific to space. But, even in a spatial environment, it is not the case, as O'Keefe and Nadel (1978, p. 242) suggest, that 'in the absence of the hippocampus all forms of exploratory behaviour . . . disappear from the animal's repertoire'. The lesioned animal still explores and indeed learns its way about. The chief difference from normal behaviour is that its pattern of exploration is less flexible, less well adapted to ensuring that all parts of the environment are visited. I shall consider how these effects can be explained within the present theory later (see Scenario 3).

Scenario 2: just checking

In this scenario there is a set of expectations, already established, and these continue to be verified by current sensory input. It is necessary first to distinguish two subvarieties of this case. In the first, the animal does nothing much to change its environment, and this simply lives up to expectation (as, for example, in a habituation or classical conditioning experiment). In the second, the animal has a familiar response routine (e.g. running in an alley or complex maze, pressing a bar). The second of these is more interesting and has been subjected to more intensive empirical study, so we shall take it for our principal object of analysis. Consider as a concrete example a rat running in an alley for a food reward on a simple CRF schedule. That the hippocampus is active under these conditions is indicated by the continuous high-frequency theta which is observed as the rat runs to the goal; and the data from single-unit experiments make it probable that a probe inserted into the hippocampus during this behaviour would encounter what O'Keefe and Nadel (1978) call 'place' and 'displace' units (Chapter 7). Yet we know that a rat without a hippocampus or without the septal area (and so the theta rhythm) runs just as efficiently as an intact animal. We must suppose, therefore, that the hippocampus is not controlling this behaviour; it is 'just checking'.

It is worth speculating in more detail exactly how it might do this checking.

Following the arguments outlined above (Fig. 10.1), the hippocampus must generate a prediction about the next event (e.g. the rat's nose crossing a photo-beam placed half way down an alley when it has travelled a further 10 centimetres) on the basis of information about the current state of the world, information about intended movements, stored regularities relating successive sets of stimuli along the alley, and stored regularities relating these stimuli to the animal's movements. As these regularities are not stored in the hippocampus itself, the information concerning them has to be fetched from somewhere else. Information about intended movements must presumably be fetched in the same way. Information about the current state of the world is presumed to enter the hippocampus via the perforant path. But, as already indicated, this information is likely to be highly selected under hippocampal control. Thus the hippocampus must also send instructions to the entorhinal area concerning the particular sensory information it is seeking. Once these items of information are all available, they can be used to generate a prediction (in our example, the one about the nose and the photo-beam). This prediction must arrive in the comparator at the right time to be matched with the next item of incoming sensory information; as we have seen, this implies that the prediction has to be time-tagged. The matching sensory input must similarly be selected to arrive at this time, again by hippocampal control over the perforant path input. We may now begin to see why, as I put it in Chapter 3, the septo-hippocampal system is remarkably well-equipped for talking to itself.

Can we make any guesses about its internal telephone lines?

To simplify matters a little we suppose (as illustrated in Fig. 10.1) that the same neural message that identifies the current state of the world, once it has been matched successfully with the relevant prediction, also serves as information to help generate the next prediction. Thus we need to look for a place where an incoming message which started out in the entorhinal cortex can both: (i) terminate a loop, by identifying the current state of the world which has to be matched against a prediction which has already circled round the loop; and (ii) initiate a loop, to commence generation of the next prediction. The subicular area appears ideally suited for this purpose (Fig. 10.2). Information reaches it from CA 1 after passage around the basic hippocampal circuit (Fig. 3.5), i.e. from the entorhinal area to the dentate gyrus via the perforant path, thence to CA 3 via the mossy fibres, and on to CA 1 via the Schaffer collaterals. It is then recirculated through the fornix to the mammillary bodies, the anteroventral thalamus, the cingulate cortex, and back to the subicular area; in addition, there is a smaller loop providing direct two-way connections between the subiculum and the anteroventral thalamus. Thus a plausible hypothesis accords the status of comparator to the subicular area: the input from CA 1 identifies the current state of the world (though we shall need to qualify this assumption later); its recirculation around the 'su-

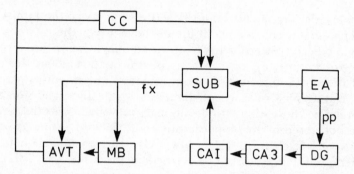

Figure 10.2. Connections of the subicular area which might allow it to function as a comparator. AVT, anteroventral thalamus; CC, cingulate cortex; DG, dentate gyrus; MB, mammillary bodies; SUB, subicular complex; fx, fornix; pp, perforant path.

bicular loop' just described forms part of the process of prediction generation; and arrival in the subicular area of the input from the cingulate cortex (perhaps in conjunction with the direct input from the anteroventral thalamus) constitutes the prediction.

Although this proposal is obviously speculative, it can draw support from certain observations already in the literature. Vinogradova (1975) reports that neurons in two way-stations on the subicular loop (the mammillary bodies and the anteroventral thalamus) extrapolate features of regularly repeated stimuli and fire as though an accustomed stimulus had been presented even when this has been changed in some way or even totally omitted. This is precisely what would be expected of a mechanism whose function is to generate predictions. In the cingulate cortex there are two reports of unit responses which are also consistent with this hypothesis. Niki and Watanabe (1976) recorded unit responses during the delay period while monkeys performed a delayed behavioural response; cingulate units fired in relation to the cue (no longer physically present) or the direction of the impending response. Gabriel, Miller, and Saltwick (1977) recorded multiple-unit responses in rabbits during a discriminated active avoidance response in a running wheel. The rabbit's task was to run in response to S+ but not to S− (tones of different frequencies). After acquisition the significance of S+ and S− was interchanged. In both the cingulate cortex and the anteroventral thalamus unit responses differentiated between S+ and S− during acquisition, firing at a greater rate to S+. At the start of reversal learning neuronal firing in both structures showed an even stronger discrimination between the two stimuli, and this continued to be appropriate to the *old* learning. Behavioural reversal was accomplished with no change in the pattern of unit responses in the cingulate cortex, and only incomplete reversal of the pattern of firing of thalamic neurons.* Thus these data support a role for the subicular loop in the generation of predictions from old learning. At the same time, they suggest that action in response to mismatch is accomplished after information has already circulated round this loop, presumably in the subicular area itself.

Following arguments outlined above, if the subicular loop subserves in this way the generation of predictions, it must have access to stored regularities concerning the environment and concerning the relations between the animal's responses and the environment. It is possible that these stored regularities take the form of changed probabilities of the firing of neurons at different points in the subicular loop itself, in the general manner suggested by Horn (1967, 1970) in discussing neuronal models of habituation. But more elaborate machinery is almost certainly required. It is plausible to see the anteroventral thalamus as a point of access for response-independent environmental regularities; the general importance of the thalamus in the organization of sensory information is well known. Where response-independent regularities are concerned, it is possible that the cingulate cortex, which has close relations with motor systems (Domesick 1969; Swanson 1978), plays this role. A generator of predictions must have information, not only about past dependencies between responses and outcomes, but also about current and intended responses. This information might also be available in the cingulate cortex, where it could function as part of the subicular loop. Alternatively, this region or the prefrontal cortex (see Chapter 13) might send relevant motor information to the entorhinal area, to which both project. In that case information about current and intended movements would form part of the description of the world which initiates the generation of predictions. Conceivably both routes are used, current movements entering into the entorhinal description of the world, intended movements taking part in the generation of predictions as the subicular loop sweeps past the cingulate cortex.

In the preceding paragraph I described the anteroventral thalamus and the cingulate cortex as 'points of access' to stored regularities. This deliberately vague phrase is compatible with two interpretations. According to the first, the relevant information is stored locally in these regions; according to the second, it is stored elsewhere and is simply activated by messages originating in the thalamus and cingulate area. This second point of view is implicit in the assumption made earlier (Scenario 1) that, after the hippocampus has analysed a new environment, it sends relevant information (concerning, for example, stimulus–stimulus or response–stimulus associations) for storage in the temporal lobe. Note that the temporal lobe projects directly to the subicular area (Van Hoesen *et al.* 1979).

Note added in proof: Gabriel *et al.* (1980) have recently reviewed these and many other findings reported by this group. Many of their observations, and some features of the theory they advance to explain them, are consistent with the general account offered here.

Thus we should perhaps expand our notion of the subicular loop to include a further way-station (concerned especially with storage) in the temporal lobe. A prediction arriving in the subicular area might then be made up of elements arriving from the thalamus, the cingulate cortex, the temporal lobe, and the prefrontal cortex in any of several possible combinations.

If we pursue this line of thought we must next ask how the system effects the selection of the sensory inputs which are used both to verify and initiate predictions. Since such selection is likely to depend critically on whether or not the last prediction was confirmed or disconfirmed, it would be reasonable to seek it in a pathway emerging from the comparator itself. It is natural also to expect that this pathway will terminate in the region from which the sensory input to the system starts out. This argument leads us to postulate a pathway from the subicular area to the entorhinal cortex; fortunately, this pathway is already known to exist (Köhler *et al.* 1978; Segal 1977*e*). Thus it can be proposed that the subiculo-entorhinal projection is responsible for sensory selection under one of the two conditions we distinguished above, namely, when the control of motor behaviour remains with other systems.

There is one feature of this model which is so far ill-motivated. Why should the neural message representing the current state of the world be sent all round the hippocampal circuit (Fig. 3.5) to the subicular area, when it could just as well go by way of the direct entorhinal-subicular projection (Van Hoesen *et al.* 1979)? The hippocampal circuit must surely do more than act as a simple four-synapse relay between the entorhinal and subicular areas.

It is in fact in these four synapses that Vinogradova (1975) places the basic comparator function which she attributes to the hippocampal formation. The single-unit evidence, both her own and that of others, as well as the research which has followed evoked potentials around the hippocampal circuit (Chapter 7), gives strong support to her hypothesis that the function of this circuit is to habituate or preserve from habituation (depending on the importance of the message) signals emanating from the entorhinal cortex and destined for the subicular area. However, rather than seeing this function in isolation, we may regard it as a further part of the selection process whereby the subicular comparator receives only those items of information about the world which are important to its task. As we saw in Chapter 7, there appears to be a 'gate' located between the dentate gyrus and CA 3. This gate passes on stimuli which are novel, but not those which are familiar and lacking in behavioural significance (Vinogradova 1975); however, familiar stimuli are also passed on, if they have been associated (by classical conditioning) with events of primary biological importance, or if they are important in guiding the animal's responses.

Note, however, that the phrase 'passes on' in this formulation is imprecise. Vinogradova's experiments make it clear that the information which is processed in CA 3 is of a very non-specific kind. As she puts it, 'the neuronal reactions in CA 3 do not code (and consequently cannot transmit) information about the quality of their sensory input. Their activity appears to be a strong generalized regulatory signal, which may possibly exert modulatory effects on the output structures' (Vinogradova 1975, p. 10). It follows that, if the postulated subicular comparator depends only on information that reaches it via CA 3 to identify the current state of the world, it will be able to do at best only a crude job. A way out of this dilemma, and at the same time to allocate plausible functions to still other pathways in the complex network of hippocampal neurons, is to suppose that the dentate–CA 3 gate works in conjunction with the direct pathway from the entorhinal cortex to the subicular area. On this hypothesis, sensory information is sent simultaneously from the entorhinal cortex to the dentate gyrus and the subicular area. However, this sensory information is used by the subicular area for matching against predicted sensory input and for generating the next prediction, only if it also receives an 'enabling' signal from CA 1. This enabling signal is sent on only in connection with stimuli that are of importance to the animal; otherwise they are habituated (filtered out) during their passage through the dentate–CA 3 gate. In short, the direct input to the subicular area from the entorhinal cortex* describes the current state of the world, the input via the hippocampus determines whether this description is treated as important.

We saw in Chapter 7 that passage through the dentate–CA 3 gate is facilitated by both the noradrenergic and the serotonergic inputs to the hippocampus. We shall consider the possible behavioural roles played by these inputs in Chapter 11. For the moment let us note simply that, if the above analysis is correct, they increase the probability that a particular stimulus will pass through the hippocampal circuit to be presented to the subicular comparator. Thus they tag the stimulus with a label saying, as it were, 'important, needs checking'.

If we confine our attention to conditions which preserve a stimulus from habituation within the hippocampal circuit, we risk giving the impression that habituation is itself a passive process. Vinogradova's (1975) experiments make it clear that this is not so. As we saw in Chapter 7, she reports that disruption of either the entorhinal or the septal input to CA 3 prevents habituation of the neuronal responses in this region.

---

*It is also possible that the projection from the temporal lobe to the subicular area (Van Hoesen *et al.* 1979) plays this role, either in addition to the entorhino–subicular projection or instead of it. This would simply put the process described here one synapse earlier, with the temporal lobe now at the origin of both the sensory input to the subicular area and the enabling signal via the hippocampus. Still another possibility would place the description of the current state of the world in the direct entorhinal–CA 1 projection (Steward 1976), with the enabling signal passing from the entorhinal area to CA 1 via the dentate gyrus and CA 3; this would be consistent with Vinogradova's (1975) single-unit observations (see Chapter 7). Neither of these accounts changes the essential features of the present theory.

This implies that habituation depends on some kind of matching of these two inputs in CA 3. If we consider her findings in more detail, it seems that the changes which give rise to habituation take place on both the septal and the entorhinal sides of CA 3, but in rather different ways.

On the entorhinal side there is a gradual build-up of responses to repeated, unimportant stimuli in both the dentate gyrus and the entorhinal area itself. The build-up of response in these regions takes about the same number of stimulus presentations (2–12 in the entorhinal area, 15–20 in the dentate gyrus) as does habituation in CA 3 (8–15). This pattern of change illustrates the great selectivity with which the hippocampus is supplied with information. It is a form of selectivity, moreover, which fits well with the hypothesis that entorhinal inputs to the hippocampus are controlled by the output of the subicular predictive device. In agreement with this view, responses build up in the same way in the cingulate cortex, again taking about 8–15 trials to reach their maximum size. Indeed, such augmentation of unit responses seems to be a feature of the whole subicular loop (Fig. 10.3). This pattern of results suggests that 'familiarity' is generated by repeated passage of the same neural message around the subicular loop and back into the entorhinal area (Vinogradova 1975). This, of course, is exactly the kind of function we would expect our postulated predictive device to perform.

This formulation places the burden of habituation on the entorhinal side of the CA 3 gate. However, there is evidence that the septal area also plays an active role in the process of habituation. Unit responses in the medial septal area (the origin of the septo-hippocampal afferents) neither augment nor show much habituation. However, since the theta rhythm, which is controlled by medial septal neurons, is initially elicited by novel stimuli and then undergoes habituation, some changes must take place in the medial septal input to the hippocampus during this time. Lateral septal unit responses undergo habituation, which appears shortly after habituation in CA 3 neurons. Sectioning the fornix-fimbria disrupts normal habituation of CA 3 responses (Vinogradova 1975; Vinogradova and Brazhnik 1978); instead there is a gradual build-up of responses. Habituation in the lateral septal area is similarly replaced by augmenting responses after lesions of the fornix-fimbria. Since this lesion interrupts both the medial septal projection to the hippocampus and the hippocampal projection to the lateral septal area, it is not possible to determine whether normal habituation depends on the one projection, the other, or both. In a more complex experiment Hirsh (1973b) made similar observations: fornix-fimbria section increased the number of hippocampal unit responses to stimuli presented in a pseudoconditioning paradigm.

One interpretation of the overall pattern of results described above is that the medial septal input to the hippocampus is a signal of novelty (Vinogradova 1975), and that habituation depends in part on changes which travel from CA 3 to the lateral septal area, from thence to the

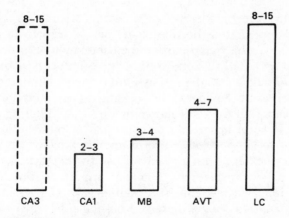

Figure 10.3. The rate of augmentation of unit responses in structures connected to the septo-hippocampal system. The structures are indicated below the bars: MB, mammillary bodies; AVT, anteroventral nucleus of the thalamus; LC, limbic (cingulate) cortex. Numbers above the bars indicate the mean number of repeated presentations of sensory stimuli necessary for responses to reach their maximum size. At the left, the rate of response habituation in field CA3 is shown by the broken line. (From Vinogradova (1975).)

medial septal area, and finally back to CA 3 (Fig. 10.4). It is consistent with this model that lesions confined to the medial septal area reduce motor orienting responses (Senba and Iwahara 1974) and spontaneous alternation, which may be interpreted as a response to the less familiar arm of the T-maze (Clody and Carlton 1969). McNaughton and Feldon (1980) have shown that the latter effect is not produced by lateral septal lesions, which leave the hippocampal theta rhythm intact, but is produced by medial septal lesions which abolish theta. Also consistent with the model is the report by Köhler (1976*b*) that lateral but not medial septal

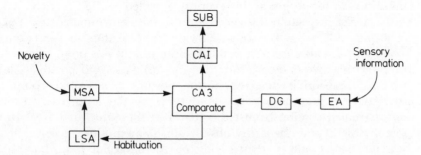

Figure 10.4 Vinogradova's CA3 comparator of novelty. See text for explanation. DG, dentate gyrus; EA, entorhinal area; LSA, lateral septal area; MSA, medial septal area; SUB, subicular area.

lesions retarded the habituation of a motor orienting response. This worker also demonstrated the role of the perforant path in habituation, since transection of this tract retarded the habituation of locomotor exploration of a closed box (Eriksson, Köhler, and Sundberg 1976).

From the present point of view, as we have seen, Vinogradova's CA 3 comparator serves an auxiliary role, passing novel stimuli along for the particular attention of the subicular comparator and filtering out familiar stimuli. But the latter action can be overcome by other influences if the familiar stimuli are important. However, though familiar, important stimuli and novel ones are both passed on for further action, the type of action they provoke is different. Familiar, important stimuli are simply sent forward for checking. But novel stimuli take us over into the third scenario distinguished above: there is a mismatch between expected and actual events and the septo-hippocampal system assumes direct control over behaviour.

Scenario 3: mismatch

It is implicit in the argument so far that there are, in fact, two different varieties of this scenario. A mismatch can arise either because there is a novel stimulus which is matched by no expectation or because there is an expectation matched by no stimulus. Vinogradova (1975) seems to allot the detection of both kinds of mismatch to the CA 3 comparator. But since she reports that neither dentate nor medial septal cells fire when a familiar signal is predicted but fails to occur, it is difficult to see how CA 3 cells can detect the second kind of mismatch. There are several possible ways round this difficulty, none of them fully satisfactory. In considering them we shall pay particular attention to the special case in which the omitted stimulus is a reward. The reason for this will be apparent from the lesion experiments reviewed in Chapter 6: the behavioural abnormalities of septal and hippocampal animals are especially marked when reactions to non-reward are measured.

One possible way round the problem of detecting the omission of a stimulus is to suppose that this event is signalled to the CA 3 comparator by the direct projection this receives from the entorhinal cortex. For this to be plausible we would require evidence that units in the entorhinal area detect the absence of a familiar stimulus. On this point the evidence is largely negative (Vinogradova 1975, p. 26). A second possibility is that stimulus omission is detected in the postulated subicular comparator when a prediction, circulated round the subicular loop, fails to meet a sensory match coming from either CA 1 or the entorhinal area. In support of this hypothesis is the observation (Vinogradova 1975) that neurons in at least one structure lying on the subicular loop, namely, the mammillary bodies, respond when a stimulus is omitted from a regular series by firing at the time the stimulus would have been expected to occur.

The trouble with both these hypotheses is that they allocate no role in the detection of missing stimuli to the septal area. But, if we take the special case of non-reward, there is strong evidence that this region plays an important role in the control of reactions to stimulus omission. We saw in Chapter 6 that large septal lesions attenuate behavioural responses to non-reward under a wide variety of conditions, and that they do so in essentially the same manner as hippocampal lesions. These effects of large septal lesions are reproduced by lesions confined to the medial septal area (Donovick 1968; Clody and Carlton 1969; Gray, Quintão, and Araujo-Silva 1972; Pompi 1974; Ellen, Makohon, and Richardson 1978; Feldon and Gray 1979a, b; and see Grossman 1978 for a review of related studies). Consistent with these findings, there is a reliable hippocampal theta response to non-reward (Gray and Ball 1970; Kimsey, Dyer, and Petri 1974), though this may be related to the behaviour elicited by this event rather than to its detection (Morris and Black 1978). These various results provide strong grounds for allocating to the medial septal area a role in behaviour elicited by non-reward analogous to its role in the detection of novelty (Fig. 10.4).

One solution to this problem is to adopt the second hypothesis suggested above, namely, that stimulus omission is detected in the subicular area, but to suppose in addition that this information is then passed along to the septal area. Such a subiculo-septal projection is known to exist (Swanson 1978). Unfortunately, it appears to terminate in the lateral septal area, and there is little anatomical evidence for terminals in the medial septal area, which is where we need to find them. There is, however, electrophysiological evidence for hippocampal efferents to the medial septal area (De France 1976b); and De France, Yoshihara, and Chronister (1978) attribute to these fibres a route in the fornix and an origin in the dorsal subiculum. One way to reconcile the anatomical and physiological data is suggested by the observation (Swanson and Cowan 1976) that the dendrites of many medial septal cells extend for considerable distances beyond the cytoarchitectonic boundaries of the nuclei to which they belong. Subicular fibres might therefore terminate on such dendrites in the lateral septal region and thus affect the firing of medial septal cells.

But if the whole point of the CA 3 comparator is to feed information to the subicular area, what is the point of then sending it back to the hippocampus via the medial septal area? A little reflection provides a good behavioural justification for what might otherwise seem like a wiring diagram gone wild.

Non-reward differs from other, more neutral kinds of stimulus omission (and from novelty generally) in that habituation must not be allowed to take place too quickly; indeed, it must be allowed to take place at all only under rather special conditions, such as those provided by a partial reinforcement schedule (Amsel 1962). Otherwise the animal would habituate to non-reward on, say, the first seven or eight trials of extinction and then continue indefinitely to make the non-rewarded, and so mala-adaptive, response. Thus some special apparatus is required to ensure that the animal continues to treat the omission of reward as a mismatch that requires attention and action, until either the non-rewarded response is abandoned or a more successful response put in its place. In agreement with this inference, there is behavioural evidence that, if the right kind of reinforcement schedule is used, the animal goes on reacting more or less indefinitely to non-reward (Feldon *et al.* 1979, Experiment 3). It is possible that the projection from the subiculum to the (medial?) septal area is re-sponsible for this immunity to habituation. On this hypothesis the subic-ular area ensures that its own alarm bell is rung by activating the medial septal input to CA 3 with no matching entorhinal input. For this to be useful, the alarm must be rung only under appropriate conditions, that is, when the omitted stimulus is an important one (of which one of the best examples is a reward). This hypothesis is consistent with Vinogra-dova's (1975) failure to observe medial septal responses to stimulus omis-sion, since she used only unimportant stimuli. We need add no further assumptions to give the subicular area a means of discriminating between the two types (important and unimportant) of stimulus omission. For we have already postulated that important stimuli are tagged as such on their passage through the dentate–CA 3 gate. Provided the 'important' tag is entered into the subicular predictive loop, the subicular comparator is automatically informed whether the omitted stimulus matters or not.

There are certain conditions, however, in which it is adaptive for reac-tions to non-reward to habituate, namely, those provided by a PRF sched-ule. On such a schedule, as in a simple habituation experiment, the ani-mal's most adaptive strategy is to become accustomed to the novel event (i.e. non-reward) and continue with its initial behavioural programme (e.g. running in an alley) as though nothing had changed. If this parallel is more than superficial, the development of tolerance for non-reward (i.e. the partial reinforcement extinction effect) should depend on the same circuitry as simple habituation. Thus, arguing from Fig. 10.4, we might expect the PREE to depend on the passage of information from CA 3 to the lateral septal area. The effects of lesions to the septo-hippocampal system on the PREE are in general agreement with this ex-pectation. Thus the PREE is disrupted by hippocampal (Amsel *et al.* 1973; Rawlins *et al.* 1980*b*) and large septal (Henke 1974, 1977; Feldon and Gray 1979*a*) lesions. In these cases the lesions produce both increased resistance to extinction after CRF training and decreased resistance to extinction after PRF training. The increased resistance to extinction after CRF training is the only one of these effects reproduced by lesions con-fined to the medial septal area, and these lesions sometimes also increase resistance to extinction after PRF training (Feldon and Gray 1979*a, b*). This is consistent with the role in the detection of non-reward allotted above to the medial septal area. Decreased resistance to extinction after

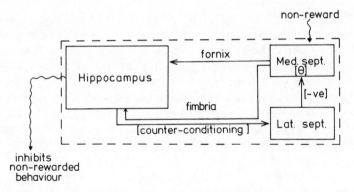

Figure 10.5. Gray *et al.*'s (1978) counter-conditioning model. (See text for explanation.)

PRF training is produced only by lesions to the lateral septal area (Feldon and Gray 1979*a, b*).

These findings are consistent with Vinogradova's (1975) experiments on habituation, and with the model presented in Fig. 10.5 (Gray *et al.* 1978). According to this model the medial septal area is the recipient of information concerning the imminence of non-reward. This information is conveyed to the hippocampus by way of the theta-producing fibres which travel in the fornix and fimbria. The hippocampus has the job of inhibiting the non-rewarded behaviour while determining the best behavioural strategy in the changed circumstances (these notions are elaborated below). Under conditions in which the best strategy is in fact to continue with the original behaviour (as on a PRF schedule), the hippocampus sends a message to the lateral septal area which, in turn, via septal interneurons inhibits or otherwise alters the medial septal input to the hippocampus. The operation of this hippocampo-septal pathway underlies the development of tolerance for non-reward ('counter-conditioning', in Amsel's 1962 term), just as it underlies simple habituation as studied by Vinogradova (1975).

This model implies that, if one could section the hippocampal projection to the lateral septal area, the PREE would be disrupted. This projection is thought to travel largely in the fimbria. Rawlins *et al.* (1980*b*) therefore examined the effect of fimbrial section on the PREE. There was no change in the behaviour of either CRF or PRF groups. Given the detailed similarities between the effects of septal (Henke 1974), lateral septal (Feldon and Gray 1979*b*), and hippocampal (Rawlins *et al.* 1980*b*) lesions on resistance to extinction in PRF-trained animals in these experiments, this negative result is difficult to explain. It is possible that a proportion of the hippocampal projection to the septal area travels in the dorsal fornix (De France 1976*b*; De France *et al.* 1978; Meibach and Siegel 1977*b*), which was not sectioned by Rawlins *et al.* (1980*b*).

On the view just developed the projection from CA 3 to the lateral septal area is a means of dampening down or perhaps even cancelling the medial septal alarm bell. It is brought into play during habituation of simple responses to novelty and during the learning of tolerance for non-reward. But what happens before it is brought into play? *Ex hypothesi* the visible behavioural outputs of the septo-hippocampal system occur at times when the subicular area, in its capacity as comparator, declares 'mismatch'. What then ensues? The present theory answers this question in the following ways.

1. Behavioural inhibition   There is an immediate inhibition of any motor programme which is in the course of execution. In the example we have been considering in most detail, this has been a learned response such as running in an alley. There is no reason in principle to suppose that matters would be different if the animal were in the middle of an unlearned programme (grooming, say, or drinking); but this is a point to which we shall need to return later. It is not proposed that the septo-hippocampal system directly inhibits descending motor pathways; it is not equipped with the connections necessary for this purpose. It is possible that the messages which eventuate in motor inhibition pass by way of the lateral septal area to the hypothalamus, following the route described by Albert and his collaborators in their work on the hyper-reactivity syndrome (Chapter 8). This pathway could be activated via the subicular projection to the lateral septal area. In addition, in cases where novelty is first detected in CA 3 (i.e. in response to the novel presentation rather than omission of a stimulus), the projection from this region to the lateral septal area might be used.

An alternative possibility is that motor inhibition results from messages which pass in the first instance along the direct projection from the subicular area to the cingulate cortex described by Meibach and Siegel (1977c). As pointed out by Swanson (1978), access to the cingulate cortex allows the septo-hippocampal system to influence, albeit indirectly, activity in the striato-thalamo-motor cortical system, the prefrontal cortex (see Chapter 13) and the cerebellum. In this connection, it is worth recalling the multiplicity of routes by which septo-hippocampal influences can be brought to bear on the cingulate cortex: in addition to the direct subiculo-cingulate projection just mentioned, the subiculum, lateral and medial septal areas all project to the cingulate cortex via the mammillary bodies and the anteroventral thalamus. Whichever route is used, it is envisaged that the type of inhibition produced by the septo-hippocampal system occurs at the level of planning motor programmes (Miller, Galanter, and Pribram 1960; Brooks 1979), not that of the execution of particular movements. This is more likely to involve neocortical sites of action (cingulate or frontal).

2. *The 'faulty' tag* The motor programme which was in the course of execution at the time that mismatch was declared is tagged with an indication which, in English, might read 'faulty, needs checking'. This has two consequences.

(i) On future occasions the revelant programme is executed with greater restraint (more slowly, more easily interrupted by hesitations for exploratory behaviour, more readily abandoned in favour of other programmes, etc.). This could come about either because the septohippocampal system alters once for all whatever systems are responsible for motor programmes; or because the septo-hippocampal system itself interferes with the smooth running of the tagged motor programme each time it occurs. Given the other consequences of the 'faulty' tag (see below), the latter alternative is more plausible. Note that the interruption of 'faulty' motor programmes occurs (after the first occasion on which mismatch was declared) in advance of the point at which mismatch was detected. This is equivalent, within the theory presented here, to the postulate that the behavioural inhibition system is activated by conditioned, not unconditioned, aversive stimuli (Chapter 1).

(ii) The tagged motor programme is given enhanced attention in the subicular comparator. This is the heart of the theory. For the most important function it attributes to the septo-hippocampal system is that of scrutinizing motor programmes that have gone wrong.

During such scrutiny the full powers of the subicular comparator circuits are brought into play. Stimuli in the environment, but particularly those that constitute or are closely related to the mismatch, are subjected to an analysis that ranges over as many dimensions as possible (e.g. brightness, hue, position, size, relation to other stimuli, repetition rate, etc.). The dependencies between the animal's responses and the results of its behaviour are subjected to a similar multidimensional analysis (e.g. a turn in a maze can be classified as left-going, white-approaching, alternating, moving along the longitudinal axis of the experimental room that surrounds the maze, etc.). This process of analysis is closely connected to the initiation and execution of certain types of exploratory behaviour described below. The two together — analysis and exploration — make up the process described by Kimble (1975) as hypothesis generation and testing. Their efficiency depends on the capacity of the septo-hippocampal system flexibly to control the entry of stimuli at the dentate–CA 3 gate. This capacity underlies the phenomenon of 'instructed habituation', discussed above in connection with Kamin's blocking effect, and its obverse, 'instructed dishabituation'. By selective, sequential opening of the dentate gate to different stimuli or stimulus attributes and to different responses or response attributes, the septo-hippocampal system is able successively to examine alternative descriptions of the behaviour that has eventuated in the mismatch and alternative means to circumvent it.

The process of enhanced stimulus and response analysis just described can in principle be prospective or retrospective. The former case offers no particular problem. It implies that, on the occasion when mismatch is declared, the faulty motor programme is simply tagged as such; enhanced analysis then commences only on the next occasion when the tagged programme is initiated. The second, retrospective case is more problematic. It requires that, when mismatch is declared, the motor programme that has just been interrupted and the stimuli associated with it (both those that were predicted to occur and those that actually occurred) should be 'replayed' by the comparator loops so that enhanced analysis can commence immediately. In human terms this is the process known as 're-hearsal'. This is usually taken to be verbal in form. But there is no reason in principle why rehearsal should be limited to a verbal mode or to a linguistic species. Indeed, Wagner (1978) has recently used the concept of rehearsal with considerable success to account for a number of phenomena in animal learning. It is a central assumption of Wagner's (1978) theory that rehearsal is a more likely consequence of surprising than expected events; this is isomorphic to the hypothesis, within the present theory, that rehearsal is initiated by mismatch. Among the phenomena to which Wagner (1978) has applied his theory is Kamin's blocking effect, which, as we know, is disrupted by hippocampal lesions (Solomon 1977; Rickert *et al.* 1978). These coincidences may be no more than that; but they encourage the belief that it is not absurd to attribute rehearsal to dumb animals. Further encouragement lies in the usual picture of rehearsal as a process that circles round a loop: as we know, there are loops a-plenty in the septo-hippocampal system.

The postulation of such 'subicular' rehearsal may offer an account of the experiments in which post-trial hippocampal or septal theta-driving stimulation has been observed to facilitate retention (Chapter 8). Conceivably the electrode placements and stimulation parameters used in these experiments succeeded in activating retrospectively the process of enhanced stimulus and response analysis described above. This would have the consequence that the information whose intake preceded the stimulation would be subjected to a more extensive analysis than usual and might therefore be more effectively retrieved later.

3. Exploratory-investigative behaviour   The third form of action undertaken by the septo-hippocampal system when mismatch is declared is the initiation of specific exploratory and investigatory behaviour designed to answer particular questions that arise from the operation of the comparator loops. If one confines the discussion to spatially extended environments, this process is essentially the same as the one postulated by O'Keefe and Nadel (1978, p. 242). As we saw in Scenario 1, during initial exploration of a new environment regularities relating stimuli to each other and responses to stimuli are analysed and stored (not in the hippocampus) for future use; this is the process O'Keefe and Nadel (1978) describe as the construction of a spatial map. When there is a mismatch, there is specific exploration of the novel element or the context that contained a now-missing element. For O'Keefe and Nadel (1978) a 'map' is necessary for this type of specific exploration to be initiated. This assumption seems unwarranted, as is the assumption that animals attempt to resolve spatial mismatches differently from other kinds. Thus, on the present hypothesis, the septo-hippocampal system reacts to mismatches in all modalities in the same way.

We can distinguish three types of situation in which the resulting exploratory behaviour can help to solve the animal's problem. The first arises when the mismatch consists in a novel element which does not disrupt completion of the animal's motor programme. In this case exploration of the novel element will re-establish a familiar environment (by habituating the septo-hippocampal response to novelty). The second arises when the mismatch is inherent in the existing motor programme, which therefore is no longer adaptive (e.g. during extinction of a once-rewarded response). In this case a search for progressively earlier indications of mismatch will allow the behaviour to be abandoned sooner and more completely. A search for signals of failure along these lines will produce, for example, the familiar pattern in which extinction in an alley occurs soonest in the goal and is then chained progressively back to the run and start sections. The third arises when environmental outcomes are ambiguous and the subicular comparator, during the process of hypothesis generation, poses specific questions which can be resolved by means of exploratory and investigative behaviour. For example, the output of the comparator may suggest that there is a difference in the brightness of the walls of a T-maze on occasions on which left-turning leads to food and those on which it does not. To gain further information on this point the comparator would command appropriate exploratory behaviour (concerned with the brightness of the walls and the direction of the animal's turn) coupled with appropriate sensory selection. This part of the theory is essentially the same as Kimble's (1975) proposal that the hippocampus is concerned with testing the animal's hypotheses.

The first of the three situations distinguished in the preceding paragraph probably arises also when an animal first explores a novel environment (Scenario 1). Presumably the intact animal habituates at different rates to different parts of such an environment. Thus there will come a time at which a relatively novel stimulus in a partially familiar context will provoke a reaction of mismatch in the septo-hippocampal system, giving rise to the diversified pattern of exploration described above. Damage to the septo-hippocampal system, by eliminating the mismatch reaction, will give rise to a less flexible pattern of exploratory behaviour, as observed (Chapter 6, Section 6.12). This analysis is similar to O'Keefe and Nadel's (1978), but without the special connotation they give to spatial maps.

Note that it is not proposed that the septo-hippocampal system itself contains the motor programmes for exploratory behaviour, but rather (as for the other functions it discharges) that it modulates the use of those contained elsewhere. It is possible that the subicular area gains access to systems that control exploratory behaviour (locomotion, eye-movements, vibrissae movements, etc.) via its projection to the cingulate cortex (Meibach and Siegel 1977c). It has already been postulated that sensory selection is controlled by the subicular projection to the entorhinal cortex. For maximal efficiency it would be expected that these two subicular outputs would be closely coordinated.

Scenario 4: disengagement

Mismatch engages the septo-hippocampal system. Eventually, it must disengage. What happens then? We consider four cases.

The first arises when the mismatch is of no fundamental consequence to the animal. This is the case studied in Vinogradova's (1975) experiments on habituation. We have already considered the machinery that is brought into play in this relatively simple case (Fig. 10.4). The outcome is that the dentate–CA 3 gate shuts to the increasingly familiar and unimportant stimulus, the subicular comparator disengages, and behaviour reverts to the control of other systems. Much the same analysis applies to exploration of a novel environment. A more complex, but essentially similar example, is that of the PREE, also discussed above (see Fig. 10.5).

The second case arises when the mismatch is important, and continued performance of the plan which eventuated in the mismatch cannot solve the problem it poses for the animal. Under these conditions, the subicular comparator will ensure that the 'faulty' programme is executed with increasing hesitation, that exploratory activities are undertaken, and that behaviour is varied in the attempt to light upon a more effective programme. If alternative response strategies are possible (e.g. taking a different turn in a maze), the comparator will instruct them to be tried out. If one of these alternative response routines is successful (e.g. leads consistently to food reward again), the subicular comparator will cease interrupting and revert to the 'just checking' mode. If none of them is successful, exploratory diversification of behaviour none the less eventually comes to an end, the animal then typically engaging in some form of unlearned behaviour (e.g. grooming, sleeping). Again, therefore, we must suppose that the septo-hippocampal system reverts to 'just checking'.

The third case arises when the solution to the animal's problem requires new and more complex distinctions to be made between environmental stimuli and their relation to its responses. Empirically this is the kind of problem posed by a conditional discrimination or by a spatial maze with many similar choice points requiring different responses. Theoretically it is the kind of problem analysed by Hirsh (1974) in his contextual retrieval model of hippocampal function (Chapter 9). Like Hirsh, we suppose that the task of the septo-hippocampal system is to discriminate between contexts in which each of several competing responses is correct and tag information (stored, as before, elsewhere) with an appropriate 'contextual label'. Absence of this function, as in an animal with hippocampal damage, would lead to excessive susceptibility to interference from competing responses, as is observed (Chapter 9). The most likely site of storage of the updated information, labelled for context, is in the temporal lobe, to which the subiculum has access via the entorhinal cortex. How contextual labelling might occur in physiological terms is at present a mystery; although, in a different connection, Kinsbourne (1981) makes some valuable suggestions. When the labelling is complete, the septo-hippocampal system can presumably once more disengage from active control of behaviour.

In the fourth case to be considered, it is not clear that the septo-hippocampal system can ever disengage without disrupting performance. Most of the impairments produced by septal or hippocampal lesions are relative: the animal is slow to extinguish, but extinguishes in the end; it is poor at passive avoidance, but it learns eventually to avoid the place in which it is punished; it is slow to develop a PREE, but does so if given enough training trials; and so on. Thus we must postulate other mechanisms besides the septo-hippocampal system which can mediate these kinds of behaviour. It is in keeping with this imperative that the present theory allots to the septo-hippocampal system a role in the control of behaviour which is, under most circumstances, temporary, a role which boosts the animal's capacity to cope with change but does not provide the whole of that capacity. But some deficits produced by septo-hippocampal damage are apparently absolute, that is, they show little if any sign of recovery even over prolonged periods of testing (Olton *et al.* 1979*a*). Thus we must suppose that, in this sort of task, the septo-hippocampal system is an indispensable tool for adequate performance.

The best example of tasks of this kind come from Olton's work with the radial-arm maze (Olton *et al.* 1979*a*; Olton, Walker, and Gage 1978) and Gaffan's (1977*a, b*) experiments on recognition memory (see Chapter 9). The most obvious feature these tasks have in common is the use of an ever-changing list from which the animal must choose the correct alternative, itself ever changing. The critical difference between tasks of this fourth kind and those susceptible to an analysis in terms of contextual labelling is probably that now even the context cannot be specified in absolute terms. Compare a conditional discrimination with Gaffan's (1977*a*) experiment in which monkeys had to respond to the second appearance of each of a list of 25 pictures (Chapter 9). In a conditional discrimination it is possible to label the correct responses once and for all: e.g. go left if the walls of the maze are white, go right if they are black. But in Gaffan's experiment only the general rùle (respond always to the second appearance of a slide) can be stored permanently, and this is useless as a guide to action unless the particular list of pictures to be responded to is also constructed afresh each time they occur.

This analysis has much in common with Olton's (1978a) in terms of working memory (see Chapter 9); conversely, the model he has proposed to account for performance in the radial-arm maze (Fig. 10.6) has much in common with the theory developed here. 'The system begins with sensory input that enters into a temporary register. A comparison process attempts to match the contents of the temporary register with each of the items in working memory. A match indicates that the choice in question (of one of the arms of the maze) has already been made and should not be repeated; information in the temporary register is deleted, a decision made as to whether to reset working memory, a search is initiated for a new choice, and new sensory input is obtained. A failure to match the contents of the temporary register and some item in working memory indicates the choice in question has not been made previously and ought to be made now. Running down the arm produces reward. The information defining the choice which was in the temporary register is stored in working memory so that the choice will not be repeated, the temporary register is cleared, the reset decision made, a search for another choice is initiated, and new sensory input is obtained' (Olton 1978a, pp. 363–4).

The similarities between this model and the general theory of hippocampal function presented here will be obvious: the central role played by the comparison of actual with stored sensory information; the use made of 'instructed habituation' ('information in the temporary register is deleted'); and the close interplay between the decisions made by the comparator and the execution of exploratory behaviour. To be sure, the details of Olson's model are different; this is not surprising, since they were closely modelled on the requirements of a particular task. But the circuitry I have described in this chapter needs little modification to perform the functions of Olton's working memory. The comparison process would proceed as before in the subicular area; the 'temporary register' is equivalent to the input from the entorhinal cortex, and 'working memory' to the operation of the subicular loop. 'Instructed habituation' could be produced via the subicular projection to the lateral septal area (Swanson 1978), acting as a kind of booster to the circuit shown in Fig. 10.5. 'Instructed dishabituation' (deletion of all items in working memory at the start of a new trial in the radial-arm maze) could be produced via the projection from the subiculum to the medial septal area which we have needed to postulate already to deal with the case of non-reward. Indeed, as pointed out above, non-reward shares with the arms of Olton's maze the property that the responses it elicits must not normally be allowed to habituate. It is parsimonious, therefore, to suppose that this common problem has been given the same neural solution.

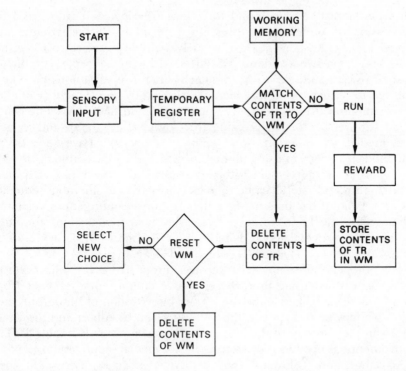

Figure 10.6. Olton's (1978*a*) model of the memory processes underlying performance in the radial-arm maze. (For explanation, see text.) TR, temporary register; WM, working memory.

Passive avoidance

I have so far said nothing about how the present theory handles punishment and passive avoidance. Consideration of this apparently simple form of behaviour has been left till now because it turns out to pose some rather special problems of its own. The first of these concerns the route by which information about punishment enters the septo-hippocampal system.

As we saw earlier in this chapter, the medial septal area appears to act as an important station on the route by which both novelty and non-reward affect the activity of the septo-hippocampal system. Thus, given the overall similarities between the effects of anti-anxiety drugs (Chapter 2) and septal and hippocampal lesions (Chapter 6) on responses to non-reward and punishment, respectively, one might have expected information about the latter event also to enter the septo-hippocampal system by this route. Alas for parsimony, it does not. There are several lines of evidence which implicate the *lateral* rather than the medial septal area in responses to punishment. High-frequency electrical stimulation of the lateral septal area has been found to reduce freezing, defecation, and the suppression of punished bar-pressing or drinking (Schwartzbaum and Donovick 1965; Kasper 1964); conversely, neither punished drinking nor step-through passive avoidance was affected by medial septal stimulation (Kasper 1964; Landfield 1977). Similarly, lateral septal lesions have been reported to reduce the suppression of drinking by punishment (Hamilton 1970; Hamilton, Kelsey, and Grossman 1970) and on-the-baseline conditioned suppression of bar-pressing (McGowan *et al.* 1972), and in both cases medial septal lesions were without effect. We have recently re-examined this problem using animals in which the hippocampal EEG was also recorded. In agreement with the results cited above, rats with intact theta rhythm and lateral septal damage showed a considerable reduction in suppression of bar-pressing by either response-contingent or response-independent shock; in contrast, rats with near-total loss of the theta rhythm due to medial septal damage showed almost normal levels of response suppression (Feldon, Rawlins, and Gray, in press *a*)*.

Since the lateral septal area receives input from the hippocampus rather than transmitting to it, the effects of lateral septal lesions on passive avoidance are likely to be due to the interruption of an output pathway. This may be the same as the one described by Albert and his collaborators in their studies of the hyper-reactivity syndrome (Chapter 8). This syndrome too is produced by lateral but not medial septal lesions (Paxinos 1976; Albert and Richmond 1976; Albert *et al.* 1978*a;* Grossman 1978; Clody and Carlton 1969; Gray 1971*c*). Medial septal stimulation has no effect on hyper-reactivity produced by hypothalamic lesions, while lateral septal stimulation inhibits it (Brayley and Albert 1977*a, b;* Albert *et al.* 1978*a*). Thus it would be parsimonious to assume that a single pathway, descending to the ventromedial hypothalamus via the lateral septal area (Chapter 8), mediates the suppression of both hyper-reactivity and punished responding. There are two observations, however, which weaken this hypothesis. First, in the experiments of Schwartzbaum and Donovick (1965) and Kasper (1964), lateral septal stimulation acted like a lesion, reducing response suppression, whereas in the experiments of Albert and his collaborators it acted in the opposite manner to a lesion, increasing response suppression. Second, experiments in which drugs have been injected into the septal area indicate a cholinergic synapse in the system suppressing punished responses (Hamilton, McCleary, and Grossman 1968) but not in the system suppressing hyper-reactivity (Albert and Richmond 1977).

After meeting so many parallels between punishment and non-reward in their general behavioural effects (Wagner 1966; Gray 1967, 1975), their drug sensitivities (Chapter 2) and their sensitivity to large septal and hippocampal lesions (Chapter 6), it is disconcerting to find that their anatomical bases within the septal area are not only different, but apparently diametrically opposed. Medial septal lesions increase resistance to

*See additional references.

extinction but have no effect on resistance to punishment. Even worse, lateral septal lesions increase resistance to punishment but under certain conditions (if the animal has been trained on a partial reinforcement schedule) actually decrease resistance to extinction. Once one has reached this conclusion, however, it is not difficult to see a reason why information about these two events should take different routes to arrive in the hippocampus. Like novelty, non-reward (according to the hypotheses developed in this chapter) depends for its recognition upon events within the septo-hippocampal system. Both 'novelty' and 'non-reward' are conclusions which can only be reached after a process of comparison has been undertaken, a process attributed to the CA 3 and subicular comparators respectively. But a painful stimulus speaks for itself. Thus there is no reason why it should not simply announce its own arrival at the entrance to the septo-hippocampal system.

There remains the question, which entrance? There appear to be two possibilities, not mutually exclusive. The first is that painful stimuli enter the septo-hippocampal system directly via the entorhinal area. This is supported by evidence that entorhinal lesions disrupt passive avoidance when rats are shocked for drinking (Ross *et al.* 1973) or for stepping into a box containing food (Van Hoesen, Wilson, MacDougall, and Mitchell 1972), or when cats are shocked through their feeding dish (Entingh 1971). The second possibility is that painful stimuli affect hippocampal activity via monoaminergic afferents. Segal (1977*a, b, c, d*) showed that the late negative potential to a contralateral hippocampal pulse is enhanced if the pulse is applied concurrently with a CS for foot-shock, and that similar effects can be produced by increasing the noradrenergic or serotonergic inputs to the hippocampus (see Chapter 7). However, CSs for food had the same effect as CSs for shock; thus these influences appear to tag intra-hippocampal events with the label 'important' rather than 'aversive' or 'appetitive'. But the theory developed here demands very different reactions in the subicular area depending on whether the message it receives is appetitive or aversive. In the former case the message is important, but requires only checking; in the latter, the subicular area should assume direct behavioural control and operate the routines described above under Scenario 3. Thus the fact that there is apparently little intrahippocampal differentiation between the two types of message (Fuster and Uyeda 1971; Segal and Olds 1973; see Chapter 7) is an embarrassment for the theory.

A second embarrassment comes to light when we ask how the activities of the lateral septal area and the hippocampal formation, both of which (according to the lesion evidence) are concerned with the control of passive avoidance behaviour, are co-ordinated. The natural place to look is in the hippocampal projection to the lateral septal area which travels in the fimbria and originates in CA 3 and the subiculum. Unfortunately, the evidence for any disruption of passive avoidance after transection of the

fimbria is scant. Most of the relevant experiments have in fact used animals in which the entire fornix-fimbria is transected, thus severing, in
addition to the hippocampo-septal pathway, the rest of the output from
the subiculum as well as the septo-hippocampal projection; however,
given the absence of change in passive avoidance after medial septal lesions, the last of these pathways can probably be ignored.

The effects of transection of the fornix-fimbria appear to depend on
the nature of the passive avoidance task used. Passive avoidance has been
reported normal when drinking (Myhrer and Kaada 1975; Ross, Grossman, and Grossman 1975) or eating in a two-box apparatus (Van Hoesen,
MacDougall, and Mitchell 1969; Van Hoesen, Wilson, MacDougall, and
Mitchell 1972; De Castro and Hall 1975) has been punished. Results with
punished extinction of one-way active avoidance have also been largely
negative (Thomas and McCleary 1974b; Liss 1968), though Liss found a
deficit at the longer of the two ITIs (10 minutes and 5 seconds) he used.
When running in an alley is punished, more clearly positive results are
obtained (Greene and Stauff 1974; Okaiche *et al.* 1978). This pattern of
results is similar to that seen after hippocampal lesions (Chapter 6, Section 6.2), although in that case (perhaps because there are many more
published reports) the differences between tasks are less stark. But the
effects of fornix-fimbria lesions are probably due to transection of the
fornix. First, in the experiment by Okaiche *et al.* (1978), the passive avoidance deficit was present in animals in which the lateral fimbria had been
left intact. Second, Jarrard (1976) transected the fimbria only and observed normal behaviour when running in the alley was punished. Myhrer
(1975a), also studying rats with the fimbria transected, actually observed
increased passive avoidance when drinking was punished. Further analysis of this surprising result showed that it could be attributed to section of
fibres in the medial rather than lateral fimbria. If this effect is general, it
might sometimes have masked an impairment in passive avoidance due to
transection of the fornix (which lies medial to the medial fimbria).

These results indicate that an impairment in passive avoidance, similar
to that seen after hippocampal or lateral septal lesions, is produced by
dorsal fornix but not by fimbrial lesions. Since medial septal lesions do
not impair passive avoidance, this effect cannot be due to transection of
the septo-hippocampal projection. It is also unlikely to be due to transection of the hippocampo-septal projection, since efferents from CA 3 and
the subiculum destined for the lateral septum travel largely in the fimbria; although this possibility is not totally excluded, since some of these
fibres may also travel in the dorsal fornix (Meibach and Siegel 1977b; De
France 1976b; De France *et al.* 1978). Thus the effects of fornix section
on passive avoidance are probably due to disruption of the subicular outflow to other regions.

This conclusion implies that, though the lateral septal area is the recipient of the hippocampo-septal projection, this projection has nothing to

do with the passive avoidance deficit produced by hippocampal and lateral septal lesions alike. How, then, if at all, do the hippocampus and the septal area co-ordinate their control of punished behaviour, if they use neither the hippocampal projection to the septal area nor the septal projection to the hippocampus (Grossman 1978)? It is possible that this co-ordination is assured outside the septo-hippocampal system itself, at a common target or common afferent or both. On the input side, both the septal area and the hippocampus receive noradrenergic and serotonergic projections; these are discussed further in Chapter 11. On the output side, the mammillary bodies receive projections from both the hippocampus and the lateral septal area. A further common target which may be important is the ventromedial hypothalamus. This is apparently the destination of the descending inhibitory pathway from the lateral septal area described by Albert's group in their experiments on the hyper-reactivity syndrome (Chapter 8); in addition, it receives a major projection from the ventral subiculum (Fig. 3.17).

If the ventral subicular outflow plays a role of this kind, one would expect lesions confined to the ventral (temporal) portion of the hippocampal formation to disrupt passive avoidance. This expectation is by and large supported by the available data. Such lesions have been found to increase the rate of punished drinking (Holdstock 1972); approach to the arm of a T-maze containing water and the threat of shock (Landfield *et al.* 1973); and approach to the goal-box of a Y-maze (Andy *et al.* 1967), two-compartment apparatus (Best and Orr 1973) or alley (Kimura 1958; Fried 1972*a*) containing food and the threat of shock. Punished extinction of one-way active avoidance, however, was not affected by ventral hippocampal lesions in the experiments by Coscina and Lash (1969) or Nadel (1968). Liss (1968) found the same pattern of effects in this task as he did with fornix-fimbria lesions, that is, an impairment with a 10-minute but not a 5-second ITI. On-the-baseline conditioned suppression of bar-pressing again gives positive results: McGowan *et al.* (1972) and Molino (1975) both report an alleviation of suppression after ventral hippocampal lesions but no change after dorsal lesions. Furthermore, the results reported by McGowan *et al.* (1972) paralleled the findings in the same experiment with lateral septal (like ventral hippocampal) and medial septal (like dorsal hippocampal) lesions.

It is possible, therefore, that the similarity between the effects on passive avoidance of lesions to the lateral septal area and hippocampus, respectively, is due at least in part to the projections from both these regions to the ventromedial hypothalamus. But there is little reason to give these projections an equal importance in the control of behavioural responses to non-reward. Thus neither at the input to the septo-hippocampal system nor at its output do punishment and non-reward appear to act on the same pathways. What, then, is left of the hypothesis that these events are equivalent (Wagner 1966; Gray 1967, 1975)?

It should be emphasized that the discovery that different particular neurons mediate the detection of and response to punishment and non-reward, respectively, does not by itself speak against the *functional* equivalence of these two events. This hypothesis supposes that the brain handles information concerning punishment and non-reward in essentially the same ways and organizes similar patterns of response in the two cases; it does not entail that identical neurons do these jobs. There must in any case be some differences between the neuronal messages that non-reward and punishment evoke since, though animals generalize between these two kinds of event, they also discriminate between them and the generalization is not perfect (Brown and Wagner 1964). None the less, the remarkable similarities in the drug sensitivities of behaviour controlled by punishment and non-reward respectively (Chapter 2; Gray 1977) is a strong indication that there is considerable physiological (as well as functional) overlap between the systems that generate this behaviour. Thus what is called into question by the data discussed in this section is the hypothesis that this physiological overlap occurs at the level of the septo-hippocampal systems (Gray 1970a).

Here too we must distinguish between functional and neuronal identity. For most purposes of the theory developed in this book it is sufficient if the septo-hippocampal system handles information about non-reward and punishment in essentially the same manner; and this proposal continues to be supported by the evidence (Chapter 6) that behaviour controlled by punishment or non-reward, respectively, is disrupted in much the same ways by large septal and hippocampal lesions. There are, to be sure, exceptions to this rule, but for the most part it remains a sound one. It is then of less importance that, within the septo-hippocampal system or even at the level of its afferents and efferents, different particular pathways deal with information about the two kinds of aversive event. It is possible that these differences arise because painful stimuli act upon an older and more vital set of structures than does non-reward. Perhaps information about punishment and anticipated punishment is dealt with more urgently than, but in the same way as, information about non-reward and anticipated non-reward. This view is both plausible and consistent with the closer relations to hypothalamic systems which (given the arguments above implicating lateral septal and ventral subicular projections to the ventromedial hypothalamus) are apparently possessed by the septo-hippocampal structures which mediate responses to punishment. We should not in any case overstress the differences between the septo-hippocampal circuits that deal with non-reward and punishment. Both apparently make use of the same subicular outputs (see the discussion of the effects of fornix lesions on passive avoidance, above); and, as we shall see in the next chapter, it is possible that they depend in similar ways on the noradrenergic and serotonergic afferents to the septo-hippocampal system.

Before we leave the topic of punishment we should give some thought to the way the septo-hippocampal system might treat the special event of non-punishment, that it, the omission of a punishment (which otherwise would have been delivered) contingent upon the animal's response. Since, by definition, non-punishment is at least initially a mismatch between expected and actual events, it should activate the septo-hippocampal system. Should we not therefore expect septo-hippocampal damage to disrupt active avoidance (which depends on the detection of non-punishment; Gray 1975, Chapter 10)? In fact, however, with the exception of a deficit in one-way active avoidance which may be confined to septal lesions and is perhaps due to disruption of the septal output to the habenular nuclei (Grossman 1978; see Chapter 6), such a disruption does not occur.

A little reflection shows that there is no real contradiction here. The function we have attributed to the septo-hippocampal system is that of calling in faulty motor programmes for checking when a *maladaptive* mismatch is detected. When non-punishment is detected there might be a momentary activation of the subicular output (behavioural inhibition, investigation, etc.) in virtue of the surprising aspects of this event; but this would rapidly be followed by confirmation of the motor programme which led to it and disengagement of the septo-hippocampal system from direct behavioural control. Thus it is only in situations of conflict that we would expect to see effects of damage to the septo-hippocampal system; and, following arguments already developed in terms of the conflict between passive and active avoidance, these would be expected to take the form of facilitation, as is observed (see Chapter 6, Sections 6.6 and 6.7).

The theta rhythm

There remains one major phenomenon to incorporate into the theory: the enigmatic theta rhythm. Following Vinogradova (1975) and O'Keefe and Nadel (1978) we suppose that this plays a role in timing and quantizing the passage of information around the septo-hippocampal system. In support of this assumption is the evidence that hippocampal neurons fire preferentially in particular phases of the locally recorded theta wave (e.g. Fig. 4.5); and that the population spikes recorded in the dentate in response to entorhinal stimulation, and in CA 1 in response to contralateral hippocampal stimulation, are both maximal at a particular phase of the theta rhythm recorded simultaneously in the dentate gyrus (Rudell *et al.* 1980; see Chapter 4). In O'Keefe and Nadel's (1978, p. 220) model, theta plays a role in determining which neurons store the information that constitutes a spatial map and subsequently in retrieving this information when it is needed. Since we have rejected the spatial theory, this model must be rejected with it. Nor can we extend the model to cover information processing in non-spatial modalities, since we have also rejected the notion that the hippocampus is concerned with any kind of storage. O'Keefe and Nadel's (1978) model in any case suffers from an unsatisfactory time scale. They suppose (as does Vinogradova) that the function of theta is to time the passage of successive neural messages around the basic four-synapse hippocampal circuit (entorhinal area, dentate gyrus, CA 3, CA 1, subiculum). But even fast theta entails an interval of about 100 ms between corresponding points on successive waves; and this looks about an order of magnitude too long to cope with four synapses.

An alternative hypothesis, which would give the septo-hippocampal system more work to do during the period of a theta wave, is that theta paces the passage of successive items of information round all three loops which constitute this system: from the entorhinal area round the hippocampal circuit to the subicular area and thence back to the entorhinal cortex; from the medial septal area to CA 3 and the dentate gyrus and back from CA 3 to the lateral and thence medial septal area; and round the subicular loop (mammillary bodies, anteroventral thalamus, cingulate cortex, and back to the subicular area). Parmeggiani, Azzaroni, and Lenzi (1971) have estimated the conduction time for information to travel round the last of these loops to be about 50–60 ms in the curarized cat; this value is about the right order of magnitude, given the other tasks the system must perform, to be paced by the theta rhythm. If this general approach is correct, it is clear that the overall system requires considerable co-ordination. The medial septal area is well placed to perform this function, since it projects not only to all fields of the hippocampal formation (dentate gyrus, CA 1, and CA 3), but also to the subicular and entorhinal areas and the mammillary bodies. Thus it could co-ordinate the passage of information around the basic hippocampal circuit with that round and subicular loop, and the entry of information into the perforant path with both. Further co-ordination may be provided by CA 3, via its projections back to the dentate gyrus, the entorhinal area, and the lateral septal area. Vinogradova (1975) has suggested in addition that some units in the mammillary bodies may serve a timing function, since they fire at extremely regular rates that are stably maintained over long periods of time.

It will be recalled (see Chapter 7) that there appear to be two rather different kinds of theta rhythm, one related to movement, the other not (Vanderwolf *et al.* 1975, 1978). These two types of theta find a natural counterpart in the distinction already made between two modes of operation of the septo-hippocampal system: 'just checking' and 'control'. On this hypothesis, movement-related (atropine-resistant; high-frequency) theta is associated with the checking of motor programmes that are in the course of smooth execution. The frequency of theta seen during this checking activity would be expected to vary with the rate at which items of information controlling the behaviour are received. This gives a natural explanation (similar to the one advanced, in the context of their own theory, by O'Keefe and Nadel 1978, p. 226) for the observed positive correlation between the frequency of movement-related theta and the speed of movement (Chapter 7). If, however, smooth motor programming is interrupted by a mismatch, lower-frequency theta (not related to movement) is generated, allowing slower, and thus more detailed analysis of the information passing at each 'theta sweep' around the septo-hippocampal system.

The particular frequency of theta seen under the latter conditions might depend to some extent on the nature of the information entering via the sensory systems. As Komisaruk (1970) and Macrides (1975) have shown, for example, theta and vibrissae movements sometimes become phase-locked for short periods. At times like this theta frequency may ensure that successive chunks of information reaching the septo-hippocampal system from the vibrissae, or via olfactory channels closely coupled to the vibrissae, arrive at the optimal time for analysis. A more interesting possibility is that different theta frequencies may determine which loops in the system achieve priority, by matching the period of a theta wave to the time taken for information to circulate in a particular loop. This possibility is supported by the observations of Parmeggiani, Lenzi, and Azzaroni (1974), who investigated the passage of neural messages around the subicular loop as a function of the frequency of stimulation of the hippocampus in curarized cats. Multiple-unit responses in the mammillary bodies and the anteroventral nucleus of the thalamus were a function of stimulus intensity only; but the response recorded in the anteromedial thalamic nucleus showed a sharp resonance at about 7 Hz, response magnitude falling rapidly as stimulation frequency rose above this value.

Parmeggiani *et al.* (1974) interpret these results as indicating that the anteromedial nucleus acts as a gate, circulating information of hippocampal origin to the neocortex (to which it projects) only at frequencies below 7 Hz in the cat (Fig. 10.7). A mechanism such as this might play a role in selecting information of neocortical origin which is then fed back to the septo-hippocampal system in the entorhinal area. In this way different frequencies of theta might determine, not only the rate at which the septo-hippocampal system processes information, but also *which* information is processed. This might account for the marked behavioural effects of septal theta-driving stimulation (Chapter 8), although the evidence that these are frequency dependent is as yet slight (Glazer 1974b). It might also be possible along these lines to understand the different characteristic frequency bands of Vanderwolf's two types of theta, and the apparently special properties of 7.7-Hz theta (Chapter 7). In this connection, it would be particularly valuable to have data on how information circulates round the interlinked loops of the septo-hippocampal system when theta is at this frequency, above, or below it.

Conclusion

This completes the presentation of the theory, which is summarized in Fig. 10.8. It can account for much of the data. Since it is largely based on these data, this is not surprising; only future experimental test will tell

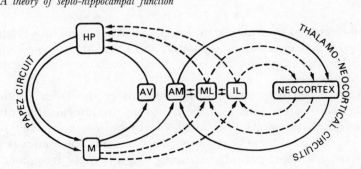

Figure 10.7. A model proposed by Parmeggiani *et al.* (1974) to account for inter-actions between the Papez circuit and thalamo-neocortical circuits. AM, antero-medial nucleus of thalamus; AV, anteroventral nucleus of thalamus; HP, hippo-campus; IL, intralaminar nuclei of thalamus; M, mammillary body; ML, midline nuclei of thalamus. (For further explanation, see text.)

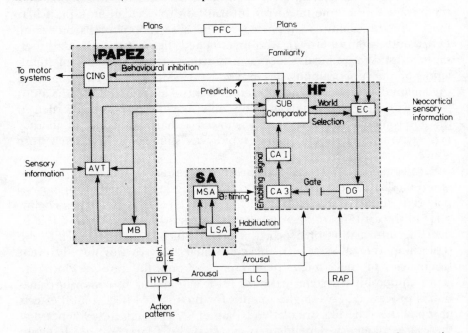

Figure 10.8. A summary of the theory developed in this book. The three major building blocks are shown in heavy print: HF, the hippocampal formation, made up of the entorhinal cortex, EC, the dentate gyrus, DG, CA 3, CA 1, and the subicular area, SUB; SA, the septal area, containing the medial and lateral septal areas, MSA and LSA; and the Papez circuit, which receives projections from and returns them to the subicular area via the mammillary bodies, MB, anteroventral thalamus, AVT, and cingulate cortex, CING. Other structures shown are the hy-pothalamus, HYP, the locus coeruleus, LC, the raphe nuclei, RAP, and the pre-frontal cortex, PFC. Arrows show direction of projection; the projection from SUB to MSA lacks anatomical confirmation (see p. 275). Words in lower case show postulated functions; beh. inh., behavioural inhibition. (For further explanation, see text.)

whether it has any real merit. It has borrowed much from other theories. This is also not surprising; after the massive investment of research into the septo-hippocampal system over the last quarter of a century, it would be something of a disaster if none of the insights gleaned by earlier workers was worth preserving. Those who dislike the way I have put these borrowings together will find the result a patchwork quilt, no stronger than its patches and weaker for the seaming.

A more favourable view might be that the present theory has distilled what is general to earlier proposals and the data on which they have rested. Central to this distillation is the notion that the septo-hippocampal system serves as a comparator between expected and actual stimulation, proposed in different ways by Vinogradova (1975), O'Keefe and Nadel (1978), and Olton (1978a). From Kimble (1975) I have taken the view that the septo-hippocampal system generates and tests hypotheses under conditions of environmental uncertainty; from Hirsh (1974) the idea of contextual labelling; and from Butters and Cermak (1975) the importance of multidimensional stimulus analysis. But while the theory developed here owes much to these newer concepts, it has not abandoned the earlier view of the septo-hippocampal system as playing an essential role in the inhibition of maladaptive behaviour (McCleary 1966; Douglas 1967). Many workers in this field appear to believe that one has to choose between a model in which the septo-hippocampal system analyses stimuli and one in which it acts on responses (see, e.g, the discussion in Elliott and Whelan 1978, p. 306). But this choice is not only unnecessary, it distorts the problem. On the view developed here, the information-processing and behaviour-inhibitory roles of the septo-hippocampal system are, functionally speaking, two sides of the same coin (which is not to say that they may not be discharged by different particular neurons).

Since the theory is a patchwork quilt, it is, I hope, unnecessary to make a detailed analysis of all the findings summarized in previous chapters to see how well it can account for them. Some of these findings have been used explicitly to. develop the theory. Others were discussed in terms of particular theoretical patches when they were reviewed. Thus, to the extent that the data can be accommodated by supposing that the septo-hippocampal system inhibits motor responses when the animal is exposed to novelty or the threat of punishment (Chapter 6, Sections 6.2, 6.6, 6.7, 6.9, 6.10, and 6.13); or replaces non-rewarded responses by new ones (Chapter 6, Sections 6.17, 6.20, 6.22); or varies responding so as to increase information intake under conditions of novelty (Chapter 6, Section 6.12); or is concerned with the simultaneous analysis of several competing sources of information (Chapter 6, Sections 6.19 and 6.22; Chapter 9); or is necessary for the ordering of items in lists (Chapter 9, discussion of Olton's and Gaffan's experiments): to that extent the theory presented here is also supported. Conversely, the data that at each point fail to fit these hypotheses pose a threat to the theory.

At some points the recalcitrant data can be better accommodated by the overall theory than by the particular hypotheses that it ties together. Consider as an example the factors that influence the effects of septal and hippocampal lesions on passive avoidance behaviour.

As we saw in Chapter 6 (Section 6.2), the effects of these lesions are magnified if there is a prolonged period of rewarded training before the introduction of shock and reduced if there is prolonged experience with shock prior to the lesion. This pattern of results is what one would expect if the function of the septo-hippocampal system is to call in faulty motor programmes for checking. Long training before shock ensures that such a programme exists to be checked; prolonged experience with shock before the lesion would have the effect that the septo-hippocampal system has already done its job before it is removed (recall that, once it has done what it can to deal with changed circumstances, the septo-hippocampal system reverts to 'just checking'). On this view, punished drinking or eating with minimal locomotion are relatively insensitive to hippocampal damage for two reasons. First, it is common in such experiments for pre-shock experience to be small; second, the motor programme established by such experience is exiguous. It is perhaps for this reason (rather than because of any major differences in circuitry) that the inhibition of learned behaviour appears to be more dependent on the integrity of the septo-hippocampal system than that of innate responses.*

This analysis can also make sense of the varying effects of septal and hippocampal lesions (as well as anti-anxiety drugs; Chapter 2) on passive avoidance, on the one hand, and tests of conditioned fear, on the other (Chapter 6, Sections 6.2 and 6.3). An analysis of this pattern of effects in terms of the difference between classical and instrumental conditioning has consistently run into difficulties (Gray 1977; Gray, Rawlins, and Feldon 1979; Rawlins, Feldon, and Gray 1980*a*; Rawlins, Feldon, Salmon, Gray, and Garrud 1980*c*). These difficulties are by-passed by the hypothesis that, upon the occurrence of an aversive stimulus (such as an electric shock), ongoing motor programmes are tagged 'faulty' and called in for checking the next time they occur. For this predicts that septal or hippocampal lesions should disrupt punishment-produced response suppression or on-the-baseline conditioned suppression (since in both cases there is a motor programme in the course of execution at the time of shock), but not off-the-baseline conditioned suppression (since, in principle, there is no motor programme common to the conditions of acquisition and

---

*As we saw in Chapter 6 (Section 6.2) septal lesions produce a more robust deficit in passive avoidance than hippocampal lesions, especially where simple, unlearnt responses are involved. It is possible that this is because septal lesions directly interrupt the output pathway from the lateral septal area to the hypothalamus (see above). Conversely, if the output from the ventral subiculum is indeed important in the control of passive avoidance, this will have been left largely intact in many of the published experiments on the effects of hippocampal lesions. These factors may also account for the different effects of septal and hippocampal lesions on tests of fearfulness (Chapter 6, Section 6.14).

test). As for aversive Pavlovian conditioning, there should be no effect of septal or hippocampal lesions on this, since simple learning is not a function of the septo-hippocampal system, and there is usually no pre-existing set of expectations to be disrupted in this type of experiment. These predictions are in general confirmed by the available data (Chapter 6, Sections 6.2 and 6.3).

A further feature of the data on passive avoidance which can be accommodated by the present theory concerns the locus of the effect of hippocampal lesions with respect to the point of punishment. It is pointed out by Black *et al.* (1977) that, in experiments in the alley, the disinhibitory effect of these lesions tends to be greater, the further the animal is from the goal (Chapter 6, Section 6.2). These authors interpret this phenomenon as reflecting the loss of the capacity to form a spatial map. But there is no reason to treat the spatial aspect of these findings às other than incidental. It has been stressed throughout the present treatment that the behavioural inhibition system (Chapters 1 and 2) is concerned with reactions to stimuli which warn of punishment, not with reactions to punishment itself. This view has now been encompassed by the proposal that maladaptive motor programmes are tagged as 'faulty' by the subicular comparator, and are then interrupted to allow exploration and enhanced stimulus–response analysis when they are next initiated. Thus the occurrence of anticipatory hesitations at points far from the locus of shock in normal but not hippocampal (Winocur and Black 1978) or fornical (Okaiche *et al.* 1978) animals is consistent with the theory developed here.

The passive avoidance deficit seen after septal and hippocampal lesions is, as it were, at one end of the spectrum of data that this theory must account for; at the other lies the human amnesic syndrome. In dealing with this we can call on several features of the theory. Most important are the roles attributed to the septo-hippocampal system in the multiple sorting of lists, and in the multidimensional analysis of stimuli, responses, and stimulus–response relationships.* It is clear enough that the need to cope with renewable lists, or to subject mutually interfering stimuli or responses to simultaneous analysis along many dimensions, is a more prominent feature of normal human life than of the rat's laboratory existence. It is no doubt for this reason that the deficit displayed by the human amnesic when he has to recognize items in a list came to light sooner than the apparently comparable deficit shown by monkeys (Gaffan 1977*a*, *b*) or

---

*Another factor which may contribute to the human amnesic syndrome is the loss of the capacity for rehearsal. Amnesic patients can sometimes retain material which they would otherwise forget if they are allowed the use of overt verbal rehearsal (Sidman *et al.* 1968). This may compensate for an inability to rehearse covertly, perhaps in a nonverbal mode. This would be consistent with the rehearsal function attributed to the subicular comparator above (Scenario 3). On the theory developed here, rehearsal is paced by the theta rhythm. It is consistent with this hypothesis that the rate of human internal rehearsal (in the verbal mode) is about 10 syllables per second (Broadbent, personal communication), a value which lies satisfactorily in the frequency range of the theta rhythm.

rats (Olton 1978*b*) which have sustained lesions to the septo-hippocampal system. But it is possible, I believe, to encompass within a single theory this deficit, whether it occurs in animals or man, and the great variety of other deficits observed in lesioned animals tested on simpler tasks.

It is also relatively easy to extend the theory at this point to the more purely human features of the amnesic syndrome. Butters and Cermak (1975) have already taken the most important step in this respect, when they suggest that the semantic encoding deficit sometimes observed in Korsakoff patients (Chapter 9) is the result of an impairment in multidimensional stimulus analysis. In terms of the present theory we may suppose that, after such analysis, the outputs of the subicular comparator are normally fed into the cortical systems which, uniquely in man, are specialized for language functions. There they are given their verbal labels by which, owing to the overwhelming role played by language in human life, we mainly know them. But corresponding powers of analysis, or nearly so, appear also to exist in animals which lack language, as Gaffan's (1977*a, b*) experiments on recognition memory in monkeys show.

This, then, is our theory of septo-hippocampal function. Is it also a theory of anxiety? This step is not yet warranted.

Although, as we saw in Chapter 6, there are abundant similarities between the behavioural effects of septo-hippocampal damage and those of the anti-anxiety drugs, there are many tasks for which we have data on the effects of lesions but none on those of drugs. Moreover, some of these tasks have played a critical role in determining the form of the theory of septo-hippocampal function developed in this chapter. Thus, if we are to transform this theory into one of anxiety, it is necessary first to study the effects of anti-anxiety drugs on behaviour in these tasks, especially those which tap the more 'cognitive' aspects of septo-hippocampal function. But this type of research has barely begun. Sahgal and Iversen (1978) have shown that chlordiazepoxide impairs the ability of pigeons to make a same-difference judgement; and in the radial-arm maze this drug impairs performance in the same way as a hippocampal lesion, though less completely (S. Brookes, personal communication). However, the septo-hippocampal syndrome may yet turn out to be wider than the one created by anti-anxiety medication. Indeed, if it has anything to do with amnesia, it must be wider, since this is at least not an obvious feature of the behaviour of patients treated with anti-anxiety drugs.* Conversely, as we saw in Chapter 6, there is no evidence that septal or hippocampal lesions eliminate the increment in arousal level elicited by conditioned aversive stimuli (Dickinson 1974), although this effect is clearly produced by the anti-anxiety drugs (Chapter 2). Thus anxiety may be based on structures that

---

*But note that, used in large doses to induce relaxation as part of anaesthetic procedures, the benzodiazepines have been reported several times to cause anterograde amnesia for material memorized at that time (Lecrubier 1976); these reports have not been controlled, however, for state dependency.

are more wide-spread in the brain than the septo-hippocampal system alone.

The safest conclusion for the moment, then, is that 'the septo-hippocampal system, among its functions, includes participation in the behavioural inhibition system; and the behavioural inhibition system, among its neural structures, includes the septo-hippocampal system' (Gray *et al.* 1978). This 'partial overlap' hypothesis leaves the septo-hippocampal system free to subserve such relatively emotion-free activities as learning lists of words in a psychological laboratory; provided of course that it has not been pre-empted by matters of greater urgency. In such calmer moments it is likely that the function of the septo-hippocampal system is dominated by its relations with the neocortex, and in man perhaps especially by language systems. But when emergency threatens, the messages received from older structures located in the brainstem take precedence. In the next chapter we shall take a closer look at these messages.

The role of the ascending projections to the septo-hippocampal system

The similarities between the behavioural effects of the anti-anxiety drugs and those of septal and hippocampal lesions, reviewed in Chapter 6, make out a strong *prima facie* case for the view that these drugs act *in some way* on the septo-hippocampal system. Other observations are consistent with this inference. For example, it has been known for many years that the anti-anxiety drugs alter the normal electrical activity of the hippocampal formation. The frequency of the theta rhythm observed in anaesthetized or free-moving animals is reduced by benzodiazepines (Randall *et al.* 1961; Gekiere *et al.* 1980), barbiturates (Stumpf 1965; Gray and Ball 1970; Kramis, Vanderwolf, and Bland 1975) and alcohol (Whishaw 1976). If the theta rhythm is elicited by electrical stimulation of the reticular formation, barbiturates lower the slope of the function relating stimulus intensity to theta frequency (Stumpf 1965; McNaughton and Sedgwick 1978); and, if theta is elicited by septal stimulation, barbiturates, benzodiazephines, and alcohol all eliminate the minimum at 7.7 Hz in the theta-driving curve (Gray and Ball 1970; McNaughton *et al.* 1977; see Fig. 7.1). These effects are all more or less specific to the anti-anxiety drugs. At higher doses the barbiturates eliminate theta entirely (Stumpf, Petsche, and Gogolak 1962). Lanoir and Killam (1968) reported that theta during paradoxical sleep disappeared when cats were injected with diazepam or nitrazepam. More recently, Whishaw (1976) found that alcohol at a moderately high dose (2 g kg^{-1}) abolished movement-related theta (see Chapter 7) in the rabbit, while only lowering the frequency of immobility-related theta. Changed rates or patterns of single-unit firing have also been observed in the septal area after barbiturate administration (Stumpf *et al.* 1962), and in the hippocampus after benzodiazepines (Chou and Wang 1977) or alcohol (Klemm *et al.* 1976).

However, none of these observations speaks unequivocally to the possibility that the action of the anti-anxiety drugs on the septo-hippocampal system is direct, or that it is related to their effects on behaviour. One way to examine this problem is to see how these drugs affect behaviour in animals with lesions to the septo-hippocampal system. Presumably, if one has removed the structure on which the drug normally acts, its behavioural effects should be abolished, or at any rate altered. However, experiments along these lines have yielded ambiguous results.

Two experiments have been concerned with response suppression. Graeff and Rawlins (1980) injected chlordiazepoxide to rats in which bar-pressing for food had been punished by foot-shock. The drug alleviated response suppression in animals with small, mainly lateral, septal lesions as in controls; but the extent of the drug effect was reduced by the lesion.

This finding is consistent with the hypothesis that the lesion damaged the substrate on which the drug acts to alleviate response suppression, but did not destroy it entirely. This is hardly surprising, since only a small portion of the septo-hippocampal system was removed. But in a more elaborate experiment Feldon, Rawlins, and Gray (in press *b*)* saw no interaction between the effects of chlordiazepoxide and septal lesions. We used the design described in Chapter 2 (Section 2.3) in which rats learn a discrimination between response-contingent and response-independent shock presented while they bar-press for food. Chlordiazepoxide impaired this discrimination and alleviated response suppression (Rawlins, Feldon, and Gray 1980*a*), and neither of these effects was altered by lateral or medial septal lesions.

Two experiments have examined the extinction of rewarded behaviour, obtaining more complex results.

Gray and Araujo-Silva (1971) injected sodium amylobarbitone to rats with small, mainly medial, septal lesions during extinction of a running response. The drug, unusually, decreased resistance to extinction, perhaps because the subjects had a complex training history, functionally equivalent to a partial reinforcement schedule; animals trained on such schedules sometimes respond to sodium amylobarbitone given during extinction by running slower (Gray 1969). Far from being reduced by septal lesions, the effect of the drug was actually greater in the lesioned animals. To account for this pattern of results, and for certain details of their findings, Gray and Araujo-Silva (1971) proposed the model shown in Fig. 11.1. According to this model, the anti-anxiety drugs act both on the septo-hippocampal system and on ascending pathways that increase the level of arousal; we shall consider this suggestion in more detail later in the chapter.

Feldon and Gray (1981*b*; Feldon 1977), studying the effects of chlordiazepoxide on resistance to extinction after continuous and partial reinforcement schedules in the alley, also needed to postulate two sites of action of the drug to account for its interactions with septal lesions. However, in this case, the two sites were both within the septo-hippocampal system, namely, the medial and lateral septal areas; and the results of their experiment could be incorporated within the model of septo-hippocampal function illustrated in Fig. 10.5. It will be recalled that, according to this model, the roles of the medial and lateral septal areas in determining resistance to extinction are opposed to each other (the medial septum facilitating extinction, the lateral counteracting it). Feldon and Gray's (1981*b*) results suggested that, after medial septal lesions, chlordiazepoxide acts principally on the lateral septal area; by inhibiting the latter structure, it acts to restore the balance that medial lesions have disrupted. After lateral septal lesions, the converse processes would be expected to occur; but this was less clearly substantiated by Feldon and Gray's results.

*See additional references.

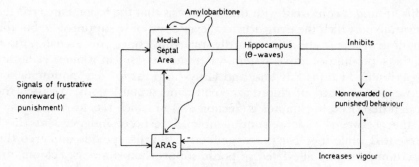

Figure 11.1. Gray and Araujo-Silva's (1971) model to account for the effects of sodium amylobarbitone on running speed under conditions of extinction. During extinction the septo-hippocampal system inhibits previously rewarded behaviour and also inhibits the ascending reticular activating system (ARAS). The latter increases the vigour of ongoing behaviour. Sodium amylobarbitone depresses activity both in the septo-hippocampal system and in the ARAS.

At best, these experiments offer only limited support for the hypothesis that the anti-anxiety drugs alter behaviour via a direct action on the septo-hippocampal system. For a stringent test of this hypothesis, it is true, it would be necessary to remove the septo-hippocampal system in its entirety before administering the drug. Such an experiment has not been attempted, so the hypothesis cannot be rejected outright. But there are other reasons to look outside the septo-hippocampal system for the critical sites of action of the anti-anxiety drugs. The most important of these is that actions on other pathways are known to occur. Furthermore, there are independent grounds for believing that at least some of these pathways play an important role in anxiety. But before taking a closer look at these pathways, we must first examine the role played by the recently discovered 'benzodiazepine receptor'.

The benzodiazepine receptor and the role of GABA

Both benzodiazepines (Costa and Greengard 1975; Macdonald and Barker 1978) and barbiturates (Ransom and Barker 1976; Barker and Ransom 1978) facilitate the action of the inhibitory neurotransmitter, γ-aminobutyric acid (GABA). In recent years much progress has been made in understanding how the benzodiazepines produce this effect. The key advance was the discovery of a specific, high-affinity receptor for the benzodiazepines located on neurons in the central nervous system (Squires and Braestrup 1977; Möhler and Okada 1977; Skolnick *et al.* 1979*b*; Lippa *et al.* 1978*b*; Guidotti *et al.* 1979). This receptor appears to be closely related to the postsynaptic receptor for GABA. Observations reported by Guidotti, Toffano, and Costa (1978) suggest that, when a benzodiazepine binds to its specific receptor, this has the effect of increasing the affinity of the nearby GABA receptor for GABA, thus increasing the net effect of transmission along GABA-ergic pathways (see Fig. 11.2). It is possible that this effect is due to the displacement of an endogenous ligand ('GABA-modulin') for the benzodiazepine receptor, whose normal function would be to inhibit the postsynaptic response to GABA (Guidotti *et al.* 1978). There are several candidates for this ligand (Skolnick *et al.* 1979*a*; Squires *et al.* 1979; Lippa *et al.* 1979*b*; Braestrup and Nielsen 1980), but none is yet firmly established. If it exists, it may be a naturally occurring anti-anxiety agent, analogous to the endogenous opiate analgesics (Hughes *et al.* 1975). Alternatively, if facilitated GABA-ergic transmission has an anti-anxiety effect (a hypothesis we discuss below), the putative endogenous ligand for the benzodiazepine receptor becomes a 'pro-anxiety' agent.

It is clear that the benzodiazepine receptor is a critical link in the chain by which the benzodiazepines themselves affect behaviour; but there are reasons to doubt that it is centrally related to anxiety. First, the benzodiazepine receptor does not bind the barbiturates or alcohol (Squires and Braestrup 1977; Möhler and Okada 1977); it follows that there are other ways into those parts of the brain that mediate anxiety than via the ben-

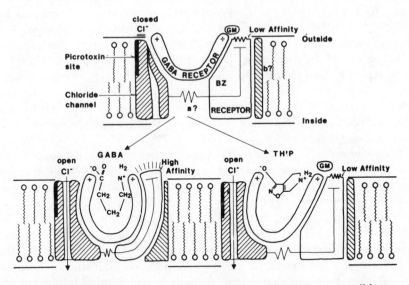

Figure 11.2. Braestrup and Nielsen's model to illustrate a possible coupling among GABA receptors, chloride channels and benzodiazepine receptors in the double lipid layer of neuronal plasma membranes. GABA-modulin (GM) may interfere with both the GABA and the benzodiazepine receptors. Furthermore, there is a link between the chloride channels and the benzodiazepine receptor (a). Since not all the effects of benzodiazepines are clearly linked to the GABA system it is also likely that the benzodiazepine receptor is coupled to a third, as yet unidentified, mechanism (b). THIP is a partial GABA agonist which is thought to induce less conformational change in the GABA receptor than does GABA itself. (From Braestrup and Nielsen (1980).)

zodiazepine receptors. Second, the distribution of the benzodiazepine receptor is not what one would expect if these are specific to brain systems that are exclusively related to anxiety. It is true that the density of benzodiazepine receptors is quite high in the limbic system, including the septal area and hippocampus (Braestrup and Squires 1977; Williamson, Paul, and Skolnick 1978). But so it is in many other regions of the central nervous system which are unlikely to play much part in anxiety. Thus the cerebellum and the spinal cord are both rich in benzodiazepine receptors, and the neocortex is richer than the hippocampus (Braestrup and Squires 1977; Williamson *et al.* 1978; Möhler and Okada 1977; Robertson, Martin, and Candy 1978).

Recently it has been reported that there are two distinct classes of benzodiazepine receptor (Squires *et al.* 1979; Lippa *et al.* 1979*b*; Klepner *et al.* 1979; Sieghart and Karobath 1980), so one might hope for a solution to the second of these problems from this direction. However, the data reported so far do not encourage this hope. Lippa *et al.* (1979*a*) distinguish between Type I and Type II receptors, showing that a new class of anti-anxiety drugs (the triazolopyridazines) disinhibits punished responding, is relatively free of the depressant and ataxic effects of the benzodiazepines, and binds only to Type I receptors (whereas the benzodiazepines bind equally to Type I and Type II receptors). The two types of receptor are differently distributed throughout the brain. Thus, if (as Lippa *et al.* 1979*a* propose) the Type I receptor is responsible for the anti-anxiety action produced by benzodiazepines and triazolopyridazines alike, we might expect to find that its distribution maps better onto neural systems likely on other grounds to be concerned with anxiety. Instead we find Type I receptors to be particularly dense in the cerebellum (Lippa *et al.* 1981), a structure which (so far as is known) is largely concerned with the control of movement.

Since neither type of benzodiazepine receptor binds the other anti-anxiety drugs, they cannot form the common link in the chain of action which leads to the behavioural effects of these agents. An alternative possibility is that the common link is the facilitation of GABA-ergic transmission which results from occupancy of the benzodiazepine receptor (Guidotti *et al.* 1978). This 'GABA' hypothesis of anti-anxiety drug action (Costa and Greengard 1975) receives strong support from the fact that the barbiturates also facilitate GABA transmission (Ransom and Barker 1976; Barker and Ransom 1978), though by other means. Recent evidence has thrown some light on how the barbiturates produce this effect. GABA, and drugs (such as muscimol) which have the same range of effects as the neurotransmitter, appear to act by changing the conformation of the GABA receptor, with the consequence that a chloride 'channel' opens in the postsynaptic membrane, hyperpolarizing and inhibiting the firing of the cell (Braestrup and Nielsen 1980). The convulsant drug, picrotoxin, binds to a site which is separate from the GABA receptor, and it appears to antagonise GABA by a direct action on the chloride channel (Olsen *et al.* 1978*a*, *b*; Braestrup and Nielsen 1980). The barbiturates also bind to the picrotoxin receptor (perhaps owing their anticonvulsant activity to this effect), and are thought to potentiate or prolong the effect of GABA on the chloride channel to which the GABA receptor is coupled (Olsen *et al.* 1978*b*; Ticku and Olsen 1978). Some of these complex interactions between the GABA, picrotoxin, and benzodiazepine receptors are illustrated in Fig. 11.2).

However, the GABA hypothesis of anti-anxiety drug action runs into some of the same difficulties as the proposal that the critical step is occupancy of the benzodiazepine receptor. Like benzodiazepine receptors, GABA-ergic neurons and receptors are distributed too widely in the brain for it to be plausible that their chief function is to regulate anxiety. Given the important role that GABA plays as an inhibitory neurotransmitter, one would expect that a drug which facilitates its action would act as a general sedative rather than a specific anti-anxiety agent. Alternatively, given the known relationship between lowered GABA function and the occurrence of convulsions (Meldrum 1975), one might expect such a drug to be an anticonvulsant. These descriptions fit both the benzodiazepines and the barbiturates (Simon and Soubrié 1979; Schallek *et al.* 1972; Randall and Kappell 1973; Browne and Perry 1973). Thus the facilitated GABA-ergic transmission produced by these drugs might underlie their sedative and anticonvulsant properties rather than their effects on anxiety.

This possibility is supported by Lippa *et al.*'s (1980) observations. These workers studied the effects of benzodiazepines and triazolopyridazines on two kinds of convulsion, one produced by drugs that reduce GABA-ergic transmission (bicuculline, isoniazid), the other by drugs that lack this effect (pentylenetetrazole). In agreement with earlier reports, the benzodiazepines antagonized both kinds of convulsion; but the triazolopyridazines blocked only convulsions not associated with reduced GABA transmission. Recall that the triazolopyridazines reduce the response suppression caused by punishment (Lippa *et al.* 1979*a*), one of the best available animal analogues of anti-anxiety action. Thus the results reported by Lippa *et al.* (in press) suggest that the pathway by which the benzodiazepines and triazolopyridazines reduce anxiety is independent of any effect on GABA transmission.

Efforts to examine more directly the hypothesis that GABA-ergic systems are involved in anxiety have met with only equivocal success.

Soubrié, Thiébot, and Simon (1979) studied the effects of picrotoxin — a GABA antagonist which (as we have seen) is thought to operate by 'shutting' a chloride channel normally 'opened' by GABA (MacDonald and Barker 1978; Olsen *et al.* 1978*a*; Simmonds 1980) — on three types of behavioural inhibition: suppression of food or water intake by novelty; suppression of bar-pressing by foot-shock; and suppression of bar-pressing by extinction or a shift from CRF to FR 4. Provided the suppression observed in controls was not too great, picrotoxin increased it, a result opposite to that produced by anti-anxiety drugs, and therefore in agreement with the hypothesis that GABA-ergic systems have an endogenous anti-anxiety influence on behaviour. Similarly, Soubrié, Thiébot, and Jobert (1978b) found that picrotoxin improved performance on a DRL schedule (recall that anti-anxiety drugs impair performance on this task). Results consistent with these have been reported in experiments using drug 'cocktails'. Thus Stein, Belluzzi, and Wise (1977) and Billingsley and Kubena (1978) used picrotoxin successfully to reverse the alleviation of response suppression produced by benzodiazepines. Conversely, Soubrié, Thiébot, and Jobert (1978b) reversed the effect of picrotoxin on DRL performance with diazepam.

Picrotoxin, then, generally has the effects predicted by the GABA hypothesis of anti-anxiety action. But experiments in which GABA action has been in some way increased have so far drawn a complete blank. Using a range of tasks suitable to demonstrate anti-anxiety action, Soubrié (1978), Thiébot, Jobert, and Soubrié (1979), and Thiébot (1979) found no effect of amino-oxyacetic acid (which increases central levels of GABA), muscimol* (a GABA receptor agonist), and several other drugs with similar modes of action. Other negative results have been reported by Cook and Sepinwall (1975). Thiébot (1979) also reports that she was unable to potentiate the anti-anxiety effects of diazepam by simultaneously administering drugs which facilitate GABA transmission. Thus it is possible that the positive findings with picrotoxin (see above) are due to some action of this drug other than its blockade of the postsynaptic effect of GABA.

A further way to investigate the possible involvement of benzodiazepine receptors or GABA-ergic systems in anxiety is to measure relevant aspects of brain biochemistry either after the imposition of a stress or in groups of animals known to respond differently to stress. Working along these lines Lippa *et al.* (1978a) and Thiébot (1979) have investigated changes in benzodiazepine receptor binding after stress (foot-shock and approach-avoidance conflict in Lippa's experiment, cold stress in Thiébot's). The trouble with this kind of experiment is that, on the hypothesis that these receptors bind an endogenous 'pro-anxiety' agent, one can predict equally well that stress will give rise to increased or to decreased receptor binding (as one can also on the opposite hypothesis, that the putative endogenous ligand is an anti-anxiety agent). To begin with, one does not know whether increased receptor binding indicates increased or decreased functional capacity in the system concerned. And, in any case, one might

---

*It is possible that the doses of muscimol used by Thiébot and Soubrié were too high. Using the theta-driving curve (Fig. 11.3), Mellanby *et al.* (1981) have found a maximal effect of this drug at 0.00125 mg kg^{-1}, which then falls off as the dose is increased. The lowest dose used by Thiébot (1979) was 0.03 mg kg^{-1}.

expect with equal plausibility that, after stress, an endogenous pro-anxiety substance should be *more* active (since the animal is presumably made anxious by the stress) or *less* (allowing the animal to keep relatively calm and so cope with the situation). This confusion in prediction is matched by confusion in the data, since Lippa *et al.* (1978*a*) report reduced benzodiazepine binding to neocortical tissue taken from stressed rats, and Thiébot (1979) increased binding. In the same study, Thiébot found no change in cerebellar benzodiazepine binding; since Type I receptors strongly predominate in the cerebellum (Lippa *et al.* 1980), this observation is inconsistent with the hypothesis that these receptors are particularly closely related to anxiety (Lippa *et al.* 1979*a*), although on other, more general grounds it is not unexpected.

In spite of the discrepancy between the findings of Lippa *et al.* (1978*a*) and Thiébot (1979), it is encouraging for the hypothesis that benzodiazepine receptors are somehow related to anxiety that there are at least some changes in their functioning after stress. However, electroconvulsive shock is also able to change (increase) benzodiazepine binding (Paul and Skolnick 1978); thus the benzodiazepine receptor may be related to the anticonvulsant effects of the benzodiazepines rather than, or as well as, their anti-anxiety action. This possibility also clouds the otherwise encouraging finding that benzodiazepine binding is higher in Maudsley Nonreactive than in Maudsley Reactive rats (Robertson *et al.* 1978), since the Nonreactive strain, as well as being less fearful than the Reactive (Broadhurst 1960; Gray 1971*a*), is more susceptible to seizures (Gray 1964*b*).

So far we have treated seizures as an annoyance, coming between us and our real object of interest, anxiety. But it is just possible that the relation between convulsions and anxiety goes deeper than this. It is intriguing that Hall (1951) and Broadhurst (1960), in their independent selective breeding programmes, both found an association between low emotionality and high seizure susceptibility (Gray 1964*b*); and that both major groups of anti-anxiety drugs also have anticonvulsant properties (but note that low anxiety now goes with *low* seizure susceptibility). More direct evidence relating stress to seizure susceptibility is to be found in Thiébot's (1979) doctoral dissertation. She demonstrated that, after rats had been exposed to a number of different stressful situations (a swim in cold water, foot-shock, a conditioned suppression task, frustration imposed by placing a barrier between the subject and reward), the threshold for provocation of seizures by certain drugs was raised. The drugs affected in this way were of a kind which interfere either with GABA-ergic transmission (isoniazid, thiosemicarbazide, picrotoxin) or with benzodiazepine binding (pentylenetetrazole); the threshold for the induction of seizures by drugs with other mechanisms of action (bemegride, strychnine) was unchanged. Thus these results suggest that stress increases the effectiveness of GABA-ergic transmission, so lowering the animal's susceptibility to seizures. It is possible that the increased GABA-

ergic transmission serves as a feedback mechanism, temporarily controlling the level of anxiety elicited by stress. But, if so, it is the Type II
benzodiazepine receptor (which apparently mediates the convulsive effects of pentylenetetrazole: Lippa *et al.* 1980), not the Type I receptor, as
predicted by Lippa *et al.*'s (1979*a*) hypothesis, which is involved.

These various findings make it almost certain that GABA and the benzodiazepine receptor will have roles to play in the final story of anxiety;
but it is unlikely that they will be central roles. For there remains too
great a contrast between, on the one hand, the considerable specificity of
the behavioural effects of the anti-anxiety drugs (Chapter 2) and, on the
other, the non-specific changes (lowered seizure susceptibility, general
sedation) that are likely to be the principal effect of a general facilitation
of GABA mechanisms throughout the brain. One is tempted, therefore,
to seek ways in which the benzodiazepine receptor–GABA link can be
inserted into a more localized neuronal chain.

There are many points in the septo-hippocampal system at which an
alteration in GABA function might critically affect the way this system
does its job. McLennan and Miller (1974*b*), for example, have described
a GABA-ergic synapse in the lateral septal area, perhaps forming part of
the hippocampo-septal projection. The hippocampus itself has an extensive, intrinsic GABA-ergic interneuronal system (Storm-Mathisen 1978).
And there is evidence for GABA-ergic terminals on both major cell
groups which give rise to monoaminergic afferents to the septo-hippocampal system, the locus coeruleus (Iversen and Schon 1973; Guyenet
and Aghajanian 1979), and the raphe nuclei (Belin *et al.* 1979); furthermore, benzodiazepines have been shown to increase the inhibitory effects
of GABA on raphe cell bodies (Gallager 1978). There is no clear reason,
however, why these GABA-ergic synapses should be particularly favoured
by the attentions of the anti-anxiety drugs; and, indeed, the binding studies (which place benzodiazepine receptors all over the brain) indicate
rather strongly that they are not. It is possible that, given the great number of GABA-ergic neurons in the brain, the effects of enhanced GABA
transmission may simply cancel out at many points in the brain, leaving
net effects for change only in a few systems which happen to be critical
for anxiety (McNaughton, personal communication); but this suggestion
lacks supporting evidence.

The dorsal ascending noradrenergic bundle

If we have to seek some special part of the brain, in which a particular
group of GABA-ergic neurons or benzodiazepine receptors is conveniently embedded, as the critical site on which the anti-anxiety drugs act,
we may as well forget about receptors and GABA (at least temporarily)
and seek it directly. The noradrenergic pathway originating in the locus
coeruleus, and ascending in the dorsal noradrenergic bundle to innervate
much of the forebrain, has many attractions as a starting point in this

search. As mentioned above, there are GABA-ergic terminals in the locus coeruleus (Iversen and Schon 1973), while the septal area and hippocampus are major targets for its efferents (see Chapter 3, Figs. 3.10 and 3.11). Thus it is possible that impulses reaching the septo-hippocampal system from the dorsal noradrenergic bundle influence the way in which this system processes information; and that the anti-anxiety drugs counteract this influence by increasing GABA-ergic inhibition on the cell-bodies in the locus coeruleus. Furthermore, as we saw in Chapter 4, there is evidence that one function of these impulses is to boost the passage of signals around the hippocampal circuit (Fig. 3.5), a function which (according to the theory developed in Chapter 10) may carry the significance of a label, destined for the subicular comparator and reading 'important, check carefully.' A function of this kind is likely to be of particular importance under conditions of threat, that is, in states of anxiety. It is consistent with this view that, as we shall now see, stress increases impulse traffic in the dorsal noradrenergic bundle; that the anti-anxiety drugs impair conduction in the dorsal bundle; that this impairment is seen especially under conditions of stress; and that it is produced by all classes of anti-anxiety drug.

Stone (1975, Table IV) has reviewed a large number of experiments in which the turnover of noradrenalin in the brain (thought to reflect the rate of impulse transmission in noradrenergic neurons) has been observed to rise after foot-shock, cold or heat stress, immobilization, forced exercise, handling, or various other stressful procedures. The same effect is produced by exposure to a CS for shock without the shock itself (Tilson, Rech, and Sparber 1975). Stress has also been reported (De Pottier *et al.* 1976) to increase the release into cerebrospinal fluid of dopamine-β-hydroxylase, the enzyme which catalyses the formation of noradrenalin from dopamine; this is probably released from nerve terminals along with noradrenalin itself. The general increase in noradrenergic activity seen in the whole brain under conditions of stress has also been demonstrated to occur specifically in the dorsal noradrenergic bundle. Thus Corrodi *et al.* (1971) and Lidbrink *et al.* (1972) showed that immobilization or shock increases noradrenalin turnover in forebrain tissue dissected out from the rest of the brain. Furthermore — and this is a critical observation for the thesis developed here — the increased turnover of noradrenalin is prevented by the administration of barbiturates, benzodiazepines, alcohol, or meprobamate (Corrodi *et al.* 1971; Lidbrink *et al.* 1972, 1973; Taylor and Laverty 1973). In agreement with these observations, Segal (1978*b*) has reported that aversive stimuli (e.g. a pinch of the tail or leg) increases firing rates in locus coeruleus neurons; and, conversely, Pohorecky and Brick (1977) report that alcohol decreases coerulear firing rates. The stress-induced increase in noradrenergic activity can be detected within the hippocampus itself. Thus the activity of tyrosine hydroxylase (the rate-limiting enzyme for the synthesis of noradrenalin) is elevated in synaptosomes (pinched-off nerve terminals) prepared from hippocampi dissected from the brains of rats shocked or handled shortly before death (Fillenz, Graham-Jones, and Gray 1979).

Observations of this kind have given rise to the hypothesis that the dorsal ascending noradrenergic bundle plays a role in anxiety, and that the anti-anxiety drugs affect behaviour in virtue of an action on this pathway (Lidbrink *et al.* 1973; Fuxe *et al.* 1975). The same hypothesis has been proposed independently by two other groups. Redmond *et al.* (1976) stimulated the locus coeruleus in conscious stump-tailed monkeys and noted similarities between the behaviour evoked by this stimulation and behaviour emitted spontaneously when a monkey is threatened; this led them to suggest that stimulation of the locus coeruleus evokes a central state akin to anxiety. The experiments of Gray *et al.* (1975) were concerned with the theta-driving curve described in Chapter 4 (Fig. 4.7), that is, the relation between the threshold septal stimulating current able to drive hippocampal theta and stimulation frequency. As we saw in Chapter 7, the minimum found at 7.7 Hz when this function is measured in the free-moving male rat is absent in the Maudsley Nonreactive strain, which has been selectively bred for low fearfulness, and in female rats, which are generally less fearful than males (Drewett *et al.* 1977); moreover, in male outbred rats it is eliminated by a range of anti-anxiety drugs (Gray and Ball 1970; McNaughton *et al.* 1977). These findings, and others discussed in Chapters 7 and 8, give some reason to link the absence of a minimum at 7.7 Hz in the theta-driving curve to a lowered level of anxiety. Thus the observation that destruction of the dorsal noradrenergic bundle eliminates the 7.7-Hz minimum in the theta-driving curve (Gray *et al.* 1975; McNaughton, Kelly, and Gray 1980*b*), thereby mimicking the effects of the anti-anxiety drugs, again suggested a role for the dorsal bundle in anxiety.

As pointed out by Fuxe *et al.* (1975), the benzodiazepines may impair transmission in the dorsal noradrenergic bundle by facilitating a GABA-ergic inhibitory input to the locus coeruleus (see above). In support of this inference, Mellanby, Gray, Holt, Quintero, and McNaughton (1981) have shown that the effect of chlordiazepoxide on the theta-driving curve is prevented by simultaneous administration of the GABA blocker, picrotoxin, while the GABA agonist, muscimol, acts on the theta-driving curve in the same way as the anti-anxiety drugs (Fig. 11.3). The effect of chlordiazepoxide was not blocked by another GABA antagonist, bicuculline. This pattern of drug action is characteristic of a putative GABA presynaptic receptor which acts to reduce monoamine release in the forebrain (Bowery *et al.* 1980). Thus it is also possible that the effect of the benzodiazenines on the theta-driving curve is mediated by presynaptic GABA receptors on noradrenergic terminals in the septo-hippocampal system itself.

Since the barbiturates also facilitate GABA-ergic transmission (Ransom

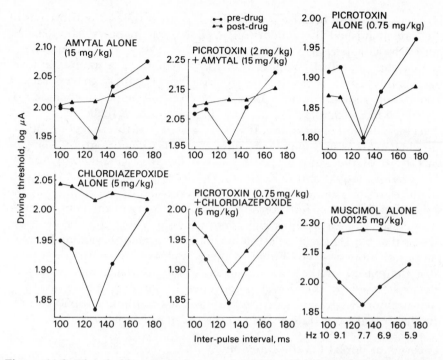

Figure 11.3. Threshold currents for septal driving of hippocampal theta rhythm as a function of inter-pulse interval in the free-moving male rat before and after systemic administration of the drugs shown. The minimum threshold at 130 ms (= 7.7 Hz) in the pre-drug curve is abolished by both sodium amylobarbitone (amytal) and chlordiazepoxide, and picrotoxin blocks only the latter effect. Muscimol, a GABA agonist, acts like the two anti-anxiety drugs. Note that the abscissa displays inter-pulse interval (an equivalent Hz scale is shown at the bottom right) and is reversed from Figs. 4.7 and 7.1. (Data from Mellanby *et al.* (1981).)

and Barker 1976; Barker and Ransom 1978), they too might impair transmission in the dorsal noradrenergic bundle or septo-hippocampal system in the same way. However (Fig. 11.3), picrotoxin failed to alter the influence of sodium amylobarbitone on the theta-driving curve (Mellanby *et al.* 1981). Thus the barbiturates appear to act at a different point in the neural chain than the GABA-ergic synapses onto the locus coeruleus or in the septo-hippocampal system, although they perhaps act at these synapses as well.

The hypothesis proposed by Gray *et al.* (1975) goes one step further than those put forward by Fuxe's group (Lidbrink *et al.* 1973) and by Redmond *et al.* (1976) in that it specifies that the important projection of the dorsal bundle (insofar as anxiety is concerned) is to the septo-hippocampal system, as distinct from, say, the amygdala or neocortex. This hypothesis can be related to the theory developed in Chapter 10 in the following way. As we saw in Chapter 7, the special role played by 7.7-

Hz theta may arise because it is a balance point between the two types of theta distinguished by Vanderwolf *et al.* (1975); in particular, data reported by Graeff *et al.* (1980) suggest that 7.7 Hz is the maximum frequency up to which Vanderwolf's low-frequency, atropine-sensitive, immobility-related theta is able to rise. In Chapter 10 we related Vanderwolf's low-frequency theta to the 'control' mode of operation of the septo-hippocampal system, and high-frequency theta to the 'just checking' mode. Furthermore, it was suggested that the function of theta in either mode is to quantize the passage of information around the various loops of the septo-hippocampal system, as originally proposed by Vinogradova (1975) and O'Keefe and Nadel (1978). In that case, 7.7 Hz might represent the maximum rate of transmission of information by the septo-hippocampal system consistent with its staying in the control mode of operation. A further possibility, not necessarily incompatible with the first, is that 7.7-Hz theta reflects a maximum degree of hesitation between policies of 'stop' and 'go.' Either of these modes of functioning is a plausible component of the state of anxiety. Thus the facilitation of 7.7-Hz theta exercised by the dorsal noradrenergic bundle (Gray *et al.* 1975; McNaughton, Kelly, and Gray 1980*b*) has a natural link to anxiety within the theoretical context developed in the previous chapter.

Theories of dorsal bundle function

There is a clear *prima facie* case, then, for supposing that the dorsal noradrenergic bundle has something to do with anxiety. But there are several rival hypotheses which attribute to the dorsal bundle quite different kinds of function. Furthermore, the 'anxiety' hypothesis of dorsal bundle function can itself take several different forms. Thus, before we consider the behavioural data which can alone decide the issue, let us try to clarify what the different theories are.

The anatomy of the locus coeruleus and its efferent fibres places severe constraints on the functions that can plausibly be attributed to the dorsal bundle (Ungerstedt 1971; Lindvall and Björklund 1978; Moore and Bloom 1979). There are only about 1500 cells in the locus coeruleus in the rat, and these innervate widespread regions of the brain, including the olfactory bulb, much of the neocortex, the hippocampus, septal area and amygdala, some thalamic and hypothalamic nuclei, the geniculate bodies and colliculi, the cerebellum, and the spinal cord. To achieve this feat, each cell body gives rise to several bifurcating axons (Olson and Fuxe 1971; Pickel, Krebs, and Bloom 1973). These observations seem to exclude the possibility that the dorsal bundle conveys any specific or selective information to its target areas, suggesting, rather, a very general message used simultaneously by many structures. Some variety in the content or at least intensity of this message may perhaps be achieved by presynaptic local regulation in particular terminal zones (McNaughton and Mason 1980); and recent evidence indicates a degree of specificity in the sets of terminal areas innervated by particular groups of locus coeruleus neurones (Mason and Fibiger 1979g). McNaughton and Mason (1980) suggest that this element of specificity can perhaps be enhanced by the action of recurrent collaterals in the locus coeruleus, which are able to modulate the firing of adjacent cells in that structure by release of noradrenalin (Aghajanian *et al.* 1977; Shimizu *et al.* 1978; Watabe and Satoh 1979). But it remains unlikely that the dorsal bundle conveys precise or detailed information, of the kind, say, carried by the primary sensory pathways. This impression is reinforced by two other features of its anatomy: the diffuse and ramifying pattern of its terminal projections within a given structure; and its relative lack of specialized synaptic terminals (Descarries *et al.* 1977; Shimizu *et al.* 1979), although this has been questioned, at least in the hippocampus (Koda *et al.* 1978).

One hypothesis which is consistent with these features of dorsal bundle morphology attributes to it a role in the control of the blood supply locally in the brain (Raichle *et al.* 1976; Harik *et al.* 1979). This would be in accord with the vascular functions exercised by peripheral noradrenergic neurons, and is further supported by the reported occurrence of noradrenergic terminals on or near blood vessels in the brain (Swanson, Connelly, and Hartman 1977; Hartman and Udenfriend 1972). Note, however, that, even if this hypothesis is correct, it does not terminate the quest for the *behavioural* functions of the dorsal bundle. It might be, for example, that the dorsal bundle carries the signal 'this is important' to the septo-hippocampal system precisely *by* increasing local blood flow (and hence the capacity for neuronal activity) in this one of its terminal areas; and comparable proposals could be made to fit other hypotheses which we shall consider below. The evidence that the dorsal bundle regulates blood supply is in any case not strong (Dahlgren and Lindvall 1980), and it is even less likely that this is all it does. That the locus coeruleus acts directly on neurons in its target organs is indicated both by observations of at least some specialized synapses on its terminals (Koda *et al.* 1978; Swanson *et al.* 1978), and by experiments in which iontophoretically applied noradrenalin has altered the firing rate of neurons in regions to which the dorsal bundle projects (Segal and Bloom 1974a). It is, of course, possible that the dorsal bundle acts simultaneously in two ways, conveying a relatively gross functional message and at the same time regulating the local blood supply to the relevant target organ so that it can deal with this message more effectively. In any event, our interest lies in the content of the functional message, so we shall not consider the vascular hypothesis further.

Until recently the most widely received hypothesis concerning the nature of the information carried by the dorsal bundle has been that it subserves reward or reinforcement. This hypothesis was suggested in the first instance by the results of experiments on electrical self-stimulation of the brain (Rolls 1975). Central noradrenergic mechanisms were implicated in this phenomenon by two major lines of evidence. Pharmacological experiments suggested that it was necessary and sufficient to block noradrenergic transmission for self-stimulation to be interrupted; and mapping experiments suggested that sites located either along the dorsal bundle or in the locus coeruleus itself were particularly likely to sustain self-stimulation.

Both these generalizations remain controversial (Wauquier and Rolls 1976; Wise 1978), but it is not my intention to review here the evidence that relates to them. I choose to duck this issue because I am not convinced that self-stimulation tells us anything very directly about the brain structures that mediate normal reward. It is usually inferred from the fact that an animal works to stimulate a particular region of the brain that this region contains neurons (cell-bodies or fibres of passage) which participate in the control of behaviour directed to the attainment of conventional rewards (food, water, etc.). Certainly, it is this inference that has been applied to the dorsal bundle: the self-stimulation data have prompted the hypothesis that this pathway forms part of a system which governs approach behaviour (Stein 1968) or learning in general (Kety 1970; Crow 1973; Fillenz 1973). The inference is plausible; yet there is overwhelming evidence that it is unsound. Time and again it has been shown that destruction of regions of the brain that support self-stimulation causes no impairment in the learning or performance of conventionally rewarded behaviour. An example that is easy to hand is that of the septal area. As we saw in Chapter 6, far from impairing rewarded behaviour or learning, septal lesions may even increase the effects of incentives on performance. Yet the septal area sustains high rates of self-stimulation, and indeed was among the first sites shown to do so (Olds and Milner 1954). Other examples are the frontal cortex (Routtenberg and Santos-Anderson 1977; Rosenkilde 1979) and the dorsal bundle itself, as we shall see.

From one point of view the reward hypothesis of dorsal bundle function is almost diametrically opposed to the anxiety hypothesis. For, as we know, the anti-anxiety drugs antagonize the behavioural effects of *non-reward*, or, more precisely, those of stimuli associated with non-reward (Chapter 2); thus on a strong interpretation of the anxiety hypothesis, it follows that the dorsal bundle mediates the behavioural effects of these stimuli. It is not easy, however, to reconcile this interpretation of the anxiety hypothesis with the anatomy of the dorsal bundle. The 1500 cells that make up the locus coeruleus require some remarkable properties if, all alone, they are to perform the comparison of expected and actual stimulation which results in the detection of non-reward. Nor does it appear likely that this information reaches them from the regions so far demonstrated to project to the locus coeruleus, namely, the central nucleus of the amygdala, the bed nucleus of the stria terminalis, a number of hypothalamic nuclei, parts of the insular cortex, the dorsal raphe, the substantia nigra, central grey substance, contralateral locus coeruleus, and various pontine and spinal regions (Sakai *et al.* 1977*b;* Cederbaum and Aghajanian 1978); although it is possible that the amygdaloid projection or the one from the bed nucleus of the stria terminalis (which itself receives a projection from the ventral subiculum) could play this role. Information about reward, in contrast, might easily reach the locus coeruleus from the hypothalamus or the amygdala, both structures which appear to play a genuine role in rewarded learning, as distinct from merely sustaining self-stimulation (Rolls 1975).

There is, however, a further possibility, one that represents a compromise between the seemingly irreconcilable reward and anxiety hypotheses of dorsal bundle function. On this view the dorsal bundle indeed carries messages about reward, but these are used by the septo-hippocampal system for the detection of non-reward (Boarder, Feldon, Gray, and Fillenz 1979). That such messages are potentially conveyed to the septo-hippocampal system via the dorsal bundle is indicated by two findings. First, there is the report that locus coeruleus stimulation and CSs for food exert similar facilitatory effects on transmission round the hippocampal circuit (Segal 1977*a, d;* see Chapter 7). Second, Boarder *et al.* (1979) measured tyrosine hydroxylase activity in hippocampal synaptosomes taken from the brains of rats that had been trained on either CRF or PRF schedules of food reward in the alley. Compared to handled but untrained controls, the CRF-trained rats had elevated levels of enzyme activity. This may indicate (Boarder and Fillenz 1978, 1979) an increased rate of impulse traffic in hippocampal noradrenergic terminals just before the animal's death (which occurred at the time and under the conditions associated with entry into the alley). The PRF-trained rats displayed levels of enzyme activity which were significantly lower than those seen in the CRF group and which did not differ from those in the handled controls. Since the same pattern of results was observed with two training paradigms involving widely differing numbers and distributions of acquisition trials (6 trials day^{-1} for 8 days and 1 trial day^{-1} for 12 days), this suggests that the non-rewarded trials actively returned the levels of tyrosine hydroxylation to the baseline from which rewarded trials raised them. Thus the level of tyrosine hydroxylation in hippocampal synaptosomes was perhaps proportional to the degree to which the animal expected reward in these experiments (Boarder *et al.* 1979). Since, as we shall see, destruction of the dorsal bundle attenuates the effects of non-reward in this kind of paradigm without altering learning about reward (Owen *et al.* 1977, 1981), a signal of this kind could not have been concerned principally with the direct control of rewarded behaviour but might play a role in the detection of non-reward.

If it were the case that the dorsal bundle carries messages which code expected reward in this way, one might account for self-stimulation along this pathway, in the regions to which it projects, and in the locus coeruleus itself, along the following lines (Gray, Owen, Davis and Tsaltas, 1983). As we have seen, each cell-body in the locus coeruleus appears to innervate several different terminal areas (Olson and Fuxe 1971; Pickel *et al.* 1973). Thus the same information which is used by the septo-hippocampal system to detect non-reward might also be used by other terminal areas (e.g. the amygdala or the cerebellum) in the organization of responses to reward. Stimulation of other dorsal bundle terminals would antidromically excite the cell-bodies in the locus coeruleus and then orthodromically excite this putative 'reward' target area, so giving rise to the phenomenon of self-stimulation. But only in the reward target area itself would such self-stimulation be a good index of normal function; and there would be no way of telling from self-stimulation studies alone which area is truly concerned with reward.

In this way, then, it is possible to reconcile the view that the dorsal bundle is an important focus of self-stimulation (Stein 1968; Crow 1973) with the hypothesis that it conveys to the septo-hippocampal system a signal that is important in anxiety and used for the detection of nonreward. The controversy concerning the role of the dorsal bundle in self-stimulation is, however, far from resolution, and recent evidence tends to weaken the case for such a role (Wise 1978). In particular, Clavier, Fibiger, and Phillips (1976) have shown that destruction of the dorsal bundle does not affect self-stimulation in the locus coeruleus. It is possible that, in this case, self-stimulation was maintained by noradrenergic fibres destined for the cerebellum or even the spinal cord; but it is clear from this result that the ascending noradrenergic fibres originating in the locus coeruleus are not essential for self-stimulation even in this organ itself. Thus the fact that the 'reward signal' hypothesis of dorsal bundle function can be reconciled with the view that the dorsal bundle is an important focus for self-stimulation may turn out to be a dubious virtue.

A further possible view is that the dorsal bundle sends to the septo-hippocampal system information concerning punishment. This view cannot easily be reconciled with the self-stimulation data, assuming these are to be trusted; for it is difficult to see how either orthodromic or antidromic excitation of fibres carrying signals about punishment could be positively reinforcing. But it can be derived from the anxiety hypothesis of dorsal bundle function in exactly the same way as the supposition that this pathway subserves the detection of nonreward: the anti-anxiety drugs antagonize the behavioural effects of stimuli associated with punishment, so the dorsal bundle mediates these effects. This view can find support in Segal's (1977*a*, *d*) report that CSs associated with punishment facilitate transmission round the hippocampal circuit in the same manner as does stimulation of the locus coeruleus (Chapter 7). And there is no great problem about getting the relevant information to the locus coeruleus. Segal (1978*b*) reports that painful stimuli activate locus coeruleus neurons. This effect could be mediated by afferents from the central grey, the dorsal raphe, or the amygdala, all of which have been implicated in the behavioural effects of pain, or it might depend on a direct input from pain-sensitive neurons in the dorsal horns of the spinal cord (Sakai *et al.* 1977*b*; Cederbaum and Aghajanian 1978).

By combining the hypotheses that the dorsal bundle conveys to the septo-hippocampal system information about reward and about punishment, we come close to the position adopted in Chapter 10, namely, that the function of the noradrenergic afferents to the hippocampal formation is to tag stimuli simultaneously entering the system from the entorhinal cortex with the label, 'important, check carefully'. McNaughton and Mason (1980) and Segal (1980) suggest a neurophysiological mechanism which might underlie this function. As they point out, a number of investigators have shown that stimulation of the locus coeruleus, or direct application of noradrenalin to a target organ served by the dorsal bundle, has two effects: the spontaneous firing rate of neurons in the projection areas of the locus coeruleus is reduced, but their response to other afferents is increased (Foote *et al.* 1975; Siggins and Hendriksen 1975; Freedman *et al.* 1976; Moises *et al.* 1978; Woodward and Waterhouse 1978; Waterhouse *et al.* 1978); in consequence the signal-to-noise ratio with respect to the non-noradrenergic afferent is increased. This phenomenon has been observed within the hippocampal formation and, in particular, in response to stimulation of the perforant path (Segal and Bloom 1976; Assaf 1978; Assaf, Mason, and Miller 1979; see Chapter 4). On the theory proposed in Chapter 10, it is plausible to see such an increase in signal-to-noise ratio as the equivalent of a boosted presentation of the current entorhinal input to the subicular comparator, that is to say, the addition of an 'important' tag.

There is, however, a problem attached to the hypothesis that the dorsal bundle labels entorhinal inputs simply as 'important' in this way. As we saw in Chapter 7, neither the single-unit experiments nor Segal's investigations of the late negative potential in the commissural evoked response suggest that the hippocampus differentiates between stimuli associated with appetitive and aversive events, respectively; both kinds of association seem to be equally effective in facilitating transmission round the hippocampal circuit. Yet, both on the evidence from lesion experiments (Chapter 6) and on the theory developed in Chapter 10, the septo-hippocampal system responds to these two kinds of stimuli in quite different manners. Somehow, then, it must be instructed that a given 'important' stimulus belongs to one or other of these two classes. One way in which this might happen is by means of an interaction between the noradrenergic and serotonergic afferents to the septo-hippocampal system. This possibility is particularly attractive since, as we shall see, the evidence from lesion experiments rather strongly suggests that the dorsal noradrenergic bundle plays a relatively greater role in behaviour controlled by non-reward and the ascending serotonergic pathways, a relatively greater role in behaviour controlled by punishment. But we shall leave discussion of this issue until the lesion studies have been reviewed.

So far we have considered hypotheses attributing to the dorsal bundle various functions in situations involving reward, non-reward, or punishment. It remains to consider the case of novelty, the third major input (besides stimuli associated with punishment and non-reward) to the behavioural inhibition system described in Chapter 1. The simple anxiety hypothesis predicts that, after destruction of the dorsal bundle, animals will show reduced responses to novelty in the same way as after injections of anti-anxiety drugs (Chapter 2). A rather different suggestion has been made by Segal and Bloom (1976) on the basis of their electrophysiological experiments (Chapter 7) and by Mason and Iversen (1977c, 1979) on the basis of the behavioural effects of dorsal bundle lesions reviewed below. This hypothesis proposes that the dorsal bundle plays a role in inhibiting attention to irrelevant stimuli. Note that this is essentially the same as Douglas's (1967) theory of hippocampal function. Unfortunately, as is often the case when the concept of attention is introduced in a physiological context (though not necessarily when it is used in an appropriate psychological theory), the application of this hypothesis to the data has largely been *ad hoc* and lacking in precision. Thus it is not always possible to tell whether the 'attention' and anxiety hypotheses make different predictions.*

Both these hypotheses face the difficulty that, anatomically, the locus coeruleus does not appear to have the information-processing capacity to discriminate between novel and familiar (or relevant and irrelevant) stimuli. Nor do any of the known afferents to the locus coeruleus look likely as the origin of this type of information. This, of course, is the same problem that we faced earlier in the more specific form of the detection of non-reward. However, there is some evidence that locus coeruleus neurones increase their firing in response to novel stimuli (Jones, Foote, Segal, and Bloom 1978; Foote, Bloom, and Schwartz 1978). Thus they must receive information about novelty from somewhere or manufacture it themselves. Given the role the hippocampus appears to play in the analysis of novelty (Vinogradova 1975; see Chapter 10), the relevant messages may originate there and reach the locus coeruleus by a round-about route.

If we ignore this difficulty and attribute to the dorsal bundle the function of boosting the hippocampal analysis of all classes of stimuli which activate the behavioural inhibition system, i.e. those associated with non-reward (or perhaps, along the lines set out above, with reward), those associated with punishment, and novel stimuli, we arrive at a position — the 'checking' version of the anxiety hypothesis — which is in some ways

*See the discussion, later in the chapter, of the 'checking' version of the anxiety hypothesis.

close to the old notion of the ascending reticular activating system (Magoun 1963; Gray 1964a; Segal 1980).

The dorsal noradrenergic bundle is now known to play a central role in the ascending functions of the reticular formation (Hobson and Brazier 1980), though the nature of this role remains obscure. It was proposed by Jouvet (1969, 1972), on the basis of pharmacological and lesion evidence, that the locus coeruleus is responsible for rapid-eye-movement (REM) or paradoxical sleep. Recent findings, however, indicate that neither the locus coeruleus nor the dorsal noradrenergic bundle are in any way essential for normal REM sleep, although they may play some kind of a modulatory role (Jacobs and Jones 1978). It is even possible that the locus coeruleus inhibits REM sleep (McCarley 1980). Single-unit recordings indicate that the firing rate of locus coeruleus cells is at a low point during REM sleep, reaches intermediate values during slow-wave sleep, and is at its highest point during waking (McCarley 1980; Segal 1980). This is consistent with a general arousal function; but we have seen enough of the pitfalls attached to inferences drawn from recording experiments not to take this consistency too seriously. None the less, an increase in the level of arousal is one output of the behavioural inhibition system described in Chapter 1, and one moreover which seems not to be mediated by the septo-hippocampal system itself (Chapter 6). Thus it would neatly fill a hole in our puzzle if we could conclude that the dorsal bundle increments arousal level under conditions which activate the behavioural inhibition system.

We have now set out the different hypotheses which we shall need to bear in mind as we consider the behavioural effects of damaging the dorsal bundle. On the 'reward' hypothesis (Stein 1968), destruction of the dorsal bundle should selectively impair the learning and performance of rewarded behaviour. On the 'learning' hypothesis (Kety 1970; Crow 1973; Fillenz 1973), it should impair the acquisition of all forms of learned responses, irrespective of the nature of the reinforcement. On the general 'anxiety' hypothesis (Lidbrink *et al.* 1973; Redmond *et al.* 1976; Gray *et al.* 1975), the effects of dorsal bundle lesions should map perfectly onto those of the anti-anxiety drugs. On the 'reward signal' hypothesis (which is a restricted version of the anxiety hypothesis) the dorsal bundle carries signals of reward to the septo-hippocampal system which uses them to detect non-reward (Boarder *et al.* 1979); this predicts that dorsal bundle lesions should mimic the effects of the anti-anxiety drugs only in tasks which involve non-reward. On the 'attention' hypothesis (Segal and Bloom 1976; Mason and Iversen 1977c, 1979), destruction of the dorsal bundle should increase the spread of attention to irrelevant stimuli. Finally, on the 'arousal' hypothesis (also a restricted version of the anxiety hypothesis) the dorsal bundle mediates only the arousal-incrementing function of the behavioural inhibiton system, and this should therefore be selectively disrupted after dorsal bundle lesions. (Predictions from the 'checking' version of the anxiety hypothesis are considered later in the chapter.)

Lesion methods

In considering how these various hypotheses fare when confronted with the data we shall for the most part confine our attention to experiments in which the selective neurotoxin, 6-hydroxydopamine (6-OHDA), has been injected into the region of the dorsal bundle in such a way as to destroy only the noradrenergic fibres which take this route to the forebrain (Ungerstedt 1968).

The cytotoxic action of 6-OHDA takes place in two stages. It is taken up into catecholamine-containing fibres (dopaminergic or noradrenergic) by the selective membrane uptake system responsible for the recapture of catecholamines after their release; it is this that produces the neurochemical specificity of the effect. Within the fibre various oxidation products are then formed which cause its destruction (Jonsson and Sachs 1975). Further localization of the toxic effect of 6-OHDA can be attained by injecting it in a region traversed by no other catecholamine-containing fibres than those it is intended to destroy. It is fortunate for experimental purposes that, as shown in Fig. 3.11, the dorsal noradrenergic bundle briefly follows a path that is somewhat separate both from the ascending dopaminergic fibres and from the ventral noradrenergic bundle (which carries fibres from brainstem nuclei other than the locus coeruleus). This fact makes it possible by careful aim to confine the toxic action of the drug largely to the dorsal bundle. It is less fortunate, however, that the dorsal bundle carries fibres to many regions of the brain besides the septo-hippocampal system. Thus it has not yet proved possible to selectively destroy only the noradrenergic innervation of the septal area or the hippocampus. The locus coeruleus is the sole source of noradrenergic innervation of the hippocampal formation. Thus one can use the technique of injection of 6-OHDA into the dorsal bundle to produce (in the best case) a virtually complete destruction of this input to the hippocampus. But the septal area receives only 50 per cent of its noradrenergic innervation from the locus coeruleus, the remainder originating in two cell groups (A 1 and A 2) in the medulla oblongata whose fibres travel in the ventral bundle (Moore 1978; Lindvall and Stenevi 1978); thus, in this region one can hope only for a partial denervation by injecting 6-OHDA into the dorsal bundle.

It is, of course, necessary to verify the success of the lesion *post mortem.* This is usually done by assaying discrete regions of the brain for their content of noradrenalin and dopamine. Results from a series of such studies undertaken in Oxford (Owen, Boarder, Gray, and Fillenz, 1982) are presented in Table 11.1. It can be seen that, using this technique, it is possible to reduce levels of noradrenalin in the forebrain (neocortex, hip-

Table 11.1. Change in regional levels† of noradrenalin (NA), dopamine (DA), and serotonin (5-HT) after injection of 6-hydroxydopamine into the dorsal ascending noradrenergic bundle. (Data from Owen *et al.* (1982))

		Sham	Lesion	t	p	% Loss
	Olfactory lobes	209± 38 (8)	10± 4 (8)	5.2	<.001	95
	Septum	699± 90 (8)	330± 72 (8)	3.2	<.01	52
	Hippocampus	368± 48 (8)	25± 17 (8)	6.7	<.001	93
NA	Cortex	228± 40 (7)	31± 16 (8)	4.6	<001	86
	Striatum	354± 85 (8)	180± 47 (7)	1.8	<.1(NS)	49
	Amygdala	510± 54 (7)	101± 26 (6)	6.8	<.001	80
	Hypothalamus	1194± 89 (7)	765±106 (6)	3.1	<.02	36
	Cerebellum	168± 30 (7)	325± 34 (8)	3.5	<.01	+93*
	Septum	433±102 (6)	416± 93 (7)	0.1	NS	4
DA	Striatum	8140±990 (8)	7570±940 (8)	0.4	NS	7
	Hypothalamus	464± 45 (7)	374± 56 (6)	1.3	NS	19
5-HT	Hippocampus	257.1±15.8 (4)	239.1±27.8 (4)	0.5	NS	4
	Hypothalamus	576.8±98.2 (4)	606.2±45.2 (4)	0.3	NS	+4*

†ng g^{-1}± standard error; number of rats in brackets.
*Increase.

pocampus) by about 90 per cent, implying that most of the noradrenergic fibres innervating these regions have been destroyed. Dopamine levels in brain regions innervated by dopaminergic fibres (e.g. the corpus striatum) are barely affected. The fall in noradrenalin levels in structures receiving both dorsal and ventral bundle fibres is consistent with destruction only of the dorsal bundle (approximately 50 per cent in the septal area and 35 per cent in the hypothalamus). Serotonin levels in the hippocampus are unchanged. Mason and Iversen (1979) report a closely comparable pattern of change, and in addition find no change in serotonin levels in the cortex or hypothalamus, and no change in choline acetyltransferase or glutamic acid decarboxylase levels in a number of brain regions. Nonspecific damage around the cannula tip is not generally large; but it should be noted that injection of the vehicle (a mixture of saline and ascorbic acid), normally regarded as the optimum control procedure, may also cause a fall in forebrain noradrenalin levels of 30–35 per cent (Owen 1979). An interesting feature of the data shown in Table 11.1 is that levels of noradrenalin in the cerebellum show a substantial rise, as though the neurotransmitter, unable to flow along the damaged axons towards the forebrain, heads off along the collaterals to the cerebellum instead.

The results shown in Table 11.1, or in Mason and Iversen's (1979) Table 1, show how effective a 6-OHDA injection into the dorsal bundle can be in producing a selective lesion of the noradrenergic innervation of the forebrain. But the pattern of results is not always so clear. Even when the same experimenter uses the same co-ordinates for injection, the effects can differ from occasion to occasion, as we have found in our own experience; and in many of Mason's experiments the reported falls in hypothalamic noradrenalin reach 70 per cent (e.g. Mason and Fibiger 1978*a*, *c*), indicating substantial encroachment on the ventral noradrenergic bundle. Even when the lesion is 'clean', the effects it produces on behaviour appear to depend to a remarkable degree on the size of the depletion it causes in forebrain noradrenalin. For example, Owen *et al.* (1982) were able to abolish the PREE completely with lesions which reduced hippocampal noradrenalin by more than 90 per cent, but lesions that reduced it by only 77 per cent had little effect on the PREE. The effects of dorsal bundle lesions may be counteracted by the development of supersensitivity in the denervated receptors to the action of noradrenalin released from residual nerve terminals (Segal and Bloom 1974*a;* Sporn *et al.* 1976). Furthermore, the amount of noradrenalin available for release is apparently increased by a rise in the activity of tyrosine hydroxylase in hippocampal terminals spared after injection of 6-OHDA (Acheson *et al.* 1980). These mechanisms may produce a large element of redundancy in the connections of the dorsal bundle, as suggested by Crow *et al.* (1977). Such redundancy, like the peculiar anatomical features of the dorsal bundle discussed above, is difficult to reconcile with any precise form of information transmission. An alternative possibility is that other pathways substitute to some degree for the missing dorsal bundle. Assuming that, at least where the PREE is concerned, the critical target area for the dorsal bundle is the septo-hippocampal system, one such pathway may be the supply to the septal area from the ventral noradrenergic bundle. Another may be the serotonergic innervation of the hippocampus; for, as we saw in Chapter 7, the effects of serotonin on transmission around the hippocampal circuit appear to be qualitatively the same as those of noradrenalin.

Whatever the explanation of the dependence of the behavioural effects of dorsal bundle lesions on the size of the noradrenalin depletion they produce, it makes interpretations of negative findings in such experiments very difficult. One cannot even determine to treat as significant only negatives seen after depletions of forebrain noradrenalin greater than, say, 90 per cent; for such a percentage depletion depends on the sensitivity of the assay used, and this varies from time to time even under apparently constant conditions. Thus the only negative findings that it is safe to accept as such are probably those obtained from animals in which a positive effect of the lesion is also observed. Since there are rather a large number of negative findings after dorsal bundle lesions, we shall need to bear these points in mind as we review the literature. It is, of course, undesirable to insulate oneself in this way against the impact of negative findings; but results such as those in Owen's (1979; Owen *et al.* 1982) experiments on the PREE leave one little choice.

Even with these limitations, the method of 6-OHDA injection into the dorsal bundle is at present the best one available. We shall therefore supplement the data that have been obtained using this method only when information from other sources is particularly relevant. We shall largely ignore the results of experiments in which 6-OHDA has been injected into the ventricles, since the pattern of destruction produced by this method is too difficult to interpret with respect to the issues that concern us here. We shall, however, take into account some of the results of experiments in which the locus coeruleus has been destroyed electrolytically. This method has the disadvantage, as compared to that of intracerebral injection of 6-OHDA, that its effects are not confined to fibres and cells utilizing a catecholamine neurotransmitter. On the other hand, it is clear that, if the locus coeruleus has been totally destroyed, this removes the noradrenergic innervation of the hippocampus and much of the innervation of the septal area.

A further method which has been used with success in the study of dorsal bundle function is that of systemic injection of 6-OHDA to neonates. In the adult the neurotoxin does not cross the blood–brain barrier, so systemic injections damage only peripheral noradrenergic neurones. In the neonate, however, the blood–brain barrier is evidently permeable to 6-OHDA, and systemic injections of the neurotoxin cause (besides peripheral damage) similar depletions of noradrenalin in the neocortex and hippocampus to those seen after injection locally in the dorsal bundle of the adult animal. However, hypothalamic noradrenalin levels are not reduced by this treatment, implying that the ventral noradrenergic bundle, and perhaps also the hypothalamic projection from the dorsal bundle, are left intact (Mason and Iversen 1978*b*). Mason and Iverson (1978*b*) have made use of this fact to triangulate the critical lesions responsible for the changed behaviour patterns seen after 6-OHDA injected systemically to adult and neonate animals and into the dorsal bundle of adult animals, respectively.

Finally, some of the experiments we shall consider below have looked at the behavioural effects of combining dorsal bundle lesions with adrenalectomy. As we shall see, the results of these experiments suggest that, to some degree, the adrenal gland (presumably by way of one or other of its hormonal secretions) is able to substitute for a lesioned dorsal bundle. If so, the site of the interaction between adrenal hormones and noradrenergic neurones may lie in the hippocampus. Cells in the hippocampus are known to concentrate injected corticosterone (McEwen, Weiss, and Schwartz 1969), and this hormone affects the firing rates of hippocampal cells (Pfaff, Silva, and Weiss 1971). Corticosterone injections also affect the theta-driving curve, shifting the minimum from its normal value of 7.7 Hz to one of 6.9 Hz (Valero *et al.* 1977); frequencies in this range are found in association with strong freezing behaviour when the rat is presented with a stimulus associated with shock (Whishaw 1976;

Graeff *et al.* 1980). The same change in the theta-driving curve is seen for a period of about 30 minutes after undrugged animals are subjected to footshock (Valero and Gray, unpublished). Thus it is possible that corticosterone, which is of course liberated from the adrenal cortex in response to a wide range of stressors, carries an alternative signal of punishment to the hippocampus which can under some conditions substitute for the signal carried (on the anxiety hypothesis) by the dorsal bundle. An alternative possibility is that corticosterone directly facilitates the functioning of dorsal bundle fibres which remain intact in the lesioned animal, since the hormone has been shown to facilitate noradrenalin synthesis (Iuvone *et al.* 1977).

The behavioural effects of dorsal bundle lesions

These, then, are the major methods used to gather the data against which we shall test the various hypotheses discussed above. We shall consider these data within the same general framework already used in Chapters 2 and 6 to encompass the effects of anti-anxiety drugs and septo-hippocampal lesions. However, there are far fewer results to consider, since the tools needed to study the dorsal noradrenergic bundle have been available for only a short time. Inevitably, therefore, there are many lacunae in the data (for a recent review, see McNaughton and Mason 1980).

1. Rewarded behaviour

Anlezark, Crow, and Greenway (1973) reported that running speed for food reward in an L-shaped alley was reduced in rats that had sustained electrolytic lesions to the locus coeruleus. This observation was greeted as a major source of support for the theory that the dorsal bundle mediates reward and/or learning. But, as the data summarized in Table 11.2 make clear, there is now no doubt that simple rewarded behaviour is normal in animals that have sustained massive destruction of the dorsal bundle (see also the review by Mason and Iversen 1979).

The original observation using locus coeruleus lesions has been replicated (Sessions, Kant, and Koob 1976; Koob, Kelley, and Mason 1978), though not always (Roberts, Price, and Fibiger 1976). But experiments in which forebrain noradrenalin has been severely depleted by 6-OHDA have almost universally found no change in rewarded running (Table 11.2). This is not because locus coeruleus lesions are a more effective way of destroying the forebrain noradrenergic projection. On the contrary, in several of the experiments using the neurotoxin the resulting loss of forebrain noradrenalin has been considerably in excess of that reported after locus coeruleus lesions (e.g. Mason and Iversen 1977c; Owen *et al.* 1982). The only impairment noted in alley-running after 6-OHDA injections into the dorsal bundle occurred in one of Owen's (1979; Owen *et al.*, 1982)* experiments. She examined the effects of this treatment in rats

*See additional references.

Table 11.2. Effects of lesions to the dorsal ascending noradrenergic bundle on behaviour controlled by reward

Task	Lesion*	Outcome†	Reference
	LC	–	Anlezark *et al.* (1973)
	LC	–	Sessions *et al.* (1976)
Alley, CRF	LC	–	Koob *et al.* (1978)
(run speed)	LC	o	Roberts *et al.* (1976)
	DB	o	Roberts *et al.* (1976)
	DB	o	Mason and Iversen (1977*c*)
	DB	o	Owen (1979)‡
	DB	–	Owen (1979)‡
	DB	o	N. M. Davis (1979*a*)
	LC	o	Koob *et al.* (1978)
	LC	o	Sessions *et al.* (1976)
	DB	o	Price *et al.* (1977)
	DB	o	Mason and Iversen (1977*a*)
Bar-pressing, CRF	DB	o	Mason and Iversen (1977*c*)
(response rate)	DB	o	Mason and Iversen (1978*a*)
	DB	o	Mason and Fibiger (1978*a*)
	DB	o	Mason and Fibiger (1979*h*)
	DB	o	Mason (1979)
	NN	o	Thornton *et al.* (1975)
	NN	o	Mason and Iversen (1978*a*)
Bar-pressing, VI	DB	o	Price *et al.* (1977)
(response rate)	DB	–	Owen and Salmon (personal communication)
	NN	o	Peterson and Laverty (1976)
Bar-pressing, FI	DB	o	Mason and Iversen (1978*c*)
(response rate)	DB	o	Mason (1979)
	DB	+	Owen and Valero (personal communication)
Bar-pressing, FR	DB	o	Mason (1979)
(response rate)	NN	+	Peterson and Laverty (1976)
Bar-pressing, VR	DB	o	Price *et al.* (1977)
(response rate)	DB	o	Mason and Fibiger (1978*a*)
	DB	o	Mason and Robbins (1979)
Push/pull ball	DB	o	Mason and Iversen (1977*b*)
	NN	o	Mason and Iversen (1977*c*)

* LC = electrolytic lesion of locus coeruleus; DB = injection of 6-hydroxydopamine in the vicinity of the dorsal bundle; NN = neonatal systemic injection of 6-hydroxydopamine.

† –, impairment; o, no effect; +, facilitation.

‡ No effect with pre-training; impairment with no pre-training. See Owen *et al.* (1982) in additional references.

given either normal pre-training (handling, habituation to the alley, and to the reward pellets) or no pre-training. Only in the latter case were running speeds reduced in the lesioned animals. (We shall consider this finding again when we come to deal with responses to novelty.) Pre-training has not been explicitly investigated as a possible variable influencing the effects of locus coeruleus lesions. Anlezark *et al.* (1973) apparently gave their animals no pre-training, but Sessions *et al.* (1976) used fairly standard (though not excessive) pre-training procedures, and in both cases the lesioned animals had lower running speeds.

It can be concluded from the data summarized in Table 11.2 that, if there is a genuine effect of locus coeruleus lesions on rewarded running as such, this cannot be due to destruction of the dorsal bundle. It is possible that the effect is due to destruction of the cerebellar or spinal noradrenergic projections (which are spared after 6-OHDA injections into the dorsal bundle or neonatal systemic 6-OHDA, but destroyed by locus coeruleus lesions). Alternatively, it may be due to destruction of non-noradrenergic fibres or cells in the vicinity of the locus coeruleus. In any case, the effect of locus coeruleus lesions is due neither to the rewarded nature of the task nor to the need for learning. Thus, in Koob *et al.*'s (1978) experiment, rats which showed a deficit in the L-shaped alley were normal in the acquisition of a spatial discrimination in the T-maze and rewarded bar-pressing. It is possible that the deficit is motoric in nature. Thus Amaral and Foss (1975) and Eison *et al* (1977) observed motor impairments after electrolytic lesions of the locus coeruleus. This slowed running speed in Amaral and Foss's experiment; but when choice of arm in a T-maze discrimination task was scored, the lesioned animals did not differ from intact controls.

It is not only in the alley that rewarded behaviour is normal after extensive destruction of the dorsal bundle. Normal acquisition and performance has been observed in rats rewarded for bar-pressing on schedules of CRF, VI, FI, FR, or VR or for pushing or pulling a ball through a small tube (Table 11.2). The latter task (Mason and Iversen 1977*b*) requires a degree of fine motor co-ordination; so, whatever effect locus coeruleus lesions have on motor skills, it seems unlikely that destruction of the dorsal bundle affects them. There is one report (Price *et al.* 1977) of reduced VI rates after dorsal bundle lesions; but this was not seen by Owen and Salmon (personal communication) after these lesions, nor by Peterson and Laverty (1976) after neonatal systemic 6-OHDA. Effects of these lesions have been observed when discrimination behaviour is studied or the pattern of schedule-controlled operant behaviour examined, but we shall leave these findings until later (Sub-sections 5 and 6).

These results virtually rule out the reward or general learning hypotheses of dorsal bundle function. Since some of the experiments used a relatively long ITI (24 hours) and still found no effect of dorsal bundle lesions on the acquisition of a running response (Owen 1979; N. M. Davis

1979*a*), any general role in the consolidation of memory is also probably ruled out. In addition, Mason and Robbins (1979) report a test of conditioned reinforcement in the Skinner-box: the reinforcing effects of a clicker or light associated with primary food reward were unchanged by dorsal bundle lesions. Since, in several of the experiments summarized in Table 11.2, the same animals which showed normal rewarded learning showed impairments in other behaviour, the lesions cannot have been insufficiently extensive. Thus, if the dorsal bundle carries a signal about reward to the forebrain, it cannot be used principally in the acquisition or execution of simple rewarded behaviour.

2. *Passive avoidance*

The effects of dorsal bundle lesions on passive avoidance behaviour constitute a critical test of the general anxiety hypothesis. The anti-anxiety drugs regularly impair this kind of behaviour (Gray 1977; Chapter 2), and this effect is often treated as the best single index of anti-anxiety activity. Unfortunately, the majority of experiments in which passive avoidance has been tested after dorsal bundle lesions have employed a step-down task. As we saw in Chapter 6 (Section 6.2), this task appears to be relatively insensitive to the effects of hippocampal lesions. On the assumption, then, that the role of the dorsal bundle in anxiety is expressed via its connections to the septo-hippocampal system, step-down passive avoidance is not a very appropriate tool with which to study the effects of lesions to this tract. As for the anti-anxiety drugs, in spite of the voluminous literature on their effects on passive avoidance (Gray 1977), only two of the relevant experiments appear to have used the step-down task. Of these, Holloway (1972) found an effect of alcohol only if the drug was given in training but not during testing, suggesting a state-dependent effect rather than a direct action of the drug. More positive results were reported by Waddington and Olley (1977; see Chapter 2), who found that chlordiazepoxide impaired step-down passive avoidance provided there was no escape component (climbing back to the platform to terminate shock). But, as pointed out in Chapter 6 (Section 6.2), the presence of an escape component in the step-down task seems to play exactly the opposite role where hippocampal lesions are concerned, increasing the passive avoidance deficit.

Given this background, it is not altogether surprising that the majority of experiments on step-down passive avoidance have found no effect of dorsal bundle lesions (Table 11.3). There are, however, several exceptions to this rule. Crow and Wendlandt (1976) shocked rats after their third step-down trial and then retested them one minute and three days later. A group injected with 6-OHDA just anterior to the locus coeruleus were impaired (i.e. stepped down more quickly than controls) at the three-day test, but not when tested one minute after the shock. Crow and Wendlandt (1976) interpret this pattern of results as indicating a role for

Table 11.3. Effects of lesions to the dorsal ascending noradrenergic bundle on passive avoidance

Task	Lesion*	Outcome†	Reference
Step-down, with escape	DB	o	Roberts and Fibiger (1977a)
	DB	o	Mason and Fibiger (1978b)
	DB	o	Mason and Fibiger (1979a)‡
	DB	–	Mason and Fibiger (1979a)‡
	DB + VB + ADX	–	Roberts and Fibiger (1977a)
Step-down, no escape	DB	o	Crow and Wendlandt (1976)§
	DB	–	Crow and Wendlandt (1976)§
	DB	o	Mason and Fibiger (1979a)
	DB	o	Wendlandt and File (1979)
	DB + ADX	–	Wendlandt and File (1979)
Step-through, with escape	LC	o	Zornetzer and Gold (1976)
Step-through, no escape	DB	o	Kovacs et al. (1979)‖
	DB	–	Kovacs et al. (1979)‖
Punished active avoidance	LC	o	Sessions et al. (1976)
Punished bar-pressing	DB	–	Tsaltas (personal communication)*
Punished running in alley	DB + VB	–	N. M. Davis (personal communication)

*Abbreviations as for Table 11.2; also, VB = injection of 6-hydroxydopamine in the vicinity of the ventral noradrenergic bundle, and ADX = adrenalectomy.

†Conventions as for Table 11.2.

‡Impairment with 4 mA, not 1 mA, shock with immediate test; no impairment at either shock intensity with test 24 hours after training.

§Impairment with test at 24 hours after training, not with immediate test.

‖Impairment with test at 48 hours after training, not with test at 24 hours after training.

the dorsal bundle in long-term retention. However, since behaviour at the one-minute test trial is presumably at least to some extent under the control of the immediate after-effects of shock (unaffected by the anti-anxiety drugs; see Chapter 2), it is impossible to distinguish within the context of their experiment between this interpretation and the hypothesis that the lesion weakens control over behaviour by signals of punishment, but not by punishment itself. Wendlandt and File (1979) were in any case unable to replicate these findings in rats in which intracerebral 6-OHDA had

*See Tsaltas et al. (1984) in additional references.

been used to damage both the dorsal bundle and the cerebellar projection from the locus coeruleus. They did find, however, that rats treated in this way and also adrenalectomized displayed the same pattern of behaviour as Crow and Wendlandt's (1976) rats given intracerebral 6-OHDA alone: impaired passive avoidance at three days and normal performance at one minute after shock.

A second attempt to replicate Crow and Wendlandt's (1976) findings was reported by Mason and Fibiger (1979a) using rats with simple dorsal bundle lesions. Lesioned animals were indistinguishable from vehicle-injected controls when tested for retention either 24 or 72 hours after training. It may be relevant that, unlike Crow and Wendlandt (1976) who shocked their rats after their third step-down trial, Mason and Fibiger (1979a) gave no pre-training before their single shock trial. The septal and hippocampal deficits in passive avoidance are magnified by pre-training on the to-be-punished response (Chapter 6, Section 6.2); indeed, the lack of pre-training in the standard step-down paradigm may be an important reason for its insensitivity to septo-hippocampal damage. That the effects of dorsal bundle lesions on passive avoidance may be sensitive to the same variables as those of hippocampal lesions is suggested by a second experiment in Mason and Fibiger's (1979a) report, in which an escape component was included, the rat having to escape back to the safe platform after descent to the shock grid. During training the animal was required to meet an acquisition criterion (staying up on the platform for three minutes). Dorsal bundle lesioned animals stepped down twice as often as controls before reaching this criterion (a significant difference) if the shock level was 4 mA; with a weaker shock (1 mA) the groups did not differ. Contrary to Crow and Wendlandt's (1976) retention hypothesis, there was no significant effect of the dorsal bundle lesion in a 24-hour retention test, whichever shock level was used, though there was a clear trend for the lesioned animals to be impaired in the 4 mA shock condition. Using an identical procedure and a 1 mA shock, Fibiger, Roberts, and Price (1975), Roberts and Fibiger (1977), and Mason and Fibiger (1978b) all found no effect of dorsal bundle lesions on either the acquisition or the 24-hour retention of step-down avoidance. Roberts and Fibiger (1977a), however, did find a passive avoidance deficit, both during acquisition and at the retention test, in animals which had sustained lesions to both the dorsal and ventral noradrenergic bundles, as well as adrenalectomy.

These confusing data point, then, to two sets of conditions in which a deficit may be seen in step-down passive avoidance in animals with dorsal bundle lesions (apparently enhanced in each case by adrenalectomy): the first (Crow and Wendlandt 1976) involves no escape component, a certain amount of pre-training on the to-be-shocked response, and a relatively long retention interval; the second (Mason and Fibiger 1979a) involves an escape component, a high shock level, and a very short retention interval. Without further experimental work it is difficult to make much theoretical sense out of these variables.

If we consider passive avoidance tasks other than step-down, there are regrettably few data (Table 11.3). There is a single experiment on punished drinking (Saari and Pappas 1973), in which a deficit in passive avoidance was observed; but this was after neonatal systemic injections of 6-OHDA, and might therefore have resulted from the destruction of the sympathetic nervous system which is produced by this treatment in addition to dorsal bundle damage. Two experiments (Kovacs *et al.* 1979; Zornetzer and Gold 1976) have employed a step-through task, which is better than step-down but still far from optimal in displaying the hippocampal deficit in passive avoidance (Chapter 6, Section 6.2). Both obtained results broadly in agreement with Crow and Wendlandt's (1976) retention hypothesis.

Thus Kovacs *et al.* (1979) report an impairment in step-through passive avoidance when dorsal bundle animals were tested 48 hours after a single-shock trial, but no effect in a 24-hour retention test. In addition, these workers showed that the effects on retention of the peptide hormone, arginine vasopressin, depend on an intact dorsal bundle. Replicating previous findings from the same laboratory, they demonstrated that this hormone, if injected immediately after the single learning trial, facilitates retention both 24 and 48 hours later (i.e. step-through latency is increased). This effect has been intensively studied, and there is much reason to suppose that the hormone genuinely enhances memory (De Wied and Bohus 1979). Destruction of the dorsal bundle eliminated the effect of vasopressin at both retention intervals (Kovacs *et al.* 1979). These results are all the more striking in that the percentage reduction of hippocampal noradrenalin was very much smaller than has been reported in many other experiments after dorsal bundle lesions, only 44 per cent. This suggests that the procedure used by Kovacs *et al.* (1979) is relatively sensitive to the changes produced by dorsal bundle lesions.

A finding which is in some respects the mirror image of those obtained by Kovacs *et al.* (1979) was reported by Zornetzer and Gold (1976), also using step-through but with an escape component. Mice with electrolytic lesions of the locus coeruleus were not different from controls on a 48-hour retention test (the lesion was made immediately after acquisition via previously implanted electrodes); but the period during which post-trial electroconvulsive shock produced a retention deficit was extended by the lesion, now lasting at least up to 40 hours after the single training trial. No biochemical data were reported in this paper, and it is impossible to be sure that the critical focus of the lesion was indeed in the locus coeruleus. But if we take the results at face value, they join with those of Kovacs *et al.* (1979) in suggesting that lack of the forebrain noradrenergic pathways somehow renders memory traces more labile: they are apparently less easily enhanced by vasopressin and more easily disrupted by electro-convulsive shock.

A classic test used to display the passive avoidance deficit after septal or hippocampal lesions, as well as after administration of anti-anxiety drugs, is to punish locomotion in the alley. Surprisingly, there are apparently no published reports using this technique after dorsal bundle lesions. In an unpublished experiment in my own laboratory (N. M. Davis 1979*a*; Davis and Gray, in preparation) we found that such lesions produced a clearcut deficit in passive avoidance (with no acquisition deficit) when running pre-viously acquired for food reward was punished by foot-shock in the goal. Unfortunately, in this particular experiment there was also much non-specific damage around the cannula tip and considerable reductions in noradrenalin levels in regions innervated by the ventral bundle and even in dopamine levels; thus, until the experiment is repeated, the particular damage responsible for the effect must remain in doubt. Another classic test is punished bar-pressing, which has been used extensively with the anti-anxiety drugs (Gray 1977). Again, there is no published report of the effects of dorsal bundle lesions on this behaviour. In unpublished exper-iments from my own laboratory (Tsaltas and Gray, in preparation)* we have found that a 'clean' dorsal bundle lesion reliably delays the acquisi-tion of suppression of bar-pressing and lessens its extent, provided the shock used is not too intense (> 0.2 mA).

These data encourage the Scottish verdict, 'not-proven'. It would be a bold man who affirmed, in the light of the evidence so far, that there is a passive avoidance deficit in dorsal bundle lesioned animals. On the other hand, there are more signs of a positive effect of the lesion than in the case of rewarded behaviour; and, as we have seen, most of the experi-ments have used tasks which, in the light of other data, are probably ill-chosen to display a passive avoidance deficit after destruction of afferents to the septo-hippocampal system.

3. Classical conditioning of fear

Since neither the anti-anxiety drugs (Chapter 2) nor septal or hippocam-pal lesions (Chapter 6) have consistent effects on off-the-baseline condi-tioned suppression, there are no grounds for predicting from the anxiety hypothesis that dorsal bundle lesions will affect this behaviour. This neg-ative expectation has been confirmed by Mason and Fibiger (1979*e*). Pre-diction for on-the-baseline conditioned suppression is more complex, since the results obtained after both drugs and lesions are variable (Chap-ters 2 and 6, Section 6.3); but, on the whole, we would expect to find that this is disrupted by dorsal bundle lesions. Lorden *et al.* (1979) failed to find such an effect. In experiments in my own laboratory (Tsaltas and Gray, in preparation), however, we have found a small, but reliable, re-duction in the level of suppression reached by dorsal bundle lesioned an-imals. There are no clear predictions for taste aversion, since this is de-

*See Tsaltas *et al.* (1984) in additional references.

creased by hippocampal lesions but apparently not by septal lesions, and no relevant data exist on the effects of the anti-anxiety drugs; it is in any case by no means clear that taste aversion is in any way related to conditioned fear. In the event, neither injections of 6-OHDA into the dorsal bundle, nor neonatal systemic 6-OHDA, nor electrolytic lesions of the locus coeruleus affect the acquisition of conditioned taste aversions (Mason and Iversen 1978*b*; Mason and Fibiger 1979*c, e*; Sessions *et al.* 1976), except in the apparently special case in which the UCS is morphine (Roberts and Fibiger 1977*b*).

4. *Escape and one-way active avoidance*

On the anxiety hypothesis, given the effects of the anti-anxiety drugs and septal and hippocampal lesions, neither escape nor one-way active avoidance should be affected by dorsal bundle lesions. This was the case in the single experiment on escape (in the shuttle-box), although escape latency was increased if dorsal bundle lesions were combined with adrenalectomy (Ögren and Fuxe 1974). The expected negative result was also obtained in three experiments on one-way active avoidance in a two-box apparatus, one after electrolytic locus coeruleus lesions (Sessions *et al.* 1976), the others after dorsal bundle injections of 6-OHDA (Fibiger and Mason 1978; Ögren and Fuxe 1977). In Ögren and Fuxe's (1977) experiment, one-way avoidance was impaired when adrenalectomy was added to the dorsal bundle lesion.

5. *Two-way and non-spatial active avoidance*

The anti-anxiety drugs and septal and hippocampal lesions all improve two-way active avoidance and avoidance in the Skinner-box; on the anxiety hypothesis, therefore, we would expect to see the same effects after dorsal bundle lesions. In the one experiment on Sidman avoidance in the Skinner-box, this prediction was not upheld, dorsal bundle lesions being without effect (Mason and Fibiger 1979*e*). However, shuttle-box avoidance was found to be improved by dorsal bundle lesions in experiments by Ögren and Fuxe (1977) and Mason and Fibiger (1979*b*). Mason and Fibiger (1979*b*) also report that inter-trial crossings and resistance to extinction of the shuttling response were increased by the lesion; these effects are also seen after damage to the septo-hippocampal system (Chapter 6, Section 6.7). Note, however, that in this experiment hypothalamic noradrenalin was reduced in the lesioned animals to 18 per cent of control values, indicating a substantial destruction of the ventral as well as the dorsal noradrenergic bundle (Ögren and Fuxe 1977 do not present biochemical results).

As against these positive findings Wendlandt and File (1979) found no effect of dorsal bundle lesions on shuttle-box avoidance. Although the reported noradrenalin depletions were high (down to 7 per cent of control), it should be noted that the lesioned animals in this study were also indistinguishable from controls on several other tests, including one (rearing) which has been reliably impaired by dorsal bundle lesions in other experiments (see below). When adrenalectomy was added to dorsal bundle damage in this study an increase in inter-trial crossings was seen, but this was confined to a retention test given 10 days after training. A rather more startling result was reported by Ögren and Fuxe (1977) when they added adrenalectomy to dorsal bundle damage. The combined lesion gave rise to a profound impairment in shuttle-box avoidance, the opposite result to that seen after dorsal bundle lesions alone (adrenalectomy alone also impaired performance, but not to the same degree). In an earlier experiment in which the combined lesions were made after acquisition of shuttle-box avoidance, the lesioned rats showed no sign of relearning the task, although neither dorsal bundle damage nor adrenalectomy on its own had any effect (Ögren and Fuxe 1974). Note that the results of this experiment are not discordant with the effects of septal or hippocampal lesions; for these too, if made after acquisition, do not facilitate and may sometimes impair shuttle-box avoidance (Chapter 6, Section 6.7).

6. Responses elicited by aversive stimuli

Neither the flinch, jump, nor vocalization thresholds to electric shock are altered by dorsal bundle lesions, nor is the pain threshold as measured by the hotplate test (Fibiger and Mason 1978; Mason and Fibiger 1979b; Wendlandt and File 1979, Ögren and Fuxe 1974). The only positive finding is that of reduced freezing during a session in which responses to shock were measured (Mason and Fibiger 1979b). The latter observation is as we would expect, given the septo-hippocampal syndrome described in Chapter 6. In addition, Ögren and Fuxe (1974) found that combined dorsal bundle lesions and adrenalectomy elevated the pain threshold in the hotplate test. This finding may account for the impaired escape, one-way and two-way active avoidance, and passive avoidance seen after the combined lesion (Ögren and Fuxe 1974, 1977; Wendlandt and File 1979).

7. Responses to novelty

Neither overall activity level nor locomotion in a novel environment is generally affected by dorsal bundle damage, no matter how it is produced. This conclusion is based on observations in the open field, various boxes, and the 'hole-board', a floor with holes into which the animal can poke its head (Table 11.4). The exceptions to this rule include one report of reduced activity in the hole-board test (Wendlandt and File 1979), which was not seen in another experiment from the same laboratory (Crow *et al.* 1978); mixed findings in an environment consisting of a series of interconnected alleys (dorsal bundle rats were slower to exit from the start-box, but then entered more alleys; Mason, Roberts, and Fibiger 1978); one report (Kovacs *et al.* 1979) of reduced ambulation in the open field which has no obvious features to distinguish it from the five negative reports using this apparatus; and two reports that systemic neonatal 6-OHDA (Robinson, Vanderwolf, and Pappas 1977) or locus coeruleus lesions (Eison *et al.* 1977) reduced running in an activity wheel, a finding which recalls the reduced activity seen after hippocampal lesions only in this apparatus (Chapter 6, Section 6.11). Rearing in the open field, however, is consistently reduced by damage to the dorsal bundle (Table 11.4). In two experiments where this result was not obtained with dorsal bundle lesions alone, it was none the less produced when adrenalectomy was added (Ögren and Fuxe 1974; Wendlandt and File 1979).

When responses to specific novel stimuli are investigated, more positive results are obtained. In the T-maze dorsal bundle lesions eliminate both spontaneous alternation, and the choice of an arm whose brightness has been changed in Ison, Glass, and Bohmer's (1966) design, discussed in Chapter 2, Section 2.10 (Owen 1979; Owen, Boarder, McNaughton, Fillenz, and Gray, in preparation)*; these effects are the same as those produced by anti-anxiety drugs (Chapter 2, Section 2.10) or septo-hippocampal damage (Chapter 6, Section 6.12) and suggest an impaired response to novelty. But Mason and Fibiger (1977) and Mason, Roberts, and Fibiger (1978) report an apparent *increase* in responsiveness to novel stimuli after dorsal bundle lesions, in that the time spent in contact with a novel object was increased (although the latency to contact the object was unchanged). This pattern of results may perhaps indicate retarded habituation in the lesioned animals. However, Wendlandt and File (1979) failed to replicate these observations, using animals which had sustained dorsal bundle lesions, destruction of the cerebellar efferents from the locus coeruleus, and adrenalectomy. There was also no effect of dorsal bundle damage alone (Crow *et al.* 1978) or combined with destruction of the cerebellar projection from the locus coeruleus (Wendlandt and File 1979) on object exploration in the hole-board test; but when adrenalectomy was added to the latter lesion, there was a retardation of within-session habituation.

8. Distraction experiments

The anxiety and attention (Mason and Iversen 1977*c*, 1979) hypotheses make different predictions for the results of distraction experiments. On the hypothesis that the dorsal bundle screens out irrelevant stimuli from attention, animals with lesions to this tract should clearly be more distractible than normal. The predictions from the anxiety hypothesis are more complex (see the discussion in Chapter 6, Section 6.10), but in general we would expect dorsal bundle lesions to reduce distractibility. The data offer little support to either hypothesis. In agreement with the attentional hypothesis, Roberts *et al.* (1976) found increased distraction (greater slowing of running speeds) when dorsal bundle rats trained to run for food in an alley were exposed to flashing overhead lights and a change in floor covering; the increased distraction was most evident on the first trial. In

*See McNaughton *et al.* (1984) in additional references.

Table 11.4. Effects of lesions to the dorsal ascending noradrenergic bundle on tests of exploration and activity

Task	Lesion*	Outcome*	Reference
Exploration of hole-board	DB	o	Crow et al. (1978)
	DB	o	Wendlandt and File (1979)
Exploration of alleys	DB	+	Mason et al. (1978)
	LC	o	Sessions et al. (1976)
	LC	o	Koob et al. (1978)
	DB	o	Mason and Iversen (1977a)
Open-field ambulation	DB	o	Wendlandt and File (1979)
	DB	o	Owen et al. (in preparation)†
	DB	–	Kovacs et al. (1979)
	NN	o	Mason and Iversen (1977a)
Emergence	LC	–	Eison et al. (1977)
	LC	o	Koob et al. (1978)
	DB	o	Ögren and Fuxe (1974)
	DB	o	Wendlandt and File (1979)
	DB	–	Kovacs et al. (1979)
	DB	–	Owen et al. (in preparation)†
Rearing	DB + VB	–	Leconte and Hennevin (1981)
	DB + ADX	–	Ögren and Fuxe (1974)
	DB + ADX	–	Wendlandt and File (1979)
	NN	–	Robinson et al. (1977)
Activity in running wheel	LC	–	Eison et al. (1977)
	NN	–	Robinson et al. (1977)
	DB	o	Crow et al. (1978)
Activity on hole-board	DB	–	Wendlandt and File (1979)
	DB + ADX	–	Wendlandt and File (1979)
	LC	–	Amaral and Foss (1975)
	LC	o	Koob et al. (1978)
	DB	o	Crow and Wendlandt (1976)
Activity in cage or box	DB	o	Mason and Iversen (1977a)
	DB	o	Mason et al. (1978)
	DB + VB	o	Leconte and Hennevin (1981)
	NN	o	Mason and Iversen (1977a)

*Conventions and abbreviations as in Tables 11.2 and 11.3.
†See McNaughton et al. (1984) in additional references.

a similar experiment using locus coeruleus lesions, Koob *et al.* (1978) found no effect on the first distraction trial, but the lesioned animals were slower to habituate to the distractor than controls. In the Skinner-box, however, there has generally been no difference between dorsal bundle and control animals in the response to a novel stimulus presented during rewarded bar-pressing (Mason and Fibiger 1978c, 1979e; Owen 1979). Mason and Fibiger (1978c) found greater distraction in the lesioned animals only when an overhead light was used as the distractor; with tones there was no lesion effect, and with a light on the front panel there was a trend to *reduced* distraction in the lesioned rats. The authors manage to interpret all these findings in terms of the attention hypothesis, but it is doubtful that many would find their *post hoc* arguments convincing. The direction of the significant findings in the above experiments is always towards increased distractibility in the lesioned animals; and Owen's (1979)* observation that dorsal bundle rats ran more slowly than controls only in an alley to which they had not previously been habituated may be an instance of the same phenomenon. But even this consistency is lost when we include a report (Crow *et al.* 1978) that suppression of licking by a tone distractor was significantly less in dorsal bundle rats than controls. This finding is as predicted by the anxiety hypothesis; but it is the only one of its kind.

9. Habituation

If we consider these various experiments on responses to novelty for what they have to tell us about habituation rates, there is again little consistency. No effect of dorsal bundle damage was seen on habituation of ambulation in the open field (Owen 1979; Owen *et al.*, in preparation)† or head-dips in the hole-board test (Wendlandt and File 1979; Crow *et al.* 1978), nor any effect of locus coeruleus lesions on habituation of the acoustic startle response (Davis *et al.* 1977) or activity in a photo-cell cage (Koob *et al.* 1978). Crow *et al.* (1978) report that not only was habituation of distraction of licking normal in dorsal bundle rats, so also was dishabituation and retention of habituation between tests. As against these negative findings, there are three reports of retarded habituation in lesioned animals, when time in contact with a novel object (Mason and Fibiger 1977; Mason *et al.* 1978) or distraction in the alley (Koob *et al.* 1978) were measured. But, using the last test, Fibiger *et al.* (1975) found faster habituation in the lesioned rats.

10. Fearful behaviour

Neither defecation nor grooming in the open field is affected by dorsal bundle lesions (Wendlandt and File 1979; Kovacs *et al.* 1979; Owen *et al.*, in preparation)†; and Koob *et al.* (1978) found no effect of locus coeruleus lesions on the time to emerge from a box into an open field. These findings suggest that the fear produced by exposure to novel environments is

---

*See Owen *et al.* (1982) in additional references.
†See McNaughton *et al.* (1984) in additional references.

intact in dorsal bundle animals. This inference is supported by the report (Crow *et al.* 1978) that dorsal bundle lesions are without effect in File's (1980) test of social behaviour: pairs of lesioned male rats interacted in an unfamiliar environment and under bright lights (conditions under which the anti-anxiety drugs increase social contact) at the same low level as controls. These are important points against the anxiety hypothesis of dorsal bundle function.

11. Non-reward: resistance to extinction

The most consistent finding after dorsal bundle lesions is that the resistance to extinction of a previously rewarded response is increased (Table 11.5), as first reported by Mason and Iversen (1975). This general result has been reported after running or bar-pressing has been acquired on a CRF schedule; after bar-pressing has been acquired on FI or single alternation schedules; after VR reinforcement for pressing on two levers; and after rats have learned to push or pull a ball through a small tube. The neurochemical specificity of the effect has been confirmed in several ways. Mason and Iversen (1978*a*) showed that resistance to extinction of bar-pressing was increased by injection of 6-OHDA into the dorsal bundle or by systemic injection of the neurotoxin in neonatal but not adult rats. Given the different patterns of damage produced by these treatments (see above), it is reasonable to conclude that an effect common to the first two but not the third is due to destruction of the noradrenergic innervation of the forebrain but not the hypothalamus. Consistent with this interpretation, it has been shown that the site of injection along the dorsal ascending bundle is not crucial for the effect; that treatment with desimipramine before 6-OHDA injection (to block uptake of the neurotoxin into noradrenergic neurones) blocks the effect; and that injection of either kainic acid (to destroy cell bodies but not fibres) or 5,7-dihydroxytryptamine (a neurotoxin which is specific for serotonergic fibres) in the vicinity of the dorsal bundle does not produce the effect (Mason and Iversen 1979; Mason and Fibiger 1979*h*). We shall postpone discussion of the psychological interpretation of the increased resistance to extinction until later.

Increased resistance to extinction is not seen after all types of acquisition schedule. The clearest exception is the case of a random PRF schedule in the alley. Given the effects of anti-anxiety drugs and lesions to the septo-hippocampal system on the PREE (Chapters 2, 6, and 10), the anxiety hypothesis makes relatively clear predictions for the effects of dorsal bundle lesions in comparable conditions. However, since the effects of the drugs and of septo-hippocampal damage depend in different ways on experimental parameters, the detailed predictions vary according to the model chosen. The effects of septal lesions have been studied most carefully, so we shall use them, at least temporarily, as our guide (Gray, Quintão, and Araujo-Silva 1972; Henke 1974, 1977; Feldon and Gray 1979*a*, *b*).

Table 11.5. Effects of lesions to the dorsal ascending noradrenergic bundle on resistance to extinction of previously rewarded responses

Task	Lesion*	Outcome*	Reference
	LC	o	Koob *et al.* (1978)
	DB	+	Mason and Iversen (1977*c*)
Alley, CRF	DB	+	Owen *et al.* (1982)†
	DB	o	Owen *et al.* (1982)†
	NN	+	Thornton *et al.* (1975)
Alley, PRF	DB	–	Owen *et al.* (1982)‡
	DB	o	Owen *et al.* (1982)‡
	DB	+	Mason and Iversen (1977*c*)
	DB	+	Mason and Iversen (1978*a*)
	DB	+	Mason and Fibiger (1978*a*)
Bar-pressing,	DB	+	Mason (1979)§
CRF	DB	o	Mason (1979)§
	DB	+	Mason and Fibiger (1979*d*)‖
	DB	o	Mason and Fibiger (1979*d*)‖
	NN	+	Mason and Iversen (1978*a*)
Bar-pressing, VI	DB	o	Price *et al.* (1977)
Bar-pressing, VR	DB	o	Mason and Fibiger (1978*a*)
	DB	+	Mason and Robbins (1979)
Bar-pressing, FI	DB	+	Mason and Iversen (1978*c*)
	DB	+	Mason (1979)
Bar-pressing, FR	DB	o	Mason (1979)
	NN	o	Peterson and Laverty (1976)
Bar-pressing, successive discrimination	DB	o	Mason (1978)
Bar-pressing, repeated extinction	DB	o	Mason (1978)
Bar-pressing, single alternation	DB¶	+	Tremmel *et al.* (1977)
Bar-pressing, resistance to satiation	DB	o	Mason (1979)
Push/pull ball	DB	+	Mason and Iversen (1977*b*)

*Conventions and abbreviations as in Tables 11.2 and 11.3.

†Increased resistance to extinction after 50 acquisition trials at short inter-trial interval (ITI); no effect after 100 acquisition trials at short ITI or (Owen 1979) with 24-hour ITI.

‡Decreased resistance to extinction after 50 acquisition trials; no effect after 100 trials.

§Increased resistance to extinction with food as reinforcer; no effect with water.

‖Increased resistance to extinction if lesion before acquisition; no effect if lesion after acquisition.

¶Radio-frequency lesion of dorsal bundle.

From the effects of septal lesions, then, we would predict that, if a short ITI (several minutes) is used, resistance to extinction after PRF training should be reduced by dorsal bundle lesions with about 50 acquisition trials, and that the PREE should be abolished in part because of this change and in part because of an increase in resistance to extinction in CRF-trained rats. This is the result obtained (Owen 1979; Owen *et al.* 1977, 1982). We next predict that, if the number of acquisition trials is increased to about 100, dorsal bundle lesions should no longer have any effect on resistance to extinction after PRF training and the PREE should be intact; if we take our cue from the effects of large septal lesions (Henke 1974), we predict that resistance to extinction after CRF training will still be increased by dorsal bundle lesions with 100 acquisition trials, but from the effects of small lateral or medial septal lesions (Feldon and Gray 1979*b*) we predict no effect of the dorsal bundle lesion. The results show, as expected, an intact PREE in dorsal bundle rats tested after 100 acquisition trials, and no change in resistance to extinction in either the PRF or the CRF condition (Owen *et al.* 1979, 1982). Finally, if the experiment is run with a 24-hour ITI and 16 acquisition trials, we predict that dorsal bundle lesions will abolish PREE in the same way as at 50 short-ITI acquisition trials. Now, however, the prediction fails to be verified: under these conditions we have failed to obtain more than a slight attenuation of the PREE using dorsal bundle lesions (Owen 1979). This negative result must make one doubt the reliability of the positive finding at 50 short-ITI acquisition trials. But when this experiment was repeated, except that extinction was carried out in the first half of a double runway, the PREE was again abolished by dorsal bundle lesions in the same manner as before (Owen 1979; Owen *et al.* 1982). Thus, with the important exception of the result in the 24-hour ITI experiment, all these findings are in general consistent with the hypothesis that dorsal bundle lesions affect responses to stimuli associated with non-reward in the same way as administration of anti-anxiety drugs or damage to the septo-hippocampal system.

The role of number of acquisition trials in determining the effects of dorsal bundle damage on resistance to extinction in the CRF condition in these experiments is consistent with other data from the alley. Thus, with 50 CRF acquisition trials Mason and Iversen (1977*c*) found increased resistance to extinction after dorsal bundle lesions; but with 100 acquisition trials Koob *et al.* (1978) found no effect of locus coeruleus lesions on resistance to extinction.

In the Skinner-box resistance to extinction has been reported to be normal in dorsal bundle rats after training on FR, VR, and VI schedules; after successive periods of acquisition, extinction, and re-acquisition; and after a successive discrimination (Table 11.5). In addition Mason (1979) has reported that dorsal bundle lesions do not increase resistance to extinction of bar-pressing rewarded on CRF with water, whereas with food the usual increase in resistance to extinction is obtained. The significance of these findings, especially the last, is obscure. Mason and Iversen (1979) attempt to relate them to their theory of attention, which we shall consider in more detail below. Some of them may relate to the effects obtained with PRF schedules in alleys; but it is difficult to extrapolate from discrete-trial alley tasks to free-operant schedules. In any case, it appears that the dorsal bundle extinction effect is narrower than the effects of damage to the septo-hippocampal system, and especially septal damage (Chapter 6, Section 6.17). This produces increased resistance to extinction after a wide variety of operant schedules and is no less effective when water rather than food is the reward.

Mason has reported findings which, he believes, rule out an explanation of the dorsal bundle extinction effect in terms of a change in the detection of non-reward (Mason and Iversen, 1979).

First, he finds that resistance to extinction is not increased if the lesion is made after acquisition of a bar-press response rather than before (Mason 1979; Mason and Fibiger 1979*d*). From this he deduces that the dorsal bundle lesion affects processes occurring during acquisition rather than during extinction itself. This is perhaps the case, but there are weaknesses in the argument. To begin with, the experiments did not control for state dependency: it is possible that the dorsal bundle lesion had its usual effect of increasing resistance to extinction but that this was opposed by an effect of changed state (resulting from the loss of the dorsal bundle) working to reduce resistance to extinction. Septal lesions made after acquisition also fail to increase resistance to extinction (Gray, Quintão, and Araujo-Silva 1972), and sometimes even decrease it (Carey 1967). It is not yet possible to evaluate the contribution of state dependency to any of these results. In addition, there is a strange feature of the results reported by Mason (1979) and Mason and Fibiger (1979*d*) which casts some doubt on the validity of the inferences they draw from them. The difference between the effects of dorsal bundle lesions made before and after acquisition was due, not to changes in the lesioned animals (which behaved very similarly in the two conditions), but to changes in the controls, which were apparently more resistant to extinction after a 10-day interval between acquisition and extinction than when extinction followed immediately upon acquisition. Since an identical pattern of results is reported by Mason (1979) and Mason and Fibiger (1979*d*), something systematic is evidently going on, though it is not clear what. Thus it seems that, rather than failing to alter resistance to extinction, dorsal bundle lesions made after acquisition may block whatever process is responsible for the different patterns of behaviour shown by the controls in the two conditions of the experiment.

Second, Mason and Iversen (1979) point out that increased resistance to extinction has been seen after dorsal bundle lesions in tasks involving negative reinforcers, in which of course extinction does not depend on non-reward. Thus these lesions have been reported to retard the extinction of step-down passive avoidance (Mason and Fibiger 1978*b*) and off-the-baseline conditioned suppression (Mason and Fibiger 1979*e*). However, Tsaltas, and Gray (in preparation)† have made contrary observations: extinction of the suppression of bar-pressing produced by punishment was unaffected by dorsal bundle lesions, and extinction of on-the-baseline conditioned suppression was significantly facilitated. In accounting for the discrepancy between these results, it may be important that Mason and Fibiger's (1978*b*) step-down task included an escape component which was not present in Tsaltas and Gray's punishment paradigm. Mason and Fibiger (1979*b*) also report increased resistance to extinction of two-way active avoidance in the shuttle-box after dorsal bundle lesions. This effect, however, which is seen also after septal and hippocampal lesions (Chapter 6, Section 6.7), is likely simply to reflect the general facilitation of shuttle-box performance produced by dorsal bundle lesions. There remain two reports of increased resistance to extinction of taste aversion (Mason and Fibiger 1979*c*) and one-way active avoidance (Fibiger and Mason 1978); as against these Mason and Fibiger (1979*e*) found no effect of dorsal bundle lesions on extinction of Sidman bar-press avoidance. The variability of these effects makes it difficult at present to apply inferences drawn from them to the more robust increase in resistance to extinction seen after dorsal bundle lesions when reward is discontinued.

There is one report of the effects of dorsal bundle lesions on resistance to satiation, which is increased by both hippocampal (Kimble 1969) and septal (Henke 1975) lesions; dorsal bundle lesions, however, had no effect (Mason 1979). It is difficult to evaluate the significance of this finding. If responses are eliminated during satiation because the animal discovers that the reward is no longer positively reinforcing (Morgan 1974), one would expect on most theories that resistance to satiation and resistance to extinction would co-vary after dorsal bundle lesions. Conversely, if the elimination of responses during satiation does not depend in this way on a comparison between expected and actual reward, it is not clear why resistance to satiation is increased by septal and hippocampal lesions.

12. *Non-reward: schedule effects*

We consider in this section a mixed bag of findings from experiments in which intermittent or changing schedules have been employed and variables other than resistance to extinction measured.

Using a PRF schedule in the alley Owen (1979; Owen *et al.* 1982) made two observations which had been predicted on the anxiety hypothesis of dorsal bundle function. First, in two separate experiments with 50 acquisition trials, dorsal bundle lesions eliminated the partial reinforcement acquisition effect.* Like the anti-anxiety drugs (Chapter 2, Section 2.7) they

---

*In Owen's (1979) experiment with 100 acquisition trials the controls did not show a partial reinforcement acquisition effect; thus it is not known whether elimination of this effect by dorsal bundle lesions depends on number of training trials in the same way as elimination of the PREE.

†See Tsaltas *et al.* (1984) in additional references.

did this by selectively reducing running speeds in the PRF group which, if not drugged, ran faster than animals trained on CRF. Second, the frustration effect in the double runway was unchanged by the lesion; this is the same negative result that is seen after anti-anxiety drug administration (Chapter 2, Section 2.9) or septal or hippocampal lesions (Chapter 6, Section 6.23). The failure to alter the frustration effect was not due to an incomplete lesion, since the same animals showed reduced resistance to extinction when subsequently extinguished in the first half of the double runway. Since Henke (1977) has shown that septal lesions produce exactly this pattern of results (as does sodium amylobarbitone; Gray and Dudderidge 1971), whereas amygdaloid lesions impair the frustration effect but leave the PREE intact, Owen *et al.*'s (1982) findings suggest that the innervation of the amygdala by the dorsal bundle is less important in determining the behavioural functions exercised by this pathway than is its innervation of the septo-hippocampal system. A further prediction from the anxiety hypothesis was that dorsal bundle lesions should reduce the Crespi depression effect when a large reward is changed to a small one in the alley, since this is observed after administration of the anti-anxiety drugs (Gray 1977). This prediction, however, was not verified, dorsal bundle lesions being without effect (Owen 1979).

Results in Skinner-box experiments have been less encouraging for the anxiety hypothesis. From the effects of the anti-anxiety drugs (Chapter 2, Section 2.7) we would predict that dorsal bundle lesions should increase FI and FR response rates by increasing response rates in the period just after reinforcement. FI response rates, however, have been reported to be normal in dorsal bundle lesioned rats by Mason and Iversen (1978c) and Mason (1979). Owen (1979) found increased FI response rates after dorsal bundle lesions, but this was due to an unexpected *increase* in the FI scallop, i.e. rates increased differentially more in the lesioned animals as the time of the next reinforcement approached. This is the same result that Haddad and Rabe (1969) and Jackson and Gergen (1970) reported after hippocampal lesions, although the effects of septal lesions are generally like those of the anti-anxiety drugs (Chapter 6, Section 6.18). FR response rates have also been reported to be normal after dorsal bundle lesions by Mason (1979). However, Peterson and Sparber (1974) and Peterson and Laverty (1976) found elevated response rates after intraventricular and neonatal systemic 6-OHDA, respectively, and this was in part due, as predicted, to a reduction in the post-reinforcement pause; the common biochemical effect of these two treatments is likely to have been a destruction of forebrain noradrenergic terminals.

A further prediction from the effects of all three of our reference treatments, drugs (Chapter 2, Section 2.7) and septal and hippocampal lesions (Chapter 6, Section 6.18), is that DRL responding should be impaired after damage to the dorsal bundle. Mason and Iversen (1977a), however, found no effect of dorsal bundle lesions on DRL responding acquired *de* *novo*, and when DRL was preceded by training on CRF (which brings out the hippocampal deficit in DRL performance) the dorsal bundle animals were actually superior to controls. The behavioural results of this experiment, however, are reported in very little detail, and it is by no means clear that either group had learned to time their responses as a DRL schedule requires. The experiments were terminated after 25 days of training (which is very short for DRL), at which time the controls but not the lesioned animals were showing an accelerating learning curve. Thus this negative result must be treated with caution. Using the β-noradrenergic blocking drug, propranolol, administered systemically, Salmon (personal communication)* has produced a marked disruption in the DRL performance of intact animals. This indicates the involvement of noradrenergic mechanisms in this behaviour, but not necessarily, of course, the dorsal bundle.

Other negative results in the Skinner-box are less surprising.

Mason and Fibiger (1978a) shifted rats from CRF to VR 2 and then to VR 4, and measured the increment in response rate that this produced relative to a group maintained on CRF; this increment did not differ between dorsal bundle and control rats. The authors treat this paradigm as the equivalent of a PRF schedule in the alley and the increment in response rate as equivalent to a partial reinforcement acquisition effect. This interpretation is unacceptable. On a free-operant VR schedule there is a direct relationship between the rate of response and the rate of reinforcement. Thus, in order to maintain reinforcement rate constant, an animal shifted from CRF to VR 2 must double its response rate and, when shifted to VR 4, double it again. It follows that the increment in response rate produced by this schedule is best regarded as a simple manifestation of the law of effect, with no necessary relation to the behavioural consequences of non-reward as such. This consideration does not apply to running speed measured in a discrete-trial paradigm. The relationship between running speed and reinforcement rate is identical for CRF and PRF conditions, since it holds within a single trial. Thus the increased start and run speeds demonstrated by PRF-trained animals (Goodrich 1959; Haggard 1959) are *excess* consequences of non-reward *not* accounted for by the law of effect. This view is supported by much empirical and theoretical research (Amsel 1962; Gray 1975); but it cannot be applied to the paradigm used by Mason and Fibiger (1978a). Thus the failure of dorsal bundle lesions to affect behaviour in this paradigm does not, as claimed by the authors, conflict with the prediction from the anxiety hypothesis that the partial reinforcement acquisition effect should be abolished by dorsal bundle lesions.

Mason and Iversen (1978c), in another experiment which purports to test this hypothesis, studied the FI omission effect which was developed as an operant analogue of the double-runway frustration effect (see Chapter 6, Section 6.23). As we have seen, the frustration effect in the

---

*See Salmon and Gray (1985) in additional references.

double runway is not affected by dorsal bundle lesions (Owen *et al.* 1982), nor is it predicted to be (Gray 1977; Chapter 2, Section 2.9). Thus, if the FI omission effect were a good analogue of the double-runway frustration effect, we would not expect it to be altered by dorsal bundle lesions. In fact, it appears to be rather a poor analogue of the frustration effect (Staddon, 1970, 1972). Empirically, septal and hippocampal lesions have been reported either to leave the FI omission effect unaltered or to increase it (Chapter 6, Section 6.23); thus this is probably the best prediction we can make for the effects of dorsal bundle lesions. The result of Mason and Iversen's (1978c) experiment — seen by the authors to conflict with the predictions of the anxiety hypothesis — was in reasonable agreement with this analysis: the FI omission effect was initially the same in dorsal bundle and control animals but increased over days in the lesioned group while decreasing in controls.

In a second experiment in this paper Mason and Iversen (1978c) examined the possibility that dorsal bundle lesions decrease the aversiveness of stimuli associated with non-reward. For this purpose they gave rats an opportunity to terminate exposure to the S− of a successive discrimination by pressing a second ('time-out') lever in the operant chamber. There was no effect of dorsal bundle lesions on the response rate on the time-out lever. Unfortunately, the authors present no evidence that responding on the time-out lever was maintained by the opportunity to escape from S−, and such evidence is essential for the interpretation of an experiment of this kind (see the discussion of Henke's 1976 experiment in Chapter 6, Section 6.23).

A final negative result is Peterson and Laverty's (1976) report that neonatal systemic 6-OHDA failed to affect responding on a progressive ratio schedule in the Skinner-box. This is surprising, given the close similarities between a progressive ratio schedule and extinction. But it can perhaps be attributed to the incompleteness of the lesion: cortical noradrenalin was reduced by only 55 per cent.

13. Discrimination learning: simultaneous

Given the effects of the anti-anxiety drugs (Chapter 2, Section 2.8) and damage to the septo-hippocampal system (Chapter 6, Section 6.19), we would not expect dorsal bundle lesions to affect simultaneous discrimination learning. In accord with this expectation simple position learning in the T-maze is normal after injection of 6-OHDA into the dorsal bundle (Roberts *et al.* 1976), and olfactory discrimination is normal after electrolytic lesions to the locus coeruleus (Amaral and Foss 1975). Brightness discrimination in the T-maze is similarly unaffected by dorsal bundle lesions (Owen and McNaughton, personal communication) or by neonatal intraventricular 6-OHDA (Oke and Adams 1978). An impairment in a visual simultaneous discrimination has, however, been reported by Leconte and Hennevin (1981). The animal's task was to choose between three doors which were black, white, or striped black and white (black was always positive). However, the injection site in this experiment was caudal to the point at which the dorsal and ventral noradrenergic bundles diverge; thus, although the authors report only cortical noradrenalin depletions, it must be assumed that both bundles were damaged.

14. Discrimination learning: successive

From both the drug and lesion background (Chapter 2, Section 2.8; Chapter 6, Section 6.20) we would expect damage to the dorsal bundle to impair successive discrimination performance by increasing responding in the presence of the negative stimulus. This result has been reported in experiments in the Skinner-box by Mason and Iversen (1977c, 1978b), using a multiple schedule of CRF and extinction, and by Salmon and Owen (personal communication) using a Mult VI/EXT schedule. Using the same task as Mason and Iversen (1977c, 1978b), however, Koob et al. (1978) found no effect of electrolytic lesions of the locus coeruleus. Cortical noradrenalin was depleted to 14 per cent in this experiment, but this may have been insufficient. Tremmel et al. (1977) found no effect of dorsal bundle lesions on single alternation responding in the Skinner-box. Although one might predict in principle (from the hypothesis of an impaired capacity to withhold non-rewarded responses) that dorsal bundle lesions should disturb this behaviour, experiments with hippocampal lesions have yielded very mixed results in this paradigm (Chapter 6, Section 6.20), and the parameters used by Tremmel et al. (1977) — a retractable lever and an ITI of 20 seconds — are the same as those which, in the hands of Walker et al. (1972), failed to show any effect of hippocampal lesions.

15. Discrimination learning: spatial

Leconte and Hennevin (1981) showed that intracerebral 6-OHDA impaired performance in a multiple-T-maze, significantly so on a measure of speed of traversing the maze, non-significantly on a measure of errors. This result would be expected, given the effects of septal and hippocampal lesions on performance in complex mazes (Chapter 6, Section 6.21). But because of the injection site used by these workers (see above), this result cannot with confidence be attributed to specifically dorsal bundle damage. The effects of septal and hippocampal lesions also lead one to expect that left-right alternation in a T-maze will be impaired by dorsal bundle lesions; this finding has been reported by Mason and Fibiger (1978d).

In their experiment using the multiple-T-maze Leconte and Hennevin (1981) also measured the duration of slow-wave and REM sleep in the period immediately after the daily learning session. It is well established that, during the time when learning is proceeding fastest, there is a brief augmentation of REM sleep shortly after the end of each training session

(Bloch, Hennevin, and Leconte 1978). Leconte and Hennevin (1981) report the striking finding that their lesion eliminated both the accelerated phase of the learning curve (speed of traversal of the maze) and the augmentation of REM sleep which, in the controls, accompanied this phase. These results (assuming that the critical focus of their lesion lay in the dorsal bundle) fall into place alongside the observations of Kovacs *et al.* (1979) and Zornetzer and Gold (1976) using step-through passive avoidance (see above, subsection 2). In each case the experimental observations suggest that the dorsal bundle plays a role in strengthening the effects of at least certain learning experiences.

16. Reversal learning

A final prediction from the effects of septo-hippocampal damage (Chapter 6, Section 6.22) is that dorsal bundle lesions should impair reversal learning. The few experiments reported so far do not encourage belief in this prediction. Mason and Iversen (1978*b*) found that dorsal bundle lesions impaired the reversal of their operant successive discrimination (see above); but, since the impairment took the same form (increased response rates during S−) as the impairment during acquisition of the discrimination, it cannot with confidence be attributed to the reversal element itself. Position reversal in the T-maze (which has been very successful in bringing out both the septal and the hippocampal deficits) is unaffected by dorsal bundle (Roberts *et al.* 1976) or locus coeruleus (Amaral and Foss 1975) lesions. Preliminary data from our laboratory (Owen and McNaughton, personal communication) suggest a similar lack of effect of dorsal bundle lesions in a brightness reversal task in the T-maze. Finally, Mason and Iversen (1977*b*) found no effect of dorsal bundle lesions on the reversal from pulling to pushing a ball through a tunnel or vice versa. However, in contrast to these negative results with lesions, Segal (1980) reports that electrical stimulation of the locus coeruleus improved position reversal without affecting initial acquisition of the position habit.

Functions of the dorsal noradrenergic bundle

None of the hypotheses of dorsal bundle function considered earlier in this chapter emerges unscathed from contact with the data. Before attempting to resolve the problem of interpretation this creates, let us address a more empirical issue: what features of the dorsal bundle syndrome are common also to the anti-anxiety drug and septo-hippocampal syndromes? A best guess (for there are many gaps and inconsistencies in the data) is presented in Table 11.6.

There are several features of this table that are worth noting.

First, the dorsal bundle syndrome appears to be considerably narrower than the other three to which it is compared; there are far more null effects to its credit. This cannot be a matter of simple extent of lesion. On the contrary, there are very few experiments on hippocampal lesions where the damage is as much as even 80 per cent of the total tissue making up this structure; yet there are many negative findings with dorsal bundle lesions of greater than 90 per cent, judging by forebrain noradrenalin depletion. It is possible, as suggested earlier, that the dorsal bundle has a specially great redundancy; but this in turn implies that it can carry information only of a rather gross kind.

Second, when lesions of the dorsal bundle do have effects, they are almost invariably of the same kind as those seen after one or more of the other treatments (which, of course, usually resemble one another). The only exception to this rule which is at all clear (and even in this case the data on dorsal bundle lesions are not entirely consistent among themselves) concerns reactions to distractors: both septal and hippocampal lesions (Chapter 6, Section 6.10) decrease the distractibility of ongoing motor behaviour, dorsal bundle lesions more commonly increase it.

Third, there is a greater tendency for the dorsal bundle lesion to produce behavioural effects, the more clearcut and concordant among themselves are the effects of the other three treatments. Thus if one considers the cases in which entries for the anti-anxiety drugs, septal and hippocampal lesions are all of the same kind, one finds that the same entry usually appears in the column of dorsal bundle effects. The exceptions to this rule are: (i) the lack of effect of dorsal bundle lesions on reversal learning; (ii) their lack of effect on open-field ambulation; (iii) their lack of effect on intermittently rewarded bar-pressing; (iv) their lack of effect on Sidman avoidance in the Skinner-box, but this is based on a single report (Mason and Fibiger 1979e); and (v) their lack of effect on DRL performance, but I have commented above on the inadequacy of the data presented in the single relevant paper (Mason and Iversen 1977a).

Fourth, the positive effects of dorsal bundle lesions cluster most strongly in tasks which involve non-reward. However, any hypothesis which seeks to limit its role to this type of task must conflict with the positive findings in experiments using shock (two-way active avoidance, sometimes passive avoidance) or stimuli of no certain reinforcing effect (spontaneous alternation and response to stimulus change in the T-maze).

Finally, there is no apparent tendency for the effects of dorsal bundle lesions to resemble any one of the three comparison treatments more closely than any other. Overall, this pattern of results suggests that the function of the dorsal bundle is closely related to, but narrower than, that of the septo-hippocampal system.

It is harder to determine what that function might be. The various hypotheses outlined earlier in the chapter must be judged according to their success in accounting for the dorsal bundle syndrome summarized in Table 11.6. If we leave aside behaviour for which the data are too scanty or inconsistent to allow conclusions to be drawn, the major features of this syndrome are the following: the learning and performance of simple rewarded responses is normal; there are sometimes slight impairments in

Table 11.6. Comparison between the dorsal bundle, anti-anxiety drug, and septo-hippocampal syndromes.*

Section			Task	dorsal bundle lesions	Effects of anti-anxiety drugs	septal lesions	hippocampal lesions
Ch. 2	Ch. 6	Ch. 11					
1	1	1	rewarded running, CRF	o	o	o	o
1	1	1	rewarded bar-pressing, CRF	o	o	+	o
7	1	1	rewarded bar-pressing, intermittent reinforcement	−†	+	+	+
2	2	2	passive avoidance	−†	−	−	−
3	3	3	on-the-baseline conditioned suppression	o	?o	?	?o
3	3	3	off-the-baseline conditioned suppression	o	?	?	−
3	3	3	taste aversion	o			o
4	4	4	skilled escape	o	o	o	o
5	5	4	one-way active avoidance	o	o	−	o
5	6	5	non-spatial active avoidance	o‡	+	+	+
5	7	5	two-way active avoidance	+	+	+	+
6	8	6	threshold of detection of shock	o	o	o	o
	11	7	general activity	o	?	?	+
10	12	7	exploration of novel stimuli	?	−	−	−
10	12	7	spontaneous alternation	−	−	−	−
10	12	7	open-field ambulation	o	+§	+§	+
10	12	7	rearing	−	−	−	−

10		8	distraction	?+	?	—	—
10	13	9	habituation rate	o	?	?—	?—
10	13	10	open-field defecation	o	?	—	o
10	13	10	emergence time	+	—	—	?—
7	17	11	resistance to extinction	—	+	+	+
7	17	11	partial reinforcement extinction effect	o¶	—	—	—
7		12	partial reinforcement acquisition effect	o	—	?o‖	?—
7	18	12	performance on DRL schedule	o	—	—	?+
7	18	12	fixed-interval scallop	—	o	o	o
8	19	13	simultaneous discrimination	—	—	o	—
8	20	14	successive discrimination	—	—	—	—
	21	15	spatial discrimination	o	—	—	—
8	22	16	reversal learning	o	o	—	o
9	23	12	double runway frustration effect	o	o	o	o
7	23	12	Crespi depression effect	o	—	—	?—

*This comparison is based on the information contained in the sections of this chapter and Chapters 2 and 6, as listed in the left-hand column. +, facilitation; —, impairment; o, no consistent change; ?, insufficient data.

†See Tsaltas et al. (1984) in additional references.

‡Based on only one report (Mason and Fibiger 1979e).

§Septal lesions reduce ambulation upon early exposure to the open field but increase ambulation with continued exposure; the pattern of change with anti-anxiety drugs is the reverse.

‖Feldon and Gray (1979a,b).

¶Based on only one report (Mason and Iversen 1977a).

passive avoidance; there is no change in conditioned taste aversion; off-the-baseline conditioned suppression is normal, but there is a slight impairment in on-the-baseline suppression; escape and one-way active avoidance are normal; shuttle-box avoidance is improved; pain thresholds are unchanged; overall activity and locomotion in a novel environment are unchanged, but rearing is reduced; responses to specific novel stimuli in spatial contexts are reduced (spontaneous alternation and response to stimulus change in the T-maze); distractibility is sometimes increased; habituation is sometimes retarded; tests of fearfulness show no change; resistance to extinction is reliably increased, but not under all conditions; under appropriate conditions the partial reinforcement extinction effect is eliminated; the partial reinforcement acquisition effect is also eliminated; the double-runway frustration effect and the Crespi depression effect are unchanged; simultaneous discrimination is normal; successive discrimination learning is impaired, owing to an increased probability of response in the presence of S−; spatial discrimination learning is impaired; and reversal learning is normal. How well do the different hypotheses explain this syndrome?

The reward hypothesis can be ruled out, since the learning and performance of simple rewarded behaviour is normal in dorsal bundle rats. The general learning hypothesis is ruled out by the same data, and by the evidence of efficient learning in several other tasks (e.g. shuttle-box avoidance). A role in the general consolidation of memory is ruled out by the evidence that dorsal bundle rats can learn and retain a response over periods of up to 24 hours in appetitive tasks (Owen 1979) and 72 hours in avoidance tasks (Mason and Fibiger 1979a). On the other hand, the results from several experiments suggest that the dorsal bundle may under some conditions facilitate retention (Crow and Wendlandt 1976; Kovacs *et al.* 1979; Zornetzer and Gold 1976; Leconte and Hennevin 1981). Noradrenalin has been implicated in retention processes in a variety of experiments using pharmacological means to manipulate neurotransmitter function, often by post-trial injection (e.g. Randt *et al.* 1971; Cohen and Hamburg 1975; Stein, Belluzzi, and Wise 1975; Meligeri *et al.* 1978; Izquierdo *et al.* 1979). Since it is not possible in these experiments to localize the effects obtained to any particular central noradrenergic pathway (nor often to exclude the possibility of peripheral effects), it is not my intention to discuss these data here; but they serve as a further reason not to exclude the possibility that the dorsal bundle plays a facilitatory — though certainly not an essential — role in the retention of acquired information.

The general anxiety hypothesis is not clearly ruled out by the data summarized in Table 11.6. But there are several apparent discrepancies between the effects of dorsal bundle damage and anti-anxiety drugs which weaken this hypothesis. First, although dorsal bundle lesions sometimes affect passive avoidance in the predicted manner (Subsection 2), they have so far proved to have less definite disinhibitory effects than the anti-anxiety drugs. As we have seen, however, hardly any of the relevant experiments have used the most appropriate behavioural techniques. Second, as pointed out above, there are several cases in which dorsal bundle lesions apparently fail to produce effects which are clearly seen after administration of the anti-anxiety drugs. Since discrepancies of this kind are rare when one compares the effects of the anti-anxiety drugs and those of septo-hippocampal damage, it is difficult to believe that the drugs affect the septo-hippocampal system exclusively by way of an action on its noradrenergic afferents. This line of argument encourages one to seek an account of the effects of dorsal bundle lesions which would attribute to this pathway a role, but a restricted one, in the neural mechanisms by which the anti-anxiety drugs act.

Before trying to define this role more closely, let us see how Mason and Iversen's (1977c, 1979) attentional hypothesis fares. This holds that animals with dorsal bundle lesions are unable to screen out irrelevant cues. Since it has grown out of the data on dorsal bundle lesions, one might suppose that it would be able to explain them tolerably well. But this closeness to the data turns out to be a weakness rather than a strength. For the most part, the Mason and Iversen hypothesis is too ill specified to have predictive power. In particular, it is usually impossible to know in advance what is a 'relevant' or 'irrelevant' stimulus.

As an example of this imprecision, consider Owen's (1979; Owen et al., in preparation)* finding that dorsal bundle lesions eliminate the response to stimulus change. In this experiment the animal is placed in the stem of a T-maze of which one arm is white and one black and left there, separated from the arms by transparent partitions, for three minutes. It is then taken out, the arms are changed so that both are now black or both white, the partitions are removed, and the rat is returned to the stem of the maze. Normal rats enter the changed arm about 75 per cent of the time; dorsal bundle lesioned rats — like rats drugged with sodium amylobarbitone (Ison et al. 1966; Owen 1979)* — choose at random. Can this result be predicted from Mason and Iversen's (1979) hypothesis? Evidently, the answer to this question depends on whether the brightness of the arms of the T-maze is relevant or irrelevant (to what?). If it is 'relevant', the lesioned animal might be expected to respond less to the change in brightness than controls (because it is busy responding to other 'irrelevant' stimuli). If it is 'irrelevant', the lesioned animal would presumably respond more than controls to a change in brightness. Thus the experimental finding can be explained, *post hoc*, by deciding that the brightness of the arms is 'relevant'; but in advance of the experiment this point is indeterminate. The same arguments apply to the finding (Owen et al., in preparation)* that spontaneous alternation in the T-maze is eliminated by dorsal bundle lesions. A further example of the dangerous flexibility of the attentional hypothesis comes from a paper by Mason and Fibiger

*See McNaughton et al. (1984) in additional references.

(1978c). When they find that dorsal bundle animals are more distracted by an overhead light, less distracted by a light in front of their eyes, and not different from controls when the distractor is auditory, these authors are able to include *all* these results within the attentional theory by postulating different initial values of salience for the three stimuli in controls.

Mason and Iversen (1979) have attempted to increase the power of their approach by wedding it to the Sutherland and Mackintosh (1971) general theory of selective attention. But the one case to which they have so far fully applied this analysis fails to square with their predictions. This is the blockade of the PREE by dorsal bundle lesions (Owen *et al.* 1977, 1982).

Mason and Iversen (1979) argue that the increased resistance to extinction produced by dorsal bundle lesions in CRF-trained animals arises because the lesioned animals attend to more stimuli, and so attach the instrumental response to more stimuli than controls. In intact animals such a broadening of attention can be produced by PRF training, and this phenomenon might be responsible for the PREE (Sutherland and Mackintosh 1971). Thus, on the Mason and Iversen (1979) analysis, a CRF-trained dorsal bundle rat is equivalent to a PRF-trained intact rat. It follows that the PREE should be blocked by dorsal bundle lesions, as it is; but the predicted pattern is for the lesion to increase resistance to extinction in CRF-trained rats up to the level shown by animals trained on PRF, and not to affect resistance to extinction in the latter at all. Mason and Fibiger (1978a) claimed to obtain just this result in an experiment discussed in subsection 10, above, in which rats were trained in the Skinner-box on CRF or VR 4 and then extinguished. But there is little reason to regard extinction after a free-operant VR schedule as the equivalent of a PREE in the discrete-trial alley task; and in any case the different response rates recorded at the end of acquisition by Mason and Fibiger's (1978a) groups trained on CRF and VR 4 make it impossible to distinguish between the effects of the VR schedules on acquisition and on resistance to extinction, respectively. In the only experiments in which dorsal bundle lesions have been shown to block a genuine PREE, this has been due to a fall in resistance to extinction in the PRF condition in addition to a rise in the CRF condition (Owen *et al.* 1977, 1982), and the attentional hypothesis is clearly contradicted by this pattern of results (N. M. Davis 1979b).

Mason and Iversen's (1979) more developed form of the attention hypothesis makes some further interesting predictions for the effects of dorsal bundle lesions. Three of these are reported to have been experimentally verified: loss of Kamin's blocking effect (Lorden *et al.* 1979), loss of latent inhibition and improved non-reversal shift learning (Mason and Fibiger 1979f). But these reports have appeared so far in abstract only, so it is not possible to judge how well the data fit with the detailed predictions of the theory. Note that in any case two of these findings might be predicted in general terms from the gross empirical similarities between dorsal bundle and septo-hippocampal lesion effects, since both latent inhibition and Kamin's blocking effect are disrupted by damage to the septo-hippocampal system (Chapter 6, Section 6.3).

If one wished to specify 'relevance' more clearly than is done in Mason and Iversen's (1977c, 1979) theory, a definition which would fit with the general approach adopted in this book might be 'associated with reward, associated with punishment, or novel'. This analysis has the advantage that it is consistent with the physiological data reviewed in Chapter 7, and notably with Segal's (1977a, b, c, d) experiments showing that an association with either reward or punishment facilitates the passage of stimuli round the hippocampal circuit in the same way as priming stimulation of the locus coeruleus. In terms of the theory developed in the last chapter, facilitation of the transmission of information around the hippocampal circuit is the equivalent of a tag, reading 'important, check carefully'. The hypothesis that the dorsal bundle exercises this kind of function bears obvious similarities to Mason and Iversen's (1979) view that this pathway picks out stimuli that are particularly relevant to the animal's activities and sees that they are given special attention. But it differs from Mason and Iversen's view in one important respect: it supposes that the dorsal bundle boosts attention to relevant stimuli, not generally, but *within the septo-hippocampal system*. Thus the predictions this hypothesis makes for the effects of dorsal bundle damage on a particular form of behaviour depend on the manner in which that behaviour is controlled by the septo-hippocampal system (Chapter 10).

On this 'checking' hypothesis, how would we expect behaviour to be affected when the septo-hippocampal system is robbed of its normal noradrenergic input?

Consider first the case in which relevance arises from an association with reward. In the intact animal we suppose that the dorsal bundle is responsible for boosting the hippocampal presentation of such relevant stimuli to the subicular comparator, whose job it is to keep track of them and use them to detect non-reward, should this occur. Since the septo-hippocampal system does not control rewarded behaviour, the loss of the dorsal bundle signal would leave this unchanged, as observed. But the stimuli and response-patterns associated with reward would be less clearly specified within the septo-hippocampal system. In consequence, non-reward would be less easily detected by the subicular comparator, giving rise to the deficits in response to non-reward which are the major feature of the dorsal bundle syndrome. Note that, on this view, the report that dorsal bundle lesions do not increase resistance to extinction if they are carried out after acquisition (Mason 1979; Mason and Fibiger 1979d) — assuming that it is reliable (see subsection 11) — does not pose any particular problem. On the contrary, this finding can be predicted, though with no great rigour: once the signals of reward have entered the septo-hippocampal system, the task performed by the dorsal bundle is complete. It is also possible that we can account along these lines for the influence of acquisition length on the effect of dorsal bundle lesions on resistance to extinction after training on CRF. As we saw in subsection 11, the lesion increases resistance to extinction after 50, but not after 100, CRF training trials (Owen *et al.* 1979, 1982). If the role of the dorsal bundle is to enhance — rather than provide — the specification of reward-associated stimuli within the septo-hippocampal system, it is perhaps understandable that a sufficient number of rewards can compensate for its absence.

This much of the argument is identical to the narrower 'reward signal' hypothesis (Boarder *et al.* 1979). The case of novelty is more complicated. As pointed out earlier in the chapter, the anatomy of the locus coeruleus does not encourage the belief that it can itself detect novelty. Presumably, therefore, if it plays any role in the control of responses elicited by novel stimuli (and the evidence summarized in subsections 7, 8, and 9 suggests that it does), it must receive this information from somewhere else, perhaps from the septo-hippocampal system itself, though apparently not by a direct route (Sakai *et al.* 1977*b;* Cederbaum and Aghajanian 1978). Once having received information about novel stimuli (on the view proposed here), the task of the locus coeruleus is to boost their passage through the hippocampal circuit and their consequent presentation to the subicular comparator, exactly as in the case of reward-associated stimuli. Without the extra boost from the dorsal bundle, therefore, we would expect that the novel stimulus will be less efficiently analysed by the subicular comparator. If we now imagine a set of such initially novel stimuli, constituting a complete novel environment, it follows that these will eventually provide a less well-defined familiar background against which the subicular comparator is called on to compare further novel stimuli. In this way, specific novel stimuli presented against a familiar background might be expected to be detected less efficiently after dorsal bundle lesions, as in fact observed in Owen's (1979; Owen *et al.*, in preparation)* experiments in the T-maze (abolition of spontaneous alternation and of the response to stimulus change). If this analysis is correct, the lesioned animal's deficit could be overcome by sufficiently long exposure to the initial configuration of the maze in these experiments. A second prediction — provided one could control for state dependency — is that, just as the dorsal bundle extinction effect is absent if the lesion is made after acquisition (Mason 1979; Mason and Fibiger 1979*d*), so the altered responses in the T-maze would not be manifest if the lesion were made after exposure to the initial configuration.

The data suggesting that the dorsal bundle may enhance the stability of memory traces (Crow and Wendlandt 1976; Kovacs *et al.* 1979; Zornetzer and Gold 1976; Leconte and Hennevin 1981) can perhaps be accounted for in a similar manner by supposing that, as a result of the noradrenergic input to the septo-hippocampal system, incoming stimuli are character-

*See McNaughton *et al.* (1984) in additional references.

ized more fully in the predictive circuits associated with the subiculum, along the lines discussed in Chapter 10 in connection with the human amnesic syndrome. Such an account would be consistent with the report of a reduction of metabolites of noradrenalin in the cerebrospinal fluid of Korsakoff patients (McEntee and Mair 1978). Note also that all four of the experiments cited above made use of tasks — passive avoidance or spatial maze-learning — which are sensitive to the effects of hippocampal dysfunction.

If we take this account seriously, and ally it to the report that dorsal bundle lesions simultaneously impair learning of a complex maze and the augmentation of REM sleep that is normally associated with such learning (Leconte and Hennevin 1981), it might be deduced that one of the functions of REM sleep is to re-circulate recently acquired information around the subicular loop. In this connection, recall that hippocampal theta is a prominent feature of REM sleep; furthermore, its frequency in the rat is in the range — 6.5–8.5 Hz (O'Keefe and Nadel 1978, Table A11, b; Robinson, Kramis, and Vanderwolf 1977) — associated with both noradrenergic activation of the septo-hippocampal system (Gray *et al.* 1975; McNaughton *et al.* 1977; McNaughton, Kelly, and Gray 1980*b*) and active exploratory behaviour in the waking state (Chapters 7 and 10). Thus it is possible that the occurrence of this theta rhythm during sleep is associated with the circulation of information around the subicular loop. It would stretch speculation too far to wonder what this might have to do with the extraordinary phenomena of dreams, which are known to be closely related to REM sleep in man.

The 'checking' version of the anxiety hypothesis, then, can handle much of the data. But it has its problems.

First, it clearly predicts that there should be a deficit in reversal learning after dorsal bundle lesions. If, as argued above, increased resistance to extinction is due to a failure to detect non-reward, such a failure should also impair the animal's capacity to detect the change in reinforcement conditions at the onset of reversal. But reversal learning is apparently normal after dorsal bundle lesions (subsection 14). Note, however, that, as would also be predicted, Segal (1980) was able to improve reversal learning by stimulation of the locus coeruleus.

Second, the same arguments that lead to the prediction of the loss of response to stimulus change after dorsal bundle lesions (see above) also predict reduced distractibility; but the bulk of the evidence suggests (though not very clearly) the opposite effect (subsection 8).

A third problem has consequences that are perhaps more far-reaching. It concerns the partial reinforcement acquisition effect, i.e. the faster running speeds seen when animals are trained on PRF as compared to CRF in the alley (Goodrich 1959; Haggard 1959). This is abolished by dorsal bundle lesions (Owen 1979; Owen *et al.* 1982) and anti-anxiety drugs (Gray 1977; Chapter 2, Section 2.7), both of which reduce speeds selectively in the PRF group. The drug effect has been interpreted as a blockade of the arousal produced by conditioned frustrative stimuli (Amsel 1962; Gray 1977), and it is tempting to extend this interpretation to the effect of dorsal bundle lesions. But we cannot do this and stay within the bounds of the checking version of the anxiety hypothesis. For it is unlikely that the role played by the dorsal bundle in the partial reinforcement acquisition effect is exercised via the septo-hippocampal system. This phenomenon is apparently intact after septal lesions (Feldon and Gray 1979*a*, *b*); there are no relevant data on hippocampal lesions. More generally, there is no evidence that septal or hippocampal lesions alter the arousing effects of conditioned frustrative or punishing stimuli, and some evidence that they do not (Dickinson 1974, 1975; Raphelson *et al.* 1965; see the discussion at the end of Chapter 6). Thus, even when we have an effect of the dorsal bundle lesion which is clearly as predicted by the general anxiety hypothesis, to account for it we must apparently take into consideration projections of the dorsal bundle to structures other than the septo-hippocampal system.

In the case of the partial reinforcement acquisition effect, the dorsal bundle lesion does too much to be accomodated within the checking version of the anxiety hypothesis. When we turn to the case of punishment, it does too little. As we have seen, with the exception of the improvement in shuttle-box avoidance, the effects of dorsal bundle lesions in tasks involving aversive stimuli are generally rather weak. In particular, there is only little sign of reduction in behavioural inhibition as such (weak impairments in passive avoidance, punishment-induced suppression, and on-the-baseline conditioned suppression). This conclusion is also suggested by the data on responses to novel environments or stimuli. There is a clear motor disinhibition when these responses are measured in animals with septal or hippocampal lesions (Chapter 6, Section 6.9–6.14), but this has not been seen after dorsal bundle lesions. There is, for example, a definite discrepancy between the effects of dorsal bundle or septohipocampal damage, respectively, on behaviour in the open field: ambulation is increased by hippocampal lesions consistently and by septal lesions inconsistently (Chapter 6, Section 6.12), but by dorsal bundle lesions not at all (subsection 7, above). Thus the findings in experiments using both aversive and novel stimuli suggest that systems directly concerned with the inhibition of motor responses are intact in animals with dorsal bundle lesions. This inference is not necessarily inconsistent with the arguments pursued so far. For, in Chapter 10, this role was allocated to the pathways from the subiculum to the cingulate cortex and from the lateral septal area to the hypothalamus; and there is no reason to suppose that these would be affected by dorsal bundle lesions. None the less, if the dorsal bundle boosts hippocampal analysis of stimuli associated with punishment, we would expect that, after dorsal bundle lesions, the septo-hippocampal system would be less ready to operate the efferent pathways of

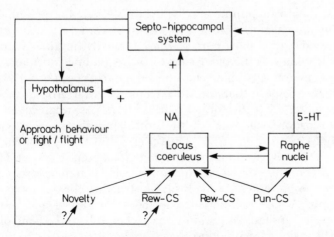

Figure 11.4. The extended checking hypothesis. NA, noradrenalin; 5-HT, 5-hy-droxytryptamine (serotonin); +, facilitates; −, inhibits; Pun-CS, signals of punishment; Rew-CS, signals of reward; $\overline{\text{Rew}}$-CS, signals of non-reward. The question marks indicate that no pathway has been established as carrying information about novelty or non-reward from the septo-hippocampal system to the locus coeruleus. (See text for further explanation.)

motor inhibition. So, on the checking version of the anxiety hypothesis, we would expect a better match between the effects of septo-hippocampal and dorsal bundle lesions on passive avoidance than is in fact obtained.

To deal with these problems it is necessary to extend the checking hypothesis. The extension has five facets. The first two are required by the data on the partial reinforcement acquisition effect, the last three by the data on behavioural inhibition. At the same time they attempt to deal with a problem raised earlier in the chapter: that of instructing the septo-hippocampal system whether a stimulus is important because it is associated with reward or with punishment, respectively. Extended in this way, the hypothesis becomes the model shown in Fig. 11.4.

First, we suppose that the locus coeruleus receives information about non-reward. This step is not a great one, since the data from both lesion (subsections 7, 8, and 9) and recording (Cederbaum and Aghajanian 1978; Jones *et al.* 1978; Foote *et al.* 1978) experiments have already required us to postulate that it receives information about novelty, of which, of course, non-reward is a special case. As in the case of novelty, the source of this information is unknown. We continue to suppose that the dorsal bundle is also activated by stimuli associated with reward, since there is evidence that this is so from Segal's experiments (Chapter 7) and from Boarder *et al.*'s (1979) observations of changes in tyrosine hydroxylase activity in hippocampal synaptosomes taken from animals trained on CRF or PRF respectively (see above). Thus, on the extended checking

hypothesis, the dorsal bundle is activated by all events of potential importance to the animal's survival: it is a general alerting or alarm system (see
also Redmond 1979). This part of the extended checking hypothesis is
essentially the same as the older view of the ascending reticular activating
system as a general arousal mechanism (Magoun 1963; Gray 1964a).

Second, we suppose that the dorsal bundle is an arousal mechanism
also in the sense that it invigorates behaviour, that is, whatever the animal
does, it does more vigorously if the dorsal bundle is active (Gray and
Smith 1969; Gray 1964a, 1975). Thus it executes the 'increment arousal'
output of the behavioural inhibition system (Chapters 1 and 2). However,
as we have seen, this part of its function is unlikely to be exercised via the
septo-hippocampal system. A likely target structure for this purpose is the
hypothalamus, which is innervated by both the dorsal and the ventral
noradrenergic bundles. This region plays a key role in the control of both
approach behaviour (of the kind that is invigorated by conditioned frustrative stimuli to produce the partial reinforcement acquisition effect),
and the fight/flight behaviour which appears to be simultaneously primed
and inhibited when an animal is exposed to conditioned aversive stimuli
(Gray 1971a, 1972a). Note that, since one of the pathways of motor inhibition that is efferent from the septo-hippocampal system passes from the
lateral septal area to the ventromedial hypothalamus (see Chapters 8 and
10), this postulate leads to a model that is similar to the one deduced by
Gray and Araujo-Silva (1971) from the effects of sodium amylobarbitone
on resistance to extinction in septal-lesioned rats (see Fig. 11.1).

Third, we suppose that the dorsal bundle plays little or no role in the
facilitation or execution of behavioural inhibition as such. Thus, of the
three outputs of the behavioural inhibition system — increased arousal,
increased attention, and behavioural inhibition — the dorsal bundle plays
an important role in the first two, but not in the last.

Fourth, we suppose that behavioural inhibition, particularly in response
to stimuli associated with punishment, is facilitated by the ascending serotonergic input to the septo-hippocampal system.

Fifth, we suppose that the noradrenergic input to the septo-
hippocampal system says merely, 'this is important, check carefully', while
a joint noradrenergic, serotonergic, and cholinergic input signifies 'this is
important and associated with punishment'. The fourth and fifth assumptions are closely linked, and neither can properly be discussed until we
have considered the data on the behavioural effects of lesions to the ascending serotonergic pathways, as we do below.

Note that both the functions attributed to the dorsal bundle — that of
boosting hippocampal analysis of its other simultaneous inputs, and that
of amplifying hypothalamic outputs producing approach or fight/flight
behaviour — are consistent with McNaughton and Mason's (1980) hypothesis that noradrenergic neurons increase the signal-to-noise ratio of
the cells on which they impinge. Thus, at the physiological level, the

model shown in Fig. 11.4 assumes that this is the underlying mode of action of noradrenergic neurons. Their *behavioural* function then depends on the characteristics of the target organs which they innervate. The important targets, for the problems considered in this book, are the septo-hippocampal system and (much more tentatively) the hypothalamus.

On the hypothesis illustrated in Fig. 11.4 activity in the dorsal bundle has two consequences: it sends a signal to the septo-hippocampal system reading 'important, check carefully'; and it primes motor systems (perhaps via the hypothalamus) to be ready for particularly vigorous action. Imagine now that such a mechanism becomes, for whatever reason, acutely or chronically overactive, requiring the animal to scrutinize carefully all kinds of stimuli that it would ordinarily neglect and to remain in a constant state of motor readiness. Would this not correspond rather well to the state that human beings experience as anxiety? And might not the capacity of the anti-anxiety drugs to reduce this kind of activity in the dorsal bundle (Lidbrink *et al.* 1973; Pohorecky and Brick 1977) plausibly underlie their clinical effects?

Owen's (1979) thesis provides some evidence that the behavioural effects of the anti-anxiety drugs indeed proceed by way of the dorsal bundle. In several of her experiments she injected sodium amylobarbitone to animals which had sustained dorsal bundle lesions. In every case the behavioural effects of the drug were altered by the lesion. Thus, in the T-maze test of response to stimulus change, both the drug and the lesion independently reduced the choice of the changed arm, and the drug had no effect at all in lesioned animals.* This, however, could have been a 'floor' effect, since both the lesion and the drug alone gave rise to random choices. In the open-field test the drug increased ambulation in sham-operated animals, but was without effect in lesioned rats; the lesion alone did not alter ambulation levels.* And in a one-trial-a-day partial reinforcement experiment dorsal bundle lesions *attenuated* the increase in resistance to extinction caused by the drug in CRF-trained animals and *produced* an increase in resistance to extinction in PRF-trained animals given the drug. Considerably more work along these lines will be needed to ascertain the precise way in which dorsal bundle lesions change the effects of anti-anxiety drugs; but the fact that they reliably do so is itself in good agreement with the hypothesis that the behavioural effects of these agents are produced, at least in part, by an action on the dorsal bundle.

Other approaches to noradrenergic function

The model shown in Fig. 11.4 allots a critical role to the ascending serotonergic innervation of the septo-hippocampal system. But, before we look at the evidence relating to this feature of the model, there remain important data to consider from experiments in which central noradrenergic function has been manipulated pharmacologically.

Stein's group (Wise, Berger, and Stein 1973) has reported a series of

*See McNaughton *et al.* (1984) in additional references.

experiments in which noradrenalin and a variety of other substances were injected into the cerebral ventricles of rats while they performed various rewarded and/or punished responses in the Skinner-box. Intraventricular noradrenalin did not increase the suppression of punished bar-pressing, as might be predicted from the general anxiety hypothesis of dorsal bundle function, but rather decreased it. This finding is consistent with an increase in the approach (rewarded) component of the approach–avoidance conflict in which the animals found themselves, and therefore with the reward hypothesis of dorsal bundle function. Since, however, this hypothesis must be rejected, given the effects of dorsal bundle lesions reviewed earlier in this chapter, some other account must be offered for Wise *et al.*'s (1973) results.

There are two possible such accounts.

The first is that intraventricular noradrenalin acts on structures other than the septo-hippocampal system. The bulk of the noradrenergic innervation of the hippocampal formation is located in the hilus of the dentate gyrus, some way from the ventricles. It is possible that other dorsal bundle terminals are more easily reached by intraventricular noradrenalin and that these indeed play a role in mediating behavioural responses to reward, as postulated by Stein (1968). One possible site is the amygdala. Consistent with this possibility, Margules (1968, 1971) showed that noradrenalin injected directly into the amygdala alleviated punishment-produced suppression of bar-pressing.

The second possible account of the effects of intraventricular noradrenalin is that they are due to an action on presynaptic receptors. Wise *et al.*'s (1973) experiments showed that noradrenalin produced its effects via an alpha- not a beta-noradrenergic receptor. Now, alpha-noradrenergic receptors in the brain have usually been identified as presynaptic (Starke 1979). Since the effect of a noradrenergic agonist at a presynaptic receptor is to decrease (by homeostatic feedback) the output of the noradrenergic neuron to the postsynaptic receptor (Langer 1979), this account of Wise *et al.*'s (1973) findings completely reverses the interpretation placed upon them by these authors. The fact that intraventricular noradrenalin decreased the suppression of punished behaviour would now be consistent with the hypothesis that forebrain noradrenalin mediates the effects of punishment; for the decreased behavioural suppression would arise from reduced activity at postsynaptic receptors. If this account is correct, it should be possible to abolish the effects observed by Wise *et al.* (1973) by destroying the noradrenergic fibres on which the presynaptic alpha-receptors are located (e.g. by injecting 6-OHDA into the dorsal bundle) before injecting noradrenalin into the ventricles.* This experiment has not been performed.

---

*This prediction arose from a discussion with Dr L. Stein at a symposium held at the Eastern Psychological Association in Philadelphia in the spring of 1979.

In one or other of these ways, then, it may be possible to reconcile the observations reported by Wise *et al.* (1973) with the theory proposed here. It is in any case unlikely that the effects they observed were due to an action of intraventricular noradrenalin on the hippocampus, since the postsynaptic receptor in this structure is of the 'beta' variety (Segal and Bloom 1974*a;* Atlas and Segal 1977), as it apparently is also in the cingulate cortex (Melamed, Lahar, and Atlas 1977; Dillier *et al.* 1978). Thus Wise *et al*'s (1973) data do not provide any compelling reason to abandon the view that the dorsal bundle forms part of a system mediating anxiety and is an important site of action of the anti-anxiety drugs.

The anti-anxiety drugs are apparently not alone in their affinity for the noradrenergic system originating in the locus coeruleus. Recent evidence suggests that opiates, such as heroin and morphine, also exert a powerful effect on coerulear neurons.

Understanding of the mechanisms of opiate addiction has been revolutionized by the discovery, a few years ago, of the endogenous opiates and the receptors on which they act (Hughes *et al.* 1975; Kuhar *et al.* 1973). The locus coeruleus is particularly rich in these receptors (Pert and Snyder 1973; Pert *et al.* 1975). Axonal terminals containing one of the endogenous opiates, met-enkephalin, have been demonstrated on dendrites in this structure (Pickel *et al.* 1979), and iontophoretic experiments have shown that both morphine and naturally occurring opiates depress the firing rate of coerulear neurones (Guyenet and Aghajanian 1977; Young, Bird, and Kuhar 1977; Bird and Kuhar 1977). The latter observation is the basis of an interesting account of the distressing symptoms seen during opiate withdrawal, proposed by Gold, Redmond, and Kleber (1978). According to these authors exogenous opiates reduce activity in the dorsal bundle. Thus, when the opiate is withdrawn from an addicted individual, there ensues a rebound hyperactivity in coerulear neurons, or in the receptors that are postsynaptic to terminals from these neurons; this hyperactivity gives rise to the withdrawal syndrome.

In support of this hypothesis it has been demonstrated that clonidine, a drug which also inhibits the firing of neurons in the locus coeruleus (Cederbaum and Aghajanian 1976; Tang *et al.* 1979), eliminates the symptoms of opiate withdrawal in man (Gold, Redmond, and Kleber 1978, 1979). Clonidine is itself an alpha-noradrenergic agonist. The receptor on which it acts (different from the opiate receptor: Simon, cited by Gold *et al.* 1979) is located (among other places) on locus coeruleus neurons. This receptor appears normally to mediate feedback inhibition of the firing of coerulear cells in response to noradrenalin liberated by collaterals of the principal axons of these cells themselves (Aghajanian, Cederbaum, and Wang 1977). Thus clonidine acts by a different molecular mechanism than the opiates, but produces the same final effect: reduced activity in locus coeruleus neurons.

If opiate withdrawal symptoms are due to hyperactivity in the locus coeruleus system, and if (as proposed here) activity in this system is equivalent to anxiety, it follows that the opiate withdrawal syndrome is a form of anxiety, perhaps a particularly intense form. This inference is supported by a consideration of the actual symptoms that make up the syndrome. These include (Gold, Poltash, Sweeney, and Kleber 1979) 'anxiety, yawning, perspiration, lacrimation, goose flesh, tremors, hot and cold flashes, increased blood pressure, insomnia, increased respiratory rate and depth, increased pulse rate, and restlessness', along with other features less easily associated with anxiety (e.g. aching bones and muscles, nausea, and vomiting). Note that, if the opiate withdrawal syndrome is equivalent to intense anxiety, and if it is due to hyperactivity in coerulear neurones or the receptors on which they act, we at last have a clue where to look for the autonomic symptoms of anxiety, which for the most part have eluded us so far in our travels through the brain. It will be recalled that open-field defecation, which has been an excellent index of fearfulness in genetic experiments (Broadhurst 1960; Gray 1971a), is unaffected by either hippocampal or dorsal bundle lesions. The opiate withdrawal syndrome, however, is rich in autonomic symptoms, and these were all suppressed by clonidine treatment in the studies reported by Gold, Redmond, and Kleber (1978, 1979). It is possible, therefore, that the descending projections from the locus coeruleus (which are left intact by dorsal bundle lesions) play a role in the production of these symptoms. These projections perhaps act in conjunction with a descending projection from the septal area to the hypothalamus (since septal lesions do reduce autonomic signs of fearfulness: see Chapter 6, Section 6.14). It should be borne in mind, however, that, as with any other purely pharmacological experiment, it is difficult to be sure where in the brain clonidine acts to produce its behavioural effects. Not only may it act on other noradrenergic nuclei besides the locus coeruleus, but it might also influence adrenergic neurons, i.e. ones that use adrenalin as their neurotransmitter (Cederbaum and Aghajanian 1976).

A further deduction from the arguments pursued above is that clonidine should act like an anti-anxiety drug. Davis, Redmond, and Baraban (1979) have reported findings consistent with this deduction. They used the potentiated startle response, which is blocked by benzodiazepines (M. Davis 1979; see Chapter 2, Section 2.3). The startle response was elicited by a loud tone which, on some trials, was preceded by a light which had previously been paired with foot-shock. Clonidine in a dose of 10 μg kg^{-1} had no effect on the unconditioned startle response to the tone, resembling in this respect electrolytic lesions of the locus coeruleus (Davis, Cederbaum, Aghajanian, and Gendelmann 1977). But the potentiation of the startle response produced by the light was attenuated by the drug. Conversely, the alpha-noradrenergic antagonists, piperoxane and yohimbine, while also having no effect on the unconditioned startle response, enhanced the potentiated response. Finally, propranolol, a beta-noradrenergic antagonist, reduced the potentiated startle response, again without altering the unconditioned response. These results, then, are highly systematic: increased activity in noradrenergic neurones (presumably produced by the alpha-antagonists) gave rise to an increase in the potentiated startle response; decreased noradrenergic activity (whether produced by the alpha-agonist or the beta-antagonist) gave rise to a decrease in the potentiated startle response. Anti-anxiety-like effects have also been seen after propranolol injection by Salmon (personal communication)*, working in my own laboratory (impaired DRL performance and increased response rates during the negative stimulus of a successive discrimination). These results with animals are consistent with reports that, in man, yohimbine (Holmberg and Gershon 1961) and piperoxane (Goldenberg *et al.* 1947; Soffer 1954) produce feelings of anxiety; while propranolol is sometimes used as an anti-anxiety agent (Redmond 1979). However, neither in the animal experiments (Salmon, personal communication) nor in the clinical literature (Gottschalk *et al.* 1974; Tyrer 1976) has the possibility that these drugs work by a peripheral action been ruled out.

Davis, Redmond, and Baraban's (1979) experiment has important implications for our understanding of the role played in anxiety by the dorsal bundle (if we accept for the moment that this was the structure which mediated the effects of the drugs they studied). First, in agreement with other data considered earlier in this book, their results show that anxiety is concerned with reactions, not to a primary aversive event (here, a 110-decibel tone) but to stimuli that warn of such events (a light previously paired with shock and now preceding the tone). Second, their results are consistent with the hypothesis adopted in Fig. 11.4 in showing that the heightened arousal which is one of the behavioural changes elicited by secondary aversive stimuli (Chapter 1) has a noradrenergic basis.

The ascending serotonergic system

The evidence reviewed above established a reasonably strong case for the proposition that central noradrenergic mechanisms, and particularly the projection from the locus coeruleus to the septo-hippocampal system, play an important role in anxiety. Much of this evidence can be accommodated by two hypotheses: first, that the dorsal noradrenergic bundle alerts the septo-hippocampal system to check carefully on particularly important stimuli (apparently those that are associated with reward, punishment, novelty, or non-reward); second, that the dorsal bundle mediates the increased arousal that is one output of the behavioural inhibition system when it is challenged by its adequate stimuli (Chapter 1). It is also possible that, via its descending projections, the locus coeruleus is responsible for some of the autonomic signs of anxiety. However, we should not suppose that the dorsal noradrenergic bundle is the only ascending monoaminergic pathway involved in anxiety. This would be a mistake for two reasons. On the negative side, we have as yet given the septo-hippocampal

*See Salmon and Gray (1985, 1986) in additional references.

system no way of differentiating between signals of reward and signals of punishment; yet, without this distinction, it cannot perform the tasks we have allotted to it. On the positive side, there is good evidence that ascending serotonergic pathways also play an important role in the control of certain patterns of behaviour which have been treated in this book as diagnostic of anxiety. Interestingly, this evidence is particularly strong for behaviour suppressed by punishment (which, as we have seen, is affected only slightly by dorsal bundle lesions). Perhaps, then, we can find in the activities of the ascending serotonergic pathways the missing signal the septo-hippocampal needs if it is to distinguish punishment from reward.

The anatomy of the serotonergic pathways that innervate the septo-hippocampal system was described in Chapter 3. These pathways, which originate in the median and dorsal raphe nuclei (mainly the median), follow similar routes to those taken by fibres from the locus coeruleus and, like these, innervate the septal area and hippocampus extensively but diffusely (Figs. 3.12 and 3.13). These anatomical similarities are apparently paralleled by functional ones. Stimulation of the raphe nuclei facilitates the passage of neural messages round the hippocampal circuit, and this effect is blocked by antiserotonergic drugs (Segal 1977a; Assaf and Miller 1978); this effect is similar to that seen after locus coeruleus stimulation (Segal 1977a; Chapters 4 and 7). Stress increases the turnover of forebrain serotonin less consistently than that of forebrain noradrenalin (Curzon and Green 1969; Fuxe *et al.* 1970; Lidbrink *et al.* 1973), but it also increases the activity of tryptophan hydroxylase (Azmitia and McEwen 1974, 1976), a key enzyme in the biosynthetic pathway responsible for the formation of 5-hydroxytryptamine (serotonin). The anti-anxiety drugs reduce the turnover of serotonin as of noradrenalin, although the doses at which this has been observed are somewhat elevated and likely to cause sedation (Lidbrink *et al.* 1973; Chase, Katz, and Kopin 1970; Wise, Berger, and Stein 1972; Stein *et al.* 1973). Stein *et al.* (1973) report that the decline in serotonin turnover caused by oxazepam (a benzodiazepine) persisted with repeated administration of the drug, whereas the effect on noradrenalin turnover gradually disappeared. Since the anti-anxiety effects of the benzodiazepines are maintained with repeated administration but the sedative effects weaken, these workers suggest that the former are more closely related to changes in serotonergic than noradrenergic function.

It is clear, then, that many of the reasons that led to the proposal of a role in anxiety for the noradrenergic output to the septo-hippocampal system are equally valid for its serotonergic afferents. Just this hypothesis, but robbed of its specific connection to the septo-hippocampal system, has been proposed by several investigators on the basis of psychopharmacological experiments which have shown that the suppression of behaviour by punishment is reversed by systemic administration of putative serotonin receptor blockers (Graeff and Schoenfeld 1970; Graeff 1974; Winter 1972; Stein *et al.* 1973; Geller *et al.* 1974; Cook and Sepinwall 1975). Among the drugs used successfully in this way is methysergide (e.g. Graeff and Schoenfeld 1970; Stein *et al.* 1973). In iontophoretic experiments this drug has been shown to antagonize the effects of serotonin in the hippocampus (Segal 1975a, 1976) but not in a number of other brain areas (Haigler and Aghajanian 1974); thus, if methysergide reverses punishment-produced response suppression by an antiserotonergic action, this is most likely exercised at serotonergic terminals in the hippocampus.

The response suppression produced by punishment is also lessened by systemic administration of *p*-chlorophenylalanine (PCPA), which blocks the synthesis of the immediate precursor of serotonin, 5-hydroxytryptophan, by inhibiting tryptophan hydroxylase (Robichaud and Sledge 1969; Geller and Blum 1970; Wise, Berger, and Stein 1973). The antiserotonergic nature of the action of PCPA in these experiments was confirmed by the demonstration that it is reversed by a subsequent injection of 5-hydroxytryptophan. The conditioned suppression of an operant response has also been reported to be alleviated by PCPA (Hartmann and Geller 1971). However, experiments with PCPA do not always produce such clearcut results. Thornton and Goudie (1978) were able to block stepdown passive avoidance with this drug, but the reversal of this effect by subsequent 5-hydroxytryptophan was only slight; Blakely and Parker (1973) found no effect of PCPA on punished bar-pressing; and Winocur and Bagchi (1974) actually found an increased effect of punishment on running in the alley after PCPA.

With these few exceptions, however, the data are consistent in showing that serotonergic antagonists reduce the suppression of behaviour by punishment. Conversely, serotonergic agonists directly produce behavioural suppression. This was first shown by Aprison and Ferster (1961) in an experiment in which the levels of serotonin were increased by administration of 5-hydroxytryptophan together with a monoamine oxidase inhibitor to delay the catabolism of serotonin after its release. Similar findings were reported by Graeff and Schoenfeld (1970) and Stein *et al.* (1973) using the long-lasting serotonergic receptor agonist, alpha-methyltryptamine.

These effects have been related to the serotonergic pathways which innervate the forebrain in experiments in which the dorsal and median raphe nuclei have been stimulated directly. Stein *et al.* (1973) report that chemical stimulation of the dorsal raphe (with the cholinomimetic agent, carbachol) suppressed both punished and unpunished behaviour in the Skinner-box, and that this effect could be reversed by systemic administration of oxazepam. The opposite pattern of interaction was shown in an experiment in which serotonin, injected into the cerebral ventricles, decreased the antipunishment effects of oxazepam (Stein *et al.* 1973). The dorsal raphe has also been implicated in behavioural suppression by Thiébot, Jobert, and Soubrié (1980). These workers demonstrated that the suppression of bar-pressing produced by a signal associated with shock could be reversed by injection of either chlordiazepoxide or GABA directly into this nucleus; unpunished responding was unaffected by these treatments. Other work also implicates the median raphe. Thus Graeff and Silveira Filho (1978) stimulated this nucleus electrically. The stimulation suppressed rewarded operant behaviour and at the same time elicited obvious signs of fear (crouching, defecation, urination, and piloerection). The serotonergic nature of these effects was confirmed by the demonstration that they could be blocked by PCPA; in one rat the effect of PCPA was then itself reversed by further injection of 5-hydroxytryptophan.

In contrast to this consistent pattern of findings, Fibiger, Lepiane, and Phillips (1978) found that stimulation of the dorsal raphe during acquisition of a one-trial step-down passive avoidance task disrupted retention of this response 24 hours later. This effect, like Graeff and Silveira Filho's, was blocked by PCPA, but it is apparently opposite in sign to theirs. However, as pointed out in Chapter 8, there is at least as much reason to expect stimulation to act like a lesion as to suppose that it will activate the stimulated pathway in a more or less physiological manner. Thus the discrepancy may reflect a different fit between the stimulation parameters and the functional characteristics of the fibres or cells stimulated in the two experiments. A further possibility is that the effect reported by Fibiger *et al.* (1978) was due to state dependency, since stimulation was applied only during the learning trial.

Further evidence for the existence of a serotonergic mechanism responsible for the suppression of punished behaviour comes from experiments which have used the neurotoxins, 5,6- and 5,7-dihydroxytryptamine (DHT), which are selective for serotonergic fibres in much the same way that 6-OHDA is selective for catecholaminergic ones. Stein, Wise, and Belluzzi (1975) report that intraventricular 5,6-DHT released punished behaviour (in the Skinner-box) from suppression; however, this effect lasted only for three or four days. More permanent changes of the same kind, also in the Skinner-box, were reported by Tye, Everitt, and Iversen (1977) after injections of 5,7-DHT into the ascending serotonergic fibre pathways. Increased resistance to punishment has also been observed in the alley after intracerebral 5,7-DHT (N. M. Davis 1979a)*. Fuxe *et al.* (1978) similarly observed increased resistance to the punished extinction of a one-way active avoidance response after this treatment; the lesioned animals were not deficient in the acquisition of the response. Lorens *et al.* (1976) were unable to produce this effect by injecting 5,7-DHT directly into the raphe nuclei themselves; however, these workers did obtain a deficit in the punished extinction of one-way active avoidance in animals which had sustained electrolytic lesions of the median (but not dorsal) raphe (Srebro and Lorens 1975). In agreement with the latter observa-

*See Davis and Gray (1983) in additional references.

tion, Thornton and Goudie (1978) found that an electrolytic lesion of the median raphe impaired step-down passive avoidance.

These converging lines of evidence add up to a convincing case that the ascending serotonergic pathways originating in the raphe nuclei are concerned in the production of the behavioural inhibition seen when an animal is exposed to aversive stimuli. The coherence of these data stands in sharp contrast to those that relate to almost every other form of behaviour that has so far been investigated after comparable treatments. In these other cases the extent of disagreement between the results obtained with different methods (systemic drug injection, electrical stimulation, neurotoxic or electrolytic lesions, etc.) is usually so great that it is of little value to examine them here (for recent partial reviews, see Lorens 1978, and N. M. Davis 1979a). I shall confine my attention, therefore, to a few relevant points which the available data, in spite of their confusion, allow one to make.

First, it is clear that the reduction in response suppression seen in animals with impaired forebrain serotonergic function is not due to a loss of sensitivity to the primary aversive reinforcer. On the contrary, sensitivity to painful stimuli is, if anything, increased in such animals (Lorens 1978). As in the comparable case of septal and hippocampal lesions (Chapter 6, Section 6.8), this change seems to be one of motor disinhibition rather than in pain sensitivity as such. Thus the threshold for increased activity or jumping in response to shock is lowered by PCPA (an effect which is reversed by subsequent injection of 5-hydroxytryptophan), but the threshold for the detection of shock is unchanged (Harvey and Lints 1971; Sheard and Davis 1976; Fibiger, Mertz, and Campbell 1972). Hole *et al.* (1976) and Fuxe *et al.* (1978) report no change in pain sensitivity as measured by the hot-plate test after intracerebral 5,7-DHT. It is not clear whether this negative result is due to the method used to destroy central 5-HT fibres or to the behavioural test. The latter is more likely, since the hot-plate test is essentially a measure of the time taken to detect pain. The results of experiments using electrolytic raphe lesions have been inconsistent. Harvey *et al.* (1974) and Hole.and Lorens (1975) found no effect of this treatment, but Vergnes and Penot (1976a) found a pattern of change similar to that seen after PCPA, i.e. a reduction in the jump but not the flinch threshold to shock. It is not certain, however, that Vergnes and Penot's (1976a) results were due to a disruption in serotonergic function, especially since they were able to reverse the effect of their raphe lesion by administering the cholinergic drug, physostigmine (recall that the raphe nuclei probably contain cholinergic as well as serotonergic cellbodies).

The observations of increased motor reactivity to foot-shock after PCPA or raphe lesions raise the possibility that these treatments produce a general motor disinhibition rather than a specific disruption of punishment-produced response suppression. This possibility is strengthened by evidence that PCPA and raphe lesions may both sometimes increase motor activity in, for example, the open field or stabilimeter cages.

The effects of PCPA observed in such experiments have been variable (N. M. Davis 1979a). One important factor appears to be the level of stimulation. Brody (1970) has shown in the open field that the drug increases activity when the animal is tested with bright lights and noise, but decreases activity when these conditions are absent. This is consistent with an alleviation of the response suppression which is induced by exposure to a novel environment and associated with a high level of fear (see the discussion in Chapter 2, Section 2.10). Increased motor activity is seen more reliably after electrolytic raphe lesions (Srebro and Lorens 1975; Lorens *et al.* 1976; Vergnes and Penot 1976b; Jacobs *et al.* 1974, 1975; Geyer *et al.* 1976; Asin *et al.* 1979). Again, however, the effect is observed particularly clearly under conditions likely to suppress activity in intact controls, namely, when the environment is novel (Lorens *et al.* 1971; Geyer *et al.* 1976) or after a change in lighting conditions (Srebro and Lorens 1975). Increased motor activity has been seen after damage to the median raphe, alone or in combination with dorsal raphe damage, but not usually after damage limited to the dorsal raphe (Jacobs *et al.* 1974, 1975; Steranka and Barrett 1974; Geyer *et al.* 1976; Srebro and Lorens 1975; Asin *et al.* 1979). This implicates the serotonergic projection to the hippocampus, an inference which is supported by evidence that the increase in activity is inversely correlated with the level of hippocampal serotonin (Jacobs *et al.* 1974) and by the findings that neither PCPA nor median raphe lesions alter activity after removal of the hippocampus (Jacobs *et al.* 1975), while destruction of hippocampal serotonergic afferents (by injection of 5,7-DHT into the fornix-fimbria) increases activity to a degree that is highly correlated with the ensuing loss of hippocampal 5-HT uptake (Williams and Azmitia 1981). However, injection of 5,7-DHT into the ascending serotonergic fibre pathways had no effect on motor activity in Lorens's (1978) hands, and actually reduced activity in an experiment by Hole *et al.* (1976). Furthermore, Vergnes and Penot (1976b) found that physostigmine differentially reduced open-field activity in raphe-lesioned rats relative to controls, implying that the increased activity produced by the raphe lesion may have been due to damage to cholinergic cells.

Further aspects of the rather general loss of behavioural inhibition which appears to flow from disruption of forebrain serotonergic function are perhaps the hyper-reactivity to mild tactile stimuli (airpuff, tail pinch) which has been reported after both PCPA injection (Dalhouse 1976) and raphe lesions (Vergnes and Penot 1976b; Geyer *et al.* 1976); and the increased aggressive response to foot-shock sometimes also observed after these treatments (Sheard and Davis 1976; Jacobs and Cohen 1976; Vergnes and Penot 1976a). Both these effects are similar to those seen

after septal lesions (Chapter 6, Section 6.15). Indeed, the similarity between the effects of raphe and septal (particularly lateral septal) lesions
extends to several other features of the two syndromes. Vergnes and
Penot (1976*b*) studied these similarities directly, and also investigated the
interaction between the two types of lesion. Raphe (dorsal and median)
and septal lesions resembled each other in giving rise to hyper-reactivity
to tactile stimuli, increased motor activity, increased killing of mice, and
increased ambulation in the open field; in addition, the septal (but not
the raphe) lesion reduced open-field defecation and rearing. The effects
of the raphe lesion were all blocked or reduced by septal lesions carried
out a month earlier. As we have seen, hippocampal lesions have also been
shown to eliminate the increased motor activity otherwise produced by
PCPA or median raphe lesions (Jacobs *et al.* 1975). Thus it seems that the
septal area and the hippocampus are both important in mediating the
behavioural functions of raphe efferents.

The data so far reviewed in this section indicate that pharmacological
or surgical interference with forebrain serotonergic systems is able, under
a variety of conditions, to cause a loss of behavioural inhibition. It is not
clear whether these conditions include exposure to non-reward. Some evidence of impaired responses to non-reward has been reported after systemic administration of PCPA. Thus Thornton and Goudie (1978) found
a reduction in the suppression of bar-presssing when this was put on a
DRO schedule (i.e. reward for anything other than bar-pressing); there
was no effect of the drug on response rate on the VI schedule which
preceded DRO. Beninger and Phillips (1979) similarly found that PCPA
retarded extinction after CRF training, but the extinction of a response
acquired on an RI schedule was unaffected. Gray, Rickwood, and Stewart
(unpublished) were also able to retard the extinction of a running response by injecting PCPA between acquisition and extinction; furthermore, the effect of PCPA was reversed when 5-hydroxytryptophan was
injected before each extinction session. These experiments with PCPA are
paralleled by a single experiment on extinction after raphe lesions: Asin
et al. (1979) report retarded extinction in the alley after median but not
dorsal raphe damage.

These results encourage the belief that the role of the serotonergic efferents from the raphe extends to the case of non-reward. But when this
proposition has been examined by the most appropriate experimental
procedure at present available — injection of 5,7-DHT into the ascending
serotonergic pathways — the results have been negative. Tye *et al.* (1977)
found no effect of this treatment on responding in the extinction component of a multiple schedule in the Skinner-box; and Davis and Gray (in
preparation*; N. M. Davis 1979*a*), no effect on resistance to extinction in
the alley or on the PREE. One might attempt to dismiss these negative
results as being due to an insufficiently thorough lesion, since intracerebral 5,7-DHT usually produces only a subtotal loss of hippocampal sero-

*See additional references.

tonin (70–80 per cent). However, in both these experiments the same lesion produced a clear disinhibition of punished responding; and in Tye *et al.*'s (1977) report this was in the same animals which showed normal suppression of responding during extinction.

In the light of these data it is difficult to conclude either that forebrain serotonergic pathways play a role in responses to non-reward or that they do not. But it is reasonably clear that, if they do play such a role, it is less central than the one they play in the suppression of punished responses. In this respect the forebrain serotonergic pathways appear to be the mirror image of the dorsal noradrenergic bundle, which, as we saw earlier in the chapter, plays an unequivocal role in determining responses to non-reward, but is only ambiguously concerned with responses to punishment. These symmetries suggest the attractively simple hypothesis that the dorsal noradrenergic bundle carries signals of reward (to be used in the detection of non-reward) and the serotonergic fibres signals of punishment. However, this hypothesis is probably ruled out by the evidence that noradrenergic mechanisms play at least some part in the organization of responses to punishment, and serotonergic mechanisms similarly some part in responses to non-reward; for the distinction between punishment and non-reward is sufficiently clearcut for us to expect a corresponding clarity in the data.

Thus it appears more fruitful to look for the distinction between noradrenergic and serotonergic function on the output rather than the input side of the behavioural inhibition system. Most of the data are consistent with a specialization of the ascending serotonergic fibres for the promotion of behavioural inhibition in the narrow sense (that is, suppression of motor responses), and a corresponding specialization of the dorsal noradrenergic bundle for the arousal and attentional functions of the behavioural inhibition system as discussed earlier in this chapter. A distinction of this kind is likely then to map fuzzily onto the experimental difference between tasks involving punishment and those involving non-reward. For it is usually the case that response suppression (becoming in the extreme freezing) is a more prominent feature of the behaviour of an animal threatened with, say, shock than it is in an animal threatened only with the loss of reward. If this hypothesis is correct, it should be possible to control the extent to which lesions of the ascending serotonergic and noradrenergic pathways affect the animal's behaviour by varying the requirement for response suppression while holding the kinds and amounts of reinforcement constant.

Whatever functions the ascending serotonergic and noradrenergic pathways discharge separately, it seems likely that they often act together. Co-ordination between them could take place within the septo-hippocampal system to which they both project. But it could also be mediated by the reciprocal connections which exist between the raphe nuclei and the locus coeruleus. Serotonergic terminals have been demonstrated in the locus coeruleus (Pickel, Joh, and Reis 1977; Leger and Descarries 1978) and their origin shown to be in the dorsal raphe (Sakai *et al.* 1977*b*; Segal 1978*b*). The locus coeruleus in turn projects, although sparsely, back to the dorsal and median raphe (Chu and Bloom 1974; Aghajanian and Wang 1977; Sakai *et al.* 1977*a*). There are also possibilities for more complex loops to the septo-hippocampal system and back, since the raphe nuclei receive afferents from the lateral habenular nucleus (which itself receives a projection from the triangular and septo-fimbrial nuclei: Fig. 3.14) and from the nucleus of the diagonal band (Aghajanian and Wang 1977).

There is probably further co-ordination between the ascending monoaminergic pathways and ascending cholinergic fibres, although we shall have only little to say on this topic here. As noted earlier in the chapter, the median raphe, in particular, appears to contain both serotonergic (Fuxe and Jonsson 1974) and cholinergic (Shute and Lewis 1967) cell-bodies.

We have recently studied the relationship between the behavioural effects of electrical stimulation of the median raphe (which appear to be largely mediated by serotonergic mechanisms) and the effects of this stimulation on the electrical activity of the hippocampus (which appear to be largely cholinergic). As shown by Graeff and Silveira Filho (1978), median raphe stimulation gives rise to response suppression and overt signs of fear (see above); these effects are blocked by PCPA. Simultaneously there appears in the hippocampus a theta rhythm whose maximum frequency lies close to 7.7 Hz (see Fig. 7.2); this response is unaffected by antiserotonergic drugs but is blocked by scopolamine (Graeff *et al.* 1980). Both the type of theta and the behaviour produced by median raphe stimulation resemble the responses produced by exposing the rat to a stimulus previously paired with foot-shock (Graeff *et al.* 1980). It is possible that the association between the cholinergic theta response and the serotonergic behavioural response to raphe stimulation is an artefact of the method of electrical stimulation. However, the fact that the same association occurs in response to a CS paired with shock (Whishaw 1976; Graeff *et al.* 1980) and that the same pharmacological profiles are seen under these conditions (Hartman and Geller 1971; Graeff *et al.* 1980) suggests a physiological relationship between the two responses. This point of view is supported by the observation that the anti-anxiety drugs, sodium amylobarbitone and chlordiazepoxide, both raise the threshold for the low-frequency theta response to raphe stimulation and reduce the low-frequency theta which is elicited by a CS paired with shock (Graeff *et al.* 1980). Thus these drugs appear to antagonize both the serotonergic mechanism responsible for behavioural inhibition (Stein *et al.* 1973) and the cholinergic mechanism responsible for the low-frequency theta associated with this type of behaviour.

If the arguments advanced in Chapter 10 are correct, the appearance of low-frequency theta, favoured by the cholinergic projection from the median raphe (though not only by this: Robinson and Vanderwolf 1978), facilitates in some way septo-hippocampal information processing concerned with the need to alter existing motor programmes. Thus we might propose that the ascending serotonergic projection is predominantly related to the output side of the behavioural inhibition system, along the lines discussed above, and its cholinergic partner to the input side. This view is in general agreement with the analysis of the behavioural effects of antiserotonergic and anticholinergic drugs recently advanced by Warburton (1977). (That behavioural inhibition can, under some conditions, be disrupted by anticholinergics has been known since the pioneering work of Carlton 1963.) Warburton's (1977, p. 422) analysis leads him to conclude that a cholinergic system mediates 'the selection, from the mass of impinging stimuli, of the relevant stimuli which set the occasion for the . . . response and those which set the occasion for inhibiting irrelevant responses'. This formulation is similar to the description of septo-hippocampal function adumbrated in Chapter 10. Thus Warburton's 'cholinergic system' may consist of the cholinergic septo-hippocampal projection and/or the ascending cholinergic projection responsible for Vanderwolf *et al.*'s (1978) atropine-sensitive, low-frequency theta.

The site at which the latter affects the frequency of theta is not known. Given the basic role of the medial septal area in controlling theta frequency, a septal site would seem likely. It has been suggested on histochemical grounds that the lateral septal area contains cholinoceptive neurons (Srebro *et al.* 1976). The serotonergic projection from the raphe nuclei also terminates in this general area (Chapter 3). It is possible, therefore, that the lateral septal area is an important target for both serotonergic and cholinergic efferents from the raphe. This might account for the similarities, noted above, between some of the behavioural effects of lateral septal and raphe lesions.

Conclusion

This completes our survey of the functions, as best they can be judged, of the ascending projections to the septo-hippocampal system. There is no need to summarize *in extenso* the conclusions we have been able to reach, since in the main these have already been encapsulated in the model illustrated above in Fig. 11.4. The view we have adopted for the ascending noradrenergic projection is essentially the same as that proposed by Redmond (1979): it functions as a general alarm bell, enhancing the scrutiny (within the septo-hippocampal system) of all important or potentially important stimuli, and increasing motor readiness. To the extent that, alongside this noradrenergic mechanism, ascending serotonergic and cholinergic pathways are also activated, there is added a corresponding degree of motor inhibition; and we may suppose that the septo-hippocampal system, depending on the balance between the noradrenergic, cholinergic, and serotonergic influences to which it is subjected, is thereby able to distinguish between the different types of 'important' stimuli which reach it (from the entorhinal area), and particularly between those associated with reward and punishment respectively. At this point in the argument, then (but it is not the last), we may conceive of 'anxiety' as activity in the septo-hippocampal system that is provoked or boosted by the projections (noradrenergic, serotonergic, and cholinergic) that this system receives from the brainstem.

Before we attempt to refine this concept further, it is necessary to consider what happens when the activity of these ascending projections, and especially activity in noradrenergic pathways, is excessive or prolonged. What are the effects, in other words, of intense or chronic anxiety? These questions are addressed in the next chapter.

12

Long-term effects of stress: the relation between anxiety and depression

As we saw in the last chapter, there is much evidence that, acutely, stress increases the activity of noradrenergic neurons in the central nervous system (Stone 1975, Table IV). This, indeed, was one of the links in the chain of argument we used to relate the dorsal noradrenergic bundle to anxiety. But there is evidence that, after excessive or prolonged stress, the changes that take place in central noradrenergic function are more complex than this. In the present chapter we examine these effects and the problems they raise for the theory of anxiety proposed in this book.

The noradrenergic neuron

It will help if we first take a closer look at the noradrenergic neuron (Fillenz 1977). Until now the approach adopted in this book has taken the neuron — and more often whole populations of neurons — as the smallest unit of analysis. But, like any other cell, the neuron is itself a complex chemical factory, whose activities are closely controlled by a large number of interacting mechanisms. Some of these mechanisms assume a particular importance when we consider the long-term effects of exposure to stress.

Like other substances released by neurons, noradrenalin is stored in special organelles — the synaptic vesicles — from which it is released by exocytosis on arrival of a nerve impulse. Synaptic vesicles in noradrenergic neurons, however, have the special feature that they are responsible not only for the storage and release of the neurotransmitter, but also for its synthesis. For this purpose they contain the enzyme, dopamine-β-hydroxylase (DBH), which catalyses the last step in the synthesis of noradrenalin (Fig. 12.1). The synaptic vesicles are themselves synthesized in the cell-body of the neuron and transported to the nerve terminal along the axon ('axoplasmic transport') at a velocity of around 10 mm h^{-1}. The vesicles have only a limited life span, since they cannot refill with noradrenalin after they have undergone exocytosis (Fillenz and West 1976). Thus, in order to maintain the stores of releasable noradrenalin in the terminals, there has to be a constant supply of new vesicles by axoplasmic transport.

Another requirement for maintaining the stores of noradrenalin in the nerve terminal is the replacement of released noradrenalin by new synthesis of the neurotransmitter itself. This is controlled by the enzyme, tyrosine hydroxylase (TH), which catalyses the rate-limiting step in noradrenalin synthesis. As we saw in Chapter 11, acute stress leads to an increased release of noradrenalin from neurons in the brain. The same thing occurs in peripheral noradrenergic neurons. Experiments on pe-

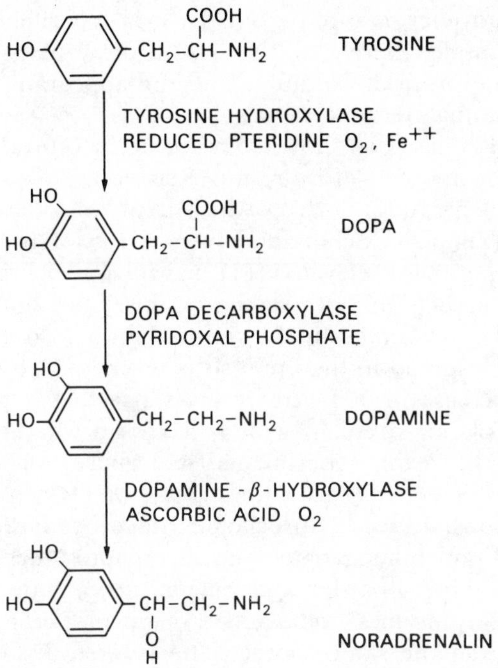

Figure 12.1 Biosynthesis of noradrenalin from tyrosine.

ripheral nerves have shown that the increased release of noradrenalin can be maintained for a limited period of time, since there is a rapid acceleration of noradrenalin synthesis to replace the lost transmitter (Alousi and Weiner 1966; Salzman and Roth 1980*a, b*). When the store of functional vesicles becomes depleted, however, noradrenalin release begins to fall (Benedict, Fillenz, and Stanford 1977). At the same time, however, the stimulus which causes neurons to release noradrenalin also sets in train an increase in the rate of synthesis of both TH and DBH. This phenomenon is known as 'transneuronal enzyme induction' (Thoenen 1975; Fillenz 1977). Increased levels of enzyme begin to appear in the cell-body 16–18 hours after the original stimulus and remain elevated for a number of days (Thoenen 1975). In order to exert an effect on releasable transmitter, however, the enzymes have to reach the nerve terminal. This introduces a further delay, which is different for the two enzymes, since they are transported along the axon at different rates: 10 mm h^{-1} for DBH, which is bound to the vesicles, and 5–10 mm day^{-1} for TH, which is largely in solution in the cytoplasm. Thus elevated enzyme levels appear in the nerve *terminals* only long after the original stimulus has ceased. Furthermore, the delay in the rise in enzyme levels varies with the distance of the nerve terminal from the cell-body (I. B. Black 1975). In the case of the noradrenergic input from the locus coeruleus to the hippo-campus, for example, there is likely to be a delay of 6–7 days between exposure to an appropriate stimulus and the appearance of higher TH levels in hippocampal nerve terminals.

Induction of TH has been shown to occur in the central nervous system in response to the injection of reserpine (Reis, Joh, Ross, and Pickel 1974; Boarder and Fillenz 1979), a drug which depletes catecholamine stores, and cold stress (Zigmond, Schon, and Iversen 1974). In Boarder and Fil-lenz's (1979) experiment, elevated TH activity was observed in the hip-pocampus and cerebellum (both served by the dorsal bundle) and in the hypothalamus (largely served by the ventral bundle), so the phenomenon is apparently widespread in the brain. It is not known, however, whether the observed increase in TH activity gives rise to the possibility of in-creased release of noradrenalin. Nor is it known whether the increased TH activity which, in the experiments cited above, was detected in ho-mogenized brain tissue reflects a true increase in TH activity under phys-iological conditions. Indeed, dissociations have been reported between TH activity in brain homogenates and in synaptosomes prepared from the same tissue. Thus Boarder and Fillenz (1979) found increased TH activity after reserpine in a homogenate of rat hippocampus, but not in synaptosomes from the same source. The reverse dissociation can also occur, that is, increased hippocampal synaptosomal TH activity with un-changed TH in a fully solubilized preparation of hippocampal tissue (Fil-lenz, Graham-Jones, and Gray 1979). None the less, it seems probable that induction of TH provides the noradrenergic neuron with an in-creased capacity to meet extreme demands on its functioning.

If this assumption is correct, we can envisage three stages in the func-tioning of noradrenergic neurons when they are called upon for sus-tained intense activity. Initial exposure to a stressor would cause an in-creased level of activity, as reported in both the periphery and the brain (Stone 1975; Lidbrink *et al.* 1973; Ritter and Ritter 1977). If the demands imposed on noradrenergic impulse traffic by the stressor are too severe, there will then be a fall in the level of noradrenalin available for release; this too has been observed both in the periphery and in a number of brain regions (Stone 1975; Fillenz 1977; Weiss and Glazer 1975; Ritter and Ritter 1977). Finally, the increased noradrenergic impulse traffic (or the conditions which give rise to it) will also set in motion a chain of events which results in increased noradrenalin synthesis and an increased avail-ability of the neurotransmitter for release at nerve terminals. In agree-ment with this account, Stone (1975), in an extensive review of the exper-imental evidence, concludes that, although noradrenalin decreases in most brain regions with acute stress, it 'either shows no change or tends to rise if the same stress is repeated several times in periods lasting more than 24 hours, or if the stress is given chronically'. This same pattern appears to hold for peripheral noradrenalin, although in this area there are fewer data. Stone (1975) also points out that, although the altered noradrenalin levels are restored at least to normal as a chronic stress continues, the increased *turnover* of noradrenalin which is elicited by stressors does not habituate. Thus, when adaptation to chronic stress is complete, equilibrium between release and synthesis of the transmitter is maintained at a higher level.

Note that the changes in noradrenergic functioning just described are consistent with Selye's (1952) model of the 'general adaptation syndrome'. According to this hypothesis, there are three stages in the adaptation of endocrine and autonomic reactions to stress (see Gray 1971a): an initial 'alarm' reaction, when existing reserves are utilized; a stage of 'resistance', during which additional reserves are mobilized to deal with the continuing stress; and a final stage of 'exhaustion' if the stress is so severe or prolonged that even the additional reserves are inadequate. The changes in noradrenergic functioning noted above conform well to the first two of these stages. Thus Selye's (1952) notion of the general adaptation syndrome may apply also to the brain's adaptation to prolonged stress.

These are not the only mechanisms involved in the adaptation of central noradrenergic neurons to prolonged activity. As we saw in the last chapter, when considering the action of clonidine, it is necessary also to take into account the feedback control over noradrenalin release exercised by receptors (apparently usually alpha-receptors) located on the pre-synaptic terminal or on the cell-body of the noradrenergic neuron (Langer 1977, 1979; Aghajanian, Cederbaum, and Wang 1977). This feedback acts on a short time-scale to restrain increases in noradrenalin release. On a slower time-scale (hours or days) both pre- and postsynaptic noradrenalin receptors have been shown to undergo systematic changes in number (Molinoff *et al.* 1978) and sensitivity (Kebabian *et al.* 1975). These changes in receptor function will be of importance when we come to deal with the mode of action of antidepressant drugs later in the chapter; for the moment, however, we shall leave them aside.

Helplessness

In the preceding section we noted three stages in the activity of central noradrenergic neurons under conditions of prolonged stress: an initial increase in noradrenalin release; a subsequent fall in noradrenalin levels if release is sufficiently intense and prolonged; and a final restoration of noradrenalin to levels able to subserve sustained increased release of the neurotransmitter. To what behaviour, if any, do these phenomena correspond? Recent research has begun to provide a plausible answer to this question. Much of it grew out of concern with a rather different issue, that of so-called 'learned helplessness' and its relation to clinical depression (Seligman 1975). Given the importance of the relation between depression and anxiety for the themes developed in this book, it is worth tracing this background in some detail before we consider more directly the relevance of this research to our immediate concerns.

The key observation in the literature on learned helplessness was reported by Overmier and Seligman (1967) and Seligman and Maier (1967). These workers showed that dogs, exposed in a first phase of the experiment to electric shocks which they could neither escape nor avoid, later failed to escape shock in a different situation in which escape was possible. Subsequently, the same effect was demonstrated in cats, mice, fish, and even that ubiquitous citizen of the psychological laboratory, the rat, though it was initially harder to do so with this species (Maier and Seligman 1976; Anisman and Sklar 1979). It is important to note that the deficit in escape behaviour is not seen when animals receive, in the first phase of the experiment, equivalent experience of shock but which they can control (i.e. escape) by making an appropriate instrumental response. The experimental paradigm used to establish these conclusions has come to be dignified by the appellation, 'triadic design'. That is to say, there are three basic experimental conditions: a group which can terminate each shock by an instrumental response; a 'yoked' group, in which each animal is paired with one in the first group and receives the same shocks as its 'master' independently of its own behaviour; and an unshocked group which is otherwise treated identically to the yoked group. Using this design it is observed that, when escape is possible for all animals in the second phase of the experiment, the yoked group is impaired relative to both the others (Maier and Seligman 1976). It is this impairment, or comparable effects when other instrumental responses are measured in the second phase of the experiment, that constitutes 'learned helplessness'.

Since much of the controversy which has surrounded this phenomenon has turned on what, if anything, is learned, to term it 'learned helplessness' begs many important questions. To circumvent this problem, Glazer and Weiss (1976a) proposed instead the term 'interference effect'. This is suitably neutral, but can easily be confused with the hundreds of other interference effects with which psychology abounds. I shall therefore preserve the term 'helplessness' (stripped of 'learned'), but use it in a strictly descriptive manner, to refer to the class of phenomena in which initial exposure to uncontrollable aversive events gives rise to subsequent deficits in instrumental responding.

Helplessness is a sufficiently striking phenomenon in its own right to account for the experimental attention that it has received in the decade since Seligman and his collaborators published their first reports; but this attention has been all the more intense since Seligman (1975) proposed it as a model of clinical depression in man. We shall leave examination of this claim till later in the chapter.

To account for the phenomenon of helplessness Maier and Seligman

(1976) propose a 'learned helplessness' hypothesis. It argues that 'when events are uncontrollable the organism learns that its behaviour and outcomes are independent, and that this learning produces the motivational, cognitive, and emotional effects of uncontrollability'. These three kinds of effect are: the failure to initiate escape responses (motivational); an impairment in the 'organism's tendency to perceive contingent relationships between its behaviour and outcomes' (cognitive); and the feelings that human beings experience as depression (emotional). In later developments of the theory, especially when applied to man, the cognitive member of this trio has achieved ever more prominence (e.g. Abramson, Seligman, and Teasdale 1978). Thus, in its most extreme form, Seligman's theory emphasizes cognitive processes with regard both to the necessary and sufficient conditions for producing helplessness (the opportunity to learn that behaviour does not control events) and to the principal feature of helplessness (loss of the capacity to perceive contingent relationships even when they exist).

In opposition to this cognitive theory, Weiss, Glazer, and Pohorecky (1976) proposed that uncontrollable aversive events produce a central noradrenergic deficiency that impairs the animal's ability to initiate motor behaviour. At one level, this opposition is a real one, namely, when it proposes that the psychological impairment in helpless animals is a deficit in motor activation rather than in the detection of instrumental contingencies. But at another level it is quite spurious, namely, in pitting a psychological theory (that of learned helplessness) against a neurochemical one (the putative deficit in noradrenergic functioning). *This* controversy is rather like arguing whether the stuff that comes out of the bathroom tap is water or H_2O. Cognitions, no matter how abstract, have to be based on some brain process or other; and there is no reason to rule out *a priori* impaired noradrenergic function as a candidate for the cognition, 'life is awful and nothing can be done about it'.

Sadly, much of the disagreement between the protagonists in this controversy has been at the second, spurious level, and it need not detain us here. The issues which do concern us are these: what is the psychological nature of helplessness; and is it mediated by a fall in central noradrenalin? Unfortunately, simple answers to these questions are virtually ruled out by the evidence that there is probably more than one kind of helplessness (Glazer and Weiss 1976a). Since our main concern is with anxiety, and since we related this in the previous chapter to noradrenalin, we shall devote most attention to the kind of helplessness which appears to be intimately associated with this neurotransmitter. This means that we shall do scant justice to the view that 'real' helplessness is *not* related to noradrenalin (Maier and Seligman 1976). But, so long as the reader bears in mind the purpose to which the argument is directed, this bias will perhaps be of little importance.

What, then, is the evidence that helplessness can at least sometimes be due to an alteration in the functional capacity of central noradrenergic neurons?

The evidence is, in fact, substantial. Much of it comes from Weiss's group in New York. These workers (Glazer and Weiss 1976*a*, *b*) distinguish between two types of helplessness, or interference as they prefer to call it. The experiments supporting this distinction were performed with rats exposed to one of two inescapable shock régimes. The first of these employed a relatively low shock intensity (1 mA) and gave rise to a long-term interference effect (escape-avoidance learning was impaired at times ranging from 3 hours to 1 week after inescapable shock). The second employed a very high shock intensity (4 mA) and gave rise to a short-term interference effect (present only at 30 minutes after the end of the inescapable shock session). Other points of difference between the two kinds of effect were: the long-term effect was *not* present if escape-avoidance learning was tested 30 minutes after inescapable shock; the long-term effect appeared only if the duration of inescapable shock was at least 5 seconds, whereas the short-term effect was obtained with a shock duration of 2 seconds; the short- but not the long-term effect could be prevented by multiple sessions of inescapable shock (a phenomenon considered in more detail below); and the short- but not the long-term effect was accompanied by a fall in the level of noradrenalin in the brain at the time that helplessness occurred.

Given the theme of this chapter, it is Glazer and Weiss's (1976*a*) short-term interference effect which has first claim on our attention. We have already met the first item of evidence (Weiss *et al.* 1975, 1976) that suggests a noradrenergic basis for this phenomenon: 30 minutes after the session of inescapable shock the levels of noradrenalin were reduced in the hypothalamus, brainstem, and forebrain; the reduction was greatest in the hypothalamus, a point to which we shall return. This observation joins many others (Stone 1975; Anisman and Sklar 1979; Schütz *et al.* 1979; Ritter and Ritter 1977) in showing that acute stress gives rise to a fall in central noradrenalin, presumably reflecting a level of activity in noradrenergic neurons which exceeds their immediate capacity to synthesize new releasable transmitter (see above). As it stands, however, it is merely a correlation between neurochemical and behavioural observations; by itself it is insufficient to establish a causal connection between them. Several other findings, however, suggest that such a causal connection exists.

First, helplessness and the fall in central noradrenalin are affected by the same behavioural parameters. Most importantly, in Weiss's experiments the level of noradrenalin fell only in rats which were exposed to uncontrollable shock. Rats which received identical experience of shock but could control its duration showed no change in hypothalamic or forebrain noradrenalin levels, and in the brainstem there was actually an increase (Weiss, Stone, and Harrell 1970; Weiss *et al.* 1975). That this was not an artefact of the different amounts of movement which occurred in the two groups was demonstrated by using two different escape responses, one requiring movement, the other requiring the animal to hold still; the yoked animals (exposed to uncontrollable shock) had lower hypothalamic noradrenalin levels than their masters in both cases (Weiss *et al.* 1976).

Somewhat similar data were reported by Schütz *et al.* (1979). In their experiment rats were exposed to one of four conditions in a shuttle-box: pseudoconditioning, i.e. a random intermixture of shocks and buzzers; classical conditioning, i.e. the buzzer predicted the shock, but no avoidance response was possible; an instrumental avoidance procedure in which the shock followed the buzzer at unpredictable intervals but could be avoided by shuttling; and a standard signalled avoidance procedure. Only the pseudoconditioning task produced a fall in noradrenalin levels (in the hypothalamus, amygdala, and nucleus accumbens), measured immediately after the end of the single training session. Thus the fall in noradrenalin levels produced by unpredictable unavoidable shocks (in the pseudoconditioning group) was blocked *either* by giving the animal instrumental control over the shocks, *or* by making them predictable (in the classical conditioning group).

Note that the shock parameters used by Schütz *et al.* (1979) were rather different from those found by Glazer and Weiss (1976*a*) to be critical for their short-term interference effect. First, they were of lower intensity (1.5 mA). Second, and more important, they were *escapable* in all four experimental conditions. Thus 'control' appears to be a continuous variable, not a dichotomy. In Weiss's experiments inescapable but not escapable shocks produced a fall in central noradrenalin levels; in Schütz *et al.*'s (1979), unavoidable, unpredictable escapable shocks, but not predictable escapable or avoidable escapable shocks, produced such a fall. Presumably, the particular values of shock intensity, duration, etc., that must be used to affect noradrenalin levels are then a function of other features of the experimental situation. Thus it may be premature to accept the neat distinction proposed by Glazer and Weiss (1976*a*) between two types of interference effect, one associated with a fall in central noradrenalin levels and the other not; and in any event the shock parameters which these workers used to differentiate between the two effects evidently cannot be generalized to other tasks.

A second line of evidence which suggests that a fall in central noradrenalin levels may underlie helplessness comes from experiments in which drugs are used to manipulate the neurotransmitter. Thus Glazer *et al.* (1975) produced a deficit in escape-avoidance performance in the shuttle-box by injecting tetrabenazine, a drug which depletes all monoamines (noradrenalin, dopamine, and serotonin) in the brain. They describe this deficit as being closely similar to that seen after a session of inescapable shock. Similar findings have been reported by Anisman *et al.* (1979*a*, *b*), working with mice and an escape task in the shuttle-box. They too produced a deficit in escape (resembling that seen after inescapable shock) by injecting drugs which impair monoaminergic function. Furthermore, their results permit a clearer identification of the monoamines involved. The escape deficit was seen after injections of drugs which affect both noradrenalin and dopamine (α-methyl-p-tyrosine, which inhibits TH and so blocks the synthesis of both transmitters; see Table 12.1); drugs which affect only noradrenalin (FLA-63, which blocks noradrenalin synthesis by inhibiting DBH); and also drugs which affect only dopaminergic transmission (the dopamine receptor blockers, haloperidol and pimozide). Blockade of the synthesis of serotonin by PCPA, however, did not give rise to helplessness. Thus these experiments implicate both noradrenalin and dopamine in helplessness. Schütz *et al.* (1979) also found that their pseudoconditioning procedure (see above) caused a fall in dopamine levels in the nucleus accumbens and the caudate nucleus, and that this was partially reversed by their other training conditions. In general, however, brain levels of dopamine are more resistant to alteration by acute stress than those of noradrenalin (Stone 1975).

These findings, depending as they do on the similarity of the behaviour seen after dissimilar treatments, are at best circumstantial evidence that the same brain processes are involved in the two cases. Somewhat more direct evidence comes from experiments in which interactions between drug treatments and inescapable shock are investigated.

Some of these experiments have depended on the demonstration by Seligman and Maier (1967) that training with escapable shock before a session of inescapable shock blocks the development of helplessness. Maier and Seligman (1976) believe that this 'immunization' effect arises because 'prior experience with controllable shock should proactively interfere with the subject's learning that shock is uncontrollable and should also allow the subject to discriminate between the places where shocks are controllable and uncontrollable'. This hypothesis is much weakened, however, by the observation that helplessness induced by a swim in cold water (Weiss and Glazer 1975; see below) or by antinoradrenergic or antidopaminergic drugs (Anisman *et al.* 1979*b*) is also blocked by prior experience with escapable shock. In these experiments a behavioural treatment is able to block the effect of a drug. It has also been shown that the two kinds of treatment can facilitate each other. Thus Anisman and Sklar (1979) showed that if, in the first phase of a helplessness experiment, the number of inescapable shocks was 15 or less, helplessness was not produced, nor was there a fall in central noradrenalin levels. But combining five shocks with sub-threshold doses of either α-methyl-p-tyrosine or FLA-63 during the inescapable shock session caused both helplessness and a fall in the level of noradrenalin.

In a further variant of this type of experiment it has been shown that drug treatments which affect monoamine transmission and/or reverse pharmacologically induced helplessness can similarly reverse helplessness induced behaviourally. In the first demonstration of this kind Glazer *et al.* (1975) used the monoamine oxidase inhibitor (MAOI), pargyline. Mono- amines released at the presynaptic membrane are taken back into the cell and destroyed by monoamine oxidase (though this is not the only way they are catabolized). Glazer *et al.* (1975) argued, therefore, that a MAOI would attenuate the depletion of noradrenalin produced by inescapable shock and thus block helplessness. In accordance with this prediction they report that pargyline, given before the inescapable shock session, elimi- nated their short-term interference effect. Although this result does not distinguish between the different monoamines that might be involved, it has another importance. Since pargyline is widely used as an antidepres- sant, it offers some evidence that helplessness is indeed a model of human depression, as suggested by Seligman (1975).

More precise identification of the catecholamines as critical in this kind of effect comes from data reported by Anisman *et al.* (1979*a, b;* Anisman and Sklar 1979). These workers showed that the catecholamine precursor, L-DOPA, reversed the helplessness produced by both α-methyl-*p*-tyrosine and FLA-63; similarly, given in conjunction with inescapable shock, it blocked the helplessness normally seen after this treatment. These find- ings are consistent with an effect on noradrenergic mechanisms, especially as L-DOPA blocked the effect of the specific inhibitor of DBH, FLA-63. However, other findings reported by Anisman's group also implicate do- pamine. Thus the helplessness produced by haloperidol (a dopamine re- ceptor blocker) was reversed by the anticholinergic drug, scopolamine, and this drug also reversed the helplessness seen after inescapable shock (Anisman *et al.* 1979*b*).

A third line of evidence which suggests a causal role for central norad- renergic mechanisms in helplessness comes from experiments in which animals are exposed to multiple sessions of inescapable shock.

As pointed out above, this treatment blocks Glazer and Weiss's (1976*a*) short-term but not their long-term interference effect. These workers re- port that, when a single session of inescapable shock of 4 mA intensity was preceded by 14 daily sessions of the same treatment, the helplessness usually observed 30 minutes later was totally absent. This 'toughening up', as Neal Miller (1976) called it in a characteristically gritty phrase, is also seen when the final inescapable shock session is preceded by exposure to repeated stress of other kinds. Thus Weiss *et al.* (1975) showed that 14 days' exposure to a swim in cold (2 °C) water blocked the helplessness otherwise produced by a single session of inescapable shock. The same 'cross-tolerance' between these two stressors could be demonstrated when the relations between them were reversed. Thus Weiss and Glazer (1975) reported that a single session of cold swim produced helplessness in an escape-avoidance task 30 minutes later, an effect that was very similar to the helplessness produced by inescapable shock. Like inescapable shock, moreover, the cold swim loses its capacity to produce helplessness if it is repeated for 14 days. And, just as repeated exposure to a cold swim blocks the helplessness produced by inescapable shock, so repeated exposure to inescapable shock blocks the helplessness produced by the cold swim (Weiss *et al.* 1975).

Several observations implicate noradrenergic mechanisms in toughening up.

First, the fall in noradrenalin which was seen 30 minutes after a single session of inescapable shock was not evident when the animal was killed after the fifteenth such session (Weiss *et al.* 1975). At the same time, there was an increase in the activity in the brain of tyrosine hydroxylase, the rate-limiting enzyme in the synthesis of noradrenalin (Table 12.1). Additionally, repeated inescapable shock sessions led to a fall in the uptake of noradrenalin by brain slices. Since, as pointed out above re-uptake of noradrenalin after release plays a major role in the termination of the synaptic effect of the transmitter, this change, like the increase in TH activity, probably reflects an increase in the effective output of noradrenergic neurons. It is possible, therefore, as suggested by Weiss *et al.* (1975), that toughening up results from such an increase in effective noradrenergic output.

The findings in animals which had been repeatedly exposed to a cold swim were, however, less consistent with this hypothesis. In these animals the fall in hypothalamic noradrenalin after a single session of inescapable shock was identical to that seen in animals not pre-exposed to cold swims, and there was no increase in TH activity. Since helplessness in response to inescapable shock *was* blocked by repeated cold swims, it seems that induction of TH and a return to normal levels of noradrenalin are not necessary conditions for the occurrence of toughening up. There were, however, certain changes in the animals repeatedly exposed to a cold swim which were consistent with the hypothesis of a noradrenergic basis to toughening up. In the forebrain, although inescapable shock gave rise to a fall in noradrenalin levels in these animals, it was less than that seen in animals not pre-exposed to cold swims, and indeed it was non-significant. Furthermore, brain slices taken from these animals showed a decrease in the uptake of noradrenalin, although this was not so great as the decrease seen in animals pre-exposed to repeated shock. Thus it is possible that repeated cold swims also gave rise to an increase in the functional capacity of central noradrenergic neurons, but to a smaller degree and perhaps by different mechanisms and with a different distribution in the brain than repeated shock.

A final experiment in this series also provided support for an involvement of monoamines (though not necessarily noradrenalin) in toughening up: repeated injection for 14 days of the monoamine-depleting drug, tetrabenazine, blocked not only the helplessness produced by a single injection of this drug, but also the helplessness normally seen after a single session of inescapable shock (Glazer *et al.* 1975).

Reports from other laboratories also suggest that noradrenergic mechanisms are involved in toughening up. As already noted, it is very generally the case that, whereas acute stress often causes a fall in brain noradrenalin levels, chronic stress either does not change or even increases them. At the same time, there is apparently an increase in the turnover of noradrenalin during chronic, as well as acute, exposure to stress. Findings published since Stone's (1975) thorough review continue to support these generalizations. Östman and Nybäck (1976), for example, found a 26 per cent increase in the level of noradrenalin in the brain, together with increased turnover, in rats required to swim regularly in warm water for a period of 17 weeks. If the hypothesis advanced by Weiss *et al.* (1975) is correct, these animals should also have developed increased tolerance for stress, thus perhaps demonstrating a noradrenergic basis for the Latin tag, *mens sana in corpore sano*.

Ritter *et al.* (1978; Ritter and Ritter 1977) have also reported observations which fit well with those made by Weiss's group. They studied feeding in response to an injection of 2-deoxyglucose, an analogue of glucose which cannot be metabolized and therefore acts like a rapid-onset starvation. If rats were exposed to a single session of cold stress or foot-shock, there was an acute fall of hypothalamic and forebrain noradrenalin. When hypothalamic noradrenalin fell by about 25 per cent, feeding in response to 2-deoxyglucose ('glucoprivic' feeding) disappeared; this is consistent with other evidence that noradrenergic synapses in the hypothalamus play an important role in the control of eating (Hoebel 1977). Inescapable shock for 14 days, however, blocked the fall in hypothalamic noradrenalin produced by a single shock session (as in Weiss's experiments) and restored a normal glucoprivic feeding response. Conversely, 14 injections of 2-deoxyglucose blocked the fall in hypothalamic and forebrain noradrenalin otherwise produced by a single session of inescapable shock. Thus there was cross-tolerance between foot-shock and 2-deoxyglucose, just as, in Weiss's experiments, between foot-shock, cold swim, and tetrabenazine injections.

Although they are not conclusive, these various experiments make a strong case for the view that, at least under some conditions, helplessness is caused by an acute fall in the levels of noradrenalin in the brain; and that toughening up is due to a restoration of noradrenalin levels as noradrenergic neurons develop an extra functional capacity (Weiss *et al.* 1975; Miller 1976; Gray, Davis, Feldon, Owen, and Boarder 1981). However, it is possible that other monoamines, especially dopamine, are also involved in these phenomena.

Recent reports also suggest that in part helplessness may reflect a conditioned analgesic response, perhaps mediated by the enkephalins. Thus Chance *et al.* (1978) exposed rats for 8 days to inescapable shock in a distinctive apparatus and then measured the threshold heat stimulus which (in the same apparatus) elicited a flick of the tail. Compared to handled controls the shocked rats had a higher threshold; in addition, when the binding of leu-enkephalin (one of the endogenous opiates) was measured in a brain homogenate, there was less binding in the shocked group, suggesting that they may have had higher levels of an endogenous ligand for the enkephalin receptor. It is not possible to tell whether the shock schedule used by Chance *et al.* (1978) would have produced behavioural helplessness, but a report by Jackson, Maier, and Coon (1979) establishes a connection between this and conditioned analgesia. These workers demonstrated a raised threshold for pain, again to a heat stimulus, in rats exposed to a schedule of inescapable shock which also produced a deficit in shuttle-box escape behaviour. Furthermore, the analgesic response did not appear in a group of rats which had escapable shock in the first phase of the experiment, although it was present in their yoked, inescapable-shock counterparts; and it only appeared if the rats were tested in the shuttle-box before sacrifice. Thus it appears that inescapable shock gives rise to an incipient analgesia which, however, requires further exposure to shock to be realised.

These findings raise the possibility that helplessness is a consequence of analgesia: the animal fails to escape shock because it feels it as less painful than controls. Various arguments were marshalled by Maier and Seligman (1976) against this 'adaptation hypothesis'. Many of these arguments are by-passed by the demonstration of an analgesia that is reinstated by exposure to shock (Jackson *et al.* 1979), but some of them still stand, notably the observation that helplessness is not overcome by raising shock intensity during the escape phase of the experiment (Seligman and Maier 1967). In any case, the methods by which pain thresholds are measured have the consequence that any explanation of helplessness in terms of analgesia is circular; for one might just as well say that the pain threshold (the intensity of heat at which the animal moves its tail) is raised because the animal is helpless (unable to escape) as the converse.

An involvement of endogenous opiate mechanisms is not necessarily at variance with the noradrenergic hypothesis of helplessness. No behaviour depends on only one set of neurons in the central nervous system; and we have already seen (Chapter 11) that there is a close connection between the endogenous opiates and at least one noradrenergic nucleus, the locus coeruleus. Other findings that suggest interactions between opiates and central noradrenergic mechanisms are reviewed by McNaughton and Mason (1980). In addition, the observation that the analgesic response produced by a régime of inescapable shock requires further appropriate experience before it becomes manifest in behaviour (Jackson *et al.* 1979) has an interesting parallel in Anisman and Sklar's (1979) experiments on the effects of inescapable shock on brain noradrenalin levels. These workers report that 24 hours after a session of 60 inescapable shocks there was no change in brain noradrenalin levels in mice, confirming Weiss *et al.*'s (1975, 1976) observations in the rat. However, if 10 further shocks were given just before killing (a régime not sufficient to have effects by itself), noradrenalin levels fell in the hypothalamus, a result which was also obtained if the mice were killed immediately after the initial inescapable shock session (Anisman and Sklar 1979). Thus inescapable shock may sensitize the animal to the later effects of shock in such a way that there is both a more rapid mobilization of noradrenergic neurons (with a consequent fall in the level of noradrenalin as the neurotransmitter is used up), and an endogenous analgesic response. It is not known whether these two phenomena are related; however, the observation that destruction of the dorsal noradrenergic bundle with intracerebral 6-OHDA potentiates the analgesic response to exogenous morphine (Price and Fibiger 1975) suggests that they may be.

If we accept that the helplessness observed in the experiments reported by Weiss's and Anisman's groups is in large part mediated by an acute fall in the level of central noradrenalin, can we make any headway in describing the psychological nature of this effect? Unfortunately, there is a paucity of data directly relevant to this question.

If Glazer and Weiss (1976*a, b*) are right in supposing that there are two kinds of interference effect, only one of which is based on noradrenergic mechanisms, we are forced to ignore all data on the psychology of helplessness gained in experiments where the noradrenergic basis of the effect was not simultaneously demonstrated. Since Anisman's experiments have not been directed to psychological issues, this leaves in practice only those from Weiss's laboratory. Weiss's group itself favours the 'motor inactivation' hypothesis, that is, they believe that the acute fall in central noradrenalin levels leaves the animal able to engage in only a limited amount of motor activity (Weiss and Glazer 1975). In effect, they propose that lowered levels of noradrenalin produce a kind of central fatigue. In accordance with this hypothesis they predict that the deficit in escape produced by prior inescapable shock, cold swims and the like will be a positive function of the amount of movement the escape response requires of the animal. In agreement with this deduction Weiss and Glazer (1975) report that raising the height of the barrier in a shuttle-box from 2 to 4 inches (5 to 10 cm) (a manipulation which has no effect on the performance of normal animals) increased the escape-avoidance deficit produced by a cold swim. Conversely, when an escape response requiring little motor activity (poking the nose through a hole) was used, neither a cold swim nor inescapable shock caused any deficit in escape or avoidance (Weiss and Glazer 1975).

This pleasingly simple hypothesis has some merit if we wish to treat 'noradrenergic' helplessness as a model for depression. For a central symptom in this condition is so-called psychomotor fatigue, the feeling that almost any effort is beyond one's forces, appearing behaviourally as a paucity and slowness of movement ('motor retardation'; Jouvent *et al.* 1980). Allied to this is a loss of appetite and a consequent fall in body weight. These symptoms too have their parallels in 'noradrenergic' helplessness. Thus anorexia and loss of body weight are marked in rats exposed for a day or two to foot-shock, but are much diminished (toughening up?) after 9 daily one-hour exposures to this stress (Stone 1978). As we have seen, Ritter's experiments (Ritter *et al.* 1978; Ritter and Ritter 1977) suggest that these effects reflect an alteration, probably at hypothalamic level, in noradrenergic control over feeding in response to glucose deprivation. Thus, following Weiss and Glazer (1975), we might suppose that the core of depression is a rather generalized apathy, and that this is due to impaired function in central noradrenergic mechanisms.

There is, however, a problem with Weiss and Glazer's (1975) hypothesis. We have supposed (on good grounds) that a fall in noradrenalin levels occurs when the rate of firing of noradrenergic neurons outstrips their capacity to synthesize new transmitter. This implies that, during the first phase of a helplessness experiment, noradrenergic neurons are extremely active. This in turn implies that, if the role of noradrenergic neurons is to initiate and maintain motor activity (as suggested by Weiss and Glazer 1975), the animal is very busy moving at this time. But that, of course, is just what it is not doing. In Weiss's own experiments, for example, the rat exposed to inescapable shock is more or less totally immobile inside a small tube. Furthermore, such an animal manifests a fall in central noradrenalin levels relative to other animals which receive escapable shock, irrespective of whether the escape response requires the latter to move or to hold still (Weiss *et al.* 1976). It is difficult, therefore, to suppose that movement as such has anything to do with the conditions which activate noradrenergic neurons during the first phase of an experiment on helplessness. Indeed, Weiss and his colleagues have not claimed that movement does play a role in this part of the experiment; but the general logic of their hypothesis implies that they should have made this claim.

Weiss's motor inactivation hypothesis is derived from the behaviour of the animal that has been made helpless, but it has trouble in dealing with the conditions which make it helpless. What if we reverse the chain of argument and look for a hypothesis which fits the conditions that cause helplessness? This, essentially, is what Seligman (1975) did in deriving his 'learned helplessness' theory. It is uncontrollability of shock that produces helplessness, so the animal (according to this theory) learns about uncontrollability.

At first sight this hypothesis does not look at its best when confronted with the kind of data gathered by Weiss and Anisman. It makes one uneasy to suppose that a drug such as tetrabenazine or FLA-63 can produce the cognition, 'there is nothing I can do about anything'. But, as I have already said, this is mere prejudice. All cognitions depend on some brain state or other. To be sure, a fall in central noradrenalin levels is a very gross neurochemical change, and any cognition it supports must be correspondingly crude. But the cognition, 'there is nothing I can do about anything', *is* crude, as is the state of depression to which, according to Seligman, it gives rise. So the mere fact that helplessness can be produced by drug treatments, cold swims and the like, is not evidence against Seligman's theory (although both Seligman and Weiss seem agreed that it is). If this much is accepted, it is striking how very 'cognitive' are the conditions which affect the level of brain noradrenalin. The experiments of Weiss *et al.* (1976) and Schütz *et al.* (1979) concur in indicating that it is *uncertainty* (uncontrollability plus unpredictability) that causes a fall in the level of noradrenalin: inescapable shock has a bigger effect than escapable shock; unavoidable, than avoidable shock; and predictable, than unpredictable shock. Thus the same reasoning that led Seligman (1975) to propose that behavioural helplessness is associated with learning that one has no control over events can be applied with equal validity to its neurochemical concomitants.

If one searches for a better reason to reject the learned helplessness hypothesis for 'noradrenergic' helplessness, the only relevant findings are those already cited by which Weiss and Glazer (1975) support their motor inactivation hypothesis, namely, the fact that helplessness is increased by raising the height of the barrier in the shuttle-box and eliminated by using an escape-avoidance response (nose-poking) that requires little effort. These authors argue that, if the main problem for a helpless animal is to detect the contingency that connects its responses to outcomes, it should make little difference whether the instrumental response is effortful or not. While not conclusive, this argument has some merit. Note that Weiss and Glazer's (1975) findings also pose difficulties for the hypothesis that helplessness is due to analgesia (Jackson *et al.* 1979; Chance *et al.* 1978). For, if the animal fails to escape shock because it no longer feels it to be very painful, this should affect all responses equally, regardless of the amount of effort involved.

Weiss's hypothesis, then, deals well with the behaviour of the helpless animal, while Seligman's has a natural application to the conditions that give rise to this behaviour. Can these qualities be combined? A possible account, within the general theoretical framework developed in this book, requires that we suppose, not that noradrenergic neurons are directly concerned with the execution of motor behaviour, but rather that they in some way increase the readiness for motor behaviour. This account was adumbrated in a different context in the previous chapter. It will be easier to apply it to the problems examined here, if we first decide which noradrenergic neurons we are talking about.

Until now, in keeping with the literature on helplessness, I have been deliberately vague on this point. Some of the experiments in this field have been concerned with noradrenalin in the whole brain; and when regional levels have been reported, they have generally shown only little differentiation between brain areas (although, as we shall see, these data contain important clues as to which mechanisms are particularly important in helplessness). But when we consider the behavioural changes that accompany alterations in the level of brain noradrenalin, and especially if we bear in mind the data summarized in the previous chapter on the behavioural effects of dorsal bundle lesions, it is not difficult to narrow the field. As we have seen, the principal behavioural measure of helplessness is a deficit in escape and/or active avoidance, especially in the shuttle-box; and this occurs at a time when central noradrenergic functioning is apparently impaired. These facts seem to exclude the dorsal bundle as a major pathway underlying helplessness. For, as we saw in Chapter 11 (subsections 4 and 5), dorsal bundle lesion generally *improve* avoidance in the shuttle-box and have no effect on escape or one-way active avoidance. Thus it is more likely that the phenomena observed by Weiss, Anisman, and their collaborators are due in the main to alterations in noradrenalin levels in the terminal areas of the ventral bundle. This point of view finds support in the experiments by Ritter *et al.* (1978; Ritter and Ritter 1977) on glucoprivic feeding (see above), since this is most likely mediated at a hypothalamic level (Hoebel 1977; Leibowitz 1972). It is also supported by the fact that, in several of the relevant experiments, the alterations in noradrenalin level were more marked in the hypothalamus (which receives no more than about 30 per cent of its noradrenergic terminals from the locus coeruleus) than elsewhere in the brain (Weiss *et al.* 1975, 1976; Ritter *et al.* 1978; Ritter and Pelzer 1978; Anisman and Sklar 1979).

It may be concluded, then, that, insofar as the behavioural phenomena of helplessness are concerned, the important changes in noradrenalin levels are in the hypothalamus and perhaps other terminal areas largely served by the ventral noradrenergic bundle. Armed with this assumption, let us return to the question of the psychological nature of 'noradrenergic' helplessness. The hypothesis I shall propose was originally advanced at the level of the conceptual nervous system, and based on purely behavioural data (Gray and Smith 1969; Gray 1975). As shown in Fig. 12.2, it holds that presentation of a warning signal for punishment activates two related mechanisms, one which inhibits ongoing behaviour and another which increases the level of arousal so that whatever behaviour the animal next initiates is undertaken with especially great vigour. In earlier chapters in this book we have identified the first of these mechanisms with the septo-hippocampal system, primed (Chapter 11) by ascending serotonergic and cholinergic mechanisms. In addition, in the previous chapter (Fig. 11.4), we attributed control over the level of arousal to the dorsal noradrenergic bundle. We are now in a position to elaborate this proposal and bring out more clearly the arousal functions of the brain's noradrenergic neurons.

We suppose that, under conditions of threat (such as those presented by repeated, unpredictable, and inescapable shock), the noradrenergic in-

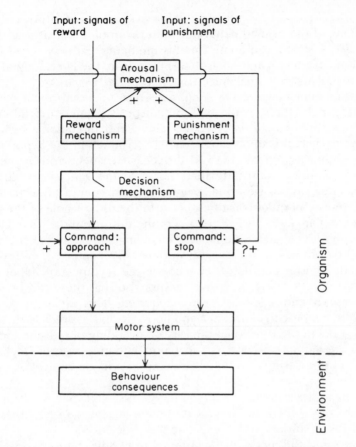

Figure 12.2. Gray and Smith's (1969) model for conflict behaviour. Presentation of a stimulus associated with punishment activates the 'punishment mechanism' with two consequences: (1) via the 'decision mechanism' there is an increased likelihood of inhibition ('command: stop') of ongoing behaviour; (2) via the 'arousal mechanism' there is a boost to 'command: approach' so that whatever behaviour occurs next is carried out with increased vigour.

put to diencephalic, and perhaps particularly hypothalamic, structures primes mechanisms which subserve those behavioural patterns which are most likely to be needed if and when there is anything the animal can do at all. In a rat exposed to inescapable shock these are likely to be the kinds of behaviour called 'species-specific defense' (Bolles 1971) or 'fight–flight' (Cannon 1932; Gray 1971a) reactions. There is evidence that the hypothalamus plays an important role in the co-ordination of this type of behaviour (de Molina and Hunsperger 1962). At the same time, we suppose that the septo-hippocampal system (perhaps acting in response to ascending serotonergic and cholinergic influences, as discussed in the previous chapter) activates a descending inhibitory pathway which prevents initiation of any of the primed behaviour patterns until it is clear that they will be of use. A strong candidate for this inhibitory pathway is the one described in Chapters 8 and 10 as descending from the lateral septal area to the ventromedial hypothalamus (e.g. Albert *et al.* 1978a).

If this model (shown in Fig. 12.3) is correct, hypothalamic mechanisms subserving fight–flight would be simultaneously primed and inhibited; it is perhaps this struggle between excitation and inhibition which places such severe demands upon noradrenergic terminals in the hypothalamus. These terminals originate both in the locus coeruleus and in the brainstem nuclei which contribute their fibres to the ventral noradrenergic bundle. Thus, on this view, the ascending noradrenergic fibres in the dorsal and ventral bundles constitute between them the whole of the arousal mechanism illustrated in Fig. 12.2. Via the dorsal bundle, they alert the septo-hippocampal system to analyse incoming stimuli and check existing motor programmes, in the manner outlined in Chapter 10; and, via both dorsal and ventral bundles, they increase the readiness of hypothalamic mechanisms controlling defensive reactions so that these can be set into action rapidly and vigorously when required. This theory is consistent with Weiss's motor inactivation hypothesis, in that it predicts that, when there is a fall in the functional capacity of ascending noradrenergic mechanisms, the animal will be less capable of initiating vigorous behaviour; but it does not attribute to these mechanisms a direct control over movement.

This hypothesis, then, can account for the behaviour of the helpless animal in much the same way as the motor inactivation hypothesis. But what of the conditions which give rise to helplessness?

At first sight the model is ill-equipped to handle these conditions. For I have previously allocated to the behavioural inhibition system (to which the ascending noradrenergic fibres, *ex hypothesi*, now belong) the task of responding to signals of aversive events, not to these events themselves. Yet, when a rat is exposed to repeated inescapable and unsignalled shock, there is no explicit warning signal. But this objection misses the point that, in the experiments of Weiss *et al.* (1975, 1976) and Schütz *et al.* (1979), it was precisely *not* the shocks that determined the effects observed, either at the behavioural level (helplessness) or at the neurochemical (the fall in central noradrenalin). The determining factors were the degree to which the shocks were controllable and predictable, as in other work in this field (Maier and Seligman 1976). And the role played by these factors can be deduced from the general theory of the behavioural inhibition system developed in this book.

The argument turns on the fact that, in classical conditioning experiments, it has been shown that, the less definitely an aversive UCS is signalled by explicit CSs, the more the general experimental environment acquires the characteristics of an undifferentiated cluster ('background

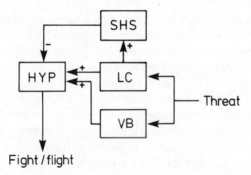

Fight / flight

Figure 12.3. A model for simultaneous excitatory and (via the septo-hippocampal system, SHS) inhibitory effects of threatening stimuli on hypothalamic (HYP) fight/flight mechanisms mediated by noradrenergic fibres ascending in the dorsal bundle from the locus coeruleus (LC) and in the ventral bundle (VB) from other noradrenergic brainstem nuclei.

stimuli') of aversive CSs (Odling-Smee 1975). This relationship has not been shown so clearly for instrumental responses. But it has been shown that instrumental responses and Pavlovian CSs can compete with each other for attention in Kamin's blocking paradigm (Mackintosh and Dickinson 1979) and other situations (e.g. Garrud *et al.* 1981; St. Claire-Smith 1979); while Odling-Smee's (1975) experiment shows that background stimuli and explicit CSs interact in the same manner. It seems likely, therefore, that instrumental responses and background stimuli also compete for attention. It then follows that, the less an aversive UCS is *either* predictable *or* controllable, the more the general environment will acquire secondary aversive characteristics. Since background stimuli, unlike explicit CSs, are present all the time, the behavioural inhibition system, as this was defined in Chapter 1, will be most intensely active precisely under those conditions which give rise to helplessness —unpredictable and uncontrollable shocks.

It seems possible, then, to arrive at a reasonably coherent account of the psychology and physiology of 'noradrenergic' helplessness within the general framework adopted in this book. What of 'non-noradrenergic' helplessness?

Glazer and Weiss (1976a) and Maier and Seligman (1976) are agreed that there are two kinds of helplessness, one noradrenergic and the other not, though there is very little else on which they agree. But their consensus on this point may not be justified. The evidence that some helplessness is related to a fall in central noradrenalin stores is, as we have seen, strong. But there is as yet no compelling reason to suppose that there is another kind of helplessness based on other neural machinery.

The clearest apparent differentiation between two kinds of helplessness lies in Glazer and Weiss's (1976a, b) description of their short- and long-term interference effects. The short-term effect seems clearly to be nor-adrenergic. But the possibility that the long-term effect also has a noradrenergic basis has barely been examined. Glazer and Weiss (1976a) state that no 'gross biochemical disturbance' has been observed in animals exposed to their low-shock (1 mA) régime. But, precisely because a fall in the level of noradrenalin *is* a gross biochemical change, this does not mean that other and more subtle impairments in noradrenergic functioning are not caused by this shock schedule. Furthermore, it is possible that this schedule *does* cause a latent fall in noradrenalin stores, but one that requires further exposure to shock to become apparent, as in Anisman and Sklar's (1979) experiment (see above).

Maier and Seligman (1976) use as an argument against the generality of the noradrenergic account of helplessness the fact that Glazer and Weiss's (1976a) short-term interference effect is present only 30 minutes after exposure to inescapable shock, whereas in many other experiments (including, of course, those demonstrating Glazer and Weiss's own long-term effect) helplessness has been observed at much longer delays after inescapable shock. But since then, as we have seen, Anisman *et al.* (1979*b*) have described helplessness in mice which lasts at least 7 days but appears to have a basis in noradrenergic and dopaminergic functioning in the brain. Thus, in the absence of direct investigation of the neurochemical basis of a given instance of helplessness, one cannot conclude from the experimental parameters or the behavioural observations that it is *not* noradrenergic. Maier and Seligman (1976) also argue that, although a neurochemical explanation of helplessness can be applied to a short-term interference effect, it cannot naturally be applied to long-term effects, since a neurochemical depletion can be expected to put itself right (as indeed it usually does). But this argument has lost much of its force with the demonstrations that both the reduced levels of noradrenalin and the analgesia (due perhaps to altered functioning in endogenous opiate mechanisms) produced by inescapable shock can be conditioned, or at least sensitized so that they occur with extreme rapidity (Anisman and Sklar 1979; Chance *et al.* 1978; Jackson *et al.* 1979). Thus it remains possible that all, or at any rate most, instances of helplessness depend in part on changes in noradrenergic systems in the brain; though, to be sure, many more data are required to lift this proposition above the level of speculation.

This is not to say that, behaviourally, all instances of helplessness need fit the mold we have deduced from those experiments which most clearly implicate central noradrenalin. Certainly, there are some reports which cannot easily be reconciled to Weiss's motor inactivation hypothesis or the modification of that hypothesis proposed above. Perhaps the clearest of these is an experiment by Jackson, Maier, and Rapoport (1978) in which it was shown that pre-exposure to inescapable shock reduced the suppressant effects of response-contingent shock on bar-pressing. Since the same treatment had no effect on the response-suppressant effects of response-independent shock (in a conditioned suppression paradigm), Jackson *et al.* (1978) argue that inescapable shock made the rat less sensitive to the instrumental contingencies linking the bar-pressing response to shock, as predicted by Seligman's (1975) learned helplessness theory. Whether or not this is the correct interpretation of their results, it is clear that they cannot be attributed to motor inactivation, since the rats previously exposed to inescapable shock bar-pressed *more* than controls when their responses were punished. Thus it is probable that inescapable shock produces other changes in behaviour besides a reduced readiness to engage in motor behaviour, and these may include an impairment in learning about the consequences of one's own responses (Jackson *et al.* 1978; Maier and Seligman 1976); but the neural basis of these other changes remains unknown.

Before we close this discussion of helplessness and toughening up, note that, if these effects are due to changes in noradrenergic neurons, we might expect them to be attenuated by treatment with anti-anxiety drugs. These antagonize the stress-induced increase in noradrenalin turnover (Lidbrink *et al.* 1973; see Chapter 11). They should therefore reduce the fall in noradrenalin levels caused by inescapable shock, cold swims, and other similar treatments. If so, and if helplessness is a direct result of the fall in noradrenalin levels, this too should be reduced by the anti-anxiety drugs. Furthermore, if it is necessary for noradrenalin stores to be used up for the functional capacity of noradrenergic neurons subsequently to increase (though this assumption is unverified), the anti-anxiety drugs should also block this process, and with it the behavioural toughening up to which it apparently gives rise. There appear to be no published data dealing directly with this issue. It is possible, however, that the effects of the anti-anxiety drugs on the partial reinforcement extinction effect and the analogous 'partial punishment effect' are related to it.

We have discussed the increased resistance to extinction produced by a PRF schedule several times in this book. A similar paradigm is used to demonstrate the partial punishment effect. During training (in the alley) rats receive a food reward on every trial. For rats in the control group, this is the only experimental contingency. Those in the 'partial punishment' group receive in addition a foot-shock in the goal-box which is initially of low intensity but gradually increases; in the design used in my own laboratory this shock is delivered on a random 50 per cent of trials. Subsequently the animals from both groups are tested with food and high-intensity shock on every trial. The animals trained on the partial punishment schedule show greater resistance to punishment (i.e. run faster to the goal-box) than those trained on simple CRF (Miller 1960; Brown and Wagner 1964). By analogy with the PREE this can be called the 'partial punishment effect'.

There is cross-tolerance between the two effects: a PRF schedule pro-

duces increased resistance to punishment and a partial punishment schedule, increased resistance to extinction (Brown and Wagner 1964). This is
similar to the cross-tolerance which, we have seen, holds between foot-
shock and other forms of stress in the experiments on toughening up
(Weiss *et al.* 1975; Ritter *et al.* 1978). This similarity is reinforced by the
observation that inescapable shock, given before any runway training in a
régime comparable to those used to produce helplessness and toughening
up, can increase subsequent resistance to extinction (Chen and Amsel
1977). Both the PREE and the partial punishment effect are susceptible
to the influence of anti-anxiety drugs, although the changes observed depend on the parameters of the experiment. The clearest effects are obtained at a 24-hour inter-trial interval. Under these conditions the PREE
is abolished by sodium amylobarbitone (Feldon *et al.* 1979) and chlordiazepoxide (Feldon and Gray 1981*a*), and the partial punishment effect is
abolished by chlordiazepoxide (Davis *et al.* 1981). The detailed pattern of
change produced by the drug is the same in the two paradigms: there is
increased resistance to punishment (or extinction) in the CRF group if
the drug is given during the test phase of the experiment; there is decreased resistance to punishment (or extinction) in the partial punishment
(or PRF) group if the drug is given during training; and if the drug is
given throughout both training and test phases, both effects are seen.
Thus, assuming that these phenomena are related to toughening up, they
respond to the anti-anxiety drugs according to the predictions set out
above.

It would be valuable to have data on the effects of these drugs on the
type of phenomenon studied by Weiss and his collaborators. If the anti-
anxiety drugs generally antagonize behavioural adaptation to stress, as
they do in the particular instances of the partial reinforcement and partial
punishment effects, this would severely limit their clinical usefulness and
perhaps even render them, under certain conditions, counter-productive.
This is a topic to which we shall return in Chapter 15.

Anxiety and depression

In the discussion so far I have implicitly treated helplessness as though it
were related to anxiety. Yet it is usually treated as an analogue of depression. There is not necessarily a contradiction between these two points of
view. Clinically, symptoms of anxiety and depression co-exist more often
than either is found in the pure state (Roth *et al.* 1976). Thus it would not
be surprising if experimentally induced stress gave rise to both types of
symptom. On common sense grounds it is almost a contradiction in terms
to suppose that it is possible to expose an animal to a régime of unpredictable and uncontrollable shock *without* making it anxious; and Roth
(1979*a*) points out that some of the symptoms displayed by Seligman's
experimental animals would indicate anxiety if they were seen in human
subjects. Thus the onus is rather on proponents of the view that helpless-

ness is an analogue of depression to offer evidence for this proposition.

In fact, though much indirect evidence has been offered from studies of the behaviour of both animals and normal or clinically depressed human subjects (Seligman 1975; Miller and Norman 1979; Abramson *et al.* 1978), the case for this view is not overwhelming. The most convincing data are probably those from experiments which have investigated the effects on helplessness in animals of treatments that are effective in alleviating human depression. Surprisingly, I have come across only two reports of this kind. One is the observation by Glazer *et al.* (1975), mentioned earlier, that the antidepressant drug, pargyline (an inhibitor of monoamine oxidase), given before a session of inescapable shock, blocked helplessness measured in a subsequent escape-avoidance task. However, the drug was given in a single acute dose and, clinically, antidepressants do not become effective until they have been administered chronically for some 10–20 days (van Praag 1978), a fact which will be important for the discussion later in the chapter. The second relevant experiment investigated the effects of electroconvulsive shock (ECS). This too is an effective antidepressant treatment if it is given some six or seven times over a period of days (Royal College of Psychiatrists 1977). Dorworth and Overmier (1977) report that a treatment of this kind alleviated helplessness in dogs when it was given before the animals were tested in the shuttle-box.

These two experiments offer some support, then, for the view that helplessness is a valid analogue of clinical depression. This is not the place to review the rest of the abundant literature that deals with this problem (see Seligman 1975; Maier and Seligman 1976; Abramson *et al.* 1978; Miller and Norman 1979). Although the issue is far from settled, there continue to be plausible parallels between helplessness and many features of the clinical picture. It is worth considering, therefore, how anxiety and depression might be expected to interact, on the assumption that both are consequences of exposure to inescapable aversive events. In pursuing this speculation I shall assume that 'noradrenergic' helplessness is the relevant analogue for human depression. This is not the position adopted by those who have argued most strongly for the validity of this analogy. Seligman (1975) and Maier and Seligman (1976) argue *both* that 'learned' helplessness is an analogue for depression *and* that the neurochemical phenomena described by Weiss's group are unrelated to this kind of helplessness. But Seligman's position flavours of paradox at this point. For (as we shall see) there is abundant evidence that all treatments which are effective in clinical depression alter the activity of monoaminergic neurons in the brain. Thus, if helplessness (of whatever variety) is an analogue of human depression, we would expect precisely the kind of relation between this phenomenon and monoaminergic function that has been reported by Weiss, Anisman, and their collaborators.

In this and the previous chapter it has been suggested that, under conditions of threat, there occurs an increased noradrenergic, serotonergic, and cholinergic input to the septo-hippocampal system, and an increased noradrenergic input to hypothalamic mechanisms controlling defensive and aggressive behaviour. The effects of these events will include the following: (i) there will be increased activity in the septo-hippocampal system of the kind described in Chapter 10; (ii) there will be increased readiness for defensive and/or aggressive behaviour; and (iii) there will be increased inhibition (from the septo-hippocampal system downstream to the hypothalamus) of this same defensive/aggressive behaviour. As stress continues there is a temporary exhaustion of the functional capacity of noradrenergic neurons, which is apparently most marked in hypothalamic terminals; it is this exhaustion which gives rise to helplessness as this is measured in escape-avoidance behaviour. If we take increased activity in the septo-hippocampal system to correspond to anxiety, and helplessness to correspond to depression, this sequence of events implies that, under conditions of moderately prolonged stress, the initial reaction will be dominated by anxiety but with time there will be an increasing admixture of depression. This general sequence has been proposed by Seligman (1975) and Engel and Schmale (1972) on other grounds, and is in agreement with clinical observation (Roth 1979a). It has been suggested by Engel and Schmale (1972) that the onset of depressive symptoms when escape or other coping behaviour is not possible has an adaptive function, in that it conserves bodily resources (by eliminating useless struggling, etc.) for a time when escape may once more be possible. Jackson *et al.* (1979) similarly suggest that this might be the adaptive function of the increased analgesia they observe after inescapable shock.

Note that, according to this analysis, anxiety and depression are not mutually exclusive: not only are they allowed to co-exist, under many conditions they would be expected to do so. These conditions would be those in which there is simultaneously a strong noradrenergic input to the septo-hippocampal system and some degree of exhaustion in the noradrenergic input to the hypothalamus. Such conditions would be expected to occur rather often, given that there is increased noradrenalin turnover (and therefore increased neuronal functioning) even when the level of noradrenalin is reduced (Stone 1975). Furthermore, since *ex hypothesi* the noradrenergic activation of hypothalamic mechanisms is simultaneously opposed by descending inhibition from the septo-hippocampal system, an incipient exhaustion of the functional capacity of noradrenergic neurons is likely to be felt sooner at a hypothalamic level than in the septo-hippocampal system. None the less, if the exhaustion of noradrenergic functional capacity deepens, we would expect activity in the latter system also to diminish as the booster it normally receives from the dorsal bundle is reduced. At this time, anxiety would begin to lessen, leaving a purer state of depression. Thus, if stress is prolonged at a sufficiently high level, we predict (after an initial passage from anxiety only to anxiety-plus-depression) a further passage to depression only. Such a progression has been suggested several times before (e.g. Seligman 1975; Engel and Schmale 1972), and is consistent with clinical impression (Roth 1979a).

If stress acts to produce anxiety and depression in this manner, how might one design a drug to reverse these conditions? If our analysis so far has been correct, there is no easy answer to this question. It will depend on the point in the temporal evolution of anxiety and depression in response to prolonged stress that has been reached at the time when the drug is applied; on the site in the brain at which the drug produces its maximal effect; and (a point that is elaborated below) on the individual characteristics of the stressed subject.

It is clear that, if we wished to combat anxiety, we would use a drug which reduces the activity of noradrenergic neurons, especially those that innervate the forebrain; and, as we saw in the last chapter, this seems to be an accurate description of the action — or at least part of the action — of the anti-anxiety drugs. But the position is more complicated when it comes to the symptoms of depression. If we equate these to the behaviour that accompanies, and is perhaps caused by, a fall in the level of hypothalamic noradrenalin, one can make out an equally good case for saying that the drug of choice should reduce noradrenergic activity or increase it. By reducing activity in hypothalamic noradrenergic terminals, one might protect the levels of transmitter from falling or allow them to recover if they have fallen already. On the other hand, a drug which increased noradrenergic activity might reinstate the capacity of hypothalamic noradrenergic terminals to perform their functions. If such a drug also acted in the forebrain, the ensuing relief in depression might, however, be purchased at the cost of an increase in anxiety.

It can hardly be counted a credit to our theory that such opposing therapeutic hypotheses can be derived from it. It might be possible to improve on this situation if, in a given case, we knew the balance between heightened noradrenergic activity in the forebrain, heightened activity in the hypothalamus, and exhaustion of noradrenergic function at both these sites; and, no doubt, if would help even more if we could design a drug which acted specifically at one site rather than the other. But neither of these advantages is likely soon to be in our hands. In default of theory, then, let us turn to the data.

When we do so, we find no less confusion. The classic theory of antidepressant action is that these drugs facilitate the functioning of either noradrenalin (Schildkraut 1965) or serotonin (Ashcroft *et al.* 1966). This view is supported by much biochemical evidence relating to both major groups of antidepressant drugs, the tricyclics and the monoamine oxidase inhibitors. The tricyclics block the re-uptake of these transmitters after their release into the synaptic cleft and the MAOI prevent their intraneuronal inactivation, thus increasing in both cases the amount of transmitter available at the postsynaptic junction (Sulser 1978; van Praag 1978). But these effects occur acutely, whereas the therapeutic action of the drug is not felt for several weeks. Thus the therapeutic effect of the antidepressants is either unrelated to the changes they produce at the nerve terminal or, more likely, it is related to adaptations the neuron makes to these changes.

We saw earlier in the chapter how very adaptable the noradrenergic neuron, in particular, is. Evidence that this adaptability is important in mediating the behavioural effects of the antidepressant drugs has been reviewed by Sulser (1978) and Stone (1979a). Following chronic (Schildkraut *et al.* 1970, 1971; Roffler-Tarkov *et al.* 1973) but not acute (Sulser *et al.* 1962, 1964) administration of tricyclics there is a decrease in the level of brain noradrenalin. This may be due to changes in the activity of tyrosine hydroxylase, which has been shown to be reduced in the locus coeruleus and the forebrain after administration of the tricyclic, desimipramine, over a period of 8 days, although no change was seen 24 hours after drug treatment commenced (Segal, Kuczenski, and Mandell 1974). The decreased levels of noradrenalin and TH seen after chronic tricyclic treatment are accompanied by decreased turnover of the neurotransmitter (Rosloff 1975; Rosloff and Davis 1978). These changes are of a kind which would tend to re-establish homeostasis, that is, lower the increased level of noradrenergic function initially created by antidepressant treatment. Other changes with similar effects take place in the postsynaptic receptor. After chronic administration of tricyclics or MAOI there is reduced binding of ligands by β-noradrenergic receptors (Stone 1979a), and a reduced response to noradrenalin applied to brain tissue, as measured by the generation of cyclic adenyl monophosphate (cAMP) (Vetulani, Stawarz, Dingell, and Sulser 1976a; Vetulani and Sulser 1975; Vetulani, Stawarz, and Sulser 1976b; Stone 1979a). The effect of the tricyclics appears to be relatively specific to β-noradrenergic (postsynaptic) receptors, since they do not apparently alter binding to α-noradrenergic, serotonergic, or dopaminergic receptors in the central nervous system (Stone 1979a).

Chronically, therefore, the blockade of noradrenalin re-uptake and degradation produced by the tricyclics and MAOI, respectively, is balanced by other changes which tend to cause a net reduction in the output of noradrenergic neurons. These observations have led Sulser (1978) and Stone (1979a) to stand the classic hypothesis of antidepressant action on its head and propose instead that this is due to a *reduction* in noradrenergic function. If this view is correct, it suggests a fundamental similarity between the mode of action of anti-anxiety drugs and antidepressants, the major difference now being that the former act acutely, the latter chronically.

In line with this approach, Stone (1979a) has also proposed an interesting new look at the phenomenon of toughening up. According to his hypothesis this is based, not on a restoration of initially lowered levels of noradrenalin (and hence an increased functional capacity in central noradrenergic systems), but on subsensitivity of the postsynaptic noradrenergic receptor (giving rise to a decreased functional output from these systems). On this hypothesis, toughening up and antidepressant drugs work via the same underlying mechanism. The effect of initial antidepressant medication or, say, of initial exposure to foot-shock is to liberate noradrenalin at central terminals; but the effect of prolonged medication or repeated sessions of foot-shock is to create subsensitive postsynaptic noradrenergic receptors. In support of this hypothesis, Stone (1978, 1979*b*) has shown that repeated foot-shock over a period of 9 days caused a reduced cAMP response to noradrenalin applied to slices of cerebral cortex. This reduced response to noradrenalin was not seen after acute shock; and in the animals chronically shocked the reduction was about the same size as that seen in rats given chronic desimipramine.

By now the need for double vision imposed by the arguments pursued in this chapter is perhaps creating a sense of dizziness. It appears to be possible to treat depression and its laboratory analogue, helplessness, as being due to either decreased (Weiss *et al.* 1976) or increased (Stone 1979*a*) noradrenergic activity; and antidepressant therapy and toughening up inversely as increasing (Schildkraut 1965; Weiss *et al.* 1976) or decreasing (Sulser 1978; Stone 1979*a*) noradrenergic function. Thus, on the view of anxiety developed in this book, this condition becomes more or less identical to depression if we adopt the Sulser–Stone position, and more or less its exact opposite if we stand with Schildkraut and Weiss. Clearly, both points of view cannot be correct; or at least they cannot be correct at the same time, in the same brain region and the same individual.

The Sulser–Stone position is supported by the fact that the time-course of the therapeutic effects of the antidepressants is better correlated with the signs of lowered than with those of increased noradrenergic function. It can also find comfort in the observation that the tricyclic antidepressant, iprindole, does not block noradrenalin uptake or alter its turnover (Rosloff and Davis 1978), yet it shares with other tricyclics the capacity to reduce the postsynaptic cAMP response to noradrenalin (Vetulani *et al.* 1976*a*). However, if antidepressant action is due to reduced noradrenergic function, and especially to subsensitivity in β-noradrenergic receptors, it should be possible to treat depression with β-noradrenergic blockers, such as propranolol. But these drugs do not appear to have any antidepressant action (van Praag 1978; A. R. Green, personal communication); rather, they reduce anxiety (Redmond 1979). Thus it is unlikely that antidepressant activity is explicable *simply* in terms of lowered noradrenergic function. Nor is it likely that such activity is due *simply* to increased noradrenergic function; for, if it were, antidepressants should act much more quickly than they do.

We have already sketched a way out of this dilemma, in considering the possibility that there might be simultaneously heightened noradrenergic activity in the forebrain (corresponding to anxiety) and some degree of functional exhaustion in noradrenergic terminals in the hypothalamus (corresponding to depression). But before we can pursue this possibility further it is necessary to consider the differences that are found between individual patients, all of whom are diagnosed as suffering in one way or another from depression. For it is clear that depressions are not all of the same kind.

We touch here on an argument which has exercised psychiatrists and psychologist alike for many decades. Roughly, there are three positions which have been adopted. According to the first, there is one kind of depression, and the differences seen between different patients are superficial only. According to the second, there are quite distinct categories of depression, although those who hold this position do not necessarily agree among themselves as to the number or nature of the categories. According to the third, there is a smooth continuum along which depressions and depressive individuals vary. Those who hold this last position give different names to the poles which define the extremes of the continuum, but there is a good deal of agreement about the symptoms and other characteristics to be found at each pole. The literature dealing with this problem is large and highly technical, and I do not intend to review it here. The conclusions I shall present are largely based on the work of Roth's group in Newscastle and their recent reviews (Roth *et al.* 1976; Roth 1979 *a*, *b*), although they are not entirely identical to the conclusions these workers draw themselves.

The position that depression is a completely undifferentiated syndrome can certainly be rejected. It is harder to choose between the other two alternatives (separate syndromes or a continuum). It is, in fact, not essential for the purposes of the present argument to do so. This is fortunate, since the best description of the available data is that they form a kind of lumpy continuum.

Depressive patients or syndromes (the terms are largely interchangeable, since, when they present with repeated illnesses, patients usually run true to form) can be ordered along a continuum which has no definite breaks. The poles of this continuum are variously labelled 'neurotic' vs. 'psychotic' or 'reactive' vs. 'endogenous'. Neither pair of terms is satisfactory. There is little evidence that 'reactive' depression requires more environmental stress than 'endogenous' depression (Brown and Harris 1978; Brown, Ni Bhrolchain, and Harris 1979), and the relation of 'psychotic' depression to other psychoses remains unclear. I shall speak here of 'neurotic' (= 'reactive') and 'psychotic' (= 'endogenous') depression. At the neurotic pole of this dimension one finds such features as autonomic signs of anxiety, obsessional symptoms, irritability, restlessness, and difficulty in falling asleep; at the psychotic pole, marked slowing of responses (retardation), early morning wakening, depressed mood particularly pronounced in the morning, weight loss, feelings of hopelessness, and tendencies to be male and older. These differences are quantitative, not absolute, as befits the notion of a continuum. However, Roth's group has shown that, if one chooses the items which best differentiate between extreme neurotic and psychotic depressions, weights them in such a way as to maximize this differentiation, and uses a scale so made up (a 'discriminant function') to give each individual a score indicating his position between the extreme poles, one then obtains a bimodal distribution of individuals. It is in this sense that the neurotic–psychotic dimension is 'lumpy'. But the lumpiness falls well short of a complete differentiation between two types of depression. Thus it appears that depressions come in all shades between neurotic and psychotic, but with some tendency to hug the extremes.

It will not have escaped the reader's notice that the items that define the neurotic pole of this continuum include symptoms that are also found in states of anxiety (see Chapter 14). Is neurotic depression, then, simply anxiety under another name? Not quite. For Roth's group has performed a similar exercise to distinguish between anxiety and depression. Again there is a definite continuum relating the two conditions, with no empty space along it; but it is once more possible, using discriminant function analysis, to produce a bimodal distribution of patients, some with predominantly anxious symptoms, others with predominantly depressive ones. When the symptoms which distinguish the two poles of this anxiety–depression continuum are examined, however, they resemble very closely those which discriminate between neurotic and psychotic depression, as shown in Fig. 12.4. This presents the results of a principal component analysis (Harman 1960) of more than 300 variables scored on a cohort of 145 individuals 'judged on clinical grounds to be suffering from a primary mood disorder of anxiety, depression or both combined' (Roth *et al.* 1976). It can be seen, for example, that retardation and early morning waking mark out the extreme 'depression' pole of this continuum (the first principal component), just as they mark out the 'psychotic depression' pole of the neurotic–psychotic continuum. Thus it would seem that our lumpy continuum stretches from anxiety through neurotic to psychotic depression.

It is possible to relate this continuum to the broader framework provided by the description of personality in normal individuals (see Chapter 16). For, as shown in Fig. 12.3, there is a clear relation between the personality space described by H. J. and S. B. G. Eysenck (1969) and the anxiety–depression continuum. At the anxiety pole one finds high neuroticism (N) and low extroversion (E) scores; at the depression pole, the reverse. Essentially the same loadings on these dimensions of personality are found if one considers only the part of this continuum which runs from neurotic to psychotic depression: the neurotic depressive has higher N and lower E scores than the psychotic depressive (Kerr *et al.* 1970; Paykel 1971). This is a topic to which we return in Chapter 16.

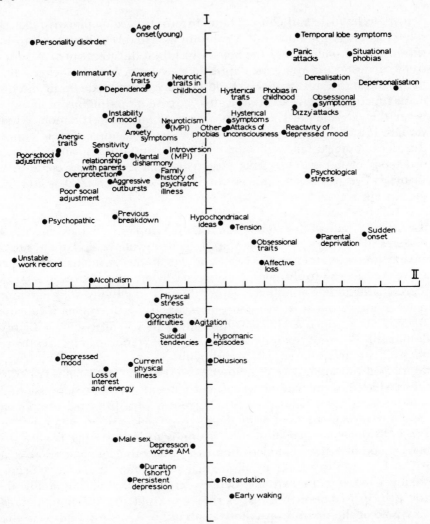

Figure 12.4. Plot of 58 items on Roth *et al.*'s (1976) first two principal components derived from an analysis of the scores of 145 patients suffering from anxiety, depression, or both. The first principal component (I) extends from anxiety (up) to depression (down).

We are now in a position to return to the main concern of this section: what is the relation between anxiety and depression? Given the continuum, lumpy or not, that we have just described, we must answer differently for neurotic and psychotic depression. Neurotic depression shades over into anxiety in such a manner that it is difficult if not impossible to say where one begins and the other ends; but psychotic depression is clearly different from, and perhaps even opposed to, anxiety. This conclusion must make one wonder whether it is, after all, necessary to choose between the two opposite views of depression and antidepressant medication which, as we saw above, have been proposed on the one hand by Schildkraut (1965) and Weiss *et al.* (1976) and, on the other, by Sulser (1978) and Stone (1979*a*). They could both be right, but at different points along the anxiety–depression continuum just described.

It has been suggested above that, as stress is prolonged, one first sees symptoms of anxiety in a relatively pure state (increased forebrain noradrenergic activity); then a mixture of anxiety and depression, as functional exhaustion begins to occur in hypothalamic noradrenergic terminals; and finally a relatively pure state of depression as functional exhaustion sets in also at the level of forebrain terminals. I have described this progression along a temporal dimension in the same individuals. But one might also expect to see it along a dimension of individual differences. Thus one might suppose that, under identical conditions of stress, individuals with a relatively great functional capacity in noradrenergic neurons would display predominantly symptoms of anxiety; those with a moderate functional capacity, mixed symptoms of anxiety and depression; and those with a weak functional capacity, symptoms predominantly of depression.

There is some evidence from animal experiments for individual differences of this kind. The Maudsley Nonreactive strain of rats has been bred to be less fearful than the Maudsley Reactive strain (Broadhurst 1960, 1975; Gray 1971*a*). Furthermore, evidence from the shape of the theta-driving curve (Chapter 7) suggests that there is a less powerful noradrenergic signal to the septo-hippocampal system in Nonreactive relative to Reactive rats (Drewett *et al.* 1977). We would therefore predict that Nonreactive rats would be more prone to 'depression' (as defined above) than Reactives. Consistent with this prediction, Franklin and Broadhurst (1979) found greater helplessness (impairment of shuttle-box avoidance by prior inescapable shock) in the Nonreactive than in the Reactive strain.

We may now bring this putative neurochemical dimension into contact with the psychiatric dimension already described. For this we require simply the hypothesis that the anxious pole of the anxiety–depression continuum consists of individuals with a high reactivity in central noradrenergic neurons (which would increase their susceptibility to anxiety) and also a high functional capacity in these neurons (giving a high resistance to depression); conversely, the depressive pole consists of individuals with low reactivity and a low functional capacity in central noradrenergic neurons. There are several lines of evidence which are consistent with this hypothesis.

First, the characteristic symptoms that define the two poles of the anxiety–depression continuum are as one would expect. Detailed discussion of the symptoms of anxiety will be left till Chapter 14. As to the symptoms of psychotic depression, these — especially motor retardation and weight loss — are similar to those which, as we have seen, can be created in animals by exposure to inescapable shock and which are apparently due to lowered noradrenergic function (Weiss *et al.* 1976; Stone 1979*a*).

Second, age is positively associated with vulnerability to psychotic depression (Fig. 12.3). This suggests that age increases the risk of functional exhaustion in central noradrenergic neurons. Consistent with this inference, Ritter and Pelzer (1978) report that the fall in central noradrenalin levels in rats exposed to inescapable shock is greater, the older the animal.

Third, individuals occupying different positions along the anxiety–depression continuum respond differently to antidepressive therapies. This suggests that different brain mechanisms underlie the conditions they display (Roth *et al.* 1976; Roth 1979*a, b*). This point is more substantial than the first two, and requires more detailed exposition.

It is clear, to begin with, that some patients classified as depressive respond to treatments which are also effective in anxiety. Thus such typical antianxiety drugs as chlordiazepoxide have been found to reduce self-reported depression as much as they reduce anxiety, and they produce much the same degree of improvement in patients whose predominant complaint is depression as in those whose predominant complaint is anxiety (Kellner *et al.* 1979; Frith *et al.* 1979; Johnstone *et al.* 1980). These studies were conducted with out-patients, who therefore consisted principally of neurotic rather than psychotic depressives. Another treatment which is as effective in depression as in anxiety is psychosurgery (see Chapter 13): both prefrontal (Kelly *et al.* 1972; Ström-Olsen and Carlisle 1971) and cingulate (Mitchell-Heggs *et al.* 1976; Powell 1979) lesions have been reported to reduce anxiety and depression to the same extent. The patients who are submitted to these operations are typically extremely neurotic and introverted, as measured for example by the Maudsley Personality Inventory. After surgery there is a considerable fall in the N score and a smaller rise in the E score (Powell 1979). Thus the patients who benefit from frontal and cingulate lesions are preoperatively close to the neurotic or anxious pole of the anxiety–depression continuum, and they appear to move away from this pole after surgery. The simplest interpretation of these findings is that there is no essential difference between the syndromes of anxiety and neurotic depression: they respond in the same manner to anti-anxiety drugs and prefrontal or cingulate lesions because they constitute one, not two, disorders.

If we turn to treatments regarded principally as effective in depression, these string out in three positions along the anxiety–depression continuum (Roth *et al.* 1976; Roth 1979*a, b*). The MAOI were introduced as antidepressants, but in fact they have little effect in cases of psychotic depression. In contrast, they have been reported to be definitely effective, not only in cases of depression in which anxiety figures prominently, but even for such classical anxiety symptoms as phobias (Paykel *et al.* 1979). The tricyclics are most effective in psychotic depression, but they have some lesser effects in the neurotic variety. Rachman *et al.* (1979) report that chlorimipramine, one of this group of drugs, is valuable in the treatment of obsessional patients; but the effect was on depressive mood as such, and neither extended to obsessive–compulsive symptoms nor interacted with the changes produced in these by behavioural treatment. Finally, electroconvulsive therapy (ECT) seems to be clearly more effective in psychotic depression than in other affective illnesses.

The differences between the types of illness that respond to the MAOI and tricyclics, respectively, would not be predicted by either the Schildkraut or the Sulser–Stone hypothesis taken alone. It is possible that, in the case of the MAOI, postsynaptic receptor subsensitivity outweighs the decreased catabolism of noradrenalin; conversely, the net effect produced by the tricyclics is perhaps weighted towards the activation of noradrenergic transmission resulting from decreased re-uptake of the transmitter. A further possibility is that the brain sites at which these effects are strongest differ between the two classes of drug. Investigations of peripheral structures indicate that subsensitivity of the response to noradrenalin after antidepressant treatment may occur in some tissues but not others (Stone 1979a). There is evidence that such subsensitivity can be found *in vivo* in the terminals of locus coeruleus fibres. Thus Korf, Sebens, and Postema (1978) report that the rise in cAMP levels produced in the cerebral cortex by stimulation of the locus coeruleus is reduced by chronic administration of tricyclics. On the theory advanced here, this would be expected to have an anti-anxiety effect, while an increase in noradrenergic function in the hypothalamus would be expected to antagonize depression. If the former effect is relatively greater after treatment with MAOI and the latter after treatment with tricyclics, this could account for the predominantly anti-anxiety effects of the former class of drugs and the predominantly antidepressant effect of the latter. These hypotheses are obviously speculative, but they are readily open to experimental test.

If we turn finally to the mode of action of ECT, there is some evidence that this treatment, like the antidepressant drugs, reduces the postsynaptic β-noradrenergic response (Vetulani and Sulser 1975; Vetulani *et al.* 1976a), an effect which, on the arguments pursued above, we would certainly not predict. However, there is also evidence pointing to a different mode of action. Modigh (1976) gave rats ECS on a schedule which is clinically effective in man and observed a sustained increase in the activity of tyrosine hydroxylase in regions of the brain that are rich in noradrenalin, together with a small and transient increase in noradrenalin turnover. The same worker (Modigh 1975) also reports an increase in the postsynaptic response to dopamine after ECS; while Green and Grahame-Smith confirm this effect and also find an increased postsynaptic response to serotonin (Evans *et al.* 1976; Green *et al.* 1977; Costain *et al.* 1979; Green and Deakin 1980). The increased sensitivity of dopamine and serotonin receptors seen after ECS is mediated by noradrenergic mechanisms, since it is blocked in animals in which the dorsal and ventral noradrenergic bundles have first been destroyed by local injection of 6-OHDA (Green and Deakin 1980). None of these effects is seen if ECS is given singly, rather than on a schedule mimicking the clinically effective treatment in man. Thus it is possible that the therapeutic effect of ECT is due to the development of enhanced monoaminergic transmission rather generally in the brain, and that the increased activity in noradrenergic systems observed by Modigh (1976) plays a key role in this development. This mode of action would be in general agreement with the classic theory of antidepressant action (Schildkraut 1965). If, however, as Stone (1979*a*) suggests, ECT works by reducing the postsynaptic receptor response to noradrenalin, and if this is also the mechanism of action of the MAOI, some other explanation must be sought for the very different kinds of patients who respond to each of these treatments.

Clearly, this issue is far from resolved, and there are likely to be many further discoveries before we fully understand the mode of action of any of these treatments. Crews and Smith (1978), for example, report that long-term administration of antidepressants gives rise to subsensitivity in peripheral presynaptic α-noradrenergic receptors, and (unlike the corresponding changes in β-receptors) this would tend to *increase* noradrenergic transmission. None the less, it seems probable that there is one kind of depression which is found in neurotic introverts, which is closely related to anxiety, and which responds to the same types of therapy as anxiety; and another kind which is found in stable extroverts, which is not so closely related to anxiety, and which responds to different types of therapy than does anxiety. A more parsimonious conclusion is that there exist only two states: anxiety, found especially in neurotic introverts, and depression, found especially in stable extroverts; and that these occur in varying mixtures as a function of position along the personality continuum that links these two extremes. In addition, it can be proposed that anxiety is due in part to excessive activity in forebrain noradrenergic systems, and depression to underactivity in diencephalic noradrenergic systems; and that anti-anxiety drug action is due in part to a reduction in the former, and antidepressant action to an increase in the latter.

13

The role of the prefrontal cortex

Much of the argument pursued in this book is derived from the action of the anti-anxiety drugs. The effects of drug therapy are temporary; more positively speaking, they are reversible. There is, however, another approach to the therapy of anxiety whose effects are irreversible. This approach is exemplified by the animal experiments on the effects of lesions to the septo-hippocampal system (Chapter 6) and its monoaminergic afferents (Chapter 11): one can modify anxiety by destroying part of the brain systems that produce it. This drastic technique has also been applied to cases of human anxiety. But the target areas have been different: the prefrontal and cingulate regions of the neocortex. Damage to these areas has served successfully as a treatment of last resort for chronic, severe, and disabling states of anxiety (Marks 1969; Powell 1979). What are the implications of this fact for the theory of anxiety developed here?

It is simpler to start with the cingulate cortex. In the theory of septo-hippocampal function developed in Chapter 10, several important roles were attributed to this region. First, it lies on the loop which subserves the generation of predictions for entry into the subicular comparator. As we saw, single-unit studies support this hypothesis by demonstrating that, during reversal learning, cingulate neurons fire in relation to the contingencies that were correct during acquisition of the initial discrimination (Gabriel *et al.* 1977). Second, it may contribute information about the next intended motor response, to be used in determining the content of the next subicular prediction. In accordance with this hypothesis, some cingulate units fire during the delay period of a delayed-response task in relation to the direction of the following response (Niki and Watanabe 1976). Third, it is possible that the efferent projection from the subiculum to the cingulate cortex plays a role in inhibiting the execution of ongoing motor programmes when the subicular comparator detects mismatch.

From these postulates it follows that destruction of the cingulate cortex should have profound effects on the functioning of the septo-hippocampal system. Since the generation of predictions is impaired, it should be harder for the subicular comparator to detect mismatch; and, if mismatch were none the less detected, the execution of behavioural inhibition is likely to be impaired. In behavioural terms, this implies that someone with a cingulate lesion will be less likely to notice failure, absence of reward, etc., and less able to activate the various routines attributed to the septo-hippocampal system in its 'control' mode (Chapter 10). Among these routines is the active search for stimuli associated with mismatch; thus someone with a cingulate lesion should search the environment less actively for threat. In emotional terms, this should appear as a reduction in anxiety, an inference which will become clearer when we discuss the symptoms of anxiety in the next chapter.

The data from several recent studies of the effects of cingulate lesions, reviewed by Powell (1979), are consistent with this deduction. The majority of patients treated in this way were suffering from chronic and severe obsessive–compulsive symptoms or anxiety state (see Chapter 14). The success rate has been good. Thus Mitchell-Heggs *et al.* (1976) report a follow-up of 15 cases of anxiety state and 27 obsessional patients who had had severely disabling symptoms for an average of 11 years. Sixteen months after the operation 89 per cent of the obsessionals and 66 per cent of the patients with anxiety state showed improvement. This improvement was found on a variety of measures of anxiety and obsessional behaviour, it was highly significant statistically, and on many measures it was quantitatively substantial. The other studies reviewed by Powell (1979) agree with the report by Mitchell-Heggs *et al.* (1976). Thus there seems little doubt that the operation indeed reduces subjective anxiety and the behavioural symptoms associated with this. Furthermore, the operation is apparently very free from side-effects (Powell 1979); there is no impairment in intelligence, nor any of the apathy which is one consequence of prefrontal lesions.

This seems, then, to provide a satisfactory fit between theory and observation. But in a way the fit is too good. On the theory developed in this book, anxiety has in effect been defined as that state which is susceptible to the action of the anti-anxiety drugs. Development of the notions, first, of the behavioural inhibition system and then of its neural counterpart has been based on that definition. But the operation of cingulectomy, not unnaturally, has been used to treat patients whose condition is *resistant* to pharmacotherapy. For example, Laitinen and Vilkki (1972) produced cingulate lesions in 20 patients suffering from drug-resistant anxiety; all but two of them benefited from the operation. It is possible that resistance to the action of anti-anxiety drugs is due to the development of tolerance, given the long duration of illness before a patient would normally be considered a candidate for the drastic option of psychosurgery. But there is an alternative possibility: neocortical structures may play, at least in man, a role in the production of anxiety which goes beyond that which we have so far attributed to them. This is a possibility to which we shall return after considering the effects of prefrontal lesions.

The use of prefrontal lesions (prefrontal lobotomy, or the fibre-cutting operation known as 'leucotomy') has a longer, richer, and far more alarming history than that of cingulectomy. It was originally introduced as a treatment for schizophrenia, for which, many thousands of gratuitous operations later, it was found to be of absolutely no use (Willett 1960). But it turns out to alleviate those same symptoms of anxiety, obsessions, and depression upon which cingulate lesions act (Marks 1969; Kelly *et al.* 1972; Tan *et al.* 1971; Ström-Olsen and Carlisle 1971). This too is apparently a satisfactory fit between theory and observation, since the first statement of the model elaborated in this book (Gray 1970b) attributed to the prefrontal cortex the role of cortical representation of the behavioural inhibition system. It is not clear, however, that the much greater development that that model has now undergone still allows the prefrontal cortex to fit so neatly into place in the overall puzzle.

We have considered the relation of the prefrontal cortex to the arguments pursued in this book at several points. Anatomically (Chapter 3) there are undoubtedly close connections between the prefrontal cortex and the septo-hippocampal system. In monkeys there are prefrontal projections to the entorhinal cortex (Van Hoesen *et al.* 1972, 1975; Van Hoesen and Pandya 1975), to the hippocampus (Leichnetz and Astruc 1976), to the cingulate cortex (Pandya, Dye, and Butters 1971), to the septal area (Johnson, Rosvold, and Mishkin 1968; Tanaka and Goldman 1976) and to the mammillary bodies (Jacobson, Butters, and Tovsky 1978). Functionally, the prefrontal cortex was tentatively allotted (Chapter 10) the task of providing the septo-hippocampal system with information about the motor programmes controlling the animal's behaviour at any particular moment. It was suggested that this function could be performed either by way of the fronto-cingulate projection, in which case the information so transmitted would contribute to the formation of predictions about the next expected event; or by way of the fronto-entorhinal projection, in which case the relevant information would form part of the description identifying the current state of the sensory world; and both these routes might be used.

This is a much more detailed theory than the one I advanced in 1970. The lines of the puzzle have become sharper and more clearly outlined, with the consequence that it is much harder to fit extra pieces into it. It is no longer sufficient to note that, in animal experiments, some of the behavioural effects of prefrontal lesions resemble those produced by septal or hippocampal lesions (Gray 1970b), a generalization that has in any case been questioned (Passingham 1970). We should now be able to make more precise predictions as to which particular behavioural changes should be observed after prefrontal lesions.

If the theory so far is correct, damage to the prefrontal cortex should have the consequence that the septo-hippocampal system is inadequately informed of the motor programme which currently controls behaviour. It should therefore be impaired in its normal functions of (i) detecting occasions on which the goal of a motor programme is not achieved (failure), and (ii) comparing alternative programmes, including alternative descriptions of the same motor response ('turn left', 'approach white', 'alternate', etc.), to determine which, if any, is able to circumvent failure. From this it follows that prefrontal lesions should impair the subject's ability to detect failure and correct plans. But does it follow that such lesions should reduce anxiety? On the theory so far, not necessarily. This would depend on the nature of the stimuli which, in a given instance, evoke anxiety. If these are themselves the consequence of a failure to carry out a planned action programme, prefrontal lesions might be expected to reduce anxiety because of the reduced detectability of failure. But if they have other origins — e.g. innate fear stimuli or stimuli associated with an aversive UCS (Chapter 14) — a reduction in anxiety would not be expected. Indeed, if anxiety consists in the entry of an alarm signal (of noradrenergic, serotonergic, or intrahippocampal origin) into the septo-hippocampal system, as proposed in Chapters 10 and 11, the consequence of a lesion which leaves the alarm bells ringing but weakens the capacity of the septo-hippocampal system to deal with the problem that rings them ought, at least under some circumstances, to be an *increase* in anxiety.

Even in the case in which anxiety is caused by a failure to carry out a planned action programme, we must distinguish between two ways in which this can happen. The first is when failure consists in an *intrinsic* discrepancy between the intended and the executed action. Take, for example, an obsessional patient for whom a compulsive ritual (e.g. the ubiquitous hand-washing routine) has become a source of relief (Chapter 14). For such a patient failure to complete the ritual in the self-prescribed manner can itself produce a further access of anxiety. In such a case one might expect prefrontal lesions to impair the detectability of failure and thus to reduce anxiety stemming from this source. The second way in which failure can occur is for a source of reinforcement *extrinsic* to the action programme to be missing, even though the intended action has itself been completed correctly. A simple example of this is the omission of a food reward during extinction of an instrumental response, as in a typical animal experiment. There is no reason, on the theory, to suppose that prefrontal lesions will reduce the detectability of non-reward as such. This has been attributed to the joint action of the subicular comparator, the septo-hippocampal connections, and the ascending noradrenergic innervation of the septo-hippocampal system (Chapter 10 and 11). However, we would expect prefrontal lesions to impair the capacity to alter behaviour to take account of the changed reinforcement contingencies. Thus, in the case considered, resistance to extinction would be increased because the animal is less able to identify the motor programme that needs emendation. In emotional terms, this might well correspond again to an increase in anxiety: the animal can detect that reward is absent, but it is unable to do anything about the conditions that lead to this unfortunate state of affairs.

The prediction we make, therefore, is that prefrontal lesions will reduce anxiety only under conditions in which the stimuli eliciting anxiety constitute a mismatch between the intended outcome of a motor programme and its actual, intrinsic outcome, that is, completion of the motor programme itself. Is a prediction constrained in this way able to account for the beneficial effects of prefrontal lesions as a therapy for human anxiety? To some extent, perhaps. Thus prefrontal leucotomy has been reported to benefit obsessive–compulsive patients (Tan, Marks, and Marset 1971). This finding can probably be accommodated within the analysis advanced above, as the hand-washing example shows. A similar account can be applied without too much strain to many other compulsive rituals. To take just one further example, rituals concerned with tidyness and orderliness must almost certainly be weakened if the capacity to detect and react to discrepancies between intended and executed outcomes of motor programmes is impaired. More abstractly — and thus more dangerously — one may speculate that such an impairment weakens the tendency, commonly found in both obsessive and neurotic depressive patients, to evaluate one's own conduct generally and continually against a set of internalized, often very high, standards. But agoraphobia also benefits from prefrontal lesions (Marks, Birley, and Gelder 1966). If this is a form of passive avoidance behaviour (see Chapter 14), it is difficult to see why it should disappear when the capacity to judge the intrinsic outcomes of motor programmes is impaired.

Thus, as in the case of cingulate damage, the therapeutic effects of prefrontal lesions, while not completely unexpected, are a little too good to be encompassed by the theory as it has so far been developed. Let us turn, therefore, to the experimental literature on prefrontal lesions, to see whether this can take us any further.

The behavioural effects of prefrontal lesions

Unfortunately, research in this field is fraught with multiple difficulties of interpretation. The first concerns the very meaning of the term 'prefrontal cortex'. Until now I have deliberately avoided breaking this concept up into portions corresponding to more specific regions of the cortical mantle. This is because it is by no means clear how such a parcellation should be carried out, particularly if one wishes simultaneously to encompass findings that have been made in man, monkeys, and rodents. In discussing the behavioural functions of the hippocampus we had one inestimable advantage: the anatomy of this structure is well worked out, and in a way which is independent of behavioural findings. The problem with which we are now faced is so far different that a recent review of the literature divides the prefrontal cortex of the monkey (the most extensively studied family of species) into 5–7 separate regions exclusively on behavioural grounds (Rosenkilde 1979). Thus, where the prefrontal cortex is concerned, behavioural research runs ahead of anatomical observations, and these are sought after the event in order to make sense out of the functional parcellation already set up. The trouble with this kind of bootstrapping operation is that it is hard to know when it has stopped. Thus the prefrontal cortex has gone from two functionally defined regions in

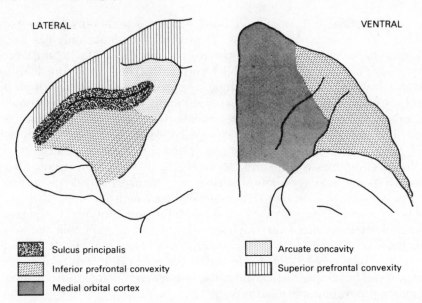

Figure 13.1. Division of the monkey prefrontal cortex into five regions on functional grounds by Rosenkilde (1979).

1965 to seven in 1979, and both the boundaries of these regions and the functions attributed to them change from experiment to experiment (Brutkowski 1965; Rosenkilde 1979; see Fig. 13.1).

These difficulties become still greater if we extend the compass of our interest beyond the monkey. Thus, in the rat, the prefrontal cortex as a whole was not even clearly defined until Leonard (1969) established which regions receive projections from the mediodorsal nucleus of the thalamus that are similar to those which innervate the prefrontal cortex in the monkey. On the basis of these connections it was possible tentatively to identify two regions in the rat's rostral cortex as corresponding to monkey prefrontal cortex (Fig. 13.2). One of these is thought to be roughly equivalent to monkey dorsolateral prefrontal cortex (Brutkowski 1965); in the rat it lies dorsomedially, extending ventrally into the medial walls of the hemispheres and caudally into a supra-callosal region which was earlier treated as belonging to the cingulate cortex. The second is thought to be roughly equivalent to monkey orbitofrontal cortex (Brutkowski 1965); in the rat it lies ventrolaterally, along the upper lip of the rhinal sulcus. Confirmation of these equivalences has been provided by the observation that, in both rat and monkey, these same regions receive a dopaminergic projection from nucleus A 10 (Dahlström and Fuxe 1965) in the ventral tegmental area (Divac *et al.* 1978; Emson and Koob 1978). The change

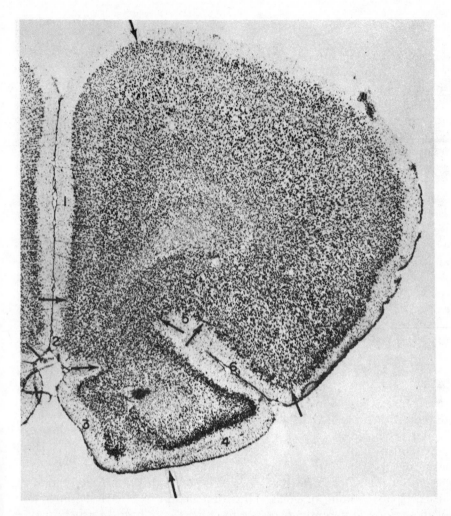

Figure 13.2. Photographs of Nissl-stained frontal section of rat brain showing, *inter alia*, the areas to which the mediodorsal nucleus of the thalamus (MD) projects, i.e. regions 1 and 6, each demarcated by arrows. Region 1 lies along the midline, region 6 just above the rhinal sulcus. Region 1 probably corresponds to dorsolateral prefrontal cortex in the monkey and region 6, to the orbitofrontal cortex. (From Leonard (1969).)

AC = anterior commissure;   AD = anterodorsal nucleus;
AM = anteromedial nucleus;   AS = anterior segment of MD;
AV = anteroventral nucleus;   CC = corpus callosum;
ES = external segment of MD;   F = fornix;
Hl = habenula: lateral nucleus   Hm = habenula: medial nucleus;
IS = internal segment of MD;   OB = olfactory bulb;
PF = parafascicular nucleus;   PV = periventricular nuclei;
SM = stria medullaris;   Vd = Vic d'Azyr's bundle (mammillo-thalamic tract);   VM = ventromedial nucleus of the thalamus.

that these observations have wrought in our conception of the functional anatomy of the rat's prefrontal cortex is so great that little of the research on the behavioural effects of frontal lesions in this or related species now lends itself readily to interpretation if it was carried out more than about 10 years ago.

If we attempt to pass from monkey to man, the situation is, if anything, still worse. In man we must again rely heavily on behaviour-based anatomy, and, of course, generally with very unsystematic lesions to which to relate behaviour. What is more, at those points at which comparison between simian and human behaviour seems most possible, there is apparently a major divergence between the cortical locations of different functions. Thus reversal learning is most markedly impaired in the monkey after damage to parts of the orbital frontal cortex (Rosenkilde 1979; Deuel and Mishkin 1977), as defined by Brutkowski (1965; see Fig. 13.1), whereas in man apparently similar deficits follow upon dorsolateral frontal damage (Milner 1963, 1964).

Given these difficulties, it is premature to attempt a complete survey of the experimental literature on the behavioural effects of prefrontal lesions. I shall confine myself, therefore, to a few general observations which bear either on the theory of prefrontal involvement with the septo-hippocampal system developed above or on the observed effects of prefrontal damage in man.

Several of the conclusions reached by Rosenkilde (1979) in his review of the behavioural effects of lesions to the different regions of monkey prefrontal cortex shown in Fig. 13.1 are consistent with the hypothesis that the functions discharged by this part of the brain are in part related to the organization of motor programmes. The region of most importance in this respect lies dorsolaterally and includes the sulcus principalis and the superior prefrontal convexity (Fig. 13.1). Rosenkilde (1979) suggests that the sulcus principalis is concerned with the representation of absent spatial stimuli or goals. Thus destruction or electrical stimulation of this region apparently gives rise to deficits only in tasks which involve both spatial stimuli and a delay, such as spatial delayed response and spatial delayed alternation. As to the superior prefrontal convexity, this may be concerned with the perception or storage of information regarding the subject's own responses. Thus Passingham (1978) and Manning (1978) find impairments after dorsolateral lesions in the monkey's ability to use movement-produced cues (in a counting task) to control a choice response; Passingham (1978) showed that the focus for this deficit was not in the sulcus principalis. Another task which depends on the use of movement-produced cues is single (go no-go) alternation. It is consistent with Passingham and Manning's observations, therefore, that Goldman *et al.* (1971) found a substantial impairment in this task after dorsolateral prefrontal lesions; and as in Passingham's (1978) experiment, lesions confined to the sulcus principalis did not have this effect. Single-unit evidence is also consistent with a role for dorsolateral prefrontal cortex in the organization of motor programmes (Fuster 1973; Kubota and Niki 1971; Niki and Watanabe 1976). Thus Niki and Watanabe (1976) trained monkeys on a conditional discrimination in which the position of a stimulus (left or right) signalled the correct direction for a response (up or down). Some units responded to the position of the cue (only to left or only to right) and others to the impending direction of response (only if up or only if down).

These observations suggest, then, that the prefrontal cortex (and especially that part of it which, in the monkey, lies dorsolaterally) has access to the kind of information it needs if it is to instruct the septo-hippocampal system about current motor programmes. But it is unlikely that the prefrontal cortex serves only such an auxiliary function. It is probable, rather, that it takes an active part in the control of motor programmes, or in their selection. Such a function takes the prefrontal cortex out of the orbit of anxiety, as that notion has been analysed in this book; for this comes into play only when motor programmes go wrong. It may be this active function of the prefrontal cortex which accounts for one of the major undesirable side-effects seen after prefrontal leucotomy, namely, apathy and inertia (Powell 1979). These effects are apparently not seen after cingulate damage (Tow and Whitty 1953; Powell 1979). This suggests that information about current motor programmes is transferred from systems which actually control them to ones which merely monitor them by passing from the prefrontal to the cingulate cortex.

The behavioural effects of dorsolateral prefrontal damage in the monkey, then, are consistent with the function we allotted to the prefrontal cortex in Chapter 10 — the provision of information about plans. But this does not solve the problem we identified above: namely, that the theory developed in Chapter 10 does not predict such substantial effects of prefrontal or cingulate lesions on human anxiety as are actually observed. For a possible solution to this problem we must turn to other data, obtained in studies of the behaviour of human subjects after prefrontal lesions. These bring into the discussion a factor which, in the nature of things, could not emerge from experiments using non-human subjects: the verbal control of behaviour.

In several studies of the effects of prefrontal damage in man it has been observed that there is a dissociation between, on the one hand, the patient's ability (intact) to describe the requirements or contingencies of the task he is set and, on the other, his ability (impaired) to control his behaviour in accordance with this description (Rosenkilde 1979).* Dissociations of this kind have been reported in a go no-go discrimination

---

*Note that this dissociation is opposite in sign to the one observed in the amnesic syndrome. Here memory is sometimes behaviourally intact, but the patient cannot describe the contingencies which control his behaviour (see Chapter 9).

(Drewe 1975*a, b;* Toczek 1960) and on the Wisconsin card sorting test (Milner 1963, 1964), in which the subject has to sort multidimensional stimuli according to principles which are changed every now and then without warning. Note that both of these are tasks which one would expect to be susceptible to septo-hippocampal damage (Chapter 6). It is consistent, therefore, with the theory developed here that they are also impaired after prefrontal lesions, due presumably to the consequent degradation of the information about motor programmes that is made available to the septo-hippocampal system. But the fact that the patients were able correctly to describe the contingencies of reinforcement operative in these experiments, yet could not use this knowledge to control their behaviour, suggests in addition a new principle, namely, that in man the prefrontal cortex serves as a way station by which language systems normally *can* contribute to the correction of behavioural error.

Such a development would make good evolutionary sense. The septo-hippocampal system, as that concept has been developed here, has the task of examining carefully the relations between motor programmes and outcomes when things go wrong. This is the sort of problem to which, typically, human beings bring to bear their full powers of verbal analysis. Thus it would not be surprising if, in the human brain, some sort of liaison were established between the language systems of the temporal and frontal cortex (Lenneberg 1967) and the septo-hippocampal system, so as to arrange, as it were, mutual co-operation. This could take place by way of septo-hippocampal activation of appropriate language circuits, by way of descending cortical control over the septo-hippocampal system, or both. The fact that prefrontal lesions leave verbal descriptions of behavioural contingencies intact, while behaviour itself fails to adapt to these contingencies, suggests that the prefrontal cortex lies athwart the second of these routes. This inference is supported by the studies of Homskaya (1964), who showed that, in normal subjects or patients with other brain lesions, the galvanic skin response and vasomotor orienting response (Sokolov 1960) appear and disappear rapidly in response to verbal instruction (e.g. that a stimulus will, or will no longer, be followed by pain), but that these responses to verbal stimuli are absent in patients with prefrontal damage. Conditioning and extinction of the GSR and vasomotor response to non-verbal stimuli, while not entirely normal, did take place in these patients. Thus the disturbance produced by prefrontal lesions was relatively selective to verbal control over orienting responses.

These observations suggest an explanation of the powerful effects of prefrontal and cingulate lesions on human anxiety. For this we require the assumption that a circuit connecting, by way of the prefrontal cortex, language mechanisms and the septo-hippocampal system permits activation of the latter by verbally coded descriptions of threats. The cingulate cortex might also form part of this circuit; alternatively cingulate lesions may disrupt fibre pathways projecting from the prefrontal cortex to the septo-hippocampal system. These pathways would constitute an alternative alarm bell acting instead of, or in tandem with, the phylogenetically older monoaminergic afferents to the septo-hippocampal system. If this hypothesis is correct, one would expect the 'cortical' alarm to be of relatively little importance in the anxiety elicited by so-called 'prepared' stimuli (Seligman 1971; see Chapter 14), such as snake or spider phobias. Conversely, it would play a relatively large role in phobic or compulsive behaviour that depends heavily on such processes as semantic generalization (Razran 1971), verbal self-description of potential threats, or the perception of situations as threatening only in virtue of their verbal description (e.g. the possibility that one will fail to meet a self-imposed deadline at work). These considerations are *consistent* with — but the argument is too general to permit a stronger term — the type of patient who has been reported to benefit from psychosurgery: extreme neurotic introverts displaying obsessional symptoms, widely generalized phobic behaviour or anxiety states (Powell 1979; Marks *et al.* 1966; Tan *et al.* 1971).

The fact that we have adopted the hypothesis of a descending cortical alarm mechanism travelling by way of the prefrontal cortex does not eliminate the possibility that there is also traffic in the other, corticopetal direction. Such a direction of flow has indeed already been adumbrated in Chapter 10, when we suggested that one route by which the subicular area might take direct control over behaviour is via its projection to the cingulate cortex (Meibach and Siegel 1977c). The same direction of flow is contained in the suggestion, also made in Chapter 10, that the subicular area exercises selective control over sensory input to the hippocampus by way of its projection to the entorhinal area (Köhler *et al.* 1978; Segal 1977e). Either or both of these routes may allow the septo-hippocampal system to gain access to and manipulate cortical information about threats. This is an issue to which we return in the next chapter. For the moment, note simply that, if the source of threat (e.g. a self-imposed deadline) and the information relevant to the threat (e.g. the intellectual operations that must be performed to meet the deadline) are both verbally coded, the role of the ascending monoaminergic pathways afferent to the septo-hippocampal system, which play a critical role in the organization of responses to phylogenetically older varieties of threat (Chapter 11), may become vestigial. Since an important part of the effects of the anti-anxiety drugs is apparently due to an action on these pathways, this may account for the existence of anxiety syndromes which are resistant to pharmacotherapy, yet responsive to cortical (prefrontal, cingulate) lesions (e.g. Laitinen and Vilkki 1972). In this way, though the behavioural effects of the anti-anxiety drugs provided the corner-stone of the theory built in this book, it may be possible to remove it without pulling down the entire edifice.

If these arguments are correct, the role of cortical structures in anxiety has become much greater in man; and common-sense considerations make this conclusion in any case almost a truism. But there is evidence that the prefrontal cortex plays a role in the control of emotional behaviour also in animals in which anxiety is presumably less encephalized than it is in man.

In monkeys there appears to be an especially close involvement with emotional behaviour in the orbitofrontal cortex, i.e. the segments which Rosenkilde (1979) terms the inferior prefrontal convexity and the medial orbital cortex, particularly the latter (see Fig. 13.1). Stimulation of the medial orbital cortex produces a variety of changes in vegetative and autonomic responses, including slowing or arrest of respiration, changes in blood pressure, inhibition of peristalsis, pupillary dilation, salivation, changes in body temperature, increased plasma cortisol, and decreased levels of circulating eosinophils (Rosenkilde 1979). These changes are generally consistent with the occurrence of a stress reaction. As is always the case with such experiments, however, it is not possible to tell whether the electrical stimulus acts as a functional lesion or excites the performance of functions normally discharged by the stimulated neurons. Experiments in which this region of the prefrontal cortex has been ablated go some way to resolve this issue, since increased fear has been seen after large prefrontal lesions when the response to another monkey was observed (Deets *et al.* 1970), and after orbitofrontal lesions when the aversive response to a doll, a model snake, or a human stare was measured (Butter, Mishkin, and Mirsky 1968; Butter and Snyder 1972; Butter, Snyder, and McDonald 1970). The most plausible interpretation of these data is that the orbitofrontal cortex normally exerts an inhibitory influence over fearful behaviour (stimulation then acting as a functional lesion).

The trouble with this interpretation, of course, is that it runs directly counter to the observed clinical effects of prefrontal lesions in man. There are various possible reasons for this discrepancy. First, as we have seen, it is possible that the geographical location in the cortical mantle of different functional subregions of the prefrontal cortex differs in monkeys and man. Second, the lesions carried out in experimental work on monkeys are very different from those practised for therapeutic ends in man. Third, if the hypotheses developed in this chapter are correct, we would expect prefrontal lesions to reduce anxiety in a non-verbal organism only to the extent that anxiety is provoked by a mismatch between a motor programme and its intrinsic outcome (in the sense defined earlier). It is clear that this description does not cover reactions to dolls, stares, snakes, or other monkeys.

Any or all of these reasons might account for the failure usually to observe decreased fear after orbitofrontal lesions in monkeys; but they do not account for an actual increase in fear. The theory developed above predicts such an effect only if the animal is also faced with the need to cope with threat by correcting an inadequate motor programme; and in the experiments cited above this was not the case. Thus we must consider the possibility that, in the monkey, the orbitofrontal cortex exercises an inhibitory control over fear but that, in man, this is overriden under certain conditions by verbally coded controls emanating from other regions of the neocortex. Indeed, one might then see such verbal controls as increasing anxiety by simple disinhibition in the prefrontal cortex. In man prefrontal lesions would therefore increase the basal level of anxiety, but this would be amply compensated in, say, an obsessional patient by removal of the pathway by which internal speech can enhance anxiety. Something of this sort appears to take place in the case of intractable pain, a condition which is also helped by prefrontal lesions. Patients treated in this way report that the pain of which they formerly complained is still present, but no longer bothers them; at the same time, the threshold to externally imposed pain is actually lowered (Chapman *et al.* 1948).

A second possibility, however, is that the relation between prefrontal lobe function and fearful behaviour in primates is exactly the reverse of the one just suggested, and that descending fibres from this region directly excite lower brain centres involved in anxiety rather than serving an inhibitory function. This hypothesis would account for certain aspects of the orbitofrontal syndrome in monkeys that resemble the septo-hippocampal syndrome (Chapter 6) in rodents: increased resistance to extinction (Butter 1969), impaired reversal learning (McEnaney and Butter 1969; Deuel and Mishkin 1977) and impaired single alternation (Butters, Butter, Rosen and Stein 1973; Iversen and Mishkin 1970); although these deficits do not all follow from the same lesions within the general orbitofrontal area (Rosenkilde 1979). On this view, the reaction to dolls, stares, snakes and other monkeys observed in the experiments in which fear has seemed to increase after orbitofrontal lesions do not relate to anxiety, as this term is understood here.* To resolve this issue we would need data relating these reactions to the better understood measures of emotional behaviour used in experiments on the rat, or to the effects of the anti-anxiety drugs, and such data do not seem to exist.

Note, however, that we need not interpret the increased resistance to extinction or impaired reversal and single alternation learning seen after orbitofrontal lesions (see above) as signs of reduced fear. For, as we have seen, on the hypothesis that the prefrontal cortex is concerned with the control of motor programmes and the transmission of information about such programmes to the septo-hippocampal system, it is possible for a lesion in this region to impair the capacity to adjust motor programmes to failure, and simultaneously to increase the emotional response to failure. Thus, in the monkey, orbitofrontal lesions might increase fear while

---

*This move runs into difficulties, however, with the prevalence of snake phobia in human beings, and the widespread use of this type of phobia in the experimental study of anxiety and its treatment in man (see Chapters 14 and 15).

none the less producing some of the same effects as septo-hippocampal damage.

In the absence of further data there is little point in pursuing this discussion further. The best we can conclude is that the primate prefrontal cortex is *somehow* involved in fearful behaviour. Recent experiments show that the same is true in rodents.

Many of these experiments have been concerned with the dopaminergic innervation of the prefrontal cortex originating in nucleus A 10 in the ventral tegmentum (Divac *et al.* 1978; Emson and Koob 1978). This innervation seems to be necessary for the normal functioning of the prefrontal cortex, as shown in an experiment by Brozoski *et al.* (1979) with rhesus monkeys. As we have seen, destruction of the region of the sulcus principalis in this species produces a severe impairment in spatial delayed alternation; Brozoski *et al.* (1979) were able to reproduce this effect by selective destruction of the dopaminergic terminals in the sulcus principalis, achieved by local injection of 6-OHDA. In the rat, Lavielle *et al.* (1978) showed that the turnover of dopamine in the prefrontal and cingulate cortices rose sharply in response to foot-shock. This effect was not seen in other dopaminergically innervated structures (septal area, nucleus accumbens, corpus striatum, amygdala). Furthermore, it was blocked by injections of chlordiazepoxide or diazepam. It seems, therefore, that stress selectively increases the turnover of dopamine in the prefrontal and cingulate cortices, a change which (given the findings reported by Brozoski *et al.* 1979) would probably facilitate the normal function of these regions; and that this effect can plausibly be related to anxiety, since it is blocked by anti-anxiety drugs. The effect of these drugs may be secondary to an action on efferents from the locus coeruleus to A 10 (Lindvall and Björklund 1978; Simon *et al.* 1979). In support of this possibility J. Glowinski (personal communication) has observed decreased dopamine turnover in the prefrontal cortex after destruction of noradrenergic terminals in the ventral tegmental area.

Other work from this group also implicates the prefrontal cortex in anxiety. Thus the increased turnover of prefrontal cortical dopamine after either foot-shock (Hervé *et al.* 1979) or exposure to an open field (Tassin *et al.* 1980) is greater in the more emotional of two strains of mice. In addition, performance on that classic test of anxiety, passive avoidance (step-down, with six training trials before the introduction of shock), was impaired in rats in which the dopaminergic projection from A 10 had been destroyed by local injection of 6-OHDA (Le Moal, Galey, and Cardo 1975). Other evidence implicates the target area of this projection more directly. Thus Lippa *et al.* (1978*b*, 1979) showed that exposure of rats to an approach–avoidance conflict altered the binding of benzodiazepines to tissue taken from the prefrontal cortex (see Chapter 11), and that ablation of the same area, like administration of benzodiazepines, reduced the response-suppressant effects of punishment n this task. It seems possible, therefore, that the prefrontal cortex and its dopaminergic projection play a role in anxiety which is in some ways analogous to that of the septo-hippocampal system and its noradrenergic and serotonergic projections. These roles, furthermore, may be co-ordinated, along with the rest of the activities of the septo-hippocampal system, by means of the theta rhythm (Chapters 4 and 10). For Le Moal and Cardo (1975) have recorded theta in the ventral tegmental area, in the vicinity of A 10, and, like hippocampal theta, this was abolished by medial septal lesions.

These experiments suggest, therefore, that we should expand our concept of the sites of action of the anti-anxiety drugs to include all the monoaminergic systems which innervate structures subserving anxiety-related behaviour, i.e. the dopaminergic innervation of the prefrontal and cingulate cortices as well as the noradrenergic and serotonergic innervation of the septal area and hippocampus; although it remains unclear how the anti-anxiety drugs achieve this selectivity of action (see Chapter 11). They show, in addition, that the relation between the prefrontal cortex and anxiety is phylogenetically old, since it appears to be present in rats and mice as well as primates. However, it seems probable that the role of cortical structures in anxiety has expanded at the primate level. This is suggested by the increased anatomical relationship between the septo-hippocampal system and the prefrontal and cingulate cortices which is observed among monkeys. Thus connections have been shown in the monkey between the prefrontal cortex and the hippocampus (Leichnetz and Astruc 1976) and septal area (Johnson *et al.* 1968; Tanaka and Goldman 1976), and between the cingulate cortex and the septal area (Kemper, Wright, and Locke 1972), but there is no evidence for these connections in the rat. On the theory advanced here, this may indicate that, as primates evolved, it became increasingly important to detect departures from relatively elaborate motor programmes, a development which has presumably gone even further in man. This allows us to conclude — along with common sense — that failure, or the potential failure, of one's plans correspondingly becomes a particularly important source of anxiety at the human level.

14

The symptoms of anxiety

The theory of anxiety that has been developed in this book is based largely on data from animal experiments, psychological and physiological. But its major aim is to provide a new perspective within which to view the manifestations of this condition in man. It is time to see how well it achieves this aim.

We entered on the task of constructing a theory of anxiety armed, at the psychological level, with the concept of the behavioural inhibition system outlined in Chapter 1. This concept was based largely on the results of purely behavioural experiments (Gray 1975), although the behavioural effects of the anti-anxiety drugs also played an important part in its formulation (Gray 1967, 1977). Most of this book has been concerned with a search for the neural structures which might subserve the functions allotted to the behavioural inhibition system. It is perhaps surprising that, as a result of this search, it has been necessary to define more sharply and deeply the *psychological* content of the concept of the behavioural inhibition system; but this is no isolated example of the fruitful interaction which is possible between the two halves of physiological psychology — provided the practitioners of this hybrid discipline pursue their researches with a sufficient regard for theory.

This psychological development has had the consequence that the model of the behavioural inhibition system presented in Chapter 1 (Fig. 1.1) now looks a little threadbare, although none of the postulates that it encapsulates need be abandoned. The behavioural inhibition system can still be regarded as responding to its adequate inputs (stimuli which warn of punishment, stimuli which warn of non-reward, novel stimuli, and innate fear stimuli) with its major kinds of output (inhibition of ongoing behaviour, increased attention to environmental stimuli, and increased level of arousal). But the need to specify how the brain might discharge these functions has forced us to define more clearly the kinds of information processing it must undertake. Thus, to see how adequate an account of anxiety is now provided by the notion of 'activity in the behavioural inhibition system', we must first recapitulate certain features of the theory of septo-hippocampal function developed in Chapter 10.

As argued there, the chief function of our system is to compare, quite generally, actual with expected stimuli, checking that outcomes coincide with expectations and motor programmes (or 'plans', as Miller, Galanter, and Pribram 1960 call them). So long as expectations are fulfilled, the system does nothing actually to control behaviour. But this does not mean that, at such times, it is inactive. On the contrary, it is kept extremely busy, using incoming sensory information, combined where necessary with information about intended patterns of movement, either to predict the next likely sensory event or to lay the foundations which will enable such predictions to be made on subsequent occasions, as well as to check predictions already made. To these ends the system exercises selective control over the sensory information that reaches it, and tags it as 'important' or filters it out as unimportant (depending on the presence or absence of associations with reinforcers) before allowing it to be stored elsewhere.

In this comparator or monitoring capacity ('just checking') the behavioural inhibition system functions continuously; but it controls behaviour directly only under special conditions. These conditions ('mismatch') are those in which expectations are not fulfilled, either because an unpredicted environmental event occurs, or because a predicted event fails to occur; and also those in which the predicted event is aversive. In this 'control' mode, the system at once interrupts ongoing motor programmes in the manner that initially gave rise to the name 'behavioural inhibition system'. Such programmes are now tagged 'faulty' and called in for careful inspection. When they next occur they are interrupted so that the system can determine whether alternative programmes lead to more satisfactory outcomes. To enable such checking to be carried out, the system is capable of evaluating descriptions of stimuli and/or response patterns simultaneously along several dimensions (e.g. colour, orientation and position of a stimulus; or left-turning, white-approaching, and rough-avoiding as descriptions of a response). In addition, the system can take control over exploratory and investigative behaviour, either by selecting among stimulus inputs to which the organism is in any case exposed by motor programmes controlled elsewhere, or by actively directing exploratory motor behaviour. The latter case includes diversification of alternative motor programmes which may bypass the disruption. In all cases, the system takes active control over behaviour upon receipt of stimuli which have preceded (on a previous occasion) the disruptive event (novelty, non-reward, punishment, innate fear stimuli); only in this way is it possible to try out alternative motor programmes which may bypass the disruption. (This is equivalent to the postulate, in earlier formulations of the theory, that the behavioural inhibition system responds to conditioned, but not unconditioned, aversive stimuli; see Chapter 1.) Consequently, when the system is 'just checking', a particularly careful watch is maintained for such warning stimuli.

Under most conditions the active behavioural role of the behavioural inhibition system ceases when one of three results is achieved: either the disruption is relatively unimportant and the initial motor programme is resumed (habituation); or an alternative motor programme is found which is successful; or the goal to which the initial motor programme was directed is abandoned and the subject engages in other behaviour. But certain tasks seem to require that the system continually participate in the control of behaviour. These are tasks which contain multiple sources of interference that can be overcome only by maximum use of the system's capacity for multidimensional comparison of stimuli and response patterns.

This, then, is the core of the theory. The major facts that it is called on to explain fall into three classes, relating to the *symptoms* and *therapy* of anxiety, and to the *personality* of the anxious individual; although it is impossible to keep discussions of these three classes of data entirely separate from one another. In the present chapter we consider principally the symptoms of anxiety.

Symptoms of one kind of behavioural disorder do not come with convenient labels distinguishing them from those of other conditions, or from behaviour that is a symptom of nothing at all. Indeed, the problem of classification of behavioural disorders is one of the most difficult that psychiatry faces. Many different approaches to this problem have been proposed. I do not intend to discuss this issue here, but I should make my biasses clear. These favour (certainly where anxiety is concerned) the kind of dimensional approach advocated, for example, by Eysenck (1960). On this view most psychiatric problems are not usefully regarded as analogous to physical diseases, with the attendant dichotomy of 'well' or 'ill'. Rather, there are continuous distributions of behavioural propensities which run through the entire population, and those individuals who need psychiatric attention are simply located near the extreme pole of one or other of these 'dimensions'. It is then possible to distinguish different types of behavioural disorder by their location in the multidimensional space so created. We have already seen an example of this approach, in the discussion of the relations between anxiety and neurotic and psychotic depression which engaged our attention in Chapter 12.

Note that the space used to locate psychiatric syndromes in this way is one of which the axes are dimensions of normal personality (H. J. and S. B. G. Eysenck 1969). Thus this solution to the problem of classification in psychiatry is inextricably bound up with the problem of describing personality in psychology. Fortunately, there is now considerable agreement about the number and general nature of the major dimensions of personality that are needed to define the 'anxious' person (Eysenck and Eysenck 1969; Morris 1979), although, as we shall see in Chapter 16, there are major issues that still require resolution. There is also general agreement among psychiatrists, whether or not they share the dimensional approach to classification, as to which syndromes and symptoms are due to heightened anxiety and which to other conditions (Mayer-Gross, Slater, and Roth 1969). Thus the list of anxiety symptoms given here is unlikely to differ in major respects from similar lists given elsewhere.

From a dimensional point of view, anxiety symptoms are those that are found in individuals whose personality lies in the neurotic introvert portion of the multidimensional personality space described by Eysenck and Eysenck (1969) or the equivalent portions of the spaces described by Cattell or Guilford (Morris 1979). This description is not meant to imply that the best account of the personality of the neurotic introvert and his susceptibility to symptoms of anxiety is the one proposed by Eysenck (e.g. 1957, 1967), nor even that the best location of the axes of the relevant personality space is the one adopted by Eysenck and Eysenck (1969). Indeed, we shall have occasion to question both these parts of Eysenck's overall theory of neurosis (Chapter 16). But we need a map of personality space within which to situate the individuals we are discussing, and the one developed by the Eysencks (1969) is simple, well described, and well known. It is based on the two orthogonal dimensions of introversion–extroversion (E) and neuroticism (N), to which later work has added a less well-defined dimension, orthogonal to the first two, known (perhaps misleadingly) as 'psychoticism' (P) (H. J. and S. B. G. Eysenck 1976). Within this framework we can define the symptoms that concern us as those which are found predominantly in individuals who are high on N, low on E (i.e. introverted) and low on P (Eysenck 1957). Note that, for the purposes of the argument pursued in this book, it is an important advantage that this definition makes no reference to the anti-anxiety drugs. Thus there is no circularity in testing our theory (based as it is on the behavioural effects of the anti-anxiety drugs) by its capacity to account for anxiety symptoms.

Detailed descriptions of the syndromes and symptoms of anxiety can be found elsewhere (Mayer-Gross *et al.* 1969; Marks 1969; Beech 1974; Lader 1975; Rachman and Hodgson 1979); here I shall do no more than list them. At the syndromal level it is useful to distinguish between phobias, obsessive–compulsive neurosis, and the anxiety state. But it should be noted that the key symptoms of each of these different syndromes are often found together, so that it is unlikely that they correspond to fundamental differences at the level of process (but see Marks 1979). To these syndromes, by the criteria we have adopted (presence in the neurotic introvert), we must add that of neurotic depression (Kerr *et al.* 1970; Paykel 1971). We have already discussed the relations between this condition and anxiety in Chapter 12.

At the level of symptoms it has become common to distinguish between behavioural, cognitive, and physiological aspects of anxiety (Lang 1970; Rachman 1978). This division is useful, so long as it is not taken to correspond in any simple manner to separate systems in the brain. Behaviourally, the chief symptom of the phobias is avoidance of the phobic stimulus. This is something which is not objectively dangerous. In many cases, however, it evokes fear quite widely in the normal population (e.g. spiders, snakes). In other cases, the phobic stimulus is more idiosyncratic (e.g. cats, a special pattern of wallpaper). In the most crippling cases the phobic stimuli are widespread and can be avoided only at great cost to normal social life (agoraphobia, social phobia). The obsessive–compulsive neurosis is more complex. In the majority of cases there is a ritual behavioural act ('compulsion') which makes no obvious sense (the excessive washing of already clean hands is a common example); prevention of this ritual gives rise to a sharp increase in the subjective experience and physiological signs of anxiety (Röper and Rachman 1976). At the cognitive level, most such patients also experience 'obsessions', that is 'intrusive, repetitive thoughts, images or impulses that are unacceptable and/or unwanted and give rise to subjective resistance; the person finds them difficult to dismiss or control' (Rachman 1978). The cognitive aspects of the phobias are not so dramatic, and in practice often boil down to the self-report of anxiety, or even a tick placed at an appropriate point on an adjective check list. In all the anxiety syndromes there are easily detectable peripheral physiological signs: raised skin conductance with an increased rate of spontaneous fluctuations in conductance level, raised heart rate, increased blood-flow in the forearm, etc. (Lader 1975). These signs become particularly prominent during panic attacks (Lader and Mathews 1970), which may occur when a phobic patient is exposed to the phobic stimulus or an obsessional patient is prevented from carrying out his accustomed ritual. In the anxiety state panic attacks become a major symptom, and physiological measures also reveal a chronically raised level of activity in the autonomic nervous system between such attacks (Lader and Wing 1966; Lader 1967). Raised autonomic activity is also seen in many phobic patients, especially in cases of agoraphobia and social phobia, though not in patients with animal phobias (Lader 1967). Thus the different types of symptom — behavioural, cognitive, and physiological — are prominent to differing degrees in different syndromes; but all are present in each condition.

The phobias

Previous theories of anxiety derived from the animal laboratory have emphasized at the experimental level conditioned fear or passive avoidance and, clinically, phobias with few and clearly delineated precipitating stimuli (Eysenck and Rachman 1965; Gray 1971a). Although such phobias are of relatively little clinical importance (Marks 1969), the fact that these theories could apparently account for them in terms of a well-defined experimental model gave them considerable plausibility. Recently, however, it is just at this point that they have come in for increasing attack. Although, as we shall see, the strengths of the present theory are most apparent when it is applied to the obsessive–compulsive neurosis, the historical importance that the phobias have had in the development of the subject give them a claim to priority of treatment.

According to the 'standard' conditioning theory of phobias, usually attributed in the first instance to Watson and Rayner (1920), there are a few stimuli which are innately capable of eliciting fear reactions (Watson listed loud noise, pain, and sudden loss of support). The strange panoply of adult human phobias is then thought to arise through Pavlovian conditioning between these (as UCSs) and a random assortment of conditioned stimuli that happen to achieve the right temporo-spatial association with them. Eysenck (1979) has recently summarized the objections to this theory. The most important are: (i) The stimuli that elicit phobias are not a random sample of stimuli; some (e.g. closed spaces) are greatly over-represented, others (e.g. cars) that are associated with objective dangers are under-represented. (ii) Phobic stimuli unaccompanied by their UCSs ought to undergo extinction; of course, they do not, or phobias would not constitute a psychiatric problem. To these two objections we may add a third (Gray 1979b). (iii) The times of onset of phobias are not a random sample of ages; there is a predominance of onsets in early adult life (Marks 1969).

In an effort to deal with objections (i) and (ii), Eysenck (1979) has made use of Seligman's (1971) concept of 'preparedness' and allied it to a new theory of his own. According to this theory some stimuli are 'prepared' (by Darwinian evolution) to enter into an association with aversive UCSs; furthermore, once such an association has been formed, the phobic power of the prepared CS, far from extinguishing, can be further increased by presentation *without* a following UCS (a process termed 'incubation').

Now, while the difficulties for the standard conditioning theory of phobias briefly outlined above are real, Eysenck's solution to them is unsatisfactory (Gray 1979b). First, it does not meet objection (iii) above. Second, the experimental evidence for incubation is poor (Bersh 1980). Third, the concept of preparedness for conditioning is unacceptable. This last point requires justification; especially since recent data from Öhman's group in Uppsala apparently offer strong support both for the concept of preparedness and for its relevance to the genesis of phobias. Closer inspection of these data shows, however, that they are not quite what they seem.

Öhman's experiments

The major experimental paradigm used by Öhman and his collaborators is that of differential classical conditioning of autonomic responses (usually the skin conductance response, SCR) with an aversive UCS (usually a mild electric shock) and visual stimuli (presented as slides) as CSs. The experiments are conducted with normal human subjects, most often undergraduates. The key innovation lies in the choice of CSs. It is difficult to describe this feature of Öhman's design, however, in a way that does not prejudge the theoretical issues we have to face later. Clinically speaking, they consist of pictures of stimuli which are either commonly found as objects of phobias (snakes and spiders) or rarely if ever play this role (flowers and mushrooms, circles and triangles). In the context of preparedness theory, the first kind of stimulus is prepared to enter readily into an association with aversive UCSs, the second kind is not. Following Öhman (e.g. 1979), we shall call them 'fear-relevant' or 'fear-irrelevant' stimuli respectively.

Let us first present Öhman's findings as seen from the perspective of the preparedness hypothesis (Seligman 1971; Öhman 1979). According to this view, phobias develop when prepared stimuli are followed by an aversive UCS. The resulting conditioned fear response is said to be formed very rapidly, indeed on one trial; to be extremely resistant to extinction; and to be resistant to control by rational argument. Prepared stimuli are those which have constituted potentially dangerous objects or situations through millennia of human and pre-human evolution (e.g. closed spaces, wide open spaces, snakes, spiders). That is why, on the theory, these stimuli are over-represented among the phobias of modern man. From these arguments it follows that Öhman's fear-relevant stimuli should be more potent CSs for the conditioned SCR, provided an aversive UCS is used, than his fear-irrelevant stimuli. The CR to fear-relevant stimuli should be formed more readily, it should be more resistant to extinction, and it should be less open to cognitive control.

With the exception of the first (speed of acquisition), these predictions are in general confirmed by the results of Öhman's experiments. When a shock UCS is used, the differential conditioned SCR (that is, the difference in the magnitudes of the responses elicited by a CS+ and a CS−, respectively) is more resistant to extinction if the stimuli are relevant rather than irrelevant to fear (e.g. Öhman, Fredrikson, Hugdahl, and Rimmö 1976). Furthermore, if, at the start of extinction, instructions are given that there will be no more shocks, the differential conditioned SCR disappears at once when fear-irrelevant stimuli are used as CSs, but shows considerable resistance to extinction when fear-relevant stimuli are used (Hugdahl and Öhman 1977). Thus, when an aversive (shock) UCS is used, conditioning with fear-relevant stimuli produces responses that are more resistant to extinction and less open to cognitive control, as predicted. On the other hand (again as predicted), if the SCR is measured in a non-aversive task (in response to a warning signal in a reaction-time experiment), there is apparently no difference between fear-relevant and fear-irrelevant stimuli; although this demonstration (Öhman *et al.* 1976) is flawed by a lack of evidence that any conditioning took place in either experimental condition. Nor was there any difference in a shock-conditioning paradigm between fear-irrelevant stimuli and stimuli (revolvers and rifles) which, although *relevant* to fear, could not have been *prepared* by evolutionary development to be so (Hodes, Öhman, and Lang 1977, cited by Öhman 1979). Finally, although Öhman's group does not normally find differences in the acquisition of the conditioned SCR as a function of the stimuli used as CSs, they none the less report, as predicted by the preparedness hypothesis, that there is one-trial learning of this response (Öhman, Erickssson, and Olofsson 1975).

This pattern of results seems to offer strong support for the preparedness hypothesis. But closer examination reveals several curious aspects of Öhman's findings which fit ill with the central assertion of preparedness theory, namely, that prepared (fear-relevant) stimuli are more readily *associated* with aversive UCSs.

Note first that the bulk of the data have been obtained with the SCR. It is well known that this response participates in the orienting reflex (Sokolov 1960). Although the orienting reflex can be conditioned, it is not clear that this depends on the same processes as other forms of Pavlovian conditioning; and, in any case, the preparedness theory is concerned with conditioned fear, not conditioned orienting. Öhman, Fredrikson, and Hugdahl (1978) have attempted to meet this objection by arguing that the SCR observed in response to a fear-relevant CS for a shock UCS is a conditioned defensive reaction (Sokolov 1960). Their evidence consists in certain differences between the SCRs measured on the dorsal and palmar surfaces of the hand respectively; but the data they report are complex and by no means all in agreement with the conclusion they reach. Furthermore, a second attempt to substantiate the same conclusion by measuring heart rate in conjunction with the SCR was unsuccessful (Fredrikson and Öhman 1979).

Other features of Öhman's data also suggest that the response he measures is directed at the CS (as is a conditioned orienting response) rather than being anticipatory of the UCS, as is commonly the case in classical conditioning (Pavlov 1927). In most of his experiments the CS is presented for 8 seconds and the CR is measured separately during the first and second halves of this interval. It is only the response measured during the first half of the CS period which behaves according to the predictions of preparedness theory; the response measured in the second half of this period is unaffected by the major experimental manipulations (e.g. Öhman et al. 1976). This is quite unlike a normal CR, which is usually maximal just prior to UCS onset (Pavlov 1927). Furthermore, Öhman (1971) has himself presented evidence that the SCR measured during the first 4 seconds of the CS period behaves like an orienting response. Thus the most plausible interpretation of the findings in experiments in which a fear-relevant CS is paired with a shock UCS is that this *causes particular attention to be paid to the CS*.

Now this conclusion might be acceptable to proponents of the preparedness theory, since it could be said that I have done no more than redescribe the conditioned response: rather than conditioned fear, it is now conditioned attention to the CS. But there are other features of Öhman's results which are inconsistent with the notion that prepared stimuli are more ready to enter into an association with aversive UCSs, no matter how we then describe the conditioned response.

If normal conditioning is involved, it is in the first place surprising that the conditioned SCR elicited by fear-relevant stimuli is insensitive to several experimental parameters which affect other forms of conditioning quite powerfully: number of acquisition trials (Öhman et al. 1975), the difference between trace and delay procedures, and the CS–UCS interval (Hugdahl and Öhman 1980). In rebuttal of this point, proponents of preparedness theory might claim that, although prepared stimuli undergo conditioning, it is a special kind of conditioning (Seligman 1971).

How very special becomes apparent when we consider in more detail the response that Öhman measures. The major apparent support for the preparedness hypothesis has come from a within-subject differential conditioning paradigm (e.g. Öhman *et al.* 1976). In this design one group of subjects is presented with only fear-relevant stimuli, of which one is CS+ and the other CS− for shock, the two stimuli (e.g. snakes and spiders) being counter-balanced in this assignment; a second group of subjects similarly sees only fear-irrelevant stimuli (flowers and mushrooms in most of the experiments). The most robust finding in these experiments is that the group exposed to fear-relevant stimuli is more resistant to extinction as measured by *the difference in the size of the SCR on CS+ and CS− trials respectively.* But a little reflection shows that this result is *not* predicted by preparedness theory. This theory holds that prepared stimuli are more ready to enter into a positive association with an aversive UCS. But the difference between the SCRs given to the CS+ and the CS− is a function of both these responses. If preparedness theory predicts anything for this situation, it is that the differentiation between snakes and spiders should take place at a higher overall level of skin conductance than that between mushrooms and flowers; but it has no reason to predict that it should be easier to *discriminate* between prepared than between unprepared stimuli.

At the best, preparedness theory might predict a better discrimination between prepared stimuli provided this is entirely due to higher responding to the prepared than to the unprepared CS+, with no difference between the responses to the CS−s. Unfortunately, an evaluation of this possibility requires a between-group comparison, and Öhman's group appears to have reported quantitative data allowing such a comparison on only one occasion (Öhman *et al.* 1976, Table 2, first-interval responses). In this experiment there were three groups, one given snakes and spiders as CSs, one mushrooms and flowers, and the third circles and triangles. The comparison between the first two groups supports preparedness theory, in that there was a significantly superior discrimination in the fear-relevant condition and this was due entirely to higher responding to the CS+. But subjects in the circle–triangle condition were only non-significantly worse than the snake–spider group, and this was due to higher responding to the CS− as well as lower responding to the CS+. Inspection of the graphs published in other papers from Öhman's laboratory shows that the findings often support preparedness theory (e.g. Öhman and Dimberg 1978, Fig. 3; Hugdahl, Fredrikson, and Öhman 1977, Fig. 1). But this pattern is not invariable. For example, Hugdahl and Öhman (1980) found superior discrimination between snakes and spiders than between mushrooms and flowers at three CS–UCS intervals: at 2 and 8 seconds, this was due to stronger CS+ responding in the fear-relevant group, as predicted by preparedness theory, but at 16 seconds it was due to weaker CS− responding. Similarly, in Hygge and Öhman's (1978) experiment (in which fear was elicited by exposure to a fearful human model, rather than by the usual shock UCS), superior discrimination in the fear-relevant condition was due as much to reduced CS− responding as to increased responding to the CS+.

The fact that a reliable superiority of the discrimination between fear-relevant CSs can be demonstrated even under conditions where this is apparently not due to stronger *positive* fear conditioning makes one seek an alternative explanation for Öhman's very interesting findings. A possible account is suggested by observations which show that there is a greater SCR to fear-relevant than to fear-irrelevant stimuli even when *no association with an aversive UCS is involved at all.*

To begin with, fear-relevant stimuli elicit a greater SCR when simply presented repeatedly in a habituation paradigm (e.g. Öhman *et al.* 1974; Hugdahl *et al.* 1977). Furthermore, if a fear-relevant stimulus follows another fear-relevant stimulus in such a habituation paradigm, the SCR is potentiated, a phenomenon not seen with fear-irrelevant stimuli (Hygge and Öhman 1978). More directly related to shock-conditioning experiments is the observation (Öhman *et al.* 1974) that the difference between the unconditioned skin conductance responses to fear-relevant and fear-irrelevant stimuli, respectively, is considerably magnified if the subject is given experience with a mild electric shock before the stimuli are presented and is told simply that shocks will be delivered during the experiment. In the light of this observation, it is not surprising that the response to fear-relevant stimuli is particularly prone to sensitization when shocks are in fact delivered, but in a random relationship to the stimuli (Öhman *et al.* 1975). In this experiment separate groups of subjects were exposed to pictures of either snakes or houses in a stimulus-only condition, to a truly random control procedure (pictures and shocks randomly intermixed), or to a classical conditioning procedure (pictures predicting shocks). During acquisition the SCR in the first half of the CS period was significantly larger to snakes than houses in the truly random and classical conditioning groups, but not in the stimulus-only condition; furthermore, the truly random and classical conditioning groups did not differ from each other.

These results must make one suspect that the phenomena observed by Öhman's group are largely due to sensitization, and have nothing at all to do with conditioning as this is usually understood, especially since the experiment reported by Öhman *et al.* (1975), described above, is apparently the only time they have controlled for this possibility. However, in the extinction phase of the same experiment, the pattern of results was consistent with a true conditioning effect specific to the fear-relevant stimulus: the response was significantly greater in the fear-relevant conditioning group than in the fear-relevant truly random controls, and significantly greater in the fear-relevant than in the fear-irrelevant conditioning group (Öhman *et al.* 1975). Thus it appears that fear-relevant stimuli elicit greater SCRs initially, and that their capacity to elicit such responses is differentially potentiated by shock or the threat of shock, even though this is not specifically associated with them; but that this capacity is *also* differentially potentiated by associative conditioning, at least when measures are taken during extinction. But preparedness theory predicts only the last of these findings.

Innate fear stimuli

The findings reported by Öhman's group, then, justify the conclusion that fear-relevant stimuli come to elicit more persistent SCRs in consequence of an association with an aversive UCS; and, given the lack of a similar effect when fear-relevant but phylogenetically novel stimuli (rifles and revolvers; Öhman 1979) are used as CSs, it is justifiable to replace the term 'fear-relevant' by the more theoretically loaded term 'prepared'. But, given the other features of Öhman's results described above, it is implausible that the special characteristic of prepared stimuli is that they can more readily become conditioned fear stimuli as the result of a Pavlovian conditioning process. This hypothesis leaves too many other observations unexplained: the fact that the special nature of prepared stimuli becomes manifest particularly in the first half of the CS period; the special affinity of prepared stimuli for the SCR rather than other response measures; their tendency to elicit strong SCRs in the absence of any conditioning; their susceptibility to sensitization effects; the fact that prepared stimuli are particularly easily differentiated into positive *and* negative fear stimuli; and the fact that their putative high associability affects resistance to extinction, but not acquisition. We should seek instead for a unified account which can explain all, or at any rate most, of these findings.

We can begin on the construction of such an account by noticing that the concept of preparedness is in many respects an amalgam of two other notions: those of innate reactions to unconditioned stimuli, and of conditioning proper. It is an amalgam, moreover, which is both unnecessary and confusing. The whole point of the concept of conditioning, as Pavlov noted at the outset of his research on this phenomenon (Gray 1979c), is to make sense of those cases in which there is *no* biologically prepared connection between the stimulus and the response it elicits. Once there is such a connection, it is hard to see what role conditioning can play.

A simpler move is to treat spiders, snakes, and the like as innate stimuli for fear, requiring no conditioning at all. This accounts for the selectivity with which only certain stimuli commonly elicit phobic reactions along the same, evolutionary lines as the preparedness hypothesis, and thus shares the main advantage that this has over the standard conditioning theory. There is plenty of evidence for innate fears of a wide variety of stimuli in a diversity of species (Gray 1971a), including fear of snakes in monkeys never before exposed to them (Hebb 1946). One of the interesting features of such fears is that they are often subject to maturation; that is, they appear *without learning* at a given stage in ontogeny. This concept, which is well supported in the animal literature (Gray 1971a, Chapter 2), seems eminently well suited to cope with the evidence that some phobias appear in human beings rather consistently at certain ages (Marks 1969). To account for this age distribution the preparedness hypothesis must postulate that conditioning experiences involving the relevant stimuli also cluster at these ages. But this is no more plausible than the postulate required of the standard conditioning theory that conditioning experiences happen especially often when spiders or snakes are around.

The supposition that the fear-relevant stimulus used by Öhman's group are, quite simply, innate stimuli for fear in our species makes immediate sense of several of the findings this group reports. The heightened response to fear-relevant stimuli *before* any conditioning is exactly what one would expect of an innate stimulus for fear. So, plausibly, is the exaggeration of this tendency seen when there are other threatening elements in the situation (previous experience of shock, the threat of shock, or shocks occurring in random association with the stimulus). These other threatening elements can be presumed to increase the overall reactivity of the central mechanisms which process fear stimuli, in a way that will be specified more clearly when we discuss the obsessive-compulsive syndrome. On this view, a fear-relevant 'CS' elicits the SCR in its own right, rather than as a predictor of the UCS, and that is why the response is most marked at CS onset rather than at the time the UCS is expected to occur.

Other features of Öhman's findings, however, call for a more elaborate account. This account requires us to link the concept of innate fear stimuli to the behavioural inhibition system.

At first sight the concept of the behavioural inhibition system may appear to be as closely wedded to Pavlovian conditioning as the standard conditioning theory of phobias which we are trying to replace. After all, it has been stressed throughout this book that the behavioural inhibition system is specialized to respond to threats of unconditioned aversive stimuli, not to these stimuli themselves. But this is not to say that the behavioural inhibition system produces Pavlovian CRs. On the contrary, since the earliest development of this concept, I have pointed out that responses to stimuli that warn of aversive UCSs possess certain features which sharply differentiate them from Pavlovian CRs (Gray 1971a, 1975; see also Razran 1971). Physiological experiments are consistent with this point of view. Neither anti-anxiety drugs (Chapter 2) nor septal or hippocampal lesions (Chapter 6) affect the formation or expression of Pavlovian CRs, even when these are based on aversive UCSs, except in the case where presentation of the CS causes disruption of an ongoing motor programme, a case which was discussed in Chapter 10.

It does no violence to the theory developed here, then, to suppose that innate stimuli for fear act on the behavioural inhibition system (Gray 1976). Indeed, this is a natural extension of the theory. It has failed to emerge in earlier chapters simply because there is virtually no relevant experimental work in the animal literature we have reviewed.

Such evidence as there is relates to social behaviour. Stimuli that arise in the course of social interaction are among the most important innate stimuli for fear in many animal species (Gray 1971a); and their continuing importance in our own species is attested by the fact that the most widespread and crippling of the phobias, agoraphobia, and social phobia (Marks 1969), appear to be responses to such stimuli. Their relevance to Öhman's laboratory analogue of phobic behaviour was demonstrated in an interesting experiment by Öhman and Dimberg (1978), who showed that pictures of angry faces are fear-relevant and pictures of faces with neutral or happy expressions, fear-irrelevant by the same criteria (resistance to extinction of the SCR) as pictures of snakes compared to pictures of flowers. It was proposed by Gray (1976) that 'stimuli arising in the course of dominance interactions' are among the kinds of stimulus which activate the behavioural inhibition system; Öhman and Dimberg's (1978) findings, taken with the rest of the argument pursued in this section, are consistent with this suggestion. Also consistent with it is the evidence that septal (Chapter 6, Section 6.16) and locus coeruleus (Eison *et al.* 1977) lesions increase gregariousness; this is perhaps due to a reduction in the avoidance behaviour elicited in intact animals by stimuli arising during social interaction. There are insufficient data to determine the effects of hippocampal lesions. Anti-anxiety drugs increase social interaction when this is suppressed by bright light and an unfamiliar environment (File 1980), although there is one report (Crow *et al.* 1978) that this effect is not produced by lesions of the dorsal ascending noradrenergic bundle.

This is clearly a field that calls for much more experimental work. The best we can say for the moment is that the available data do not preclude the hypothesis that innate fear stimuli act via the behavioural inhibition system. If we therefore adopt this hypothesis, we are able to account for two further features of Öhman's data on which the preparedness theory stumbles: the ease with which fear-relevant (relative to fear-irrelevant) stimuli are discriminated into CS+ and CS−; and the fact that CRs to such stimuli are not formed more easily, but are more resistant to extinction.

The first of these findings arises directly from the properties we have given to the behavioural inhibition system. Recall that one of the functions of this system is to carry out a multidimensional analysis of the stimuli encountered in a threatening environment. Thus it is sufficient to suppose that pictures of snakes and spiders innately activate the behavioural inhibition system to generate the prediction that such stimuli will be better discriminated from each other than more neutral stimuli, such as flowers and mushrooms; and this, of course, is what Öhman and his colleagues find to be the case (see above). The fact that this superior discrimination is allied to greater resistance to extinction can also be derived from this approach, if we bear in mind the evidence (Sutherland and Mackintosh 1971) that resistance to extinction increases as a positive function of the number of stimulus dimensions to which the subject attends during training. If activation of the behavioural inhibition system causes an increase in multidimensional stimulus analysis, it follows that there should also be an increase in the resistance to extinction of a differential CR.

The role played by the SCR in these experiments is also consistent with the position adopted here. As we have seen, there are a number of reasons to consider the SCR as an orienting response, unconditioned, sensitized or conditioned, and probably (in many of the cases studied by Öhman's group) a mixture of all three. If this is so, it provides a further reason to link Öhman's observations to the operation of the behavioural inhibition system. First, the general theory developed in this book supposes that the behavioural inhibition system is concerned with orienting-investigative behaviour under conditions of threat, as set out in Chapter 10. Second, such evidence as there is from animal experiments is consistent in showing that the galvanic skin response is reduced after septal lesions (Holdstock 1969, 1970) and benzodiazepine or barbiturate administration (Marcy and Quermonne 1974). Finally, Fowles (1980) has reviewed much of the relevant human literature and concludes that 'electrodermal activity increases when there is an activation of the behavioural inhibition system'. Thus the findings reported by Öhman's group may depend critically on their choice of measure, as suggested also by their failure to obtain similar results using heart rate (Fredrikson and Öhman 1979), a measure which is apparently unrelated to the activities of the behavioural inhibition system (Fowles 1980).

What, then, remains of the case for prepared conditioning? The major finding from Öhman's laboratory which is not yet accounted for by the above analysis is the report that, in a between-subject paradigm, classical conditioning of a snake CS to a shock UCS produced increased resistance to extinction over and above that produced by a truly random association between these stimuli, an effect not observed when a house was used as CS (Öhman *et al.* 1975). This suggests a true preparedness to enter into an association. Note, however, that Hygge and Öhman (1978) observed an increase in the SCR when fear-relevant stimuli merely followed one another in a habituation paradigm. The line that separates such mutual sensitization between fear-relevant stimuli from true conditioning between a fear-relevant CS and a shock UCS is hard to draw. If a real line exists, it is still not necessary to call upon a special process of prepared conditioning. For it has been shown (in experiments in which preparedness appears to play no part) that conditioning is facilitated by similarity between the events that are associated (Rescorla 1978). If the capacity to elicit fear provides a dimension along which such similarity can act, this principle could account for the greater ease of association between two innately fear-eliciting stimuli, be they two pictures of potentially phobic objects (snakes, spiders), or one such picture and an electric shock. Thus there is no need to call upon preparedness, as proposed by Seligman (1971) and Eysenck (1979), to account even for the extra associability of such pairs of stimuli.

The preparedness hypothesis took from conditioning the central role in the genesis of phobias allotted to it by Watson and Rayner (1920) and in Eysenck's (e.g. 1957) earlier treatment of the problem. The present approach reduces this role still further. On this view the chief determinant of phobias and other symptoms of anxiety is the reactivity of the behavioural inhibition system. This is primarily a matter of personality, a matter we deal with in Chapter 16. That is to say, an individual is endowed with a behavioural inhibition system which is more or less likely to respond, and/or likely to respond more or less intensely, to the adequate stimuli for anxiety. Since this endowment continues (though undoubtedly with fluctuations) throughout life, there is no need to look for an explanation of anxiety in specific childhood learning experiences, as do both Freud and Eysenck — strange bedfellows — in their different ways. It is sufficient to suppose that adequate stimuli for anxiety exist in the patient's environment at the time he is anxious — as, indeed, is normally the case.

This is not to deny, however, all influence to conditioning and learning. On the contrary, these processes play at least three important roles.

First, experience plays a part in the formation of the personality which predisposes to anxiety. Studies both of phobic individuals (Torgersen 1979) and of the personality traits of neuroticism and extroversion (Young *et al.* 1980) estimate the contribution of heredity to these conditions at about 50 per cent of the variance. But that means, of course, that another 50 per cent of the variance remains to be accounted for; and it is likely that learning (of as yet unknown kinds) plays a determining role in this respect.

Second, there are cases in which phobic stimuli cannot in any manner be described as prepared or, by the same token, as reflecting only innate fears (Rachman and Seligman 1976). Some of these clearly require an account in terms of conditioning, along the lines originally advocated by Watson and Rayner (1920). H. J. Eysenck (1977), for example, describes a case in which a man developed a phobic reaction to a pattern of wallpaper which had been on the walls of a bedroom in which he had been set upon by an irate husband. Cases such as these, however, appear to comprise only a minority of phobias. They offer no problem for the theory developed here. This treats conditioned and innate fear stimuli as acting upon the same system (which does not, however, mediate reactions to unconditioned painful stimuli, such as electric shocks).

Third, conditioning undoubtedly plays a role in extending phobic reactions. Thus someone who is afraid of spiders may curtail activities which will bring him into contact with stimuli only secondarily associated with spiders. These associations may spread along the intricate network of routes offered by stimulus and semantic (Razran 1971) generalization. A particularly important way in which this process can come into play lies in the development of a fear of situations associated with the physiological consequences of fear itself. In this manner, a person who experiences a panic attack in a particular environment may develop a conditioned phobic reaction to that environment; associational spread of this response may then contribute to the development, for example, of agoraphobia. These various possibilities call for no new theoretical apparatus.

It seems, then, that application of the present theory to the phobias is relatively simple. It requires only the assumption that anxiety consists of heightened activity in the behavioural inhibition system. The central behavioural symptom in the phobias then yields readily to an analysis in terms of passive avoidance of the phobic object or situation. (Recall that blockade of passive avoidance is a central feature of the action of anti-anxiety drugs, on which the concept of the behavioural inhibition system is partly based.) This simplicity is, of course, possible only because of the considerable amount of theory construction that has gone before; without this, we would be engaged in the vacuous exercise of defining the behavioural inhibition system as that which underlies anxiety, and anxiety as the state produced by activity in the behavioural inhibition system.

Such complications as arise concern the origin of the phobic stimulus (innate, prepared, or conditioned), rather than its effects on behaviour. We have by no means exhausted these complications. Most of the relevant experimental material, as we have seen, concerns in fact only a minority of the phobias, and a clinically unimportant minority at that — the simple animal phobias (Marks 1969). This concentration stems from the ease with which spider or snake phobias can be brought into the laboratory. The much more crippling agoraphobias or social phobias are unfortunately not so tractable. Thus there are virtually no experimental data relating to the origin of the phobic stimuli in these cases. Given the phylogenetic continuity with which stimuli that arise during social interaction elicit fearful behaviour (Gray 1971a), it is probable that the social phobias will yield to the same general type of analysis as that which has been applied above to the animal phobias; and the demonstration that angry facial expressions behave in the SCR conditioning paradigm in the same manner as pictures of snakes or spiders (Öhman and Dimberg 1978) encourages this belief. The importance of stimuli of social interaction in agoraphobia suggests that the same approach may also be fruitful in this connection. These are problems ripe for attack with the increasingly ingenious techniques of experimental social psychology. But, to my knowledge, that attack has not yet been made, so there is little point in discussing these issues further here.

The obsessive–compulsive syndrome

The phobias constitute a relatively low hurdle for theories of anxiety. A much higher hurdle is posed by the obsessive–compulsive syndrome. To start with, from a common-sense point of view the symptoms are more mysterious. If you say you are frightened of spiders or travelling on trains you will be regarded at worst as excessively nervous; but say you must wash your hands exactly eighty-four times and you risk being considered quite mad.

For laboratory-based theories of anxiety obsessive–compulsive behaviour has also seemed much less tractable than the phobias. When it is dealt with at all, it is usually as an extension from the base provided by a model of phobic behaviour. Thus the obsessional ritual (e.g. hand-washing, checking that there are no sharp objects around) may be construed as *active* avoidance, in contrast to the passive avoidance of phobias (Gray 1971a; Hodgson and Rachman 1972). On this analysis, at its simplest, there are fear-eliciting stimuli in the environment (possible sources of contamination, objects that may cut); anxiety is consequently increased; performance of the compulsive ritual is followed by a decrease in anxiety, and it is thus acquired and maintained as an active avoidance response. This account has much to recommend it, and direct tests have provided experimental support for certain of its major assumptions. Thus it is indeed possible in many cases to identify environmental stimuli which provoke the compulsive ritual; and, as demanded by the active-avoidance model, exposure to these stimuli without performance of the ritual increases subjective anxiety, and performance of the ritual is followed by a decrease in anxiety (Hodgson and Rachman 1972; Röper and Rachman 1976).

Extension of this type of model to obsessional symptoms is, not surprisingly, more difficult. It has been pushed furthest by Rachman (1978). He treats obsessions — e.g. the *thought* of homosexual acts, the *impulse* to jump out of the window, or the *image* of dead people in an open coffin (Rachman and de Silva 1978; Rachman 1978) — as noxious internal stimuli which, like phobic objects, give rise to anxiety and attempts at avoidance behaviour. Such behaviour may be overt. So, one who is troubled by an impulse to jump out of windows may (passively) avoid windows. Or a compulsive ritual may be used as an active avoidance response. Rachman (1978), for example, describes a patient who was troubled by intrusive aggressive and sexual thoughts and was able to gain some relief by going through a hand-washing ritual. Alternatively, the avoidance behaviour, like the obsession, may remain internal. Thus the same patient could obtain temporary relief from his obsessions if he constructed a 'good thought' and then repeated the action which had been interrupted by the 'bad' one (Rachman 1978); or a patient troubled by an image of a child in danger may succeed in 'putting things right' by forming a counter-image of the child safe and sound (Rachman 1976).

Rachman's (1978) attempt to treat obsessions in this way is a valiant one. But the strain that behavioural concepts suffer when they are pushed like this into the mind is difficult to hide. It is also inevitable. Cognitive phenomena are not behaviour, they are part of the systems that control behaviour, a part that (for whatever mysterious reason) happens to reach consciousness and is therefore open to introspective account. To suppose that the systems that control behaviour follow the same laws as behaviour itself is the same kind of mistake as the belief that the neural display on the visual cortex is inspected by a second pair of eyes inside the head. Obsessions call for a different type of account than this.

Even at the level of behaviour, in its account of the overt rituals that occupy so much of the patient's day, the active-avoidance hypothesis leaves many crucial phenomena unexplained. In some ways the weaknesses of this hypothesis are similar to those of the standard conditioning theory of phobias: the *selectivity* of obsessional–compulsive behaviour goes unexplained. The rituals seen in this syndrome are not a random sample of the kinds of behaviour that could just happen to precede the reduction in anxiety by which they are supposedly reinforced; nor are obsessions a random sample of ideas which could be threatening. On the contrary, there is a great regularity in the kinds of ritual and obsession observed in widely differing places. In New Delhi (Akhtar *et al.* 1975) as in England (Rachman 1978), the commonest obsessional preoccupation is with dirt, disease, or contamination (50–60 per cent of reported obsessions), followed by orderliness and aggression (35 and 19 per cent, respectively, in England, 23 and 25 per cent in India), and then by religion and sex (10 and 13 per cent in England, 10 and 5 per cent in India). Behavioural rituals similarly consist in the great majority of cases of cleaning, tidying up, and checking that various potential threats (dirt, germs, etc.) are absent. Some account of this selectivity is needed.

Also unexplained by the active-avoidance hypothesis is the intrusive nature of obsessions and the repetitive nature of compulsions. It is reasonable to describe the obsessions reported by most people as 'noxious'; and, as Rachman (1978) points out, there is experimental evidence that the physiological reactions that accompany the obsessional experience are similar to those elicited by phobic stimuli. But in that case why do they occur at all? If we treat internal events as behaviour, would we not expect noxious thoughts to be avoided passively, that is, not occur? Contrary to this expectation, of course, obsessions occur not only once, but repeatedly and intrusively. And, since they are precisely *not* external stimuli, this can happen only because the patient's brain is actively producing them; but the active-avoidance hypothesis does not tell us why. Similarly, if compulsions are active avoidance responses, one would expect them to occur once, perhaps, but why repetitively? Active avoidance responses studied in the laboratory, like other motor responses reinforced in any of the usual ways, are typically no more effortful than they need to be. Of course, since the putative reinforcement for compulsive behaviour (an internal reduction in anxiety) is not open to inspection, we cannot tell how effortful a ritual must be to produce it. But it is strange that hand-washing, checking that the door is locked, and so on, are hardly ever sufficient to reduce anxiety in these patients if they are done once; and it is commonly found that they must be done tens or even hundreds of times. The similarity between the repetitiveness of compulsions and obsessions, respectively, makes one seek a common explanation; but the active-avoidance hypothesis does not offer one.

Previous laboratory-based theories of anxiety, then, experience increasing strain as they move from phobias to compulsions and finally to obsessions. In contrast, the account of anxiety developed here is in some ways applied most naturally to the obsessive–compulsive syndrome.

As set out at the beginning of the chapter, the chief function of the behavioural inhibition system is to monitor ongoing behaviour, checking continuously that outcomes coincide with expectations. In this role, it scans incoming sensory information for threatening or unexpected events and, if they occur, brings all other behaviour to a halt so as to evaluate the nature of the threat. Certain stimuli are tagged 'important' and searched for with particular care. Now, if such a system becomes hyperactive, if it tags too many stimuli as 'important', if it searches for them too persistently, is it not obsessive–compulsive behaviour that it will produce?

Had it not been derived from quite independent sources of data, this description might seem too close to the phenomena to count as an explanation at all. It treats obsessive–compulsive behaviour much as does common sense. The patient scans his environment to an excessive degree for potential threats: dirt, bacteria, sharp objects, and the like. Much of this scan is carried out overtly, in the form of checking rituals. The exact form of the ritual depends, naturally, on the threat the patient is attempting to exclude. If this is a scratch, he searches for sharp objects; if disorder, for objects out of place. Some rituals may both serve this kind of checking function and act as avoidance responses in the manner proposed by Hodgson and Rachman (1972) and Gray (1971a). Thus that most common of rituals, hand-washing, is at once an effective means of searching for dirt and a way to remove it. But, if it were only an active-avoidance response, it would not be expected to occur over and over again; its repetitiveness derives from its checking function.

The functions we have attributed to the behavioural inhibition system also offer a natural account of the cognitive symptoms of the obsessive–compulsive patient. There are two ways these can arise.

First, the scan for potential threats in the external environment can extend to internal repositories of information concerning such threats. Such internal repositories are likely to be verbally coded in many cases; and we have the testimony of the patient that obsessions often take a verbal form (Rachman and de Silva 1978). Presumably, information of this kind is stored in the language areas of the temporal lobe (Lenneberg 1967; Ojemann and Mateer 1979). The subicular area has easy access to this region of the neocortex by way of its projection to the entorhinal area, as does the hippocampus itself (Chapter 3). This is therefore perhaps the route used when one who is anxious, say, about cutting himself checks his memory to verify where he disposed of a razor blade, or wonders whether he saw a splinter of glass on a table. It is easy to see how an internal scan of this kind could also involve imagining the relevant scene. In this way, a person whose greatest fear is of harming her own child might imagine scenes in which she has done just that (Rachman and de Silva 1978).

Second, there are some threats which are themselves of purely internal origin. Take, for example, someone who is afraid of his own impulses. Rachman and de Silva (1978) describe several cases of this kind, involving impulses to jump out of the window, to utter swear words, to look at buttocks, etc. How is the behavioural inhibition system to check on threats of this nature? Evidently this can be achieved only by some sort of internal scan of the systems that produce the behaviour of which the patient is afraid. But at this point the principle of ideo-motor action (James 1890) is likely to come into play: that is, the thought of a particular action itself primes the systems that produce it. Thus checking whether one has a dangerous impulse will increase the probability of experiencing it. The intrusive and repetitive nature of obsessional impulses could in this way arise from the very checking process which attempts to ensure that they are absent; and a similar analysis can be applied to obsessional thoughts or images.

The selectivity of rituals and obsessions also finds a reasonably natural explanation within the theory.

Rituals are for the most part fairly obvious examples of checking behaviour. The very frequent choice of hand-washing as the compulsive ritual, however, suggests that in this case other factors may also be at work. As pointed out above, it may be that hand-washing can conveniently serve simultaneously as a checking ritual and an active avoidance response. In the latter capacity its use may be favoured by early learning that it is an effective way of removing parental anger, along the lines discussed by Gray (1971a, p. 237). There may also be an evolutionary continuity between the human use of soap and water and more ancient forms of grooming behaviour, which has sometimes been observed to increase when animals are fearful (Willingham 1956); but this excursion into what we might call 'response preparedness' is obviously speculative. This speculation is encouraged, however, by the fact that, as a counterpart to the privileged status of hand-washing among compulsive rituals, so dirt is the commonest of obsessional preoccupations (Akhtar *et al.* 1975; Rachman 1978). Thus natural selection may have favoured fear of dirt and its attendant grooming behaviour as much as fear of snakes or enclosed spaces; certainly, the danger to survival is no less great.

The other common obsessional preoccupations require somewhat different explanations. The need for orderliness may spring from the fact that disorder produces novel arrays of stimuli, which *ex hypothesi* activate the behavioural inhibition system. Obsessions with aggressive and sexual impulses or thoughts arise naturally from the internal origin of these drives, the danger of retribution attendant upon their illicit satisfaction, and the way that (as set out above) the behavioural inhibition system checks up on them. As to obsessions with religion, the amalgam of concerns that religion invests in cleanliness, sex, and aggression probably makes these parasitic on the rest.

The obsessions are the most cognitive of the symptoms of anxiety. It is encouraging to see them yield up some of their mystery to an analysis which is based on the results of behavioural and physiological experiments on animals; and, if one result of the approach adopted here is to blur the lines between 'behaviourist' and 'cognitive' psychology, or those between emotion and thought, that will be no small gain. It is evident that the functions attributed to the behavioural inhibition system are in the highest order cognitive. Yet the nature of the stimuli that activate it give it a clear role to play under conditions which provoke (if any do) emotion. This is as it should be. We do not stop thinking when we are emotionally aroused, nor use different machinery with which to think. Nor do we *only* think at such times: we also act (or interrupt action) and feel. The theory developed here correspondingly binds thought and action, cognition and emotion, into a single whole.

If something is missing, it is that part of the dimension of feeling that starts out in the periphery: the tense stomach, sweaty hands, and pounding heart which is the stuff of the James–Lange theory of emotion (Gray 1971a). This has been under-emphasized for the simple reason that, at the animal level, there are very few useful data. Rodent psychophysiology is a poorly developed discipline, so there are few points of contact with the much better known psychophysiology of anxiety in man (e.g. Lader and Wing 1966; Lader 1975). In consequence our physiologically based theory has little or nothing to offer by way of analysis of the physiological symptoms of anxiety. It was suggested in Chapter 11 that the autonomic manifestations of anxiety might depend in part upon descending fibres from the locus coeruleus, perhaps working in conjunction with a septal projection to the hypothalamus, but on slender evidence. Other links to the behavioural inhibition system are provided by observations that septal lesions (Holdstock 1969, 1970) and anti-anxiety drugs (Marcy and Quermonne 1974) reduce the galvanic skin response. But these scattered facts bring little insight into the role played by the autonomic nervous system in the overall psychology of anxiety. As to the remainder of the dimension of feeling, that is shrouded in the mystery of how the brain becomes conscious of its own doings (Gray 1971d), a mystery that is neither more nor less acute for anxiety than it is for the rest of psychology.

15

The treatment of anxiety

In the previous chapter it was shown that the standard conditioning theory of the genesis of phobic anxiety is no longer tenable (Eysenck 1979). An alternative approach was sketched, in which anxiety is seen simply as hyperactivity in the behavioural inhibition system when the subject is exposed to any of the adequate stimuli for anxiety. To the list of such stimuli with which this book has been principally concerned — secondary punishing, secondary frustrative, and novel stimuli — we added certain innate fear stimuli. These include those which Gray (1971a) termed 'stimuli of special evolutionary dangers' and Seligman (1971) analysed in terms of preparedness for conditioning, and (of particular importance) stimuli which arise during the course of social interaction. Applying this approach to the symptoms of obsessive–compulsive neurosis, we saw these as reflecting principally a hyperactivity of the checking functions of the behavioural inhibition system. Thus, although the role played in the present theory by conditioning and learning is still significant, it is much reduced from the status it occupied in many earlier accounts of anxiety.

Behaviour therapy

Anyone familiar with the successes of behaviour therapy in the treatment of phobias (e.g. Mathews 1978) and the kinds of theoretical account that have been given for these successes (e.g. Eysenck and Rachman 1965), could by now be forgiven a certain sense of bewilderment. For these successes have been gained by treating phobias as though they *were* conditioned reactions and then subjecting them to extinction or counter-conditioning. If this assumption is wrong, then what is the efficacy of behaviour therapy due to?

Recent evidence, however, suggests that the efficacy of behaviour therapy has rather little to do with the theories on which the therapeutic methods were based. For details of therapeutic procedure that these theories would suggest to be of critical importance — e.g. the ordering of the sequence of presentation of phobic items, the presence or absence of relaxation after presentation of an item — turn out to play an insignificant role, if any. All that seems to matter (to a first approximation) is the total amount of time for which the patient is exposed to the phobic stimulus — the greater the exposure, the greater the therapeutic effect (Marks 1973; Gelder *et al.* 1973; Teasdale 1977; Levis and Hare 1977). Now this poses something of a dilemma. If one gets better by being exposed to the phobic stimulus, why did one get ill by being exposed to it in the first place? And why does one not get better in the natural course of exposure in the real world, without the help of a therapist?

An answer to these questions which is consistent with the theory developed in this book was proposed by Lader (Lader and Wing 1966; Lader and Mathews 1968) and later elaborated by Watts (1971, 1979). According to these workers, the common element in methods of behaviour therapy which are superficially very different from one another is that they allow responses to the phobic stimulus to habituate. This view fits naturally with the arguments advanced in the previous chapter. If much of the behaviour of the anxious person consists of innate reactions to stimuli to which he is particularly sensitive, it follows that the disappearance of such reactions is perhaps due to habituation of the kind described by Sokolov (1960; Horn and Hinde 1971). And, if habituation underlies the effects of behaviour therapy, the most important variable would be expected to be — as it seems in fact to be — total exposure time.

Before examining this view in closer detail, let us pause to consider what is involved in two of the methods of behaviour therapy most often used with phobic patients: systematic desensitization and flooding. We shall take extreme versions of the two methods, so as to contrast them more effectively.

In systematic desensitization stimuli are first graded into a hierarchy according to their capacity to elicit fear. They are then presented to the subject (usually by asking him to imagine them) in a sequence which corresponds to gradually increasing phobic power. Each stimulus presentation is typically short, since it is terminated as soon as the patient signals that he is beginning to feel anxious. As soon as the stimulus is terminated, the patient is instructed to relax deeply, using techniques in which he has been trained before therapy commences. This, essentially, is the method developed by Wolpe (1958). It is based on the notion of 'reciprocal inhibition' of anxiety by relaxation: 'if a response antagonistic to anxiety can be made to occur in the presence of anxiety evoking stimuli so that it is accompanied by a complete or partial suppression of the anxiety responses, the bond between these stimuli and the anxiety responses will be weakened'. This will be recognized as the same concept that we have called 'counter-conditioning' (Amsel 1962) earlier in the book (see Fig. 10.5, and the discussion of the partial reinforcement extinction and partial punishment effects in Chapter 2, Section 2.9, and Chapter 12). Relaxation serves the same function, theoretically, as food reward in these paradigms. The graded hierarchy of phobic power and the short stimulus presentation are intended to keep the level of anxiety down so that counter-conditioning is facilitated.

In flooding or implosive therapy (Stampfl 1970; Levis and Hare 1977), the patient is again asked to imagine aversive stimuli. But now the therapist attempts to maximize emotional arousal by describing the stimuli as vividly as he can and by opposing any attempt on the part of the patient to elude them. Apart from the fact that this all occurs in imagination, it is tantamount to throwing a child who is frightened of water into the deep end of a swimming pool. In this respect flooding is diametrically opposed to the step-by-step gradualism of systematic desensitization. Like Wolpe's

(1958) technique, however, it is based on the assumption that phobias are conditioned fears, and its purpose is to eliminate them. This is supposed to occur by simple extinction: 'the presentation of fear cues is expected to elicit a strong emotional response at first, but with repetition the emotional responding should subside' (Levis and Hare 1977). From this point of view, the brief and mild elicitation of fear on which systematic desensitization is based would be a slow and inefficient way to produce extinction.

Given the very different procedures used in these two therapies and the different theoretical analyses on which they are based, it would be reasonable to expect that, if one worked well, the other would not. Quite the opposite is the case: they both work fairly well, and attempts to discriminate between their therapeutic effects have by and large failed (Teasdale 1977; Levis and Hare 1977; Mathews 1978). This suggests that neither of them works quite in the way it is thought to do.

The habituation model of the treatment of phobias proposed by Lader and Mathews (1968) was intended to apply only to the method of systematic desensitization, since the flooding technique was not yet widely known. According to this model, anxiety is primarily a state of over-arousal in the central nervous system with consequently high levels of activity in the autonomic nervous system. This view is close to the one advocated here, if we substitute 'overactivity in the behavioural inhibition system' for over-arousal. This substitution is not a difficult one to make: arousal is one of the functions we have attributed to the behavioural inhibition system; and the level of skin conductance, taken by Lader and Mathews (1968) as a measure of arousal, appears to be under at least partial control by the behavioural inhibition system (Fowles 1980; and see the discussion in the previous chapter). The theory proposed by Lader and Mathews (1968) goes on to treat systematic desensitization as 'habituation occurring when the rate of habituation is maximal; that is, when the level of arousal is as low as possible consistent with clear consciousness'. On this view, the role of relaxation and the presentation of stimuli low in the phobic hierarchy for only short periods is to maintain arousal level as low as possible, this being thought to facilitate habituation of the phobic response. Theoretically, this approach is closer to the arguments used by proponents of flooding, since it is difficult to distinguish between the concept of habituation as used by Lader and Mathews (1968) and that of extinction as used by Levis and Hare (1977). In practice, however, the method Lader and Mathews (1968) argue for is systematic desensitization. This is no doubt largely due to the fact that, at the time, this was the only method in wide and successful use. This is a warning against taking too seriously the *post hoc* application of a theory to the known facts: an exercise in which we are, of course, engaged.

Recently, Watts (1979) has returned to the theme of habituation. He discards the 'maximal habituation' model of Lader and Mathews (1968) on the basis of both clinical evidence and advances in our understanding of the process of habituation. The hypothesis he proposes himself is, however, a natural extension of Lader and Mathews's. He follows Groves and Thompson (1970) in supposing that the reactions to a repeatedly presented stimulus are determined by the interaction of two processes, one decremental (habituation, properly speaking), the other incremental (sensitization). The net effect observed on any given trial then depends on the properties attributed to these two processes. Habituation is seen as relatively specific to the particular response elicited by a particular stimulus, and to depend on the formation of a 'neural model of the stimulus' after the manner proposed by Sokolov (1960). It is independent of stimulus intensity and grows with repeated training sessions. Sensitization, in contrast, is non-specific, affecting the general level of responsiveness only; it is positively related to stimulus intensity; and it at first grows, but then decays, especially over repeated sessions. In the short term (that is, immediately after a particular stimulus presentation), both habituation and sensitization are thought to decay over time, but sensitization decays more rapidly.

Watts (1979) specifically relates this model to the behavioural inhibition system as described by Gray (1975, 1976). As he points out, this system is activated both by novel stimuli (to which the concepts of habituation and sensitization are applicable) and by secondary aversive (including phobic) stimuli. Thus it becomes parsimonious to treat the loss of reaction to phobic stimuli during behaviour therapy as a species of habituation. The more completely developed model of the behavioural inhibition system presented in this book maps even better onto Watts's (1979) hypothesis. As we have seen, this model includes both a septo-hippocampal circuit for habituation (Chapter 10) and an ascending noradrenergic pathway of arousal (Chapter 11). We may therefore think of the decremental process in Watts's theory as taking place in the former circuit and the incremental process in the latter. Note further that, by so doing, we perhaps by-pass the theoretical issue which divides Wolpe's (1958) counter-conditioning (reciprocal inhibition) model of ' behaviour therapy from the habituation/extinction models of Lader and Mathews (1968) and Levis and Hare (1977). For, as we saw in Chapter 10 (see Figs. 10.4 and 10.5), the same septo-hippocampal circuitry which handles habituation (Vinogradova 1975) seems also to deal with counter-conditioning, at least where non-reward and the PREE are concerned (Gray *et al.* 1978).

It is one thing to narrow the gap between the counter-conditioning and habituation theories of behaviour therapy, but quite another to explain the equal success of two such different therapies as systematic desensitization and flooding. However, Watts's (1979) article also opens up a useful line of attack on this problem.

He argues that two different combinations of conditions can be derived from his model as being therapeutically effective. On the one hand one

can attempt to minimize the effects of sensitization, while allowing habituation to exert its beneficial effects. For this one would choose stimuli of
low phobic power and present them for short enough periods so that
sensitization does not occur to any great extent. This, of course, is the
method of systematic desensitization. Relaxation, as in Lader and
Mathews's (1968) treatment, is also seen as preventing sensitization
(arousal increment). In addition, since habituation but not sensitization is
stimulus specific, it should aid therapy if the stimulus is clearly perceived.
In support of this deduction, Watts cites an experiment of his own (Watts
1974) which showed that a careful description of the stimulus, each time
the subject was instructed to imagine it, enhanced the amount of long-
term reduction in anxiety produced by systematic desensitization. (Note
the congruence between this argument and the function of multidimensional stimulus analysis, attributed to the septo-hippocampal system in
Chapter 10.) In contrast to this combination of conditions, found in systematic desensitization, Watts (1979) proposes that flooding depends for
its therapeutic success on the fact that, although it maximizes sensitization, it also (by keeping the subject exposed to the phobic stimulus for
long periods) allows sensitization time to decay.

From this theory Watts (1979) is able to derive a number of specific
predictions which palliate a *tour de force* that is otherwise disturbingly *post
hoc*. Some of these predictions seem to be supported by existing data,
though these are scanty. Thus, for flooding to work, long sessions should
be essential, a deduction supported by the observations of Stern and
Marks (1973). Conversely, the optimal conditions for desensitization
should be short stimulus presentations together with relaxation. In accordance with this deduction, Proctor (1969) found 5-second stimulus presentations to be superior to 20-second presentations if the subject was
required to relax; but without relaxation the relationship between these
stimulus durations was reversed. Sue (1975) similarly found 5-second presentations to be superior to 30-second presentations with relaxation, but
observed no effect of stimulus duration without relaxation. Testing his
own theory, Watts (1971) found that, as predicted, anxiety reduction was
greater for items low in phobic power if 5-second presentations were used
rather than 30-second presentations; while for items high in phobic
power this relation was reversed. This was the pattern of results on a
short-term measure of anxiety reduction. But when long-term measures
are taken, it seems generally to be the case that anxiety reduction is directly proportional to exposure duration (Mathews 1978), and this was
observed in Watts's (1971) experiment even in the condition (low-intensity
stimuli) in which, on the short-term measure, short durations produced a
better effect. Watts (1979) suggests that this may be due to the more lasting effects of habituation relative to sensitization. Another finding consistent with the theory is that shortening the interval between stimulus
presentations weakened the anxiety reduction observed with high-

intensity stimuli, but had no effect with stimuli of low intensity (Watts 1973); this could be due to greater summation of sensitization over short inter-stimulus intervals when high-intensity stimuli are used (Watts 1979).

Clearly, this theory requires further confirmation. But it is well enough specified to lend itself readily to experimental test; and it handles the existing data as well as any of its competitors. From the present point of view it has the great merit of fitting snugly with our theory of anxiety, both psychologically and physiologically. Thus, jointly, the two theories hold out the promise of a coherent conceptual framework extending from the anatomical basis of anxiety in the rat to its treatment by behavioural methods in man.

Drug therapy

We have concentrated in this chapter on the methods of behaviour therapy. The other major method of treating anxiety is with drugs (psycho-surgery was dealt with in Chapter 13). Since the corner-stone of the theory developed earlier in the book has been the assumption that drugs such as the benzodiazepines and the barbiturates reduce anxiety, we cannot use the fact they do (Rickels 1978) as evidence in favour of the theory.

Note, however, that it is consistent with the evidence concerning the behavioural effects of these drugs in animals (Chapter 2) that they act only temporarily to suppress anxiety (Lader and Marks 1972): they do not eliminate the patient's reaction to anxiogenic stimuli as, in the best of cases, does behaviour therapy. Indeed, it is even possible that, under some conditions, the anti-anxiety drugs antagonize the beneficial effects of behaviour therapy on the long-term reduction of anxiety. This might be expected to occur, given that barbiturates and benzodiazepines sometimes block the PREE and the partial punishment effect (Gray 1977; Feldon et al. 1979; Feldon 1977; Feldon and Gray 1981a; Davis et al. 1981; Willner and Crowe 1977; see Chapter 2, Section 2.9, and Chapter 12). If these effects are construed as habituation to non-reward and punishment, respectively, and if behaviour therapy is construed as guided habituation to phobic stimuli, it follows that the anti-anxiety drugs may also block the effects of behaviour therapy.

The literature relevant to this deduction is small and inconsistent (Marks 1976; Mathews 1978). Several findings, however, suggest that the deduction is correct.

Taub et al. (1977) report the results of an experiment with rats deliberately designed to mimic combinations of flooding and pharmacotherapy common in the clinic. They trained rats on a one-way avoidance task (jumping to a retractable ledge). There was then a single 10-minute session of exposure to the grid floor without shock and with the ledge retracted, equivalent in conception to a flooding session. Drugs were given only during this session. Three days later the rats were tested without shock to see to what extent their avoidance response had been affected by 'flooding'. There was a significant reduction in avoidance in undrugged, flooded rats relative to controls not given a flooding session. This effect (equivalent to anxiety reduction, if the model is valid) was attenuated in rats given chlordiazepoxide, amylobarbitone, or meprobamate, as would be predicted from the argument above. It is not certain, however, that this was due to a direct action of the drug, since state dependency may have played a role (no drug was administered before the test session). From a clinical point of view, of course, this theoretical nicety is unimportant, since the hope is to finish up with a patient free of both anxiety and drugs. In any case, both direct and state-dependent drug effects may contribute to the same end result (weakened habituation), as in the case of the PREE (Gray 1969; Feldon *et al.* 1979).

Clinical findings point in the same direction. Thus Hafner and Marks (1976) treated agoraphobics by 'exposure *in vivo*', that is, by placing them in the real-life situation which elicited their anxiety. Exposure occurred after a placebo, or after diazepam given one or four hours previously (the 'peak' and 'waning' diazepam conditions, respectively). There was no effect of the drug if improvement was measured during or immediately after treatment. But at follow-up six months later the peak diazepam group was significantly worse than the placebo controls on measures of susceptibility to panic attacks and subjective anxiety, and non-significantly worse on measures of mood and somatic anxiety; and the waning diazepam group was not different from the placebo controls, but significantly superior to the peak diazepam group on three of these four measures. These results are in accord with expectation, both in that the deleterious effect of the drug was found in that condition (peak diazepam) which maximizes the likelihood of state dependency, and in that it affected specifically long-term improvement. An earlier study by the same group (Marks *et al.* 1972) used essentially the same design with patients suffering from specific phobias (of blood, spiders, etc.), but there was no long-term follow-up. In this experiment the immediate therapeutic effect of flooding *in vivo* was greater in the waning diazepam condition than in either of the other two. But this could have been due to differences in the amount of exposure, since the patients were tested individually and the speed of touching the phobic object was faster in the drugged subjects; as we have seen, increased exposure time would be expected to facilitate behaviour therapy. In the Hafner and Marks (1976) experiment, in contrast, patients were exposed in groups mixed with respect to drug condition, so this variable was controlled.

Thus there are probably two effects of the drug. One, beneficial, works by increasing the patient's exposure to the phobic object; the other, harmful, blocks the habituation that results from this exposure. In addition, of course, there is an acute reduction in anxiety while the drug continues to act directly. The interaction between these different effects may account for the mixed results obtained in other experiments of this kind (Hussain

1971; Johnston and Gath 1973; Chambless *et al.* 1979). But it is clear that anti-anxiety medication may sometimes attenuate or even reverse the benefits of behaviour therapy (Hafner and Marks 1976; Chambless *et al.* 1979). Given that the habituation which is specifically manipulated by behaviour therapy may occur in a less systematic manner also in the absence of therapy, so producing the high spontaneous recovery rate observed in anxiety syndromes, long-term maintenance on anti-anxiety drugs is usually contra-indicated as a therapeutic strategy. The best use of these drugs is probably as a short-term crutch, either to aid coping with a particularly threatening situation or to facilitate exposure to phobic stimuli during behaviour therapy. But, at least in the present state of the art, simple drug therapy should generally yield priority to behavioural methods of treatment.

16

The anxious personality

We do not all run equal risks of developing phobias, obsessive–compulsive behaviour, and so on. Certain kinds of people are much more likely to manifest these symptoms than others. We used this fact in Chapter 14 to define 'anxious' symptoms as those displayed by people of this kind, namely, neurotic introverts as these are described within the multidimensional personality space of Eysenck and Eysenck (1969). But this definition raises the futher question: what is the nature of the neurotic introvert, and how does this predispose him to anxiety?

From one point of view this question can be given a simple, almost trivial, answer within the theoretical framework developed in this book: a neurotic introvert is an individual with a highly sensitive or reactive behavioural inhibition system. This, by definition, makes him highly susceptible to anxiety. But even though this answer is axiomatic, it carries with it consequences which force a new look at the personality correlates of anxiety.

In the first place, since the behavioural inhibition system, as we have described it, functions as a unity (albeit one with differentiated parts), it is natural to locate anxious individuals at the pole of a single personality dimension, rather than in a quadrant bounded by two, as does Eysenck's 'neurotic introvert' location. I have considered this issue before (Gray 1970*b*) and proposed the rotation of Eysenck's axes shown in Fig. 16.1. This preserves two orthogonal axes in the space defined by Eysenck's dimensions of E and N, but now has one of them run from his neurotic introvert to his stable extrovert quadrant. Schematically, one can represent this as a 45° rotation of Eysenck's axes. But the fact that cingulectomy and prefrontal lesions reduce neuroticism more than introversion (Powell 1979), coupled with the observed correlations between the Eysenckian dimensions and scales intended directly to measure the trait of anxiety (Gray 1970*b*), suggests that a rotation which located the resulting dimension of 'Anxiety' (the negative diagonal in Fig. 16.1) closer to Eysenck's dimension of Neuroticism would be more appropriate (Gray 1981). The dimension thus rotated is close to the trait of anxiety found in the work of Cattell (e.g. 1965) and Taylor (1953).

Note that the techniques of factor analysis, used both by the Eysencks (1969) and Cattell (1965), can establish how many factors or dimensions there are in a given space, but not where they should be located. Thus, if any location of these axes reflects underlying causal influences (and it is entirely possible that none does), this cannot be established by factor-analytic techniques alone but must be justified by other considerations, empirical or theoretical. The rotation of Eysenck's axes shown in Fig. 16.1 can be justified in part in terms of parsimony: we now have to suppose that the effective physical therapies for anxiety (drugs and prefrontal or

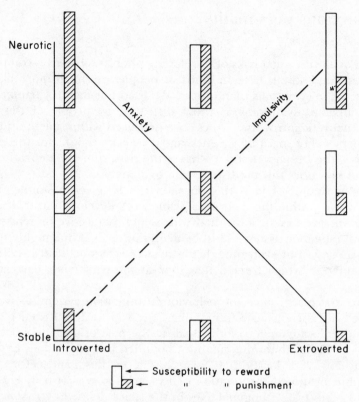

Figure 16.1. Rotation of Eysenck's dimensions of neuroticism and introversion–extroversion proposed by Gray (1970*b*). The dimension of trait Anxiety represents the steepest rate of growth in susceptibility to signals of punishment (and other adequate inputs to the behavioural inhibition system); the dimension of Impulsivity represents the steepest rate of growth in susceptibility to signals of reward. Introversion–extroversion now becomes a derived dimension, reflecting the balance of susceptibility to signals of punishment and reward, respectively; and neuroticism similarly reflects the sum of these two types of susceptibility to signals of reinforcement.

cingulate lesions) alter the functioning of only one biological system rather than two (Gray 1970*b*). Other reasons for making the rotation, germane more to personality theory than to anxiety as such, can be found in Gray (1970*b*, 1981) and Gray, Owen, Davis, and Tsaltas (1983).

Having rotated Eysenck's axes in this way, we can see more clearly the axiomatic nature of the answer I have so far offered to the question, what is the anxious personality? For the model shown in Fig. 16.1 states that an anxious individual is one who is highly susceptible to the adequate stimuli for anxiety (i.e. threats of punishment, of failure, etc., as discussed earlier in the book). And this is perilously close to circularity. But we are saved from circularity by the theoretical elaboration of the behavioural inhibition system that has gone before. This permits the derivation of many new predictions not contained in the description of an anxious person simply as one who is sensitive to anxiogenic stimuli. Furthermore, like any other aspect of personality, trait anxiety is a continuing disposition, present at all times; and scores on the dimension of Anxiety are continuously distributed in the normal population. It thus becomes possible to test predictions by seeking appropriate behavioural differences under laboratory conditions between normal individuals with differing levels of trait anxiety. This, of course, is the same strategy that Eysenck (1967), Cattell and Scheier (1961), and Spence and Spence (1966) have employed to test their several theories of anxiety.

Far from being trivial, then, the link between anxiety and the anxious personality opens up the theory developed here to experimental attack across a far wider range of data than would otherwise be possible. Indeed, so vast is the reach of these data that to measure the theory against them calls, not for a chapter, but another book. For the present, therefore, I can do no more than hint at some of the themes such a book should address.

Many of the relevant observations have been reviewed by Eysenck (1957, 1967, 1981) and incorporated within his developing theory of personality. Although this theory has many striking successes to its credit, the strains imposed on it by a number of key experimental findings made during the last 15 years or so are in my view too great for it to survive in its present form (Gray 1981). But, like any good scientific theory, its demise will eventually come at the hands of a better theory, rather than the experimental findings alone. Whether the present theory, suitably extended into the field of personality, provides a viable alternative to Eysenck's cannot be determined without a thorough analysis of the existing data from the new vantage point it offers, and we cannot attempt this here. But, as argued elsewhere (Gray, 1981), it seems in principle to be able to get round some of the problems with which Eysenck's theory is faced. Furthermore there are certain areas of data for which the two theories make conflicting predictions and the present theory is upheld.

The most notable of these concerns Eysenck's (1957) conditioning postulate, i.e. the hypothesis that introverts (and especially neurotic introverts) form conditioned reflexes more readily than extroverts. This postulate forms a critical link in the chain of argument by which Eysenck deduces that the neurotic introvert will be especially likely to manifest symptoms of anxiety (Gray 1970*b*; see Fig. 16.2). In contrast, the model presented in Fig. 16.1 postulates that introverts (and especially neurotic introverts) are particularly sensitive to secondary aversive stimuli, but relatively *in*sensitive to secondary positive reinforcers. Thus, if aversive conditioning is studied, both theories predict that introverts will out-perform extroverts; but, if appetitive stimuli are used, Eysenck's theory predicts

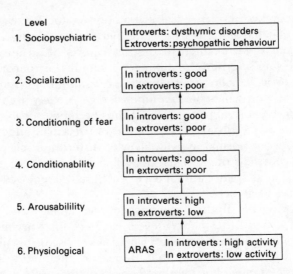

Figure 16.2. The structure of Eysenck's (1967) theory of the development of dysthymic behaviour in neurotic introverts and psychopathic behaviour in neurotic extroverts. Each level is thought to give rise causally to the next level above. ARAS, ascending reticular activating system. (From Gray (1970*b*).)

superior conditioning in introverts, whereas Gray's (1970*b*) predicts an extrovert superiority. The data lend support to the author's theory at this critical point (Gray 1970*b*, 1981; McCord and Wakefield 1981). The failure of Eysenck's conditioning postulate leaves him unable to predict the greater susceptibility to anxiety of the neurotic introvert (Gray 1970*b*); and this, from the present point of view, is the central problem in this area of personality theory.

The best way to determine the usefulness of a new approach to an old problem is usually to subject it to direct experimental test, rather than re-examine existing data. With a few exceptions (Nicholson and Gray 1972; Nicholson 1975; Seunath 1975; Gupta and Nagpal 1978; Kantorowitz 1978; McCord and Wakefield 1981), and these directed towards an earlier and simpler formulation, the present theory has yet to be tested directly at the level of personality. The description of the behavioural inhibition system that has been given in this book should permit the derivation of numerous predictions which can be examined experimentally at this level.

In any endeavour of this kind, however, there is a major practical problem that must be borne in mind. The concept of the behavioural inhibition system is based on the behaviour of animals in situations in which there is little doubt that the animal's first concern is with the task that the experimenter has set it (to avoid a shock, to obtain food, etc.). From observations of this kind there has emerged a view of anxiety as something *useful*, a process that serves the adaptive function of steering the animal away from danger or eliminating useless responses. This is in stark contrast to the view of anxiety that emerges from studies of human beings, whether in the psychiatric clinic or the experimental laboratory. Here, anxiety appears as a disruptive influence that prevents the subject from getting on with other things. In the laboratory, this situation probably arises because the tasks that are set a human subject are most unlikely, in the majority of cases, to become his first concern. While the experimenter wishes him to learn a list of nonsense syllables, his mind (if he is anxious) is on other things (am I being evaluated?, will I pass my examination tomorrow?, are there going to be electric shocks in this laboratory?). This problem has been discussed by Mandler and Sarason (1952), who accordingly distinguish between task-relevant and self-oriented responses (see M. W. Eysenck 1977, Chapter 10). Many of the predictions that can be derived from the concept of the behavioural inhibition system are applicable only if the subject's behaviour is largely dominated by task-relevant concerns.

To take one example, it is clear from the description of the behavioural inhibition system given in this book that an individual in whom this system is particularly efficient (*ex hypothesi* one high in trait anxiety) should be better at reversal learning than an individual low in trait anxiety. This is the exact reverse of the hypothesis derived by Spence and Spence (1966) from a Hullian analysis of anxiety. These workers deduce that anxious subjects should have particular difficulty in learning the correct response under conditions in which it is first necessary to inhibit a high-probability incorrect response to the same stimulus; and, by and large, the data support this deduction (M. W. Eysenck 1977, Chapter 10). But these data have been gained typically in paired-associate learning tasks; and it is reasonable to suppose, with Mandler and Sarason (1952), that such a task leaves plenty of emotional room for the intrusion of task-irrelevant concerns which, by competing for cognitive space, are likely to disrupt the performance of anxious individuals more than that of individuals low in anxiety. If anxious individuals are genuinely worse at reversal learning, it is strange that, in animals, anti-anxiety drugs impair the ability to suppress dominant incorrect responses and thus hinder reversal learning (Chapter 2). But the response the animal has to reverse is of overwhelming importance to its well-being. Thus the correct comparison is with the reversal of a response that is similarly important for human subjects and so likely to engage the behavioural inhibition system. It is not easy to see, however, how this can be achieved within the usual constraints of laboratory experiments.

Many similar predictions can easily be generated from the theory developed in this book, though usually hedged by the same practical qualifications. A more or less mechanical way of generating them is to make use of the effects of the anti-anxiety drugs described in Chapter 2: as a drugged animal is to a sober one, so an individual low on trait anxiety should be to one high on this trait. Others can be derived from the more abstract description of the behavioural inhibition system given in the later chapters of this book (see especially Chapter 10). For example, the capacity for multidimensional stimulus scanning attributed to the behavioural inhibition system implies that anxious individuals should learn more about the different aspects of a set of stimuli than individuals low in anxiety — provided, as before, that they are anxious *about* the stimuli rather than attending to other things. Such data as exist on this point are again negative: M. W. and M. C. Eysenck (1979) found that, with N scores equated, introverts had greater difficulty than extroverts in scanning verbal material simultaneously for physical and semantic features. Again, however, there is no reason to suppose that the task was of a kind to engage the behavioural inhibition system.

Before we bring this chapter to a close, there is one other problem in the field of personality which briefly requires our attention. The model shown in Fig. 16.1 places the Anxiety dimension in such a way that its other pole is located in Eysenck's stable extrovert quadrant. This location follows automatically so long as one stays within a two-dimensional space. Furthermore, it turns out to have certain advantages when one uses the model to account for the behaviour of primary psychopaths (Hare and Cox 1978), who appear to have stable extrovert personalities and (as predicted by the model) a specific deficit in passive avoidance learning (Gray, Owen, Davis, and Tsaltas, 1983). However, recent developments within Eysenck's personality theory (H. J. and S. B. G. Eysenck 1976; S. B. G. and H. J. Eysenck 1977, 1978) have forced this into a three-dimensional space, even when it deals with phenomena — notably, impulsivity, and psychopathy — which, in earlier versions of the theory, seemed to be encompassed by just two dimensions. Cattell (1965), of course, has long argued that many more dimensions than this are required. But it is sufficient to have three for quite new questions to arise concerning the correct location of the pole opposite to the one corresponding to high anxiety. Indeed, it is no longer clear that there is just one such 'opposite pole'; there could be several. One possibility is particularly relevant to the theme of this book: the dimension running from anxiety through neurotic to psychotic depression (see Chapter 12). In addition, there remain many attractions in the notion of a dimension running from high anxiety to primary psychopathy (Gray, Owen, Davis, and Tsaltas, 1983). But, if we are to postulate the existence of both these dimensions, many new questions arise concerning their interrelations.

Proper consideration of these issues would take us far beyond the scope of this book; nor was it my intention to do more than point to their existence, in the hope that they may be followed up at a later time.

17

Résumé

We have had a long and sometimes bumpy ride. This final chapter looks back over the road we have travelled and attempts to map, summarily, the theory we have constructed to answer two interrelated questions: what is the psychology of anxiety, and what is its neurology? But the arguments we have pursued have been too complex, the data too varied and abundant, for a summary to serve in any way as a substitute for reading the book. Thus the presentation here will be brief and dogmatic, indicating (not recapitulating) what has gone before.

1. Relying on data from behavioural and psychopharmacological experiments, we first postulated a behavioural inhibition system (Chapters 1 and 2). Activity in this system constitutes anxiety. The anti-anxiety drugs affect anxiety by impairing this activity. The major inputs to the behavioural inhibition system (and thus the adequate stimuli for anxiety) are: stimuli that warn of punishment or non-reward, novel stimuli, and innate fear stimuli (including those that arise during social interaction with conspecifics). The major outputs of the system are: inhibition of ongoing motor behaviour, increased level of arousal and increased attention to the environment, and especially to novel elements in the environment. In addition, there are changes in the activity of the autonomic nervous system which have figured very little in this book. The mode of operation of the behavioural inhibition system has been deduced from a consideration of data on the brain structures presumed to constitute this system (see below).

2. Data obtained in physiological and behavioural experiments (Chapters 3–8) suggest that the neural structures which make up the behavioural inhibition system include: the septal area, the hippocampal formation, and their interconnections (i.e. the septo-hippocampal system); the 'Papez circuit', running from the subicular area in the hippocampal formation to the mammillary bodies, anterior thalamus, cingulate cortex, and back to the subicular area; the neocortical inputs to the septo-hippocampal system from the entorhinal area and prefrontal cortex; the ascending noradrenergic and serotonergic inputs to the septo-hippocampal system; the dopaminergic ascending input to the prefrontal cortex; an ascending cholinergic input to the septo-hippocampal system; the noradrenergic innervation of the hypothalamus; and perhaps (underlying the autonomic outflow of the behavioural inhibition system) the descending noradrenergic fibres of the locus coeruleus (Chapters 10–13). This list is not necessarily exhaustive; nor is it implied that these structures do not participate in other functional systems.

3. Within this overall framework, the septo-hippocampal system, together with the entorhinal area and the 'subicular loop' (Papez's circuit)

has the task of predicting the next sensory event to which the animal will be exposed and checking whether it actually does occur; of operating the outputs of the behavioural inhibition system either if there is a mismatch between the actual and predicted events or if the predicted event is aversive; and of testing out alternative strategies (including alternative multidimensional descriptions of stimuli and/or responses) which may overcome the difficulty with which the animal is faced. Detailed proposals about the neural machinery involved in fulfilling these tasks are made in Chapter 10 (see Fig. 10.8). Among the outputs of the behavioural inhibition system, increased attention to and exploration of the environment are executed via the entorhinal area and cingulate cortex, and behavioural inhibition is executed via the cingulate cortex and a descending projection from the lateral septal area to the hypothalamus. The hippocampal theta rhythm quantizes and paces the flow of information around this system.

4. The role of the ascending noradrenergic projection to the septo-hippocampal system is to tag certain stimuli (entering the septo-hippocampal system from the entorhinal area) as 'important', i.e. requiring particularly careful checking; that of the ascending serotonergic projection is to add to this 'important' tag the information that the stimulus is associated with punishment and/or to bias the operation of the septo-hippocampal system more strongly towards the inhibition of motor behaviour; that of the ascending cholinergic projection is to facilitate stimulus analysis; and that of the noradrenergic projection to the hypothalamus is to mediate the increased arousal output of the behavioural inhibition system by priming hypothalamic motor systems (especially those involved in fight and flight behaviour) for rapid action when required (Chapters 11 and 12).

5. The prefrontal cortex (Chapter 13) plays two roles. It transmits to the septo-hippocampal system information about ongoing motor programmes to be used in the making of predictions about the next expected sensory events; and, in man, it allows neocortical control, using verbally coded information, of the activities of the septo-hippocampal system. The cingulate cortex may also participate in these functions.

6. The septo-hippocampal system does not store information, but it has access to and may modify information stored elsewhere. The most likely site of storage is in the temporal lobe, to which the septo-hippocampal system has access via the entorhinal area. In man the stored information to which the septo-hippocampal system has access is in part in verbal form. The bidirectional relations between the septo-hippocampal system and neocortical language areas (this and the previous paragraph) allow it to function under certain conditions independently of its ascending in-

puts. It is this interaction between language areas and the septo-hippocampal system which permits the latter to play a major role in human cognitive function even when this is not emotionally coloured (Chapter 9); in this role the capacity for multidimensional analysis of stimuli and responses (paragraph 3) is particularly important.

7. Under conditions of prolonged stress there are biphasic changes in the functioning of noradrenergic neurons (Chapter 12), a temporary exhaustion being followed by restored or even increased functional capacity. Exhaustion of the noradrenergic arousing input to the hypothalamus (paragraph 4) underlies the phenomena of helplessness in animals and the experience of depression in man. In man individual differences in the reactivity and tendency towards functional exhaustion of central noradrenergic neurons underlie the personality dimension running from susceptibility to anxiety to susceptibility to, successively, neurotic and psychotic depression.

8. The symptoms of anxiety in man (Chapter 14) arise from excessive activity in the behavioural inhibition system as described above. Phobias are most often due to exposure to innate fear stimuli, but secondary aversive stimuli are also sometimes important. Obsessive–compulsive symptoms are due to excessive checking activities in the behavioural inhibition system. The cognitive phenomena of the obsessive–compulsive syndrome arise from the interaction of the septo-hippocampal system and cortical language systems (paragraphs 5 and 6).

9. The therapeutic action of the anti-anxiety drugs is principally due to a reduction in the activity of ascending monoaminergic projections (noradrenergic and serotonergic to the septo-hippocampal system, noradrenergic to the hypothalamus, and dopaminergic to the prefrontal cortex). This may be secondary to an increase in the activity of GABA-ergic neurons afferent to the monoaminergic systems. A direct action in the hippocampus is also not excluded (Chapters 11–13).

10. Prefrontal and cingulate lesions (Chapter 13) are effective treatments for anxiety which is largely controlled by descending neocortical (linguistic) projections to the septo-hippocampal system (paragraphs 5, 6, and 8). For the same reasons, the conditions in which these lesions are effective are often resistant to pharmacotherapy.

11. Behaviour therapy is effective (Chapter 15) because it permits systematic habituation of the septo-hippocampal response to anxiogenic stimuli. The process of habituation is built in to the circuits described in Chapter 10.

12. Individuals who are especially susceptible to anxiety have highly reactive behavioural inhibition systems (Chapter 16). To allow this simple

description of the personality correlates of anxiety, the axes of Eysenck's personality space are rotated so that one dimension runs through high trait anxiety. However, personality is dealt with only briefly; this aspect of the theory will be developed elsewhere.

*   *   *

Our map is complete; whether it will serve as a useful guide to that portion of the Janus continent of mind and brain that is anxiety, only time and experiment will tell.

References

Abramson, L. Y., Seligman, M. E., and Teasdale, J. D. (1978). Learned helplessness in humans: critique and reformulation. *J. abnorm. Psychol.* **87**, 49–74.

Acheson, A., Zigmond, M. J., and Stricker, E. M. (1980). Compensatory increase in tyrosine hydroxylase activity in rat brain after intraventricular injections of 6-hydroxydopamine. *Science, N.Y.* **207**, 537–40.

Ackil, J. E., Mellgren, R. L., Halgren, C., and Frommer, G. P. (1969). Effects of CS pre-exposures on avoidance learning in rats with hippocampal lesions. *J. comp. physiol. Psychol.* **69**, 739–47.

Adey, W. R. (1967). Hippocampal states and functional relations with corticosubcortical systems in attention and learning. In *Progress in Brain Research* (ed. W. R. Adey and T. Tokizane) Vol. 27, pp. 228–45. Elsevier, Amsterdam.

—— Dunlop, C. W., and Hendrix, C. E. (1960). Hippocampal slow waves: distribution and phase relations in the course of approach learning. *Archs neurol., Chicago* **3**, 74–90.

Aghajanian, G. K., Cedarbaum, J. M., and Wang, R. Y. (1977). Evidence for norepinephrine-mediated collateral inhibition of locus coeruleus neurons. *Brain Res.* **136**, 570–7.

—— and Wang, R. Y. (1977). Habenular and other midbrain raphe afferents demonstrated by a modified retrograde tracing technique. *Brain Res.* **122**, 229–42.

Ahmad, S. S. and Harvey, J. A. (1968). Long-term effects of septal lesions and social experience on shock-elicited fighting in rats. *J. comp. physiol. Psychol.* **66**, 596–602.

Ahtee, L. and Shillito, E. (1970). The effect of benzodiazepines and atropine on exploratory behaviour and motor activity of mice. *Br. J. Pharmac.* **40**, 361–71.

Akhtar, S., Wig, N., Varma, O., Pershad, D., and Verma, S. (1975). A phenomenological analysis of symptoms in obsessive–compulsive neurosis. *Br. J. Psychiat.* **127**, 342–8.

Albert, D. J., Brayley, K. N., and Milner, J. A. (1978*a*). Connections from the lateral septum modulating reactivity in the rat. *Physiol. Behav.* **21**, 761–7.

—— —— —— (1978*b*). Medial hypothalamic electrical stimulation is ineffective in suppressing septal lesion induced hyperreactivity. *Physiol. Behav.* **21**, 135–9.

—— and Richmond, S. E. (1976). Neural pathways mediating septal hyperreactivity. *Physiol. Behav.* **17**, 451–5.

—— —— (1977). Reactivity and aggression in the rat: induction by alpha-adrenergic blocking agents injected ventral to anterior septum but not into lateral septum. *J. comp. physiol. Psychol.* **91**, 886–96.

—— and Wong, R. C. K. (1978). Hyperreactivity, muricide and intraspecific aggression in the rat produced by infusion of local anesthetic into the lateral septum or surrounding areas. *J. comp. physiol. Psychol.* **92**, 1062–73.

Alger, B. E. and Teyler, T. J. (1976). Long-term and short-term plasticity in the CA1, CA3 and dentate regions of the rat hippocampal slice. *Brain Res.* **110**, 463–80.

Alousi, A. and Weiner, N. (1966). The regulation of norepinephrine synthesis in sympathetic nerves: effect of nerve stimulation, cocaine and catecholamine releasing factors. *Proc. natn. Acad. Sci. USA* **56**, 1491–6.

Altman, J., Brunner, R. L., and Bayer, S. A. (1973). The hippocampus and behavioral maturation. *Behav. Biol.* **8**, 557–96.

Alvarez-Leefman, F. J. (1977). A structural and electrophysiological study of the synaptic mechanisms which affect the excitation of the granule cells of the

dentate gyrus of the rabbit. Unpublished Ph.D. thesis, London University.
—— and Gardner-Medwin, A. R. (1975). Influences of the septum on the hippocampal dentate area which are unaccompanied by field potentials. *J. Physiol., Lond.* **244,** 14–15P.

Amaral, D. G. and Foss, J. A. (1975). Locus coeruleus lesions and learning. *Science, N.Y.* **188,** 377–9.

Amsel, A. (1962). Frustrative nonreward in partial reinforcement and discrimination learning: some recent history and a theoretical extension. *Psychol. Rev.* **69,**306–28.

—— (1972). Behavioural habituation, counterconditioning, and a general theory of persistence. In *Classical conditioning II: current research and theory* (ed. A. H. Black and W. F. Prokasy) pp. 409–26. Appleton-Century-Crofts, New York.

—— Glazer, H., Lakey, J. R., McCuller, T., and Wong, P. T. P. (1973). Introduction of acoustic stimulation during acquisition and resistance to extinction in the normal and hippocampally damaged rat. *J. comp. physiol. Psychol.* **84,** 176–86.

—— and Roussel, J. (1952). Motivational properties of frustration. I. Effect on a running response of the addition of frustration to the motivational complex. *J. exp. Psychol.* **43,** 363–8.

Anchel, H. and Lindsley, D. B. (1972). Differentiation of two reticulo-hypothalamic systems regulating hippocampal activity. *Electroenceph. clin. Neurophysiol.* **32,** 209–26.

Andersen, P. (1978). Long-lasting facilitation of synaptic transmission. In *Functions of the septo-hippocampal system.* Ciba Foundation Symposium 58 (New Series) (ed. K. Elliott and J. Whelan) pp. 87–102. Elsevier, Amsterdam.

—— Bland, B. H., and Dudar, J. D. (1973). Organization of the hippocampal output. *Expl Brain Res.* **17,** 152–68.

—— —— Myhrer, T., and Schwartzkroin, P. A. (1979). Septo-hippocampal pathway necessary for dentate theta production. *Brain Res.* **165,** 13–22.

—— Bliss, T. V. P., and Skrede, K. K. (1971). Unit analysis of hippocampal population spikes. *Expl Brain Res.* **13,** 208–21.

—— Sundberg, S. H., and Sveen, O. (1977). Specific long-lasting potentiation of synaptic transmission in hippocampal slices. *Nature, Lond.* **266,** 736–7.

—— Teyler, T., and Wester, K. (1973). Long-lasting change of synaptic transmission in a specialised cortical pathway. *Acta physiol. scand.* Suppl. 396, 34.

Andy O. J., Peeler, D. F., and Foshee, D. P. (1967). Avoidance and discrimination learning following hippocampal ablation in cat. *J. comp. physiol. Psychol.* **64,** 516–19.

Anisman, H., Irwin, J., and Sklar, L. S. (1979a). Deficits of escape performance following catecholamine depletion: implications for behavioral deficits induced by uncontrollable stress. *Psychopharmacology* **64,** 163–70.

—— Remington, G., and Sklar, L. S. (1979b). Effect of inescapable shock on subsequent escape performance: catecholaminergic and cholinergic mediation of response initiation and maintenance. *Psychopharmacology* **61,** 107–24.

—— and Sklar, L. S. (1979). Catecholamine depletion in mice upon reexposure to stress: mediation of the escape deficits produced by inescapable shock. *J. comp. physiol. Psychol.* **93,** 610–25.

Anlezark, G. M., Crow, T. J., and Greenway, A. P. (1973). Impaired learning and decreased cortical norepinephrine after bilateral locus coeruleus lesions. *Science, N.Y.* **181,** 682–4.

Antelman, S. M., and Brown, T. S. (1972). Hippocampal lesions and shuttlebox avoidance behavior: a fear hypothesis. *Physiol. behav.* **9,** 15–20.

Apostol, G. and Creutzfeldt, O. D. (1974). Crosscorrelation between the activity of septal units and hippocampal EEG during arousal. *Brain Res.* **67,** 65–75.

Aprison, M. H., and Ferster, C. B. (1961). Neurochemical correlates of behavior: II. Correlation of brain monomine oxidase activity with behavioral changes after iproniazid and 5-hydroxytryptophan. *J. Neurochem.* **6**, 350–7.

Archer, J. (1973). Tests for emotionality in rats and mice: a review. *Anim. Behav.* **21**, 205–35.

Arnolds, D. E. A. T., Lopes da Silva, F. H., Aitiak, J. W., and Kamp, A. (1979a). Hippocampal EEG and behaviour in dog. I. Hippocampal EEG correlates of gross motor behaviour. *Electroenceph. clin. Neurophysiol.* **46**, 552–70.

—— —— —— —— (1979b) Hippocampal EEG and behaviour in dog. II. Hippocampal EEG correlates with elementary motor acts. *Electroenceph. clin. Neurophysiol.* **46**, 571–80.

—— —— —— —— (1979c) Hippocampal EEG and behaviour in dog. III. Hippocampal EEG correlates of stimulus–response tasks and of sexual behaviour. *Electroenceph. clin. Neurophysiol.* **46**, 581–91.

Ashcroft, G. W., Crawford, T. B. B., Eccleston, D., Sharman, D. F., McDougall, E. J., Stanton, J. B., and Binns, J. K. (1966). 5-Hydroxyindole compounds in the cerebro-spinal fluid of patients with psychiatric or neurological diseases. *Lancet* **ii**, 1049–52.

Asin, K. E., Wirtshaffer, D., and Kent, E. W. (1979). Straight alley acquisition and extinction and open field activity following discrete electrolytic lesions of the mesencephalic raphe nuclei. *Behav. neural Biol.* **25**, 242–56.

Assaf, S. Y. (1978). Electrical activity in the hippocampal formation of the rat: role of ascending monoamine systems. Unpublished Ph.D. thesis, University of British Columbia.

—— Mason, S. T., and Miller, J. J. (1979). Noradrenergic modulation of neuronal transmission between the entorhinal cortex and the dentate gyrus of the rat. *J. Physiol., Lond.* **292**, 52P.

—— and Miller, J. J. (1978). Neuronal transmission in the dentate gyrus: role of inhibitory mechanisms. *Brain Res.* **151**, 587–92.

Atlas, D. and Segal, M. (1977). Simultaneous visualization of noradrenergic fibres and beta-adrenoreceptors in pre- and postsynaptic regions in rat brain. *Brain Res.* **135**, 347–50.

Atnip, G. and Hothersall, D. (1975). Response suppression in normal and septal rats. *Physiol. Behav.* **15**, 417–21.

Azmitia, E. C. and McEwen, B. S. (1974). Adrenalcortical influence on rat brain tryptophan hydroxylase activity. *Brain Res.* **78**, 291–302.

—— —— (1976). Early response of rat brain tryptophan hydroxylase activity to cycloheximide, puromycin and corticosterone. *J. Neurochem.* **27**, 773–8.

—— and Segal, M. (1978). An autoradiographic analysis of the differential ascending projections of the dorsal and median raphe nucleus in the rat. *J. comp. Neurol.* **179**, 641–68.

Azrin, N. H. (1967). Pain and aggression. *Psychol. Today* **1**, 26–33.

Baddeley, H. (1981). Amnesia: a minimal model and an interpretation. In *Human memory and amnesia* (ed. L. Cermak). Erlbaum, Hillsdale, NJ.

Baenninger, R. (1967). Contrasting effects of fear and pain on mouse killing by rats. *J. comp. physiol. Psychol.* **63**, 298–303.

Ball, G. G. and Gray, J. A. (1971). Septal self-stimulation and hippocampal activity. *Physiol. Behav.* **6**, 547–9.

Baltzer, V., Huber, H., and Weiskrantz, L. (1979). Effects of various drugs on behavioral contrast using a double-crossover procedure. *Behav. neural Biol.* **27**, 330–41.

—— and Weiskrantz, L. (1970). Negative and positive behavioural contrast in the same animals. *Nature, Lond.* **228**, 581–2.

Barker, J. L. and Ransom, B. R. (1978). Pentobarbitone pharmacology of mammalian central neurones grown in tissue culture. *J. Physiol., Lond.* **280,** 355–72.

Barry, H. H. and Miller, N. E. (1965). Comparison of drug effects on approach, avoidance and escape motivation. *J. comp. physiol. Psychol.* **59,** 18–24.

Baumgarten, H. G., Klemm, H. P., and Lachenmayer, L. (1978). Mode and mechanism of action of neurotoxic indoleamines: a review and a progress report. *Ann. NY Acad. Sci.* **305,** 3–24.

Beatty, W. W., Beatty, P. A., Obriant, D. A., Gregoire, K. C., and Dahl, B. L. (1973). Factors underlying deficient passive-avoidance behavior by rats with septal lesions. *J. comp. physiol. Psychol.* **85,** 502–14.

—— Bengelloun, W. A., Vilberg, T. R., Klepac, R. K., and Steiner, J. M. (1975). Differential effects of CS intensity and flooding on the acquisition and extinction of one-way active avoidance responding in female rats with septal lesions. *Behav. Biol.* **13,** 311–21.

—— and Schwartzbaum, J. S. (1968). Commonality and specificity of behavioral dysfunctions following septal and hippocampal lesions in rats. *J. comp. physiol. Psychol.* **66,** 60–8.

Beckstead, R. M. (1978). Afferent connections of the entorhinal area in the rat as demonstrated by retrograde cell-labelling with horseradish peroxidase. *Brain Res.* **152,** 249–64.

Beech, R. (ed.) (1974). *Obessional states.* Methuen, London.

Belin, M. F., Aguera, M., Tappaz, M., McRae-Deguerce, A., Bobillier, P., and Pujol, J. F. (1979). GABA-accumulating neurons in the nucleus raphe dorsalis and periaqueductal gray in the rat: a biochemical and autoradiographic study. *Brain Res.* **170,** 279–97.

Benedict, C. R., Fillenz, M., and Stanford, S. C. (1977). Plasma noradrenaline levels during exposure to cold. *J. Physiol., Lond.* **269,** 47–48P.

Bengelloun, W. A. (1979). Elimination of the septal deficit in one-way active avoidance. *Physiol. Behav.* **22,** 615–19.

—— Burright, R. G., and Donovick, P. J. (1976a). Nutritional experience and spacing of shock opportunities alter the effects of septal lesions on passive avoidance acquisition by male rats. *Physiol. Behav.* **16,** 583–7.

—— —— —— (1977). Septal lesions, cue availability, and passive avoidance acquisition by hooded male rats of two ages. *Physiol. Behav.* **18,** 1033–7.

—— Nelson, D. J., Zent, H. M., and Beatty, W. W. (1976b). Behavior of male and female rats with septal lesions: influence of prior gonadectomy. *Physiol. Behav.* **16,** 317–30.

Beninger, R. J. and Phillips, A. G. (1979). Possible involvement of serotonin in extinction. *Pharmac. Biochem. Behav.* **10,** 37–42.

Bennett, T. L. and French, J. (1977). Electrical activity of the cat hippocampus during the species-typical gape response: evidence against the voluntary movement hypothesis. *Behav. Biol.* **21,** 432–7.

—— —— and Burnett, K. N. (1978). Species differences in the behavior correlates of hippocampal RSA. *Behav. Biol.* **22,** 161–77.

Berger, T. W. and Thompson, R. F. (1978a). Neuronal plasticity in the limbic system during classical conditioning of the rabbit nictating membrane response. I. The hippocampus. *Brain Res.* **145,** 323–46.

—— —— (1978b). Neuronal plasticity in the limbic system during classical conditioning of the rabbit nictating membrane response. II Septum and mammillary bodies. *Brain Res.* **156,** 293–314.

Bersh, P. J. (1980). Eysenck's theory of incubation: a critical analysis. *Behav. Res. Ther.* **18,** 11–17.

Best, P. J. and Orr, J. (1973). Effects of hippocampal lesions on passive avoidance and taste aversion conditioning. *Physiol. Behav.* **10,** 193–6.

Bignami, G., De Acetis, L., and Gatti, G. L. (1971). Facilitation and impairment of avoidance responding by phenobarbital sodium, chlordiazepoxide and diazepam — the role of performance baselines. *Pharmac. exp. Ther.* **176**, 725–32.

Billingsley, M. L. and Kubena, R. K. (1978). The effects of naloxone and picrotoxin on the sedative and anti-conflict effects of benzodiazepines. *Life Sci.* **22**, 897–906.

Bindra, D. and Reichert, H. (1967). The nature of dissociation: effects of transitions between normal and barbiturate-induced states on reversal learning and habituation *Psychopharmacologia* **10**, 330–44.

Bird, S. J. and Kuhar, M. J. (1977). Iontophoretic application of opiates to the locus coeruleus. *Brain Res.* **122**, 523–33.

Black, A. H. (1975). Hippocampal electrical activity and behavior. In *The Hippocampus*, Vol. 2, *Neurophysiology and behaviour* (ed. R. L. Isaacson and K. H. Pribam) pp. 129–67. Plenum, NY.

—— Nadel, L., and O'Keefe, J. (1977). Hippocampal function in avoidance learning and punishment. *Psychol. Bull.* **84**, 1107–29.

—— and Young, G. A. (1972). The electrical activity of the hippocampus and cortex in dogs operantly trained to move and to hold still. *J. comp. physiol. Psychol.* **79**, 128–41.

—— —— and Batenchuk, C. (1970). Avoidance training of hippocampal theta waves in flaxedilized dogs and its relation to skeletal movement. *J. comp. physiol. Psychol.* **70**, 15–24.

Black, I. B. (1975). Increased tyrosine hydroxylase activity in frontal cortex and cerebellum after reserpine. *Brain Res.* **95**, 170–5.

Blackman, D. (1968). Conditioned suppression or facilitation as a function of the behavioural baseline. *J. exp. Anal. Behav.* **11**, 53–61.

Blackstad, T. W. (1956). Commissural connections of the hippocampal region in the rat, with special reference to their mode of termination. *J. comp Neurol.* **105**, 417–537.

Blakeley, T. A. and Parker, L. F. (1973). The effects of parachlorophenylalanine on experimentally induced conflict behavior. *Pharmac. Biochem. Behav.* **1**, 609–13.

Blanchard, D. C., Blanchard, R. J., Lee, E. M. C., and Nakamura, S. (1979). Defensive behaviors in rats following septal and septal-amygdala lesions. *J. comp. physiol. Psychol.* **93**, 378–90.

—— —— Takahashi, L. K., and Takahashi, T. (1977). Septal lesions and aggressive behavior. *Behav. Biol.* **21**, 157–61.

Blanchard, R. J. and Blanchard, D. C. (1972). Effects of hippocampal lesions on the rat's reaction to a cat. *J. comp. physiol. Psychol.* **78**, 77–82.

—— —— and Fial, R. A. (1970). Hippocampal lesions in rats and their effect on activity, avoidance, and aggression. *J. comp. physiol. Psychol.* **71**, 92–102.

—— and Fial, R. A. (1968). Effects of limbic lesions on passive avoidance and reactivity to shock. *J. comp. physiol. Psychol.* **66**, 606–12.

Bland, B. H., Andersen, P., and Ganes, T. (1975). Two generators of hippocampal theta activity in rabbits. *Brain Res.* **94**, 199–218.

—— —— —— and Sveen, O. (1980). Automated analysis of rhythmicity of physiologically identified hippocampal formation neurons. *Expl Brain Res.* **38**, 205–19.

—— Sainsbury, R. S., and Creery, B. L. (1979). Anatomical correlates of rhythmical slow wave activity (theta in the hippocampal formation of the cat. *Brain Res.* **161**, 199–209.

—— and Vanderwolf, C. H. (1972a). Diencephalic and hippocampal mechanisms of motor activity in the rat: effects of posterior hypothalamic stimulation on behaviour and hippocampal slow wave activity. *Brain Res.* **43**, 67–88.

—— —— (1972*b*). Electrical stimulation of the hippocampal formation: Behavioural and biolectric effects. *Brain Res.* **43**, 89–106.

—— and Whishaw, I. Q. (1976). Generators and topography of hippocampal theta (RSA) in the acute and freely moving rabbit. *Brain Res.* **118**, 259–80.

Bliss, T. V. P. (1980). Hippocampal function: a review of *The hippocampus as a cognitive map* by J. O'Keefe and L. Nadel. *Nature, Lond.* **283**, 230–1.

—— and Gardner-Medwin, A. R. (1973). Long-lasting potentiation of synaptic transmission in the dentate area of the unanaesthetised rabbit following stimulation of the perforant path. *J. Physiol., Lond.* **232**, 357–74.

Bloch, V. (1970). Facts and hypotheses concerning memory consolidation. *Brain Res.* **24**, 561–75.

—— Hennevin, E., and Leconte, P. (1978). Relationship between paradoxical sleep and memory processes. *Brain mechanisms in memory and learning: from the single neuron to man* (ed. M. A. B. Brazier) pp. 329–43. Raven Press, New York.

Boarder, M. R., Feldon, J., Gray, J. A., and Fillenz, M. (1979). Effect of runway training on rat brain tyrosine hydroxylase: differential effect of continuous and partial reinforcement schedules. *Neurosci. Lett.* **15**, 211–15.

—— and Fillenz, M. (1978). Synaptosomal tyrosine hydroxylation in the rat brain: comparison of activity from hippocampus and hypothalamus with activity from striatum. *J. Neurochem.* **31**, 1419–25.

—— —— (1979). Absence of increased tyrosine hydroxylation after induction of brain tyrosine hydroxylase following reserpine administration. *Biochem. Pharmac.* **28**, 1675–7.

Boast, C. A., Zornetzer, S. F., and Hamrick, M. R. (1975). Electrolytic lesions of various hippocampal subfields in the mouse: differential effects on short- and long-term memory. *Behav. Biol. 14*, 85–94.

Bobillier, P., Seguin, S., Petitjean, F., Salvert, D., Touret, M., and Jouvet, M. (1976). The raphe nuclei of the cat brainstem: a topographical atlas of their efferent projections as revealed by autoradiography. *Brain Res.* **113**, 449–86.

Boissier, J. R., and Simon, P. (1969). Evaluation of experimental techniques in the psychopharmacology of emotion. *Ann. NY Acad. Sci.* **159**, 898–914.

Boitano, J. J. and Isaacson, R. L. (1967). Effects of variation in shock-intensity on the behavior of dorsal-hippocampectomized rats in two passive-avoidance situations. *Am. J. Psychol.* **80**, 73–80.

—— Lubar, J. F., Auer, J., and Furnald, M. S. (1968). Effects of hippocampectomy on consummatory behavior and movement inhibition in rats. *Physiol. Behav.* **3**, 901–6.

Bolles, R. C. (1971). Species-specific defence reactions. In *Aversive conditioning and learning* (ed. F. R. Brush) pp. 183–233. Academic Press, New York.

—— (1972). The avoidance learning problem. In *The psychology of learning and motivation* (ed. G. H. Bower) Vol. 6, pp. 97–145. Academic Press, New York.

—— Stokes, L. W., and Younger, M. S. (1966). Does CS termination reinforce avoidance behaviour? *J. comp. physiol. Psychol.* **62**, 201–7.

Booth, C. L., Meyer, P. M., and Abrams, J. (1979). Changes in social behavior of mice with septal lesions. *Physiol. Behav.* **22**, 931–7.

Bowery, N. G., Hill, D. R., Hudson, A. L., Doble, A., Middlemiss, D. N., Shaw, J., and Turnbull, M. (1980). (−) Baclofen decreases neurotransmitter release in the mammalian CNS by an action at a novel GABA receptor. *Nature, Lond.* **283**, 92–4.

Brady, J. V., and Nauta, W. J. H. (1953). Subcortical mechanisms in emotional behavior: affective changes following septal forebrain lesions in the albino rat. *J. comp. physiol. Psychol.* **46**, 339–46.

—— —— (1955). Subcortical mechanisms in emotional behavior: the duration of affective changes following septal and habenular lesions in the albino rat. *J. comp. physiol. Psychol.* **48**, 412–20.

Braestrup, C. and Nielsen, M. (1980). Benzodiazepine receptors. *Arzneimittelforsch.* **30**, 852–7.

—— and Squires, R. F. (1977). Specific benzodiazepine receptors in rat brain characterized by high-affinity [³H]-diazepam binding. *Proc. natn. Acad. Sci. USA* **74**, 3805–9.

Braggio, J. T. and Ellen, P. (1976). Cued DRL training: effects on the permanence of lesion-induced over-responding. *J. comp. physiol. Psychol.* **90**, 694–703.

Brayley, K. N. and Albert, D. J. (1977a). Suppression of VMH-lesion-induced reactivity and aggressiveness in the rat by stimulation of lateral septum, but not medial septum or cingulate cortex. *J. comp. physiol. Psychol.* **91**, 290–9.

—— —— (1977b). Suppression of VMH-lesion-induced reactivity and aggressiveness by electrical stimulation ventral to the anterior septum in the rat. *Physiol. Behav.* **18**, 567–71.

Brazier, M. A. B. (1968). Studies of the EEG activity of limbic structures in man. *Electroenceph. clin. Neurophysiol.* **25**, 309–18.

Breglio, V., Anderson, D. C., and Merrill, H. K. (1970). Alteration in footshock threshold by low-level septal brain stimulation. *Physiol. Behav.* **5**, 715–19.

Broadbent, D. E. (1971). *Decision and stress*. Academic Press, London.

Broadhurst, P. L. (1960). Applications of biometrical genetics to the inheritance of behaviour. In *Experiments in personality*, Vol. 1 *Psychogenetics and psychopharmacology* (ed. H. J. Eysenck) pp. 1–102. Routledge Kegan Paul, London.

—— (1975). The Maudsley reactive and nonreactive strains of rats: a survey. *Behav. Genet.* **5**, 299–319.

Brody, J. F. (1970). Behavioural effects of serotonin depletion and *p*-chlorophenylalanine (a serotonin depletor) in rats. *Psychopharmacologia* **17**, 14–33.

Brooks, V. B. (1979). Motor programs revisited. In *Posture and movement* (ed. R. E. Talbott and D. R. Humphrey) pp. 13–49. Raven Press, New York.

Brown, B. B. (1968). Frequency and phase of hippocampal theta activity in the spontaneously behaving cat. *Electroenceph. clin. Neurophysiol.* **24**, 53–62.

Brown, G. W. and Harris, T. (1978). *Social origins of depression*. Tavistock, London.

—— Ni Bhrolchain, M., and Harris, T. O. (1979). Psychotic and neurotic depression. Part 3: Aetiological and background factors. *J. affect. Disord.* **1**, 195–211.

Brown, J. S. (1961). *The motivation of behavior*. McGraw Hill, New York.

Brown, M. W. (1982). The effect of context on the response of single units recorded from the hippocampal region of behaviourally trained monkeys. In *Neuronal plasticity and memory formation: Proc. VIth Int. Neurobiol. Symp. Learning Memory* (ed. C. Ajmone Marsan and H. Matthies). Raven Press, New York.

Brown, P. L. and Jenkins, H. M. (1968). Auto-shaping of the pigeon's key-peck. *J. exp. Anal. Behav.* **11**, 1–8.

Brown, R. T. and Wagner, A. R. (1964). Resistance to punishment and extinction following training with shock or non-reinforcement. *J. exp. Psychol.* **68**, 503–7.

Brown, T. S., Kaufman, P. G., and Marco, L. A. (1969). The hippocampus and response perseveration in the cat. *Brain Res.* **12**, 86–98.

Browne, T. R. and Perry, J. K. (1973). Benzodiazepines in the treatment of epilepsy. *Epilepsia* **14**, 277–310.

Brozoski, T. J., Brown, R. M., Rosvold, H. E., and Goldman, P. S. (1979). Cognitive deficit caused by regional depletion of dopamine in prefrontal cortex of Rhesus monkey. *Science, N.Y.* **205**, 929–32.

Brücke, F., Petsche, H., Pillat, B., and Deisenhammer, E. (1959). Die Beeinflussung der 'Hippocampus-arousal-Reaktion' beim Kaninchen durch elektrische Reizung im Septum. *Pflügers Arch. ges. Physiol.* **269**, 319–38.

Brunner, R. L. and Rossi, R. R. (1969). Hippocampal disruption and passive avoidance behavior. *Psychon. Sci.* **15**, 228–9.

——— Stutz, R. M., and Roth, T. G. (1970). Memory loss following posttrial electrical stimulation of the hippocampus. *Psychon. Sci.* **18**, 159–60.

Brutkowski, S. (1965). Functions of prefrontal cortex in animals. *Physiol. Rev.* **45**, 721–46.

Buddington, R. W., King, F. A., and Roberts, L. (1967). Emotionality and conditioned avoidance responding in the squirrel monkey following septal injury. *Psychon. Sci.* **8**, 195–6.

Bunnell, B. N. and Smith, M. H. (1966). Septal lesions and aggressiveness in the cotton rat. *Psychon. Sci.* **6**, 443–4.

Buño, W. Jr and Velluti, J. C. (1977). Relationships of hippocampal theta cycles with bar pressing during self-stimulation. *Physiol. Behav.* **19**, 615–21.

Butter, C. M. (1969). Perseveration in extinction and in discrimination reversal tasks following selective frontal ablations in *Macaca mulatta*. *Physiol. Behav.* **4**, 163–71.

——— Mishkin, M., and Mirsky, A. F. (1968). Emotional responses toward humans in monkeys with selective frontal lesions. *Physiol. Behav.* **3**, 213–15.

——— and Snyder, D. R. (1972). Alterations in aversive and aggressive behaviors following orbital frontal lesions in Rhesus monkeys. *Acta neurobiol. exp.* **32**, 525–65.

——— ——— and McDonald, J. A. (1970). Effects of orbital frontal lesions on aversive and aggressive behaviors in Rhesus monkeys. *J. comp. physiol. Psychol.* **72**, 132–44.

Butters, N., Butter, C., Rosen, J., and Stein, D. (1973). Behavioral effects of sequential and one-stage ablations of orbital prefrontal cortex in the monkey. *Expl Neurol.* **39**, 204–14.

——— and Cermak, L. S. (1975). Some analyses of amnesic syndromes in brain-damaged patients. In *The hippocampus*, Vol. 2 *Neurophysiology and behaviour* (ed. R. L. Isaacson and K. H. Pribram) pp. 377–409. Plenum Press, New York.

Byzsakaki, G., Grastyan, E., and Lenard, L. (1978). Hippocampal inhibition and the fornix. *Behav. Biol.* **22**, 67–76.

Calderazzo Filho, L. S., Moschorakis, A., and Izquierdo, I. (1977). Effect of hippocampal lesions on rat shuttle responses in four different behavioral tests. *Physiol. Behav.* **19**, 569–72.

Cannon, W. B. (1932). *The wisdom of the body*. Norton, New York.

Capaldi, E. J. (1967). A sequential hypothesis of instrumental learning. In *The psychology of learning and motivation* (ed. K. W. Spence and J. T. Spence) Vol. 1, pp. 67–156. Academic Press, New York.

Caplan, M. (1973). An analysis of the effects of septal lesions on negatively reinforced behavior. *Behav. Biol.* **9**, 129–67.

Capobianco, S., Macdougall, J. M., and Foster, S. M. (1977). Direct neurobehavioral comparisons within the septohippocampal system. *Physiol. Psychol.* **5**, 215–20.

Carder, B. (1971). Effects of septal stimulation on active avoidance in rats. *Physiol. Behav.* **6**, 503–6.

Carey, R. J. (1967). A retention loss following septal ablations in the rat. *Psychon. Sci.* **7**, 307–8.

Carlson, N. R., Carter, E. N., and Vallante, M. (1972). Runway alternation and discrimination of mice with limbic lesions. *J. comp. physiol. Psychol.* **78**, 91–101.

——— and Norman, R. J. (1971). Enhanced go, no-go single-lever alternation of mice with septal lesions. *J. comp. physiol. Psychol.* **75**, 508–12.

——— and Vallante, M. A. (1974). Enhanced cue function of olfactory stimulation in mice with septal lesions. *J. comp. physiol. Psychol.* **87**, 237–48.

Carlton, P. (1963). Cholinergic mechanisms in the control of behavior by the brain. *Psychol. Rev.* **70**, 19–39.

Cattell, R. B. (1965). *The scientific analysis of personality.* Pelican, Harmondsworth.

—— and Scheier, I. H. (1961). *The meaning and measurement of neuroticism and anxiety.* Ronald, New York.

Caul, W. F. (1967). Effects of ambarbital on discrimination acquisition and reversal. *Psychopharmacologia* **11**, 414–21.

Cedarbaum, J. M. and Aghajanian, G. K. (1976). Noradrenergic neurons of the locus coeruleus: inhibition by epinephrine and activation by the alpha-antagonist piperoxane. *Brain Res.* **112**, 413–19.

—— —— (1978). Afferent projections to the rat locus coeruleus as determined by a retrograde tracing technique. *J. comp. Neurol.* **178**, 1–16.

Cermak, L. S. and Butters, N. (1972). The role of interference and encoding in the short-term memory deficits of Korsakoff patients. *Neuropsychologia* **10**, 89–95.

—— —— and Gerrein, J. (1973). The extent of the verbal encoding ability of Korsakoff patients. *Neuropsychologia* **11**, 85–94.

—— —— and McReines, J. (1974). Some analyses of the verbal encoding deficit of alcoholic Korsakoff patients. *Brain Lang.* **2**, 141–50.

Chambless, D. L., Foa, E. B., Groves, G. A., and Goldstein, A. J. (1979). Flooding with Brevital in the treatment of agoraphobia: counter-effective? *Behav. Res. Ther.* **17**, 243–52.

Chance, W. T., White, A. C., Krynock, G. M., and Rosecrans, J. A. (1978). Conditioned fear-induced antinociception and decreased binding of [³H]N-leu-enkephalin to rat brain. *Brain Res.* **141**, 371–74.

Chapman, W. P., Rose, A. S., and Solomon, H. C. (1948). Measurements of heat stimulus producing motor withdrawal reaction in patients following frontal lobotomy *Res. Publs. Ass. Res. nerv. ment. Dis.* **27**, 754–62.

Chase, T. N., Katz, R. I., and Kopin, P. J. (1970). Effect of diazepam on fate of intracisternally injected serotonin-C14 *Neuropharmacology* **9**, 103–8.

Chen, J. S. and Amsel, A. (1977). Prolonged, unsignalled, inescapable shocks increase persistence in subsequent appetitive instrumental learning. *Anim. Learn. Behav.* **4**, 377–85.

Cherry, C. T. (1975). Variability and discrimination reversal learning in the open field following septal lesions in rats. *Physiol. Behav.* **15**, 641–6.

Chi, C. C. (1965). The effect of amobarbital sodium on conditioned fear as measured by the potentiated startle response in rats. *Psychopharmacologia* **7**, 115–22.

Chin, T., Donovick, P. J., and Burright, R. G. (1976). Septal lesions in rats produce reversal deficits in a simultaneous visual discrimination. *J. comp. physiol. Psychol.* **90**, 1133–43.

Chou, D. T. and Wang, S. C. (1977). Unit activity of amygdala and hippocampal neurons: effects of morphine and benzodiazepines. *Brain Res.* **126**, 427–40.

Chu, N. S. and Bloom, F. E. (1974). The catecholamine-containing neurons in the cat dorsolateral pontine tegmentum: distribution of the cell bodies and some axonal projections. *Brain Res.* **66**, 1–21.

Church, R. M., Wooten, C. L., and Matthews, T. J. (1970). Discriminative punishment and the conditioned emotional response. *Learn. Motiv.* **1**, 1–17.

Clavier, R. M., Fibiger, H. C., and Phillips, A. G. (1976). Evidence that self-stimulation of the region of the locus coeruleus in rats does not depend upon noradrenergic projections to telencephalon. *Brain Res.* **113**, 71–81.

Clody, D. E. and Carlton, P. L. (1969). Behavioral effects of lesions of the medial septum of rats. *J. comp. physiol. Psychol.* **67**, 344–51.

Cogan, D. C., Posey, T. B., and Reeves, J. L. (1976). Response patterning in hippocampectomized rats. *Physiol. Behav.* **16**, 569–76.

—— and Reeves, J. L. (1979). Passive avoidance learning in hippocampectomized rats under different shock and intertrial interval conditions. *Physiol. Behav.* **22**, 1115–21.

Cohen, J. S. (1970). Exploration in the hippocampal-ablated albino rat. *J. comp. physiol. Psychol.* **73**, 261–8.

Cohen, R. P. and Hamburg, M. D. (1975). Evidence for adrenergic neurons in a memory access pathway. *Pharmac. Biochem. Behav.* **3**, 519–23.

Collier, T. J. and Routtenberg, A. (1978). Entorhinal cortex electrical stimulation disrupts retention performance when applied after, but not during, learning. *Brain Res.* **152**, 411–17.

Cook, L. and Davidson, A. B. (1973). Effects of behaviorally active drugs in a conflict-punishment procedure in rats. In *The benzodiazepines* (ed. S. Garattini, E. Mussini, and L. O. Randall) pp. 327–45. Raven Press, New York.

—— and Sepinwall, J. (1975). Behavioral analysis of the effects and mechanisms of action of benzodiazepines. In *Mechanisms of action of benzodiazepines* (ed. E. Costa and P. Greengard) pp. 1–28. Raven Press, New York.

Corkin, S. (1968). Acquisition of motor skill after bilateral medial temporal-lobe excision. *Neuropsychologia* **6**, 255–65.

Corrodi, H., Fuxe, K., Lidbrink, P., and Olson, L. (1971). Minor tranquilizers, stress and central catecholamine neurons. *Brain Res.* **29**, 1–16.

Coscina, D. V. and Lash, L. (1969). The effects of differential hippocampal lesions on a shock versus shock conflict. *Physiol. Behav.* **4**, 227–33.

—— —— (1970). Extinction of active avoidance as a measure of passive avoidance in hippocampectomized rats. *Psychon. Sci.* **18**, 35–6.

Costa, E. and Greengard, P. (eds.) (1975). *Mechanism of action of benzodiazepines* Raven Press, New York.

Costain, D. W., Green, A. R., and Grahame-Smith, D. G. (1979). Enhanced 5-hydroxytryptamine-mediated behavioural responses in rats following repeated electroconvulsive shock: relevance to the mechanism of the antidepressive effect of electroconvulsive therapy. *Psychopharmacology* **61**, 167–70.

Crespi, L. P. (1942). Quantitative variation of incentive and performance in the white rat. *Am. J. Psychol.* **55**, 467–517.

Crews, F. T. and Smith, C. B. (1978). Presynaptic alpha-receptor subsensitivity after long-term antidepressant treatment. *Science, NY* **202**, 322–4.

Crow, T. J. (1972a). A map of the rat mesencephalon for electrical self-stimulation. *Brain Res.* **36**, 265–73.

—— (1972b). Catecholamine-containing neurones and electrical self-stimulation. I. A review of some data. *Psychol. Med.* **2**, 414–21.

—— (1973). Catecholamine neurones and self-stimulation. II. A theoretical interpretation and some psychiatric implications. *Psychol. Med.* **3**, 66–73.

—— Deakin, J. F. W., File, S. E., Longden, A., and Wendlandt, S. (1978). The locus coeruleus noradrenergic system: evidence against a role in attention, habituation, anxiety and motor activity. *Brain Res.* **155**, 249–61.

—— Longden, A., Smith, A., and Wendlandt, S. (1977). Pontine tegmental lesions, monoamine neurones and varieties of learning. *Behav. Biol.* **20**, 184–96.

—— and Wendlandt, S. (1976). Impaired acquisition of a passive avoidance response after lesions induced in the locus coeruleus by 6-hydroxydopamine. *Nature, Lond.* **259**, 42–4.

Crowne, D. P. and Riddell, W. I. (1969). Hippocampal lesions and the cardiac component of the orienting response in the rat. *J. comp. physiol. Psychol.* **69**, 748–55.

Curtis, D. R., Felix, D., and McLennan, H. (1970). GABA and hippocampal inhibition. *Br. J. Pharmac.* **40**, 881–3.

Curzon, G. and Green, A. R. (1969). Effects of immobilization on rat liver tryptophan pyrrolase and brain 5-hydroxytryptamine metabolism. *Br. J. Pharmac.* **37**, 689–97.

Dabrowska, J. and Drzewiecka, B. (1975). Comparison of the septal lesion effects on visual and spatial discrimination in rats. *Acta Neurobiol. exp.* **35**, 255–74.

Dahlgren, N. and Lindvall, O. (1980). Effects of locus coeruleus lesions on cerebral blood flow and oxygen consumption in the rat brain. *Abstr. 12th CINP Congr.* pp. 120–1 (Suppl. to *Prog. Neuropsychopharmac.*). Pergamon, Oxford.

Dahlstrom, A. and Fuxe, K. (1964). Evidence for the existence of monoamine-containing neurons in the central nervous system. I. Demonstration of monoamines in the cell bodies of brain stem neurons. *Acta physiol. scand.* **62**, Suppl. 232, 1–55.

—— —— (1965). Evidence for the existence fo monoamine neurons in the central nervous system. II. Experimentally induced changes in the intraneuronal amine levels of bulbospinal neuron systems. *Acta physiol. scand.* **64**, Suppl. 247, 1–36.

Dalby, D. A. (1970). Effect of septal lesions on the acquisition of two types of active-avoidance behavior in rats. *J. comp. physiol. Psychol.* **73**, 278–83.

Dalhouse, A. D. (1976). Social cohesiveness, hypersexuality and irritability induced by *p*-CPA in the rat. *Physiol. Behav.* **17**, 679–86.

Dalland, T. (1970). Response and stimulus perseveration in rats with septal and dorsal hippocampal lesions. *J. comp. physiol. Psychol.* **71**, 114–18.

—— (1976). Response perseveration of rats with dorsal hippocampal lesions. *Behav. Biol.* **17**, 473–84.

Dantzer, R. and Mormede, P. (1976). Fear-dependent variations in continuous avoidance behavior of pigs. I. Lack of effect of diazepam on performance of discriminative fear conditioning. *Psychopharmacology* **49**, 69–73.

—— —— and Favre, B. (1976). Fear-dependent variations in continuous avoidance behavior of pigs. II. Effects of diazepam on acquisition and performance of Pavlovian fear conditioning and plasma corticosteroid levels. *Psychopharmacology* **49**, 75–8.

Davis, M. (1979). Diazepam and flurazepam: effects on conditioned fear as measured with the potentiated startle paradigm. *Psychopharmacology* **62**, 1–7.

—— Cedarbaum, J. M., Aghajanian, G. K., and Gendelman, D. S. (1977). Effects of clonidine on habituation and sensitization of acoustic startle in normal, decerebrate and locus coeruleus lesioned rats. *Psychopharmacology* **57**, 243–53.

—— Redmond, D. E. Jr, and Baraban, J. M. (1979). Noradrenergic agonists and antagonists: effects on conditioned fear as measured by the potentiated startle paradigm. *Psychopharmacology* **65**, 111–18.

Davis, N. M. (1979*a*). The role of serotonergic and other mechanisms in behavioural responses to punishment. Unpublished D. Phil. thesis, University of Oxford.

—— (1979*b*). Attentional hypothesis in question. *Trends Neurosci.* **2**, 170–1.

—— Brookes, S., Gray, J. A., and Rawlins, J. N. P. (1981). Chlordiazepoxide and resistance to punishment. *Q Jl exp. Psychol.* **33B**, in press.

Davison, C., Lowther, W. R., and Allen, J. D. (1975). Effect of septal lesions on behavioral contrast. *Physiol. Psychol.* **3**, 179–82.

Dawson, R. G., Conrad, L., and Lynch, G. (1973). Single and two-stage hippocampal lesions: a similar syndrome. *Expl Neurol.* **40**, 263–77.

De Castro, J. and Hall, T. W. (1975). Fornix lesions: effects on active and passive avoidance behavior. *Physiol. Psychol.* **3**, 201–4.

De France, J. F. (ed.) (1976a). *The septal nuclei* Plenum, New York.
—— (1976b). A functional analysis of the septal nuclei. In *The septal nuclei* (ed. J. F. DeFrance) pp. 185–227. Plenum, New York.
—— Yoshihara, H., and Chronister, R. B. (1978). Electrophysiological studies of the septal nuclei: II. The medial septal region. *Expl Neurol.* **58**, 14–31.
De Molina, A. F. and Hunsperger, R. W. (1962). Organization of the subcortical system governing defense and flight reactions in the cat. *J. Physiol., Lond.* **160**, 200–13.
De Noble, V. and Caplan, M. (1977). Enhanced response acceleration or suppression produced by response-independent food presentations in rats with septal lesions. *J. comp. physiol. Psychol.* **91**, 107–19.
De Pottier, W. P., Chanh, C. P.-H., De Smet, F., and De Schaepdryver, A. F. (1976). The presence of dopamine beta-hydroxylase in the cerebrospinal fluid of rabbits and its increased concentration after stimulation of peripheral nerves and cold stress. *Neuroscience* **1**, 523–9.
De Wied, D. and Bohus, B. (1979). Modulation of memory processes by neuropeptides of hypothalamic neurohypophyseal origin. In *Brain mechanisms in memory and learning: from the single neuron to man* (ed. M. A. B. Brazier) pp. 139–49. Raven Press, New York.
Deadwyler, S. A., Dunwiddie, T., and Lynch, G. (1978). Short lasting changes in hippocampal neuronal excitability following repetitive synaptic activation. *Brain Res.* **147**, 384–9.
—— West, M., and Lynch, G. (1979). Synaptically identified hippocampal slow potentials during behavior. *Brain Res.* **161**, 211–25.
Deets, A. C., Harlow, H. F., Singh, S. D., and Blomquist, A. J. (1970). Effects of bilateral lesions of the frontal granular cortex on the social behavior of Rhesus monkeys. *J. comp. physiol. Psychol.* **72**, 452–61.
Descarries, L., Watkins, K. C., and Lapierre, Y. (1977). Noradrenergic axon terminals in the cerebral cortex of rat: III. Topometric ultrastructural analysis. *Brain Res.* **133**, 197–222.
Destrade, C. and Jaffard, R. (1978). Post-trial hippocampal and lateral hypothalamic electrical stimulation: facilitation on long-term memory of appetitive and avoidance-learning tasks. *Behav. Biol.* **22**, 354–74.
—— —— Desminière, J.-M., and Cardo, B. (1976). Effets de la stimulation de l'hippocampe sur la réminiscence chez deux lignées de souris. *Physiol. Behav.* **16**, 237–43.
—— Soumireu-Mourat, B., and Cardo, B. (1973). Effects of posttrial hippocampal stimulation on acquisition of operant behaviour in the mouse. *Behav. Biol.* **8**, 713–24.
Deuel, R. and Mishkin, M. (1977). Limbic and prefrontal contributions to somesthetic learning in monkeys. *Brain Res.* **132**, 521–35.
Dickinson, A. (1973). Septal lesions in rats and the acquisition of free-operant successive discriminations. *Physiol. Behav.* **10**, 305–13.
—— (1974). Response suppression and facilitation by aversive stimuli following septal lesions in rats: a review and model. *Physiol. Psychol.* **2**, 444–56.
—— (1975). Suppressive and enhancing effects of footshock on food-reinforced operant responding following septal lesions in rats. *J. comp. physiol. Psychol.* **88**, 851–61.
—— (1980). *Contemporary animal learning theory.* Cambridge University Press.
—— and Morris, R. G. M. (1975). Conditioned acceleration and free-operant wheel-turn avoidance following septal lesions in rats. *Physiol. Psychol.* **3**, 107–12.
—— and Pearce, J. M. (1977). Inhibitory interactions between appetitive and aversive stimuli. *Psychol. Bull.* **84**, 690–711.

Dillier, N., Laszlo, J., Muller, B., Koella, W. P., and Olpe, H.-R. (1978). Activation of an inhibitory noradrenergic pathway projecting from the locus coeruleus to the cingulate cortex of the rat. *Brain Res.* **154**, 61–8.

Divac, I., Björklund, A., Lindvall, O., and Passingham, R. E. (1978). Converging projections from the mediodorsal thalamic nucleus and mesencephalic dopaminergic neurons to the neocortex in three species. *J. comp. Neurol.* **180**, 59–72.

Dokla, C. P. J. (1979). Effects of hippocampectomy in a one-trial electroconvulsive shock paradigm. *Physiol. Psychol.* **7**, 53–8.

Domesick, V. B. (1969). Projections from the cingulate cortex in the rat. *Brain Res.* **12**, 296–320.

Donovick, P. J. (1968). Effects of localized septal lesions on hippocampal EEG activity and behavior in rats. *J. comp. physiol. Psychol.* **66**, 569–78.

—— Burright, R. G., and Fink, E. A. (1979). Discrimination behavior of rats with septal lesions in a cue addition–deletion paradigm. *Physiol. Behav.* **22**, 125–31.

—— —— Sikorsky, R. D., Stamato, N. J., and McLaughlin, W. W. (1978). Cue elimination effects on discrimination behavior of rats with septal lesions. *Physiol. Behav.* **20**, 71–8.

—— and Schwartzbaum, J. S. (1966). Effects of low-level stimulation of the septal area on two types of discrimination reversal in the rat. *Psychon. Sci.* **6**, 3–4.

—— and Wakeman, K. A. (1969). Open-field dominance and 'septal hyperemotionality'. *Anim. Behav.* **17**, 186–90.

Dorworth, T. R. and Overmier, J. B. (1977). On 'learned helplessness': the therapeutic effects of electroconvulsive shocks. *Physiol. Psychol.* **5**, 355–8.

Douglas, R. J. (1967). The hippocampus and behavior. *Psychol. Bull.* **67**, 416–42.

—— Barrett, T. W., Pribram, K. H., and Cerny, M. C. (1969). Limbic lesions and error reduction. *J. comp. physiol Psychol.* **68**, 437–41.

—— and Pribram, K. H. (1966). Learning and limbic lesions. *Neuropsychologia* **4**, 197–219.

—— —— (1969). Distraction and habituation in monkeys with limbic lesions. *J. comp. physiol. Psychol.* **69**, 473–80.

—— and Truncer, P. C. (1976). Parallel but independent effects of pentobarbital and scopolamine on hippocampus related behavior. *Behav. Biol.* **18**, 359–67.

Drewe, E. A. (1975a). An experimental investigation of Luria's theory on the effects of frontal lobe lesions in man. *Neuropsychologia* **13**, 421–9.

—— (1975). Go-no go learning after frontal lobe lesions in humans. *Cortex* **11**, 8–16.

Drewett, R. F., Gray, J. A., James, D. T. D., McNaughton, N., Valero, I., and Dudderidge, H. J. (1977). Sex and strain differences in septal driving of the hippocampal theta rhythm as a function of frequency: effects of gonadectomy and gonadal hormones. *Neuroscience* **2**, 1033–41.

Dudai, Y. and Segal, M. (1978). Alpha-bungarotoxin binding sites in rat hippocampus: localization in post-synaptic cells. *Brain Res.* **154**, 161–71.

Duncan, P. M. (1971). Effect of temporary septal dysfunction on conditioning and performance of fear responses in rats. *J. comp. physiol. Psychol.* **74**, 340–8.

—— (1972). Effect of septal area damage and base-line activity levels on conditioned heart-rate response in rats. *J. comp. physiol. Psychol.* **81**, 131–42.

—— and Duncan, N. C. (1971). Free-operant and T-maze avoidance performance by septal and hippocampal-damaged rats. *Physiol Behav.* **7**, 687–93.

Dunwiddie, T., Madison, D., and Lynch, G. (1978). Synaptic transmission is required for initiation of long-term potentiation. *Brain Res.* **150**, 413–17.

Eichelmann, B. S. (1971). Effect of subcortical lesions on shock-induced aggression in the rat. *J. comp. physiol. Psychol.* **74**, 331–9.

Eison, M. S., Stark, A. D., and Ellison, G. (1977). Opposed effects of locus coeruleus and substantia nigra lesions on social behavior in rat colonies. *Pharmac. Biochem. Behav.* **7**, 87–90.

Elazar, Z. and Adey, W. R. (1967). Spectral analysis of low frequency components in the electrical activity of the hippocampus during learning. *Electroenceph. clin. Neurophysiol.* **23**, 225–46.

Ellen, P., Dorsett, P. G., and Richardson, W. K. (1977). The effect of cue-fading on the DRL performance of septal and normal rats. *Physiol. Psychol.* **5**, 469–476.

—— Gillenwater, G., and Richardson, W. K. (1977). Extinction responding by septal and normal rats following acquisition under four schedules of reinforcement. *Physiol. Behav.* **18**, 609–15.

—— Makohon, L., and Richardson, W. K. (1978). Response suppression on DRL by rats with septal damage. *J. comp. physiol. Psychol.* **92**, 511–21.

—— and Powell, E. W. (1962). Effects of septal lesions on behaviour generated by positive reinforcement. *Expl Neurol.* **6**, 1–11.

—— and Wilson, A. S. (1963). Perseveration in the rat following hippocampal lesions. *Expl Neurol.* **8**, 310–17.

Elliott, K. and Whelan, J. (eds.) (1978). Functions of the septo-hippocampal system. Ciba Foundation Symposium 58 (New Series). Elsevier, Amsterdam.

Ely, D. L., Greene, E. G., and Henry, J. P. (1976). Minicomputer monitored social behavior of mice with hippocampus lesions. *Behav. Biol.* **16**, 1–29.

—— —— —— (1977). Effects of hippocampal lesion on cardiovascular, adrenocortical and behavioural response patterns in mice. *Physiol. Behav.* **18**, 1075–83.

Emson, P. C. and Koob, G. F. (1978). The origin and distribution of dopamine-containing afferents to the rat frontal cortex. *Brain Res.* **142**, 249–67.

Endröczi, E. and Nyakas, C. (1971). Effect of septal lesion on exploratory activity, passive avoidance learning and pituitary–adrenal function in the rat. *Acta physiol. hung.* **39**, 351–60.

Engel, G. L. and Schmale, A. H. (1972). Conservation-withdrawal: a primary regulatory process for organismic homeostasis. In *Physiology, emotion and psychosomatic illness* (ed. R. Porter and J. Knight) Ciba Symposium 8 (New Series), pp. 57–75. Elsevier, Amsterdam.

Entingh, D. (1971). Perseverative responding and hyperphagia following entorhinal lesions in cats. *J. comp. physiol. Psychol.* **75**, 50–8.

Eriksson, H. E., Köhler, C., and Sundberg, H. (1976). Exploratory behavior after angular bundle lesions in the albino rat. *Behav. Biol.* **17**, 123–30.

Estes, W. K. and Skinner, B. F. (1941). Some quantitative properties of anxiety. *J. exp. Psychol.* **29**, 390–400.

Evans, J. P. M., Grahame-Smith, D. G., Green, A. R., and Tordoff, A. F. C. (1976). Electroconvulsive shock increases the behavioural responses of rats to brain 5-hydroxytryptamine accumulation and central nervous system stimulant drugs. *Br. J. Pharmac.* **56**, 193–9.

Eysenck, H. J. (1957). *The dynamics of anxiety and hysteria.* Praeger, New York.

—— (1960). Classification and the problem of diagnosis. In *Handbook of abnormal psychology* (ed. H. J. Eysenck) pp. 1–31. Pitman, London.

—— (1967). *The biological basis of personality.* Thomas, Springfield, Ill.

—— (1977). *You and neurosis.* Temple Smith, London.

—— (1979). The conditioning model of neurosis. *Behav. Brain Sci.* **2**, 155–66.

—— (ed.) (1981). *A model for personality.* Springer, New York.

—— and Eysenck, S. B. G. (1969). *The structure and measurement of personality.* Routledge and Kegan Paul, London.

—— —— (1976). *Psychoticism as a dimension of personality*. Hodder and Stoughton, London.

—— and Rachman, S. (1965). *The causes and cures of neurosis*. Knapp, San Diego.

Eysenck, M. W. (1977). *Human memory: theory, research and individual differences*. Pergamon, Oxford.

—— and Eysenck, M. C. (1979). Memory scanning, introversion–extraversion and levels of processing. *J. Res. Pers.* **13**, 305–15.

Eysenck, S. B. G. and Eysenck, H. J. (1977). The place of impulsiveness in a dimensional system of personality description. *Br. J. soc. clin. Psychol.* **16**, 57–68.

—— —— (1978). Impulsiveness and venturesomeness: their position in a dimensional system of personality description. *Psychol. Rep.* **43**, 1247–55.

Falk, J. L. (1971). The nature and determinants of adjunctive behaviour. *Physiol. Behav.* **6**, 577–88.

Fallon, D. and Donovick, P. J. (1970). Low resistance to extinction in rats with septal lesions under inappropriate appetitive motivation. *J. comp. physiol. Psychol.* **73**, 150–6.

Fantie, B. D. (1979). Septal modulation of perforant path-evoked activity in the fascia dentata of the rat. Unpublished MA thesis, Dalhousie University.

Feder, R. and Ranck, J. B. Jr (1973). Studies on single neurons in dorsal hippocampal formation and septum in unrestrained rats. II. Hippocampal slow waves and theta cell firing during bar pressing and other behaviours. *Expl Neurol.* **41**, 532–55.

Feigley, D. A. and Hamilton, L. W. (1971). Response to novel environment following septal lesions or cholinergic blockade in rats. *J. comp. physiol. Psychol.* **76**, 496–504.

Feldon, J. (1977). The effects of anti-anxiety drugs and selective lesions of the septo-hippocampal system on behavioural responses to non-reward and punishment. Unpublished D.Phil. thesis, University of Oxford.

—— and Gray, J. A. (1979a). Effects of medial and lateral septal lesions on the partial reinforcement extinction effect at one trial a day. *Q. Jl exp. Psychol.* **31**, 653–74.

—— —— (1979b). Effects of medial and lateral septal lesions on the partial reinforcement extinction effect at short inter-trial intervals. *Q. Jl exp. Psychol.* **31**, 675–90.

—— —— (1981a). The partial reinforcement extinction effect after treatment with chlordiazepoxide. *Psychopharmacology* **73**, 269–75.

—— —— (1981b). The partial reinforcement extinction effect: influence of chlordiazepoxide in septal-lesioned rats. *Psychopharmacology*, **74**, 280–9.

—— Guillamon, A., Gray, J. A., De Wit, H., and McNaughton, N. (1979). Sodium amylobarbitone and responses to nonreward. *Q. Jl exp. Psychol.* **31**, 19–50.

Ferraro, D. P. and York, K. M. (1968). Punishment effects in rats selectively bred for emotional elimination. *Psychon. Sci.* **10**, 177–8.

Fibiger, H. C., Lepiane, F. G., and Phillips, A. G. (1978). Disruption of memory produced by stimulation of the dorsal raphe nucleus: mediation by serotonin. *Brain Res.* **155**, 380–6.

—— and Mason, S. T. (1978). The effects of dorsal bundle injections of 6-hydroxydopamine on avoidance responding in rats. *Br. J. Pharmac.* **64**, 601–5.

—— Mertz, P. H., and Campbell, B. A. (1972). The effect of para-chlorophenylalanine on aversion thresholds and reactivity to foot shock. *Physiol. Behav.* **8**, 259–63.

—— Roberts, D. C. S., and Price, M. T. C. (1975). On the role of telencephalic noradrenaline in learning and memory. In *Chemical tools in catecholamine research*, Vol. 1 (ed. G. Jonssen, T. Malinfors, and C. Sachs) pp. 349–56. North Holland, Amsterdam.

File, S. E. (1976). A comparison of the effects of ethanol and chlordiazepoxide on exploration and on its habituation. *Physiol. Psychol.* **4**, 529–32.

—— (1980). The use of social interaction as a method for detecting anxiolytic activity of chlordiazepoxide-like drugs. *J. neurosci. Meth.* **2**, 219–38.

Fillenz, M. (1973). Hypothesis for a neuronal mechanism involved in memory. *Nature, Lond.* **238**, 41–3.

—— (1977). The factors which provide short-term and long-term control of transmitter release. *Prog. Neurobiol.* **8**, 251–78.

—— Graham-Jones, S., and Gray, J. A. (1979). The effect of foot-shock on synaptosomal tyrosine hydroxylation in rat brain regions. *J. Physiol., Lond.* **296**, 97–8P.

—— and West, D. P. (1976). Fate of noradrenaline storage vesicles after release. *Neurosci. Lett.* **2**, 285–7.

Flaherty, C. F., Capobianco, S., and Hamilton, L. W. (1973). Effect of septal lesions on retention of negative contrast. *Physiol. Behav.* **11**, 625–31.

—— and Hamilton, L. W. (1971). Responsivity to decreasing sucrose concentrations following septal lesions in the rat. *Physiol. Behav.* **6**, 431–7.

—— Powell, G., and Hamilton, L. W. (1979). Septal lesion, sex, and incentive shift effects on open field behavior of rats. *Physiol. Behav.* **22**, 903–9.

Foote, S. L., Bloom, F. E., and Schwartz, A. (1978). Behavioral and electroencephalographic correlates of locus coeruleus neuronal discharge activity in the unanaesthetized squirrel monkey. *Soc. Neurosci. Abst.* **4**, 848.

—— Freedman, R., and Oliver, A. P. (1975). Effects of putative neurotransmitters on neuronal activity in monkey auditory cortex. *Brain Res.* **86**, 229–42.

Fowles, D. (1980). The three arousal model: implications of Gray's two-factor learning theory for heart rate, electrodermal activity and psychopathy. *Psychophysiology* **17**, 87–104.

Fox, S. E. and Ranck, J. B. Jr (1975). Localization and anatomical identification of theta cells and complex spike cells in dorsal hippocampal formation of rats. *Expl Neurol.* **49**, 299–313.

Franchina, J. J. and Brown, T. S. (1970). Response patterning and extinction in rats with hippocampal lesions. *J. comp. physiol. Psychol.* **70**, 66–72.

Frank, L. H. and Beatty, W. W. (1974). Effects of septal lesions on passive avoidance behavior using ice water as the aversive stimulus. *Physiol. Behav.* **12**, 321–3.

Franklin, R. V. and Broadhurst, P. L. (1979). Emotionality in selectively bred strains of rats mediates prior shock effects on escape-avoidance conditioning. *Behav. Res. Ther.* **17**, 349–54.

Fredrikson, M. and Öhman, A. (1979). Cardiovascular and electrodermal responses conditioned to fear-relevant stimuli. *Psychophysiology* **16**, 1–7.

Freedman, P. E., Hennessy, J. W., and Groner, D. (1974). Effects of varying active/passive shock levels in shuttle box avoidance in rats. *J. comp. physiol. Psychol.* **86**, 79–84.

Freedman, R., Hoffer, B. J., Puro, D., and Woodward, D. J. (1976). Noradrenaline modulation of the responses of the cerebellar Purkinje cell to afferent synaptic activity. *Br. J. Pharmac.* **57**, 603–5.

Freeman, F. G., Kramarcy, N. R., and Lee, J. (1973). Discrimination learning and stimulus generalization in rats with hippocampal lesions. *Physiol. Behav.* **11**, 273–5.

—— Mikulka, P. J., and D'Auteuil, P. (1974). Conditioned suppression of a licking response in rats with hippocampal lesions. *Behav. Biol.* **12**, 257–63.

Fried, P. A. (1969). Effects of septal lesions on conflict resolution in rats. *J. comp. physiol. Psychol.* **69**, 375–80.

—— (1972*a*). Conflict resolution by septal, dorsal hippocampal or ventral hippocampal lesioned rats with pre- or post-operative approach training. *Br. J. Psychol.* **63**, 411–20.

—— (1972*b*). Septum and behavior: a review. *Psychol. Bull.* **78**, 292–310.

—— and Goddard, G. V. (1967). The effects of hippocampal lesions at different stages of conflict in rat. *Physiol Behav.* **2**, 325–30.

Frith, C. D., Johnstone, E. C., Owens, D., and McPherson, K. (1979). The phenomenological, pharmacological and psychophysiological characteristics of neurotic outpatients to whom no diagnosis has been applied. In *Neuropsychopharmacology* (ed. B. Saletu, P. Berner, and L. Hollister) pp. 473–7. Pergamon, Oxford.

Fukuda, S. and Iwahara, S. (1974). Dose effects of chlordiazepoxide upon habituation of open-field behavior in white rats. *Psychologia* **17**, 82–90.

Fuller, J. L. (1970). Strain differences in the effects of chlorpromazine and chlordiazepoxide upon active and passive avoidance in mice. *Psychopharmacologia* **16**, 261–71.

Fuster, J. M. (1973). Unit activity in prefrontal cortex during delayed-response performance: neuronal correlates of transient memory. *J. Neurophysiol.* **36**, 61–78.

—— and Uyeda, A. A. (1971). Reactivity of limbic neurons of the monkey to appetitive and aversive signals. *Electroenceph. clin. Neurophysiol.* **30**, 281–93.

Fuxe, K., Agnati, L. F., Bolme, P., Hökfelt, T., Lidbrink, P., Ljungdahl, A., Perez de la Mora, M., and Ögren, S.-O. (1975). The possible involvement of GABA mechanisms in the action of benzodiazepines on central catecholamine neurons. In *Mechanism of action of benzodiazepines* (ed. E. Costa and P. Greengard) *Adv. Biochem. Pharmac.*, Vol. 14, pp. 45–61. Raven, New York.

—— Corrodi, H., Hökfelt, T., and Jonsson, G. (1970). Central monoamine neurons and pituitary–adrenal activity. *Prog. Brain Res.* **32**, 42–56.

—— and Jonsson, G. (1974). Further mapping of central 5-hydroxytryptamine neurons: studies with the neurotoxic dihydroxytryptamines. In *Serotonin: new vistas* (ed. E. Costa, G. L. Gessa, and M. Sandler) *Adv. Biochem. Psychopharmac.* Vol. 10, pp. 1–12.

—— Ögren, S.-O., Agnati, L. F., Jonsson, G., and Gustafsson, J.-A. (1978). 5,7-Dihydroxytryptamine as a tool to study the functional role of central 5-hydroxytryptamine neurons. *Ann NY Acad. Sci.* **305**, 346–69.

Gabriel, M., Foster, K., Orona, E., Saltwick, S. E., and Stanton, M. (1980). Neuronal activity of cingulate cortex, anteroventral thalamus, hippocampal formation and discriminative conditioning: encoding and the extraction of the significance of conditional stimuli. *Prog. Psychobiol. physiol. Psychol.* (ed. J. M. Sprague and A. Epstein), vol. 9, pp. 125–231. Academic Press, New York.

—— Miller, J. D., and Saltwick, S. E. (1977). Unit activity in cingulate cortex and anteroventral thalamus of the rabbit during differential conditioning and reversal. *J. comp. physiol. Psychol.* **91**, 423–33.

Gaffan, D. (1972). Loss of recognition memory in rats with lesions of the fornix. *Neuropsychologia* **10**, 327–41.

—— (1973). Inhibitory gradients and behavioural contrast in rats with lesions of the fornix. *Physiol. Behav.* **11**, 215–20.

—— (1974). Recognition impaired and association intact in the memory of monkeys after transection of the fornix. *J. comp. physiol. Psychol.* **86**, 1100–9.

—— (1977*a*). Monkeys' recognition memory for complex pictures and the effect of fornix transection. *Q. Jl exp. Psychol.* **29**, 505–14.

—— (1977b). Recognition memory after short retention intervals in fornix-transected monkeys. *Q. Jl exp. Psychol.* **29,** 577–88.

Gage, F. H., Olton, D. S., and Bolanowski, D. (1978). Activity, reactivity and dominance following septal lesions in rats. *Behav. Biol.* **22,** 203–10.

Gallager, D. W. (1978). Benzodiazepines: potentiation of a GABA inhibitory response in the dorsal raphe nucleus. *Eur. J. Pharmac.* **49,** 133.

Gallup, G. G. (1965). Aggression in rats as a function of frustrative nonreward in a straight alley. *Psychon. Sci.* **3,** 99–100.

Garber, E. E. and Simmons, H. J. (1968). Facilitation of two-way avoidance performance by septal lesions in rats. *J. comp. physiol. Psychol.* **66,** 559–62.

Garrud, P., Goodall, G., and Mackintosh, N. J. (1981). Overshadowing of a stimulus-reinforcer association by an instrumental response. *Q. Jl. exp. Psychol.* **33B,** 123–35.

Gekiere, F., Allègre, G., Brindeau, F., and Borenstein, P. (1980). Benzodiazépines et système limbique: anxiété et vigilance. *Path. Biol., Paris* **28,** 63–7.

Gelder, M. G., Bancroft, J. H. J., Gath, D. H., Johnston, D. W., Matthews, A. M., and Shaw, P. M. (1973). Specific and non-specific factors in behaviour therapy. *Br. J. Psychiat.* **123,** 445–62.

Geller, I., Bachman, E., and Seifter, J. (1963). Effects of reserpine and morphine on behavior suppressed by punishment. *Life Sci.* **4,** 226–31.

—— and Blum, K. (1970). The effects of 5-HTP on para-chlorophenylalamine (*p*-CPA) attenuation of 'conflict' behavior. *Eur. J. Pharmac.* **9,** 319–24.

—— Hartman, R. J., Croy, D. J., and Haber, B. (1974). Attenuation of conflict behavior with cinanserin, a serotonin antagonist: reversal of the effect with 5-hydroxytryptophan and 2-methyltryptamine. *Res. Comm. chem. Path. Pharmac.* **1,** 165–74.

—— and Seifter, J. (1960). The effects of meprobamate, barbiturates, D-amphetamine and promazine on experimentally induced conflict in the rat. *Psychopharmacologia* **1,** 482–92.

Gerbrandt, L. K., Lawrence, J. C., Eckardt, M. J., and Lloyd, R. D. (1978). Origin of the neocortically monitored theta rhythm of the curarized rat. *Electroenceph. clin. Neurophysiol.* **45,** 454–67.

—— Rose, G., Wheeler, R. L., and Lynch, G. (1978). Distribution of the perforant path following selective elimination of granule cells. *Expl Neurol.* **62,** 122–32.

Geyer, M. A., Puerto, A., Menkes, D. B., Segal, D. S., and Mandell, A. J. (1976). Behavioural studies following lesions of the mesolimbic and mesostriatal serotonergic pathways. *Brain Res.* **106,** 257–70.

Glazer, H. I. (1974a). Instrumental response persistence following induction of hippocampal theta frequency during fixed-ratio responding in rats. *J. comp. physiol. Psychol.* **86,** 1156–62.

—— (1974b). Instrumental conditioning of hippocampal theta and subsequent response persistence. *J. comp. physiol. Psychol.* **86,** 267–273.

—— and Weiss, J. M. (1976a). Long-term and transitory interference effects. *J. exp. Psychol.: Anim. Behav. Proc.* **2,** 191–201.

—— —— (1976b). Long-term interference effect: an alternative to 'learned helplessness'. *J. exp. Psychol.: Anim. Behav. Proc.* **2,** 202–13.

—— —— Pohorecky, L. A., and Miller, N. E. (1975). Monoamines as mediators of avoidance-escape behavior. *Psychosom. Med.* **37,** 535–43.

Glick, S. D. and Greenstein, S. (1973). Comparative learning and memory deficits following hippocampal and caudate lesions in mice. *J. comp. physiol. Psychol.* **82,** 188–94.

—— Marsanico, R. G., and Greenstein, S. (1974). Differential recovery of function following caudate, hippocampal, and septal lesions in mice. *J. comp. physiol. Psychol.* **86,** 787–92.

Gold, M. S., Pottash, A. L. C., Sweeney, D. R., and Kleber, H. D. (1979). Clonidine detoxification: a fourteen day protocol for rapid opiate withdrawal. In *Problems of drug dependence*, NIDA Research Monograph Vol. 27, pp. 226–32. U.S. Department of Health, Education and Welfare, Rockville.

—— Redmond, D. E. Jr, and Kleber, H. D. (1978). Clonidine blocks acute opiate-withdrawal symptoms. *Lancet* ii, 599–602.

—— —— —— (1979). Noradrenergic hyperactivity in opiate withdrawal supported by clonidine reversal of opiate withdrawal. *Am. J. Psychiat.* **136**, 100–1.

Goldenberg, M., Snyder, C. H., and Aranow, H. Jr (1947). New test for hypertension due to circulating epinephrine. *J. Am. med. Ass.* **135**, 971–6.

Goldman, P. S., Rosvold, H. E., Vest, B., and Galkin, T. W. (1971). Analysis of the delayed-alternation deficit produced by dorsolateral prefrontal lesions in the Rhesus monkey. *J. comp. physiol. Psychol.* **77**, 212–20.

Goldstein, R. (1966a). Facilitation of active avoidance behavior by reinforcing septal stimulation in the rat. *Physiol. Behav.* **1**, 335–9.

—— (1966b). Effects of non-contingent septal stimulation on the CER in the rat. *J. comp. physiol. Psychol.* **61**, 132–5.

Gomer, F. E. and Goldstein, R. (1974). Attentional rigidity during exploratory and simultaneous discrimination behavior in septal lesioned rats. *Physiol. Behav.* **12**, 19–28.

Goodrich, K. P. (1959). Performance in different segments of an instrumental response chain as a function of reinforcement schedule. *J. exp. Psychol.* **57**, 57–63.

Gottlieb, D. I. and Cowan, W. M. (1973). Autoradiographic studies of the commissural and ipsilateral association connections of the hippocampus and dentate gyrus of the rat. I. The commissural connections. *J. comp. Neurol.* **149**, 393–422.

Gottschalk, L. A., Stone, W. N., and Gleser, G. G. (1974). Peripheral versus central mechanisms accounting for anti-anxiety effects of propranolol. *Psychosom. Med.* **36**, 47–56.

Graeff, F. G. (1974). Tryptamine antagonists and punished behaviour. *J. Pharmac. exp. Ther.* **189**, 344–50.

—— Quintero, S., and Gray, J. A. (1980). Median raphe stimulation, hippocampal theta rhythm and threat-induced behavioural inhibition. *Physiol. Behav.* **25**, 253–61.

—— and Rawlins, J. N. P. (1980). Dorsal periaqueductal gray punishment, septal lesions and the mode of action of minor tranquilizers. *Pharmac. Biochem. Behav.* **12**, 41–5.

—— and Schoenfeld, R. I. (1970). Tryptaminergic mechanisms in punished and nonpunished behavior. *J. Pharmac. exp. Ther.* **173**, 277–83.

—— and Silveira Filho, N. G. (1978). Behavioural inhibition induced by electrical stimulation of the median raphe nucleus of the rat. *Physiol. Behav.* **21**, 477–84.

Grastyàn, E., Karmos, G., Vereczkey, L., and Kellenyi, E. E. (1966). The hippocampal electrical correlates of the homeostatic regulation of motivation. *Electroenceph. clin. Neurophysiol.* **21**, 34–53.

—— Lissak, K., Madarasz, I., and Donhoffer, H. (1959). Hippocampal electrical activity during the development of conditioned reflexes. *Electroenceph. clin. Neurophysiol.* **11**, 409–30.

—— and Vereczkei, L. (1974). Effects of spatial separation of the conditioned signal from the reinforcement: a demonstration of the conditioned character of the orienting response or the orientational character of conditioning. *Behav. Biol.* **10**, 121–146.

Gray, J. A. (1964*a*). Strength of the nervous system and levels of arousal: a rein-
terpretation. In *Pavlov's typology* (ed. J. A. Gray) pp. 289–366. Pergamon,
Oxford.

—— (1964*b*). The relation between stimulus intensity and response strength in
the context of Pavlovian personality theory. Unpublished Ph.D. thesis, University of London.

—— (1965). A time-sample study of the components of general activity in selected
strains of rats. *Can. J. Psychol.* **19**, 74–82.

—— (1967). Disappointment and drugs in the rat. *Adv. Sci.* **23**, 595–605.

—— (1969). Sodium amobarbital and effects of frustrative nonreward. *J. comp.
physiol. Psychol.* **69**, 55–64.

—— (1970*a*). Sodium amobarbital, the hippocampal theta rhythm and the partial
reinforcement extinction effect. *Psychol. Rev.* **77**, 465–80.

—— (1970*b*). The psychophysiological basis of introversion–extraversion. *Behav.
Res. Ther.* **8**, 249–66.

—— (1971*a*). *The psychology of fear and stress.* Weidenfeld and Nicolson, London.*

—— (1971*b*). Sex differences in emotional behaviour in mammals including man:
endocrine bases. *Acta psychol.* **35**, 29–46.

—— (1971*c*). Medial septal lesions, hippocampal theta rhythm and the control of
vibrissal movement in the freely moving rat. *Electroenceph. clin. Neurophysiol.*
30, 189–97.

—— (1971*d*). The mind–brain identity theory as a scientific hypothesis. *Philosoph.
Q.* **21**, 247–52.

—— (1972*a*). The structure of the emotions and the limbic system. In *Physiology,
emotion and psychosomatic illness,* Ciba Foundation Symposium 8 (New Series)
(ed. R. Porter and J. Knight) pp. 87–130. Associated Scientific Publishers,
Amsterdam.

—— (1972*b*). Effects of septal driving of the hippocampal theta rhythm on resistance to extinction. *Physiol. Behav.* **8**, 481–90.

—— (1975). *Elements of a two-process theory of learning.* Academic Press, London.

—— (1976). The behavioural inhibition system: a possible substrate for anxiety.
In *Theoretical and experimental bases of behaviour modification* (ed. M. P. Feldman
and A. M. Broadhurst) pp. 3–41. Wiley, Chichester.

—— (1977). Drug effects on fear and frustration: possible limbic site of action of
minor tranquilizers. In *Handbook of psychopharmacology* (ed. L. L. Iversen, S. D.
Iversen, and S. H. Snyder) Vol. 8, *Drugs, neurotransmitters and behaviour,* pp.
433–529. Plenum Press, New York.

—— (1979*a*). Emotionality in male and female rodents: a reply to Archer. *Br. J.
Psychol.* **70**, 425–40.

—— (1979*b*). Is there any need for conditioning in Eysenck's conditioning model
of neurosis? *Behav. Brain Sci.* **2**, 169–71.

—— (1979*c*). *Pavlov.* Fontana, London.

—— (1981). A critique of Eysenck's theory of personality. In *A model for personality*
(ed. H. J. Eysenck) pp. 246–76. Springer, New York.

—— and Araujo-Silva, M. T. (1971). Joint effects of medial septal lesions and
amylobarbitone injections in the rat. *Psychopharmacologia* **22**, 8–22.

—— —— and Quintão, L. (1972). Resistance to extinction after partial reinforcement training with blocking of the hippocampal theta rhythm by septal stimulation. *Physiol. Behav.* **8**, 497–502.

—— and Ball, G. G. (1970). Frequency-specific relation between hippocampal
theta rhythm, behavior and amobarbital action. *Science, NY* **168**, 1246–8.

—— Davis, N. M., Feldon, J., Owen, S., and Boarder, M. (1981). Stress tolerance:
possible neural mechanisms. In *Foundations of psychosomatics* (ed. M. J. Christie
and P. G. Mellett) Vol. 1, *Behavioural approaches,* pp. 153–67. Wiley, Chichester.

—— and Dudderidge, H. (1971). Sodium amylobarbitone, the partial reinforce-

*See also additional references.

ment extinction effect and the frustration effect in the double runway. *Neuropharmacology* **10**, 217–22.

—— Feldon, J., Rawlins, J. N. P., Owen, S., and McNaughton, N. (1978). The role of the septo-hippocampal system and its noradrenergic afferents in behavioural responses to nonreward. In *Functions of the septo-hippocampal system* (ed. K. Elliott and J. Whelan) Ciba Foundation Symposium No. 58 (New Series) pp. 275–300. Elsevier, Amsterdam.

—— and Lalljee, B. (1974). Sex differences in emotional behaviour in the rat: correlation between open field defecation and active avoidance. *Anim. Behav.* **22**, 856–61.

——and McNaughton, N. (1983). Comparison between the behavioural effects of septal and hippocampal lesions: a review. *Neurosci. biobehav. Rev.* **8**, 119–88.

—— —— James, D. T. D., and Kelly, P. H. (1975). Effect of minor tranquillisers on hippocampal theta rhythm mimicked by depletion of forebrain noradrenaline. *Nature, Lond.* **258**, 424–5.

——Owen, S., Davis, N. M., and Tsaltas, E. (1983). Psychological and physiological relations between anxiety and impulsivity. In *The biological basis of impulsivity and sensation seeking* (ed. M. Zuckerman) pp. 181–217. Erlbaum, Hillsdale, N.J.

—— —— —— and Feldon, J. (1980). Associative and non-associative mechanisms in the development of tolerance for stress. In *Coping and health* (ed. S. Levine and H. Ursin) pp. 61–81. Plenum, New York.

—— Quintão, L., and Araujo-Silva, M. T. (1972). The partial reinforcement extinction effect in rats with medial septal lesions. *Physiol. Behav.* **8**, 491–6.

—— Rawlins, J. N. P., and Feldon, J. (1979). Brain mechanisms in the inhibition of behaviour. In *Mechanisms of learning and motivation* (ed. A. Dickinson and R. A. Boakes) pp. 295–316. Erlbaum, Hillsdale, NJ.

—— and Smith, P. T. (1969). An arousal-decision model for partial reinforcement and discrimination learning. In *Animal discrimination learning* (ed. R. Gilbert and N. S. Sutherland) pp. 243–72. Academic Press, London.

Gray, P. E. (1976). Disinhibition and external inhibition of response following septal lesions in rats. *Physiol. Behav.* **17**, 1015–17.

Green, A. R. and Deakin, J. F. W. (1980). Brain noradrenaline depletion prevents ECS-induced enhancement of serotonin- and dopamine-mediated behaviour. *Nature, Lond.* **285**, 232–3.

—— Heal, D. J., and Grahame-Smith, D. G. (1977). Further observations on the effect of repeated electroconvulsive shock on the behavioural responses of rats produced by increases in the functional activity of brain 5-hydroxytryptamine and dopamine. *Psychopharmacology* **52**, 195–200.

Green, J. S. and Arduini, A. (1954). Hippocampal electrical activity in arousal. *J. Neurophysiol.* **17**, 533–57.

Green, K. F. and Rawlins, J. N. P. (1979). Hippocampal theta in rats under urethane: generators and phase relations. *Electroenceph. clin. Neurophysiol.* **47**, 420–9.

Greene, E. and Stauff, C. (1974). Behavioral role of hippocampal connections. *Expl. Neurol.* **45**, 141–60.

Gross, C. G., Black, P., and Chorover, S. L. (1968). Hippocampal lesions: effects on memory in rats. *Psychon. Sci.* **12**, 165–6.

Grossman, S. P. (1978). An experimental 'dissection' of the septal syndrome. In *Functions of the septo-hippocampal system.* (ed. K. Elliott and J. Whelan) Ciba Foundation Symposium 58 (New Series) pp. 227–60. Elsevier, Amsterdam.

Groves, P. M. and Thompson, R. F. (1970). Habituation: a dual-process theory. *Psychol. Rev.* **77**, 419–59.

Grzanna, R. and Molliver, M. E. (1980). The locus coeruleus in the rat: an immunohistochemical delineation. *Neuroscience* **5**, 21–40.

Guidotti, A., Baraldi, M., Schwartz, J. P., and Costa, E. (1979). Molecular mechanisms regulating the interactions between the benzodiazepines and GABA receptors in the central nervous system. *Pharmac. Biochem. Behav.* **10**, 803–7.

—— Toffano, G., and Costa, E. (1978). An endogenous protein modulates the affinity of GABA and benzodiazepine receptors in rat brain. *Nature, Lond.* **275**, 553–5.

Gupta, B. S. and Nagpal, M. (1978). Impulsivity/sociability and reinforcement in verbal operant conditioning. *Br. J. Psychol.* **69**, 203–6.

Gustafson, J. W. (1975). Distractibility and reactivity under different response conditions following hippocampal lesions in rats. *Behav. Biol.* **15**, 479–84.

—— and Koenig, L. J. (1979). Hippocampal function in distractibility and generalization: a behavioral investigation. *Physiol. Behav.* **22**, 297–303.

Guyenet, P. G. and Aghajanian, G. K. (1977). Excitation of neurons in the nucleus locus coeruleus by substance P and related peptides. *Brain Res.* **136**, 178–84.

—— —— (1979). ACh, substance P and met-enkephalin in the locus coeruleus: pharmacological evidence for independent sites of action. *Eur. J. Pharmac.* **53**, 319–28.

Habets, A. M. M. C., Lopes da Silva, F. H., and De Quartel, F. W. (1980b). Autoradiography of the olfactory–hippocampal pathway in the cat with special reference to the perforant path. *Expl Brain Res.* **38**, 257–65.

—— —— and Mollevanger, W. J. (1980a). An olfactory input to the hippocampus of the cat: field potential analysis. *Brain Res.* **182**, 47–64.

Haddad, R. K. and Rabe, A. (1969). Modified temporal behavior in rats after large hippocampal lesions. *Expl Neurol.* **23**, 310–17.

Hafner, J. and Marks, I. (1976). Exposure *in vivo* of agoraphobics: contributions of diazepam, group exposure, and anxiety evocation. *Psychol. Med.* **6**, 71–88.

Haggard, D. F. (1959). Acquisition of a simple running response as a function of partial and continuous schedules of reinforcement. *Psychol. Rep.* **9**, 11–18.

Haigler, H. J. and Aghajanian, G. K. (1974). Peripheral serotonin antagonists: failure to antagonize serotonin in brain areas receiving a prominent serotonergic input. *J. neural Trans.* **35**, 257–73.

Hall, C. S. (1951). The genetics of behavior. In *Handbook of experimental psychology* (ed. S. S. Stevens) pp. 304–29. Wiley, New York.

Hamilton, L. W. (1970). Behavioral effects of unilateral and bilateral septal lesions in rats. *Physiol. Behav.* **5**, 855–9.

—— (1972). Intrabox and extrabox cues in avoidance responding: effect of septal lesions. *J. comp. physiol. Psychol.* **78**, 268–73.

—— Kelsey, J. E., and Grossman, S. P. (1970). Variations in behavioral inhibition following different septal lesions in rats. *J. comp. physiol. Psychol.* **70**, 79–86.

—— McCleary, R. A., and Grossman, S. P. (1968). Behavioral effects of cholinergic septal blockade in the cat. *J. comp. physiol. Psychol.* **66**, 563–8.

Hammond, G. R. and Thomas, G. J. (1971). Failure to reactivate the septal syndrome in rats. *Physiol. Behav.* **6**, 599–601.

Han, M. F. and Livesey, P. J. (1977). Brightness discrimination learning under conditions of cue enhancement by rats with lesions in the amygdala or hippocampus. *Brain Res.* **125**, 277–92.

Hare, R. D. and Cox, D. N. (1978). Clinical and empirical conceptions of psychopathy, and the selection of subjects for research. In *Psychopathic behaviour: approaches to research* (ed. R. D. Hare and D. Schalling) pp. 1–22. Wiley, Chichester.

Harik, S. I., Lamanna, J. C., Light, A. I., and Rosenthal, M. (1979). Cerebral norepinephrine: influence on cortical oxidative metabolism *in situ. Science, NY* **206**, 69–71.

Harley, C. W. (1972). Hippocampal lesions and two-cue discrimination in the rat. *Physiol. Behav.* **9**, 343–8.

—— (1979). Nonreversal and reversal shifts in the hippocampectomized rat. *Physiol. Behav.* **22**, 1135–9.

Harman, H. (1960). *Modern factor analysis*. Chicago University Press.

Harper, R. M. (1971). Frequency changes in hippocampal electrical activity during movement and tonic immobility. *Physiol. Behav.* **7**, 55–8.

Harris, E. W., Lasher, S. S., and Steward, O. (1978). Habituation-like decrements in transmission along the normal and lesion-induced temperodentate pathways in the rat. *Brain Res.* **151**, 623–31.

Hartman, B. K. and Udenfriend, S. (1972). The application of immunological techniques to the study of enzymes regulating catecholamine synthesis and degradation. *Pharmac. Rev.* **23**, 311–30.

Hartman, R. J. and Geller, I. (1971). *p*-Chlorophenylalanine effects on a conditioned emotional response in rats. *Life Sci.* **10**, 927–33.

Harvey, J. A. and Hunt, H. F. (1965). Effect of septal lesions on thirst in the rat as indicated by water consumption and operant responding for water reward. *J. comp. physiol. Psychol.* **59**, 49–56.

—— and Lints, C. E. (1971). Lesions in the medial forebrain bundle: relationship between pain sensitivity and telencephalic content of serotonin. *J. comp. physiol. Psychol.* **74**, 28–36.

—— —— Jacobson, L. E., and Hunt, H. F. (1965). Effects of lesions in the septal area on conditioned fear and discriminated instrumental punishment in the albino rat. *J. comp. physiol. Psychol.* **59**, 37–48.

—— Schlosberg, A. J., and Yunger, L. M. (1974). Effect of *p*-chlorophenylalanine and brain lesions on pain sensitivity and morphine analgesia in the rat. In *Serotonin: new vistas* (ed. E. Costa, G. L. Gessa, and M. Sandler) *Adv. Biochem. Psychopharmac.* **10**, 233–45.

Hayat, A. and Feldman, S. (1974). Effects of sensory stimuli on single cell activity in the septum of cat. *Expl Neurol.* **43**, 298–313.

Haycock, J. W., Deadwyler, S. A., Sideroff, S. I., and McGaugh, J. L. (1973). Retrograde amnesia and cholinergic systems in the caudate–putamen complex and dorsal hippocampus of the rat. *Expl Neurol.* **41**, 201–13.

Hebb, D. O. (1946). On the nature of fear. *Psychol. Rev.* **53**, 259–76.

—— (1949). *The organization of behavior*. Wiley-Interscience, New York.

Heimer, L. and Wilson, R. D. (1975). The subcortical projections of the allocortex: similarities in the neural associations of the hippocampus, the pyriform cortex, and the neocortex. In *Golgi Centennial Symp. Proc.* (ed. M. Santini) pp. 177–93. Raven Press, New York.

Hendrickson, C. W., Kimble, R. J., and Kimble, D. P. (1969). Hippocampal lesions and the orienting response. *J. comp. physiol. Psychol.* **67**, 220–7.

Henke, P. G. (1974). Persistence of runway performance after septal lesions in rats. *J. comp. physiol. Psychol.* **86**, 760–7.

—— (1975). Septal lesions and the extinction of incentive-motivation. *Physiol. Behav.* **15**, 537–42.

—— (1976). Septal lesions and aversive nonreward. *Physiol. Behav.* **17**, 483–8.

—— (1977). Dissociation of the frustration effect and the partial reinforcement extinction effect after limbic lesions in rats. *J. comp. physiol. Psychol.* **91**, 1032–8.

—— and Bunnell, B. N. (1971). Reinforcement and extinction interactions after limbic lesions in rat. *Comm. behav. Biol.* **6A**, 329–35.

Heritage, A. S., Stumpf, W. C., Sar, M., and Grant, L. D. (1980). Brainstem catecholamine neurons are target sites for sex steroid hormones. *Science, NY* **207**, 1377–9.

Herkenham, M. (1978). The connections of the nucleus reuniens thalami: evidence for a direct thalamo-hippocampal pathway in the rat. *J. comp. Neurol.* **177**, 589–609.

Herrmann, T., Black, A. H., Anchel, H., and Ellen, P. (1978). Comparison of septal and fornical lesioned rats' performance on the Maier three table reasoning task. *Physiol. Behav.* **20**, 297–302.

Hervé, D., Tassin, J. P., Barthelemy, C., Blanc, G., Lavielle, S., and Glowinski, J. (1979). Difference in the reactivity of the mesocortical dopaminergic neurons to stress in the BALB/C and C57 BL/6 mice. *Life Sci.* **25**, 1659–64.

Hesse, G. W. (1979). Chronic zinc deficiency alters neuronal function of hippocampal mossy fibers. *Science, NY* **205**, 1005–10.

Heybach, J. P. and Coover, G. D. (1976). Different passive and one-way active avoidance acquisition following medial forebrain bundle lesions in rats. *J. comp. physiol. Psychol.* **90**, 491–504.

Hill, A. J. (1978). First occurrence of hippocampal spatial firing in a new environment. *Expl Neurol.* **62**, 282–97.

Hirano, T., Best, P. J., and Olds, J. (1970). Units during habituation, discrimination learning and extinction. *Electroenceph. clin. Neurophysiol.* **28**, 127–35.

Hirsh, R. (1973*a*). Previous stimulus experience delays conditioning-induced changes in hippocampal unit responses in rats. *J. comp. physiol. Psychol.* **83**, 337–45.

—— (1973*b*). The effect of septal input upon hippocampal unit response in normal conditions in rats. *Brain Res.* **58**, 234–9.

—— (1974). The hippocampus and contextual retrieval of information from memory: a theory. *Behav. Biol.* **12**, 421–44.

Hitch, G. J. (1980). Developing the concept of working memory. In *New directions in cognitive psychology* (ed. G. Claxton) pp. 154–96. Routledge & Kegan Paul, London.

Hjorth-Simonsen, A. (1971). Hippocampal efferents to the ipsilateral entorhinal area: an experimental study in the rat. *J. comp. Neurol.* **142**, 417–37.

—— (1973). Some intrinsic connections of the hippocampus in the rat: an experimental analysis. *J. comp. Neurol.* **147**, 145–61.

Hobson, J. A. and Brazier, M. A. B. (eds.) (1980). *The reticular formation revisited.* Raven Press, New York.

Hodgson, R. and Rachman, S. (1972). The effects of contamination and washing in obsessional patients. *Behav. Res. Ther.* **10**, 111–17.

Hoebel, B. G. (1977). The psychopharmacology of feeding. In *The handbook of psychopharmacology*, Vol. 8. *Drugs, neurotransmitters and behaviour* (ed. L. L. Iversen, S. D. Iversen, and S. H. Snyder) pp. 55–129. Plenum Press, New York.

Holdstock, T. L. (1969). Autonomic reactivity following septal and amygdaloid lesions in white rats. *Physiol. Behav.* **4**, 603–7.

—— (1970). Plasticity of autonomic functions in rats with septal lesions. *Neuropsychologia* **8**, 147–60.

—— (1972). Dissociation of function within the hippocampus. *Physiol Behav.* **8**, 659–67.

Hole, K., Fuxe, K., and Jonsson, G. (1976). Behavioral effects of 5,7-dihydroxytryptamine lesions of ascending 5-hydroxytryptamine pathways. *Brain Res.* **107**, 385–99.

—— and Lorens, S. A. (1975). Response to electric shock in rats: effects of selective midbrain raphe lesions. *Pharmac. Biochem. Behav.* **3**, 307–9.

Holloway, F. A. (1972). State-dependent effects of ethanol on active and passive avoidance learning. *Psychopharmacologia* **25**, 238–61.

Holmberg, G. and Gershon, S. (1961). Autonomic and psychic effects of yohimbine hydrochloride. *Psychopharmacologia* **2**, 93–106.

Homskaya, E. D. (1964). Verbal regulation of the vegetative components of the orienting reflex in focal brain lesions. *Cortex* **1**, 63–76.

Horel, J. A. (1978). The neuroanatomy of amnesia: a critique of the hippocampal memory hypothesis. *Brain* **101**, 403–45.

Horn, G. (1967). Neuronal mechanisms of habituation. *Nature, Lond.* **215**, 707–11.
—— (1970). Changes in neuronal activity and their relationship to behaviour. In *Short-term changes in neural activity and behaviour* (ed. G. Horn and R. A. Hinde) pp. 567–606. Cambridge University Press.
—— and Hinde, R. A. (eds.) (1971). *Short-term changes in neural activity and behaviour.* Cambridge University Press.
Hsiao, S. and Isaacson, R. L. (1971). Learning of food and water positions by hippocampus damaged rats. *Physiol Behav.* **6**, 81–3.
Hugdahl, K., Fredrikson, M., and Öhman, A. (1977). 'Preparedness' and 'arousability' as determinants of electrodermal conditioning. *Behav. Res. Ther.* **15**, 345–53.
—— and Öhman, A. (1977). Effects of instruction on acquisition and extinction of electrodermal responses to fear-relevant stimuli. *J. exp. Psychol.: Hum. Learn. Mem.* **3**, 608–18.
—— —— (1980). Skin conductance conditioning to potentially phobic stimuli as a function of interstimulus interval and delay versus trace paradigm. *Psychophysiology* **17**, 348–55.
Hughes, J., Smith, T. W., Kosterlitz, H. W., Fothergill, L. A., Morgan, B. A., and Morris, H. R. (1975). Identification of two related pentapeptides from the brain with potent agonist activity. *Nature, Lond.* **258**, 577–9.
Hughes, R. N. (1972). Chlordiazepoxide modified exploration in rats. *Psychopharmacologia* **24**, 462–9.
—— and Greig, A. M. (1975). Chlordiazepoxide effects on reaction to novelty and activity with and without prior drug experience. *Psychopharmacologia* **42**, 289–92.
—— and Syme, L. A. (1972). The role of social isolation and sex in determining effects of chlordiazepoxide and methylphenidate on exploratory behaviour. *Psychopharmacologia* **27**, 359–66.
Huppert, F. A. and Iversen, S. D. (1975). Response suppression in rats: a comparison of response-contingent and non-contingent punishment and the effect of the minor tranquilizer, chlordiazepoxide. *Psychopharmacologia* **44**, 67–75.
Hussain, M. Z. (1971). Desensitization and flooding (implosion) in treatment of phobias. *Am. J. Psychiat.* **127**, 1509–14.
Hygge, S. and Öhman, A. (1978). Modeling processes in the acquisition of fears in vicarious electrodermal conditioning to fear-relevant stimuli. *J. Pers. soc. Psychol.* **36**, 271–9.
Isaacson, R. L. (1972). Neural systems of the limbic brain and behavioural inhibition. In *Inhibition and learning* (ed. R. A. Boakes and M. S. Halliday) pp. 497–528. Academic Press, London.
—— Nonneman, A. J., and Schmaltz, L. W. (1968). Behavioural and anatomical sequelae of damage to the infant limbic system. In *The neuropsychology of development: a symposium* (ed. R. L. Isaacson) pp. 41–78. Wiley-Interscience, New York.
—— Olton, D. S., Bauer, B., and Swart, P. (1966). The effect of training trials on passive avoidance deficits in the hippocampectomized rat. *Psychon. Sci.* **5**, 419–20.
—— and Pribram, K. H. (eds.) (1975). *The hippocampus.* Plenum Press, New York.
Ison, J. R., Glass, D. H., and Bohmer, H. M. (1966). Effects of sodium amytal on the approach to stimulus change. *Proc. Am. psychol. Ass.* **2**, 5–6.
Ito, M. (1966). Hippocampal electrical correlates of self-stimulation in the rat. *Electroenceph. clin. Neurophysiol.* **21**, 261–8.
Iuvone, P. M., Morasco, J., and Dunn, A. J. (1977). Effect of corticosterone on the synthesis of [^{3}H]-catecholamines in the brains of CD-1 mice. *Brain Res.* **120**, 571–6.

Iversen, L. L. and Schon, F. (1973). The use of radioautographic techniques for the identification and mapping of transmitter-specific neurons in CNS. In *New concepts of transmitter regulation* (ed. A. Mandell and D. Segal) pp. 153–93. Plenum Press, New York.

Iversen, S. D. (1976). Do hippocampal lesions produce amnesia in animals? *Int. Rev. Neurobiol.* **19**, 1–49.

—— and Mishkin, M. (1970). Perseverative interference in monkeys following selective lesions of the inferior prefrontal convexity. *Expl Brain Res.* **11**, 376–86.

Iwahara, S. and Sakama, E. (1972). Effects of chlordiazepoxide upon habituation of open-field behavior in white rats. *Psychopharmacologia* **27**, 285–92.

Iwasaki, T., Ezawa, K., and Iwahara, S. (1976). Differential effects of chlordiazepoxide on simultaneous and successive brightness discrimination learning in rats. *Psychopharmacology* **48**, 75–8.

Izquierdo, I. (1975). The hippocampus and learning. *Prog. Neurobiol.* **5**, 37–75.

—— Beamish, D. G., and Anisman, H. (1979). Effect of an inhibitor of dopamine-beta-hydroxylase on the acquisition and retention of four different avoidance tasks in mice. *Psychopharmacology* **63**, 173–8.

Jackson, F. B. and Gergen, J. A. (1970). Acquisition of operant schedules by squirrel monkeys lesioned in the hippocampal area. *Physiol. Behav.* **5**, 543–7.

Jackson, R. L., Maier, S. F., and Coon, D. J. (1979). Long-term analgesic effects of inescapable shock and learned helplessness. *Science, NY* **206**, 91–3.

—— —— and Rapaport, P. M. (1978). Exposure to inescapable shock produces both activity and associative deficits. *Learn. Motiv.* **9**, 69–98.

Jackson, W. J. and Strong, P. N. (1969). Differential effects of hippocampal lesions upon sequential tasks and maze learning by the rat. *J. comp. physiol. Psychol.* **68**, 442–50.

Jacobs, B. L. and Cohen, A. (1976). Differential behavioral effects of lesions of the median or dorsal raphe nuclei in rats: open field and pain-elicited aggression. *J. comp. physiol. Psychol.* **90**, 102–8.

—— and Jones, B. E. (1978). The role of central monoamine and acetylcholine systems in sleep–wakefulness states: mediation or modulation. In *Cholinergic–monoaminergic interactions in the brain* (ed. L. L. Butcher) pp. 271–90. Academic Press, New York.

—— Trimbach, C., Eubanks, E. E., and Trulson, M. (1975). Hippocampal mediation of raphe lesion- and PCPA-induced hyperactivity in the rat. *Brain Res.* **94**, 253–61.

—— Wise, W. D., and Taylor, K. M. (1974). Differential behavioural and neurochemical effects following lesions of the dorsal or median raphe nuclei in rats. *Brain Res.* **79**, 353–61.

Jacobson, S., Butters, N., and Tovsky, N. J. (1978). Afferent and efferent subcortical projections of behaviorally defined sectors of prefrontal granular cortex. *Brain Res.* **159**, 279–96.

Jaffard, R., Destrade, C., and Cardo, B. (1976). Effets de la stimulation de l'hippocampe sur l'évitement passif chez deux lignées de souris. *Physiol. Behav.* **16**, 233–6.

—— —— Durkin, T., and Ebel, A. (1979). Memory formation as related to genotypic or experimental variations of hippocampal cholinergic activity in mice. *Physiol. Behav.* **22**, 1093–6.

—— Ebel, A., Destrade, C., Durkin, T., Mandel, P., and Cardo, B. (1977). Effects of hippocampal electrical stimulation on long-term memory and on cholinergic mechanisms in three inbred strains of mice. *Brain Res.* **133**, 277–89.

James, D. T. D., McNaughton, N., Rawlins, J. N. P., Feldon, J., and Gray, J. A. (1977). Septal driving of hippocampal theta rhythm as a function of frequency in the free-moving male rat. *Neuroscience* **2**, 1007–17.

James, W. (1890). *Principles of psychology* Macmillan, London.

Jarrard, L. E. (1968). Behavior of hippocampal lesioned rats in home cage and novel situations. *Physiol. Behav.* **3**, 65–70.

—— (1973). The hippocampus and motivation. *Psychol. Bull.* **79**, 1–12.

—— (1975). Role of interference in retention by rats with hippocampal lesions. *J. comp. physiol. Psychol.* **89**, 400–8.

—— (1976). Anatomical and behavioral analysis of hippocampal cell fields in rats. *J. comp. physiol. Psychol.* **90**, 1035–50.

—— (1978). Selective hippocampal lesions: differential effects on performance by rats of a spatial task with preoperative versus postoperative training. *J. comp. physiol. Psychol.* **92**, 1119–27.

—— and Isaacson, R. L. (1965). Hippocampal ablation in rats: effects of intertrial interval. *Nature, Lond.* **207**, 109–10.

—— —— and Wickelgren, W. O. (1964). Effects of hippocampal ablation and intertrial interval on runway acquisition and extinction. *J. comp. physiol. Psychol.* **57**, 442–4.

Jeffery, D. R. and Barrett, J. E. (1979). Effects of chlordiazepoxide on comparable rates of punished and unpunished responding. *Psychopharmacology* **64**, 9–11.

Johnson, D. A. (1972). Developmental aspects of recovery of function following septal lesions in the infant rat. *J. comp. physiol. Psychol.* **78**, 331–48.

Johnson, T. N., Rosvold, H. E., and Mishkin, M. (1968). Projections from behaviorally-defined sectors of the prefrontal cortex to the basal ganglia, septum and diencephalon of the monkey. *Expl Neurol.* **21**, 20–34.

Johnston, D. and Gath, D. (1973). Arousal levels and attribution effects in diazepam-assisted flooding. *Br. J. Psychiat.* **123**, 463–6.

Johnstone, E. C., Owens, D. G. C., Frith, C. D., McPherson, K., Dowie, C., Riley, G., and Gold, A. (1980). Neurotic illness and its response to anxiolytic and antidepressant treatment. *Psychol. Med.* **10**, 321–8.

Jones, B. and Mishkin, M. (1972). Limbic lesions and the problem of stimulus-reinforcement associations. *Expl Neurol.* **36**, 362–77.

Jones, G., Foote, S. L., Segal, M., and Bloom, F. E. (1978). Locus coeruleus neurons in freely behaving rats exhibit pronounced alterations of firing rate during sensory stimulation and stages of the sleep–wake cycle. *Soc. Neurosci. Abst.* **4**, 856.

Jonsson, G. and Sachs, Ch. (1975). On the mode of action of 6-hydroxydopamine. In *Chemical tools in catecholamine research* (ed. G. Jonsson, T. Malmfors, and G. Sachs) Vol. 1, pp. 41–50. North-Holland, Amsterdam.

Jouvent, R., Frechette, D., Binoux, F., Lancrenon, S., and Des Lauriers, A. (1980). Le ralentissement psycho-moteur dans les états dépressifs: construction d'une échelle d'évaluation quantitative. *Encéphale* **6**, 41–58.

Jouvet, M. (1969). Biogenic amines and the states of sleep. *Science, NY* **163**, 32–41.

—— (1972). The role of monoamines and acetylcholine containing neurones in the regulation of the sleep–waking cycle. *Ergebn. Physiol.* **64**, 165–305.

Kaada, B. R. (1951). Somatomotor, autonomic and electrocortigraphic responses to electrical stimulation of 'rhinencephalic' and other structures of primates, cat and dog: a study of response from the limbic subcallosal, orbital insula, pyriform and temporal cortex, hippocampus, fornix and amygdala. *Acta physiol. scand.* **24**, 1–285.

—— Jansen, J., and Andersen, P. (1953). Stimulation of the hippocampus and medial cortical areas in unanesthetized cats. *Neurology, Minneap.* **3**, 844–57.

—— Rasmussen, E. W., and Kveim, O. (1961). Effects of hippocampal lesions on maze learning and retention in rats. *Expl Neurol.* **3**, 333–55.

—— —— —— (1962). Impaired acquisition of passive avoidance behavior by subcallosal, septal, hypothalamic, and insular lesions in rats. *J. comp. physiol. Psychol.* **55**, 661–70.

Kamin, L. J. (1968). 'Attention-like' processes in classical conditioning. In *Miami symposium on the prediction of behaviour: aversive stimulation* (ed. M. R. Jones) pp. 9–31. University of Miami Press.

—— Brimer, C. J., and Black, A. H. (1963). Conditioned suppression as a monitor of fear of the CS in the course of avoidance training. *J. comp. physiol. Psychol.* **56,** 497–501.

Kantorowitz, D. A. (1978). Personality and conditioning of tumescence and detumescence. *Behav. Res. Ther.* **16,** 117–123.

Kaplan, J. (1965). Temporal discrimination in rats during continuous brain stimulation. *Psychon Sci.* **2,** 255–6.

—— (1968). Approach and inhibitory reactions in rats after bilateral hippocampal damage. *J. comp. physiol. Psychol.* **65,** 274–81.

Kasper, P. (1964). Attenuation of passive avoidance by continuous septal stimulation. *Psychon. Sci.* **1,** 219–20.

—— (1965). Disruption of position habit reversal by septal stimulation. *Psychon. Sci.* **3,** 111–12.

Kasper-Pandi, P., Schoel, W. M., and Zysman, M. (1969). Motivation and response strength in passive avoidance deficits of septal lesioned rats. *Physiol. Behav.* **4,** 815–21.

Kebabian, J. W., Zatz, M., Romero, J. A., and Axelrod, J. (1975). Rapid changes in the rat pineal beta-adrenergic receptor: alterations in L-^{3}H-alprenolol binding and adenylate cyclase. *Proc. natn. Acad. Sci. USA* **72,** 3735–41.

Kelleher, R. T. and Morse, W. H. (1964). Escape behavior and punished behavior. *Fedn Proc. Fedn Socs exp. Biol.* **23,** 808–17.

—— —— (1968). Determinants of the specificity of behavioral effects of drugs. *Ergeb. Physiol.* **60,** 1–56.

Kellner, R., Rada, R. T., Andersen, T., and Pathak, D. (1979). The effects of chlordiazepoxide on self-rated depression, anxiety, and well-being. *Psychopharmacology* **64,** 185–91.

Kellor, K. J., Brown, P. A., Madrid J., Bernstein, M., Vernikos-Danellis, J., and Nehler, W. R. (1977). Origins of serotonin innervation of forebrain structures. *Expl Neurol.* **56,** 52–62.

Kelly, D., Walter, C. J. S., Mitchell-Heggs, N., and Sargant, W. (1972). Modified leucotomy assessed clinically, physiologically and psychologically at six weeks and eighteen months. *Br. J. Psychiat.* **120,** 19–29.

Kelsey, J. E. (1975). Role of pituitary–adrenocortical system in mediating avoidance behavior of rats with septal lesions. *J. comp. physiol. Psychol.* **88,** 271–80.

—— and Grossman, S. P. (1971). Nonperseverative disruption of behavioral inhibition following septal lesions in rats. *J. comp. physiol. Psychol.* **75,** 302–11.

Kemp, I. R. and Kaada, B. R. (1975). The relation of hippocampal theta activity to arousal, attentive behaviour and somato-motor movements in unrestrained cats. *Brain Res.* **95,** 323–42.

Kemper, T. L., Wright, S. J., and Locke, S. (1972). Relationship between the septum and the cingulate gyrus in *Macaca mulatta*. *J. comp. Neurol.* **146,** 465–78.

Kenyon, J. and Krieckhaus, E. E. (1965). Enhanced avoidance behavior following septal lesions in the rat as a function of lesion size and spontaneous activity. *J. comp. physiol. Psychol.* **59,** 466–8.

Kerr, T. A., Schapira, K., Roth, M., and Garside, R. F. (1970). The relationship between the Máudsley personality inventory and the course of affective disorders. *Br. J. Psychiat.* **116,** 11–19.

Kesner, R. P., Dixon, D. A., Pickett, D., and Berman, R. F. (1975). Experimental animal model of transient global amnesia: Role of the hippocampus. *Neuropsychologia* **13,** 465–80.

Kety, S. S. (1970). The biogenic amines in the central nervous system: their possible roles in arousal, emotion and learning. In *The neurosciences, second study program* (ed. F. O. Schmitt) pp. 324–36. Rockefeller University Press, New York.

Kimble, D. P. (1969). Possible inhibitory functions of the hippocampus. *Neuropsychologia* **7**, 235–44.

—— (1975). Choice behavior in rats with hippocampal lesions. In *The hippocampus*, Vol. 2. *Neurophysiology and behavior* (ed. R. L. Isaacson and K. H. Pribam) pp. 309–26. Plenum Press, New York.

—— Bremiller, R., Schroeder, L., and Smotherman, W. P. (1979). Hippocampal lesions slow extinction of a conditioned taste aversion in rats. *Physiol. Behav.* **23**, 217–22.

—— and Kimble, R. J. (1970). The effect of hippocampal lesions on extinction and 'hypothesis' behavior in rats. *Physiol. Behav.* **5**, 735–8.

—— Kirkby, R. J., and Stein, D. G. (1966). Response perseveration interpretation of passive avoidance deficits in hippocampectomized rats. *J. comp. physiol. Psychol.* **61**, 141–3.

Kimsey, R. A., Dyer, R. S., and Petri, H. L. (1974). Relationship between hippocampal EEG, novelty, and frustration in the rat. *Behav. Biol.* **11**, 561–8.

Kimura, D. (1958). Effects of selective hippocampal damage on avoidance behavior in the rat. *Can. J. Psychol.* **12**, 213–18.

Kinsbourne, M. (1981). Single channel theory. In *Human skills* (ed. D. R. Holding) pp. 65–89. Wiley, Chichester.

—— and Wood, F. (1975). Short-term memory processes and the amnesic syndrome. In *Short-term memory* (ed. D. Deutsch and J. A. Deutsch) pp. 258–91. Academic Press, New York.

Kirkby, R. J., Stein, D. G., Kimble, D. P., and Kimble, R. J. (1967). Effects of hippocampal lesions and duration of sensory input on spontaneous alternation. *J. comp. physiol. Psychol.* **64**, 342–5.

Klemm, W. R., and Dreyfus, L. R. (1975). Septal- and caudate-induced behavioral inhibition in relation to hippocampal EEG of rabbits. *Physiol Behav.* **15**, 561–7.

—— —— Forney, E., and Mayfield, M. A. (1976). Differential effects of low doses of ethanol on the impulse activity in various regions of the limbic system. *Psychopharmacology* **50**, 131–8.

Klepner, C. A., Lippa, S. A., Benson, D. I., Sano, M. C., and Beer, B. (1979). Resolution of two biochemically and pharmacologically distinct benzodiazepine receptors. *Pharmac. Biochem. Behav.* **11**, 457–62.

Koda, L. Y., Schulman, J. A., and Bloom, F. E. (1978). Ultrastructural identification of noradrenergic terminals in rat hippocampus: Unilateral destruction of the locus coeruleus with 6-hydroxydopamine. *Brain Res.* **145**, 190–5.

Köhler, C. (1976a). Habituation after dorsal hippocampal lesions: a test dependent phenomenon. *Behav. Biol.* **18**, 89–110.

—— (1976b). Habituation of the orienting response after medial and lateral septal lesions in the albino rat. *Behav. Biol.* **16**, 63–72.

—— Shipley, M. T., Srebro, B., and Harkmark, W. (1978). Some retrohippocampal afferents to the entorhinal cortex: cells of origin studied by the HRP method in the rat and mouse. *Neurosci. Lett.* **10**, 115–20.

Kolb, B. and Nonneman, A. J. (1974). Fronto-limbic lesions and social behavior in the rat. *Physiol. Behav.* **13**, 637–43.

Komisaruk, B. R. (1970). Synchrony between limbic system theta activity and rhythmical behaviours in rats. *J. comp. physiol. Psychol.* **70**, 482–92.

Koob, G. F., Kelley, A. E., and Mason, S. T. (1978). Locus coeruleus lesions: learning and extinction. *Physiol. Behav.* **20**, 709–16.

Korf, J., Sebens, J. B., and Postema, F. (1978). Cyclic AMP in the rat cerebral cortex: role of the locus coeruleus and effects of antidepressants. *Abst. 7th Int. Cong. Pharmac., Paris*, p. 123.

Kovacs, G. L., Bohus, B., and Versteeg, D. H. G. (1979). Facilitation of memory consolidation by vasopressin: mediation by terminals of the dorsal noradrenergic bundle? *Brain Res.* **172**, 73–85.

Kramarcy, K., Mikulka, P., and Freeman, F. (1973). The effects of dorsal hippocampal lesions on reinforcement shifts. *Physiol. Psychol.* **1**, 248–50.

Kramis, R. C., and Routtenberg, A. (1977). Dissociation of hippocampal EEG from its behavioral correlates by septal and hippocampal electrical stimulation. *Brain Res.* **125**, 37–49.

—— Vanderwolf, C. H., and Bland, B. H. (1975). Two types of hippocampal rhythmical slow activity in both the rabbit and the rat: relations to behaviour and effects of atropine, diethylether, urethane and pentobarbital. *Expl Neurol.* **49**, 58–85.

Krane, R. V., Sinnamon, H. M., and Thomas, G. J. (1976). Conditioned taste aversions and neophobia in rats with hippocampal lesions. *J. comp. physiol. Psychol.* **90**, 680–93.

Krayniak, P. F., Weiner, S., and Siegel, A. (1980). An analysis of the efferent connections of the septal area in the cat. *Brain Res.* **189**, 15–29.

Krettek, J. E. and Price, J. T. (1977). Projections from the amygdaloid complex and adjacent olfactory structures to the entorhinal cortex and to the subiculum in the rat and cat. *J. comp. Neurol.* **172**, 723–52.

Kršiak, M. (1976). Effect of ethanol on aggression and timidity in mice. *Psychopharmacology* **51**, 75–80.

Kubota, K. and Niki, H. (1971). Prefrontal cortical unit activity and delayed alternation performance in monkeys. *J. Neurophysiol.* **34**, 337–47.

Kuhar, M. J., Pert, C. B., and Snyder, S. H. (1973). Regional distribution of opiate receptor binding in monkey and human brain. *Nature, Lond.* **245**, 447.

—— and Yamamura, H. I. (1976). Localization of cholinergic muscarinic receptors in rat brain by light microscopic radioautography. *Brain Res.* **110**, 229–43.

Kurtz, R. G. and Adler, N. T. (1973). Electrophysiological correlates of copulatory behaviour in the male rat: evidence for a sexual inhibitory process. *J. comp. physiol. Psychol.* **84**, 225–39.

Kveim, O., Setekleiv, J., and Kaada, B. R. (1964). Differential effects of hippocampal lesions on maze and passive avoidance learning in rats. *Expl Neurol.* **9**, 59–72.

Lader, M. H. (1967). Palmar skin conductance measures in anxiety and phobic states. *J. psychosom. Res.* **11**, 271–81.

—— (1975). *The psychophysiology of mental illness.* Routledge & Kegan Paul, London.

—— and Marks, I. M. (1972). *Clinical anxiety.* Grune & Stratton, New York.

—— and Mathews, A. (1968). A physiological model of phobic anxiety and desensitization. *Behav. Res. Ther.* **6**, 411–21.

—— —— (1970). Physiological changes during spontaneous panic attacks. *J. psychosom. Res.* **14**, 377–82.

—— and Wing, L. (1966). *Physiological measures, sedative drugs, and morbid anxiety.* Maudsley Monographs, Vol. 18. Oxford University Press, London.

Laitinen, L. V. and Vilkki, J. (1972). Stereotaxic central anterior cingulotomy in some psychological disorders. In *Psychosurgery* (ed. E. Hitchcock, L. Laitinen, and K. Vaernet) pp. 242–63. Thomas, Springfield, Ill.

Landfield, P. W. (1976). Synchronous EEG rhythms: their nature and possible functions in memory, information transmission and behavior. In *Molecular and functional neurobiology* (ed. W. H. Gispen) pp. 387–424. Elsevier, Amsterdam.

——(1977). Different effects of posttrial driving or blocking of the theta rhythm on avoidance learning in rats. *Physiol. Behav.* **18**, 439–45.

—— and McGaugh, J. L. (1972). Effects of electroconvulsive shock and brain stimulation on EEG cortical theta rhythms in rats. *Behav. Biol.* **7**, 271–8.

—— Tusa, R. J., and McGaugh, J. L. (1973). Effects of posttrial hippocampal stimulation on memory storage and EEG activity. *Behav. Biol.* **8**, 485–505.

Lanfumey, L., Adrien, J., and Gray, J.A. (1982). Septal driving of hippocampal theta rhythm as a function of frequency in the infant male rat. *Expl. Brain Res.* **45**, 230–2.

Lang, P. (1970). Stimulus control, response control, and the desensitization of fear. In *Learning approaches to therapeutic behavior* (ed. D. J. Levis) pp. 148–73. Aldine Press, Chicago.

Langer, S. Z. (1977). Presynaptic receptors and their role in the regulation of transmitter release. 6th Gaddum Memorial Lecture. *Br. J. Pharm.* **60**, 481–97.

—— (1979). Presynaptic adrenoceptors and regulation of release. In *The release of catecholamines from adrenergic neurones* (ed. D. M. Paton) pp. 59–86. Pergamon Press, Oxford.

Lanoir, J. and Killam, E. K. (1968). Alternation in the sleep-wakefulness patterns by benzodiazepines in cat. *Electroenceph. clin. Neurophysiol.* **25**, 530–42.

Lash, L. (1964). Response discriminability and the hippocampus. *J. comp. physiol. Psychol.* **57**, 251–6.

Lau, P. and Miczek, K. A. (1977). Differential effects of septal lesions on attack and defensive-submissive reactions during intra-species aggression in rats. *Physiol. Behav.* **18**, 479–85.

Lavielle, S., Tassin, J. P., Thierry, H. M., Blanc, G., Hervé, D., Barthelemy, C., and Glowinski, J. (1978). Blockade by benzodiazepines of the selective high increase in dopamine turnover induced by stress in mesocortical dopaminergic neurons of rat. *Brain Res.* **168**, 585–94.

Lé Moal, M. and Cardo, B. (1975). Rhythmic slow wave activity recorded in the ventral mesencephalic tegmentum in the rat. *Electroenceph. clin. Neurophysiol.* **38**, 139–47.

—— Galey, D., and Cardo, B. (1975). Behavioral effects of local injection of 6-hydroxydopamine in the medial ventral tegmentum in the rat: possible role of the mesolimbic dopaminergic system. *Brain Res.* **88**, 190–4.

Leander, J. D., McMillan, D. E., and Ellis, F. W. (1976) Ethanol and isopropanol effects on schedule-controlled responding. *Psychopharmacology*, **47**, 157–64.

Lebovitz, R. M., Dichter, M., and Spencer, W. A. (1971). Recurrent excitation in the CA3 region of cat hippocampus. *Int. J. Neurosci.* **2**, 99–108.

Leconte, P. and Hennevin, E. (1981). Perturbation de l'apprentissage et suppression correlative du phénomène d'augmentation de sommeil paradoxal consécutives à une lésion des voies noradrénergiques chez le rat. *Physiol. Behav.* **26**, 587–94.

Lecrubier, Y. (1976). Benzodiazépines et amnésie. Unpublished DM thesis, Université Pierre et Marie Curie, Paris.

Leger, L. and Descarries, L. (1978). Serotonin nerve terminals in the locus coeruleus of adult rat: a radio-autographic study. *Brain Res.* **145**, 1–13.

Leibowitz, S. F. (1972). Central adrenergic receptors and the regulation of hunger and thirst. In *Neurotransmitters* (ed. I. J. Kopin) *Res. Publ. Ass. Res. nerv. ment. Dis.* **50**, 327–58.

Leichnetz, G. P. and Astruc, J. (1976). The efferent projections of the medial prefrontal cortex in the squirrel monkey (*Saimiri sciureus*). *Brain Res.* **109**, 455–72.

Lenneberg, E. H. (1967). *Biological foundations of language.* Wiley, New York.

Leonard, C. M. (1969). The prefrontal cortex of the rat: I. Cortical projections of the medio-dorsal nucleus. II. Efferent connections. *Brain Res.* **12**, 321–43.

Levine, S. (1962). Psychophysiological effects of infant stimulation. In *Roots of behavior* (ed. E. L. Bliss) pp. 246–53. Hoeber, New York.

—— (1966). UCS intensity and avoidance learning. *J. exp. Psychol.* **71**, 163–4.

Levis, D. J. and Hare, N. P. (1977). A review of the theoretical rationale and empirical support for the extinction approach of implosive (flooding) therapy. in *Progress in behavior modifivation*, Vol. 4 (ed. M. Hersen, R. M. Eisler, and P. M. Moller) pp. 299–376. Academic Press, New York.

Lewis, P. R. and Shute, C. C. D. (1967). The cholinergic limbic system: projections to the hippocampal formation, medial cortex, nuclei of the ascending cholinergic reticular system, and subfornical organ and supraoptic crest. *Brain* **90**, 521–40.

—— —— (1978). Cholinergic pathways in CNS. In *Handbook of psychopharmacology*, Vol. 9. *Chemical pathways in the brain* (ed. L. L. Iversen, S. D. Iversen, and S. H. Snyder) pp. 315–55.

Lidbrink, P., Corrodi, H., Fuxe, K., and Olson, L. (1972). Barbiturates and meprobamate: decreases in catecholamine turnover of central dopamine and noradrenaline neuronal systems and the influence of immobilization stress. *Brain Res.* **45**, 507–24.

—— —— —— —— (1973). The effects of benzodiazepines, meprobamate, and barbiturates on central monoamine neurons. In *The benzodiazepines* (ed. S. Garattini, E. Mussini, and L. O. Randall) pp. 203–23. Raven Press, New York.

Lidsky, A., Levine, M. S., and MacGregor, S. Jr (1974a). Tonic and phasic effects evoked concurrently by sensory stimuli in hippocampal units. *Expl Neurol.* **44**, 130–4.

—— —— —— (1974b). Hippocampal units during orienting and arousal in rabbits. *Expl Neurol.* **44**, 171–86.

—— and Slotnick, B. M. (1970). Electrical stimulation of the hippocampus and electroconvulsive shock produce similar amnestic effects in mice. *Neuropsychologia* **8**, 363–9.

—— —— (1971). Effects of posttrial limbic stimulation on retention of a one-trial passive avoidance response. *J. comp. physiol. Psychol.* **76**, 337–48.

Lindsley, D. B. and Wilson, C. L. (1975). Brainstem–hypothalamic systems influencing hippocampal activity and behavior. In *The Hippocampus*, Vol. 2. *Neurophysiology and behavior* (ed. R. L. Isaacson and K. H. Pribram) pp. 247–78. Plenum Press, New York.

Lindvall, O. and Björklund, A. (1978). Organization of catecholamine neurons in the rat central nervous system. In *Handbook of psychopharmacology*, Vol. 9. *Chemical pathways in the brain* (ed. L. L. Iversen, S. D. Iversen, and S. H. Snyder) pp. 139–222. Plenum Press, New York.

—— and Stenevi, U. (1978). Dopamine and noradrenaline neurons projecting to the septal area in the rat. *Cell Tissue Res.* **190**, 383–407.

Lippa, A. S., Coupet, J., Greenblatt, E. N., Klepner, C. H., and Beer, B. (1979a). A synthetic non-benzodiazepine ligand for benzodiazepine receptors: probe for investigating neuronal substrates of anxiety. *Pharmac. Biochem. Behav.* **11**, 99–106.

—— Critchett, D., Sano, M. C., Klepner, C. A., Greenblatt, E. N., Coupet, J., and Beer, B. (1979b). Benzodiazepine receptors: cellular and behavioral characteristics. *Pharmac. Biochem. Behav.* **10**, 831–43.

—— Klepner, C. A., Benson, D. I., Critchett, D. J., Sano, M. C., and Beer, B. (1980). The role of GABA in mediating the anticonvulsant properties of benzodiazepines. In *GABA neurotransmission: current developments in physiology and neurochemistry* (Brain Res. Bull. **5**, suppl. 2, ed. H. Lal and S. Fielding) pp. 861–6. ANKHO Publishing Co., Fayetteville, N.Y.

—— —— Yunger, L., Sano, M. C., Smith, W. V., and Beer, B. (1978a). Relationship between benzodiazepine receptors and experimental anxiety in rats. *Pharmac. Biochem. Behav.* **9**, 853–6.

—— Sano, M. C., Coupet, J., Klepner, C. A., and Beer, B. (1978b). Evidence that benzodiazepine receptors reside on cerebellar Purkinje cells: studies with 'nervous' mutant mice. *Life Sci.* **23**, 2213–18.

Liss, P. (1968). Avoidance and freezing behavior following damage to the hippocampus or fornix. *J. comp. physiol. Psychol.* **66**, 193–7.

—— and Lukaszewska, I. (1966). The effects of overtraining and septal lesions on the ability to switch attention between cues. *Acta Biol. exp.* **26**, 299–307.

Livett, B. G. (1973). Histochemical visualization of peripheral and central adrenergic neurones. In *Catecholamines* (ed. L. L. Iversen) *Br. med. Bull.* Suppl. **29**, 93–9.

Lockhart, M. and Moore, J. W. (1975). Classical differential and operant conditioning in rabbits with septal lesions. *J. comp. physiol. Psychol.* **88**, 147–54.

Lopes da Silva, F. H. and Kamp, A. (1969). Hippocampal theta frequency shifts and operant behaviour. *Electroenceph. clin. Neurophysiol.* **26**, 133–43.

Lorden, J. F., Rickert, E. J., Dawson, R. Jr, and Pelleymounter, M. (1979). Forebrain norepinephrine depletion attenuates the blocking effect. *Soc. Neurosci. Abst.* **5**, 342.

Lorens, S. A. (1978). Some behavioral effects of serotonin depletion depend on method: a comparison of 5,7-dihydroxytryptamine, p-chlorophenylalanine, p-chloroamphetamine, and electrolytic raphe lesions. *Ann. NY Acad. Sci.* **305**, 532–55.

—— Guldberg, H. C., Hole, K., Köhler, C., and Srebro, B. (1976). Activity, avoidance learning and regional 5-hydroxytryptamine following intra-brainstem 5,7-dihydroxytryptamine and electrolytic midbrain raphe lesions in the rat. *Brain Res.* **108**, 97–113.

—— Sorenson, J. P., and Yunger, L. M. (1971). Behavioral and neurochemical effects of lesions in the raphe system of the rat. *J. comp. physiol. Psychol.* **77**, 48–52.

Lorente de No, R. (1934). Studies on the structure of the cerebral cortex. II. Continuation of the ammonic system. *J. Psychol. Neurol. Lpz.* **46**, 113–77.

Lovely, R. H. (1975). Hormonal dissociation of limbic lesion effects on shuttle box avoidance in rats. *J. comp. physiol. Psychol.* **89**, 224–30.

—— Grossen, N. E., Moot, S. A., Bauer, R. H., and Peterson, J. J. (1971). Hippocampal lesions and inhibition of avoidance behavior. *J. comp. physiol. Psychol.* **77**, 345–52.

Lubar, J. F. and Numan, R. (1973). Behavioral and physiological studies of septal functions and related medial cortical structures. *Behav. Biol.* **8**, 1–25.

Lubow, R. E. and Moore, A. U. (1959). Latent inhibition: the effect of non-reinforced pre-exposure to the conditioned stimulus. *J. comp. physiol. Psychol.* **52**, 415–19.

Lynch, G. S., Dunwiddie, T., and Gribkoff, V. (1977). Heterosynaptic depression: a post-synaptic correlate of long term potentiation. *Nature, Lond.* **266**, 737–9.

—— Rose, G., and Gall, C. M. (1978). Anatomical and functional aspects of the septo-hippocampal projections. In *Functions of the septo-hippocampal system* (ed. K. Elliott and J. Whelan) Ciba Foundation Symposium 58 (New Series) pp. 5–20. Elsevier, Amsterdam.

Lynch, M. A., Lindsay, J., and Ounsted, C. (1975). Tranquilizers causing aggression. *Br. med. J.* No. 5952, p. 260.

Mabry, P. D. and Peeler, D. F. (1972). Effects of septal lesions on response to frustrative nonreward. *Physiol. Behav.* **8**, 909–13.

McAllister, W. R., McAllister, D. E., and Douglass, W. K. (1971). The inverse relationship between shock intensity and shuttle-box avoidance learning in rats: a reinforcement explanation. *J. comp. physiol. Psychol.* **74**, 426–33.

McCarley, R. W. (1980). Mechanisms and models of behavioral state control. In *The reticular formation revisited* (ed. J. A. Hobson and M. A. B. Brazier) pp. 375–403. Raven Press, New York.

McCleary, R. A. (1961). Response specificity in the behavioral effects of limbic system lesions in the cat. *J. comp. physiol. Psychol.* **54**, 605–13.

—— (1966). Response-modulating functions of the limbic system: initiation and suppression. In *Progress in physiological psychology* (ed. E. Stellar and J. M. Sprague) Vol. 1, pp. 209–72. Academic Press, New York.

—— Jones, C., and Ursin, H. (1965). Avoidance and retention deficits in septal cats. *Psychon. Sci.* **2**, 85–6.

McCord, P. R. and Wakefield, J. A. Jr (1981). Arithmetic achievement as a function of introversion–extraversion and teacher-presented reward and punishment. *Pers. indiv. Diff.* **2**, 145–52.

MacDonald, R. L. and Barker, J. L. (1978). Specific antagonism of GABA-mediated post-synaptic inhibition in cultured mammalian spinal cord neurons: a common mode of convulsant action. *Neurology, Minneap.* **28**, 325–30.

MacDonnell, M. F. and Stoddard-Apter, S. (1978). Effects of medial septal stimulation on hypothalamically-elicited intra-specific attack and associated hissing in cats. *Physiol. Behav.* **21**, 679–83.

McDonough, J. H., Gill, J. H., and Nielson, H. C. (1975). Impairment of fixed-interval responding during chronic alcohol drinking in rats. *Physiol. Psychol.* **3**, 417–21.

—— and Kesner, R. P. (1971). Amnesia produced by brief electrical stimulation of amygdala or dorsal hippocampus in cats. *J. comp. physiol. Psychol.* **77**, 171–8.

McEnaney, K. W. and Butter, C. M. (1969). Perseveration of responding and non-responding in monkeys with orbital frontal ablations. *J. comp. physiol. Psychol.* **68**, 558–61.

McEntee, W. J. and Mair, R. G. (1978). Memory impairment in Korsakoff's psychosis: a correlation with brain noradrenergic activity. *Science, NY* **202**, 905–7.

McEwen, B. S., Weiss, J. M., and Schwartz, L. S. (1969). Uptake of corticosterone by rat brain and its concentration by certain limbic structures. *Brain Res.* **16**, 227–41.

McFarland, D. J., Kostas, J., and Drew, W. G. (1978). Dorsal hippocampal lesions: effects of preconditioning CS exposure on flavor aversion. *Behav. Biol.* **22**, 398–404.

McGaugh, J. L. (1966). Time-dependent processes in memory storage. *Science, NY* **153**, 1351–8.

McGonigle, B., McFarland, D. J., and Collier, P. (1967). Rapid extinction following drug-inhibited incidental learning. *Nature, Lond.* **214**, 531–2.

McGowan, B. K., Garcia, J., Ervin, F. R., and Schwartz, J. (1969). Effects of septal lesions on bait-shyness in the rat. *Physiol. Behav.* **4**, 907–9.

—— Hankins, W. G., and Garcia, J. (1972). Limbic lesions and control of the internal and external environment. *Behav. Biol.* **7**, 841–52.

McGowan-Sass, B. K. (1973). Differentiation of electrical rhythms and functional specificity of the hippocampus of the rat. *Physiol. Behav.* **11**, 187–94.

Mackintosh, N. J. (1973). Stimulus selection: learning to ignore stimuli that predict no change in reinforcement. In *Constraints on learning* (ed. R. A. Hinde and J. T. Stevenson-Hinde) pp. 75–96. Academic Press, London.

—— (1974). *The psychology of animal learning.* Academic Press, New York.

—— (1978). Cognitive or associative theories of conditioning: implications of an analysis of blocking. In *Cognitive processes in animal behavior* (ed. S. H. Hulse, H. Fowler, and W. K. Honig) pp. 155–75. Erlbaum, Hillsdale, NJ.

—— and Dickinson, A. (1979). Instrumental (Type II) conditioning. In *Mechanisms of learning and motivation* (ed. A. Dickinson and R. A. Boakes) pp. 143–70. Erlbaum, Hillsdale, NJ.

MacLean, P. D. (1957). Chemical and electrical stimulation of hippocampus in unrestrained animals II. Behavioural findings. *Archs Neurol. Psychiat., Chicago* **78**, 128–42.

McLennan, H. and Miller, J. J. (1974a). The hippocampal control of neuronal discharges in the septum of the rat. *J. Physiol., Lond.* **237**, 607–24.

—— —— (1974b). Gamma-aminobutyric acid and the inhibition of the septal nuclei of the rat. *J. Physiol., Lond.* **237**, 625–33.

—— —— (1976). Frequency-related inhibitory mechanisms controlling rhythmical activity in the septal area. *J. Physiol., Lond.* **254**, 827–41.

McMillan, D. E. (1973). Drugs and punished responding. I. Rate-dependent effects under multiple schedules. *J. exp. Anal. Behav.* **19**, 133–45.

McNaughton, B. L., Douglas, R. M., and Goddard, G. V. (1978). Synaptic enhancement in fascia dentata: cooperativity among coactive afferents. *Brain Res.* **157**, 277–93.

McNaughton, N. (1977). Exploration, frustration and the electrophysiology of the septo-hippocampal theta system in the rat. Unpublished Ph.D. thesis, University of Southampton.

—— Azmitia, E. C., Williams, J. H., Buchan, A., and Gray, J. A. (1980a). Septal elicitation of hippocampal theta rhythm after localized deafferentation of serotonergic fibres. *Brain Res.* **200**, 259–69.

—— and Feldon, J. (1980). Spontaneous alternation of body turns and place: differential effects of amylobarbitone, scopolamine and septal lesions. *Psychopharmacology* **68**, 201–6.

—— James, D. T. D, Stewart, J., Gray, J. A., Valero, I., and Drewnowski, A. (1977). Septal driving of hippocampal theta rhythm as a function of frequency in the male rat: effects of drugs. *Neuroscience* **2**, 1019–27.

—— Kelly, P. H., and Gray, J. A. (1980b). Unilateral blockade of the dorsal ascending noradrenergic bundle and septal elicitation of hippocampal theta rhythm. *Neurosci. Lett.* **18**, 67–72.

—— and Mason, S. T. (1980). The neuropsychology and neuropharmacology of the dorsal ascending noradrenergic bundle — a review. *Prog. Neurobiol.* **14**, 157–219.

—— and Miller, J. J. (1979). Synapse-specific long term potentiation (LTP) in the septo-hippocampal system of the rat. *Neurosci. Lett.* Suppl. 3, S72.

—— and Sedgwick, E. M. (1978). Reticular stimulation and hippocampal theta rhythm in rats: effects of drugs. *Neuroscience* **3**, 629–32.

McNew, J. J. and Thompson, R. (1966). Role of the limbic system in active and passive avoidance conditioning in rat. *J. comp. physiol. Psychol.* **61**, 173–80.

Macrides, F. (1975). Temporal relationship between hippocampal slow waves and exploratory sniffing in hamsters. *Behav. Biol.* **14**, 295–308.

Maeda, H. (1978). Effects of septal lesions on electrically elicited hypothalamic rage in cats. *Physiol. Behav.* **21**, 339–43.

Magoun, H. W. (1963). *The waking brain,* 2nd edn. Thomas, Springfield, Ill.

Mahut, H. (1971). Spatial and object reversal learning in monkeys with partial temporal lobe ablations. *Neuropsychologia* **9**, 409–24.

Maier, S. F. and Seligman, M. E. P. (1976). Learned helplessness: theory and evidence. *J. exp. Psychol.: Gen.* **105**, 3–46.

Mair, W. G. P., Warrington, E. K., and Weiskrantz, L. (1979). Memory disorder in Korsakoff's psychosis: a neuropathological and neuropsychological investigation of two cases. *Brain* **102**, 749–83.

Malick, J. B. (1970). A behavioral comparison of three lesion-induced models of aggression in rat. *Physiol. Behav.* **5**, 679–81.

Mandel, P. and Defeudis, F. V. (eds.) (1979). *GABA: biochemistry and CNS functions*. Plenum Press, New York.

Mandler, G. and Sarason, S. B. (1952). A study of anxiety and learning. *J. abnorm. soc. Psychol.* **47**, 166–73.

Manning, F. J. (1978). Dorsolateral prefrontal cortex lesions and discrimination of movement-produced cues by Rhesus monkeys. *Brain Res.* **149**, 77–88.

—— and McDonough, J. H. (1974). Reinforcement omission, non-contingent reinforcement, and limbic lesions in rats. *Behav. Biol.* **11**, 327–38.

Marcy, R. and Quermonne, M. A. (1974). An improved method for studying the psychogalvanic reaction in mice and its inhibition by psycholeptic drugs: comparison with the effects of other pharmacological agents. *Psychopharmacologia* **34**, 335–49.

Margules, D. L. (1968). Noradrenergic basis of inhibition between reward and punishment in amygdala. *J. comp. physiol. Psychol.* **66**, 329–34.

—— (1971). Localization of anti-punishment actions of norepinephrine and atropine in amygdala and entopeduncular nucleus of rats. *Brain Res.* **35**, 177–84.

Marks, I. M. (1969). *Fears and phobias*. Heinemann, London.

—— (1973). Reduction of fear: towards a unifying theory. *Can. psychiat. Ass. J.* **18**, 9–12.

—— (1976). 'Psychopharmacology': the use of drugs combined with psychological treatment. In *Evaluation of psychological therapies* (ed. R. L. Spitzer and D. F. Klein) pp. 108–26. Johns Hopkins University Press, Baltimore.

—— (1979). Conditioning models for clinical syndromes are out of date. *Behav. Brain Sci.* **2**, 175–7.

—— Birley, J. L. T., and Gelder, M. G. (1966). Modified Leucotomy in severe agoraphobia: a controlled serial inquiry. *Br. J. Psychiat.* **112**, 757–69.

—— Viswanathan, R., Lipsedge, M. S., and Gardner, R. (1972). Enhanced relief of phobias by flooding during waning diazepam effect. *Br. J. Psychiat.* **121**, 493–505.

Marriott, A. S. and Spencer, P. S. J. (1965). Effects of centrally acting drugs on exploratory behaviour in rats. *Br. J. Pharmac.* **25**, 432–41.

Martin, L. K., Powell, B. J., and Kamano, D. K. (1966). Effects of amobarbital sodium on avoidance performance of rats differing in emotionality. *Proc. 74th ann. Conv. Am. psychol. Ass.* pp. 125–6.

Mason, S. T. (1978). Parameters of the dorsal bundle extinction effect: previous extinction experience. *Pharmac. Biochem. Behav.* **8**, 655–9.

—— (1979). Dorsal bundle extinction effect: motivation or attention? *Physiol. Behav.* **23**, 43–51.

—— and Fibiger, H. C. (1977). Altered exploratory behaviour after 6-OHDA lesion to the dorsal noradrenergic bundle. *Nature, Lond.* **269**, 704–5.

—— —— (1978a). Noradrenaline and partial reinforcement in rats. *J. comp. physiol. Psychol.* **92**, 1110–18.

—— —— (1978b). 6-OHDA lesion of the dorsal noradrenergic bundle alters extinction of passive avoidance. *Brain Res.* **152**, 209–14.

—— —— (1978c). Evidence for a role of brain noradrenaline in attention and stimulus sampling. *Brain Res.* **159**, 421–6.

—— —— (1978d). Noradrenaline and spatial memory. *Brain Res.* **156**, 382–6.

—— —— (1979a). The dorsal noradrenergic bundle and varieties of passive avoidance. *Psychopharmacology* **66**, 179–82.

—— —— (1979*b*). Noradrenaline and avoidance learning in the rat. *Brain Res.* **161**, 321–33.

—— —— (1979*c*). Noradrenaline and extinction of conditioned taste aversion in the rat. *Behav. neural Biol.* **25**, 206–16.

—— —— (1979*d*). The dorsal bundle extinction effect: dependence on subtle changes in acquisition. *Brain Res.* **166**, 341–8.

—— —— (1979*e*). Noradrenaline, fear and extinction. *Brain Res.* **165**, 47–56.

—— —— (1979*f*). Noradrenaline and selective attention. *Soc. Neurosci. Abst.* **5**, 343.

—— —— (1979*g*). Regional topography within noradrenergic locus coeruleus as revealed by retrograde transport of horseradish peroxidase. *J. comp. Neurol.* **187**, 703–11.

—— —— (1979*h*). Neurochemical basis of the dorsal bundle extinction effect. *Pharmac. Biochem. Behav.* **10**, 373–80.

—— and Iversen, S. D. (1975). Learning in the absence of forebrain noradrenaline. *Nature, Lond.* **258**, 422–4.

—— —— (1977*a*). Behavioral basis of the dorsal bundle extinction effect. *Pharmac. Biochem. Behav.* **7**, 373–9.

—— —— (1977*b*). An investigation of the role of cortical and cerebellar noradrenaline in associative motor learning in the rat. *Brain Res.* **134**, 513–27.

—— —— (1977*c*). Effects of selective forebrain noradrenaline loss on behavioral inhibition in the rat. *J. comp. physiol. Psychol.* **91**, 165–73.

—— —— (1978*a*). Central and peripheral noradrenaline and resistance to extinction. *Physiol. Behav.* **20**, 681–6.

—— —— (1978*b*). Reward, attention and the dorsal noradrenergic bundle. *Brain Res.* **150**, 135–48.

—— —— (1978*c*). The dorsal noradrenergic bundle, extinction and nonreward. *Physiol. Behav.* **21**, 1043–5.

—— —— (1979). Theories of the dorsal bundle extinction effect. *Brain Res. Rev.* **1**, 107–37.

—— and Robbins, T. W. (1979). Noradrenaline and conditioned reinforcement. *Behav. neural Biol.* **25**, 523–34.

—— Roberts, D. C. S., and Fibiger, H. C. (1978). Noradrenaline and neophobia. *Physiol. Behav.* **21**, 353–61.

Masserman, J. H. and Yum, K. S. (1946). An analysis of the influence of alcohol on experimental neuroses in cats. *Psychosom. Med.* **8**, 36–52.

Matalka, E. S. and Bunnell, B. N. (1968). Septal ablation and CAR acquisition in the golden hamster. *Psychon. Sci.* **12**, 27–8.

Mathews, A. (1978). Fear-reduction research and clinical phobias. *Psychol. Bull.* **85**, 390–404.

Mattingley, B. A., Osborne, F. H., and Gotsick, J. E. (1979). Activity changes during a conditioned aversive stimulus in rats with septal lesions. *Physiol. Behav.* **22**, 521–5.

Mayer-Gross, W., Slater, E. T. O., and Roth, M. (1979). *Clinical Psychiatry.* Baillière, Tindall, and Cox, London.

Mays, L. E. and Best, P. J. (1975). Hippocampal unit activity to tonal stimuli during arousal from sleep and in awake rats. *Expl Neurol.* **47**, 268–79.

Means, L. W. and Douglas, R. J. (1970). Effects of hippocampal lesions on cue utilization in spatial discrimination in rats. *J. comp. physiol. Psychol.* **73**, 254–60.

—— Leander, J. D., and Isaacson, R. L. (1971). The effects of hippocampectomy on alternation behavior and response to novelty. *Physiol. Behav.* **6**, 17–22.

—— Walker, D. W., and Isaacson, R. L. (1970). Facilitated single-alternation go, no-go acquisition following hippocampectomy in the rat. *J. comp. physiol. Psychol.* **72**, 278–85.

Meibach, R. C. and Siegel, A. (1977a). Efferent connections of the septal area in the rat: an analysis utilizing retrograde and anterograde transport methods. *Brain Res.* **119**, 1–20.

—— —— (1977b). Efferent connections of the hippocampal formation in the rat. *Brain Res.* **124**, 197–224.

—— —— (1977c). Subicular projections to the posterior cingulate cortex in rats. *Expl Neurol.* **57**, 264–74.

Melamed, E., Lahar, M., and Atlas, D. (1977). Beta-adrenergic receptors in rat cerebral cortex: histochemical localization by a fluorescent beta-blocker. *Brain Res.* **128**, 379–84.

Meldrum, B. S. (1975). Epilepsy and gamma-aminobutyric acid-mediated inhibition. *Int. Rev. Neurobiol.* **17**, 1–36.

Meligeri, J. A., Ledergerber, S. A., and McGaugh, J. L. (1978). Norepinephrine attenuation of amnesia produced by diethyldithiocarbamate. *Brain Res.* **149**, 155–64.

Mellanby, J., Gray, J. A., Quintero, S., Holt, L., and McNaughton N. (1981). Septal driving of hippocampal theta rhythm: a role for gamma-amino-butyrate in the effects of minor tranquillizers: *Neuroscience* **6**, 1413–21.

Mellgren, S. I. and Srebro, B. (1973). Changes in acetylcholinesterase and the distribution of degenerating fibres in the hippocampal region after septal lesions in the rat. *Brain Res.* **52**, 19–36.

Micco, D. J. and Schwartz, M. (1971). Effects of hippocampal lesions upon the development of Pavlovian internal inhibition in rats. *J. comp. physiol. Psychol.* **76**, 371–7.

Miczek, K. A. (1973). Effects of scopolamine, amphetamine and benzodiazepines on conditioned suppression. *Pharmac. Biochem. Behav.* **1**, 401–11.

—— and Barry, H. III (1977). Effects of alcohol on attack and defensive–submissive reactions in rats. *Psychopharmacology* **52**, 231–7.

—— and Grossman, S. P. (1972). Effects of septal lesions on inter- and intraspecific aggression in rats. *J. comp. physiol. Psychol.* **79**, 37–45.

—— Kelsey, J. E., and Grossman, S. P. (1972). Time course of effects of septal lesions on avoidance, response suppression and reactivity to shock. *J. comp. physiol. Psychol.* **79**, 318–27.

Middaugh, L. D. and Lubar, J. F. (1970). Interaction of septal lesions and experience on the suppression of punished responses. *Physiol. Behav.* **5**, 233–7.

Miley, W. M. and Baenninger, R. (1972). Inhibition and facilitation of interspecies aggression in septal lesioned rat. *Physiol. Behav.* **9**, 379–84.

Millenson, J. R. (1967). *Principles of behavioral analysis.* Macmillan, New York.

Miller, C. R., Elkins, R. L., Fraser, J., Peacock, L. J., and Hobbs, S. H. (1975). Taste aversion and passive avoidance in rats with hippocampal lesions. *Physiol. Psychol.* **3**, 123–6.

—— —— and Peacock, L. J. (1971). Disruption of a radiation-induced preference shift by hippocampal lesions. *Physiol. Behav.* **6**, 283–5.

Miller, G. A., Galanter, E. H., and Pribram, K. H. (1960). *Plans and the structure of behavior.* Rinehart and Winston, New York.

Miller, I. W. III and Norman, W. H. (1979). Learned helplessness in humans: a review and attribution-theory model. *Psychol. Bull.* **86**, 93–118.

Miller, J. J. and McNaughton, N. (1979). Collateral-specific long term potentiation (LTP) of hippocampal field CA_3 output in the rat. *Soc. Neurosci. Abst.* **5**, 632.

Miller, N. E. (1951). Learnable drives and rewards. In *Handbook of experimental psychology* (ed. S. S. Stevens) pp. 435–72. Wiley, New York.

—— (1960). Learning resistance to pain and fear: effects of over-learning, exposure and rewarded exposure in context. *J. exp. Psychol.* **60**, 137–45.

—— (1976). Learning, stress and psychosomatic symptoms. *Acta Neurobiol. exp.* **36**, 141–56.

—— and Barry, H. III (1960). Motivational effects of drugs: methods which illustrate some general problems in psychopharmacology. *Psychopharmacologia* **1**, 169–99.

Miller, S. W. and Groves, P. M. (1977). Sensory evoked neuronal activity in the hippocampus before and after lesions of the medial septal nuclei. *Physiol. Behav.* **18**, 141–6.

Milner, B. (1963). Effects of different brain lesions on card sorting. *Archs Neurol.* **9**, 90–100.

—— (1964). Some effects of frontal lobectomy in man. In *The frontal granular cortex and behavior* (ed. J. M. Warren and K. Akert) pp. 313–31. McGraw-Hill, New York.

—— (1968). Preface: material specific and generalized memory loss. *Neuropsychologia* **6**, 175–9.

—— (1970). Memory and the medial temporal regions of the brain. In *Biology of memory* (ed. K. H. Pribram and D. E. Broadbent) pp. 29–50. Academic Press, New York.

—— (1971). Interhemispheric differences and psychological processes. *Br. med. Bull.* **27**, 272–7.

—— Corkin, S., and Teuber, H.-L. (1968). Further analysis of the hippocampal amnesic syndrome: 14 year follow-up study of H.M. *Neuropsychologia* **6**, 215–34.

Misgeld, U., Sarvey, J. M., and Klee, M. R. (1979). Heterosynaptic postactivation potentiation in hippocampal CA3 neurons: long-term changes of the post-synaptic potentials. *Expl Brain Res.* **37**, 217–30.

Mitchell, S. J. and Ranck, J. B. Jr (1980). Generation of theta rhythm in medial entorhinal cortex of freely-moving rats. *Brain Res.* **189**, 49–66.

Mitchell-Heggs, N., Kelly, D., and Richardson, A. (1976). Stereotactic limbic leucotomy: a follow-up at 16 months. *Br. J. Psychiat.* **128**, 226–40.

Modigh, K. (1975). Electroconvulsive shock and postsynaptic catecholamine effects: increased psychomotor stimulant action of apomorphine and clonidine in reserpine pretreated mice by repeated ECS. *J. Neur. Transm.* **36**, 19–32.

—— (1976). Long-term effects of electroconvulsive shock therapy on synthesis, turnover and uptake of brain monoamines. *Psychopharmacology* **49**, 179–85.

Möhler, H. and Okada, T. (1977). Benzodiazepine receptor: demonstration in the central nervous system. *Science, NY* **198**, 849–51.

Moises, H. C., Waterhouse, B., and Woodward, D. J. (1978). Locus coeruleus stimulation potentiates Purkinje cell responses to afferent synaptic inputs. *Soc. Neurosci. Abst.* **4**, 876.

Molino, A. (1975). Sparing of function after infant lesions of selected limbic structures in the rat. *J. comp. physiol. Psychol.* **89**, 868–81.

Molinoff, P. B., Sporn, J. R., Wolfe, B. B., and Harden, T. K. (1978). Regulation of beta-adrenergic receptors in the cerebral cortex. *Adv. cyclic Nucl. Res.* **9**, 465–83.

Moore, R. Y. (1964). Effects of some rhinencephalic lesions on retention of conditioned avoidance behavior in cats. *J. comp. physiol. Psychol.* **57**, 65–71.

—— (1978). Catecholamine innervation of the basal forebrain. I. The septal area. *J. comp. Neurol.* **177**, 665–84.

—— and Bloom, F. E. (1979). Central catecholamine neuron systems: anatomy and physiology of the norepinephrine and epinephrine systems. *A. Rev. Neurosci.* **2**, 113–67.

Morgan, M. J. (1974). Resistance to satiation. *Anim. Behav.* **22**, 449–66.

Morris, L. W. (1979). Extraversion and introversion: an interactional perspective. Hemisphere, Washington.

Morris, R. G. M. and Black, A. H. (1978). Hippocampal electrical activity and behavior elicited by nonreward. *Behav. Biol.* **22**, 524–32.

—— —— and O'Keefe, J. (1976). Hippocampal EEG during a ballistic movement. (Abstract.) *Neurosci. Lett.* **3**, 102.

Mos, L. P., Lukaweski, R., and Royce, J. R. (1977). Effects of septal lesions on factors of mouse emotionality. *J. comp. physiol. Psychol.* **91**, 523–32.

Mowrer, O. H. (1947). On the dual nature of learning: a re-interpretation of 'conditioning' and 'problem-solving'. *Harv. educ. Rev.* **17**, 102–48.

—— (1960). *Learning theory and behavior.* Wiley, New York.

Moyer, K. E. and Chapman, J. A. (1966). Effect of continuous vs. discontinuous shock on shuttle box avoidance in the rat. *Psychon. Sci.* **4**, 197–8.

—— and Korn, J. H. (1964). Effect of UCS intensity on the acquisition and extinction of an avoidance response. *J. exp. Psychol.* **67**, 352–9.

Murphy, H. M. and Brown, T. S. (1970). Effects of hippocampal lesions on simple and preferential consummatory behavior in the rat. *J. comp. physiol. Psychol.* **72**, 404–15.

Murphy, L. R., Race, K. E., and Brown, T. S. (1975). Behaviors emitted by rats with limbic lesions during feeding. *Behav. Biol.* **15**, 231–7.

Myer, J. S. (1971). Some effects of noncontingent aversive stimulation. In *Aversive conditioning and learning* (ed. F. R. Brush) pp. 469–536. Academic Press, New York.

Myhrer, T. (1975a). Locomotor avoidance and maze behaviour in rats with selective disruption of hippocampal output. *J. comp. physiol. Psychol.* **89**, 759–77.

—— (1975b). Locomotor and avoidance behaviour in rats with partial or total hippocampal perforant path sections. *Physiol. Behav.* **15**, 217–34.

—— (1977). Jump avoidance acquisition and locomotor behavior in rats with the hippocampal theta rhythm disrupted. *Behav. Biol.* **19**, 361–70.

—— and Kaada, B. (1975). Locomotor avoidance and maze behaviour in rats with the dorsal fornix transected. *Physiol. Behav.* **14**, 847–53.

Nadel, L. (1968). Dorsal and ventral hippocampal lesions and behavior. *Physiol. Behav.* **3**, 891–900.

—— O'Keefe, J., and Black, A. H. (1975). Slam on the brakes: a critique of Altman, Brunner and Bayer's response inhibition model of hippocampal function. *Behav. Biol.* **14**, 151–62.

Nicholas, T., Galbraith, G., and Lewis, D. J. (1976). Theta EEG activity and memory processes in rats. *Physiol. Behav.* **16**, 489–92.

Nicholson, J. N. (1975). Behavioural indices of frustration in normal and emotionally maladjusted children. *J. Child Psychol. Psychiat.* **16**, 19–31.

—— and Gray, J. A. (1972). Peak shift, behavioural contrast and stimulus generalization as related to personality and development in children. *Br. J. Psychol.* **63**, 47–62.

Nielsen, M., Braestrup, C., and Squires, R. F. (1978). Evidence for a late evolutionary appearance of brain-specific benzodiazepine receptors: an investigation of 18 vertebrate and 5 invertebrate species. *Brain Res.* **141**, 342–6.

Niki, H. (1962). Effects of hippocampal ablation on behavior in the rat. *Jap. psychol. Res.* **4**, 139–53.

—— (1965). Effects of hippocampal ablation on inhibitory control of operant behavior in the rat. *Jap. psychol. Res.* **7**, 126–37.

—— (1966). Response perseveration following hippocampal ablation in the rat. *Jap. psychol. Res.* **8**, 1–9.

—— and Watanabe, M. (1976). Cingulate unit activity and delayed response. *Brain Res.* **110**, 381–6.

Nolan, N. A. and Parkes, M. W. (1973). The effects of benzodiazepines on the behaviour of mice on a hole-board. *Psychopharmacologia* **29**, 277–88.

Nonneman, A. J. and Isaacson, R. L. (1973). Task dependent recovery after early brain damage. *Behav. Biol.* **8**, 143–72.

—— Voigt, J., and Kolb, B. E. (1974). Comparisons of behavioral effects of hippocampal and prefrontal cortex lesions in the rat. *J. comp. physiol. Psychol.* **87**, 249–60.

Notterman, J. M., Schoenfeld, W. N., and Bersh, P. J. (1952). Conditioned heart rate response in human beings during experimental anxiety. *J. exp. Psychol.* **45**, 1–18.

Novick, I. and Pihl, R. (1969). Effect of amphetamine on the septal syndrome in rats. *J. comp. physiol. Psychol.* **68**, 220–5.

Obrist, P. A., Wood, D. M., and Perez-Reyes, M. (1965). Heart rate during conditioning in humans: effects of UCS intensity, vagal blockade and adrenergic block of vasomotor activity. *J. exp. Psychol.* **70**, 32–42.

Odling-Smee, F. J. (1975). Background stimuli and the inter-stimulus interval during Pavlovian conditioning. *Q. Jl exp. Psychol.* **27**, 387–92.

Ögren, S. O. and Fuxe, K. (1974). Learning, noradrenaline and the pituitary–adrenal axis. *Med. Biol.* **52**, 399–405.

—— —— (1977). The role of brain noradrenaline and the pituitary–adrenal axis in learning. *Brain Res.* **127**, 372–3.

Ohman, A. (1971). Differentiation of conditioned and orienting response components in electrodermal conditioning. *Psychophysiology* **8**, 7–22.

—— (1979). Fear relevance, autonomic conditioning, and phobias: a laboratory model. In *Trends in behavior therapy* (ed. P. O. Sjöden, S. Bates, and W. W. Dockens) pp. 107–33. Academic Press, New York.

—— and Dimberg, U. (1978). Facial expressions as conditioned stimuli for electrodermal responses: a case of 'preparedness'? *J. Pers. soc. Psychol.* **36**, 1251–8.

—— Eriksson, A., Fredrikson, M., Hugdahl, K., and Olofsson C. (1974). Habituation of the electrodermal orienting reaction to potentially phobic and supposedly neutral stimuli in normal human subjects. *Biol. Psychol.* **2**, 85–93.

—— —— and Olofsson, C. (1975). One-trial learning and superior resistance to extinction of autonomic responses conditioned to potentially phobic stimuli. *J. comp. physiol. Psychol.* **88**, 619–27.

—— Fredrikson, M., and Hugdahl, K. (1978). Orienting and defensive responding in the electrodermal system: palmar–dorsal differences and recovery rate during conditioning to potentially phobic stimuli. *Psychophysiology* **15**, 93–101.

—— —— —— and Rimmo, P.-A. (1976). The premise of equipotentiality in human classical conditioning: conditioned electrodermal responses to potentially phobic stimuli. *J. exp. Psychol.: Gen.* **105**, 313–37.

Oishi, H., Iwahara, S., Yang, K. M., and Yogi, A. (1972). Effects of chlordiazepoxide on passive avoidance responses in rats. *Psychopharmacologia* **23**, 373–85.

Ojemann, G. and Mateer, C. (1979). Human language cortex: localization of memory, syntax, and sequential motor-phoneme identification systems. *Science, NY* **205**, 1401–3.

Okaiche, H., Anchel, H., Barbaree, H., and Black, A. H. (1978). Punishment of runway behaviour in rats with fornical lesions. *Physiol. Behav.* **21**, 503–9.

Oke, A. F. and Adams, R. N. (1978). Selective attention dysfunctions in adult rats neonatally treated with 6-hydroxydopamine. *Pharmac. Biochem. Behav.* **9**, 429–32.

O'Keefe, J. (1976). Place units in the hippocampus of the freely moving rat. *Expl Neurol.* **51**, 78–109.

—— and Black, A. H. (1978). Single unit and lesion experiments on the sensory inputs to the hippocampal map. In *Functions of the septo-hippocampal system* (ed. K. Elliott and J. Whelan) Ciba Foundation Symposium 58 (New Series) pp. 179–92. Elsevier, Amsterdam.

—— and Dostrovsky, J. (1971). The hippocampus as a spatial map: preliminary evidence from unit activity in the freely-moving rat. *Brain Res.* **34**, 171–5.

—— and Nadel, L. (1978). *The hippocampus as a cognitive map*. Clarendon Press, Oxford.

Olds, J. and Hirano, T. (1969). Conditioned responses of hippocampal and other neurons. *Electroenceph. clin. Neurophysiol.* **2**, 159–66.

—— and Milner, P. (1954). Positive reinforcement produced by electrical stimulation of septal area and other regions. *J. comp. physiol. Psychol.* **47**, 419–27.

—— Mink, W. D., and Best, P. J. (1969). Single unit patterns during anticipatory behavior. *Electroenceph. clin. Neurophysiol.* **26**, 144–58.

Olsen, R. W., Greenlee, D., Van Ness, P., and Ticku, M. K. (1978*a*). Studies on the gamma-aminobutyric acid receptor/ionophore proteins in mammalian brain. In *Amino acids as chemical transmitters* (ed. F. Fonnum) pp. 467–86. Plenum Press, New York.

—— Ticku, M. K., Greenlee, D., and Van Ness, P. (1978*b*). GABA receptor and ionophore binding sites: interaction with various drugs. In *GABA-neurotransmitters* (ed. P. Krogsgaard-Larsen, J. Scheel-Kruger, and H. Kofod) pp. 165–78. Academic Press, New York.

Olson, L. and Fuxe, K. (1971). On the projections from the locus coeruleus noradrenaline neurons: the cerebellar innervation. *Brain Res.* **28**, 165–71.

Olton, D. S. (1972). Behavioral and neuroanatomical differentiation of response-suppression and response-shift mechanisms in the rat. *J. comp. physiol. Psychol.* **78**, 450–6.

—— (1978*a*). Characteristics of spatial memory. In *Cognitive processes in animal behavior* (ed. S. H. Hulse, H. Fowler, and W. K. Honig) pp. 341–73. Erlbaum, Hillsdale, N.J.

—— (1978*b*). The function of septo-hippocampal connections in spatially organized behaviour. In *Functions of the septo-hippocampal system* (ed. K. Elliott and J. Whelan) Ciba Foundation Symposium 58 (New Series) pp. 327–42. Elsevier, Amsterdam.

—— Becker, J. T., and Handelmann, G. E. (1979*a*). Hippocampus, space, and memory. *Behav. Brain Sci.* **2**, 313–22.

—— —— —— (1979*b*). Hippocampus, space, and memory: authors' responses. *Behav. Brain Sci.* **2**, 352–9.

—— Branch, M., and Best, P. J. (1978). Spatial correlates of hippocampal unit activity. *Expl Neurol.* **58**, 387–409.

—— and Isaacson, R. L. (1968). Hippocampal lesions and active avoidance. *Physiol. Behav.* **3**, 719–24.

—— —— (1969). Fear, hippocampal lesions and avoidance behaviour. *Commun. Behav. Biol. A* **3**, 259–62.

—— and Pappas, B. C. (1979). Spatial memory and hippocampal function. *Neuropsychologia* **17**, 669–82.

—— Walker, J. A., and Gage, F. H. (1978). Hippocampal connections and spatial discrimination. *Brain Res.* **139**, 295–308.

—— and Werz, M. A. (1978). Hippocampal function and behavior: spatial discrimination and response inhibition. *Physiol. Behav.* **20**, 597–605.

Oscar-Berman, M. O. and Samuels, I. (1973). Stimulus-preference and memory factors in Korsakoff's syndrome. Paper presented at the American Psychological Association Meetings, Montreal.

—— —— (1977). Stimulus preference and memory factors in Korsakoff's syndrome. *Neuropsychologia* **15**, 99–106.

Ostman, I. and Nyback, H. (1976). Adaptive changes in central and peripheral noradrenergic neurons in rats, following chronic exercise. *Neuroscience* 1, 41–7.

Overmier, J. B. and Seligman, M. E. P. (1967). Effects of inescapable shock upon subsequent escape and avoidance learning. *J. comp. physiol. Psychol.* 63, 28–33.

Overton, D. A. (1966). State-dependent learning produced by depressant and atropine-like drugs. *Psychopharmacologia* 10, 6–31.

Owen, S. (1979). Investigations of the role of the dorsal ascending noradrenergic bundle in behavioural responses to nonreward and novelty in the rat. Unpublished D.Phil. thesis, University of Oxford.

—— Boarder, M. R., Feldon, J., Gray, J. A., and Fillenz, M. (1979). Role of forebrain noradrenaline in reward and nonreward. In *Catecholamines: basic and clinical frontiers* (ed. E. Usdin, J. D. Barchas, and I. J. Kopin) pp. 1678–80. Pergamon, Oxford.

—— —— and Gray, J. A. (1977). The effects of depletion of forebrain noradrenaline on the runway behaviour of rats. *Expl Brain Res.* 28, R32–3.

—— —— —— and Fillenz, M. (1982). Acquisition and extinction of continuously and partially reinforced running in rats with lesions of the dorsal noradrendergic bundle. *Behav. Brain Res.* 5, 469–84.

Paiva, T., Lopes da Silva, F. H., and Mollevanger, W. (1976). Modulating systems of hippocampal EEG *Electroenceph. clin. Neurophysiol.* 40, 470–80.

Pandya, D., Dye, P., and Butters, N. (1971). Efferent cortico-cortical projections of the prefrontal cortex in the Rhesus monkey. *Brain Res.* 31, 35–46.

Papez, J. W. (1937). A proposed mechanism of emotion. *Archs Neurol. Psychiat.* 38, 725–43.

Papsdorf, J. D. and Woodruff, M. (1970). Effects of bilateral hippocampectomy on the rabbit's acquisition of shuttle-box and passive-avoidance responses. *J. comp. physiol. Psychol.* 73, 486–9.

Parmeggiani, P. L., Azzaroni, A., and Lenzi, P. (1971). On the functional significance of the circuit of Papez. *Brain Res.* 30, 357–74.

—— Lenzi, P., and Azzaroni, A. (1974). Transfer of the hippocampal output by the anterior thalamic nuclei. *Brain Res.* 67, 269–78.

Pasquier, D. A. and Reinoso-Suarez, F. (1976). Direct projections from hypothalamus to hippocampus in the rat demonstrated by retrograde transport of horseradish peroxidase. *Brain Res.* 108, 165–9.

—— —— (1977). Differential efferent connections of the brain stem to the hippocampus in the cat. *Brain Res.* 120, 540–8.

Passingham, R. E. (1970). The neurological basis of introversion–extraversion: Gray's theory. *Behav. Res. Ther.* 8, 353–66.

—— (1978). Information about movements in monkeys (*Macaca mulatta*) with lesions of dorsal prefrontal cortex. *Brain Res.* 152, 313–28.

Paul, S. M. and Skolnick, P. (1978). Rapid changes in brain benzodiazepine receptors after experimental seizures. *Science, NY* 202, 892–4.

Pavlov, I. P. (1927). *Conditioned reflexes* (trans. G. V. Anrep). Oxford University Press, London.

Paxinos, G. (1975). The septum: neural systems involved in eating, drinking, irritability, muricide, copulation, and activity in rats. *J. comp. physiol. Psychol.* 89, 1154–68.

—— (1976). Interruption of septal connections: effects on drinking, irritability and copulation. *Physiol. Behav.* 17, 81–8.

Paykel, E. S. (1971). Classification of depressed patients: a cluster analysis derived grouping. *Br. J. Psychiat.* 118, 275–88.

—— Parker, R. R., Penrose, R. J. J., and Rassaby, E. R. (1979). Depressive classification and prediction of response to phenelzine. *Br. J. Psychiat.* 134, 572–81.

Penfield, W. and Milner, B. (1958). Memory deficit produced by bilateral lesions in the hippocampal zone. *Archs Neurol. Psychiat.* **79**, 475–97.

Pert, C. B., Kuhar, M. J., and Snyder, S. H. (1975). Autoradiographic localization of the opiate receptor in rat brain. *Life Sci.* **16**, 1849–54.

—— and Snyder, S. H. (1973). Opiate receptor: demonstration in nervous tissue. *Science, NY* **179**, 111–14.

Peterson, D. W. and Laverty, R. (1976). Operant behavioural and neurochemical effects after neonatal 6-hydroxydopamine treatment. *Psychopharmacology* **50**, 55–60.

—— and Sparber, S. B. (1974). Increased fixed-ratio performance and differential D- and L-amphetamine action following norepinephrine depletion by intraventricular 6-hydroxydopamine. *J. Pharmac. exp. Ther.* **191**, 349–57.

Petsche, H. and Stumpf, Ch. (1960). Topographic and toposcopic study of origin and spread of the regular synchronised arousal pattern in the rabbit. *Electroenceph. clin. Neurophysiol.* **12**, 589–600.

—— —— (1962). Hippocampal arousal and seizure activity in rabbits: toposcopical and microelectrode aspects. In *Physiologie de l'hippocampe* (ed. P. Passouant) Editions du Centre National de la Recherche Scientifique, Paris.

—— —— and Gogolak, G. (1962). The significance of the rabbit's septum as a relay station between the midbrain and the hippocampus. I. The control of hippocampus arousal activity by the septum cells. *Electroenceph. clin. Neurophysiol.* **14**, 202–11.

Pfaff, D. W., Silva, M. T. A., and Weiss, J. M. (1971). Telemetered recording of hormone effects on hippocampal neurons. *Science, NY* **172**, 349–95.

Phillips, A. G. and Lepiane, F. G. (1980). Disruption of conditioned taste aversion in the rat by stimulation of amygdala: a conditioning effect, not amnesia. *J. comp. physiol. Psychol.* **94**, 664–74.

Pickel, V. M., Joh, T. H., and Reis, D. J. (1977). A serotonergic innervation of noradrenergic neurons in nucleus locus coeruleus: demonstration by immunocytochemical localization of the transmitter specific enzymes tyrosine and tryptophan hydroxylase. *Brain Res.* **131**, 197–214.

—— —— —— Leeman, S. E., and Miller, R. J. (1979). Electron microscopic localization of substance P and enkephalin in axon terminals related to dendrites of catecholaminergic neurons. *Brain Res.* **160**, 387–400.

—— Krebs, H., and Bloom, F. E. (1973). Proliferation of norepinephrine-containing axons in rat cerebellar cortex after peduncle lesions. *Brain Res.* **59**, 169–79.

Plotnik, R., Mollenauer, S., and Bean, N. J. (1977). Effects of hippocampal lesions on competitive behavior in rats. *Behav. Biol.* **19**, 269–77.

Plunkett, R. P. and Faulds, B. D. (1979). The effect of cue distinctiveness on successive discrimination performance in hippocampal lesioned rats. *Physiol. Psychol.* **7**, 49–52.

Plutchik, R. (1962). *The emotions: facts, theories and a new model.* Random House, New York.

Pohorecky, L. A. and Brick, J. (1977). Activity of neurons in the locus coeruleus of the rat: inhibition by ethanol. *Brain Res.* **131**, 174–9.

Pompi, K. F. (1974). Immediate effect of septal area damage on DRL performance in the rat. *J. comp. physiol. Psychol.* **86**, 523–30.

Poplawsky, A. and Cohen, S. L. (1977). Septal lesions and the reinforcer-omission effect. *Physiol. Behav.* **18**, 893–5.

Powell, B. J., Martin, L. K., and Kamano, D. K. (1967). Relationship between emotionality, drug effects, and avoidance responses in Tryon S1 and S3 strains. *Can. J. Psychol.* **21**, 294–300.

Powell, D. A., Milligan, W. L., and Buchanan, S. L. (1976). Orienting and classical conditioning of the rabbit (*Oryctolagus cuniculus*): effects of septal area lesions. *Physiol. Behav.* **17**, 955–62.

Powell, G. E. (1979). *Brain and personality.* Saxon House, London.

Price, M. T. C. and Fibiger, H. C. (1975). Ascending catecholamine systems and morphine analgesia. *Brain Res.* **99**, 189–93.

—— Murray, G. N., and Fibiger, H. C. (1977). Schedule dependent changes in operant responding after lesions of the dorsal tegmental noradrenergic projection. *Pharmac. Biochem. Behav.* **6**, 11–15.

Proctor, S. (1969). Duration of exposure to items and pretreatment training as factors in systematic desensitization therapy. In *Advances in behaviour therapy 1968* (ed. R. D. Rubin and C. M. Franks) pp. 105–16. Academic Press, New York.

Pubols, L. M. (1966). Changes in food-motivated behavior of rats as a function of septal and amygdaloid lesions. *Expl Neurol.* **15**, 240–54.

Rabe, A. and Haddad, R. K. (1968). Effect of selective hippocampal lesions in the rat on acquisition, performance, and extinction of bar pressing on a fixed ratio schedule. *Expl Brain Res.* **5**, 259–66.

Rabin, J. S. (1975). Effects of varying sucrose reinforcers and amobarbital sodium on positive contrast in rats. *Anim. Learn. Behav.* **3**, 290–4.

Rachman, S. (1976). The modification of obsessions: a new formulation. *Behav. Res. Ther.* **14**, 437–43.

—— (1978). An anatomy of obsessions. *Behav. Anal. Mod.* **2**, 253–78.

—— Cobb, J., Grey, S., McDonald, B., Mawson, D., Sartory, G., and Stern, R. (1979). The behavioural treatment of obsessional-compulsive disorders with and without clomipramine. *Behav. Res. Ther.* **17**, 467–78.

—— and De Silva, P. (1978). Abnormal and normal obsessions. *Behav. Res. Ther.* **16**, 233–48.

—— and Hodgson, R. (1979). *Obsessions and compulsions.* Prentice Hall, New York.

—— and Seligman, M. E. P. (1976). Unprepared phobias: be prepared. *Behav. Res. Ther.* **14**, 333–8.

Racine, R. J. and Kimble, D. P. (1965). Hippocampal lesions and delayed alternation in the rat. *Psychon. Sci.* **3**, 285–6.

Raichle, M. E., Eichling, J. O., Grubb, R. L., and Hartman, B. K. (1976). Central noradrenergic regulation of brain microcirculation. In *Dynamics of brain edema* (ed. H. M. Pappins and W. Feindel) pp. 11–17. Springer, Berlin.

Raisman, G. (1966). The connections of the septum. *Brain* **89**, 317–48.

—— (1969). A comparison of the mode of termination of the hippocampal and hypothalamic afferents to the septal nuclei as revealed by electron microscopy of degeneration. *Expl Brain Res.* **7**, 317–43.

—— Cowan, W. M., and Powell, T. P. S. (1966). An experimental analysis of the efferent projections of the hippocampus. *Brain* **89**, 83–108.

Ramon y Cajal, S. (1955). Histologie du système nerveux de l'homme et des vertébrates, Vol II (1911), pp. 772–9. Consejo Superior de Investigaciones Científicos Instituto Ramon y Cajal, Madrid.

Ranck, J. B. Jr (1973). Studies on single neurons in dorsal hippocampal formation and septum in unrestrained rats. *Expl Neurol.* **41**, 461–555.

Randall, L. O., Heise, G. A., Schallek, W., Bagdon, R. E., Banziger, R. E., Boris, A., Moe, R. A., and Abrams, W. B. (1961). Pharmacological and clinical studies of Valium (TM), a new psychotherapeutic agent of the benzodiazepine class. *Curr. ther. Res.* **3**, 405–25.

—— and Kappell, B. (1973). Pharmacological activity of some benzodiazepines and their metabolites. In *The benzodiazepines* (ed. S. Garattini, E. Mussini, and L. O. Randall) pp. 27–51. Raven Press, New York.

Randt, C. T., Quartermain, D., Goldstein, M., and Anagnoste, B. (1971). Norepinephrine synthesis inhibition: effects on memory in mice. *Science, NY* **172**, 498–9.

Ransom, B. R. and Barker, J. L. (1976). Pentobarbital selectively enhances GABA-mediated post-synaptic inhibition in tissue cultured mouse spinal neurons. *Brain Res.* **114**, 530–5.

Raphelson, A. C., Isaacson, R. L., and Douglas, R. J. (1965). The effect of distracting stimuli on the runway performance of limbic damaged rats. *Psychon. Sci.* **3**, 483–4.

Rawlins, J. N. P. (1977). Behavioural and physiological correlates of limbic system activity. Unpublished D.Phil. Thesis, University of Oxford.

—— (1980). Associative and non-associative mechanisms in the development of tolerance for stress: the problem of state-dependent learning. In *Coping and health* (ed. S. Levine and H. Ursin) pp. 83–6. Plenum Press, New York.

—— Feldon, J., and Gray, J. A. (1979). Septo-hippocampal connections and the hippocampal theta rhythm. *Expl Brain Res.* **37**, 49–63.

—— —— —— (1980*a*). Discrimination of response-contingent and response-independent shock by rats: effects of chlordiazepoxide HCl and sodium amylobarbitone. *Q. Jl exp. Psychol.* **32**, 215–32.

—— —— —— (1980*b*). The effects of hippocampectomy and of fimbria section upon the partial reinforcement extinction effect in rats. *Expl Brain Res.* **38**, 273–83.

—— —— Salmon, P., Gray, J. A., and Garrud, P. (1980*c*). The effects of chlordiazepoxide HCl administration upon punishment and conditioned suppression in the rat. *Psychopharmacology* **70**, 317–22.

—— and Green, K. F. (1977). Lamellar organization in the rat hippocampus. *Expl Brain Res.* **28**, 335–44.

—— Mitchell, S. J., Olton, D. S., and Steward, O. (1980*d*). Medial septal lesions and the entorhinal theta rhythm: correlating theta loss with radial arm maze learning. *Soc. Neurosci. Abst.* **6**, 192.

Razran, G. (1971). *Mind in evolution.* Houghton Mifflin, Boston.

Redmond, D. E. Jr (1979). New and old evidence for the involvement of a brain norepinephrine system in anxiety. In *Phenomenology and treatment of anxiety* (ed. W. G. Fann, I. Karacan, A. D. Pokorny, and R. L. Williams) pp. 153–203. Spectrum, New York.

—— Huang, Y. H., Snyder, D. R., and Maas, J. W. (1976). Behavioral effects of stimulation of the nucleus locus coeruleus in the stump-tailed monkey (*Macaca arctoides*). *Brain Res.* **116**, 502–10.

Reis, D. J., Joh, T. H., Ross, R. A., and Pickel, V. M. (1974). Reserpine selectively increases tyrosine hydroxylase and dopamine-beta-hydroxylase enzyme protein in central noradrenergic neurones. *Brain Res.* **81**, 380–6.

Rescorla, R. A. (1978). Some implications of a cognitive perspective on Pavlovian conditioning. In *Cognitive processes in animal behavior* (ed. S. H. Hulse, H. Fowler, and W. K. Honig) pp. 15–50. Wiley, New York.

Reynolds, G. S. (1961). Behavioral contrast. *J. exp. Anal. Behav.* **4**, 57–71.

Rich, I. and Thompson, R. (1965). Role of the hippocampo-septal system, thalamus, and hypothalamus in avoidance conditioning. *J. comp. physiol. Psychol.* **59**, 66–72.

Rickels, K. (1978). Use of anti-anxiety agents in anxious outpatients. *Psychopharmacology* **58**, 1–17.

Rickert, E. J., Bennett, T. L., Lane, P., and French, J. (1978). Hippocampectomy and the attenuation of blocking. *Behav. Biol.* **22**, 147–60.

Riddell, W. I. (1968). An examination of the task and trial parameters in passive avoidance learning by hippocampectomized rats. *Physiol. Behav.* **3**, 883–6.

—— (1972). Consolidation time of hippocampectomized rats in a one-trial learning situation. *Psychon. Sci.* **29**, 285–7.

—— Malinchoc, M., and Reimers, R. O. (1973). Shift and retention deficits in hippocampectomized and neodecorticate rats. *Physiol. Behav.* **10**, 869–78.

Ridgers, A. and Gray, J. A. (1973). Influence of amylobarbitone on operant depression and elation effects in the rat. *Psychopharmacologia* **32**, 265–70.

Ritter, S. and Pelzer, N. L. (1978). Magnitude of stress-induced brain norepinephrine depletion varies with age. *Brain Res.* **152**, 170–5.

—— —— and Ritter, R. C. (1978). Absence of glucoprivic feeding after stress suggests impairment of noradrenergic neuron function. *Brain Res.* **149**, 399–411.

—— and Ritter, R. C. (1977). Protection against stress-induced brain norepinephrine depletion after repeated 2-deoxy-D-glucose administration. *Brain Res.* **127**, 179–84.

Roberts, D. C. S. and Fibiger, H. C. (1977a). Evidence for interactions between central noradrenergic neurons and adrenal hormones in learning and memory. *Pharmac. Biochem. Behav.* **7**, 191–4.

—— —— (1977b). Lesions of the dorsal noradrenergic projection attenuate morphine- but not amphetamine-induced conditioned taste aversion. *Psychopharmacology* **55**, 183–6.

—— Price, M. T. C., and Fibiger, H. C. (1976). The dorsal tegmental noradrenergic projection: an analysis of its role in maze learning. *J. comp. physiol. Psychol.* **90**, 368–72.

Robertson, H. A., Martin, I. L., and Candy, J. M. (1978). Differences in benzodiazepine receptor binding in Maudsley reactive and Maudsley nonreactive rats. *Eur. J. Pharmac.* **50**, 455–7.

Robichaud, R. C. and Sledge, K. L. (1969). The effects of *p*-chlorophenylalanine on experimentally induced conflict in the rat. *Life Sci.* **8**, 965–9.

Robinson, T. E., Kramis, R. C., and Vanderwolf, C. H. (1977). Two types of cerebral activation during active sleep: relations to behavior. *Brain Res.* **124**, 544–9.

—— and Vanderwolf, C. H. (1978). Electrical stimulation of the brain stem in freely moving rats. II. Effects on hippocampal and neocortical electrical activity and relations to behavior. *Expl Neurol.* **61**, 485–515.

—— —— and Pappas, B. A. (1977). Are the dorsal noradrenergic bundle projections from the locus coeruleus important for neocortical or hippocampal activation? *Brain Res.* **138**, 75–98.

Roffler-Tarkov, S., Schildkraut, J. J., and Draskoczy, R. R. (1973). Effects of acute and chronic administration of desmethylimipramine on the content of norepinephrine and other monoamines in the rat brain. *Biochem. Pharmac.* **22**, 2923–6.

Rogozea, R. and Ungher, J. (1968). Changes in orienting activity of cat induced by chronic hippocampal lesions. *Expl Neurol.* **21**, 176–86.

Rolls, E. T. (1975). *The brain and reward*. Pergamon Press, New York.

Röper, G. and Rachman, S. (1976). Obsessional-compulsive checking: experimental replication and development. *Behav. Res. Ther.* **14**, 25–32.

Rosen, A. J., Glass, D. H., and Ison, J. R. (1967). Amobarbital sodium and instrumental performance following reward reduction. *Psychon. Sci.* **9**, 129–30.

Rosenkilde, C. E. (1979). Functional heterogeneity of the prefrontal cortex in the monkey: a review. *Behav. neural Biol.* **25**, 301–45.

Rosloff, B. N. (1975). Studies on mechanism of action of tricyclic anti-depressant drugs using iprindole as a tool. Unpublished Ph.D. thesis, Vanderbilt University.

—— and Davis, J. M. (1978). Decrease in brain NE turnover after chronic DMI treatment; no effect with iprindole. *Psychopharmacology* **56**, 335–41.

Ross, J. F., Grossman, L., and Grossman, S. P. (1975). Some behavioral effects of transecting ventral or dorsal fiber connections of the septum in the rat. *J. comp. physiol. Psychol.* **89**, 5–18.

—— and Grossman, S. P. (1975). Septal influences on operant responding in the rat. *J. comp. physiol. Psychol.* **89**, 523–36.

—— —— (1977). Transections of the stria medullaris or stria terminalis in the rat: effects on aversively controlled behavior. *J. comp. physiol. Psychol.* **91**, 907–17.

—— Walsh, L. L., and Grossman, S. P. (1973). Some behavioral effects of entorhinal cortex lesions in the albino rat. *J. comp. physiol. Psychol.* **85**, 70–81.

Ross, R. R. (1964). Positive and negative partial-reinforcement extinction effects carried through continuous reinforcement, changed motivation, and changed response. *J. exp. Psychol.* **68**, 492–502.

Roth, M. (1979a). A classification of affective disorders based on a synthesis of new and old concepts. In *Research in the psychobiology of human behavior* (ed. E. Meyer III and J. V. Brady) pp. 75–114. Johns Hopkins University Press, Baltimore.

—— (1979b). A new classification of the affective disorders. In *Neuropsychopharmacology* (ed. B. Saletu, P. Berner, and L. Hollister) pp. 255–73. Pergamon Press, Oxford.

—— Gurney, C., Mountjoy, G. Q., Kerr, T. A., and Schapira, K. (1976). The relationship between classification and response to drugs in affective disorder — problems posed by drug response in affective disorders. In *Monoamine oxidase and its inhibition*. Ciba Foundation Symposium 39 (New Series) pp. 297–325. Elsevier, Amsterdam.

Routtenberg, A. and Holzman, N. (1973). Memory disruption by electrical stimulation of substantia nigra, pars compacta. *Science, NY* **181**, 83–5.

—— and Santos-Anderson, R. (1977). The role of prefrontal cortex in intracranial self-stimulation: a case history of anatomical localization of motivational substrates. In *Handbook of psychopharmacology*, Vol. 8. *Drugs, neurotransmitters and behavior* (ed. L. L. Iversen, S. D. Iversen, and S. H. Snyder) pp. 1–24. Plenum Press, New York.

Royal College of Psychiatrists (1977). The Royal College of Psychiatrists memorandum on the use of electroconvulsive therapy. *Br. J. Psychiat.* **131**, 261–72.

Rudell, A. P., Fox, S. E., and Ranck, J. B. Jr (1980). Hippocampal excitability phase-locked to the theta rhythm in walking rats. *Expl Neurol.* **68**, 87–96.

Rushton, R. and Steinberg, H. (1966). Combined effects of chlordiazepoxide and dexamphetamine on activity of rats in an unfamiliar environment. *Nature, Lond.* **211**, 1312–13.

Saari, M. and Pappas, B. A. (1973). Neonatal 6-hydroxydopamine sympathectomy reduces foot-shock induced suppression of water-licking in normotensive and hypertensive rats. *Nature, Lond.* **244**, 181–3.

Sagvolden, T. (1975a). Operant responding for water in rats with septal lesions: effect of deprivation level. *Behav. Biol.* **13**, 323–30.

—— (1975b). Acquisition of two-way active avoidance following septal lesions in the rat: effect of intensity of discontinuous shock. *Behav. Biol.* **14**, 59–74.

—— (1976). Free-operant avoidance behavior in rats with lateral septal lesions: effect of shock intensity. *Brain Res.* **110**, 559–74.

—— (1979). Behavior of rats with septal lesions during low levels of water deprivation. *Behav. neural Biol.* **26**, 431–41.

Sahgal, A. and Iversen, S. D. (1978). The effects of chlordiazepoxide on a delayed pair comparison task in pigeons. *Psychopharmacology* **59**, 57–64.

Sailer, S. and Stumpf, Ch. (1957). Beeinflussbarkeit der Rhinencephalen tätigkeit des Kaninchens. *Arch. exp. path. Pharmak.* **231**, 63–77.

Sainsbury, R. S. (1970). Hippocampal activity during natural behavior in the guinea pig. *Physiol. Behav.* **5**, 317–24.

Sakai, K., Salvert, D., Touret, M., and Jouvet, M. (1977a). Afferent connections of the nucleus raphe dorsalis in the cat as visualized by the horseradish peroxidase technique. *Brain Res.* **137**, 11–35.

—— Touret, M., Salvert, D., Léger, L., and Jouvet, M. (1977b). Afferent projections to the cat locus coeruleus as visualized by the horseradish peroxidase technique. *Brain Res.* **119**, 21–41.

Salzman, P. M. and Roth, R. H. (1980a). Poststimulation catecholamine synthesis and tyrosine hydroxylase activation in central noradrenergic neurons: I. *In vivo* stimulation of the locus coeruleus. *J. Pharmac. exp. Ther.* **212**, 64–73.

—— —— (1980b). Poststimulation catecholamine synthesis and tyrosine hydroxylase activation in central noradrenergic neurons. II. Depolarized hippocampal slices. *J. Pharmac. exp. Ther.* **212**, 74–84.

Samuels, I. (1972). Hippocampal lesions in the rat: effects on spatial and visual habits. *Physiol. Behav.* **8**, 1093–8.

—— and Valian, V. (1968). Hippocampal lesions and redundant visual cues: effects on spatial reversal learning and subsequent visual discriminations. *Proc. 76th Ann. Convention Am. Psychol. Ass.* Vol. 3, pp. 321–2.

Sanders, H. I. and Warrington, E. K. (1971). Memory for remote events in amnesic patients. *Brain* **94**, 661–8.

Sanger, D. J. and Blackman, D. E. (1976). Effects of chlordiazepoxide, ripazepam and D-amphetamine on conditioned deceleration of running behaviour in rats. *Psychopharmacology* **48**, 209–15.

Sanwald, J. C., Porzio, N. R., Deane, G. E., and Donovick, P. J. (1970). The effects of septal and dorsal hippocampal lesions on the cardiac component of the orienting response. *Physiol. Behav.* **5**, 883–8.

Schallek, W., Schlosser, W., and Randall, L. O. (1972). Recent developments in the pharmacology of the benzodiazepines. *Adv. Pharmac. Chemother.* **10**, 119–81.

Schildkraut, J. J. (1965). The catecholamine hypothesis of affective disorders: a review of supporting evidence. *Am. J. Psychiat.* **122**, 509–22.

—— Winokur, A., and Applegate, C. W. (1970). Norepinephrine turnover and metabolism in rat brain after long term administration of imipramine. *Science, NY* **168**, 867–9.

—— —— Draskoczy, P. R., and Hensle, J. H. (1971). Changes in norepinephrine turnover in rat brain during chronic administration of imipramine and protriptyline: a possible explanation for the delay in onset of clinical antidepressant effects. *Am. J. Psychiat.* **27**, 72–9.

Schmaltz, L. W. and Isaacson, R. L. (1966). The effects of preliminary training conditions upon DRL performance in the hippocampectomized rat. *Physiol. Behav.* **1**, 175–82.

—— —— (1967). Effect of bilateral hippocampal destruction on the acquisition and extinction of an operant response. *Physiol. Behav.* **2**, 291–8.

—— Wolf, B. P., and Trejo, W. R. (1973). FR, DRL, and discrimination learning in rats following aspiration lesions and penicillin injection into hippocampus. *Physiol. Behav.* **11**, 17–22.

Schutz, R. A. and Izquierdo, I. (1979). Effect of brain lesions on rat shuttle behavior in four different tests. *Physiol. Behav.* **23**, 97–105.

—— Schutz, M. T. B., Orsingher, O. A., and Izquierdo, I. (1979). Brain dopamine and noradrenaline levels in rats submitted to four different aversive behavioural tests. *Psychopharmacology* **63**, 289–92.

Schwab, M. A., Javoy-Agid, F., and Agid, Y. (1978). Labeled wheatgerm agglu-tinin (WGA) as a new highly sensitive retrograde tracer in the rat brain hip-pocampal system. *Brain Res.* **152**, 145–50.

Schwartz, B. and Gamzu, E. (1977). Pavlovian control of operant behavior. In *Handbook of operant behavior* (ed. W. K. Honig and J. E. R. Staddon) pp. 53–97. Prentice-Hall, Englewood Cliffs, NJ.

Schwartzbaum, J. S. and Donovick, P. J. (1965). An artifact in the use of brain stimulation with shock-motivated behavior. *Psychon. Sci.* **2**, 183–4.

—— —— (1968). Discrimination reversal and spatial alternation associated with septal and caudate dysfunction in rats. *J. comp. physiol. Psychol.* **65**, 83–92.

—— Green, R. H., Beatty, W. W., and Thompson, J. B. (1967). Acquisition of avoidance behavior following septal lesions in the rat. *J. comp. physiol. Psychol.* **63**, 95–104.

—— and Kreinick, C. J. (1974). Visual evoked potentials during appetitive behav-ior after septal lesions in rats. *J. comp. physiol. Psychol.* **86**, 509–22.

—— and Spieth, T. M. (1964). Analysis of the response-inhibition concept of sep-tal functions in 'passive-avoidance' behavior. *Psychon. Sci.* **1**, 145–6.

Scobie, S. R. and Bliss, D. K. (1974). Ethyl alcohol: relationships to memory for aversive learning in goldfish (*Carassius auratus*). *J. comp. physiol. Psychol.* **86**, 867–74.

Scoville, W. B. and Milner, B. (1957). Loss of recent memory after bilateral hip-pocampal lesion. *J. Neurol. Neurosurg. Psychiat.* **20**, 11–21.

Segal, D. S., Kuczenski, R., and Mandell, A. J. (1974). Theoretical implications of drug-induced adaptive regulations for a biogenic amine hypothesis of affec-tive disorder. *Biol. Psychiat.* **9**, 147–50.

Segal, M. (1973a). Flow of conditioned responses in limbic telencephalic system of the rat. *J. Neurophysiol.* **36**, 840–54.

—— (1973b). Dissecting a short-term memory circuit in the rat brain. I. Changes in entorhinal unit activity and responsiveness of hippocampal units in the process of classical conditioning. *Brain Res.* **64**, 281–92.

—— (1974a). Responses of septal nuclei neurons to microiontophoretically admin-istered putative neurotransmitters. *Life Sci.* **14**, 1345–51.

—— (1974b). Convergence of sensory input on units in the hippocampal system of the rat. *J. comp. physiol. Psychol.* **87**, 91–9.

—— (1975a). Physiological and pharmacological evidence for a serotonergic pro-jection to the hippocampus. *Brain Res.* **94**, 115–31.

—— (1975b). Hippocampal conditioned responses in the absence of entorhinal input. *Physiol. Behav.* **15**, 381–4.

—— (1976). 5-HT antagonists in rat hippocampus. *Brain Res.* **103**, 161–6.

—— (1977a). The effects of brainstem priming stimulation on interhemispheric hippocampal responses in the awake rat. *Expl Brain Res.* **28**, 529–41.

—— (1977b). Changes of interhemispheric hippocampal responses during condi-tioning in the awake rat. *Expl Brain Res.* **29**, 553–65.

—— (1977c). Changes in hippocampal evoked respones to afferent stimulation during conditioning. (Abstract.) *Brain Res.* **127**, 382.

—— (1977d). Excitability changes in rat hippocampus during conditioning. *Expl Neurol.* **55**, 67–73.

—— (1977e). Afferents to the entorhinal cortex of the rat studied by the method of retrograde transport of horseradish peroxidase. *Expl Neurol.* **57**, 750–65.

—— (1978a). A correlation between hippocampal responses to interhemispheric stimulation, hippocampal slow rhythmic activity and behaviour. *Electroenceph. clin. Neurophysiol.* **45**, 409–11.

—— (1978b). Serotonergic innervation of the locus coeruleus from the dorsal raphe. *J. Physiol., Lond.* **286**, 401–15.

—— (1980). The noradrenergic innervation of the hippocampus. In *The reticular formation revisited* (ed. J. A. Hobson and M. A. B. Brazier) pp. 415–25. Raven Press, New York.

—— and Bloom, F. E. (1974*a*). The action of norepinephrine in the rat hippocampus. I. Iontophoretic studies. *Brain Res.* **72**, 79–97.

—— —— (1974*b*). The action of norepinephrine in the rat hippocampus. II. Activation of the input pathway. *Brain Res.* **72**, 99–114.

—— —— (1976). The action of norepinephrine in the rat hippocampus. IV. The effects of locus coeruleus stimulation on evoked hippocampal unit activity. *Brain Res.* **107**, 513–25.

—— and Landis, S. C. (1974). Afferents to the septal area of the rat studied with the method of retrograde axonal transport of horseradish peroxidase. *Brain Res.* **82**, 263–8.

—— and Olds, J. (1973). Activity of units in the hippocampal circuit of the rat during differential classical conditioning. *J. comp. physiol. Psychol.* **82**, 195–204.

Seligman, M. E. P. (1971). Phobias and preparedness. *Behav. Ther.* **2**, 307–20.

—— (1975). *Helplessness.* Freeman, San Francisco.

—— and Maier, S. F. (1967). Failure to escape traumatic shock. *J. exp. Psychol.* **74**, 1–9.

Selye, H. (1952). *The story of the adaptation syndrome.* Acta, Montreal.

Semba, K. and Komisaruk, B. R. (1978). Phase of the theta wave in relation to different limb movements in awake rats. *Electroenceph. clin. Neurophysiol.* **44**, 61–71.

Senba, K. and Iwahara, S. (1974). Effects of medial septal lesions on the hippocampal electrical activity and the orienting response to auditory stimulation in drinking rats. *Brain Res.* **66**, 309–20.

Sessions, G. R., Kant, G. J., and Koob, G. F. (1976). Locus coeruleus lesions and learning in the rat. *Physiol. Behav.* **17**, 853–9.

Seunath, O. M. (1975). Personality, reinforcement and learning. *Percept. motor Skills* **41**, 459–63.

Sheard, M. H. and Davis, M. (1976). Shock elicited fighting in rats: importance of intershock interval upon effect of *p*-chlorophenylalanine (PCPA). *Brain Res.* **111**, 433–7.

Shimizu, N., Katoh, Y., Hida T., and Satoh, K. (1978). The fine structural organization of the locus coeruleus in the rat with reference to noradrenaline contents. *Expl Brain Res.* **37**, 139–48.

—— Ohnishi, S., and Satoh, K. (1978). Cellular organization of locus coeruleus in the rat as studied by the Golgi method. *Archs Histol. Jap.* **41**, 103–12.

Shute, C. C. D. and Lewis, P. R. (1967). The ascending cholinergic reticular system: neocortical, olfactory and subcortical projections. *Brain* **90**, 497–520.

Sideroff, S. (1977). The relationship of seizures to retrograde amnesia in hippocampectomized rats. *Physiol. Behav.* **18**, 577–80.

—— and Bindra, D. (1976). Neural correlates of discriminative conditioning: separation of associational and motivational processes. *Brain Res.* **101**, 376–82.

—— Bueno, O., Hirsch, A., Weyand, T., and McGaugh, J. (1974). Retrograde amnesia initiated by low-level stimulation of hippocampal cytoarchitectonic areas. *Expl Neurol.* **43**, 285–97.

Sidman, M., Stoddard, L., and Mohr, J. (1968). Some additional quantitative observations of immediate memory in a patient with bilateral hippocampal lesions. *Neuropsychologia* **6**, 245–54.

Siegel, J. L. (1976). Effect of medial septal lesions on conditioned taste aversion in the rat. *Physiol. Behav.* **17**, 761–5.

Sieghart, W. and Karobath, M. (1980). Molecular heterogeneity of benzodiazepine receptors. *Nature, Lond.* **286**, 285–7.

Siggins, G. R. and Hendriksen, S. J. (1975). Analogs of cyclic adenosine monophosphate: correlation of inhibition of Purkinje neurons with proteinkinase activation. *Science, NY* **189**, 559–60.

Sikorsky, R. D., Donovick, P. J., Burright, R. G., and Chin, T. (1977). Experiential effects on acquisition and reversal of discrimination tasks by albino rats with septal lesions. *Physiol. Behav.* **18**, 231–6.

Silveira, J. M. and Kimble, D. P. (1968). Brightness discrimination and reversal in hippocampally lesioned rats. *Physiol. Behav.* **3**, 625–30.

Simmonds, M. A. (1980). A site for the potentiation of GABA-mediated responses by benzodiazepines. *Nature, Lond.* **284**, 558–60.

Simon, H., Le Moal, M., and Calas, A. (1979). Efferents and afferents of the ventral tegmental A 10 region studied after local injection of [^{3}H]-leucine and horseradish peroxidase. *Brain Res.* **178**, 17–40.

Simon, P., Fraisse, B., Tillement, J. P., Guernet, M., and Boissier, J. R. (1968). Actions de quelques substances psychotropes sur la souris en situation libre soumise à un stimulus extéroceptif. *Thérapie* **23**, 1277–85.

—— and Soubrié, P. (1979). Behavioral studies to differentiate anxiolytic and sedative activity of the tranquilizing drugs. In *Differential psychopharmacology of anxiolytics and sedatives* (ed. J. R. Boissier) *Modern problems of pharmacopsychiatry*, Vol. 14, pp. 99–143. Karger, Basel.

Simonov, P. V. (1974). On the role of the hippocampus in the integrative activity of the brain. *Acta Neurobiol. exp.* **34**, 33–41.

Singh, D. (1973). Comparison of behavioral deficits caused by lesions in septal and ventromedial hypothalamic areas of female rats. *J. comp. physiol. Psychol.* **84**, 370–9.

Sinnamon, H. M., Freniere, S., and Kootz, J. (1978). Rat hippocampus and memory for places of changing significance. *J. comp. physiol. Psychol.* **92**, 142–55.

Skinner, B. F. (1938). *The behavior of organisms.* Appleton-Century, New York.

Skolnick, P., Marangos, P. J., Syapin, P., Goodwin, F. K., and Paul, S. M. (1979*a*). CNS benzodiazepine receptors: physiological studies and putative endogenous ligands. *Pharmac. Biochem. Behav.* **10**, 815–23.

—— Syapin, P. J., Paugh, B. A., and Paul, S. M. (1979*b*). Reduction in benzodiazepine receptors associated with Purkinje cell degeneration in nervous mutant mice. *Nature, Lond.* **277**, 397–8.

Slotnick, B. M. and Jarvik, M. E. (1966). Deficits in passive avoidance and fear conditioning in mice with septal lesions. *Science, NY* **154**, 1207–8.

—— and McMullen, M. F. (1972). Intraspecific fighting in albino mice with septal forebrain lesions. *Physiol. Behav.* **8**, 333–7.

—— —— (1973). Response inhibition deficits in mice with septal, amygdala or cingulate cortical lesions. *Physiol. Behav.* **10**, 385–9.

Snyder, D. R. and Isaacson, R. L. (1965). The effects of large and small bilateral hippocampal lesions on two types of passive avoidance responses. *Psychol. Rep.* **16**, 1277–90.

Sodetz, F. J. and Koppell, S. (1972). Punishment of free-operant avoidance responding in rats with septal lesions. *Psychon. Sci.* **28**, 289–92.

Soffer, A. (1954). Reginine and benodaine in the diagnosis of pheochromocytoma. *Med. Clins N. Am.* **38**, 375–84.

Sokolov, E. N. (1960). Neuronal models and the orienting reflex. In *The central nervous system and behaviour, 3rd Conference* (ed. M. A. B. Brazier) pp. 187–276. Josiah Macy Jr Foundation, New York.

—— (1963). *Perception and the conditioned reflex.* Pergamon Press, Oxford.

Solomon, P. R. (1977). Role of the hippocampus in blocking and conditioned inhibition of the rabbit's nictating membrane response. *J. comp. physiol. Psychol.* **91**, 407–17.

—— and Moore, J. W. (1975). Latent inhibition and stimulus generalization of the classically conditioned nictating membrane response in rabbits following dorsal hippocampal ablation. *J. comp. physiol. Psychol.* **89**, 1192–203.

Soubrié, P. (1978). Behavioral approaches to study mechanisms of action of minor tranquilizers. *Proc. 10th Cong. Collegium Internationale Neuro-psychopharmacologicum* (ed. P. Deniker, C. Radouco-Thomas, and A. Villeneuve) pp. 899–906. Pergamon Press, Oxford.

—— de Angelis, L., Simon, P., and Boissier, J. R. (1976). Effets des anxiolytiques sur la prise de boisson en situation nouvelle et familière. *Psychopharmacologia* **50**, 41–5.

—— Kulkarmi, S., Simon, P., and Boissier, J. R. (1975). Effets des anxiolytiques sur la prise de nourriture de rats et de souris placés en situation nouvelle ou familière. *Psychopharmacologia* **45**, 203–10.

—— Thiébot, M. H., and Jobert, A. (1978*b*). Picrotoxin–diazepam interaction in a behavioural schedule of differential reinforcement of low rates. *Experientia* **34**, 1621–2.

—— —— and Simon, P. (1979). Enhanced suppressive effects of aversive events induced in rats by picrotoxin: possibility of a GABA control on behavioral inhibition. *Pharmac. Biochem. Behav.* **10**, 463–9.

—— —— —— and Boissier, J. R. (1977). Effet des benzodiazépines sur les phénomènes d'inhibition qui contrôlent les comportements exploratoires et le recueil de l'information chez le rat. *J. Pharmac., Paris* **8**, 393–403.

—— —— —— —— (1978*a*). Benzodiazepines and behavioural effects of reward (water) omission. *Psychopharmacology* **59**, 95–100.

Soumireu-Mourat, B., Destrade, C., and Cardo, B. (1975). Effects of seizure and subseuzure posttrial hippocampal stimulation on appetitive operant behavior in mice. *Behav. Biol.* **15**, 303–16.

Spence, J. T. and Spence, K. W. (1966). The motivational components of manifest anxiety: drive and drive stimuli. In *Anxiety and behavior* (ed. C. D. Spielberger) pp. 291–326. Academic Press, London.

Spevack, A. A. and Pribram, K. H. (1973). Decisional analysis of the effects of limbic lesions on learning in monkeys. *J. comp. physiol. Psychol.* **82**, 211–26.

Sporn, J. R., Harden, T. K., Wolfe, B. B., and Molinoff, P. B. (1976). Beta-adrenergic receptor involvement in 6-hydroxydopamine-induced supersensitivity in rat cerebral cortex. *Science, NY* **194**, 624–6.

Squires, R. F., Benson, D. I., Braestrup, C., Coupet, J., Klepner, C. A., Myers, V., and Beer, B. (1979). Some properties of brain specific benzodiazepine receptors: new evidence for multiple receptors. *Pharmac. Biochem. Behav.* **10**, 825–30.

—— and Braestrup, C. (1977). Benzodiazepine receptors in rat brain. *Nature, Lond.* **266**, 732–4.

Srebro, B. and Lorens, S. A. (1975). Behavioural effects of selective midbrain raphe lesions in the rat. *Brain Res.* **89**, 303–25.

—— Mellgren, S. I., and Harkmark, W. (1976). Acetylcholinesterase histochemistry of the septal region in the rat. In *The septal nuclei* (ed. J. F. DeFrance) pp. 65–78. Plenum Press, New York.

Staddon, J. E. R. (1970). Temporal effects of reinforcement: a negative 'frustration' effect. *Learn. Motiv.* **1**, 227–47.

—— (1972). Temporal control and the theory of reinforcement schedules. In *Reinforcement: behavioral analyses* (ed. R. M. Gilbert and J. R. Millenson) pp. 201–62. Academic Press, New York.

Stampfl, T. G. (1970). Implosive therapy: an emphasis on covert stimulation. In *Learning approaches to therapeutic behavior change* (ed. D. J. Levis) pp. 182–204. Aldine, Chicago.

Starke, K. (1979). Presynaptic regulation of release in the central nervous system. In *The release of catecholamines from adrenergic neurones* (ed. D. M. Paton) pp. 143–84. Pergamon Press, Oxford.

St. Claire-Smith (1979). The overshadowing and blocking of punishment. *Q. Jl exp. Psychol.* **31**, 51–61.

Stefanis, C. (1964). Hippocampal neurons: their responsiveness to microelectrophoretically administered endogenous amines. *Pharmacologist* **6**, 171.

Stein, D. G. and Kirkby, R. J. (1967). The effects of training on passive avoidance deficits in rats with hippocampal lesions: a reply to Isaacson, Olton, Bauer and Swart. *Psychon. Sci.* **7**, 7–8.

—— Rosen, J. J., Graziadei, V., Mishkin, D., and Brunk, J. J. (1969). Central nervous system: recovery of function. *Science, NY* **166**, 528–30.

Stein, L. (1968). Chemistry of reward and punishment. In *Psychopharmacology: a review of progress 1957–1967* (ed. D. H. Efron) pp. 105–23. US Govt Printing Office, Washington, D.C.

—— Belluzzi, J. D., and Wise, C. D. (1975). Memory enhancement by central administration of norepinephrine. *Brain Res.* **84**, 329–35.

—— —— —— (1977). Benzodiazepines: behavioral and neurochemical mechanisms. *Am. J. Psychiat.* **134**, 665–9.

—— Wise, C. D., and Belluzzi, J. D. (1975). Effects of benzodiazepines on central serotoninergic mechanisms. In *Mechanism of action of benzodiazepines* (ed. E. Costa and P. Greengard) *Adv. biochem. Pharmac.* Vol. 14, pp. 29–44. Raven Press, New York.

—— —— —— (1977). Neuropharmacology of reward and punishment. In *Handbook of psychopharmacology*, Vol. 8, *Drugs, neurotransmitters, and behaviour* (ed. L. L. Iversen, S. D. Iversen, and S. H. Snyder) pp. 25–53. Plenum Press, New York.

—— —— and Berger, B. D. (1973). Anti-anxiety action of benzodiazepines: decrease in activity of serotonin neurons in the punishment system. In *The benzodiazepines* (ed. S. Garattini, E. Mussini, and L. O. Randall) pp. 299–326. Raven Press, New York.

Steinbusch, H. W. M. (1981). Distribution of serotonin-immunoreactivity in the central nervous system of the rat — cell bodies and terminals. *Neuroscience* **6**, 557–618.

Steranka, L. R. and Barrett, R. J. (1974). Facilitation of avoidance acquisition by lesions of the median raphe nucleus: evidence for serotonin as a mediator of shock-induced suppression. *Behav. Biol.* **11**, 205–13.

Stern, R. and Marks, I. M. (1973). Brief and prolonged flooding: a comparison in agoraphobic patients. *Archs gen. Psychiat.* **28**, 270–6.

Stevens, R. (1973). Effects of duration of sensory input and intertrial interval on spontaneous alternation in rats with hippocampal lesions. *Physiol. Psychol.* **1**, 41–4.

—— and Cowey, A. (1972). Enhanced alternation learning in hippocampectomized rats by means of added light cues. *Brain Res.* **46**, 1–22.

Steward, O. (1976). Topographic organization of the projections from the entorhinal area to the hippocampal formation of the rat. *J. comp. Neurol.* **167**, 285–314.

—— White, W. F., and Cotman, C. W. (1977). Potentiation of the excitatory synaptic action of commissural, associational and entorhinal afferents to dentate granule cells. *Brain Res.* **134**, 551–60.

Stone, E. A. (1975). Stress and catecholamines. In *Catecholamines and behavior* (ed. A. J. Friedhoff) Vol. 2, pp. 31–72. Plenum Press, New York.

—— (1978). Effect of stress on norepinephrine-stimulated cyclic AMP formation in brain slices. *Pharmac. Biochem. Behav.* **8**, 583–91.

—— (1979*a*). Subsensitivity to norepinephrine as a link between adaptation to stress and antidepressant therapy: an hypothesis. *Res. Comm. Psychol. Psychiat. Behav.* **4,** 241–55.

—— (1979*b*). Reduction by stress of norepinephrine-stimulated accumulation of cyclic AMP in rat cerebral cortex. *J. Neurochem.* **32,** 1335–7.

Storm-Mathisen, J. (1978). Localization of putative transmitters in the hippocampal formation, with a note on the connections to septum and hypothalamus. In *Functions of the septo-hippocampal system* (ed. K. Elliott and J. Whelan) Ciba Foundation Symposium 58 (New Series) pp. 49–79.

Strom-Olsen, R. and Carlisle, S. (1971). Bi-frontal stereotactic tractotomy: a follow-up study of its effects on 210 patients. *Br. J. Psychiat.* **118,** 141–54.

Strong, P. N. and Jackson, W. J. (1970). Effects of hippocampal lesions in rats on three measures of activity. *J. comp. physiol. Psychol.* **70,** 60–5.

Stuble, R. G., Desmond N. L., and Levy, W. B. (1978). Anatomical evidence for interlamellar inhibition in the fascia dentata. *Brain Res.* **152,** 580–5.

Stumpf, Ch. (1965). Drug action on the electrical activity of the hippocampus. *Int. Rev. Neurobiol.* **8,** 77–138.

—— Petsche, H., and Gogolak, G. (1962). The significance of the rabbit's septum as a relay station between the midbrain and hippocampus. II. The differential influence of drugs upon the septal cell firing and the hippocampal theta activity. *Electroenceph. clin. Neurophysiol.* **14,** 212–19.

Sue, D. (1975). The effect of duration of exposure on systematic desensitization and extinction. *Behav. Res. Ther.* **13,** 55–60.

Sulser, F. (1978). Tricyclic antidepressants: animal pharmacology (biochemical and metabolic aspects). In *Handbook of psychopharmacology*, Vol. 14, *Affective disorders: drug actions in animals and man* (ed. L. L. Iversen, S. D. Iversen, and S. H. Snyder) pp. 157–97. Plenum Press, New York.

—— Bickel, M. H., and Brodie, B. B. (1964). The action of desmethylimipramine in counteracting sedation and cholinergic effects of reserpine-like drugs. *J. Pharmac. exp. Ther.* **144,** 321–30.

—— Watts, J., and Brodie, B. B. (1962). On the mechanism of antidepressant action of imipramine-like drugs. *Ann. NY Acad. Sci.* **96,** 279–86.

Sutherland, N. S. and Mackintosh, N. J. (1971). *Mechanisms of animal discrimination learning.* Academic Press, London.

Swanson, A. M. and Isaacson, R. L. (1969). Hippocampal lesions and the frustration effect in rats. *J. comp. physiol. Psychol.* **68,** 562–7.

Swanson, L. W. (1978). The anatomical organization of septo-hippocampal projections. In *Functions of the septo-hippocampal system* (ed. K. Elliott and J. Whelan) Ciba Foundation Symposium 58 (New Series) pp. 25–43.

—— Connelly, M. A., and Hartman, B. K. (1977). Ultrastructural evidence for central monoaminergic innervation of blood vessels in the paraventricular nucleus of the hypothalamus. *Brain Res.* **136,** 166–73.

—— —— —— (1978). Further studies on the fine structure of the adrenergic innervation of the hypothalamus. *Brain Res.* **151,** 165–74.

—— and Cowan, W. M. (1975). Hippocampo–hypothalamic connections: origin in subicular cortex not Ammon's horn. *Science, NY* **189,** 303–4.

—— —— (1976). Autoradiographic studies of the development and connections of the septal area in the rat. In *The septal nuclei* (ed. J. F. DeFrance) pp. 37–64. Plenum Press, New York.

—— —— (1977). An autoradiographic study of the organization of the efferent connections of the hippocampal formation in the rat. *J. comp. Neurol.* **172,** 49–84.

Tallman, J. F., Paul, S. M., Skolnick, P., and Gallager, D. W. (1980). Receptors for the age of anxiety: pharmacology of the benzodiazepines. *Science, NY* **267,** 274–81.

Tan, E., Marks, I. M., and Marset, P. (1971). Bimedial leucotomy in obsessive-compulsive neurosis: a controlled serial enquiry. *Br. J. Psychiat.* **118**, 155–64.

Tanaka, D. and Goldman, P. S. (1976). Silver degeneration and autoradiographic evidence for a projection from the principal sulcus to the septum in the Rhesus monkey. *Brain Res.* **103**, 535–40.

Tang, S. W., Helmeste, D. M., and Stancer, H. C. (1979). The effect of clonidine withdrawal on total 3-methoxy-4-hydroxyphenylglycol in the rat brain. *Psychopharmacology* **61**, 11–12.

Tassin, J. P., Hervé, D., Blanc, G., and Glowinski, J. (1980). Differential effects of a two-minute open-field session on dopamine utilization in the frontal cortices of BALB/C and C57 BL/6 mice. *Neurosci. Lett.* **17**, 67–71.

Taub, J., Taylor, P., Smith, M., Kelley, K., Becker, B., and Reid, L. (1977). Methods of deconditioning persisting avoidance: drugs as adjuncts to response prevention. *Physiol. Psychol.* **5**, 67–72.

Taylor, J. A. (1953). A personality scale of manifest anxiety. *J. abnorm. soc. Psychol.* **48**, 285–90.

Taylor, K. M. and Laverty, R. (1973). The interaction of chlordiazepoxide, diazepam and nitrazepam with catecholamine and histamine in regions of the rat brain. In *The benzodiazepines* (ed. S. Garattini, E. Mussini, and L. O. Randall) pp. 191–202. Raven Press, New York.

Teasdale, J. D. (1977). Psychological treatment of phobias. In *Tutorial essays in psychology*, Vol. 2 (ed. N. S. Sutherland) pp. 137–63. Erlbaum, Hillsdale, NJ.

Teitelbaum, H. and Milner, P. (1963). Activity changes following partial hippocampal lesions in rats. *J. comp. physiol. Psychol.* **56**, 284–9.

Tenen, S. S. (1967). Recovery time as a measure of CER strength: effects of benzodiazepines, amobarbital, chlorpromazine and amphetamine. *Psychopharmacologia* **12**, 1–7.

Teyler, T. J. and Alger, B. E. (1976). Monosynaptic habituation in the vertebrate forebrain: the dentate gyrus examined *in vitro*. *Brain Res.* **115**, 413–25.

Theios, J., Lynch, A. D., and Lowe, W. F. Jr (1966). Differential effects of shock intensity on one-way and shuttle avoidance conditioning. *J. exp. Psychol.* **72**, 294–9.

Thiébot, M. H. (1979). Benzodiazépines et acide gamma-aminobutyrique. Unpublished Doctoral dissertation, Université Paris-Sud, Centre d'Orsay.

—— Jobert, A., and Soubrié, P. (1979*b*). Effets comparés du muscimol et du diazépam sur les inhibitions du comportement, induites chez le rat par la nouveauté, la punition et le non-renforcement. *Psychopharmacology* **61**, 85—9.

—— —— —— (1980). Conditioned suppression of behavior: its reversal by intraraphe microinjection of chlordiazepoxide and GABA. *Neurosci. Lett.* **16**, 213–17.

—— Soubrié, P., Simon, P., and Boissier, J. R. (1973). Dissociation de deux composantes du comportement chez le rat sous l'effet de psychotropes: application à l'étude des anxiolytiques. *Psychopharmacologia* **31**, 77–90.

—— —— —— (1976). Spécificité d'action des tranquillisants mineurs dans le test de l'escalier: relation entre ces effets et leurs propriétés anxiolytiques. *J. Pharmac., Paris* **7**, 87–102.

Thoenen, H. (1975). Transsynaptic regulation of neuronal enzyme synthesis. In *Handbook of psychopharmacology* (ed. L. L. Iversen, S. D. Iversen, and S. H. Snyder) Vol. 3. *Biochemistry of biogenic amines* pp. 443–75. Plenum Press, New York.

Thomas, G. J. (1978). Delayed alternation in rats after pre- or postcommissural fornicotomy. *J. comp. physiol. Psychol.* **92**, 1128–36.

—— Moore, R. Y., Harvey, J. A., and Hunt, H. F. (1959). Relations between the behavioral syndrome produced by lesions in the septal region of the forebrain and maze learning of the rat. *J. comp. physiol. Psychol.* **52**, 527–32.

—— and Otis, L. S. (1958). Effect of rhinencephalic lesions on maze learning in rats. *J. comp. physiol. Psychol.* **51**, 161–6.

Thomas, J. B. (1972*a*). Non-appetitive passive avoidance in rats with septal lesions. *Physiol. Behav.* **8**, 1087–92.

—— (1972*b*). Stimulus perseveration and choice behavior in rats with septal lesions. *J. comp. physiol. Psychol.* **80**, 97–105.

—— (1973). Some behavioral effects of olfactory bulb damage in the rat. *J. comp. physiol. Psychol.* **83**, 140–8.

—— (1974). Cross-maze avoidance behavior and septal lesions in the rat. *Physiol. Behav.* **12**, 163–7.

—— and McCleary, R. A. (1974*a*). One-way avoidance behavior and septal lesions in the rat. *J. comp. physiol. Psychol.* **86**, 751–9.

—— —— (1974*b*). Fornical lesions and aversively-motivated behavior in the rat. *Physiol. Behav.* **12**, 345–50.

Thomka, M. L. and Brown, T. S. (1975). The effect of hippocampal lesions on the development and extinction of a learned taste aversion for a novel food. *Physiol. Psychol.* **75**, 281–4.

Thornton, E. W. and Goudie, A. J. (1978). Evidence for the role of serotonin in the inhibition of specific motor responses. *Psychopharmacology* **60**, 73–9.

—— —— and Bithell, V. (1975). The effects of 6-hydroxydopamine induced sympathectomy on response inhibition in extinction. *Life Sci.* **17**, 363–8.

Ticku, M. K. and Olsen, R. W. (1978). Interaction of barbiturates with dihydropicrotoxinin binding sites related to the GABA receptor-ionophore system. *Life Sci.* **22**, 1643–52.

Tilson, H. A., Rech, R. H., and Sparber, S. B. (1975). Release of ^{14}C-norepinephrine into the lateral cerebroventricle of rats by exposure to a conditioned aversive stimulus. *Pharmac. Biochem. Behav.* **3**, 385–92.

Toczek. S. (1960). Disturbances of inhibitory processes due to lesions in the frontal area of the brain in man. *Acta Biol. exp.* **20**, 103–19.

Torgersen, S. (1979). The nature and origin of common phobic fears. *Br. J. Psychiat.* **134**, 343–51.

Tow, P. M. and Whitty, C. W. M. (1953). Personality changes after operations on the cingulate gyrus in man. *J. Neurol. Neurosurg. Psychiat.* **16**, 186–93.

Trafton, C. L. (1967). Effects of lesions in the septal area and cingulate cortical areas on conditioned suppression of activity and avoidance behavior in rats. *J. comp. physiol. Psychol.* **63**, 191–7.

Tremmel, F., Morris, M. D., and Gebhart, G. F. (1977). The effect of forebrain norepinephrine depletion on two measures of response suppression. *Brain Res.* **126**, 185–8.

Tye, N. C., Everitt, B. J., and Iversen, S. D. (1977). 5-Hydroxytryptamine and punishment. *Nature, Lond.* **268**, 741–2.

Tyrer, P. (1976). The role of bodily feelings in anxiety. (Maudsley Monographs, No. 23). Oxford University Press, London.

Ungerstedt, U. (1968). 6-Hydroxydopamine-induced degeneration of central monoamine neurons. *Eur. J. Pharmac.* **5**, 107–10.

—— (1971). Stereotaxic mapping of the monoamine pathways in the rat brain. *Acta physiol. scand.* **82** Suppl. 367, 1–48.

Uretsky, E. and McCleary, R. A. (1969). Effect of hippocampal isolation on retention. *J. comp. physiol. Psychol.* **68**, 1–8.

Ursin, H. (1976). Inhibition and the septal nuclei: breakdown of the single concept model. *Acta Neurobiol. exp.* **36**, 91–115.

Valero, I., Stewart, J., McNaughton, N., and Gray, J. A. (1977). Septal driving of the hippocampal theta rhythm as a function of frequency in the male rat: effects of adreno–pituitary hormones. *Neuroscience* **2**, 1029–32.

Van Harreveld, A. and Fifkova, F. (1975). Swelling of dendritic spines after stimulation of the perforant path as a mechanism of post-tetanic potentiation. *Expl Neurol.* **49**, 736–49.

Van Hartesveldt, C. (1973). Size of reinforcement and operant responding in hippocampectomized rats. *Behav. Biol.* **8**, 347–56.

Van Hoesen, G. W., Macdougall, J. M., and Mitchell, J. C. (1969). Anatomical specificity of septal projections in active and passive avoidance behavior in rats. *J. comp physiol. Psychol.* **68**, 80–9.

—— and Pandya, D. N. (1975). Some connections of the entorhinal (area 28) and perirhinal (area 35) cortices of the Rhesus monkey. I. Temporal lobe afferents. *Brain Res.* **95**, 1–24.

—— —— and Butters, N. (1972). Cortical afferents to the entorhinal cortex of the Rhesus monkey. *Science, NY* **175**, 1471–3.

—— —— —— (1975). Some connections of the entorhinal (area 28) and perirhinal (area 35) cortices of the Rhesus monkey. II. Frontal lobe afferents. *Brain Res.* **95**, 25–38.

—— Rosene, D. L., and Mesulam, M. M. (1979). Subicular input from temporal cortex in the Rhesus monkey. *Science, NY* **205**, 608–10.

—— Wilson, L. M., Macdougall, J. M., and Mitchell, J. C. (1972). Selective hippocampal complex deafferentation and deefferentation and avoidance behavior in rats. *Physiol. Behav.* **8**, 873–9.

Van Praag, H. M. (1978). Amine hypotheses of affective disorders. In *Handbook of psychopharmacology* (ed. L. L. Iversen, S. D. Iversen, and S. H. Snyder) Vol. 13. *Biology of mood and antianxiety drugs*, pp. 187–297. Plenum Press, New York.

Vanderwolf, C. H. (1969). Hippocampal electrical activity and voluntary movement in the rat. *Electroenceph. clin. Neurophysiol.* **26**, 407–18.

—— (1971). Limbic-diencephalic mechanisms of voluntary movement. *Psychol. Rev.* **78**, 83–113.

—— Kramis, R., Gillespie, L. A., and Bland, B. H. (1975). Hippocampal rhythmical slow activity and neocortical low voltage fast activity: relations to behavior. In *The hippocampus*, Vol. 2. *Neurophysiology and behaviour* (ed. R. L. Isaacson and K. H. Pribram) pp. 101–28. Plenum Press, New York.

—— —— and Robinson, T. E. (1978). Hippocampal electrical activity during waking behaviour and sleep: analyses using centrally acting drugs. In *Functions of the septo-hippocampal system* (ed. K. Elliott and J. Whelan) Ciba Foundation Symposium 58 (New Series) pp. 199–221. Elsevier, Amsterdam.

Vanegas, H. and Flynn, J. P. (1968). Inhibition of cortically-elicited movement by electrical stimulation of the hippocampus. *Brain Res.* **11**, 489–506.

Vardaris, R. M. and Schwartz, K. E. (1971). Retrograde amnesia for passive avoidance produced by stimulation of dorsal hippocampus. *Physiol. Behav.* **6**, 131–5.

Vergnes, M. and Penot, C. (1976a). Aggression intraspecifique induite par chocs électriques et reactivité après lésion du raphé chez le rat: effects de la physostigmine. *Brain Res.* **104**, 107–19.

—— —— (1976b). Effets comportementaux des lésions du raphé chez des rats privés du septum. *Brain Res.* **115**, 154–9.

Vetulani, J., Stawarz, R. J., Dingell, J. V., and Sulser, F. (1976a). A possible common mechanism of action of antidepressant treatments: reduction in the sensitivity of the noradrenergic cyclic AMP generating system in the rat limbic forebrain. *Naunyn-Schmiedeberg's Arch. Pharmac.* **293**, 109–14.

—— —— and Sulser, F. (1976b). Adaptive mechanisms of the noradrenergic cyclic AMP generating system in the limbic forebrain of the rat: adaptation to persistent changes in the availability of norepinephrine. *J. Neurochem.* **27**, 661–6.

—— and Sulser, F. (1975). Action of various antidepressant treatments reduces reactivity of noradrenergic cyclic AMP generating system in limbic forebrain. *Nature, Lond.* **257,** 495–6.

Victor, M., Adams, R. D., and Collins, G. H. (1971). *The Wernicke–Korsakoff syndrome.* Blackwell, Oxford.

Vinogradova, O. S. (1970). Registration of information and the limbic system. In *Short-term changes in neural activity and behaviour* (ed. G. Horn and R. A. Hinde) pp. 95–140. Cambridge University Press.

—— (1975). Functional organization of the limbic system in the process of registration of information: facts and hypotheses. In *The hippocampus,* Vol. 2. *Neurophysiology and behavior* (ed. R. L. Isaacson and K. H. Pribram) pp. 1–70. Plenum Press, New York.

—— and Brazhnik, P. S. (1978). Neuronal aspects of septo-hippocampal relations. In *Functions of the septo-hippocampal system* (ed. K. Elliott and J. Whelan) Ciba Foundation Symposium 58 (New Series) pp. 145–71. Elsevier, Amsterdam.

Vom Saal, F. S., Hamilton, L. W., and Gandelman, R. J. (1975). Faster acquisition of an olfactory discrimination following septal lesions in male albino rats. *Physiol. Behav.* **14,** 697–703.

Waddington, J. L. and Olley, J. E. (1977). Dissociation of the anti-punishment activities of chlordiazepoxide and atropine using two heterogeneous passive avoidance tasks. *Psychopharmacology* **52,** 93–6.

Wagner, A. R. (1963). Conditioned frustration as a learned drive. *J. exp. Psychol.* **66,** 142–8.

—— (1966). Frustration and punishment. In *Current research on motivation* (ed. R. M. Haber) pp. 229–39. Holt, Rinehart, Winston, New York.

—— (1969). Frustrative nonreward: a variety of punishment? In *Punishment and aversive behavior* (ed. B. A. Campbell and R. M. Church) pp. 157–81. Appleton-Century-Crofts, New York.

—— (1978). Expectancies and the priming of STM. In *Cognitive processes in animal behavior* (ed. S. H. Hulse, H. Fowler, and W. K. Honig) pp. 177–209. Erlbaum, Hillsdale, NJ.

Walker, D. W. and Means, L. W. (1973). Single-alternation performance in rats with hippocampal lesions: disruption by an irrelevant task interposed during the intertrial interval. *Behav. Biol.* **9,** 93–104.

—— —— and Isaacson, R. L. (1970). The effects of hippocampal and cortical lesions on single-alternation go, no-go acquisition in rats. *Psychon. Sci.* **21,** 29–31.

—— Messer, L. G., Freund, G., and Means, L. W. (1972). Effect of hippocampal lesions and intertrial interval on single-alternation performance in the rat. *J. comp. physiol. Psychol.* **80,** 469–77.

Walker; J. A. and Olton, D. S. (1979). Spatial memory deficit following fimbria-fornix lesions: independent of time for stimulus processing. *Physiol. Behav.* **23,** 11–15.

Warburton, D. M. (1969). Effects of atropine sulfate on single alternation in hippocampectomized rats. *Physiol. Behav.* **4,** 641–4.

—— (1977). Stimulus selection and behavioral inhibition. In *Handbook of psychopharmacology,* Vol. 8. *Drugs, neurotransmitters and behavior* (ed. L. L. Iversen, S. D. Iversen, and S. H. Snyder) pp. 385–431. Plenum Press, New York.

Warrington, E. K. and Weiskrantz, L. (1968). A study of learning and retention in amnesic patients. *Neuropsychologia* **6,** 283–91.

—— —— (1970). Amnesic syndrome: consolidation or retrieval? *Nature, Lond.* **228,** 628–30.

—— —— (1974). The effect of prior learning on subsequent retention in amnesic patients. *Neuropsychologia* **12,** 419–28.

—— —— (1978). Further analysis of the prior learning effect in amnesic patients. *Neuropsychologia* **16**, 169–77.

Watabe, K. and Satoh, T. (1979). Mechanism underlying prolonged inhibition of rat locus coeruleus neurons following anti- and orthodromic activation. *Brain Res.* **165**, 343–7.

Waterhouse, B. D., Moises, H. C., and Woodward, D. J. (1978). Noradrenergic modulation of somatosensory cortical neuronal responses to iontophoretically applied putative neurotransmitters. *Soc. Neurosci. Abst.* **4**, 903.

Watson, J. B. and Rayner, B. (1920). Conditioned emotional reactions. *J. exp. Psychol.* **3**, 1–14.

Watts, F. N. (1971). Desensitization as an habituation phenomenon: stimulus intensity as determinant of the effect of stimulus lengths. *Behav. Res. Ther.* **9**, 209–17.

—— (1973). Desensitization as an habituation phenomenon: II. Studies of interstimulus interval length. *Psychol. Rep.* **33**, 715–18.

—— (1974). The control of spontaneous recovery of anxiety in imaginal desensitization. *Behav. Res. Ther.* **12**, 57–9.

—— (1979). Habituation model of systematic desensitization. *Psychol. Bull.* **86**, 627–37.

Wauquier, A. and Rolls, E. T. (eds.) (1976). *Brain-stimulation reward.* North-Holland, Amsterdam.

Webster, D. B. and Voneida, T. J. (1964). Learning deficits following hippocampal lesions in split-brain cats. *Expl Neurol.* **10**, 170–82.

Weiskrantz, L. (1978). A comparison of hippocampal pathology in man and other animals. In *Functions of the septo-hippocampal system* (ed. K. Elliott and J. Whelan) Ciba Foundation Symposium 58 (New Series) pp. 373–87. Elsevier, Amsterdam.

—— and Warrington, E. K. (1970*a*). Verbal learning and retention by amnesic patients using partial information. *Psychon. Sci.* **20**, 210–11.

—— —— (1970*b*). A study of forgetting in amnesic patients. *Neuropsychologia* **8**, 281–8.

—— —— (1975). The problem of the amnesic syndrome in man and animals. In *The hippocampus*, Vol. 2. *Neurophysiology and behaviour* (ed. R. L. Isaacson and K. H. Pribram) pp. 411–28. Plenum Press, New York.

—— —— (1979). Conditioning in amnesic patients. *Neuropsychologia* **17**, 187–94.

Weiss, J. M. and Glazer, H. I. (1975). Effects of acute exposure to stressors on subsequent avoidance-escape behavior. *Psychosom. Med.* **37**, 499–521.

—— and Pohorecky, L. A. (1976). Coping behavior and neurochemical changes: an alternative explanation for the original 'learned helplessness' experiments. In *Animal models in human psychobiology* (ed. A. Serban and A. Kling) pp. 141–73. Plenum Press, New York.

—— —— Brick, J., and Miller, N. E. (1975). Effects of chronic exposure to stressors on avoidance-escape behavior and on brain norepinephrine. *Psychosom. Med.* **37**, 522–34.

—— Stone, E. A., and Harrell, N. (1970). Coping behavior and brain norepinephrine level in rats. *J. comp. physiol. Psychol.* **72**, 153–60.

Weiss, K. R., Friedman, R., and McGregor, S. (1974). Effects of septal lesions on latent inhibition and habituation of the orienting response in rats. *Acta Neurobiol. exp.* **34**, 491–504.

Weitz, M. K. (1974). Effects of ethanol on shock-elicited fighting behavior in rats. *Q. Jl Stud. Alcohol* **35**, 953–8.

Weldon, E. (1967). An analogue of extraversion as a determinant of individual behaviour in the rat. *Br. J. Psychol.* **58**, 253–9.

Wendlandt, S. and File, S. E. (1979). Behavioral effects of lesions of the locus coeruleus noradrenaline system combined with adrenalectomy. *Behav. neural Biol.* **26**, 189–201.

Wetzel, W., Ott, T., and Matthies, H. (1977a). Hippocampal rhythmic slow activity ('theta') and behavior elicited by medial septal stimulation in rats. *Behav. Biol.* **19**, 534–42.

—— —— —— (1977b). Post-training hippocampal rhythmic slow activity ('theta') elicited by septal stimulation improves memory consolidation in rats. *Behav. Biol.* **21**, 32–40.

Whimbey, A. E. and Denenberg, V. H. (1967). Two independent behavioral dimensions in open field performance. *J. comp. physiol. Psychol.* **63**, 500–4.

Whishaw, I. Q. (1972). Hippocampal electroencephalographic activity in the Mongolian gerbil during natural behaviours and in wheel running and conditioned immobility. *Can. J. Psychol.* **26**, 219–39.

—— (1976). The effects of alcohol and atropine on EEG and behavior in the rabbit. *Psychopharmacology* **45**, 83–90.

—— Bland, B. H., and Bayer, S. A. (1978). Postnatal hippocampal granule cell agenesis in the rat: effects on two types of rhythmical slow activity (RSA) in two hippocampal generators. *Brain Res.* **146**, 249–68.

—— —— and Vanderwolf, C. H. (1972). Hippocampal activity, behavior, self-stimulation, and heart rate during electrical stimulation of the lateral hypothalamus. *J. comp. physiol. Psychol.* **79**, 115–27.

—— and Vanderwolf, C. H. (1973). Hippocampal EEG and behavior: changes in amplitude and frequency of RSA (theta rhythm) associated with spontaneous and learned movement patterns in rats and cats. *Behav. Biol.* **8**, 461–84.

White, S. R. (1974). Atropine, scopolamine and hippocampal lesion effects on alternation performance of rats. *Pharmac. Biochem. Behav.* **2**, 297–307.

White, W. F., Nadler, J. V., and Cotman, C. W. (1979). Analysis of short-term plasticity at the perforant path-granule cell synapse. *Brain Res.* **178**, 41–53.

Wickens, D. D. (1970). Encoding categories of words: an empirical approach to meaning. *Psychol. Rev.* **77**, 1–15.

Wilcock, J. and Fulker, D. W. (1973). Avoidance learning in rats: genetic evidence for two distinct behavioral processes in the shuttle-box. *J. comp. physiol. Psychol.* **82**, 247–53.

Willett, R. (1960). The effects of psychosurgical procedures on behaviour. In *Handbook of abnormal psychology* (ed. H. J. Eysenck) pp. 566–610. Pitman, London.

Williams, J. H. and Azmitia, E. C. (1981). Hippocampal serotonin reuptake and nocturnal locomotor activity after microinjections of 5,7-DHT in the fornix–fimbria. *Brain Res.* **207**, 95–107.

Williamson, M. J., Paul, S. M., and Skolnick, P. (1978). Labelling of benzodiazepine receptors *in vivo. Nature, Lond.* **275**, 551–3.

Willingham, W. W. (1956). The organization of emotional behavior in mice. *J. comp. physiol. Psychol.* **49**, 345–8.

Willner, P. J. and Crowe, R. (1977). Effect of chlordiazepoxide on the partial reinforcement extinction effect. *Pharmac. Biochem. Behav.* **7**, 479–82.

Wilson, J. R. and Vardaris, R. M. (1972). Posterior decortication potentiates retrograde amnesia from hippocampal stimulation. *Physiol. Behav.* **9**, 809–15.

Wilson, R. C. and Steward, O. (1978). Polysynaptic activation of the dentate gyrus of the hippocampal formation: an olfactory input via the lateral entorhinal cortex. *Expl Brain Res.* **33**, 523–34.

Wincour, G. (1979). Effects of interference on discrimination learning and recall by rats with hippocampal lesions. *Physiol. Behav.* **22**, 339–45.

—— (1981). The amnesic syndrome: a deficit in cue utilization. In *Human memory and amnesia* (ed. L. Cermak) Erlbaum, Hillsdale, NJ.

—— and Bagchi, S. P. (1974). Effects of bufotenine and *p*-chlorophenylalanine on reactivity to footshock. *Physiol. Psychol.* **2**, 75–9.

—— and Bindra, D. (1976). Effects of additional cues on passive avoidance learning and extinction in rats with hippocampal lesions. *Physiol. Behav.* **17**, 915–20.

—— and Black, A. H. (1978). Cue-induced recall of a passive avoidance response by rats with hippocampal lesions. *Physiol. Behav.* **21**, 39–44.

—— and Breckenridge, C. B. (1973). Cue-dependent behavior of hippocampally damaged rats in a complex maze. *J. comp. physiol. Psychol.* **82**, 512–22.

—— and Kinsbourne, M. (1978). Contextual cueing as an aid to Korsakoff amnesics. *Neuropsychologia* **16**, 671–82.

—— and Mills, J. A. (1969). Hippocampus and septum in response inhibition. *J. comp. physiol. Psychol.* **67**, 352–7.

—— —— (1970). Transfer between related and unrelated problems following hippocampal lesions in rats. *J. comp. physiol. Psychol.* **73**, 162–9.

—— and Olds, J. (1978). Effects of context manipulation on memory and reversal learning in rats with hippocampal lesions. *J. comp. physiol. Psychol.* **92**, 312–21.

—— and Weiskrantz, L. (1976). An investigation of paired-associate learning in amnesic patients. *Neuropsychologia* **14**, 97–110.

Winson, J. (1974). Patterns of hippocampal theta rhythm in the freely moving rat. *Electroenceph. clin. Neurophysiol.* **36**, 291–301.

—— (1976a). Hippocampal theta rhythm. I. Depth profiles in the curarized rat. *Brain Res.* **103**, 57–70.

—— (1976b). Topographic patterns of hippocampal theta rhythm in freely moving rat and rabbit. In *The septal nuclei* (ed. J. F. De France) pp. 463–80. Plenum Press, New York.

—— and Abzug, C. (1978). Neuronal transmission through hippocampal pathways dependent on behavior. *J. Neurophysiol.* **41**, 716–32.

Winter, J. C. (1972). Comparison of chlordiazepoxide, methysergide and cinanserin as modifiers of punished behavior and as antagonists of *N,N*-dimethyltryptamine. *Archs Int. Pharmacodyn. Ther.* **197**, 137–59.

Wise, C. D., Berger, B. D., and Stein, L. (1972). Benzodiazepines: anxiety-reducing activity by reduction of serotonin turnover in the brain. *Science, NY* **77**, 180–3.

—— —— —— (1973). Evidence of alpha-noradrenergic reward receptors and serotonergic punishment receptors in the rat brain. *Biol. Psychiat.* **6**, 3–21.

Wise, R. A. (1978). Catecholamine theories of reward: a critical review. *Brain Res.* **152**, 215–47.

Wolfe, J. W., Lubar, J. F., and Ison, J. R. (1967). Effects of medial cortical lesions on appetitive instrumental conditioning. *Physiol. Behav.* **2**, 239–44.

Wolpe, J. (1958). *Psychotherapy by reciprocal inhibition.* Stanford University Press.

Woodward, D. J. and Waterhouse, B. D. (1978). Interaction of norepinephrine with cerebrocortical activity evoked by stimulation of somatosensory afferent pathways in the rat. *Soc. Neurosci. Abst.* **4**, 909.

Woody, C. D. and Ervin, F. R. (1966). Memory function in cats with lesions of the fornix and mammillary bodies. *Physiol. Behav.* **1**, 273–80.

Wyers, E. J. and Deadwyler, S. A. (1971). Duration and nature of retrograde amnesia produced by stimulation of caudate nucleus. *Physiol. Behav.* **6**, 97–103.

Wyss, J. M. (1977). Hypothalamic and brainstem afferents to the hippocampal formation in rat. *Abst. Soc. Neurosci.* **3**, 209.

Yamamoto, C. and Chujo, T. (1978). Long-term potentiation in thin hippocampal sections studied by intracellular and extracellular recordings. *Expl Neurol.* **58**, 242–50.

Young, G. A. (1976). Electrical activity of the dorsal hippocampus in rats operantly trained to lever press and to lick. *J. comp. physiol. Psychol.* **90,** 78–90.

Young, P. A., Eaves, L. J., and Eysenck, H. J. (1980). Intergenerational stability
and change in the causes of variation in personality. *Person. indiv. Diff.* **1,** 35–
55.

Young, W. S. III, Bird, S. J., and Kuhar, M. J. (1977). Iontophoresis of methio-
nine-enkephalin in the locus coeruleus area. *Brain Res.* **129,** 366–70.

Yutzey, D. A., Meyer, D. M., and Meyer, D. A. (1964). Emotionality changes following septal and neocortical ablations in rats. *J. comp. physiol. Psychol.* **58,**
463–7.

Ziff, D. R. and Capaldi, E. J. (1971). Amytal and the small trial partial reinforcement effect: stimulus properties of early trial nonrewards. *J. exp. Psychol.* **87,**
263–9.

Zigmond, R. E., Schon, F., and Iversen, L. L. (1974). Increased tyrosine hydroxylase activity in the locus coeruleus of the rat brain after reserpine treatment
and cold stress. *Brain Res.* **70,** 547–52.

Zimmer, J. (1971). Ipsilateral afferents to the commissural zone of the fascia dentata, demonstrated in decommissurated rats by silver impregnation. *J. comp.
Neurol.* **142,** 393–416.

Zin, R., Conforti, N., and Feldman, S. (1977). Sensory responsiveness of single
cells in the medial septal nucleus in intact and hypothalamic-deafferented
rats. *Expl Neurol.* **54,** 7–23.

Zornetzer, S. F., Boast, C., and Hamrick, M. (1974). Neuroanatomic localization
and memory processing in mice: the role of the dentate gyrus of the hippocampus. *Physiol. Behav.* **13,** 569–75.

—— and Chronister, R. B. (1973). Neuroanatomical localization of memory disruption: relationship between brain structure and learning task. *Physiol. Behav.* **10,** 747–50.

—— —— and Ross, B. (1973). The hippocampus and retrograde amnesia: localization of some positive and negative memory disruptive sites. *Behav. Biol.* **8,**
507–18.

—— and Gold, M. S. (1976). The locus coeruleus: its possible role in memory
consolidation. *Physiol. Behav.* **16,** 331–6.

Zuromski, E. S., Donovick, P. J., and Burright, R. G. (1972). Bar pressing for
illumination change in albino rats with septal lesions. *J. comp. physiol. Psychol.*
78, 83–90.

Additional references

See also new references listed on pp. xii–xiii

Davis, N. M. and Gray, J. A. (1983). Brain 5-hydroxytryptamine and learned resistance to punishment. *Behav. Brain Res.* **8,** 129–37.

Feldon, J., Rawlins, J. N. P., and Gray, J. A. (1982*a*). Effects of lateral and medial septal lesions on response suppression mediated by response-contingent and response-independent shock. *Physiol. Psychol.* **10,** 145–52.

────── (1982*b*). Discrimination of response-contingent and response-independent shock by rats: effects of medial and lateral septal lesions and chlordiazepoxide. *Behav. Neur. Biol.* **35,** 121–38.

Garrud, P., Rawlins, J. N. P., Mackintosh, N. J., Goodall, G., Cotton, M. M., and Feldon, J. (1984). Successful overshadowing and blocking in hippocampectomized rats. *Behav. Brain Res.* **12,** 39–53.

Gray, J. A. (in press). *The psychology of fear and stress,* 2nd edn. Cambridge University Press, Cambridge.

Holt, L. and Gray, J. A. (1983). Septal driving of the hippocampal theta rhythm produces a long-term, proactive and non-associative increase in resistance to extinction. *Quart. J. Exp. Psychol.* **35B,** 97–118.

McNaughton, N. and Miller, J. J. (1984). Medial septal projections to the dentate gyrus of the rat: electrophysiological analysis of distribution and plasticity. *Expl. Brain Res.* **56,** 243–56.

────── (1986). Collateral specific long-term potentiation of the output of field CA3 of the hippocampus of the rat. *Expl. Brain Res.* **62,** 250–8.

──── Owen, S. R., Boarder, M. R., Gray, J. A., and Fillenz, M. (1984). Responses to novelty in rats with lesions of the dorsal noradrenergic bundle. *New Zealand J. Psychol.* **13,** 16–24.

Owen, S. R., Boarder, M.R., Gray, J. A., and Fillenz, M. (1982). Lesions of the dorsal noradrenergic bundle and rewarded running: the role of pretraining. *Behav. Brain Res.* **5,** 3–9.

Salmon, P. and Gray, J. A. (1985). Comparison between the effects of propranolol and chlordiazepoxide on timing behaviour in the rat. *Psychopharmacology* **87,** 219–24.

────── (1986). Effects of propranolol on conditioned suppression, discriminated punishment and discriminated non-reward in the rat. *Psychopharmacology* **88,** 252–7.

Tsaltas, E., Gray, J. A., and Fillenz, M. (1984). Alleviation of response suppression to conditioned aversive stimuli by lesions of the dorsal noradrenergic bundle. *Behav. Brain Res.* **13,** 115–27.

Author index

Subject index